CHOCOLATE CITY

CHOCOLATE CITY

A HISTORY OF RACE AND DEMOCRACY IN THE NATION'S CAPITAL

Chris Myers Asch & George Derek Musgrove

The University of North Carolina Press   Chapel Hill

THIS BOOK WAS PUBLISHED WITH THE
ASSISTANCE OF THE JOHN HOPE FRANKLIN FUND
OF THE UNIVERSITY OF NORTH CAROLINA PRESS.

Manufactured in the United States of America
Set in Quadraat type by Tseng Information Systems, Inc.

The University of North Carolina Press has been
a member of the Green Press Initiative since 2003.

Cover illustration by Sally Fry Scruggs

Library of Congress Cataloging-in-Publication Data
Names: Asch, Chris Myers, author. | Musgrove, George Derek, 1975– author.
Title: Chocolate City : a history of race and democracy in the nation's capital /
Chris Myers Asch and George Derek Musgrove.
Description: Chapel Hill : The University of North Carolina Press, [2017] |
Includes bibliographical references and index.
Identifiers: LCCN 2017026934 | ISBN 9781469635866 (cloth : alk. paper) |
ISBN 9781469654720 (pbk. : alk. paper) | ISBN 9781469635873 (ebook)
Subjects: LCSH: African Americans—Washington (D.C.)—History. |
Washington (D.C.)—History. | Washington (D.C.)—Race relations.
Classification: LCC E185.93.D6 A78 2017 | DDC 305.8009753—dc23
LC record available at https://lccn.loc.gov/2017026934

Portions of Chapter 13 appeared earlier in somewhat different
form in Chris Myers Asch and George Derek Musgrove, "'We Are Headed
for Some Bad Trouble': Gentrification and Displacement in Washington, D.C.,
1920–2014," in Capital Dilemma: Growth and Inequality in Washington, D.C., ed.
Derek Hyra and Sabiyha Price (New York: Routledge, 2015), 107–35.

CONTENTS

ILLUSTRATIONS AND TABLES

Illustrations

Tables

ACKNOWLEDGMENTS

This book has its origins in a canceled class. In 2009, George Derek Musgrove's African American History course at the University of the District of Columbia underenrolled, and the powers that be terminated the class on the first day. Derek was assigned a new course: "History of the District of Columbia." A Baltimore native with no background in D.C. history, he stumbled through the ensuing semester, hurriedly reading any book on the District he could get his hands on just moments before heading to class.

A lover of self-deprecating stories, Derek shared his D.C. History woes with Chris Myers Asch, a D.C. native who had returned to his hometown and taken a position at UDC. We had become fast friends not simply because we were among a tiny handful of thirty-somethings teaching at UDC but also on the strength of our shared history with Freedom Schools. Derek had worked for the Children's Defense Fund's Freedom School Program for much of the 1990s, and Chris had cofounded and run the Sunflower County Freedom Project, a nonprofit program in rural Mississippi modeled on the Freedom Schools of the 1960s.

Derek encouraged Chris to join him in tackling the D.C. History course, and we jointly rewrote the syllabus. Teaching the course and interacting with our students deepened our love for the District, a beautiful, quirky, complicated, and sometimes maddening place too often mocked and misunderstood by outsiders. Like many native Washingtonians and longtime residents, we have a fierce pride in the city, despite (and perhaps because of) its flaws and fissures, particularly along racial lines. We wanted to tell our city's story, warts and all, and we thought that the two of us—one white and one black, both historians of race in America—could write a compelling, insightful history that would help all Americans understand their nation's capital.

For six years, we have labored together on this project. Life intervened repeatedly in the writing process. Our families grew, we changed jobs, we bought and rehabilitated beat-up old houses. At times the demands became too much. For a duration, Derek had to stop writing almost entirely, leaving Chris to write the first half of the book by himself. But throughout, the project was held together by a rich friendship, our love of D.C., and a broad vision of democracy

ix

that promises self-determination for the poor as well as the rich, the woman as much as the man, the black the same as the white.

The book that you are reading now owes a tremendous debt to the many wonderful teachers we have had throughout our lives. For Chris, two teachers from his days in D.C. public schools stand out. His eighth grade English teacher at Alice Deal Junior High, Rita Miles, pushed him to think about audience, rhythm, and sentence structure more than any teacher he had in college or graduate school. Ms. Miles spent more than four decades turning unfocused middle schoolers into sharp writers. His eleventh grade AP U.S. history teacher at Wilson High, Erich Martel, gently prodded him to think critically about sources and challenged him to question his assumptions. Though soft-spoken in class, Mr. Martel has a spine of steel and has stood up for his students and his principles in countless battles against school officials. Derek must thank the journalist and student of D.C.'s go-go scene, Natalie Hopkinson, who challenged him to write for a general audience, offering biting but incisive commentary.

A book of this scope also incurs tremendous intellectual debts. We build on the work of many dedicated scholars—including Constance McLaughlin Green, Letitia Woods Brown, Howard Gillette, Kate Masur, and others—who have contributed deeply researched books, articles, and dissertations that have helped us understand the richness and complexity of race and democracy in D.C. Please read the Essay on Sources to learn more about the intellectual foundations of the book and the shifting interpretations of D.C. history in the past century.

The field of D.C. history is blessed not only with scholars but also with a wide range of students, bloggers, and local history aficionados who have spent years writing articles, interviewing community members, rummaging through old newspapers, defending local landmarks, and telling the stories that preserve our city's history. Often unsung, these local historians produce the types of fine-grained, in-depth studies that give texture and nuance to sweeping narratives such as this book.

Two extraordinary local historians deserve particular mention: Jane Freundel Levey and Kathryn Schneider Smith. Levey was the driving force behind the creation of a remarkable set of well-researched walking tours that trace the history of D.C. neighborhoods. She has been a firm (but kind) critic almost since this book's inception. Smith helped organize the team of historians who produced the first D.C. history textbook, *City of Magnificent Intentions* (1983). Smith, with Levey's help, launched *Washington History* magazine in 1989, and the two have been prolific writers and editors in the field. They have brought D.C. history to untold thousands of students, tourists, policy makers, and others.

We appreciate the ongoing work of the D.C. Public Library's Washingtoniana

Division, a treasure trove of local history; Howard University's Moorland-Spingarn Research Center, which offers remarkable oral histories, personal collections, and organizational papers essential to understanding the city; the Historical Society of Washington, D.C., whose *Washington History* remains the best source for original research on the city; and the Special Collections at George Washington University's Gelman Library, which preserve a wide range of local source material. It simply would not be possible to conduct serious local research without these resources.

We also tap into the vast pool of newspapers and other contemporary articles about the city. In academic (and political) circles, it can be fashionable to lament the supposed shallowness and simplicity of "the media." But where would we be without journalists reporting on things as they happen? Reporters don't have the luxury of time; they don't get long sabbaticals to ruminate about their work; they don't get to hash out ideas in seminars and conferences. They just write, often much better than we historians do, under ferocious pressures of time and print space, and they capture moments that otherwise would vanish from the historical record. The *National Intelligencer*, the *Evening Star*, the *Washington Bee*, the *Washington Post*, and other local newspapers take detailed snapshots of the city, offering contemporary interviews, opinions, and ideas that help us understand how people viewed the events through which they were living. We tip our hats to them.

Unsurprisingly, our most illuminating sources for the latter chapters were the participants themselves. We thank Al Hill, who straightened out the city's finances in the early 1980s; Johnny Barnes, who defended the Seaton Street tenants and worked as chief of staff to Delegate Walter Fauntroy; Jimmy Garrett, a member of the Student Nonviolent Coordinating Committee and cofounder of the Center for Black Education; Tony Lewis Jr., who grew up on Hanover Place NW; Frank Watkins and Ray Anderson, who worked for Jesse Jackson in the early 1990s; and Joyce Ladner, the SNCC veteran and member of the Financial Control Board. All of them engaged in long conversations with Derek about the events under consideration.

Many D.C. history specialists willingly gave their time to strengthen the book. Members of our D.C. writing group, including Bell Clement, Amanda Huron, Katie Wells, and Brett Williams, offered important feedback and insight on various chapters. Ken Bowling, Joseph Genetin-Pilawa, Tikia Hamilton, Kate Masur, Samir Meghelli, Al Moss, Joe Reidy, Sarah Shoenfeld, William G. Thomas, and Eric Yellin contributed their remarkable knowledge of particular eras and people to help us avoid many mistakes.

Some of the most valuable feedback came from readers who had no specialized knowledge in D.C. history. Students of Chris's "Race and Democracy in D.C." class at Colby College wrote chapter-by-chapter "Editor's Notes" of the manuscript in progress—they offered a reader's perspective that forced us to clarify and strengthen our prose. We particularly appreciated Zoë Gibson, Maggie Hojlo, Nathalie Kirsch, Ian Mansfield, and Acquib Yacoob for their thoughtful, thorough, and at times brutally honest comments. District teachers Cosby Hunt and Brian Rohal shared our work with their students and helped us make the book more accessible to a wider audience. Scholars and friends, including Terry Bouton, Kate Brown, Justin Dillon, Steve Estes, Noralee Frankel, Rachel Reinhard, Gabe Ross, Michelle Scott, and Jason Morgan Ward also offered important perspectives on our work.

Derek has enjoyed the support of the rich community of scholars in the University of Maryland Baltimore County's Department of History, particularly Marjoleine Kars, who mentored him as an undergraduate before becoming his colleague. In a nice twist, Marjoleine studied under Peter Wood as a graduate student at Duke University—and Peter has been Chris's mentor since Chris was an undergraduate at Duke. An extraordinary historian and a model mentor, Peter has been a steadfast supporter and a thoughtful critic of this book. Two of Chris's friends, Gregg Costa and Shawn Raymond, have been an important source of encouragement, insight, and debate since their Teach For America days, when they lived in an unheated house in Itta Bena, Mississippi (Marion Barry's birthplace!). Shawn read the first (often ugly) draft of each chapter; Gregg waited until the sausage was almost ready to be cooked before he weighed in.

Our families have been our rock and refuge. Our wives have endured years of squirreling away to work and helped carve out time for research trips and "writing retreats" away from the kids. Chris dedicates the book to Nana (aka his mother, Margery Myers), who grew up on Reno Road in Northwest Washington and still lives on Western Avenue NW in the house in which he grew up. She knows and loves the city deeply, and she has taught us to see the good in people and places that often are overlooked or neglected. We hope that this book helps her see her hometown in a new light. Derek dedicates the book to his two sons, George Walker Musgrove and John Freeman Musgrove, who were born in Washington and, knowing no other home, must come to terms with its history as they help to create its future.

CHOCOLATE CITY

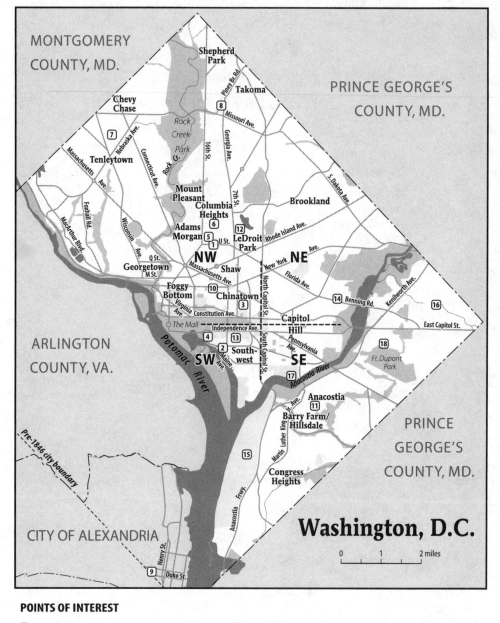

Washington, D.C.

MONTGOMERY COUNTY, MD.

PRINCE GEORGE'S COUNTY, MD.

ARLINGTON COUNTY, VA.

PRINCE GEORGE'S COUNTY, MD.

CITY OF ALEXANDRIA

Shepherd Park
Takoma
Chevy Chase
Rock Creek Park
Tenleytown
Mount Pleasant
Columbia Heights
Brookland
Adams Morgan
LeDroit Park
NW
NE
Georgetown
Shaw
Foggy Bottom
Chinatown
The Mall
Capitol Hill
SW
Southwest
SE
Ft. Dupont Park
Anacostia
Barry Farm/Hillsdale
Congress Heights

Potomac River
Anacostia River
Pre-1846 city boundary

Piney Br. Rd.
Missouri Ave.
16th St.
Georgia Ave.
7th St.
Nebraska Ave.
Massachusetts Ave.
Connecticut Ave.
Wisconsin Ave.
Foxhall Rd.
MacArthur Blvd.
Q St.
M St.
Massachusetts Ave.
U St.
Rhode Island Ave.
New York Ave.
Florida Ave.
North Capitol St.
Constitution Ave.
Virginia Ave.
Independence Ave.
Maine Ave.
South Capitol St.
Pennsylvania Ave.
Benning Rd.
Kenilworth Ave.
East Capitol St.
S. Dakota Ave.
Martin Luther King Ave.
Anacostia Frwy.
Henry St.
Duke St.

0   1   2 miles

MAP BY LARRY BOWRING CARTOGRAPHY

POINTS OF INTEREST

1. 14th & U Streets NW
2. Benjamin Banneker Park
3. Blue Jug
   (former site, now National Building Museum)
4. Bureau of Engraving and Printing
5. Busboys & Poets
6. Euclid House (former site)
7. Fort Reno
8. Fort Stevens
9. Franklin & Armfield Headquarters
   (former site, now Freedom House Museum)
10. Franklin Square
11. Frederick Douglass house
    (now Frederick Douglass National Historic Site)
12. Howard University
13. Island Hall (former site)
14. Langston Terrace Dwellings
15. Nacotchtank (former site, now Joint Base Anacostia-Bolling)
16. National Training School for Women and Girls
    (former site, now Nannie Helen Burroughs School)
17. Navy Yard
18. Sousa Junior High School (now Sousa Middle School)

Always a Chocolate City

Surely nowhere in the world do oppression and persecution based solely on the color of the skin appear more hateful and hideous than in the capital of the United States, because the chasm between the principles upon which this Government was founded, in which it still professes to believe, and those which are daily practiced under the protection of the flag, yawns so wide and deep. — MARY CHURCH TERRELL, 1906

Washington, D.C., seemed to be at its finest on August 28, 1963. Despite dire warnings of racial violence and chaos, the city welcomed more than 250,000 peaceful protesters for the "March on Washington for Jobs and Freedom." Amassing near the Lincoln Memorial, the crowd listened to an interracial lineup of inspirational speakers, culminating with the dynamic young preacher from Alabama, Martin Luther King Jr. The civil rights movement had come "to this hallowed spot," King insisted, "to make real the promises of democracy."[1]

Across the world viewers saw newsreels of King's speech and images of the smiling, sweating, sign-toting throngs who represented a broad cross-section of America—black and white, young and old, Northern and Southern, Jew and Gentile. The march was vivid evidence of vibrant American democracy in action. Beautiful, orderly, and welcoming, the nation's capital appeared to be the ideal staging ground for what King called "the greatest demonstration for freedom in the history of our nation."[2]

At the end of the day, most protesters piled onto buses to head back home, but roughly 10 percent of the march participants already *were* home. They were D.C. residents, natives of a city that was at once a shining symbol of America and a glaring rejection of democracy. Unlike other U.S. citizens, D.C. residents had no representation in Congress and lacked basic self-government. Theirs was a city run by three presidentially appointed commissioners, not locally elected officials. Washingtonians of all races had no voting rights that any elected representative anywhere was bound to respect.

King's call to "make real the promises of democracy" struck a particularly resonant chord in D.C. because it was the first majority-black major city in the nation. The crowd at the March on Washington may have epitomized an ideal of interracial unity, but D.C. itself was in a state of racial turmoil and flux. Just three years earlier, the Census Bureau had given statistical confirmation to the massive demographic transformation that was remaking the city. In 1950, D.C. claimed more than eight hundred thousand residents, almost two-thirds of them white; by 1960, the city had lost a third of its white population and was roughly 54 percent black.[3]

White neighborhoods and schools that a decade before had been protected by restrictive covenants, federal law, and social customs now were almost entirely black. As jittery white families left Washington, city planners pushed "urban renewal" plans that paved over the majority-black neighborhoods of Southwest D.C. with highways to all-white suburbs, generating racial bitterness and spawning neighborhood protest movements. A new generation of black activists and their allies challenged federal and local authorities to provide adequate housing, equal educational opportunity, and basic political rights for the black majority. To such activists, the March on Washington only highlighted the vast gulf between the ideals that Washington represented and the realities that D.C. residents faced.

As black educator Mary Church Terrell articulated at the turn of the twentieth century, no city better captures these ongoing tensions between America's expansive democratic hopes and its enduring racial realities than the nation's capital. Contentious racial issues that have challenged our nation—from slavery to civil rights to urban violence—have played out with particular symbolic and substantive power in D.C.

Yet Washington is not simply emblematic of our larger national struggle for racial equality. It is a city like no other in the country, and its racial history is a peculiarly fascinating tale. Created by constitutional fiat and controlled by Congress, the District of Columbia is the voteless capital of a democracy, a seat of government highly sensitive to shifts in national politics, a city situated in the South but torn politically and culturally between North and South. Unlike other major Eastern cities, it was planned from the beginning and grew under the watchful gaze of national leaders. Almost alone among Southern cities, D.C. was home to a strong and public abolitionist movement, and its educated free black community made the city a beacon of black opportunity even during slavery. In contrast to other urban areas, it failed to develop any meaningful industry aside from government and did not attract a substantial population of white immigrants. Cosmopolitan yet parochial, emblematic yet unique, D.C. has served as a symbol of America yet stood apart from the nation.

Chocolate City traces the political, economic, and social history of race and democracy in this extraordinary city, from its inception as a slave capital through the racially tinged mayoral election of 2010. In that time, the city experienced massive transformations—from a sparsely inhabited plantation society into a booming metropolis, from a center of the slave trade to the nation's first black-majority city, from a self-governing town to a federal fiefdom and back again. It has endured corrupt leadership and congressional meddling, weathered the Civil War and the crack epidemic, and survived urban renewal and multiple waves of gentrification.

Race is central to Washington history, so *Chocolate City* is not solely a history of D.C.'s African American community. Instead, we explore how questions of race and democracy have shaped life in the capital city for residents of all races. Thus we begin the study with the first racial battles to envelop the region, those between European settlers and Native Americans, and end with the twenty-first-century demographic revolution that is dramatically reshaping the city's racial contours.

Race, above and beyond other factors (including class, region, politics, and religion), has proven to be the most significant explanation for social, economic, and political divisions in the city. Race may be a social and historical construction with little basis in biology, but it is also a powerful lived reality that has influenced how (and where) Washingtonians of all races have lived, worked, voted, and interacted. Since the city's inception, race, racial tensions, and the changing racial demographics of the city's population have been animating forces in the lives of capital city residents.

The District's undemocratic political status has had a debilitating effect on race relations in the city. Washington is home to many marble monuments to freedom, yet it still suffers from the political tyranny that angered patriots during the American Revolution: taxation without representation. The city's lack of political power and basic self-determination has profoundly affected its history, limiting its political and economic growth, placing it at the mercy of federal lawmakers, and forcing the city's residents into a frustrating role as dependents and claimants rather than full citizens. This lack of democratic outlets has inflamed racial divisions in the city because race has been a primary factor in D.C.'s ongoing disenfranchisement.

Chocolate City examines how being the nation's capital has had both a catalyzing and at times demoralizing effect on local racial struggles. As America's capital city and home to national leaders and foreign observers, D.C. has often served as a battleground for national fights over the meaning of race and democracy, as well as a laboratory in which national ideas and agendas have been pursued on behalf (and at the expense) of local people. Washington is "the living room of the Nation," a black educator told President Dwight Eisenhower in 1953, a symbol of the country that is held to a different standard than other cities. Placed in the national microscope, its racial struggles have been magnified and distorted.[4]

This book helps explain why racial mistrust is so deeply ingrained in the nation's capital and the nation at large. Racial divisions, which parallel and accentuate lines of class, extend back to the founding of the city in the late eighteenth century; they deepened in the generations after the Civil War; they exploded during the tumultuous decades of the mid- and late twentieth century; and they continue to define life in the city in the twenty-first century. Washington has been marked by fears of racial domination, deadly race riots, and deep-seated racial bitterness. Though the election of the nation's first black president in 2008 inspired some residents to imagine a postracial society, the city's history of racial mistrust still implicates and at times envelopes newcomers and natives alike.

Yet the history of race and democracy in D.C. is not simply a litany of fears, riots, and antagonism. It is also an inspiring history of hopes, alliances, and interracial cooperation. Even as residents have struggled with racial conflict, Washington has attracted committed reformers who have worked across racial lines to build a more egalitarian city. The racial barriers that can seem so resilient have been remarkably fluid at different points in history. The extraordinary biracial movement to abolish slavery, the interracial attack on segregation, and the citywide effort to block freeways from destroying neighborhoods are examples of how Washingtonians have battled fear and mistrust to create positive change.

We are writing this book to deepen popular understanding about the ways that race and democracy interact in our city and nation. Too often, our public conversations about race lack historical awareness or an appreciation of the roots of many of our racial divisions. Contemporary racial struggles—in housing, education, law enforcement, politics, and elsewhere—are not simply phenomena that have emerged suddenly in the twenty-first century. They are the product of more than four centuries of racial conflict and mistrust that have helped create the context in which we live and interact.

The story we tell in these pages shows that racial progress is neither linear nor inevitable. It takes serious, difficult, often discomforting work, and advances can be (and often have been) reversed. We know that this story may agitate, frustrate, and anger our readers—as it should. But we hope, too, that it will inspire them to commit themselves to the struggle of building a more just, egalitarian, and democratic city that embodies the best of what our nation can be.

ONE

Your Coming Is Not for Trade, but to Invade My People and Possess My Country

A Native American World under Siege, 1608–1790

We shall by degrees chaung their barbarous natures, make them ashamed ... of their savadge nakednes, informe them of the true god, and the waie to their salvation, and fynally teach them obedience to the kings Majestie and to his Governours.
—WILLIAM STRACHEY, 1612

The Anacostia River effectively splits Washington into two separate and unequal parts. To its north and west, the hills slope upward toward the monuments of the federal city and the affluent neighborhoods of Northwest Washington. To its south and east lay the flood-prone flats and hills of "Far Southeast" and "Far Northeast." Cut off physically and psychologically from the rest of Washington, these "East of the River" communities historically have suffered from political neglect, economic deprivation, and social isolation.

The river itself reflects the area's stagnation. Up through the early nineteenth century, the Anacostia rivaled the Potomac—it was a bustling trading channel deep enough for oceangoing vessels to travel to Bladensburg, Maryland, beyond the District's northeastern border. But as tobacco-exhausted soils upstream eroded into the river, the silted Anacostia became too shallow for commercial use. The area's economy shriveled. Despite the impressive efforts of local environmental groups, in the twenty-first century the Anacostia remains a litter-strewn barrier between a flourishing capital city and its poorest, blackest neighborhoods.[1]

The word "Anacostia," a term almost synonymous with "black" and "poor" in modern Washington, has its roots in the first racial struggles in the area that we now call the nation's capital. The word emerged as a Latin pronunciation and spelling of "Nacostine," the tribe of Native Americans who lived at the confluence of the Potomac and Anacostia Rivers. Three hundred in number at the dawn of the seventeenth century, the Nacostines lived in Nacotchtank, a sprawling

5

village that dominated the river plain on which now sits Joint Base Anacostia-Bolling.[2]

Situated just below the fall line, a ragged break in the land where the Piedmont drops off to the coastal plain, Nacotchtank rested along the frontier that separated the Algonquian-speaking peoples of the Tidewater from the Iroquoian tribes of the hinterland. The two groups carried on a lucrative trade, gathering by the hundreds each year to hawk beaver pelts, copper, shell beads, and other goods. Using the natural advantage of their location, the Nacostines acted as intermediaries and profited handsomely.

The frontier brought prosperity, but it also brought danger as warriors from northern tribes such as the Susquehanock and Massawomack staged frequent and destructive raids into the upper Tidewater. Villages close to the fall line, including Nacotchtank, were particularly vulnerable to attack. They sought protection from paramount chiefdoms, entities in which a chief of chiefs commanded tribute from subject tribes in exchange for military protection.[3]

The Nacostines allied themselves with the Piscataways. From their base on the massive peninsula created by the Potomac River and the Chesapeake Bay, what today is Prince George's County, Maryland, the Piscataways held sway over roughly seven thousand people. Nacotchtank stood along its western border, and the Nacostines paid tribute to the Piscataway chief, who made his capital at Mayone, just fifteen miles downriver where Piscataway Creek empties into the Potomac.

To the south and east of Nacotchtank lay the Piscataways' rival, the mighty Powhatan Confederacy, named for its formidable leader. Based at Werowocomoco, on the York River in what is now Gloucester County, Virginia, Powhatan dominated the Tidewater from the southern shores of the Potomac all the way to the Neuse River in modern-day North Carolina. He commanded tribute from thirty subject tribes containing fifteen thousand people.[4]

When English colonists established an outpost on the James River in spring 1607, they settled amid this large, fractious, and politically sophisticated Native American population. Initially, they were interlopers in a Native American world, subject to the whims of its established rulers. Yet within just one hundred years that native-dominated world was gone, and the few Native Americans who remained in the area had become wards of the English king. In their place lived English settlers, servants, and slaves in the colonies of Maryland and Virginia. To understand how this transformation took place, we must explore the first struggles over race and democracy in the area that would become the capital of the United States.[5]

"We Shall by Degrees Chaung Their Barbarous Natures":
Native Americans Encounter European Explorers

Nacotchtank received its first European visitor, Captain John Smith, in summer 1608. Born to a family of farmers in Willoughby, Lincolnshire, Smith had, through force of will and sheer luck, transformed himself into a gentleman and adventurer. Fleeing an apprenticeship at the age of sixteen, he spent a decade as a mercenary in France, a privateer on the Mediterranean, and a slave in Turkey. On his return to England, he held the title of captain and moved in respectable circles. Still restless for adventure, Smith left London to join the Virginia Company's efforts to establish a permanent colony in the Chesapeake.[6]

By the time that Smith landed at Nacotchtank, he and other English colonists had been in the Chesapeake for well more than a year. In May 1607, they had settled nearly two hundred miles to the south, in the heart of the Powhatan Confederacy. On a low-slung, swampy island they christened Jamestown, the colonists erected a palisaded fort and set about their appointed task of building England in America. The project went poorly. By September, inept leadership, disease, hunger, and hostilities with the surrounding Native Americans had cut their numbers nearly in half.[7]

Powhatan watched from afar as the new arrivals struggled to survive. He might have left the colonists to starve or dispatched a raiding party to wipe them out, but he saw in the intruders an opportunity to expand his economic and political power. The Chesapeake Algonquians believed that copper and translucent beads acted as conduits to the spirit world, and chiefs derived their power, in part, by controlling access to these precious objects. The Jamestown colonists had brought prodigious amounts of copper and beads from England, and iron tools as well, to trade for food. Powhatan, whom one Englishman described as "of a daring spirit, vigilant, ambitious, subtle to enlarge his dominions," determined to gain exclusive access to these goods by incorporating the colonists into his paramount chiefdom.[8]

In December 1607, Powhatan commanded Smith and the colonists to leave Jamestown and settle at Capahowasick, just downriver from his capital. If they did so and provided him with "hatchets and copper," Smith wrote, Powhatan "promise[d] to give me corn, venison, or what I wanted to feed us . . . and none should disturb us."[9] Though starving and harried by their Native American neighbors, the colonists must have thought Powhatan's offer absurd and humiliating. They had crossed the Atlantic fully intending, indeed with instructions from the Virginia Company, to subjugate the natives and convert them to Christianity. "We shall by degrees chaung their barbarous natures, make

"*Virginia | Discovered and Described by Captain John Smith, 1606; Graven by William Hole.*" Published in 1612, this map shows the Chesapeake region and Native American place-names. Chief Powhatan is depicted inside a longhouse in the upper left-hand corner. *Library of Congress.*

them ashamed . . . of their savadge nakednes, informe them of the true god, and . . . teach them obedience to the kings Majestie," wrote William Strachey of the colonists' intentions. But the desperate winter of 1608 was no time for such condescension. Smith agreed to the terms, and Powhatan sent food, fulfilling his part of the bargain.[10]

The colonists, however, reneged on the deal. Not only did they remain at Jamestown, but Smith began probing the soft edges of Powhatan's territory to assess the military strength of the local population and map King James I's new domain. In June and July 1608, he made the first of two voyages up the Chesapeake and its tributaries, sailing in an open barge with a crew of fourteen. The men surveyed several river systems of the Eastern Shore before recrossing the bay to explore the Patapsco and Potomac Rivers.[11]

Unsurprisingly, Powhatan took offense and directed his subject chiefs to hound the exploring party. Along the banks of the lower Potomac, "all the woods were layd with ambuscado's to the number of three or foure thousand Salvages so strangely paynted, grimed and disguised, shouting, yelling and crying as so many spirits from hell could not have shewed more terrible," Smith wrote in his diary.[12]

The harassment ceased only when Smith passed out of Powhatan's domain to the upper Potomac, where he became the first European to explore what is now Washington, D.C. When he reached "Moyaones, Nacotchtant and Toags" in mid-July, he wrote, "the people did their best to content us." The three villages were part of the Piscataway Confederacy and likely greeted the explorers warmly because they hoped to ally themselves with the English against Powhatan, who had been expanding up the Potomac in recent years.[13]

If Powhatan initially had viewed the colonists as troublesome but nonetheless valuable allies, he now saw them as a threat. On Smith's return to Jamestown, Powhatan summoned him to a tense meeting at which the chief accused the colonists of harboring grand designs on his territory: "Your coming hither is not for trade but to invade my people and possess my country." Within a few short months, relations between the English and the confederacy deteriorated into warfare. The First Powhatan War, as the colonists and their descendants came to call it, lasted for five years and temporarily halted colonists' exploration of the Chesapeake. With the English hunkered down in Jamestown, the Nacostines saw few Europeans and experienced little disruption to their way of life in the decade after contact.[14]

"They Knew That Our Trade Might Hinder Their Benefit": English Traders Disrupt Native Networks

Though John Smith was the first Englishman to see Nacotchtank, none knew the village and its inhabitants better than the trader Henry Fleet. Born to wealth in Chatham, England, Fleet came to the Chesapeake in fall 1621 as part of the delegation accompanying his second cousin, newly appointed Virginia governor Sir Francis Wyatt. No more than twenty years old when he disembarked at Jamestown, Fleet hoped to make his fortune in the New World.

Initially, this looked to be an easy task. Wyatt and his delegation had traveled to Virginia to assume control of a growing colony seemingly at peace with its Native American neighbors. In 1614, the colonists won the First Powhatan War, and as part of the negotiated peace Powhatan agreed to supply the English with food and honor their claim to the prime farming land they had captured along the James River. Capitalizing on John Rolfe's experiments with tobacco cultivation, they used this land to raise a crop of two thousand pounds in 1615. The plant fetched a high price back in England, where it had become fashionable among the royal court. Having found the colony's cash crop, the Virginia Company imported hundreds of indentured servants, expanded cultivation, and exported forty thousand pounds in 1620. By the time Wyatt arrived, the colonists had become so focused on tobacco production that they had neglected their charge to explore the Chesapeake and convert the Native Americans to Christianity. His principal assignment was to refocus their energies.[15]

Wyatt never had the chance to implement his reforms. On the morning of March 22, 1622, just five months after Wyatt had arrived, Powhatan warriors casually walked onto the eighty-odd plantations scattered along the James River, asked to borrow hoes, shovels, and other tools, then proceeded to beat and hack their hosts to death. Within a matter of hours, they had killed 347 men, women, and children, fully one-fourth of the English population. Opechancanough, Powhatan's younger brother and the mastermind behind the assault, aimed to force the English to retreat to Jamestown and pay tribute to the confederacy.[16]

The attack brought calls for blood from London. Concluding that the natives were hopelessly savage, Virginia Company officials abandoned their dreams of assimilating and converting the local population and instead called on colonists to "destroy them who sought to destroy us."[17] Wyatt and his lieutenants launched the Second Powhatan War in 1622 and spent ten years conducting harvest raids against hostile chiefdoms. They stole corn, burned villages, and left their foes hungry and exposed on the eve of winter—a practice the English had pioneered in the Nine Years' War against the "savage" Irish. Ever aware of their economic interests, the governor and other plantation owners used the purloined corn to feed their indentured servants, who in turn devoted their labors to growing tobacco.[18]

Unlike during the First Powhatan War, Nacotchtank did not escape the violence. Scrambling for allies, the English approached the Patawomekes, an independent chiefdom that dominated the area around present-day Quantico, Virginia. The Patawomekes sought their own benefit in the hostilities, and they consented to an alliance if the English joined them in a raid on their "sworne enemies," the Piscataways to the north. The English agreed, and together they set upon Nacotchtank, killing eighteen men, plundering the food stores, and burning the houses. Among the raiders that day was Henry Fleet.[19]

The Nacostines struck back in March 1623, when Fleet returned to Nacotchtank to barter for corn. Nacostine warriors overwhelmed the English traders, killing twenty and taking Fleet hostage. Governor Wyatt sent a military expedition against the Nacostines—he bragged that they "burnt their houses & a marvelous quantity of corn"—but Fleet remained in captivity until the colonists paid a ransom for his release four years later.[20]

Ironically, Fleet's time in Nacotchtank gave him the skills necessary to establish the English as the dominant traders on the Potomac. He became intimately familiar with the geography of the river and "better proficient in the Indian language than mine own," he recalled. After his release, he and his two brothers set out to monopolize trade along the upper Potomac. In spring 1632, they scoured the area for furs, even stopping at Nacotchtank, where they came away with an impressive haul of eight hundred pelts.

Though open to trading with the Fleets, the Nacostines balked when the brothers attempted to deal directly with the tribes above Great Falls. Some years before, the Massawomacks had pushed south from above the Falls, viciously attacking the tribes of the upper Potomac. They designated the conquered Nacostines as their intermediaries who would, in Fleet's words, "convey all such English truck as commeth into this river." Determined to maintain their favored status, the Nacostines sought "to withdraw me from having any commerce with the other Indians," Fleet wrote, "because they knew that our trade might hinder their benefit." Undaunted, Fleet ignored his former captors, sailed up the Potomac, and sent his brother Edward several days' journey by foot to meet the "four kings" of the Massawomacks. Impressed by the Fleets' wares, the kings agreed to cut the Nacostines out of the upper Potomac beaver trade.[21]

The success of Virginia fur traders such as the Fleet brothers drew interest from enterprising investors in London, including the Jesuit Sir George Calvert, the first Lord Baltimore. Animated by the prospect of significant profits as well as a desire to save native souls, Calvert asked King Charles I for a charter for the land between the fortieth parallel and the Potomac River. Calvert died days before his request was granted, and proprietorship of the new colony, Maryland, passed to his son Cecilius. On his arrival in the Chesapeake in 1634, Cecilius Calvert hired Fleet to help him "conforme . . . to the Customes of the Countrey." Fleet did this and more. He introduced Calvert to the Piscataway chief Wannas, who granted the Maryland colonists the abandoned village of Yacomoco on the St. Mary's River, one hundred miles downstream from Nacotchtank, for settlement.[22]

Though their trade networks had been disrupted and English colonists now occupied a permanent settlement on the lower Potomac, the Nacostines remained upon their land, largely undisturbed by the foreigners, save a few traders and Jesuit missionaries, for another thirty years.

To "Occasion a Greater Quantity of Tobacco to Be Made": The English Supplant the Nacostines

The Nacostines' fortunes began to shift in the 1650s, when a decline in beaver prices led Maryland colonists to turn from furs back to tobacco. Tobacco required land—lots of it. The little colony, which had not grown much beyond the immediate vicinity of St. Mary's City in its first two decades, expanded rapidly in the 1650s and 1660s as planters moved north along the Potomac and cleared much of the arable land at the water's edge.[23]

Colonial settlement eventually reached the Nacostines. In 1663, Lord Calvert granted patents on the land at the confluence of the Potomac and the Anacostia (then called the Eastern Branch), including an 860-acre tract to nobleman Thomas Dent, who dubbed the estate Gisborough after his home village in Yorkshire. Under a treaty between the Maryland Assembly and the Piscataways three years later, Calvert created what came to be known as the "Reserve." Though the agreement stipulated that "the severall nacons aforesd [among them 'Anacostanck'] shall continue upon the places where they now live," Calvert centered the Reserve on the Piscataway capital Mayone, forcing the Nacostines to abandon Nacotchtank and settle several miles to the south. A small number stayed closer to home, moving to Analostan (now Roosevelt) Island in the Potomac River. The colonial government did not resist the encampment, and remnants of this group occupied the site into the next century.[24]

By 1670, colonists had claimed all the land in what would later become Washington, but they considered the area a dangerous frontier due to continued raiding by tribes from the north and east. Most of the landowners lived in St. Mary's City and left their claims untouched. In the 1680s, they began sending indentured servants and enslaved people to the area to cut tobacco fields out of the forests. Life in what were called the "Out Plantations" was lonely and difficult. Workers lived on isolated outposts with rudimentary accommodations and suffered repeated assaults from Nacostine and Piscataway warriors unwilling to accept displacement. All lived in fear of an invasion from the north. As late as 1689, rumors of an impending Seneca assault caused planter John Addison to dash off a letter to the sheriff of Charles County requesting arms, "being these parts is soe very naked and lives at soe great a distance."[25]

Addison was the first European of rank to make his home on Nacostine territory. A sailor and owner of a trading company, Addison settled in Maryland in 1677. Following his marriage to the wealthy widow Rebecca Dent, he purchased the upper half of the Gisborough tract, which covered much of the river plain on which Nacotchtank once stood. By 1688, he had built a handsome brick house on a point jutting out into the river, not far from the rotting remains of the Nacostines' old palisade.[26]

In the following decade, Addison and the colonists of the Out Plantations secured the frontier. In 1692, the Maryland Assembly commissioned forts along the colony's northern border and the movement of "white soldiers" between them. Addison directed the construction of the Charles County fort on the Potomac at Little Falls and subsequently received orders to "Raise five Men & a Captain to Range from the flails of Potomock to the falls of Petuxant or in other places where it shall be Needfull to make quest after all skulking Indians."[27] Addison and his "Rangers" patrolled the area, helping clear the way for English settlement north to present-day Bladensburg, Maryland.

Having gained the upper hand along the frontier, the colonists turned on the remaining Piscataways and Nacostines in their midst. They wanted native land to, as Governor Francis Nicholson put it, "occasion a greater quantity of Tobacco to be made." The assembly responded by carving Prince George's County out of upper Charles County, appointing Addison colonel in command of the county militia, and empowering him to "hear and determine all Personall differences that may happen or arise between the Indians & English."[28] Many of these "Personall differences" turned violent, as the Nacostines and Piscataways resisted this latest English incursion on their land and autonomy.[29]

Addison responded sternly to native assaults on colonists. A 1697 attack on one of James Stoddert's slaves drew such a threatening rejoinder that the Piscataways and the Nacostines temporarily fled the Reserve for the hills of northern Virginia. They returned, only to leave permanently in 1701 after accepting an offer from the Pennsylvania governor to settle a reservation on the lower Susquehanna River. In subsequent years they continued to move north and west, fleeing the forward line of European settlement and melding with other Native American groups until, in the late eighteenth century, they disappeared from the historical record.[30]

Back at the confluence of the Potomac and the Eastern Branch, Addison and his fellow colonists created a plantation society ruled by a landed aristocracy. By 1708, Prince George's County boasted well more than four hundred English households. Thomas Addison, who succeeded his father as colonel of the county militia, deemed the area secure enough to disband the Rangers. In the coming decades, the wealthier among these colonists turned increasingly to enslaved Africans and greatly reduced the supply of indentured servants who had served as the base of the colony's white population.[31]

In both Maryland and Virginia, the first towns on the upper Potomac were extensions of the plantations. By 1730, enslaved workers were producing so much tobacco that the Virginia colony established the Hunting Creek Warehouse on the western bank of the Potomac to gather the crop for shipment downriver. The settlement was incorporated as the town of Alexandria in 1749. Four years earlier, Maryland planter George Gordon established a tobacco inspection station at the place where a "rolling road" that stretched north to the farms of the interior met the Potomac. The area around the warehouse became "George Town" in 1751, though the Maryland legislature did not issue a charter until 1789.[32]

The landed families of the region, including the Dents, Addisons, Youngs, and Bealls, used the wealth from their plantations to dominate the region's elected offices. Their children, grandchildren, and great-grandchildren would intermarry, inherit land, assume offices, and monopolize northern Virginia and southern Maryland politics for the next century. Indeed, Addison's great-grandson, Maryland governor George Plater, signed the act of cession that deeded the territory on the Maryland side of the Potomac to the federal government for a capital city in 1791.[33]

The cumulative effects of war, disease, and subjugation decimated the Native Americans of the upper Potomac. Thousands lived in the river valley in 1608, but by 1708, just a few hundred remained—beaten, scattered, and subject to the Crown. Contact itself initially brought little change to Nacotchtank, with few Europeans visiting the village before the 1620s. With the start of the Second Powhatan War, however, the Nacostines were drawn into the violent rhythm of raid and counterraid that characterized native-white relations. The English emerged from the hostilities strengthened and eager to expand while most Native Americans, including the Nacostines, were greatly weakened. During the next thirty years, they were cut out of the valuable trade networks of the upper Potomac and made subject to the Maryland colony.

By the 1660s, the Nacostines, their numbers depleted and their trade networks disrupted, moved first south and then north and west, scrambling to distance themselves from European settlement. On their abandoned lands, the colonists created a plantation society. The few Native Americans who remained watched in anguish as their hunting grounds and corn fields were transformed by European indentured servants and enslaved Africans into tobacco farms; their trade routes made links in a transatlantic commerce joining the Chesapeake to New England and beyond to Europe. The area that would become the nation's capital, like the colonies that stretched north and south along the Atlantic seaboard, was cleared through wars of conquest and settled with coerced labor on stolen land.

When Andrew Ellicott began his survey of the ten-mile square that would become the nation's capital in 1790, the Nacostines were long gone and Nacotchtank was a distant memory—so much so, in fact, that when Thomas Jefferson inquired about the name of the Native Americans who lived along the Eastern Branch, no one could remember. Native American artifacts littered the ground on the sites of the old villages for a century after the founding of the District, but these were later gathered by Smithsonian archaeologists and amateur collectors. In the early twentieth century, the site of Nacotchtank was buried in landfill to make way for a military airstrip that became part of Joint Base Anacostia-Bolling. Today, the only remaining trace of the Nacostines is the river that bears the Latinized version of their name: Anacostia.[34]

TWO

Of Slaving Blacks and Democratic Whites

Building a Capital of Slavery and Freedom, 1790–1815

E'en here, beside the proud Potowmac's stream . . .
Who can, with patience, for a moment see,
The Medley mass of pride and misery,
Of whips and charters, manacles and rights
Of slaving blacks and democratic whites . . .
Away, away—I'd rather hold my neck
By doubtful tenure from a sultan's beck,
In climes, where liberty has scarce been named,
Nor any right but that of ruling claim'd,
Than thus to live, where bastard freedom waves
Her fustian flag in mockery over slaves.
—THOMAS MOORE, "From the City of Washington," 1808

At the southern end of the L'Enfant Promenade in Southwest Washington sits Benjamin Banneker Park, a circular expanse featuring a granite fountain and an appealing overlook of the Potomac River and wharf. Developed in the late 1960s and renamed in honor of Banneker in 1971, it was the first federal park to be named for a black person, celebrating the prominent African American astronomer who helped survey early Washington. Envisioned as part of an effort to create a vibrant waterfront connected to the National Mall, the park now is a relatively inaccessible oasis amid concrete clutter. Like much of the history of early Washington, it is easily overlooked and underappreciated.[1]

Misinformed tour guides claim with a laugh that Washington was "built on a swamp," a dismissive description that defies the geography of the place. In the late 1700s, before the city existed, the land where Banneker Park sits was coveted farmland, prime plantation country with rolling hills and gushing streams that flowed into the teeming Potomac. Barely one hundred feet from Banneker's fountain stood Notley Young's mansion, the heart of an eight-hundred-acre plantation that stretched for almost two miles along the Potomac to where it met the Eastern Branch, covering much of Southwest D.C.

16

Built about 1756, the Young mansion was perched on a raised riverbank two hundred feet from the shore, offering panoramic views from the pillared back porch. Visitors arrived via a tree-lined entrance leading to a stunning two-story brick structure that featured more than a dozen rooms and four impressive chimneys, punctuating each corner of the roof. It was "not inferior to the palaces of some European princes," remarked Irish visitor John O'Connor in 1788. Adjacent to the mansion stood a small chapel where Young, a descendant of one of Maryland's leading Catholic families, could host Mass without leaving the premises and violating the state ban on public Catholic worship.[2]

Notley Young's wealth and prominence could be measured by—and indeed derived in large part from—his status as a slave owner, one of a handful of slaveholders in Maryland who owned more than 100 slaves. Young enslaved 265 people by the time George Washington selected a ten-mile-square area centered on his plantation for the new seat of the national government. Although a handful of Young's enslaved workers lived in the "manor house," the rest stayed in wooden huts downriver. They worked the tobacco and corn fields that stretched from the riverbank hundreds of yards inland. Their labors gave Young and his descendants the wealth and time to become prominent public figures, first in Maryland and later in the budding city of Washington, where Young's son-in-law Robert Brent served as the first mayor.[3]

The area that became Washington was not a tabula rasa, not an uninhabited, swampy wilderness. It was a fully functioning slave society, a land dotted with tobacco plantations owned by powerful slaveholding families. Slavery and the aristocratic political lifestyle that accompanied it defined life in the fields of southern Maryland and northern Virginia that became the national seat of government. The city that grew atop those fields incorporated slavery into every aspect of life.

Indeed, from its inception Washington embodied the contradiction endemic to America itself, the paradoxical juxtaposition of freedom and slavery that bedeviled the nation and ultimately led to the Civil War. Washington was at once the capital of the world's first republic in more than a millennium—and a city where slave labor was integral to economic life. It was a symbol of an aspiring democratic nation—and evidence of the racial limits of American democracy. It was a "citadel of liberty"—and a center of slavery and the slave trade. Few observers could miss the enslaved people in the nation's capital. They worked on public construction projects, they were bought and sold within sight of the Capitol, they drove the hacks that crisscrossed the city, they waited on the men who ran the nation. Early Washington was a Southern city that was immersed in slavery and benefited immensely from it.

Another contradiction embedded into the fabric of the city harked back to the American Revolution. Self-government died early in the District. Not even a generation after Americans went to war to protest "taxation without representation," Congress stripped Washingtonians of democracy's basic unit of currency: the right to vote. Though citizen protests forced Congress to include a modified form of home rule, even elite Washingtonians lacked basic voting rights. The city became a political colony, a district whose fate rested not with the local people who called it home but with the national political leaders who resided there temporarily. Never just a city, Washington became a staging ground for national political battles as free black people, white elites, European immigrants, enslaved people, and national political leaders struggled to determine what "freedom" and "democracy" would mean in the new capital.

"To Sweeten It a Little": The South Wins the Capital

The three men already were legends in revolutionary America when they sat down for dinner in June 1790. One had penned the words that would come to define America and inspire freedom movements worldwide—"We hold these truths to be self-evident, that all men are created equal." Another had provided the intellectual framework for the U.S. Constitution, while the third man at the table was in the process of laying the foundation for the nation's economic system. Thomas Jefferson, James Madison, and Alexander Hamilton had helped to shape many of the fledgling nation's institutions, and over dinner at Jefferson's home in Manhattan they would add one more: the nation's capital. Before dessert was served, these three would come to a momentous agreement on where the permanent capital would be located, a compromise that would have fateful consequences for the future District of Columbia.

The dinner had been Jefferson's idea. He saw it as a way to resolve two intertwined debates that dominated the first Congress to convene after the Constitution was ratified in 1788. These debates—one over the financial power of the federal government and the other over where the federal government would be located—not only revealed the depth of the differences between the North and the South but also set the course of D.C. history by ensuring that the capital would be founded as a slave city.

The day before the dinner, Secretary of State Jefferson had been heading to a meeting with President Washington when he ran into an agitated Alexander Hamilton. A war hero now serving as secretary of the Treasury, Hamilton animatedly told Jefferson that he was growing increasingly alarmed by the nation's economic crisis, which had paralyzed Congress and threatened to rip the country apart. Not even a decade after the Revolutionary War ended in 1783, America's debt, largely incurred while fighting the war, was spiraling out of control. If the country failed to pay its debt, Hamilton feared, it could be shut off from world markets as foreign governments and individual investors, worried that their loans would never be paid back, simply refused to work with or invest in the United States. The young economy would be crippled, perhaps permanently so.[4]

To avoid default, Hamilton proposed a series of financial reforms that included "assumption"—having the federal government assume all state debts and commit itself to paying their full value. He hoped to turn the economic liability of debts into a political asset: national unity and the strengthening of the federal government. But many members of Congress, particularly from Jefferson's native South, vociferously objected to assumption, in part because many of the Southern states had already paid off their debts.[5]

Generally supported by the commerce-oriented North and opposed by the agricultural South, the "assumption" debate highlighted contrasting visions of the role of the federal government. To Hamilton and his allies, including President Washington, a dynamic trading nation required strong, centralized financial institutions and a federal government that could wield powers not specifically spelled out in the Constitution. Hamilton's opponents generally viewed such centralization as suspect, fearing an overreach of federal power and rejecting Hamilton's insistence that the Constitution's "necessary and proper" clause allowed fiscal measures of such huge scope. They believed that the federal government could wield only those powers indispensable to its existence.[6]

The issue was explosive, producing what Jefferson called "the most bitter and angry contests ever known in Congress."[7] Opponents of assumption threatened secession, and they had enough votes to block the measure. Hamilton knew that Jefferson had substantial credibility among the Southern opponents of assumption, and as he and Jefferson paced in front of the president's house, he implored the Virginian to help break the impasse. Jefferson suggested a dinner with Madison, envisioning a compromise that involved the other major political stalemate that had paralyzed Congress: where to place the national seat of government.

At least since 1783, when a band of Continental Army veterans held a raucous protest outside the Pennsylvania State House where the Congress of the Confederation was meeting, many of the nation's leaders had argued that the national seat of government should be directly under the federal government's control. The Confederation Congress had not been the target of the protest—the veterans sought back pay from the Pennsylvania Executive Council—but political leaders such as Hamilton and Madison used the incident to generate fears that the national government could be held hostage to state interests unless it had full control of its capital. Having an independent seat of government separate from existing states, they believed, would strengthen the national government and insulate it from state pressure.[8]

By 1787, this idea had become commonplace among the men who met for the Constitutional Convention. They wrote it into Article I, Section 8 of the Constitution, which authorized Congress to "exercise exclusive Legislation in all Cases whatsoever, over such District (not exceeding ten Miles square) as may, by Cession of particular States, and the acceptance of Congress, become the Seat of the Government of the United States." From this single clause grew the city we now know as Washington, D.C.

The Constitution was specific about the maximum size of the District but not its location. In late 1789, Congress began deliberating about where to locate this "Seat of Government." At the time, few people used the word "capital," a word with a sense of grandeur and scale that seemed ill-fitted to a fledgling republic. Instead of a monumental city akin to Paris or London, many Americans, including Thomas Jefferson, envisioned a humble "federal town" that would house the government and little else. Humble or not, the seat of government promised prestige, prosperity, and power for the place that claimed the prize. Jefferson himself figured that the federal city would generate roughly one million dollars in economic activity annually—more than $1 billion in twenty-first century dollars—and many observers assumed that it inevitably would become a thriving political, economic, and cultural center.[9]

Political leaders and city boosters proposed more than a dozen sites, and in 1789, the House of Representatives voted to place the seat of government on the banks of the Susquehanna River in Pennsylvania. During the next year, however, the Virginians who envisioned a Potomac River capital—including Jefferson and Madison, as well as President Washington—helped engineer a remarkable coup to reverse the House vote and persuade Congress to place the capital in the South. They sought a Southern capital for all the reasons their Northern colleagues did—power, prestige, and economic growth—but also to protect the central institution in Southern life: slavery.[10]

The three men at Jefferson's table well understood the national reach of slavery. For nearly two hundred years, since a Dutch ship first deposited twenty enslaved Africans in Jamestown in 1619, slavery had been a thoroughly national affair. By the time of the American Revolution, race-based, hereditary slavery was entrenched in all the English colonies, from Georgia to Massachusetts.

There were regional differences, however. In the North, yeoman farmers on small plots of land struggled with short growing seasons and relatively infertile soil, making slavery economically viable only on a small scale, if at all. Nearly all Northern slaveholders owned one or two slaves. By 1790, enslaved people composed just 2 percent of the Northern population, and less than 6 percent of enslaved Americans lived in the North. But slavery was critical to many Northern industries, including shipbuilding and sail-making, and Northern companies and individuals financed and dominated the African slave trade in North America.[11]

In the South, slavery flourished in the milder climate and more fertile soil. After failed attempts to subjugate local Native Americans, Southern planters turned to African slavery to provide the labor for their agricultural economy. Though most Southern slaveholders had fewer than five slaves, a significant minority owned dozens, sometimes hundreds, of enslaved people who lived and worked on massive plantations with hundreds or even thousands of acres devoted to staple crops such as tobacco and rice. Two of the three largest slave states were Maryland and Virginia, the states from which the District of Columbia would be carved. About one-third of Maryland residents were enslaved, as were about 40 percent of Virginians. Together, the two states in 1790 were home to nearly four hundred thousand enslaved people, about 55 percent of North America's slave population.[12]

Despite these differences, political leaders during the colonial era generally were committed to preserving the slave system. The Mason-Dixon Line, named for two surveyors who charted the border between Maryland and Pennsylvania, made a cartographical distinction between North and South, but it did not harden into a cultural and ideological barrier until the Revolutionary War era. In the two decades before the war broke out in 1775, an international movement began to challenge the intellectual underpinnings of slavery. For budding slavery opponents, the stirring words of the Declaration of Independence only highlighted the glaring contradiction between the freedom the new nation espoused and the bondage that about one in five of its people endured. As English writer Samuel Johnson caustically observed about American patriots who complained of British tyranny, "How is it that we hear the loudest yelps for liberty among the drivers of negroes?" Many enslaved people themselves began framing their demands in the language of the Revolution, forcing American slaveholders into the uncomfortable position of denying freedom to black people even as they fought for it for themselves.[13]

Some Americans, particularly in the North, began to see slavery as an evil anachronism in an age of freedom. Among the most committed antislavery leaders during the revolutionary period was Alexander Hamilton. The brilliant, illegitimate son of a Caribbean slaveholder, Hamilton believed that slavery "relaxes the sinews of industry, clips the wings of commerce, and introduces misery and indigence in every shape."[14] He was a founding member of the New York Society for Promoting the Manumission of Slaves, one of dozens of anti-slavery organizations that sprouted across the North in the 1780s. By the time of the Constitutional Convention in the summer of 1787, five of seven Northern states had banned slavery.

Many Revolutionary War–era leaders believed that slavery was a moribund institution that would die out of natural economic causes. The institution appeared to be on the wane, not only in the North but also in the Upper South. In Maryland and Virginia, the state legislatures altered their laws to make it easier for owners to emancipate their slaves, helping to encourage the growth of free black communities. Even many Southern slaveholders expressed concern about the institution on which their way of life depended. In his widely read 1784 essay "Notes on the State of Virginia," Jefferson fretted about the "unhappy influence" of slavery on the American people. "The whole commerce between master and slave is a perpetual exercise of the most boisterous passions, the most unremitting despotism on the one part, and degrading submissions on the other." Washington, too, felt that slavery was incompatible with a nation built on freedom. Influenced by his own experience as a slaveholder and the arguments of his vehemently antislavery friend the Marquis de Lafayette, he claimed, "There is not a man living who wishes more sincerely than I do, to see a plan adopted for the abolition" of slavery, which he considered "the only unavoidable subject of regret."[15]

For all their intellectual anguish, however, few Southern slaveholders made the leap between the abstract idea of freedom and the concrete action of emancipation. Even slaveholders sympathetic to the moral dilemmas of slavery shrank from the social ostracism and economic loss that emancipation entailed. Washington, despite his private laments, held his slaves until his death. So, too, did James Madison, who worried about the potentially revolutionary impact that freedom could have on the slave system. After having lived in Philadelphia for four years during the war, Madison feared that one of his enslaved people, Billey, was "too thoroughly tainted to be a fit companion for fellow slaves in Virginia." Though he recognized that Billey "covet[ed] that liberty for which we have paid the price of so much blood, and have proclaimed so often to be right, and worthy the pursuit, of every human being," Madison sold him.[16]

Slavery remained the bedrock of the Southern economy, and questions about its legitimacy only heightened the sense of siege that many white Southerners felt. At the Constitutional Convention, slavery lurked as an unwelcome reminder of the growing differences between the two regions. "It seemed now to be pretty well understood that the real difference of interests lay, not between the large & small but between the N. & Southn States," Madison wrote with dismay halfway through the convention. "The institution of slavery & its consequences formed the line of discrimination."[17]

That "difference of interests" revealed itself during the debate over where to place the nation's seat of government. Feeling besieged by the more populous North and the ever-expanding West, Southerners feared that placing the capital in the North—particularly anywhere near Philadelphia, the locus of the American antislavery movement—ultimately would undermine slavery and diminish Southern power. Their fears only grew in early 1790, when a group of Quakers presented Congress with two petitions demanding an end to the African slave trade. A third petition from the Pennsylvania Abolition Society (led by the esteemed Benjamin Franklin) encouraged Congress to abolish slavery altogether. The petitions triggered a tremendous backlash in Congress and stiffened Southern resolve to place the nation's seat of government within the slave South.[18]

As the spring of 1790 wore on, neither the debate over the capital nor the battle over the financial system had been resolved. Hamilton and his supporters lacked the votes they needed to get assumption through Congress, while Madison and his allies struggled to secure enough votes to put the capital on the Potomac. Jefferson, hardly a disinterested observer, stepped in to broker a deal over dinner at his rented home at 57 Maiden Lane in Manhattan.

The meal was prepared by Jefferson's enslaved chef, James Hemings, the twenty-five-year-old unacknowledged half-brother of Jefferson's late wife, Martha. Hemings recently had returned from serving Jefferson for five years in France, where he learned to speak French and witnessed the revolutionary fervor that gripped that country. His enslaved sister, Sally, soon would become Jefferson's mistress, bearing four children with a striking resemblance to the future president. Sally Hemings's children eventually would be freed, as would James himself. The only enslaved people Jefferson ever manumitted were kin to Sally Hemings. Like the issue of slavery itself, Hemings's quiet presence at the dinner was an ever-present reminder that the weighty discussions about freedom among the brightest minds of the young American nation were made possible in no small part by the enslaved laborers in their midst.[19]

At the dinner, Hamilton, Madison, and Jefferson hammered out the essence of an agreement. They came to terms first on the assumption bill. "It was observed," Jefferson recalled, "that this pill would be peculiarly bitter to the Southern States, and that some concomitant measure should be adopted to sweeten it a little to them." The "anodyne" would be to place the capital on the Potomac.

Thus, in exchange for Southern votes in favor of assumption, Hamilton would persuade his Northern allies to allow the seat of government to be located in the South. Hamilton, one of the nation's leading antislavery advocates, in effect had sacrificed his principles on slavery to pursue his national economic agenda.[20]

The legislation that emerged from the deal was titled the Residence Act of 1790, for it determined where the government would "reside." Passed in July, the law gave President Washington the power to choose a spot for the national capital along the Potomac somewhere between the mouth of the Eastern Branch and Conococheague Creek, seventy miles upstream. Maryland and Virginia would cede the necessary land to the federal government. As a sop to Pennsylvanians who had hoped for a Susquehanna River site, Congress agreed to move the federal government to Philadelphia for ten years while the new seat of government was under construction. Congress would appoint three commissioners to oversee construction and prepare for the government's arrival in 1800.

The compromise secured the nation's financial future and legitimated the doctrine of implied powers—two enormous victories for Hamilton and the Federalist Party. But the deal had devastating consequences for the future city of Washington. "I have always regretted that the Capital of the United States was moved from New York or Philadelphia," wrote D.C. civil rights leader Mary Church Terrell in 1940. "If it had been located in the North, East, or West the status of colored people would be far better than it is."[21]

Safely ensconced between two of the country's largest slave states, the new city likely would support slavery and the domestic slave trade. Instead of having its roots in the North, where the seeds of antislavery already had taken hold, Washington would be tethered to the slave South. Rather than being nurtured in a bustling, cosmopolitan, urban area, the capital would grow in plantation country and would retain its rural, Southern character for generations to come. Instead of commingling with the strong and growing free black and antislavery communities in Philadelphia, Washington residents and visitors would witness slave traders marching their coffles of enslaved men and women through the city.

The grand bargain struck over Jefferson's dinner table came with a tremendous price.

"Not Excelled for Commanding Prospect":
Visions of a Grand Capital Rising on the Potomac

For James Hoban, the proposed national capital offered the chance of a lifetime. Born in Ireland, Hoban was a skilled architect from the renowned Royal Dublin Academy who moved to America shortly after the Revolutionary War. Settling in Charleston, South Carolina, he accommodated himself to local custom, becoming a slave owner with a trusted team of enslaved carpenters. Together, they built the Charleston County Courthouse, a magnificent building that caught the attention of George Washington during a presidential visit to the port city. In 1792, President Washington and the city commissioners selected Hoban as the winner of a design competition for the president's house in the new national seat of government.[22]

Like the capital itself, Hoban depended on enslaved labor to make the most of his opportunity. He moved to the city late that year, bringing five enslaved men with him: Ben, Daniel, Harry, Peter, and Tom. Though Hoban later would sign a petition calling for an end to slavery in the city, he remained a slave owner until he died in 1831. Hoban's slaves joined with more than a dozen white carpenters, as well as dozens of unskilled laborers, white and black, to work on the massive project. Hoban particularly sought out Irish immigrants, whom he encouraged to join the local militia that he formed. Hoban's racially mixed crew of free and enslaved laborers worked feverishly to meet the timeline demanded by Washington and the commissioners.[23]

President Washington selected the site for the seat of government where Hoban and his crew worked. An austere, intimidating visionary universally revered by a grateful nation, Washington was given wide latitude to select the site and plan the capital. The president embraced the challenge with the vigor of a young lieutenant and the passionate interest of a speculator. An unabashed nationalist, he embraced Alexander Hamilton's vision of a commercial nation that would expand westward and develop into an economic power, and he viewed the Potomac as the natural opening to the West. Before he became president, he helped launch and run the Patowmack Company, which planned to turn the Potomac into a bustling waterway that connected the Atlantic to the abundant Ohio River valley.

The president saw the federal city as the embodiment of the nation's aspirations. The site on the Potomac, he believed, was a blank slate for which he envisioned a grand national capital that would outshine the cities of Europe and become a proper citadel for the growing republic. Building this symbolic city would be a fitting capstone to his own career and would help ensure the long-term survival of the nation he helped create.

Commercial considerations were at the forefront of his mind when he chose the site for the federal city. Given a range of seventy miles along the Potomac from which to select a site, Washington focused immediately on the area he knew best: the southernmost section, less than two miles from his hilltop home of Mount Vernon. The site, Washington boasted, was "not excelled for commanding prospect, good water, salubrious air, and safe harbour by any in the world." It was far enough upstream from the Atlantic Ocean to make a foreign naval invasion unlikely, and it stood just downstream from Great Falls, the northernmost extent of navigable water. "I have no doubt," he wrote to a friend, that the capital, "from the advantages given to it by nature, and its proximity to a rich interior country, and the western territory, [will] become the emporium of the United States."[24]

In January 1791, President Washington told Congress that he had selected the area at the confluence of the Potomac and Eastern Branch, including the existing port village of Georgetown, Maryland. He implored members to amend the legislation so that the seat of government also could include the town of Alexandria several miles south of the mouth of the Eastern Branch. The decision had significant implications for the racial development of the capital city. At the time, Alexandria was a growing port of more than 2,700 people, almost 20 percent of whom were enslaved. By the 1830s, its many slave dealers would help D.C. become the top slave-trading city in the nation. Incorporating the flourishing port into the boundaries of the federal district solidified the hold that slavery would have on the fledgling capital.[25]

Congress assented to Washington's selection. Maryland ceded roughly seventy square miles, Virginia ceded about twenty, and another ten were covered by the Potomac. Washington then appointed as commissioners three close friends who served as directors of the Patowmack Company and shared his vision of making the new capital a commercial center as well as a seat of government. Thomas Johnson was a feisty former governor of Maryland who had taken over the company after Washington resigned. Daniel Carroll of Rock Creek was a cosmopolitan Catholic (his brother Bishop John Carroll helped launch Georgetown College) who was among the few Southerners in Congress who had switched their votes on assumption to secure the capital on the Potomac. David Stuart was a dour Virginia planter and doctor who became the president's son-in-law when he married the widow of Martha Washington's son.[26]

All three men—like the new capital's most prominent supporters, President Washington and Secretary of State Jefferson—owned enslaved people: Johnson enslaved thirty-eight people on his Frederick, Maryland, plantation; Carroll owned more than fifty slaves on his plantation in what is now Forest Glen, Maryland; and Stuart and his wife had a one-third interest in the three hundred enslaved people who worked on their Abingdon Plantation in Alexandria, where Reagan National Airport now sits.[27]

The first order of business was to conduct a thorough survey of the area to locate boundaries for the new city. For that task the commissioners chose thirty-eight-year-old surveyor Andrew Ellicott, a Quaker and Revolutionary War veteran who came recommended by James Madison. Perhaps the nation's top surveyor, Ellicott often worked with his two brothers, but they were committed to other jobs when Jefferson summoned him to the Potomac. Needing an able assistant to accompany him, Ellicott invited Benjamin Banneker, a free, self-taught black mathematician and amateur astronomer who lived alone near Ellicott's cousin George in Baltimore County, Maryland.[28]

It was an inspired choice. Sixty years old in early 1791, the white-haired Banneker had retired from tobacco farming due to rheumatism, but he remained a sharp astronomical observer. Taught to read and write by his white grandmother, Banneker went to school for only a few weeks in his life, but he was a quick study. He learned astronomy by watching George Ellicott conduct observations. Ellicott loaned him books and instruments, and soon Banneker began conducting his own observations and detecting discrepancies in generally accepted calculations. By the time Andrew Ellicott called on him, he had spent more than a year making nightly observations and calculations. Though Ellicott was initially wary of bringing on an unschooled black man as an assistant, he hired Banneker and the two made their way to Alexandria in early February.[29]

Their task was to survey and mark the city's boundaries, battling the elements, wildlife, and skeptical property-owners along the way. Ellicott had a team of six laborers who spent two months hacking through brush, wading creeks, and charting the ten-mile sides of the diamond-shaped federal district. (After they blazed an initial border, they returned to clear twenty feet along either side of the boundary, placing stone markers every mile—thirty-six of the original markers remain visible today in or near their original spots.) Banneker, too old to do much of the heavy physical work, concentrated on the intellectual tasks of calibrating instruments, making mathematical projections, and calculating distances accurately. He spent much of his time in the observation tent using a variety of scientific instruments to observe the stars each night. During his off-hours, he worked on an almanac that he published later that year.[30]

Banneker's work earned the respect of local white people, including the commissioners. As George Ellicott's daughter recalled, "His striking superiority over all men of his race whom they had met, led them to disregard all prejudice of caste, and converse freely with him, and enjoy the clearness and originality of his remarks." The *Georgetown Weekly Ledger* claimed in March 1791 that his "abilities as a surveyor and astronomer clearly prove that Mr. Jefferson's concluding that race of men were void of mental endowments was without foundation."[31]

Banneker, however, rejected the idea that he was somehow uniquely talented and thus deserving of exceptional praise. Instead, he insisted that with freedom all black people could develop into contributing members of society. He made this argument directly to Thomas Jefferson in a remarkable August 1791 letter, which he sent to the secretary of state along with his almanac. Having himself "abundantly tasted of the fruition of those blessings which proceed from that free and unequalled liberty with which you are favoured," Banneker challenged Jefferson to extend those blessings to all black people and "eradicate that train of absurd and false ideas and opinions which so generally prevails with respect to us." Back during the Revolutionary War, Banneker reminded him, Jefferson "clearly saw into the injustice of a State of Slavery" and penned the immortal words of the Declaration of Independence. How, then, could he justify "detaining by fraud and violence so numerous a part of my brethren under groaning captivity and cruel oppression"?[32]

Impressed with Banneker's work (and perhaps by the boldness of his letter), Jefferson responded quickly, writing in a public letter, "No body wishes more than I do to see such proofs as you exhibit, that nature has given to our black brethren, talents equal to those of the other colours of men, & that the appearance of a want of them is owing merely to the degraded condition of their existence both in Africa & America." In private, however, he questioned whether Banneker had done the work himself.[33]

Banneker's accomplishments and the success of Ellicott's interracial survey team raised at least the possibility of a capital city founded on free, rather than enslaved, labor. In the afterglow of the Revolutionary War, with egalitarian rhetoric fresh in the public mind, there was nothing inevitable about the imposition of slavery in the new federal city. But the decisions of the city commissioners and the federal leaders who supervised them would soon foreclose that possibility.

As Ellicott and his team surveyed the land, Washington turned to his highly regarded wartime adviser, Peter Charles L'Enfant, to design the city. L'Enfant shared Washington's vision for a sweeping, symbolic capital that would become the center of a vast republican empire. Presented with Jefferson's draft of a simple "federal town" laid out along a familiar grid pattern, L'Enfant responded contemptuously, calling all such grids "tiresome and insipid." Instead, he developed a stunning plan for a grand city with wide boulevards, abundant parks, and diagonal streets resembling rays of light (to represent liberty and democracy) radiating out from the Capitol. Rejecting the decorative government buildings of European capitals, L'Enfant chose classic Greek architecture. He wanted to give the new city what the commissioners called a "Republican simplicity" that contrasted with the trappings of monarchy of the Old World while also communicating the timeless aesthetic appeal and values of Athenian democracy.[34]

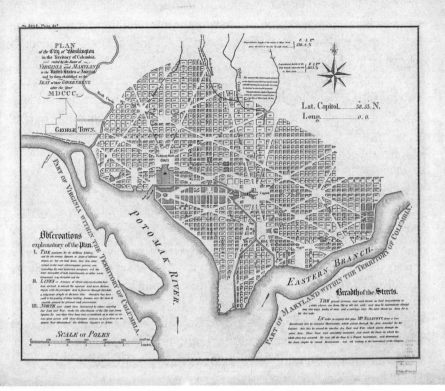

"Plan of the City of Washington in the Territory of Columbia." This facsimile of a 1792 engraving shows surveyor Andrew Ellicott's rendition of Peter L'Enfant's plan for Washington City. The plan extended as far north as Boundary Street (today's Florida Avenue). Library of Congress.

President Washington embraced the plan, but L'Enfant, impetuous and impolitic in temperament, antagonized Jefferson and others whom he might have been wise to court. When the commissioners asked for copies of L'Enfant's plan to prepare for a government land auction that would finance the construction of the city, the haughty engineer demurred. The standoff resulted in L'Enfant walking off the job, forcing Washington and the city commissioners to turn to Andrew Ellicott to develop a usable blueprint for the city. Having worked closely with L'Enfant on the plan, Ellicott (not Benjamin Banneker, as a later myth would claim) was able to re-create the original plan, to which he made some revisions.

With less than ten years in which to build the national seat of government, the commissioners hustled to attract investors, laborers, and residents to the area. Convinced that the Potomac capital would become a commercial hub, President Washington and the commissioners confidently proposed to auction off land to interested buyers. But the first land auction, held in October 1791, was a disaster—only thirty-five of ten thousand lots sold. The auction's poor results were an ominous sign that the city would not grow as rapidly or smoothly as its boosters hoped.[35]

Not only did district commissioners struggle to attract land buyers, but they also found it difficult to secure free laborers. Initially, they were bullish about the labor market. "People are on tip Toe to come [to Washington] from all parts," they wrote to Secretary of State Jefferson in April 1792. "We might probably have 2000 mechanics [and] labourers here on very short notice." Jefferson was less confident, and he urged them to consider importing workers from Germany and elsewhere in Europe.[36]

The commissioners soon recognized that there were relatively few white workers to be found in the rural area, and that scarcity only made labor more expensive. The anticipated boom in immigration of European workers simply did not materialize. As one French visitor put it, "The few available workmen are unreliable and very expensive to hire." Without significant appropriation from Congress and unable to raise sufficient money from the private lot auctions, the commissioners felt pressure to keep costs down and were unwilling to pay high wages for labor. They realized that there would not be enough white workers to get the job done at the price they wanted to pay.[37]

But they had an alternative: slaves.

"A Very Useful Check": Enslaved Workers Build the Nation's Capital

The commissioners embraced slave labor as a powerful way to control white laborers and minimize costs. "The provisioning of workmen draws after it so many Expences, and so much waste that we have hitherto left them to provide for themselves," the commissioners explained to Jefferson in early 1793. Hence, they needed to find new laborers, "a part of whom we can easily make up of Negroes and find it proper to do so. Those we have employed this Sumer have proved a very useful check & kept our Affairs Cool."[38] In other words, by offering a cheaper alternative, enslaved workers helped the commissioners keep white workers in line.

The nascent capital city committed to making enslaved labor an essential part of its workforce because it was simply too economical and expedient to do otherwise. Instead of purchasing slaves outright, the commissioners resolved "to hire good labouring negroes by the year, the masters cloathing them well and finding each a blanket, the commissioners finding them provisions and paying twenty one pounds a year" to their masters (roughly $55, equivalent to about $27,000 in twenty-first-century dollars). They instructed the city's labor supervisor, Captain Elisha Williams, "to keep the yearly hirelings at work, from sunrise to sunset, particularly the negroes." In one advertisement, they wrote: "Wanted, at the city of Washington a number of Slaves to labor in the Brick Yards, Stone quarries, &c, for which generous wages will be given. Also Sawyers to Saw by the hundred or on wages by the month or year."[39]

Williams, himself a slave owner from a nearby plantation, spent much of his time recruiting and hiring enslaved workers. By 1794, the city had contracted with plantation owners to hire at least forty-six slaves, and that number would grow to more than one hundred in the next few years. That same year, the first slave auction was held within the city limits when Edward Burrows put nine enslaved people, including a mother with two children, up for sale. Combined with the use of enslaved labor by private companies and supplies, more than three hundred enslaved workers were building the nation's capital in 1795. That August, Georgetown enacted an ordinance that banned slaves from drinking liquor and levied a $5 fine on anyone found assisting a runaway slave.[40]

Enslaved laborers worked alongside free workers and did all kinds of jobs. (There were few free black laborers, but one who made a mark on the commissioners was Jerry Holland, described by one surveyor as "justly entitled to the highest wages that is due to our hands" because he was "the best hand in the department.") On daily rations of salt meat, bread, and cornmeal, they felled trees to make way for the broad avenues and spacious federal buildings; they dug ditches to mark the planned squares, wells to support the local population, and foundations for expansive buildings; and they sawed wood, made and laid bricks, and quarried, hauled, and hoisted stone. They were so crucial to the city, Williams told his bosses in 1793, that he "could not have done without them this summer."[41]

Enslaved workers were particularly prominent in the two primary public projects of the day—about half of the two hundred laborers building the president's house and the Capitol were enslaved. When Polish visitor Julian Niemcewicz toured Washington in 1798, he noticed enslaved men working "in large number" on the new Capitol, laboring with their free white counterparts. When white workers disappeared to "drink grog" a few times a day, Niemcewicz observed, "the negroes alone work." He initially thought that the black workers were regularly paid laborers but soon discovered that "they were not working for themselves; their masters hire them out and retain all the money for themselves. What humanity! What a country of liberty. If at least they shared the earnings!"[42]

Slavery became such a powerful local institution that it proved irresistible even to newcomers with antislavery ideals. William Thornton, a British Quaker who won the competition to design the Capitol, moved with his wife, Anna, to Georgetown in 1794 to become one of Washington's commissioners. Born into a slaveholding family on the West Indian island of Tortola, Thornton was a Renaissance man—a painter, sculptor, doctor, and architect. As a young man Thornton rejected his family's embrace of slavery and became an early advocate of emancipation. As commissioner in 1795 he proposed to alleviate the city's shortage of masons by buying "50 intelligent negroes" and offering them their freedom if they agreed to work for five to six years on the Capitol.[43]

The idea went nowhere. Indeed, the longer he stayed in Washington the less antislavery Thornton became. In late 1795, he and his wife purchased a nearby farm, becoming the owners of several enslaved families in the process. Despite his professed beliefs, the economically unstable Thornton did not emancipate his slaves during his lifetime, and Anna Thornton ignored his will and chose not to free them after her husband's death in 1828. An incident at home with one of her enslaved men triggered a race riot in 1835 (see Chapter 3).[44]

Many of the enslaved workers in the city were "hirelings"—slaves hired out from their masters for a contracted period, though without any provision for future freedom. This arrangement offered advantages for the city, slave owners, and even the enslaved workers themselves. For the commissioners, hiring slaves on a short-term basis was a way to get relatively cheap and often skilled labor without bearing the full costs of ownership. Enslaved workers proved easier to manage and supervise than free ones, and their housing, medical care, and long-term employment were the responsibility of the slave owner, not the city. If an enslaved worker did not show up, then the commissioners simply docked the pay they gave to the owners. If one got sick, the commissioners could have him treated at the owner's expense.[45]

Local slave owners liked the arrangement because selling enslaved labor on a temporary basis provided income at a time when their reliance on labor-intensive tobacco farming was waning. More than a century of tobacco cultivation had depleted soils in southern Maryland and northeastern Virginia—one French visitor in the mid-1790s noted that the countryside around Washington featured "barren and bad cultivated lands." As planters shifted to different crops and farming techniques that required fewer workers, they found themselves with an excess of labor. Many families sought to preserve the status that accompanied slave ownership, so instead of selling their enslaved workers, they hired them out. With each hired slave earning between $55 and $65 a year, the practice was lucrative enough that slave owners from as far away as Charles and St. Mary's Counties in Maryland sought to hire their enslaved people out for work in the capital. Two of the commissioners and some of the city's labor overseers joined in as well.[46]

For the enslaved workers, being hired out offered a sliver of freedom in an otherwise impervious system. They often were hired for extended periods of time—months or even a full year—which required them to find housing in town. Though they worked in harsh conditions, they did so far from the oppressive oversight of the master and his minions, and they worked alongside free laborers. The prospect of working off the plantation proved tantalizing for some enslaved people, and they ran away to the city. One Maryland slaveholding family put out an ad for two slaves, Clem and Will, "who were last seen on their way to the City of Washington with their broad axes and some other tools." Clem and Will, like many black people in their time and in generations to come, may have seen Washington as a step closer to freedom.[47]

For white laborers, the turn to slavery as a source of labor in the nation's capital was an economic disaster. Slavery undermined the economic leverage that free workers could use to bargain for higher wages. As the commissioners well understood, enslaved labor provided a "very useful check" on white workers—it was difficult to fight for higher wages or better working conditions when employers could hire dirt-cheap replacements off nearby plantations.

Once established as a common source of labor, slavery created a self-perpetuating economic cycle that depressed wages and discouraged white migration to the area. Initially, with an unproven project and a limited budget, city leaders struggled to recruit sufficient free labor to get the job done. The limited supply of labor pushed wages higher, making it economically more expedient and tempting to use enslaved workers. As slaves played a larger role in building the capital, the city became even less attractive to white workers. Knowing that employers could hire enslaved competitors, white workers had to accept lower wages and harsher working conditions than they otherwise might have tolerated. These conditions, in turn, made it even harder to recruit white laborers as potential migrants avoided Washington in favor of Northern cities where they did not have to compete against slave labor.

Despite their lack of leverage, white workers in Washington regularly resisted the commissioners' efforts to keep wages low. Sometimes, their complaints revealed their resentment of their black coworkers. In 1794, white stonecutters working on the President's House demanded that they be allowed to take on only white apprentices; the commissioners acquiesced. Three years later, a group of white laborers complained that enslaved workers on public projects were overpaid; in response, the commissioners temporarily banned black carpenters from working on the Capitol or the President's House.[48]

But such collective efforts to ban enslaved and free black employment foundered on the shoals of economic incentive. For the commissioners, the black presence allowed them to build the city far more cheaply and quickly than they otherwise could have, and they would not relinquish that valuable option. Because slavery quickly became a well-used source of labor, racial divisions became embedded into the fabric of the new capital. Congress's decision to put the city on the Potomac, President Washington's selection of a site that incorporated the cities of Alexandria and Georgetown, the appointment of three slaveholders as the city's first commissioners, the commissioners' turn to slave labor—all had the effect of turning the District into a city heavily dependent on slavery.

By the time that the federal government officially moved to Washington in November 1800, the city's population had swelled to fourteen thousand, including more than three thousand enslaved residents. Within Washington City itself (not including Georgetown, Alexandria, or the unincorporated county areas), enslaved people made up more than 25 percent of the population. The presence of significant numbers of black people, both enslaved and free, shaped the contours of the new city.

"A Collection of Slaves in the Bosom of a Nation of Freemen":
D.C. Residents Challenge Taxation without Representation

For all the boosterish rhetoric about its potential, Washington remained a rural backwater when the national government moved to town. The completed President's House and north wing of the Capitol gave a glimpse of future grandeur, but the surrounding area remained undeveloped. "I look in vain for the city & see no houses," lamented Margaret Bayard Smith, a newlywed from Philadelphia whose husband, Samuel, launched the city's most prominent newspaper, the *National Intelligencer*. L'Enfant had intended for Washington to be a "city of magnificent distances," but in an era before mechanized transportation his plan made the place magnificently inconvenient. The exceptionally wide boulevards "are never repaired; deep ruts, rocks, and stumps of trees, every minute impede your progress, and often threaten your limbs with dislocation," groused one English visitor.[49]

The city was undeveloped politically as well as physically. Devised as an experiment in congressional planning and control, Washington was saddled with an ambiguous political status and an undetermined economic future. Though touted as a "citadel of liberty," it was profoundly undemocratic. As in the rest of the United States, the vast majority of the population—women, the poor, and people of color, enslaved and free—were systematically excluded from public life and decision making in the city. But what was unusual about Washington was that the poor shared their disenfranchised fate with the city elite. Almost—but not quite—from its inception, D.C. was denied the basic rights of democracy.

As Washington was being built, Congress mandated that residents abide by the laws of the states that had ceded the land. On the eastern bank of the Potomac they were governed by Maryland's laws, while on the western bank Virginia's laws ruled. The Constitution gave Congress the power to "exercise exclusive legislation" in the federal district, but few in Congress would have predicted that the citizens of the national capital would be denied the rights and privileges of residents of a state. James Madison argued in The Federalist Papers that the states that ceded land for the District would safeguard the rights of city residents and that "a municipal Legislature, for local purposes, derived from their own suffrages, will of course be allowed them." Men such as Notley Young—the white, male landowners of the city—continued to vote in local, state, and national elections through November 1800. In the presidential election of 1800, Young and other eligible Washington City residents trekked to Bladensburg, Maryland, to cast their ballots along with other free American voters.[50]

That soon would change.

The elections of 1800 brought Thomas Jefferson and his Republican allies to power, spelling the end of Federalist rule. The peaceful transition from one party to its opposition is rightfully hailed as a signal achievement in American politics, but the election exacted a heavy toll on democracy in the District. During the several months between the election and Jefferson's inauguration, the lame-duck Federalists in Congress scrambled to consolidate as much power in the federal government as possible before their small-government Republican foes took control. The two parties had spent the previous decade sparring over the scope of many of the powers enumerated in the Constitution. One last battle loomed: what to do with the District of Columbia.

Federalists interpreted the "exercise exclusive legislation" clause as broadly as possible to advance their larger agenda of centralizing federal power. An initial bill proposed by Federalist Virginian Henry Lee in December 1800 empowered Congress to serve, in essence, as the local legislature for the federal city. While Georgetown and Alexandria would retain their municipal governments, residents of Washington City would have none, and no District residents would be allowed to vote in national or federal elections.[51]

As word of the Federalist bill spread—Samuel Harrison Smith's new National Intelligencer newspaper gave residents daily reports on congressional activity—concerned white Washingtonians objected vociferously. Much of the city's white community supported having Congress remain in control of the District. A petition signed by more than two hundred residents, including Notley Young and James Hoban, called on Congress to "assume the Jurisdiction of the Territory" and to create "a Code of Laws for the government thereof." They did not want the District to remain under the jurisdiction of Maryland or Virginia, fearing that if Congress did not assume control, then Washington might lose its hold on being the seat of government—there were still plenty of members of Congress, particularly from Pennsylvania, who hoped to woo the capital back to the North.[52]

City residents, however, refused to concede that congressional control implied a loss of their rights to self-government and suffrage. Perhaps the most impassioned advocate for self-rule was a twenty-six-year-old New Yorker named Augustus Brevoort Woodward. Woodward, who would later go west and earn lasting fame as the first chief justice of Michigan and a founder of the University of Michigan, was an unforgettable character. Gangly limbed with a prominent nose, he had an eccentric manner that struck his admirers as a sign of brilliance and his detractors as evidence of pomposity. An attorney by trade but a visionary by temperament, Woodward authored a series of eight essays that began appearing in the *National Intelligencer* in late 1800, when Congress first debated how to govern the District.[53]

Woodward's essays brimmed with indignation at the idea of Congress serving as the city's local legislature. "No policy can be worse than to mingle *great* and *small* concerns," he argued. "The latter become absorbed in the former; are neglected and forgotten." Congress, he feared, would be too easily distracted by national concerns to "regard with proper attention the minute necessities of a town, a City or a District." Not only was congressional control simply bad for the District; it would also "impair the *dignity*" of federal authorities "to be occupied with all the local concerns of the Territory of Columbia." Woodward laid out in painstaking detail how the District could remain a federal city under congressional jurisdiction yet enjoy both self-government and representation in Congress.[54]

Federalists in Congress ignored such nuance. After debate on the District was interrupted by a national electoral crisis that consumed congressional attention for a month, Congress hurriedly passed the Organic Act in late February 1801, proving Woodward correct that local concerns routinely would get trumped by national issues. The bill consolidated Congress's control of the capital by placing the three developed areas of the District—Washington City, Georgetown, and Alexandria—under the exclusive control of Congress and the President. It organized the unincorporated territory within the District into two counties: the County of Washington (on the Maryland side) and the County of Alexandria (on the Virginia side).

No longer were the residents of these areas considered citizens of Maryland or Virginia; no longer could they vote for president; no longer could they help choose representatives in Congress. Instead, they were disfranchised federal subjects. Or, as Representative James Asheton Bayard of Delaware kindly explained, D.C. residents "are children, over whom it is not our wish to tyrannise, but whom we would foster and nurture."[55] Just a generation after "no taxation without representation" had been the rallying cry for the Revolutionary War, District residents lost the right to vote in all elections. Not for the last time, their rights were sacrificed for the sake of a larger national agenda.

Continued complaints from local advocates of self-rule encouraged the new Republican Congress to incorporate Washington City and establish a municipal government consisting of a mayor appointed by the president and an elected council. (Georgetown and Alexandria retained their municipal governments.) This limited home rule allowed the city's small population of white male landowners to vote, and in the election of 1802 about 90 percent of them did. Given the limitations on voting, there were only 233 votes for a slate of twenty-three candidates. Despite the concessions, the federal government remained firmly in control of the District. Not only did the president appoint the mayor, but Congress also retained veto power over any local legislation. With such restrictions on their ability to govern themselves, District residents "can regard ourselves in no higher light than a collection of slaves in the bosom of a nation of freemen," seethed Woodward.[56]

The demise of political democracy—even the District's highly restricted democracy—would haunt the city. Even the most elite Washingtonians remained supplicants who could petition, protest, and plead for congressional support and approval, but they could not hold their political patrons accountable. Within a few months of the city's birth as the national capital, not even a full generation after the Revolutionary War, the disfranchisement of District residents was codified into federal law. More than two centuries later that political impotence remained.

The lack of genuine self-government or representation in the national legislature meant not only that District residents lacked basic rights but also that the city inevitably would become a pawn in federal power struggles and a laboratory for congressional experiments. Able to control Washington directly yet unaccountable to its citizens, Congress and individual lawmakers could exert far more influence on local matters in the city than they could elsewhere. Just as

Federalists used the District's uncertain political status to advance their larger agenda about federal power, members of Congress routinely used local issues to pursue national ends. This mingling of *"great and small concerns"* would have a profound effect—though not always a negative one—on efforts to achieve racial equality long into the future.

"Most of the Inhabitants Are Low People . . . Or Negroes":
Workers, Enslaved and Free, in Early Washington

For most of the city's residents, the lack of political representation was hardly noteworthy or unusual. Most Washingtonians were neither educated like Augustus B. Woodward nor landed like Notley Young; instead, they were poor, uneducated, and landless. As Treasury Secretary Oliver Wolcott complained, "Most of the inhabitants are low people, whose appearance indicates vice and intemperance, or negroes."[57]

Secretary Wolcott may have betrayed the condescension of his class, but he had a point: most of the city's residents were low-income manual or domestic laborers. Because the city remained in a seemingly permanent state of construction, the white people whom it predominantly attracted were laborers who had to work alongside and compete with enslaved and free black workers. Of the white men whose occupations were identified in the 1800 census, 75 percent were laborers, while less than 8 percent were professionals or "gentlemen." Just 233 of 4,000 white males in the city owned real property worth $100 or more.[58]

Many of the city's white workers were Irish—about half the city's white population, according to one early observer. Although that estimate was exaggerated, Irish workers and artisans (often called "mechanics") were a vital part of the growing city and would play an important role in its racial history. Whereas the United States had broken free from its colonial masters, Ireland in the late eighteenth century remained under British control. The American Revolution inspired many Irish to flee their native land in search of opportunity across the Atlantic. As one optimistic Irish businessman proclaimed on a sign outside his business: "Peter Rodgers, saddler, from the green fields of Erin and tyranny, to the green streets of Washington and liberty."[59]

The first Irish immigrants arrived in what would become Washington in the 1780s. Like many unskilled white immigrants, they were indentured—they owed a term of service to the Patowmack Company, which paid their passage to America. About two hundred Irish workers helped dig a canal around the impassable Great Falls of the Potomac, just north of Georgetown. Unlike future generations of Irish immigrants, many of the early Irish came to America with little knowledge of English—Irish Gaelic was their native tongue, and they learned English only haltingly. They faced serious discrimination from other white people, particularly Englishmen and Scots who carried traditional animosities toward their Old World neighbors, and like other white workers they were disdained by the city elite. "The lower order of whites are a grade below the negroes in point of intelligence and ten below them in point of civility," sniffed First Lady Abigail Adams. "They look like the refuse of human nature."[60]

White workers struggled to gain an economic foothold in a city where slavery flourished. Though in time the city would become known for its strong free black community, in 1800 nearly 85 percent of Washington's black residents were enslaved. Most lived in households with a handful of enslaved people; only ten families, including Notley Young's, owned ten or more. Enslaved women (who outnumbered their male counterparts by three to two in 1800) served primarily as domestics who cooked, cleaned, and raised children in the homes of white people, while enslaved men did a variety of jobs, from manual labor to domestic service. Because many slave owners in the city had ties to nearby plantations, slaves (particularly men) often shuttled back and forth between city and country as seasonal work demanded.[61]

Washington developed a reputation among white people for being a relatively benign place to be enslaved. In D.C., wrote Englishman John Tolbert, "this unhappy class of men are treated with greater humanity than in most of the slave states." Irish writer D. B. Warden claimed that most Washington slaves were "well clad and nourished." White slave owners often prided themselves on treating their slaves well. "I find that it is not necessary to treat these people harshly in order to be well served," counseled Rosalie Stier Calvert, mistress on a plantation just outside the city. "You must only be firm."[62]

Though this reputation was self-serving, it was true in a relative sense. Compared to life on a rural plantation, slavery in the capital did indeed offer greater opportunities for enslaved people. On isolated plantations, slave owners had almost dictatorial power and could treat their slaves as they pleased; in the city, they had to submit to local authorities, as well as the unwritten pressure exerted by their neighbors' opinions. The urban environment gave enslaved people a chance to spend time beyond the gaze of their owners, and often in the company of free black people. Because city residents generally did not produce most of their own food, tools, or clothing, they bought needed items at city markets such as Center Market at Seventh Street and Pennsylvania Avenue NW. This task generally fell to enslaved women, who used their market time to visit with friends and family. Urban households typically had less work for slaves to do, so owners hired their enslaved workers out to other families in the area. These enslaved people often could live independently, and many lived in small houses along F Street NW and behind St. Patrick's Church on Tenth Street NW.[63]

Charles Ball knew firsthand that the experience of a slave in Washington could be far better than life in the country. Born enslaved on a Calvert County, Maryland, plantation, Ball was raised by his grandfather after his mother was sold away and his despondent father fled to the North. Laboring under a cruel, parsimonious owner, he and his fellow enslaved workers "suffered greatly for want of sufficient and proper food" and "very much from the cold." His owner hired him out to be a cook on a warship anchored at the Navy Yard in Washington, which proved to be an eye-opening experience for the twenty-year-old Ball.[64]

"In the enjoyment of a profusion of excellent provisions, I felt very happy," he later wrote in his 1837 memoir, *A Narrative of the Adventures of Charles Ball, a Black Man*. The officers on the ship gave him clothing and money, and "my duties, though constant, were not burthensome." Allowed "to spend Sunday afternoon in my own way," Ball roamed the streets of the city, often walking as far as Georgetown to see "the new and splendid buildings." During his two years in the city, Ball interacted with many other black people, enslaved and free. He noticed that city slaves tended to be treated better than those on the plantation because, out of a "sense of shame or pride," slave owners provided their enslaved workers "tolerably with both food and clothing, when they know their conduct is subject to the observation of persons, whose good opinion they wish to preserve."[65]

For all its relative opportunity, however, slavery in Washington remained a harsh institution driven by economic considerations and backed by violence. The institution was particularly disruptive for enslaved families. Slaveholders often separated husbands from wives and parents from children to maximize the efficiency of their workers and the profitability of their enterprise. Owners regularly transferred enslaved people from one property in the city to another in the country, splitting families up in the process. If owners' economic fortunes changed or slave prices rose, they might decide to sell off their property. Rosalie Stier Calvert, the plantation mistress who boasted about not treating her enslaved people harshly, frequently discussed selling them. "We sold your girl Lucie ... for $225," she casually informed her parents one October. The slave trade flourished in Washington. Charles Ball "frequently saw large numbers of people of my colour chained together in long trains, and driven off towards the south."[66]

Running away was difficult. "It was a rare thing to hear of a person of colour running away, and escaping altogether from his master," Ball noted. Nonethe-

A Slave-Coffle passing the Capitol.

"A Slave-Coffle passing the Capitol." Enslaved men walk in handcuffs and shackles in front of the Capitol before it was burned by the British in August 1814. Slavery was embedded in the nation's capital from its inception. Library of Congress.

less, after meeting a free black sailor whose descriptions of free life in Philadelphia "charmed my imagination," Ball began plotting an escape. Before he could flee, however, his owner appeared at the Navy Yard and informed him that he had been sold. Ball returned to plantation life and got married. But not long after his second child was born, he experienced a slave's worst nightmare—his owner sold him away from his family. "My heart died within me," he recalled, as he was padlocked into a neck collar, chained to fifty-one other slaves, and forced to walk nearly five hundred miles to an auction block in Columbia, South Carolina. (Ball eventually escaped and walked back to his family in Maryland, where he lived as a fugitive until 1830. Recaptured and returned to slavery, he escaped again and fled to Pennsylvania.)[67]

Despite the low probability of success and the harsh consequences of capture, enslaved people repeatedly attempted to run away both *from* and *to* Washington. Almost from the day it began publication, the *National Intelligencer* ran ads offering rewards for runaways. The first appeared in December 1800, for the ironically named "Negro FIDELIO, well known about the City" who was thought to be "Lurking" near the plantation where his wife lived. "Lurking" was a specialized term that flummoxed slave owners used to describe fugitive slaves who sought to disappear into the city and assume a free identity.[68]

The newspaper ran notices posted by the D.C. marshal, who often caught suspected runaways and put them in the local jail, and it listed enslaved people for sale. John Peter Van Ness, a former New York representative who later became Washington's mayor, advertised "A Negro Boy For Sale," assuring customers that the thirteen- or fourteen-year-old was "healthy, able, honest and strong."[69]

Some enslaved people, particularly women, turned to Washington's courts for redress. They took the initiative to hire white attorneys and file "freedom suits" and "freedom petitions" demanding manumission. Savvy about the context in which they lived, they timed their suits carefully to take advantage of shifting legal, political, or familial circumstances. Mina Queen was among those enslaved people who took legal action. Descended from a large family of free and enslaved Marylanders, Queen hired attorney Francis Scott Key and filed suit in January 1810. (Key was a Georgetown resident and nephew of Maryland congressman Philip Barton Key, who had represented members of the Queen family in court in the 1790s; "Frank" Key had not yet gained fame for writing the "Star Spangled Banner.")[70]

Queen claimed that her great-grandmother, Mary Queen, had been a free woman, and thus she was legally entitled to freedom. Lacking documentation for this assertion, she relied instead on family oral history establishing that she descended from free ancestors. Her owner, Washington County planter John Hepburn, countered that Mary Queen had been enslaved all her life. During the remarkable trial, Key called Simon Queen, a freeborn black man, to testify against a "free Christian white person." Despite the defense's objection, the court allowed his testimony. The jury, however, ruled against Mina Queen.[71]

Queen appealed. Her case, *Queen v. Hepburn*, eventually made it to the Supreme Court in 1813, but the justices dealt a double blow to enslaved people. Writing for the majority, Chief Justice John Marshall dismissed the use of hearsay testimony to establish one's legal status, ruling that in legal terms enslaved people were considered property. If the Court allowed such hearsay evidence, Marshall argued, "no man could feel safe in any property." Justice Gabriel Duvall gave a brief but powerful dissent. "People of color, from their helpless condition under the uncontrolled authority of a master, are entitled to all reasonable protection," Duvall wrote. "A decision that hearsay evidence in such cases shall not be admitted, cuts up by the roots all claims of the kind, and puts a final end to them, unless the claim should arise from a fact of recent date, and such a case will seldom, perhaps never, occur."[72]

The *Queen* ruling, like the Court's infamous *Dred Scott* decision in 1857, undermined the ability of enslaved petitioners to attain freedom through the courts. But enslaved Washingtonians did not abandon the fight. They continued to seek legal avenues to freedom all the way up to the Civil War. From 1800 to 1862, roughly five hundred enslaved people filed freedom suits in D.C.

Another way that enslaved people pursued freedom was through self-purchase. For economic, familial, or moral reasons, slave owners sometimes agreed to allow their slaves to earn and save money to buy their freedom; other times, slaves had to accumulate funds in secret and use white intermediaries to make the purchase. Sisters Alethia Browning Tanner and Sophia Browning Bell used both methods to become free. Born enslaved on a plantation along the Patuxent River in Prince George's County, the entrepreneurial and determined sisters capitalized on opportunities in the nascent capital to escape the hard outdoor labor of the tobacco fields and the emotionally and physically taxing inside work of the "big house" on the plantation.[73]

Sophia cultivated a small garden plot, taking her vegetables each day to market in Washington City. Unbeknownst to her mistress, she began saving a portion of her earnings. She eventually accumulated $400 (about $7,800 in twenty-first-century dollars), which she entrusted to a local Methodist minister to purchase the freedom of her husband, George Bell, who lived on a plantation nearby. George Bell later bought the freedom of his wife and their two sons, both of whom were purchased while "running"—they had fled the plantation and remained at large when their owner consented to sell them. The Bells moved into the city and became leaders in Washington's free black community.[74]

Alethia, too, turned food into freedom. With permission from her owner, she ran a produce stand near "President's Square" (today's Lafayette Square) and counted President Thomas Jefferson among her customers. By 1810, she had squirreled away more than $1,400 (about $28,000 in twenty-first-century dollars), which she used to buy her freedom through a white intermediary. With no children of her own—her husband died young and she never remarried, though she kept her married name "Tanner"—she focused on freeing her extended family and, later, her close friends. Continuing her lucrative business for another three decades, she earned enough to buy freedom for twenty-five more people, including her sixteen-year-old nephew John Cook, who would become a pioneering educator and pastor. Tanner remained active in the community all her life and owned what one observer called "a handsome property" on Fourteenth and H Streets NW, two blocks from the White House.[75]

The Browning sisters joined a small but growing free black community in Washington. As the region's tobacco industry declined and the need for slaves in the city waned, more and more enslaved people either purchased their freedom or were manumitted by their owners. The number of free black people grew much faster than the enslaved population in the early decades of the nineteenth century. Washington City had four hundred free black people at the beginning of the century, nearly double the number of eligible voters in the city. Within a decade, that number had nearly quadrupled, and free black people were more than 30 percent of the black population. Most free black people maintained close connections to their enslaved counterparts. Though their legal status was very different, free and enslaved black people did not lead separate lives in the city. They were linked through family—many free black people had spouses, siblings, parents, and even children who remained enslaved—as well as through churches and other community institutions.[76]

Free black migrants were attracted by both work opportunities and the relatively open and tolerant nature of the city. As the national capital, Washington became home to a diverse population of national and foreign government officials. Northerners and foreigners often commented about how "Southern" Washington seemed, but the city's cosmopolitan mission softened some of the harshness that black people experienced in other Southern cities, and free black people had more freedom of movement than elsewhere in the South.

One of the free black community's top priorities was education. Denied the chance to attend the public white "pauper" schools that the city had established in 1804, black Washingtonians relied instead on a small number of private schools, supported by both free black and white donors. In 1807, Sophia Browning Bell's husband, George, joined with fellow ex-slaves Moses Liverpool and Nicholas Franklin—all of whom were illiterate—to establish the Bell School at Second and D Streets SE, the first school open to black children, free or enslaved.

In the next several years, several small schools appeared, including one founded by Anne Marie Hall, a native of Prince George's County who became the city's first black teacher. An English widow named Mary Billings began allowing black children to attend her classes alongside white children. After white

TABLE 1 Washington's black population, 1800–1830

Year	Total (% of total pop.)	Free (% of black pop.)	Enslaved (% of black pop.)
1800	2,472 (30.4)	400 (16.2)	2,072 (83.8)
1810	5,126 (33.1)	1,572 (30.7)	3,554 (69.3)
1820	7,278 (31.2)	2,758 (37.9)	4,520 (62.1)
1830	9,109 (30.1)	4,604 (50.5)	4,505 (49.5)

Source: U.S. Census Bureau, "Historical Census Statistics on Population Totals by Race"

parents complained, Billings simply established a new school for black children in Georgetown. In 1820, one of Billings's students, an extraordinary black fifteen-year-old named Maria Becraft, opened a girls' school of her own. It later became a boarding school, and Becraft went on to lead the female seminary at Holy Trinity Church in Georgetown.[77]

Initially, these schools catered to both enslaved and free children. Yet, although Washington had no laws forbidding the education of slaves, white pressure forced the schools to focus exclusively on free children. The liberating potential of education—as well as the opportunity to interact regularly with free classmates—proved too much of a threat to the established order.

Schools for black children were not the only perceived threat in the early decades of the nineteenth century. The growth of the free black community, the intermingling of slaves and free black people, the founding of autonomous black institutions—all generated fear among many white Washingtonians. City leaders used the law to keep "slaves, free blacks and mulattoes" (people of mixed racial origin) in line. In 1808, with the tacit approval of Congress, the city corporation passed its first black code, adding to the slave laws of Maryland and Virginia that remained in effect in the District, and broadened it in 1812. The code required free black people to give "satisfactory evidence" of their freedom to the city register; it prohibited black people from assembling "in a disorderly or tumultuous manner"; and it imposed a curfew (10:00 p.m. during the spring and summer, 9:00 p.m. in the fall and winter) on all black people, free and enslaved. Enslaved people who violated the code faced up to thirty-nine lashes, while free black people could be imprisoned or fined $20.[78]

The black codes revealed the racial fears embedded in white Washington life. Despite the city's reputation as a relatively tolerant place for black people, Washington at its founding was a racially charged city. White workers resentful of black competition, free black people clutching at any shred of opportunity, white leaders desperate to develop and protect the city, enslaved people searching for freedom—all mingled uneasily on D.C.'s streets. Racial tension seethed below the surface of the new capital to the point where, two years into the War of 1812, Margaret Bayard Smith worried less about a British attack on the city than the potential that "the enemy at home"—slaves—would use the war as an excuse to rise up in rebellion.[79]

Not only had the nation's capital been built in part by enslaved people, but it was constructed atop the fully formed slave societies that existed on Notley Young's plantation. By 1802, when Young died and his son-in-law took the reins as Washington's first mayor, Young's former plantation was peppered with the streets, homes, and churches of a growing capital, a city that could not shed the lasting imprint of slavery.

THREE

Our Boastings of Liberty and Equality Are Mere Mockeries

Confronting Contradictions in the Nation's Capital, 1815–1836

CASH FOR 500 NEGROES
INCLUDING both sexes, from 12 to 25 years of age. Persons having likely servants
to dispose of will find it to their interest to give us a call, as we will give higher prices,
in Cash, than any other purchaser who is now, or may hereafter come into this market.
FRANKLIN & ARMFIELD
Alexandria
—Advertisement in *National Intelligencer*, 1835

The narrow, leaden gray building at 1315 Duke Street in Alexandria does not stand out much from its surroundings today. Sandwiched between two red-brick structures, the unassuming site could be mistaken for just another quaint shop in Old Town Alexandria, its tall red door and glass gas lamp exuding old-fashioned charm. But in the 1820s and 1830s, this block of D.C. real estate—Alexandria remained a part of the District until 1846—commanded the attention of slaveholders and abolitionists across the nation. It was the headquarters of Franklin & Armfield, the nation's largest and most profitable slave-trading firm. The company owned the entire block, with the three-story Duke Street office serving as the nerve center of a massive operation that sold more than one thousand enslaved people annually.

Visitors in the 1830s certainly would not have mistaken the site. It was "easily distinguished as you approach it," wrote Ethan Allen Andrews, a Yale-educated Latin professor from New England who visited Franklin & Armfield's headquarters in 1835, "by the high, white-washed wall surrounding the yards . . . giving it the appearance of a penitentiary." It was indeed a prison, a holding pen for enslaved people from across the Washington area before they were sent "down river" to slave markets in New Orleans and Natchez, Mississippi.[1]

The block-long complex featured a tailor's shop, a kitchen, and a small hospital, along with barracks where up to 150 slaves spent their nights chained together on the dirt floor. A handful of armed white men stood guard over the prisoners, who spent their days unfettered but separated by gender in two yards. The enslaved people anxiously awaited their trip south, either by water on one of Franklin and Armfield's custom-built vessels or by foot overland in a chained coffle.

Slave traders had a reputation for being, in the words of one English visitor, "sordid, illiterate, and vulgar," but Isaac Franklin and John Armfield cultivated a gentlemanly image. Armfield, a former North Carolina stagecoach driver who married Franklin's niece, ran the Alexandria office while Franklin oversaw the firm's Mississippi site. They built an innovative operation that capitalized on business advances associated with the nascent market revolution. The firm used year-round advertising to generate demand, purchased its own ships to sail its product to Southern markets, offered customers a reliable "packet" service with ships heading south on the first and fifteenth of each month, and employed the latest accounting techniques to track profits.[2]

With a modern appreciation of the power of good public relations, Armfield welcomed visitors with wine and refreshments and graciously offered tours of the Duke Street site. The firm appealed to the sophisticated slave buyer with its promises of "first class vessels" and a studied concern for the health and welfare of its property. Knowing that well-fed, well-dressed slaves fetched higher prices on the auction block, the firm gave each enslaved person two suits for the trip south and worked hard to keep their chattel relatively healthy.[3]

Their methods were extraordinarily successful. Franklin & Armfield was perfectly positioned to take advantage of the shift in American slavery away from the spent soils of the Upper South toward the flourishing fields of the Lower South. As slaveholders in Virginia, Maryland, and Delaware sold their plantations or shifted to less labor-intensive crops, they looked to Franklin & Armfield and other District slave dealers to unload what they considered surplus property—their "crop of human flesh," in the words of English abolitionist Joseph Sturge, who visited Washington in 1841.[4]

It was a lucrative business. In the 1830s, the price of slaves was "*monstrous high*," Armfield trumpeted, and they were in demand across the Deep South— children sold particularly well in the Carolinas, he noted. By the time Franklin retired to a Tennessee plantation in 1835, he was reputed to be a millionaire, while Armfield's wealth was estimated at half a million dollars (roughly $600 million in twenty-first-century dollars). Franklin & Armfield was one of the biggest businesses in the entire South, exceeded only by the largest sugar or cotton plantations. The firm's success helped to transform the District into what Sturge called "the chief seat of the American slave-trade." Indeed, the nation's capital was the largest slave-trading city in America in the 1830s, with four major slave-trading firms in Alexandria alone.[5]

Franklin & Armfield's Duke Street slave pen revealed how the nation's capital prospered from the burgeoning domestic slave trade. In the decades after the War of 1812, slavery and the slave trade in the city invited domestic and international criticism as the movement to abolish slavery focused its efforts on the District. Though some insisted that Washington should remain "the neutral ground betwixt the jarring and conflicting sections" of the nation, both the institution's defenders and its critics disagreed.[6]

For Southern slaveholders such as Senator John C. Calhoun of South Carolina, Washington was the South's Thermopylae, its "weakest point" where Southern leaders had to focus their energies—if D.C. should fall to abolitionism, then so, too, would the rest of the South. For abolitionists, Washington was, in William Lloyd Garrison's words, "the first citadel to be carried" in the battle to end slavery nationwide. As abolitionism became a national force in American politics in the 1830s, the national battle over slavery was waged in large part in and about the nation's capital, and local abolitionists, black and white, actively challenged slavery within the city itself. [7]

Washington became the national battleground over slavery not only because it was the seat of government but also because of the city's political impotence. In the capital of a budding republic, residents could not vote for representatives to the very Congress that called the city home, and they enjoyed limited powers of self-government. Because Congress had veto power over any legislation passed by the city's local council, national leaders could (and did) use Washington as a pawn in their political power struggles.

Angered by the lack of local democracy, many white Washingtonians protested for expanded political rights. The 1820s witnessed the beginning of protracted democratic agitation as poor white men clamored for the right to vote and residents of Georgetown and Alexandria sought to regain the political rights they had lost when their homes became part of the national capital. These democratic movements, combined with the local and national effort to abolish slavery in D.C., frightened elite Washingtonians and contributed to the escalating political and racial tensions that would explode in 1835.

"I Did'nt Want to Go": The First Stirrings of an
Antislavery Movement in Washington

Up until the late fall of 1815, Ann Williams had lived a relatively uneventful life. Born enslaved in Bladensburg, Maryland, she had managed to carve out a space for herself and her family within the confines of slavery. She married a man from a nearby plantation, and the couple had two daughters before she was sold to her husband's owner, uniting the family on one plantation. When the girls were aged about six and three, the owner died, and Williams's prospects changed dramatically. The owner's profligate son took over the estate and proceeded to rack up so much debt that he began selling off his assets, including his slaves. One day while her husband was working in a distant part of the plantation, a slave trader appeared and whisked Williams and her girls away. He marched them to Washington and held them in separate cells in a slave pen above George Miller's Tavern on F Street while he amassed more slaves for an overland coffle headed south.[8]

The city that Williams and her girls entered was still reeling from the devastating War of 1812. In August 1814, red-coated British soldiers had descended on the ineptly defended capital, suddenly made vulnerable after American soldiers suffered a disastrous defeat in the Battle of Bladensburg — not so much a battle, really, as an ignominious retreat that critics in the press dubbed the "Bladensburg Races." Among the British troops were soldiers from the Corps of Colonial Marines, an all-black unit of some two hundred runaway slaves from Chesapeake area plantations. The men had responded to British vice admiral Alexander Cochrane's proclamation offering freedom to any slave who supported the British; their unit served admirably, and after the war they settled in Canada and Trinidad. (The presence of black troops among the British forces particularly incensed Francis Scott Key, one of the District's militia officers who fled from the Battle of Bladensburg. When he later penned a paean to American bravery during the war, Key included a line in the third stanza that warned, "No refuge could save the hireling and slave / From the terror of flight or the gloom of the grave." Few Americans today sing this part of what is now known as the "Star Spangled Banner.")[9]

The British troops sought to punish and humiliate the upstart Americans by burning their capital city. They torched the President's House, the gleaming Capitol, and nearly all other public buildings — "the city was light and the heavens redden'd with the blaze!" wrote a terrified Margaret Bayard Smith. The Americans rebounded to defeat their former colonial masters, but the process of rebuilding the capital had barely begun by the time Ann Williams arrived in Washington. Like much of the city, the Capitol lay in ruins, a charred hulk unfit for public use.[10]

Williams and her daughters had been caught in the vortex of the growing domestic slave trade. Though George Washington and other Revolutionary War leaders expected slavery to wither away over time, Eli Whitney's invention of the

cotton gin in 1793 revitalized the institution and fueled a global textile industry that generated ever-increasing demand for cotton fiber. Slavery expanded
rapidly across the Lower South even as it declined in Maryland, Virginia, and the
Upper South. The Constitution had outlawed the importation of African slaves
in 1808, which meant that planters eager for enslaved labor turned instead to
domestic sources. The result was the rise of the domestic or internal slave trade.

Slave traders—often called "Georgia men" by Washingtonians—prowled the
fields of the Upper South in search of healthy slaves who could capture top
prices in the flourishing slave labor camps in Georgia and what would become
Alabama and Mississippi. "All the slaves here have a great dread of being sold
into Georgia & seem to consider it as much an evil, as their having been torn
from their native soil," noted one white observer. By the time of Williams's sale
in 1815, "some hundreds" of slaves were sold in Washington each year, according to Francis Scott Key.[11]

As she sat in the predawn darkness in her cell, Williams likely pondered the
future that she and her daughters faced. After a forced march of hundreds of
miles, they would be put up for auction and sold to the highest bidder—not as
a family but as individuals. They would endure endless days of toil and a high
likelihood of death in the Southern sun, separated, without each other or their
husband and father. "I did'nt want to go," she recalled later.

Williams chose an option that was at once frightful and courageous. "Confused and distracted" at the prospect of being forced to leave the world she
knew, she leaped from the third-floor window down onto F Street below. Remarkably, she survived the fall, but she broke both arms and shattered her lower
spine. As she lay sprawled on the street, her cries woke the neighbors, including
Mayor James Blake, a physician, who tended to her injuries.[12]

Williams's desperate act, which she later came to regret, did not save her
family. Arriving that morning to find her crippled, the trader simply left her behind, taking her daughters along with a coffle of strangers on the lengthy trip
south. The tavern owner, George Miller, claimed her as his slave and she lived
with him for nearly two decades. After she recovered, she reconnected with her
husband and the couple had four more children, but she never saw her eldest
girls again.

Williams was not the only slave who took desperate measures to resist
being sold that winter. An enslaved woman who lived near Francis Scott Key in
Georgetown was unexpectedly taken away by a slave trader. Described by Key as
a "faithful servant [who] had always behaved well," she slashed her own throat
on her way to George Miller's Tavern, where Williams remained. She, too, survived, but arrived at the tavern with a bloody wound that had to be sewn up. Yet

Ann Williams leaps from a third-story window to escape being sold south. She was depicted on the cover of Jesse Torrey's 1817 antislavery tract, A Portraiture of Domestic Slavery in the United States. *Library of Congress.*

another local woman, on learning that she had been sold, promptly grabbed a meat cleaver and hacked off one of her hands, rendering her unfit for sale in the eyes of the slave trader.[13]

Williams's leap and the desperate resistance of other enslaved people helped launch the long movement to ban the slave trade in Washington. In 1805, Representative William Sloan of New Jersey had introduced a bill to emancipate the District's slaves. It was soundly defeated, 77–31, with only one yes vote from a Southern state. Little progress against the institution had been made since then. A few weeks after Williams landed on F Street, she granted an interview to Jesse Torrey, a white twenty-eight-year-old physician from Philadelphia who was visiting the capital as part of an antislavery tour. Her story stunned Torrey. He later depicted Williams, who remained anonymous, jumping out of the window on the cover of his bristling 1817 denunciation of slavery, *A Portraiture of Domestic Slavery.* Torrey's book was the first antislavery tract to place Washington directly in the crosshairs of the growing movement to abolish slavery in the United States. Later that year, the *Philanthropist*, a new antislavery publication out of Ohio, joined Torrey's call to abolish slavery and the slave trade in the District.[14]

Torrey's interview with Ann Williams was only one of many disturbing incidents that he experienced during his time in Washington. As Torrey prepared to leave his lodging house near Capitol Hill one morning, a young boy burst through the door stammering, "There goes the Ge-Ge-orgy men with a drove o' niggers chain'd together two and two." Torrey followed the boy outside to investigate, and in the distance he saw "a light covered wagon, followed by a procession of men, women and children, resembling that of a funeral." Paired up and bound with ropes and iron chains, the enslaved people walked within sight of the Capitol, where Torrey caught up with them. Horrified, he stood on Pennsylvania Avenue and watched as two slave drivers marched the sullen slaves toward the Potomac River in the distance. Just then, a black hack driver (today, he would be called a cabbie) passed by. Pointing to the coffle, he cried, "See there! An't that right down *murder*? Don't you call that *right down murder*?"[15]

The words penetrated Torrey's conscience. As he passed by the blackened Capitol on his way back to his room, he thought it fitting that the grand building had been burned. In words that would be echoed half a century later in Abraham Lincoln's Second Inaugural Address, Torrey wrote, "Would it be superstitious to presume, that the sovereign Father of all nations, permitted the *perpetration* of this apparently execrable transaction, as a *fiery*, though salutary signal of his displeasure at the conduct of his Columbian children, in erecting and idolizing this splendid fabric as the temple of freedom, and at the same time oppressing with the yoke of captivity and toilsome bondage, twelve or fifteen hundred thousand of their African *brethren* . . . ?" Most incredibly, Torrey continued, "*slaves* are employed in rebuilding this sanctuary of *liberty*"—as they had helped construct it two decades before.[16]

As Torrey thundered about the symbolism of enslaved workers rebuilding the nation's emblem of freedom, rumblings of discontent arose within Congress itself. In March 1816, barely three months after Ann Williams's leap, Representative John Randolph of Virginia gave a remarkable speech condemning the slave trade in D.C. A blustery, quick-tempered slave owner who later fought a duel with Secretary of State Henry Clay, Randolph had a complicated relationship with slavery. His stepfather had penned a stunning 1796 antislavery treatise and his brother had freed all his enslaved people and given them four hundred acres of land. Randolph himself denounced slavery in private and eventually manumitted his slaves in his will, but in public he defended the institution—he believed that the federal government had no constitutional right to interfere with slavery or the slave trade in the South.[17]

The District, however, presented a different case. Because it was controlled by Congress, Randolph saw no constitutional barrier to federal action against the slave trade in the city, and he called on Congress to stop what he called "a crying sin before God and man." The existence of a thriving slave market in the nation's capital harmed America's reputation in the eyes of the world, Randolph argued. As an international city that attracted foreign dignitaries and visitors, Washington was uniquely susceptible to international outrage. Randolph recalled being "mortified" when a foreign dignitary commented that Europeans would be "horrorstruck and disgusted" by slave trading in the national capital. Visitors such as Englishman Henry Bradshaw Fearon dismissed Washington as "enfeebled . . . by the deadly weight of absolute slavery," while the esteemed Marquis de Lafayette, appalled by ads for runaway slaves in the *National Intelligencer*, condemned slavery in the capital during his highly publicized tour of the country in 1824. Foreigners' disgust with slavery and slave trading in the District would only grow in the coming decades.[18]

Randolph volunteered to chair a select committee to investigate "the inhuman and illegal traffic in slaves" in the District. The committee focused on two particularly disturbing features of the trade: the frequency with which "base, hard-hearted masters" broke families apart at selling time, and what Jesse Torrey called the "outrageous and abominable practice of seizing and selling into exile, men, women and children whose freedom and moral rights, are guaranteed by our national and state constitutions." The committee took testimony not just from Torrey—whom critics might dismiss as an emotional rabble-rouser— but also from well-respected local leaders, including Judge William Cranch, a nephew of former First Lady Abigail Adams and a stately magistrate who would serve on the U.S. Circuit Court for the District of Columbia for more than fifty years. Cranch confirmed Torrey's allegations that free black people routinely were being stolen and sold as slaves by traders eager to capitalize on the high prices being offered in the South.[19]

Another local leader who volunteered to help the committee was Georgetown attorney Francis Scott Key, who had represented Mina Queen in her freedom suit in 1810. Pious, philanthropic, and idealistic, the thirty-seven-year-old Key was the slave-owning master of the Terra Rubra ("red clay") plantation near Frederick, Maryland. He developed a reputation for being a racial humanitarian, a slaveholder who believed it was his Christian duty to protect and help enslaved people. When Randolph's committee began asking questions about the slave trade in the District, Key testified passionately about the abuses he had witnessed, including "the separations of Husband & wife, Parents & Children, & the frequent seizure of free persons who are hurried off in the night, brought to the City, & transported as slaves."[20]

Key freed seven of his slaves during his lifetime (though he still owned eight when he died), and as a lawyer he pursued dozens of cases where he could help to secure the freedom of enslaved families. One such case involved none other than Ann Williams. In 1828, thirteen years after Williams jumped from a third-story window rather than submit to being sold, Key helped her file suit for her freedom from the tavern keeper who still claimed her, George Miller. It took four more years of legal wrangling, but the court eventually brought Miller to trial. An all-white jury supported Williams's petition. She was free.[21]

To "Extinguish a Great Portion of Moral Debt": The Colonization Movement in D.C.

Francis Scott Key was no abolitionist. Though he helped individual slaves such as Ann Williams whom he deemed worthy, he wrote toward the end of his life, "I am still a slaveholder and could not, without the greatest inhumanity, be otherwise." Black people simply were not prepared for emancipation, he believed, and thus it was unjust and even immoral to free them and expect them to flourish. And yet, the man who immortalized America as the "land of the free" also recognized the fundamental contradiction that slavery presented to American democracy. The status of black people in the United States—both enslaved and free—was, in the words of Key's good friend and clerk of the Supreme Court Elias B. Caldwell, "a monument of reproach to those sacred principles of civil liberty, which constitute the foundation of all our constitutions."[22] The two men embarked on an ambitious, and controversial, effort to reconcile that contradiction.

Key and Caldwell were men of the post-Revolution era who believed that their generation had to address the contradiction implicit in a white man's democracy that contained within its borders more than a million and a half enslaved black people. "We say, in the Declaration of Independence, 'that all men are created equal,' and have certain 'inalienable rights,'" Caldwell wrote. "Yet, it is considered impossible, consistently with the safety of the state, and it certainly is impossible, with the present feelings towards these people [African Americans] that they can ever be placed upon this equality, or admitted to the enjoyment of these 'inalienable rights,' whilst they remain mixed with us."[23]

The only solution, then, was to remove black people from the country. Key and Caldwell helped Virginia slaveholder and legislator Charles Fenton Mercer write a bill calling on the national government to buy land either in the North Pacific or on the African coast where freed slaves could be resettled. The bill passed in December 1816, the first legislation to embrace what came to be known as "colonization," a movement led by Caldwell's brother-in-law, the Reverend Robert Finley.[24]

To its white supporters, colonization seemed to offer a simple solution to a vexing problem. Through congressional appropriation and private philanthropy, leading white Americans would buy land in Africa and "repatriate" free black people and former slaves (conveniently ignoring the fact that enslaved Americans were a diverse lot with roots in a variety of regions of Africa). Doing so, Key and other advocates believed, would benefit all involved. The country at last could claim, truthfully, that it was indeed a democracy; white people would be happier and more prosperous without the stressful presence of black people; and black people themselves would get to enjoy full rights and privileges as free citizens in their own land.

White supporters saw colonization as a benevolent enterprise. Ralph Randolph Gurley, a Presbyterian minister who served as chaplain of the House of Representatives, believed that colonization would "improve and regenerate" the character of black people and bring "civilization and christianity" to Africa. By helping free black people return to their homeland, white Americans could claim the moral high ground. As Speaker of the House Henry Clay of Kentucky put it: "If, instead of the evils and sufferings which we had been the innocent cause of inflicting upon the inhabitants of Africa, we can transmit to her the blessings of our arts, our civilization and our religion, may we not hope that America will extinguish a great portion of that moral debt which she has contracted to that unfortunate continent?"[25]

If the Revolution was hatched in Boston and abolitionism developed in Philadelphia, colonization grew largely out of Washington. Slave owners in Washington and the surrounding region often had excess slaves whom they could not keep, did not want to free, and felt it was inhumane to sell; they also lived in an area with a large free black population. Colonization, they believed, offered the most just and responsible way to deal with what they considered a serious and growing problem. In December 1816, Key and Caldwell helped organize the founding meeting of what would become the American Colonization Society (ACS), the nation's foremost organization for facilitating black resettlement in Africa. Half of the fifty original signers of the society's constitution lived in the city. The ACS attracted men who considered themselves "enlightened" on racial issues, including such well-respected Washingtonians as architect William Thornton, Judge William Cranch, and editor William Seaton of the National In-

telligencer. They found in colonization a compelling movement that melded practical concerns with philanthropic ideals.[26]

Though advocates of colonization brought a wide range of motivations, they generally opposed the abolition of slavery. At the founding meeting of the ACS, Key himself insisted that the organization's by-laws clearly state that it had no intention of abolishing slavery. Slave owners such as John Randolph saw colonization as essential to maintaining slavery in perpetuity. Free black people stood as "one of the greatest sources of the insecurity, and also unprofitableness, of slave property," Randolph argued. Sending free black people out of the country would "enable the master to keep in possession his own property."[27]

The colonization movement was rooted in the particular economy and paternalist impulses of the Chesapeake region, but it captured the imagination of white leaders nationwide. Prominent politicians including Presidents James Madison and James Monroe joined the movement. Within a decade (and with a $100,000 appropriation from Congress), the ACS helped establish the new colony of Liberia on the west coast of Africa and financed the migration of several thousand former slaves there.[28]

The idea of leaving America and enjoying full freedom also appealed to some black people, and the movement's white leaders worked hard to promote their opinions. William Seaton used the *National Intelligencer* to lionize Paul Cuffe, a half-black, half-Indian Massachusetts Quaker who had resettled groups of former slaves in the British colony of Sierra Leone and who was working with the ACS to coordinate resettlement voyages when he died unexpectedly in 1817. A few black Washingtonians expressed support for colonization, at least in principle. One group of "Colored Citizens of Washington City" passed a resolution arguing that leaving America was necessary because "we think it impossible for us to enjoy that Franchise Liberty which distinguishes the citizen of a free state."[29]

Yet even black people who sympathized with such arguments overwhelmingly rejected colonization, which they feared could lead to forced deportation to Liberia. If they supported leaving the United States at all, they preferred *emigration*, a voluntary, black-driven migration to Haiti, the only black-led nation in the western hemisphere. Isaac N. Cary, a prominent black abolitionist who served as a local agent for *Freedom's Journal* and other antislavery newspapers, promoted emigration to Haiti, which more than eight thousand black people did during the 1820s.[30]

In general, however, free and enslaved black Washingtonians preferred to fight for equality within the United States rather migrate elsewhere. Black leaders aggressively attacked colonization in the press and at public meetings, leading ACS leaders to complain that opponents had "prejudice[d] the minds of the free people of color against this institution, which had its origin . . . in an honest desire to promote their happiness." Former slave Thomas Smallwood initially supported colonization but later came to see the movement as an ill-disguised effort to remove black people from the country of their birth, and he worked vigorously to oppose it. He estimated that "not one in a hundred could be induced to go to Africa." Colonization, one enslaved Washingtonian told a visiting journalist, had done black people "great injury by lessening the little interest that was before felt for them, and increasing the wish to get rid of them."[31]

Black people were right to be suspicious of colonization. The movement grew out of fear—fear that antislavery agitation would eventually lead to emancipation, fear that emancipated black people could never be assimilated into American society, fear that free black people would undermine white democracy and slavery. Colonization sent a powerful message about who could and could not enjoy the blessings of American freedom. Though Liberia settled only a minuscule portion of the nearly four million enslaved people who eventually lived in the United States, colonization appealed to many generations of white Americans who believed that free black people could never have a place in their country. The American Colonization Society reached its zenith in the decades before the Civil War, but it remained active into the twentieth century, finally shuttering its doors in 1964.[32]

"The Constitution Knows No Distinction of Color": Free Black People Stake a Claim to the City

Support for colonization in Washington grew in direct proportion to the size and strength of the city's free black community. By 1820, it was clear that D.C. was becoming a magnet for free black migrants from nearby slave states. Surrounding states clamped down harshly on their free black populations as owners recognized the threat they posed to the institution of slavery—in Virginia, any slave manumitted after 1806 had one year to leave the state before having his or her freedom revoked. Washington looked more promising by contrast. The city had a thriving free black community and many black-run institutions. Free black residents lived and worked throughout the city, they enjoyed relative freedom of movement in the urban environment, and they even could watch congressional proceedings. During the debates that led to the Missouri Compromise in 1820, one newspaper noted, "the galleries were crowded with colored persons, almost to the exclusion of whites."[33]

As black migration to the city increased, so, too, did the number of manumissions through self-purchase and by last will and testament. Even after Mina Queen lost her Supreme Court decision in 1813, enslaved people filed claims and occasionally won freedom through the courts. Migration, manumission, and lawsuits sent the city's free black population soaring. It jumped 75 percent in the 1810s and another 67 percent in the 1820s—more than double the rate of the white population—while the enslaved population plateaued. By 1830, most of the city's black residents were free. Among Southern cities, only Washington, Baltimore, and St. Louis had majority-free black populations before the Civil War.[34]

Free black workers pursued a variety of economic opportunities in the city. Women, who were the majority of the black population throughout the antebellum era, served primarily as domestic workers who washed and ironed clothes and linens, delivered babies and cared for children, cooked and cleaned homes for white families, or worked as seamstresses. Men generally found employment as construction and maintenance workers on public and private building projects, as cooks, waiters, and barbers in the city's numerous restaurants, hotels, and boardinghouses, and as hack drivers, draymen, and hod carriers on city streets, particularly around the bustling area near the Navy Yard. Black workers were not able to secure well-paying clerk positions in the federal government, but only one federal agency (the Postal Service) barred their employment altogether.[35]

A small proportion of free black Washingtonians became professionals— teachers, ministers, business owners— and began to buy property in the city. Among the most successful was Beverly Snow, a confident, sharp-tongued entrepreneur from Lynchburg, Virginia, who moved to D.C. shortly after being manumitted by his owner in 1829. Trained as a chef while enslaved, Snow opened what one newspaper writer called the "stylish and excellent" Epicurean Eating House at the corner of Sixth Street and Pennsylvania Avenue NW. Offering the finest meats alongside Snow's specialty, green turtle soup, the restaurant was an astounding success, attracting crowds of well-off patrons. Other black businessmen thrived in the city as well, including Lynch Wormley, a Virginia transplant who rose from driving hacks to running a livery stable and owning property on I Street NW. Wormley and his 10 children became one of the city's most renowned free black families; several Wormleys were among more than 120 black Washingtonians who owned property by 1840.[36]

As their numbers grew, free black Washingtonians sought more autonomy in their lives and began to build their own religious institutions. During the city's early years, both enslaved and free black residents attended white churches, but they faced physical segregation and endured regular reminders of their subordination, such as when some white ministers objected to touching black children during baptism. Angered by discrimination in Montgomery Street Church in Georgetown, more than 130 black congregants broke away in 1816 to found the city's first black church, The Little Ark (renamed Mount Zion United Methodist Church in 1846). Though it was led by white pastors through the Civil War, Mount Zion played an important role in supporting Georgetown's black community. In 1820, black members of Ebenezer Church abandoned their slave-owning pastor and formed the city's first autonomous black congregation, later known as Israel Bethel Colored Methodist Episcopal Church, located on First Street SE at the foot of Capitol Hill. When Israel Bethel faced losing its building several years later, Alethia Browning Tanner and her brother-in-law, George Bell, stepped in to purchase the church.[37]

Black initiative and resources, sometimes supplemented by donations from sympathetic white residents, launched and sustained fourteen antebellum black churches, including Asbury United Methodist Church on Eleventh and K Streets NW that had more than six hundred members. (All these churches were Protestant. Black Catholics remained for a long time within white-run churches, in part because priests administered the sacraments to black and white parishioners alike; not until the Civil War did black members form their own church, St. Augustine's.) These antebellum churches became vital community institutions that nurtured racial pride, encouraged black leadership, baptized and educated children, connected free and enslaved kin, and at times offered sanctuary to fugitive slaves.[38]

Black Washingtonians also asserted their growing self-confidence by creating their own secular institutions, particularly benevolent societies. These mutual aid organizations pooled resources to help community members deal with financial distress, medical emergencies, and burials. One successful example was the Resolute Beneficial Society, founded in 1818 by a group of free black men, including George Bell. In addition to a traditional focus on illness and funerals, the society launched a school for free black children. It called on the full community to support the school through dues and subscriptions, though to assuage white concerns and "avoid disagreeable occurrences" the group pledged that no slave children would be taught. The society, like other community institutions, both reflected and nurtured black Washingtonians' emergent autonomy and sense of self-reliance.[39]

Michael Shiner embodied the hard-earned but tenuous success of many black Washingtonians. Born enslaved in 1805 near Piscataway, Maryland, Shiner later moved to D.C., where his owner hired him out as a laborer at the Navy Yard. After his owner died in 1827, he was sold as a "term slave" for $250 to Clerk of the Navy Yard Thomas Howard—Shiner was to be freed after serving a term of fifteen more years. He married an enslaved woman named Phillis, and the couple had six children. They became active members of Ebenezer Church, which offered adult Sunday school classes where Shiner likely learned to read and write. A diligent worker who earned the respect of his workmates and bosses, he began jotting down his observations of daily life in a remarkable journal that revealed fascinating insights into working-class antebellum Washington.[40]

But the Shiners could not settle comfortably into family life. After Phillis's owner died in 1833, his son paid off family debts by selling Phillis and two of the Shiners' children to the slave trading firm Franklin & Armfield. They "wher snacht away from me and sold," wrote a desperate Michael Shiner in June. "In great distress," he spent several nerve-racking days rustling up every white contact he knew to help get his family released. Shiner's persistence and his canny understanding of power paid off. He enlisted a major general from the Navy Yard, who helped get a court order that not only forced Franklin & Armfield to relent but also arranged for the manumission of Shiner's wife and children. It took a week, but the Shiners were reunited.

Shiner also tenaciously pursued his freedom. When his owner, Howard, died and the executors of Howard's will threatened to break the terms of his emancipation, Shiner challenged them in court. With the help of white attorney James Hoban Jr. (son of the first architect of the White House), he filed an 1836 freedom petition that charged that he was being "unjustly, and illegally held in bondage." He won. He thrived as a free man, working at the Navy Yard for more than two decades, accumulating property, and, after the Civil War, becoming active in local politics. "The only master I have now is the Constitution," he later declared.

Precarious though it was, the modest success of the antebellum free black population in securing employment and acquiring property helped lay the foundation for what would become the nation's largest, wealthiest, and most educated black population by the turn of the twentieth century. It also sowed the seeds of class divisions within the black community. Many free black Washingtonians had white ancestry and identified (and were classified in the census) as "mulatto" (mixed race); their lighter skin color testified to the fact that racial boundaries in Washington were more fluid and porous than fixed legal distinctions implied. With closer connections to the white community, many mixed-race residents had greater access to education and employment than their darker-skinned peers, and they often enjoyed higher status. These divisions would grow over time, particularly in the late nineteenth century.[41]

The dramatic growth and success of Washington's free black population alarmed many white residents who viewed free black people as a menace. Local writer Anne Royall complained that black people "have absolute possession of the city, and assail people with their insolence, noise, and stones." Royall blamed Congress for "preferring the black to the white people" and claimed "these negroes engross all employment and all the cash . . . and even our females," leaving nothing for "the poor starving white people." Secretary of War James Barbour believed that free people of color "are ignorant, insolent, and demoralized" and earned their keep only "from prostitution, from theft, and from begging." Getting rid of them, he said in 1824, was "an object of our first desire."[42]

The city's white leaders shared such concerns. They sought to discourage free black in-migration by passing a series of increasingly restrictive black codes. "Every imaginable form of humiliating restriction upon the personal freedom of the colored people, both bond and free, pervades these laws," noted one later observer. "It seems to have been assumed that these humble and patient beings were ready for riot, insurrection, and every species of insubordination and wickedness."[43]

After Congress granted the city council new powers in 1820, council members passed a law that gave all "free persons of colour, whether negroes or mulattoes," thirty days to appear before the mayor with "the papers of freedom or evidence of freedom," along with a certificate from three "respectable white inhabitants" who could attest that they "live peaceable and quiet lives" and are "industrious and honest" souls unlikely to become wards of the city. If the mayor accepted this evidence, then the free black applicant had to post a $20 bond promising "good, sober, and orderly conduct." Failure to abide by the provisions could lead to a $5 fine, imprisonment, and forced departure from the city.[44]

But white leaders seeking to curb free black people ran into a problem: William Costin. Costin cut a remarkable figure in early nineteenth-century D.C. He was the unacknowledged nephew and grandson of former First Lady Martha Custis Washington. His enslaved mother, Ann Dandridge, was Washington's half-sister, and she was raped by Washington's son and bore his child. Born free, Costin may have grown up on President Washington's Mount Vernon plantation. He had a rich mixture of African, European, and Native American blood, giving him a light brown complexion. With an aristocratic bearing and a steely determination to claim what he believed to be his, he was not someone to be trifled with.[45]

Well respected by both the white and black communities—no less than John Quincy Adams remarked that Costin, "though he was not white, was as much respected as any man in the District"—Costin built a home on A Street SE (now part of the Capitol grounds), worked as a messenger for the Bank of Washington, and served as president of the Resolute Beneficial Society. His seven children attended a small, integrated private school on Capitol Hill, and he purchased several relatives out of slavery.[46]

In 1821, Costin created a storm of controversy when, nearly three decades before Henry David Thoreau's celebrated act of civil disobedience, he deliberately refused to obey the city council's new law requiring him to appear before the mayor with free papers in hand. Instead, he dared authorities to enforce it. When they arrested him, he sued, arguing that the law violated both the city charter and the U.S. Constitution. "The constitution knows no distinction of color," Costin insisted. "All who are not slaves are equally free," and people of color "have a right to come here and claim all the privileges of citizenship." Rejecting the founders' racial exclusivity, Costin claimed American democracy for men of all races. His was an astounding, novel interpretation of the Constitution as a colorblind document, an argument more than a century ahead of its time.

The case found its way to Circuit Court judge William Cranch, whose enigmatic 1821 decision in *Costin v. Washington* offered both hope and frustration for the city's black community. Cranch ruled that the law "must be construed prospectively, and not retrospectively," and thus did not apply to Costin and other free black people who currently lived in the city. In its revision of the city charter, Cranch wrote, Congress did not seek "to banish old and long-established inhabitants of the city" who "can neither be reproached for, nor suspected of any crime."[47]

But the cautious judge severely limited the scope of his decision. He claimed that the city had the power to deny "to some of its citizens some of the political rights enjoyed by others," including the right to vote. The city also could take steps to target groups who threaten to "corrupt the public morals," so it was within its rights to require "security for good behavior from free persons of color, as well as from vagrants, and persons of ill-fame." Cranch's ruling was a victory for Costin personally, but not for the future free black community. The new law would not be enforced on Costin and other current black residents, but the court had affirmed the council's primary message: new black migrants were not welcome.[48]

William Costin had tried but failed to force the nation's capital to apply the Constitution to a group whom the founders had intended to exclude: free black people. The court explicitly rejected black claims to civic equality—all who were not enslaved were not equally free in the eyes of the law. Although, as Judge Cranch acknowledged, Costin and other longtime free black residents were "useful members of society" who "had contributed to the growth and improvement of the city," they were still beyond the scope of constitutional protection. The size and vitality of the city's free black community—and the willingness of black residents to stake their claims to full citizenship—generated fears among white city leaders, who then passed repressive new laws that won court approval. This cycle of black strength, white fear, and legal repression would repeat itself throughout the city's history.

"The Birthright and Inheritance of Free Men": The Push for White Democracy in Washington

As William Costin struggled to win legal protections for free black people, Thomas Carbery pushed to win political rights for another excluded group: poor white men. The son of a timber salesman, Carbery was a devout Catholic whose Irish ancestors settled in rural Maryland decades before the Revolution. Twenty-one years old when the War of 1812 erupted, he joined the military and helped man the city's defenses when the British invaded in August 1814.

Carbery was a dashing young man with a genial manner, an eye for fashionable clothing, and a burning political ambition. Shortly after the war, he built "Carbery's Wharf" near the new Washington City Canal (roughly along what is today's Constitution Avenue) and turned it into a booming business that catapulted him into social prominence. In 1818, he moved with five slaves, three sisters, a nephew, and a niece into a stately Federal mansion at Seventeenth and C Streets NW. He assumed the presidency of the National Metropolitan Bank and soon launched his political career, winning his first term in the city council in 1819. By 1822, the thirty-year-old bachelor had set his sights on the mayor's office.[49]

Carbery seemed to be precisely the kind of virtuous citizen whom the founders envisioned serving as the natural leaders of communities across the new nation. Scion of an established family, a record of patriotic military service, a distinguished business career . . . these were the makings of a political star. Carbery, however, challenged the reigning political orthodoxy by championing the common man. Like Elias Caldwell and Francis Scott Key, Carbery was a child of the post-Revolution generation, and he, too, recognized the limitations of the founders. While Caldwell and Key sought a solution to America's racial contradictions, Carbery focused on the economic contradictions embedded in the fledgling nation.

The founders had embraced a republican form of representative democracy, but they assumed that the political arena would be reserved for members of what they deemed the natural aristocracy of educated, propertied white men. Only men with property, they believed, had a stake in the long-term well-being of the community; hence, only they could be trusted with the power to rule. Carbery, by contrast, embraced General Andrew Jackson's broader vision of white democracy. Though he was relatively well off, Carbery supported the rights of the thousands of white men without property who made up the majority of Washington's male population.[50]

Carbery's view of democracy may have stemmed in part from his Catholic faith, with its emphasis on moral obligation to the poor. He was among the most visible members of Washington's small but influential Catholic community. Many Catholic families, such as the Youngs, the Brents, and the Carrolls, had been well established in Maryland for generations, and they worked diligently to assimilate into Washington's political and economic establishment. Like their Protestant counterparts, the most prosperous of these families, including the Carberys, owned slaves; indeed, slaveholding was a sign of elite status. (Some Catholic slave owners converted their enslaved people to Catholicism, both for spiritual reasons and because they believed that, as former Georgetown University president the Reverend John Grassi put it in 1818, "Catholic slaves are preferred to all others because they are more docile and faithful to their masters.")[51]

Washington's Catholics maintained their religious and cultural traditions. Even as the city's political leadership petitioned Congress in the 1810s for the right to ban vagrants from the city, the Catholic community helped poor immigrants find work and welcomed them into local congregations. Most of the Irish immigrants in the early nineteenth century arrived in town without homes or jobs. The local Catholic community offered resources such as the Washington City Hibernian Benevolent Society, formed in 1818 by Irish taverners, contractors, and workers to aid destitute Irish families. Georgetown University, founded by Bishop John Carroll in 1789, became an employer of first resort, often hiring newly arrived immigrants as cooks, tailors, or farmworkers until they could find regular employment. The experience of Irish immigrants, then, contrasted sharply with that of free black Washingtonians, who had few community resources to draw on and often were expected instead to be a source of support for their enslaved kin.[52]

As a congregant who worshiped with Irish immigrants and a builder who worked alongside manual laborers, Carbery developed a sense of shared interest with them that differentiated him from other members of the slaveholding elite. His political ascent worried more traditional leaders in the District, particularly when he ran for mayor after Congress changed the city charter in 1820. Congress expanded the powers of the city corporation and replaced the council-appointed mayor with a popularly elected one, giving District voters the chance to choose their mayor every two years. This expansion of elected self-government would last for more than half a century.[53]

Carbery ran for mayor in 1822 and won, prompting outrage among the city's elite. With legal representation from Francis Scott Key, they filed a lawsuit charging that Carbery had encouraged "unqualified" (that is, poor) voters to cast ballots. A majority of the Board of Aldermen refused to swear in the new mayor, prompting a near-riot at City Hall that required police intervention. After Carbery took office, his opponents passed a controversial "hundred dollar law" that limited voting rights to those white men who were assessed as having $100 or more in property (an economic value of more than $70,000 in twenty-first-century dollars). Carbery vetoed the bill, but the council promptly passed it again after he lost his 1824 reelection bid.[54]

Intended to keep the government the preserve of the privileged, the law angered white workers. The *United States' Telegraph*, a new Jacksonian newspaper run by an ornery former brigadier general named Duff Green, became the voice of working-class anger against the "odious and abominable $100 law" and leaders who sought "to establish a monied Aristocracy among us." Workers heartily supported Carbery when he ran again for mayor in 1826, but the voting restrictions limited his base of support. Carbery lost. The white poor would have to wait more than two decades before they could exert widespread political influence in city politics again.[55]

The Jacksonian emphasis on political power for the common man inspired calls for Alexandria and Georgetown to be "retroceded," or returned, to their original states of Virginia and Maryland, respectively. Angered by their political impotence, more and more white residents in the port cities began to question the wisdom of remaining part of the national capital.

Just a generation before, prominent leaders in both Alexandria and Georgetown had been among the most enthusiastic boosters of placing the capital on the banks of the Potomac. Before the War of 1812, the towns grew smartly and their citizens generally shared a national orientation. But the war exposed Washington's vulnerability, prompting many in Congress to talk openly of relocating the seat of government. The city's defenders defeated the relocation challenge but still struggled to win sustained attention from Congress. Though federal lawmakers committed themselves to rebuilding the Capitol and other public buildings, they routinely refused to appropriate sufficient funding for

Washington and neglected to draft a legal code for the city. In short, complained one letter writer to the *National Intelligencer* in words that echoed Augustus Woodward's arguments decades earlier, Congress was too focused on the "higher and greater interests of this immense empire" to concern itself with local matters.[56]

Many Alexandria and Georgetown residents blamed congressional neglect for their growing economic woes. Because Congress mandated that all federal buildings be built within Washington City itself, the central city blossomed as the government grew. The port cities stagnated, particularly after 1820, when the bottom dropped out of the overseas trade along the Potomac. Alexandria was especially hard hit—its population grew by less than 14 percent in the 1810s and less than 1 percent in the 1820s, while Washington City's population expanded by more than 50 percent in the 1810s and another 30 percent in the 1820s. Many Alexandrians felt increasingly isolated economically.[57]

Retrocession advocates argued that congressional neglect stemmed in part from "*the want of political freedom,*" in the words of one white Alexandrian. "It is impossible for any community, deprived of liberty, to flourish when surrounded by free states." In defiant language, retrocession supporters described their political predicament as "slavery" and bemoaned the indifference that their congressional "masters" showed. They channeled their anger into petitions (called "memorials") to Congress and letters to the editor in which they pleaded for redress from what one resident called the "state of grovelling disfranchisement and colonial vassalage." Returning Alexandria and Georgetown to their home states would not only help residents "regain those inestimable privileges, the birthright and inheritance of free men," proponents argued, but also lead to higher land values, a larger population, and more trade.[58]

But the movement for retrocession, like the struggle for white manhood suffrage, was not universally popular. Washington City leaders in particular feared that it would undermine support for keeping the capital on the Potomac. They also worried that if Congress were to allow retrocession then it might very well pull back on even the limited funding it provided for the city. In an 1822 memorial submitted by Washington's Board of Aldermen and Common Council, architect James Hoban and other city leaders flatly rejected any changes in the federal-city relationship. They preferred to "brighten the chain which binds this city to the nation, [rather] than to remove the smallest link." The District, they argued, "is more fully and ably represented than any portion of our country [because] it is represented by the whole assembled Congress."[59]

Without unified support among white people—particularly without the unqualified support of white elites—the retrocession campaign failed to make a compelling case in Congress. It was not until the movement to abolish slavery upended local and national politics in the 1830s and 1840s that retrocession would command congressional attention.

"An Evil of Serious Magnitude": The Abolitionist Movement Targets Washington

John F. Cook came of age with abolitionism. Described by one white contemporary as having a complexion "about half way between the Anglo Saxon and the doomed race," Cook was a shoemaker by trade and an educator by calling. He gained his freedom at age sixteen in 1826 when his aunt, Alethia Browning Tanner, paid $1,450 (about $36,000 in twenty-first-century dollars) to buy the freedom of his mother and his four siblings. Two years later, he enrolled in John W. Prout's Columbian Institute, one of more than 100 black students in the burgeoning school at Fourteenth and H Streets NW.[60]

Cook initially struggled with his studies. But after a shoulder injury fortuitously forced him to seek less physically strenuous labor, he read voraciously and developed into a scholar. Embracing a leadership role within the black community, he established a debating society for black people, free and enslaved, called the Young Man's Moral and Literary Society. By 1834, he was accomplished and respected enough to succeed Prout as the head of the Columbian Institute (which he renamed Union Seminary), and seven years later he founded the First Colored Presbyterian Church (later renamed Fifteenth Street Presbyterian). He enjoyed a remarkable twenty-year career in education and community uplift before his untimely death in 1855 at age forty-five.[61]

As a former slave with kin who remained enslaved, Cook despised the "peculiar" institution and eagerly imbibed the ideas of freedom and opportunity that percolated through Washington's free black community in the late 1820s. For years, free black Washingtonians quietly condemned slavery, helped individual fugitives escape to freedom, and pursued freedom suits in the courts, but few publicly supported abolition. By the time Cook gained his freedom in 1826, however, antislavery sentiment was spreading across the North, and more and more people began calling for an end to slavery altogether.[62]

Whereas most white antislavery advocates supported colonization or gradual emancipation, a new generation of free African Americans began to articulate a different vision—freedom, now, without any talk about leaving the United States. Black abolitionists in Boston formed the General Colored Association in 1826 and the nation's first black-run newspaper, *Freedom's Journal*, began publishing in New York the next year. In 1829, David Walker issued his bracing *Appeal . . . to the Coloured Citizens of the World*, which denounced slavery and colonization and challenged Americans to live up to the ideals of equality written in the Declaration of Independence. "America is more our country than it is the whites — we have enriched it with our *blood and tears*," Walker wrote. Black abolitionists' bold rhetoric and uncompromising demands fundamentally altered the course of American abolitionism, inspiring black and white antislavery advocates alike to become more militant in their demands.[63]

In his *Appeal*, Walker called on black men to use education, religion, and temperance to lead the fight for freedom; John F. Cook wove all three into his life's work. At the Columbian Institute, the teenaged Cook likely heard about and discussed this set of aggressive black leaders and the ideas they espoused. Headmaster Prout was one of the city's most outspoken black abolitionists. An authorized agent for *Freedom's Journal* from its inception, Prout was a vocal opponent of colonization and later was arrested on charges of assisting a fugitive slave. Cook shared Prout's sense of urgency. One of his first acts of community leadership was to organize a benefit for a young man "about to disenthrall himself from slavery."[64]

By 1830, free black people such as John F. Cook were the majority of the city's black population. The growing size and strength of their community worried white city leaders. In 1827, the city council passed a revised black code that imposed higher fines for breaking curfew, required all black males above age fifteen and black females above age thirteen to show evidence of freedom, and prohibited anyone from employing or harboring a black person who could not produce freedom papers. Anyone caught without papers would be assumed to be a runaway and jailed. This clause was critical, members of the House Committee of the District of Columbia explained. If black people caught without papers were assumed to be free, the city would become "the favorite resort [and] receptacle of fugitive slaves," which would be an "insupportable annoyance."[65]

The law further allowed the city jailer to sell any black prisoners whose owners did not claim them and who could not pay the jail fees — raising the possibility that free black people captured and assumed to be runaways could be sold into slavery by District authorities. Slave dealers learned to stop by the jail to see if there were any alleged fugitive slaves for sale.[66]

With such laws in place, Cook and his free black neighbors could build schools and churches, they could own their own homes and business, they could establish and lead community organizations, but they could not assume that they would be safe on the streets of the city. Though congressional leaders considered the false imprisonment of free black people as "beyond all rational possibility," the District's slave pens sometimes held free black prisoners such as Benedict Harper. Arrested in 1831 on charges of theft, Harper was taken to a slave pen rather than the magistrate. He feared that he was to be sold and managed to escape through a third-floor window of the pen.[67]

Solomon Northup was not so lucky. A free black musician from New York, Northup was visiting the city when he was ambushed and thrown into William H. Williams's slave pen on Seventh Street and B Street (now Independence Avenue) SW just south of where the Hirshhorn Museum is now located. Known as the "Yellow House" for its painted plaster walls, the two-story building "presented only the appearance of a quiet private residence," Northup later wrote, but "it was so constructed that the outside world could never see the human cattle that were herded there." Behind the ten-foot brick wall that encircled the grounds, through the iron doors, inside the twelve-foot-square cells, Northup and other prisoners faced horrific beatings, endured sleepless nights without beds or blankets, and spent miserable days and weeks before being sent south.[68]

"Strange as it may seem, within plain sight of this same house, looking down from its commanding height upon it, was the Capitol," wrote Northup ruefully. "The voices of patriotic representatives boasting of freedom and equality and the rattling of the poor slave's chains, almost commingled." Sold into slavery in Louisiana, Northup struggled for twelve years before he regained his freedom. He told his terrifying story in *Twelve Years a Slave*, published in 1853.[69]

The Yellow House sat in a thriving neighborhood of slave pens south of the National Mall. It was an ideal location for a slave trader. Just a few blocks south lay the wharf, where traders could send their chattel downriver; a few blocks north were the humming markets of Pennsylvania Avenue, where buyers and sellers could be found. Across Seventh Street and a bit south of the Yellow House was Robey's Tavern, described by abolitionist Edward Abdy as a "wretched hovel" surrounded by a fourteen-foot wooden barrier with "posts outside to prevent escape." On that same block were two more pens, one run by Joseph W. Neal and Company, the other by William H. Richards.[70]

Enslaved people also were held (and sold) along the Pennsylvania Avenue thoroughfare connecting the White House to the Capitol. James Birch, the sadistic trader who held Northup captive, often used the pens in two downtown hotels, the United States Hotel and the St. Charles Hotel, where management assured slave owners: "The Proprietor of this hotel has roomy underground cells for confining slaves for safekeeping, and patrons are notified that their slaves will be well cared for. In case of escape, full value of the negro will be paid by the Proprietor." Two blocks east of the White House were two other pens—one at Lafayette Tavern and the other in the courtyard of the Decatur House. At Center Market on Seventh Street and Pennsylvania Avenue (currently the site of the

National Archives), shoppers could buy enslaved people along with their groceries.[71]

Though not an everyday occurrence, the kidnapping of free black people in the nation's capital became a flashpoint as the debate over slavery, the slave trade, and the status of free black people in Washington intensified in the late 1820s and early 1830s. Slavery was on the wane in the city—as Washington became more of an urban area, there simply was less demand for slave labor, and many owners found it more profitable to sell or free their enslaved people rather than maintain them. The District's slave population reached its peak of 4,520 in 1820 and dropped steadily thereafter even as the rest of the city grew significantly.[72]

Yet the institution remained an inescapable part of city life. Enslaved people were highly visible as waiters in the best hotels, hack drivers on the streets, shoppers in the public markets, and sometimes prostitutes in local brothels. In the homes of elite white residents, slaves took care of cleaning, cooking, gardening, grooming, ironing, tailoring, washing, and a host of other everyday chores. Enslaved Washingtonians served prominently as servants of Southern members of Congress and at the President's House as well—of the first twelve presidents, eight were slaveholders who brought enslaved people to serve them in the nation's capital.[73]

Slave coffles regularly wended their way through downtown, and each day readers of the *National Intelligencer* could find ads from several slave traders, including Franklin & Armfield, as well as a variety of runaway notices from owners offering rewards for the capture of fugitive slaves. Not only did the slave trade enrich individuals, but it bolstered the local economy and funded civic projects. In 1834, Congress used the $400 licensing fee on slave traders to help the city fund the dredging of the Chesapeake & Ohio Canal. And it benefited private institutions as well. When Georgetown College faced financial difficulties in 1838, school officials decided to sell 272 of the enslaved people who worked the college's Maryland farms to two Louisiana planters for $115,000 (more than $60 million in twenty-first-century dollars), thereby preserving the institution.[74]

Abolitionists set their sights on the District for both symbolic and pragmatic reasons. As the nation's capital, Washington represented the highest aspirations of the American people, and abolitionists argued that it should not be tainted by the sin of slavery. "Slavery is certainly disgraceful in any part of the Union, but more particularly within the limits of the District of Columbia, under the immediate notice of Congress, and Ministers from different governments of Europe," wrote the editors of *Freedom's Journal* in 1828. "May not the latter exclaim with propriety, upon viewing the revolting scenes which daily present themselves, that all our boastings of liberty and equality are mere mockeries?" Ending slavery in Washington, abolitionists argued, would send a powerful message about the priorities and principles of the nation.[75]

From a practical political perspective, it also made sense to concentrate on Washington rather than elsewhere in the South because the federal government alone had the power to determine slavery's fate in the city. Southern slaveholders could not claim, as they did regarding slavery elsewhere, that the matter should be left to local legislatures—Congress *was* the local government. "The subject of slavery in the District of Columbia is one which is completely within the power of Congress, *acting as the legislature of the District*," abolitionist Ethan Allen Andrews wrote. "And should they even adopt a plan of general emancipation, provided the rights of their constituents in the District were regarded, the south would have no more reason to complain, than of a similar act on the part of the legislature of Virginia or Maryland."[76]

Washington—almost alone among Southern cities—buzzed with antislavery activity. By 1827, a dozen formal antislavery societies had been established in Maryland, the District, and Alexandria, according to *Freedom's Journal*. "Humanity entreats, self-interest urges, religion commands us to act" to remove "an evil so pernicious in its consequences, so disgraceful in its character," wrote the leaders of the Society for the Abolition of Slavery in the District of Columbia. White abolitionists such as Quaker Samuel Janney of the Benevolent Society of Alexandria lent their expertise and resources to freedom suits, including a successful 1827 case in which twelve black petitioners filed suit against local slave traders and won.[77]

Much abolitionist energy focused on the slave trade, which by the late 1820s had grown into a substantial and lucrative business. District slave traders, led by Franklin & Armfield, were dominant players in the industry. The graphic, everyday brutality of the slave trade fueled antislavery outrage. Antislavery writers and artists filled their journals, pamphlets, and broadsides with vivid depictions of the trade in action—manacled men and women marching through the city, auction blocks where families were ripped apart, cramped and fetid slave pens where human beings awaited a horrific fate. "While the orators in Congress are rounding periods about liberty in one part of the city, proclaiming, *alto voce*, that all men are equal, . . . the auctioneer is exposing human flesh to sale in another!" charged Scottish writer Thomas Hamilton.[78]

The slave trade did not disturb some members of Congress, however. "Although violence may sometimes be done to their feelings in the separation of families," concluded an 1829 report by the House District Committee, enslaved people sold south benefited from "a more genial and bountiful clime" and "their condition is more frequently bettered, and their minds happier by the exchange."[79]

White antislavery activists in Washington mobilized in 1828 to prepare a petition signed by more than a thousand area residents calling on Congress to abolish slavery in the city. Many signers, crowed *Freedom's Journal*, "belong[ed] to the influential classes, and some the holders of slaves," including former mayor Thomas Carbery. Slavery, the petition argued, was "an evil of serious magnitude, which greatly impairs the prosperity and happiness of this District, and casts the reproach of inconsistency upon the free institutions established among us." The petitioners called for gradual emancipation, beginning with enslaved children born on or after July 4, 1828.[80]

The petition was an extraordinary achievement for the local antislavery movement, but it masked the growing rift between abolitionists and colonizationists. Members of both groups signed the petition, but they did not share the same political goals. Samuel Janney, the white Alexandria abolitionist who helped draw up the petition, believed in immediate abolition, but "knowing the prejudice against it in the minds of the people," he acquiesced in calling for gradual emancipation. Many other signers, meanwhile, wanted to make clear that they supported gradual emancipation only on the condition that the freed slaves would be sent to Liberia.[81]

This rift was exemplified by two prominent white abolitionists who sought to make the city their home in 1830: Benjamin Lundy, the publisher of perhaps the leading antislavery journal of the day, the Baltimore-based *Genius of Universal Emancipation*, and his assistant, a brash twenty-four-year-old named William Lloyd Garrison. Slightly built but energetic, the sharp-witted Lundy courageously challenged slaveholders and slave traders in his monthly four-inch-wide tract. Like most antislavery white people at the time, he favored gradual abolition, and he saw colonization as a palatable postemancipation option for free black people.

Garrison admired Lundy, but he grew to reject his mentor's approach. Influenced by David Walker and black abolitionists whom he had met in Baltimore, the impatient Garrison was becoming known as a fiery advocate of immediate emancipation and an implacable opponent of colonization. He grew increasingly restless working under Lundy and proposed running a branch office of the *Genius* in Washington. Lundy dismissed the idea, so in early 1830 Garrison decided to start a D.C.-based paper on his own.

Proslavery leaders in Washington wanted nothing to do with him. When Garrison contemplated purchasing the printing office of the *Washington Specta-*

tor, a financially strapped, colonization-friendly paper, officials of the American Colonization Society mobilized to stop the sale. Prevented from setting up shop in Washington, Garrison instead went north to Boston, where he launched the *Liberator*, an aggressive newspaper loathed by Southern slaveholders. With his protégé thwarted and himself facing legal troubles in Baltimore, Lundy reconsidered Washington. He moved his printing operation to the city in late 1830 so that he could focus his efforts on "the question of the gradual and total abolition of slavery in the District."[82]

Lundy tried to massage the uneasy tension between abolitionists and colonizationists, but the split became irreparable after the pivotal year of 1831. Garrison began publishing the *Liberator* that January, and his blistering attacks on slaveholders and colonizationists alike helped propel the antislavery movement into a more confrontational phase, both nationally and locally. Later that spring, free black Washingtonians held a public meeting at the African Methodist Episcopal Church at which they denounced colonization. Chaired by educator John W. Prout, the group resolved that "the soil which gave them birth, is their only *true and veritable home*—and that it would be impolitic, unwise and improper for them to leave their home without the benefits of education."[83]

In August came a cataclysmic event that stymied abolitionist momentum. In Southampton County, Virginia (about 180 miles south of D.C.), a charismatic, enslaved preacher named Nat Turner led seventy slaves in a bloody rebellion, killing several dozen white people before being repulsed by the state militia. Turner's revolt, combined with a massive slave rebellion in Jamaica a few months later, triggered white fears of widespread slave insurrections across the South. That fall, the Georgetown municipal government strengthened its black code, prohibiting publications that would "excite insurrection or insubordination among the slaves or colored people, and particularly a newspaper called the *Liberator*." Local white churches, which had offered integrated Sabbath school classes, closed their doors to black children. Always wary of abolitionists, many District leaders, particularly colonizationists such as Francis Scott Key (who now served as the city's district attorney), came to see the movement as a mortal threat.[84]

Tensions escalated in the early 1830s as abolitionists called for a massive petition campaign to convince Congress to end the slave trade in Washington. Like Jesse Torrey more than a decade earlier, the abolitionists of the early 1830s used the language and imagery of democracy and freedom to highlight the hypocrisy of slavery in the nation's capital. Juxtaposing images of the Capitol with scenes of slave coffles and auction blocks, abolitionist literature challenged Americans

SLAVE MARKET OF AMERICA.

THE WORD OF GOD.

"ALL THINGS WHATSOEVER YE WOULD THAT MEN SHOULD DO TO YOU, DO YE EVEN SO TO THEM, FOR THIS IS THE LAW AND THE PROPHETS."
"AND THEY SIGHED BY REASON OF THE BONDAGE, AND THEY CRIED, AND THEIR CRY CAME UP UNTO GOD BY REASON OF THE BONDAGE, AND GOD HEARD THEIR GROANING."
"THUS SAITH THE LORD, EXECUTE JUDGMENT IN THE MORNING, AND DELIVER HIM THAT IS SPOILED OUT OF THE HANDS OF THE OPPRESSOR, LEST MY FURY GO OUT LIKE FIRE, AND BURN THAT NONE CAN QUENCH IT, BECAUSE OF THE EVIL OF YOUR DOINGS."

THE DECLARATION OF AMERICAN INDEPENDENCE.

"WE HOLD THESE TRUTHS TO BE SELF-EVIDENT,—THAT ALL MEN ARE CREATED EQUAL, THAT THEY ARE ENDOWED BY THEIR CREATOR WITH CERTAIN UNALIENABLE RIGHTS, THAT AMONG THESE ARE LIFE, LIBERTY, AND THE PURSUIT OF HAPPINESS."

THE CONSTITUTION OF THE UNITED STATES.

"THE CITIZENS OF EACH STATE SHALL BE ENTITLED TO ALL THE PRIVILEGES AND IMMUNITIES OF CITIZENS IN THE SEVERAL STATES."—Article I, Section 2.
"CONGRESS SHALL HAVE POWER TO EXERCISE EXCLUSIVE LEGISLATION, IN ALL CASES WHATSOEVER, OVER SUCH DISTRICT (NOT EXCEEDING TEN MILES SQUARE,) AS MAY, BY CESSION OF PARTICULAR STATES AND THE ACCEPTANCE OF CONGRESS, BECOME THE SEAT OF GOVERNMENT OF THE UNITED STATES."—Article I, Section 8.

CONSTITUTIONS OF THE STATES.

"EVERY CITIZEN MAY FREELY SPEAK, WRITE, AND PUBLISH HIS SENTIMENTS ON ALL SUBJECTS, BEING RESPONSIBLE FOR THE ABUSE OF THAT LIBERTY."—Constitutions of Maine, Connecticut, New York, Pennsylvania, Delaware, Ohio, Indiana, Illinois, Tennessee, Louisiana, Alabama, Mississippi, and Missouri.
"THE FREEDOM OF THE PRESS IS ONE OF THE GREAT BULWARKS OF LIBERTY, AND THEREFORE OUGHT NEVER TO BE RESTRAINED."—North Carolina.
"THE LIBERTY OF THE PRESS OUGHT TO BE INVIOLABLY PRESERVED."—Maryland.
"THE FREEDOM OF THE PRESS IS ONE OF THE GREAT BULWARKS OF LIBERTY, AND CAN NEVER BE RESTRAINED BUT BY DESPOTIC GOVERNMENTS."—Virginia. Other States nearly the same.

DISTRICT OF COLUMBIA.

"THE LAND OF THE FREE."

READING OF THE DECLARATION OF INDEPENDENCE.

THE RESIDENCE OF 7000 SLAVES.

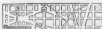

PART OF WASHINGTON CITY.

"THE HOME OF THE OPPRESSED."

CAPITOL OF THE UNITED STATES. "HAIL COLUMBIA."

RIGHT TO INTERFERE.

PUBLIC PRISONS IN THE DISTRICT.

Built by Congress with $15,000 of the People's money; perverted from the purposes for which they were built, and used by licensed Slave-dealers as depots for their victims, and by kidnappers for the imprisonment of Free Americans, seized and sold to pay their jail-fees!

JAIL IN ALEXANDRIA.

FACTS.

JAIL IN WASHINGTON—SALE OF A FREE CITIZEN TO PAY HIS JAIL FEES!

VIEW OF THE INTERIOR OF THE JAIL IN WASHINGTON—FANNY JACKSON.

FACTS.

PRIVATE PRISONS IN THE DISTRICT, LICENSED AS SOURCES OF PUBLIC REVENUE.

"For a License to trade or traffic in slaves for profit, whether as agent or otherwise, four hundred dollars;"—the Register to "deposit all monies received from taxes imposed by this act to the credit of the Canal Fund." Act to provide a revenue for the Canal Fund, approved July 29, 1831. City Laws, p. 249.

SLAVE HOUSE OF J. W. NEAL & CO.

"CASH FOR 200 NEGROES."

VIEW OF A SECTION OF ALEXANDRIA, WITH A SLAVE SHIP RECEIVING HER CARGO OF SLAVES.

"ALEXANDRIA AND NEW ORLEANS PACKETS."

FRANKLIN & ARMFIELD'S SLAVE PRISON.

"CASH FOR 400 NEGROES."

People of the United States, Congress alone possess the constitutional power to legislate for the District of Columbia; yet one hundred and sixty-three of your representatives are striving to perpetuate in the Capital of your Republic this system of robbery, cruelty and desperation.

Published by the American Anti-Slavery Society, 144 Nassau-street, New-York, 1836.

"Slave Market of America." The American Anti-Slavery Society produced this 1836 broadside during its massive petition effort to abolish slavery in Washington. The last scene on the bottom right shows enslaved people at the Alexandria, D.C., headquarters of Franklin & Armfield, the nation's largest slave-trading operation. Library of Congress.

to "flood Congress with petitions." Tens of thousands of petitions poured in to Congress, causing mailrooms to overflow.[85]

Under added scrutiny and pressure, white leaders in the District and Southern leaders in Congress abandoned the apologetic defenses of slavery so common since the American Revolution. Recasting the institution as a positive good, they charged that abolitionists were the true threat and that antislavery agitation would spark bloodshed. The question of slavery in Washington was an explosive subject, warned the editors of the *American Statesman*, and any steps must be taken "with the caution and circumspection, with which the lighted match is applied to a train of gun-powder."[86]

"I've Got Just as Much Right to Freedom as You!": The "Snow Storm" and Trial of Reuben Crandall

The explosion happened in late summer 1835. On August 4, an eighteen-year-old enslaved man named Arthur Bowen spent an evening drinking and debating with a group of free and enslaved black men at John F. Cook's debating society. Bowen was perhaps the favorite of five slaves owned by Anna Thornton, the beloved widow of famed architect William Thornton. By the time he stumbled back home after midnight, thoroughly intoxicated, Bowen's mind spun with ideas of freedom he had been discussing.[87]

He wound up standing listlessly in the doorway of Anna Thornton's bedroom with an ax in the crook of his arm, only to be confronted by his mother, Maria, who slept in the same room as Thornton. Maria managed to push her son out of the bedroom while Thornton ran out a back door to get help. Minutes later, two neighbors arrived to hear Arthur Bowen pounding on the bedroom door, shouting, "I've got just as much right to freedom as you!"[88]

Police apprehended Bowen without bloodshed later that week, but the incident unnerved Washington's white community and touched off two weeks of tumult in the nation's capital. As the city's newspapers bristled with outrage over the "most bloody tragedy," a mob of white mechanics (skilled workers) descended on the city jail in hopes of exacting revenge on Bowen. The mob, wrote Michael Shiner in his diary, hoped to "get Mrs Thortons Mullateto man out and to hang him with out Judge or juror."[89]

Many of the mechanics were primed for racial conflict. At the Navy Yard, white workers had walked off the job a week before to protest a disciplinary crackdown, but free and enslaved black workers remained on the job, angering the mechanics. The Bowen incident gave them a way to vent their rage. The situation became so dangerous that District Attorney Francis Scott Key sought federal aid, and a company of marines was sent from the Navy Yard to barricade the jail and restore order.[90]

To many local white people, Bowen was a nightmare come alive: a normally contented slave (at least according to his mistress) corrupted by free black people and their abolitionist ideas. In making their case that slavery was a positive good, slave owners argued that enslavement was a natural state of being for black people and that enslaved African Americans lacked the capacity for independent thought and action. By such logic, Bowen could not have demanded freedom and attacked his master on his own—a white abolitionist villain must be lurking behind the outburst.

With Bowen safely in prison, white leaders placed the blame squarely on the shoulders of the abolitionists and their allies. William Lloyd Garrison's American Anti-Slavery Society had sent 175,000 petitions through the mails in the previous month alone, an act of "DETESTABLE VILLAINY" that contributed to the "fanatical spirit of the day," fumed the editors of the National Intelligencer. The attack on Thornton was simply "the first fruit" of the "incendiary publications with which this city and the whole slave-holding portion of the country have been lately inundated." Bowen, many white observers alleged, had been stoked to anger by reading abolitionist literature. If the kindly Thornton could be attacked, one worried white Washingtonian wrote, then "what have the other citizens to expect from the free blacks and slaves that have congregated among us for the last twenty years?"[91]

But railing against faceless abolitionists was not enough. White accusers needed a scapegoat, and they found one in an unassuming white botanist and physician named Reuben Crandall, who had recently moved to the area. Crandall's sister, Prudence, was an outspoken abolitionist, but Reuben was not a passionate opponent of slavery—he never belonged to an antislavery organization, and he did not speak publicly in favor of emancipation. A visitor to his shop, however, had seen abolitionist literature lying about, and he warned Crandall that "such pamphlets would not do here, the latitude was too far south." The visitor borrowed a pamphlet, and rumors spread about a new abolitionist in town. Yet not until after Bowen's attack and the mob threats of the weekend did District Attorney Key act. Seeking to quell the growing discontent, he ordered Crandall's arrest and charged him with "publishing malicious and wicked libels, with the intent to excite sedition and insurrection among the slaves and free colored people of this District."[92]

Crandall's arrest triggered another spasm of violence. As Crandall was being led to jail, a man yelled, "We ought to take the damned rascal and hang him up on one of the trees," but the marines remained in formation around the jail. Unable to get their hands on either the uppity slave Bowen or the suspected abolitionist Crandall, the mob of mechanics turned instead to another community that they loathed: free black people.[93]

The mob first targeted Beverly Snow, the free black owner of the upscale Epicurean Eating House. Though Snow cultivated friends among the white elite who frequented his establishment, white workers saw him as an affront to the racial order. The purveyor of perhaps the most luxurious food in town, Snow was educated, prosperous, and perhaps a touch condescending. He was rumored to have boasted that he could "get any mechanic's wife or daughter as he pleased." That rumor, along with allegations of latent abolitionism and a general spirit of lawlessness, led an enraged mob of several hundred men and boys, in the words of one white eyewitness, "to get Snow and tar & feather him or something worse."[94]

Snow fled the city with the help of white friends. In his absence, the mob ransacked his restaurant. It then moved on to destroy John F. Cook's school, where Bowen was suspected of having been indoctrinated in abolitionism. In advance of the mob, white neighbors hurried to Cook's house on K Street and told him to "get out because [the] mob was killing all persons helping negroes. Don't stop." Cook fled to Philadelphia and did not return to the city for a year. The mob torched another school and continued its rampage through the free black community. Only the presence of federal troops and the return of President Andrew Jackson from vacation a few days later ended the "Snow Storm" and restored calm to the city.[95]

The mob's targeting of Snow, Cook, and the free black community revealed the economic dimension of the city's racial divisions. Economic resentment ran deep among white workers, particularly in the Irish community, which had burgeoned when the Chesapeake and Ohio Company recruited more than a thousand Irish immigrants to construct the C&O Canal in the late 1820s. On the canal and other projects, white workers competed against black workers, enslaved and free, and they often won out. The road between Baltimore and D.C. was laid by Irish workers even though, one observer noted, "the country which it traverses is teeming with colored men, who stand greatly in need of more profitable employment." White workers also won the contract to pave Pennsylvania Avenue with macadam in the early 1830s.[96]

Yet Washington's white workers complained that their black counterparts dominated public construction projects, and they blamed black workers for the low pay and poor working conditions that they all endured. When they acted collectively to improve their conditions, as in the Navy Yard, they often found their bosses able to turn to black workers instead. In 1834 and 1835, white workers in many Northern cities routinely rioted to register their frustration with both their bosses and their competitors. The numerous riots led one white Washingtonian to write, "We have mob-fever in the country." The "Snow Storm" in Washington was part of a string of riots that erupted in cities all along the Eastern seaboard in the summer of 1835, many of which targeted free black people and the schools that educated them.[97]

"The reason of all these attacks on the blacks is, that they enter into competition for work at a lower rate," explained the United States' Telegraph, a proslavery, workingman's paper in Washington. "Their standard of comfort being lower than that of the white laborer, they are able to underwork them." The anger that white workers felt toward free black people was a prime reason why the South should resist emancipation, argued the Telegraph. "No sooner did emancipation take place, than the North would be closed to the blacks" because Northern white workers simply would not tolerate black migration. Then Washington and other Southern cities would be stuck with a massive free black population that would destroy the white community.[98]

White workers lashed out at black people not simply because they could do so with relative impunity but also because of their frustration with pervasive market changes that undermined their autonomy and challenged their sense of independence. Like rioters in other cities during the mid-1830s, the Washington mob had grievances against their social and economic betters. It had been more than a decade since the social and economic elites of Washington had made it clear to Thomas Carbery and his supporters that men without sufficient property, whether white or not, would be excluded from the political process. In a city where upper-crust society mattered a great deal, white workers were shut out from power. Riots often substituted as a means of expressing grievances.[99]

Politically impotent, economically dependent, socially subordinated, white workers raged at the upper class, but they chose to use violence against the only groups more degraded than they—black people and their abolitionist allies. At a time of economic dislocation and racial tension, wrote the editors of a new workingman's paper, the Washingtonian, "the Abolitionists and slavery is of more importance to us than any thing else we can think of." The editors later called on Southern legislatures to "HANG every man that comes among them to interfere with their slaves."[100]

The rage of white workers and the perceived threat of free black people frightened white leaders, and during the next year they sought to reassert control over the capital city. One central figure in this process was District Attorney Francis

Scott Key. Beginning with the trial of Arthur Bowen through the prosecutions of Reuben Crandall and several members of the "Snow Storm" mob, Key sought to reestablish the order that he believed the city had lost.

Key had come a long way in two decades. As a young man, he shared the conviction that slavery was a dying institution—it certainly was in his city—and he pursued what he considered to be a noble and humane solution to the problems that would accompany slavery's demise: colonization. For a time, it seemed as if colonization could indeed work. Liberia had been founded in the early 1820s, and thousands of former slaves now lived there.

By the mid-1830s, however, colonization had been eclipsed by abolitionism, a movement that included those favoring some form of gradual emancipation and a militant minority that demanded an immediate end to slavery, with free black people remaining in the United States. Abolitionism threatened to overwhelm colonization and undermine its moral legitimacy. More and more antislavery white people came to agree with John W. Prout and other black abolitionists who denounced colonization as a devious, morally repugnant plot to strengthen slavery and remove black people.

As abolitionists became increasingly vocal, some leaders within the colonization movement sought to blunt their attacks by distancing themselves from slaveholders and other Southern supporters. Part of this effort included an 1833 attempt to remove Key (as well as Judge Cranch, *National Intelligencer* editor William Seaton, and other D.C. leaders) from the American Colonization Society's board of managers, on which they had served since the group's founding. Though the effort failed, a stung Key vigorously sought to reassert his place on the board and reestablish colonization as the most humane solution to the "problem" of free black people in America.[101]

Bowen's trial, which began in November 1836, was relatively swift and the verdict in little doubt. Though Anna Thornton sought to protect her slave and insisted that he meant no harm, other witnesses contradicted her. Key deftly convinced the judges not to allow Bowen's state of drunkenness to excuse his behavior, and he hammered away at the frightened sensibilities of the white jurors. After the defense rested, it took the jury fifteen minutes to find Bowen guilty of attempted murder. He was sentenced to death, but Thornton refused to give up on him. Using her social connections to the White House, she pleaded directly to President Andrew Jackson, who, after months of petitions and requests, acquiesced and granted Bowen a pardon. As part of the pardon deal, Bowen was sold to a friend of the president and taken from the city.[102]

Reuben Crandall's trial, by contrast, was a sensational affair. Financed by wealthy abolitionists, Crandall secured two top lawyers and made a powerful case before a courtroom crowded with congressmen and other notables. Representing the people of the city was the ubiquitous Key, who argued that this was "one of the most important cases ever tried" in Washington. His closing argument to the jury was remarkable, a keen reflection of the anxieties that drove many white Washingtonians.

The case, Key insisted, represented the clash of "two great conflicting rights: — our right, and the right of the whole slaveholding community to self-protection; and the right of others to prostrate its laws and disturb its peace." Without the power to prevent abolitionists from spreading their hateful message, local white people would have to surrender and suffer the consequences, including emancipation and race-mixing. White people who object would have to flee the city, Key thundered, "and the friends of human rights and amalgamation can come and take our places."[103]

When the defense quoted at length from Key's antislavery speeches from years past, Key responded that emancipation was "a far greater evil" than slavery itself. The true friends of black people, Key insisted, were the slaveholders themselves, particularly those who had helped establish Liberia and funded the emigration of thousands of former American slaves.[104]

Despite Key's pleas, the jury acquitted Crandall of all charges. The verdict did not necessarily reflect an embrace of abolitionism; the jurors may simply have concluded that Crandall himself had not planned on inciting Washington's black community. Though free, Crandall emerged from eight months in prison a sick and broken man. Within two years, he would be dead of the tuberculosis that he contracted in the unhygienic city jail.[105]

In the aftermath of the "riotous proceedings" of late summer 1835, many local white people grew more nervous. "We are overwhelmed with free negroes," complained one letter writer to the *Washingtonian*. The expanding free black population was a "volcano," warned another white resident, that would continue to grow "with inconceivable rapidity beneath our feet" unless new, more stringent measures were taken to discourage black migration to the city. In response to the public outcry, the next year the city council passed a harsher black code that required black people to put up a bond of $1,000 (signed by five white residents), prohibited them from holding meetings after 10:00 p.m., and barred them from getting licenses for any trade except driving carts and carriages.[106]

D.C.'s revised black code coincided with a concerted national effort to remove slavery from public discourse altogether. It was simply too dangerous, many proslavery leaders in Congress believed, to keep arguing about slavery in the public sphere. So, in May 1836, Congress passed the Pinckney Resolutions, collectively known as the "gag rule." Insisting that it "ought not to interfere in any way with slavery in the District of Columbia," Congress resolved not to take any action on "all petitions, memorials, resolutions, propositions, or papers, relating in any way, or to any extent whatever, to the subject of slavery, or the abolition of slavery."[107]

When antislavery representative Thaddeus Stevens of Pennsylvania attacked the gag rule, the editors of the *Washingtonian* fired off a response: "We, the people of the District, don't care a pin for him or his resolutions. The *niggers* are our own, and we hold them by *right* and by *might*."[108]

The *Washingtonian* editors and proslavery members of Congress may have hoped that the gag rule and D.C.'s restrictive black code would effectively silence black Washingtonians and discourage black migration to the city. But despite the vitriol, black residents refused to succumb meekly to the new restrictions. The city's free black community was too strong and deeply rooted to subdue completely. Two days after the new black code took effect, Isaac N. Cary, a free black barber and friend of Beverly Snow, applied to renew his license to sell perfume in his shop. An outspoken abolitionist, Cary was accustomed to bucking authority. After the mayor rejected his application, he defiantly kept selling perfume anyway. City officials arrested him and fined him $50.

Like William Costin a decade and a half before, Cary took the city to court—and won. The Circuit Court struck down the license restriction, calling it "repugnant to the general law of the land." Judge William Cranch, whose 1821 decision in *Costin v. Washington* had tiptoed to the edge of racial equality, offered a striking defense of black rights in *Carey v. Washington* (1836)[109]: "Although free colored persons have not the same political rights which are enjoyed by free white persons, yet they have the same civil rights. . . . Among these civil rights is the right to exercise any lawful and harmless trade, business, or occupation." Cranch's decision protected black businesses and helped preserve the city's reputation as a relatively open place for black entrepreneurs, even though the rest of the black code remained in force.[110]

Isaac Cary's resistance to—and partial triumph over—the 1836 black code laid bare a fundamental question facing the fledgling nation in the early nineteenth century: What place did black people have in American democracy? The passage of the stringent black code was in one sense a triumph of self-government. An outcry from voters prompted local elected officials to respond relatively swiftly with a new solution to a perceived problem. But that solution targeted a racial minority that was systematically excluded from the political process. Without political recourse to defend their interests or hold elected officials accountable, black Washingtonians built their own institutions and turned to the unelected judiciary to shield their community from democratic tyranny.

Francis Scott Key and other white colonizationists argued that black people simply had no place in American democracy and advocated removing them from the country entirely. But black Washingtonians refused to go. Instead, they staked a claim to "the soil which gave them birth ... their only *true and veritable home*," as abolitionist educator John Prout put it. They married, raised families, and cared for one another despite material poverty. They built churches, schools, benevolent societies, and other community institutions that bound enslaved and free black residents together and sheltered them from the harshest effects of white supremacy. They worked diligently, opened businesses, bought property, and sometimes even prospered in the face of white resistance. The District's white political leadership, like the editors of the *Washingtonian*, insisted that white people remained fully in control of the city and its institutions, but Ann Williams, John F. Cook, William Costin, Isaac Cary, and other black Washingtonians proved that such control was precariously held. White power would be tested severely in the next two decades as the issues of race and democracy, of slavery and freedom, would rip the city and the nation apart.

FOUR

Slavery Must Die

The Turbulent End to Human Bondage in Washington, 1836–1862

Whatever may be the case in the States, slavery in the District of Columbia is a national affair—our affair.—North Star, May 1848

The National Building Museum on F Street NW between Fourth and Fifth Streets is a stunning red-brick structure that consumes an entire city block across from the Judiciary Square Metro. Designed by Montgomery Meigs in the 1880s to house the Pension Bureau (which cared for veterans of the Civil War), the building was modeled on Michelangelo's Palazzo Farnese in Rome, with a massive interior Great Hall featuring seventy-five-foot marble Corinthian columns and an elegant fountain.[1]

In the 1840s and 1850s, the site where the museum now sits marked the spot of a more modest edifice: the notorious D.C. Jail. Built in 1839 on the northeast corner of the lot facing G Street, the three-story jail was derisively known as the "Blue Jug" for the hideous light-blue color of its plastered walls. It had barred windows and slatted shutters, offering cells of stone as well as an "iron cage" for more serious criminals. Back behind the jail, through what is now the Great Hall and Judiciary Square, a slimy tributary of Tiber Creek trickled toward City Hall.[2]

The Tiber has vanished from view in modern Washington, entombed in underground pipes. But it once dominated downtown, growing from a dribble near the Soldiers' Home in Northwest into an eight-hundred-foot-wide watery expanse by the time it reached the Potomac River just in front of the White House. Despite a name that appealed to antiquity (the land originally had been part of a plantation called Rome, whose owner christened the creek), by the middle of the nineteenth century the Tiber was a wretched mess. It flowed into the Washington City Canal, which was built in 1815 as part of Peter L'Enfant's plan to connect the Potomac with the Eastern Branch. One Washingtonian recalled that the Tiber "stretched in ignominious stagnation across the city, oozing at last through green scum and slime into the still more ignominious canal, which stood an open sewer and cess-pool, the receptacle of all abominations, the pest-breeder and disgrace of the city."[3]

The fetid canal symbolized the economic stagnation of the city itself, which by midcentury had clearly failed to live up to George Washington's dreams of a commercial hub. Local leaders nearly bankrupted the city in an ill-fated effort to build the Chesapeake & Ohio Canal, which they had hoped would open Washington to the markets of the West by connecting the Potomac to the Ohio River. They invested $1.5 million in public money (more than $414 million in twenty-first-century dollars) in the C&O Canal Company and borrowed to cover the interest on the city's debt, but costs spiraled out of control. By 1834, Washington City was more than $1.7 million in debt and needed a congressional bailout. The rapid rise of the Baltimore & Ohio Railroad made the canal obsolete even before it was partially completed in 1850.[4]

The silting of the Potomac River and the Eastern Branch compounded the city's economic problems, and without good transportation the city failed to generate significant private industries. Washington grew dependent on the federal government in the decades after the War of 1812, and the businesses that sprang up tended to cater to government workers and projects. Between 1820 and 1850, Washington's population more than doubled, from 23,336 to 51,687, but it failed to keep up with other urban areas in an age of stunningly rapid growth—New York's population quadrupled to more than half a million, New Orleans grew nearly sevenfold to 116,000, and Cincinnati expanded from fewer than 10,000 people to more than 115,000. Washington had been the nation's ninth largest urban area in 1820 but dropped to eighteenth three decades later.[5]

English writer Charles Dickens famously dismissed D.C. as "the City of Magnificent Intentions" on an 1842 visit. "Spacious avenues that begin in nothing, and lead nowhere; streets, mile long, that only want houses, roads, and inhabitants; public buildings that need but a public to be complete; and ornaments of great thoroughfares, which only lack great thoroughfares to ornament—are its leading features." With a minuscule population and commerce that is "scarcely worth mentioning," one Irish writer bluntly concluded in 1855, "the Federal metropolis must be considered a signal failure."[6]

The city also suffered from significant crime, particularly in some of the rough neighborhoods that grew along the canal and the Tiber, including the Irish stronghold of Swampoodle (north of today's Union Station) and the red-light district of Murder Bay (now Federal Triangle). With a steady flow of thieves, brawlers, and prostitutes plucked from the streets of the crime-ridden city, the Blue Jug was in frequent use.

But the Blue Jug was more than just a pen for petty criminals. The pale eyesore was also a central stage in the growing drama over slavery. Despite Congress's attempt to squelch public debate with the gag rule, the question of slavery in the nation's capital would not die. Frustrated abolitionists, unable to overcome what they called the "Slave Power," went "underground" to help Washington-area slaves escape to freedom. As more and more enslaved people "absconded" (the term often used in advertisements for fugitives), city leaders struggled to preserve the peculiar institution by capturing and punishing runaways.

One controversial way in which they did so was by throwing suspected fugitives into the Blue Jug—even if they were free. "In Washington," wrote an incredulous Dickens, "any justice of the peace may bind with fetters any negro passing down the street, and thrust him into gaol: no offence on the black man's part is necessary. The justice says, 'I choose to think this man a runaway:' and locks him up. Public opinion empowers the man of law, when this is done, to advertise the negro in the newspapers, warning his owner to come and claim him or he will be sold to pay the gaol fees. But supposing he is a free black, and has no owner, it may naturally be presumed that he is set at liberty. No: HE IS SOLD TO RECOMPENSE HIS GAOLER."[7]

Between 1826 and 1828, a total of 101 runaways were committed to the Blue Jug. Of those, 81 were delivered to their owners and 15 were proven to be free and discharged; the other 5 went unclaimed and were sold to recover jail fees.[8]

For abolitionists, the Blue Jug came to embody the evils of the slave system as the national debate over slavery intensified after a brief and triumphant war with Mexico ended in 1848. The question of whether to allow slavery in the newly acquired western territories could not be squelched by any gag rule, and the nation's two political parties, the Democrats and the Whigs, began to splinter along sectional lines. Slavery dominated congressional debates, leading Representative William Sawyer of Ohio to complain during one 1849 debate over the slave trade in D.C., "It is negro in the morning—the poor negro at noon—and at night again this same negro is thrust upon us."[9] With the nation tilting ominously toward civil war, slavery's opponents and its defenders placed Washington on the front lines of the struggle over human bondage in America.

"A Subterranean Railroad": The Growth of D.C.'s Biracial Antislavery Community

Thomas Smallwood and Charles T. Torrey were an unlikely pair. In an age where few people formed genuine relationships with members of another race, Smallwood and Torrey shared a mutually admiring bond. Born enslaved in Prince George's County in 1801, Smallwood learned to read and write as a child, and he scraped together enough money to purchase his freedom by age thirty. He moved to Washington and became involved in antislavery efforts, serving as the local correspondent for the Albany-based *Tocsin of Liberty*. An iconoclast and contrarian, he bristled with indignation at the timidity of local black clergy and questioned the motives of white abolitionists. He believed in more aggressive tactics to fight slavery, as did his wife, Elizabeth, a free black Virginian. Elizabeth worked in a Thirteenth Street NW boardinghouse run by an antislavery white woman named Mrs. Padgett. One of Mrs. Padgett's boarders was a white New England abolitionist named Charles T. Torrey.

Educated at Exeter and Yale, Torrey was bookish but bold, a passionate and at times intemperate young man who arrived in D.C. at age twenty-eight to serve as a local correspondent for several Northern newspapers. He immediately provoked anger among white elites by attending black churches and crashing a slaveholder convention in Annapolis in early 1842. Yanked from the convention and tossed in jail, he encountered thirteen members of a black family who were being detained until they could be transported back into slavery. With visions of becoming the next William Lloyd Garrison, Torrey wrote impassioned letters condemning slaveholders as "human hyenas" and proclaiming, "Now God has written upon the walls of Annapolis jail . . . 'Slavery must die.'" On Torrey's return to Washington, Elizabeth Smallwood arranged a meeting between the two brash activists, and they grew into committed allies as the antislavery movement moved in a new direction.[10]

Thomas Smallwood scorned most abolitionists but considered Torrey a "beloved friend." They challenged the prevailing sentiment in Washington's antislavery community. In the aftermath of the 1835 "Snow riot," the subsequent crackdown on free black people, and Congress's imposition of the gag rule in 1836, many antislavery activists in Washington saw little hope of abolishing slavery in the city in the foreseeable future. In response, some white abolitionists used funding from wealthy Northerners to purchase individual slaves and set them free. Smallwood and Torrey disdained that idea—they felt that buying slaves only legitimized and enriched an immoral institution. Instead, they sought more direct and confrontational action.

With support from Elizabeth Smallwood and Mrs. Padgett, Thomas Smallwood and Torrey planned and implemented secret escapes, helping interested slaves in the Washington area make their way to freedom in the North along a clandestine network of safe houses. "Some swear that there is a *subterranean rail road* by which they travel *under ground*," wrote abolitionist representative Joshua Giddings of Ohio, and "women & children all go whole families disappear." What came to be known as the "Underground Railroad" was not a national network coordinated by abolitionist movement leaders; rather, it consisted of countless local networks and involved small cells of black and white activists who sometimes were tied loosely to other abolitionists and philanthropists farther north.[11]

The success of the local Underground Railroad depended on the courage and connections of free and enslaved black Washingtonians, coupled with the strategic assistance of white allies. Fugitives in the Washington area often turned to local "conductors" such as Leonard Grimes, a free black hack driver who lived at the corner of Twenty-Second and H Streets NW. Light-skinned enough to pass for white, Grimes grew up in the District and often worked for white slave owners whom he drove on excursions into neighboring states. Having witnessed the horrible conditions that enslaved people endured, he committed himself to helping escapees find freedom. He helped many runaways before being arrested in northern Virginia in 1839. He served two years in prison. (The location of Grimes's home is now memorialized with a plaque on the George Washington University campus.)[12]

Smallwood and Torrey expanded the Underground Railroad in Washington. The two claimed to have helped 150 slaves escape in their two years of working together. After several harrowing brushes with the law, Torrey was arrested in Baltimore in June 1844 and charged with aiding a runaway. Imprisoned once again, he became a hero among abolitionists nationwide, but his health deteriorated quickly while he was incarcerated. He died of tuberculosis in prison in 1846. Smallwood fled the city for Canada, where he opened a hardware store, wrote an autobiography, and became a leading member of Toronto's growing black community.[13]

Though Smallwood and Torrey's partnership was cut short, the Underground Railroad endured as enslaved people continued to seek freedom from their owners throughout the 1840s and 1850s. "Slaves are running away from the District almost daily," white abolitionist Theodore Weld wrote excitedly when he arrived in the city in 1842. Fugitives sometimes found sanctuary in local churches, including Mount Zion United Methodist Church in Georgetown. Mt. Zion members hid escaping slaves in a burial vault in the church cemetery on Q Street NW, and church records noted members who were "taken away" (captured by slave patrollers), "gone away" (escaped to the North), or "lost."[14]

Fugitive slaves, as well as free black people ensnared by slave traders, often enlisted sympathetic white allies to help them escape through the Underground Railroad or the courts. A Virginia slave owner grumbled that black Washingtonians used white attorneys to "pry into every man's title to his negroes." One such lawyer was David Hall, who had come to D.C. in 1820 to study law with his mentor, colonization advocate Elias Caldwell. Hall came to reject colonization and became an antislavery activist who sometimes bought enslaved people to free them. He provided legal assistance to John Bush, a free black man who had been arrested for helping Smallwood and Torrey on an 1843 escape, and won his acquittal.[15]

Nationally prominent white abolitionists also got involved in the local Underground Railroad. Representative Joshua Giddings, a bellicose frontiersman from Ohio, was perhaps the most confrontational antislavery member of Congress. He lived with other antislavery representatives and activists in Ann Sprigg's First Street NE boardinghouse, which they dubbed "Abolition House." With their public denunciations of slavery and their personal, behind-the-scenes efforts on behalf of individual slaves, Giddings and his fellow boarders offered moral and material support to enslaved black people determined to be free.[16]

The growing strength of Washington's biracial antislavery community accelerated the calls for retrocession in Alexandria. Many residents wanted all the District land west of the Potomac to be "retroceded," or given back, to the state of Virginia. As abolitionists gained strength in the mid-1830s, as thousands of antislavery petitions deluged Congress, and as more and more enslaved people took flight, many white Alexandrians came to see retrocession as a way not only to gain political rights and prosper economically but also to protect their right to own and trade slave property from the unpredictable whims of what one Alexandria letter writer deemed "an experimenting Congress."[17]

Those two core issues—democracy and slavery—were mutually reinforcing in the minds of retrocession supporters. Because D.C. residents had no political rights, they could not defend their property rights—and in a time of the gag rule, "property" was often a euphemism for slavery. Washington had become "a field for legislative experiments ... upon the rights and property of the people," complained one retrocession advocate in the *Alexandria Gazette*. By 1840, support for retrocession had increased dramatically among white Alexandrians. A retrocession referendum that year passed by a nearly three-to-one margin.[18]

Local advocates took their case to the state House of Delegates, where the issue got caught up in political wrangling between leaders in mountainous western Virginia (where there was little slavery) and slaveholding representatives from the eastern Tidewater part of the state. Adding Alexandria would bolster the power of the eastern planters, and they helped push retrocession through the Virginia house in early 1846. Congress gave its stamp of approval that summer, and in September white voters in Alexandria voted overwhelmingly (763–222) in favor of retrocession, triggering massive celebrations.[19]

Black Alexandrians feared for their future. "As the votes were announced every quarter of an hour the suppressed wailings and Lammentations of the people of color wer constantly assending to god for help and succor," wrote free black businessman Moses Hepburn. "We expect that our school will all be broken up [and] our privelidges which we have enjoyed for so maney years will all be taken away." Indeed, within a year of retrocession, Alexandria's black schools were closed. In-migration of free black people essentially stopped, and many longtime residents left the city. By 1850, Alexandria's free black population had dropped by almost 30 percent from its 1840 high. The port's slave trade, now safe from federal interference, continued to grow as abolitionists focused instead on the truncated nation's capital.[20]

"We Can Drive Slavery Out of This District at Once!": The Pearl Escape and Its Consequences

In April 1848, Washington witnessed the largest slave escape ever attempted in the United States. The plot began with Daniel Bell, described by one contemporary as a "robust, worthy, industrious" free black carpenter who worked at the Navy Yard. Bell's wife and family (nine children, two grandchildren) were also free, but their former mistress was taking legal steps to try to get them back. In desperation, Bell approached William Chaplin, who had replaced the late Charles Torrey as D.C.'s highest-profile white abolitionist. A Massachusetts lawyer and grandson of a Revolutionary War hero, Chaplin had come to Washington to serve as the editor of the antislavery *Albany Patriot*. Working with Bell, Chaplin helped arrange financing for an elaborate escape involving a ne'er-do-well white Philadelphia ship captain named Daniel Drayton.[21]

The plan was for Drayton to sail his schooner, the *Pearl*, into Washington with a cargo of timber. After unloading the timber, he would fill the ship with escaping slaves, sail it down the Chesapeake Bay, and then head north to freedom. To recruit willing escapees, Bell found allies in Paul Jennings, a former slave of James Madison who now served as Senator Daniel Webster's valet, and Samuel Edmonson, the enslaved son of a free black farmer in Montgomery County, Maryland.[22]

The timing of the escape was symbolically rich. By early April, word had filtered across the Atlantic about the February Revolution that had brought the promise of democracy to France. As the *Pearl* docked in Washington on April 13, the Democratic Party hosted a series of celebrations in honor of the revolution. During an open-air speech, Senator Henry Foote of Mississippi exclaimed that "the age of tyrants and slavery was rapidly drawing to a close." What happened in France, Foote argued, offered the world "a promise of the universal establishment of civil and religious liberty." Enslaved Washingtonians certainly hoped so.

By the time the Pearl was ready to go before dawn on April 15th, seventy-six of them had clambered aboard, including thirteen children, at least one of former First Lady Dolley Madison's slaves, and five of Samuel Edmonson's siblings.[23]

The ship set sail early that morning and immediately ran into trouble. The wind died, the tide rolled in, and the ship drifted, squandering the head start the fugitives hoped to get on the slave catchers who would surely pursue them. When slave owners across the city awoke Sunday morning to find their enslaved workers missing, they immediately formed a posse. They gleaned key information from an enslaved black man named Diggs, who may have been angry with the escapees. Thirty men "armed to the teeth," wrote a breathless *New York Herald* correspondent, then commandeered a ship and raced after the Pearl, catching it 140 miles later as it sat in the water near Point Lookout, Maryland, where the Potomac River empties into the Chesapeake Bay. Capturing the Pearl's passengers and crew without bloodshed, they headed back to Washington.

"Their return to the capital of the Republic was hailed as a triumph," wrote one witness. "A wild joy thrilled through the city" after the ship landed at the Sixth Street Wharf and the fugitives were marched toward the Blue Jug. A white mob assailed the group, raining their wrath down particularly on Drayton and the two other white men on the Pearl's crew. Unable to prevent them from being put safely in prison, angry white Washingtonians turned their attention to other white activists assumed to be collaborators. During the following week, Representative Giddings faced repeated threats, but the mob focused primarily on the city's only antislavery newspaper, the *National Era*, which many in Washington, including some members of Congress and President James Polk himself, believed had instigated the escape.[24]

Founded a year earlier by Gamaliel Bailey, a conciliatory advocate of gradual emancipation, the *National Era* refused to vilify Southern slaveholders and boasted a wide circulation, even in the South. (The newspaper later gained national fame when it serialized Harriet Beecher Stowe's story of a slave with a Jesus-like capacity for suffering and forgiveness. First published in June 1851 and continuing until April 1852, the series proved wildly popular and Stowe published it in book form as *Uncle Tom's Cabin*.) But Bailey's relatively moderate antislavery beliefs did not soothe the mob—now several thousand strong—which attempted several times to destroy the newspaper's presses, only to be stopped by the local auxiliary guard. One splinter group aimed to tar and feather the frail Bailey, who confronted the mob on his front porch and convinced its members that he had nothing to do with the attempted escape.[25]

Bailey avoided retribution, but the fate of the captured Pearl fugitives was swift and terrible. Within just ten days, they all were "sold and scattered across the South," one antislavery reporter wrote. A few well-connected slaves managed to get bought by sympathetic white people. Daniel Bell's wife and two children were purchased and freed by local white abolitionist Thomas Blagden; two Edmonson sisters, valued higher than the other slaves ($2,400) because of their light-skinned physical beauty, inspired a massive Northern fund-raising campaign that brought in enough money to buy their freedom. For the vast majority, however, the desperate attempt to find freedom led to a life of misery in the Deep South.[26]

The "*Pearl* Affair," as the escape attempt became known, exacerbated the tensions between North and South, and many fearful slaveholders in the area jettisoned their slaves. Sales skyrocketed in the two years after the *Pearl*. "Scarcely a day passed that gangs of chained slaves did not pass through the city," William Chaplin wrote in spring 1850. The *Pearl* became a rallying cry among abolitionists. "This attempt of the 77 to 'conquer' their freedom is the grandest event for the cause of anti-slavery that has occurred in years," Chaplin wrote. "If our Abolitionists will take hold, we can drive slavery out of this District at once!" One fund-raising flyer sent throughout Boston shortly after the fugitives were captured declared: "Whatever may be the case in the States, slavery in the District of Columbia is a national affair—our affair."[27]

Led by Representative Joshua Giddings, antislavery members of Congress linked the *Pearl* to the democratic revolutions in Europe and grew more explicit in their denunciations of slavery and the slave trade in Washington. On the floor of the House, Giddings shocked Southerners by defending the right of enslaved people to use violence to protect themselves: "Were I a colored man, as I am a white man, I would not hesitate to slay any slave-catcher who should attempt to lay hands on my person to enslave me." In December 1848, Giddings introduced a bill calling for a referendum on slavery in the District to be voted on by *all* male residents, white and black, free and enslaved. Giddings's call for black suffrage frightened his colleagues in Congress, who quickly tabled the matter. The Giddings bill, chided the *National Era*'s Gamaliel Bailey, was "calculated to arouse feelings of fierce hostility."[28]

Just a few weeks after Giddings's slavery referendum died, one of his housemates at Abolition House offered a very different proposal to end both the slave trade and slavery in the District. Abraham Lincoln was a reedy, lame-duck congressman from Illinois in the last session of his first and only term. During his short time in Washington, Lincoln had seen firsthand the gruesome nature of slavery—the slave pens near the Capitol, the kidnapping of one of Abolition House's hired slaves, the sale of the *Pearl* fugitives. Though he shared Giddings's moral opposition to slavery, he favored less incendiary tactics and sought a politically feasible solution that could earn support from white District residents, as well as both Southerners and Northerners in Congress. He had long agreed with abolitionists that Congress had the power to abolish slavery in the capital, but he insisted that the power should be used only if the people of the District supported it.[29]

Lincoln proposed gradual, compensated emancipation that would take effect only after District voters approved it. His bill included an exemption for slave-holding members of Congress who would be allowed to keep enslaved people while serving in office. Before he introduced the bill, he met with District mayor William Seaton and was led to believe that Seaton and other local leaders would support it. When Lincoln later learned that Southern members of Congress had persuaded Mayor Seaton to oppose it, however, he dropped the issue. Lincoln never introduced the legislation, and instead he shifted his focus from emancipation in the District toward stopping the extension of slavery into the western territories.[30]

After Lincoln left Congress in early 1849, tensions over slavery in Washington escalated. The issue became one of the last sticking points in the negotiations that eventually led to the Compromise of 1850, a series of bills that collectively helped avert a threatened sectional war. Shepherded through Congress by a dying Senator Henry Clay of Kentucky, the Compromise of 1850 admitted California into the Union as a free state and banned the slave trade in Washington—two important concessions for the North. In return, antislavery members of Congress had to accept a stronger Fugitive Slave Law, one of the white South's top priorities. With the new law, Northerners would be held criminally liable if they were found to be aiding runaways. The law empowered slaveholders to go to the North and forcibly remove enslaved people they claimed as their own; abolitionists responded by extending the Underground Railroad into Canada.

The Compromise of 1850 rescued the Union from almost certain disaster, but it did not resolve Washington's racial questions. Though black Washingtonians and their antislavery allies rejoiced at the demise of the slave trade in the city, their triumph was limited. Washington no longer served as a depot for interstate commerce in slaves, but that meant less than it may have appeared. Slave dealers did not go defunct; they simply crossed the Potomac and continued their business on the other side. The push for white democracy that led to the retrocession of Alexandria four years earlier limited the impact of the slave trade ban. As abolitionist William Jay lamented, "Something was indeed gained to the *character* of the national capital, by prohibiting the importation of slaves for sale, but nothing to the cause of humanity, since the traffic was only transferred from Washington to Alexandria."[31]

The slave trade provision only banned the *importation* of slaves into Washington from slave states for resale elsewhere. City residents could still buy and sell *local* slaves, including at public auctions, and visitors still gawked at the occasional slave coffle trudging through the streets long after the slave trade ban took effect. Though the proportion of enslaved Washingtonians continued to decline, as it had for decades—in 1850, less than 27 percent of the black population was enslaved; by 1860, barely 22 percent—slavery remained very visible in Washington, and the institution had powerful political and economic interests behind it.[32]

The Fugitive Slave Act made running away riskier, but many enslaved people in Washington and the surrounding area nonetheless pressed for freedom by escaping. Black Washingtonians such as Anthony Bowen stepped up to help them. Born enslaved in Maryland in 1809, Bowen hired himself out from his owner and saved $425 to buy his freedom in 1830. He later purchased his wife out of bondage as well. He moved to Washington, got a job as a clerk in the U.S. Patent Office, and settled into a home at 85 E Street SW, not far from Federal Center Metro Station today. Bowen's home became a locus of black organizing activity. In 1853, he began hosting meetings for what would become the nation's first black YMCA, and three years later he started holding services for a new religious institution called the St. Paul Society (later known as St. Paul's Church). The home also became a sanctuary for fugitive slaves who arrived by boat at the Sixth Street Wharf, where Bowen would meet them and whisk them to safety.[33]

Fugitives put themselves at considerable risk. Ana Maria Weems was a fifteen-year-old enslaved girl, described by one abolitionist as "bright mulatto, well grown, smart and good-looking." She lived on a Maryland plantation just north of the city with a hard-drinking owner whose wife was "cross and peevish." Local white abolitionist Jacob Bigelow had worked with William Still, a black abolitionist from Philadelphia, to purchase Ana Maria's mother for $1,000 and her sister for $1,600 (roughly $30,000 and $50,000 in twenty-first century dollars), but the owner refused to part with Ana Maria. Fearing that she might try to run away, her owner forced her to sleep in a bedroom with him and his wife. She finally escaped in fall 1855 by dressing up as a boy with the alias "Joe Wright" and making her way to Washington, where she found Bigelow. "The city is full of incendiaries," warned Bigelow, and they had to avoid slave hunters who dangled rewards of $100 or $200 in hopes of enticing someone to betray a runaway. Bigelow smuggled Weems through the city and on to Philadelphia, where Still was waiting. He helped her get to New York and, with assistance from famed abolitionist Lewis Tappan, on to Canada.[34]

White abolitionists often shared the risks with the fugitives they sought to help, though the consequences they faced paled in comparison to what a captured black person endured. Shortly before the Fugitive Slave Law took effect, William Chaplin, one of the masterminds behind the *Pearl* escape, attempted to help two fugitive slaves, Garland White and Allen, who belonged to Georgia's two U.S. senators. As they crossed the District border into Silver Spring, Maryland, the trio encountered a posse of heavily armed police and private slave-catchers. After a dramatic gunfight, Chaplin was arrested. Wealthy abolitionist friends posted his bail, but he abandoned the city for New York and never came back. The two fugitives did not fare as well. Allen was caught and immediately sent back to his owner. White ran off, but he eventually turned himself in and authorities forced him back into slavery. (He later escaped and wound up serving as a chaplain for a black regiment in the Civil War.)[35]

Enslaved people also pursued freedom through self-purchase. Throughout the antebellum era, and particularly in the 1850s, slave families worked together to purchase the freedom of individual members. Though it took many years and often required the intervention of white intermediaries or free black kin, self-purchase offered a relatively safe and legal way for black families to remain intact and ultimately enjoy freedom together. Because the required certificates of freedom cost $50 and could be hard to obtain, family members thus purchased did not always register as legally free. In the eyes of the law they remained enslaved, but they enjoyed the privileges of freedom and lived as freemen and women. Enslaved people's initiative in pursuing their freedom by self-purchase may have helped convince Jacob Bigelow and other local white abolitionists to lay aside their personal misgivings about the practice. By the early 1850s, they began tapping the wealth of Northern abolitionists to purchase the freedom of District slaves.[36]

Washington's biracial network of antislavery activists also collaborated to improve life for free black people in the city. One example of this cooperation was the private School for Colored Girls, which opened in December 1851 with six pupils crammed into a fourteen-foot-square room in a home at Eleventh Street and New York Avenue NW. The founder of the school was a stern and sickly white New Yorker named Myrtilla Miner. Thirty-six years old, single, with a fierce stubborn streak, Miner had seen firsthand the horrors of slavery while teaching school in Mississippi in the 1840s. The experience transformed her into an abolitionist, and Miner returned home committed to educating free black girls who, she believed, would teach a future generation of the formerly enslaved how to make the most of their freedom. She chose to open a school in Washington, the southernmost city where it would be legal.[37]

Miner's plan for a school initially worried some local abolitionists. Gamaliel Bailey of the *National Era* ignored her pleas for assistance, and black educator John F. Cook—who himself had established a school for black children—feared that "any thing savouring of abolition" would meet resistance. But Jacob Bigelow offered help, and Miner launched the school with start-up money primarily from Northern abolitionists. As the school grew, she won over the city's interracial antislavery community. Despite threats from many white opponents, Miner and her interracial staff of teachers did not shy away from controversy. Students learned traditional subjects such as home economics and the three Rs as well as politics—they read Frederick Douglass's *North Star*, William Lloyd Garrison's *Liberator*, and other abolitionist literature. Local "rowdies" threatened her students on the street and sought to run Miner out of town, but she refused to be intimidated. She slept above the school with a revolver at the ready. "Mob my school! You dare not!" she yelled at one group of would-be attackers. "There is no law to prevent my teaching these people, and I shall teach them, even unto death!"[38]

Miner's School for Colored Girls, like Ana Maria Weems's courageous flight to Canada, showed the extent of interracial cooperation in the decade before the Civil War. Though not immune to the assumptions of superiority inculcated in almost all white Americans, white abolitionists such as Myrtilla Miner and Jacob Bigelow worked with and for black people in the District at a time when most of their white peers could envision black men and women only as slaves or servants. Their interracial efforts were all the more remarkable because they came at a time when the city, like the nation, endured escalating racial and political tension in the wake of the Compromise of 1850.

No "City of Refuge": White Officials Clamp Down on Free Black Washingtonians

Few white Washingtonians embraced abolitionism. More typical of the city's white leadership were men such as Walter Lenox. Born and bred in Washington, Lenox was the son of a Scottish American carpenter who made a fortune investing in D.C. real estate. After attending Yale, he returned home to practice law and pursue politics. Bearded with a slowly receding hairline, he was known as a ladies' man with a rollicking bachelor's pad that he shared with his friend (and future mayor) Richard Wallach. Lenox rose quickly in local politics. He was elected to the city council at age twenty-five, became president of the Board of Aldermen soon thereafter, and then eked out a victory in the 1850 mayoral race, at age thirty-three.[39]

Lenox's election campaign inaugurated a turbulent, partisan era in local politics. In 1848, a generation after the democratic agitation surrounding Thomas

Carbery's election and after a decades-long national push for universal white manhood suffrage, Congress removed the economic barriers to voting, extending the ballot to all white men who lived in the city for at least a year. The effect on local elections was dramatic—the number of votes cast in mayor's races more than doubled, and the elections became more partisan and contested as poor white men rushed to the polls. Lenox triumphed in 1850, but he was turned out two years later; no District mayor in the 1850s won a second term.[40]

Lenox took office amid the raucous debates that led to the Compromise of 1850. Like Senator Henry Clay of Kentucky, he was a member of the Whig Party who saw the preservation of the Union—with Washington as its capital—as the nation's top priority. But Lenox, like other white leaders in the city, also was a slaveholder with Southern sympathies. Indeed, most white Washingtonians considered themselves Southerners, and as partisan conflicts in Congress took on sectional tones, they tended to side with the South. Though some prominent figures, including Mayor Seaton, had supported a ban on the slave trade to deflect criticism of the city, they were livid at Congress for undemocratically imposing its will.

The slave trade ban raised a troubling question: If Congress had the power to outlaw D.C.'s slave trade, could slavery itself be next? Slavery in the District may not have been a growing institution, but it was a crucial barometer of Southern power. For Southerners terrified of being dominated politically and economically by the more populous and faster-growing North, a failure to defend slavery in the nation's capital would be a sign that the South was doomed to perpetual weakness. When the Georgia legislature listed the specific offenses that it would deem worthy of secession from the Union, ending slavery in Washington was number one on the list.[41]

Local white officials also feared that the ban would trigger a migration of free black people into the city. With a long-standing free black community, government jobs, a network of small but important schools, a sizable number of black-owned businesses, and a variety of black-run churches, the District already attracted free black migrants from the surrounding area. More than half of D.C.'s black residents had roots in Maryland or Virginia. In the 1840s, Washington's free black population grew by nearly 55 percent to more than ten thousand—almost 20 percent of the city's total population and nearly three-quarters of black residents. Now, with the ban in effect, white leaders such as Georgetown mayor Henry Addison worried that free black people would "flock to the District of Columbia, as to a city of refuge."[42]

The stakes could not be higher, as Tennessee senator (and future presidential candidate) John Bell explained during a last-ditch attempt to scuttle the ban

TABLE 2 Washington's black population, 1830–1860

Year	Total (% of total pop.)	Free (% of black pop.)	Enslaved (% of black pop.)
1830	9,109 (30.1)	4,604 (50.5)	4,505 (49.5)
1840	9,819 (29.1)	6,499 (66.2)	3,320 (33.8)
1850	13,746 (26.6)	10,059 (73.2)	3,687 (26.8)
1860	14,316 (19.1)	11,131 (77.8)	3,185 (22.2)

Source: U.S. Census Bureau, "Historical Census Statistics on Population Totals by Race"

on the D.C. slave trade. "If the colored population shall increase hereafter in the ratio of the last few years, it must soon become an intolerable nuisance in the District," he warned. "The white inhabitants, unless Congress shall interpose its authority, will be driven to the alternative of expelling them by force, or become a prey to continual disorder. One or the other must yield." Like many white leaders in the District, Senator Bell promised to support emancipation in the District only if there were a provision to "remove" the freed slaves from the country—the dream of colonizationists stretching back more than three decades.[43]

Unable to prevent the ban on slave trading, Mayor Lenox and D.C.'s elected officials made a concerted effort to discourage black migration into the city. Beginning in late 1850, they passed a series of amendments to the black codes to make life less attractive for free black people. Black migrants were required to register with city officials within five days of their arrival or face a fine and expulsion from the city. Secret meetings were prohibited, and any public meetings of black people had to be personally approved by the mayor. Free black residents also had to pay $50 for a certificate of freedom, a measure designed to make it prohibitively expensive for them to settle in the city—$50 represented several months' wages for skilled work.[44]

These legislative tweaks were accompanied by selective and brutal enforcement of the law. Shortly after the passage of the compromise, the Washington City Council doubled the size of its police force. Throughout the 1850s, black people were three times more likely to be arrested than white people. One incident, reported by New York journalist Frederick Law Olmsted, involved twenty-four "genteel colored men" who had been discovered in a secret meeting. "The object of their meeting appears to have been purely benevolent," Olmsted wrote, but they were arrested and hauled before the magistrate. The men were found to have a Bible, as well as a "subscription paper" to purchase the freedom of an enslaved woman. To Olmsted's horror, one of the men, who was enslaved, was sentenced to flogging, while four others were sent to the workhouse. The rest were each fined $111—more than $3,500 in twenty-first-century dollars—and set free.[45]

The black codes and increased enforcement made Washington a harsher, less tolerant city. Black migration to the city slowed in response. After decades of substantial growth, during the 1850s the free black population grew by barely one thousand, an increase of only 10 percent compared to a 60 percent increase in the white population. The enslaved population, meanwhile, declined by more than 13 percent as many owners decided to either sell or manumit their slaves rather than wait for a possible congressional ban on slavery. The percentage of black people in the city decreased to less than 20 percent by 1860—the lowest point in Washington's history, before or since.[46]

In such an environment, Myrtilla Miner's School for Colored Girls became a target. In late 1856, Miner began raising money to build a boarding school that would offer secondary education and teacher training to free black students. The planned expansion sparked a backlash that ultimately destroyed the school. Leading the charge was former mayor Walter Lenox. Lenox feared that the boarding school would attract black migrants from all over the region until, he warned in a letter to the National Intelligencer in early 1857, "our District is inundated with them." Teaching black students beyond "the primary branches" would lead to social upheaval, Lenox continued, because it would create "a restless population, less disposed than ever to fill that position in society which is allotted to them." White opposition successfully crippled the school, and Miner soon abandoned her expansion plans. Her health, never strong, deteriorated rapidly in the late 1850s, and she left the city to recuperate. Attendance dwindled in her absence, and the school closed its doors in 1860.[47]

"Worthy White Men": Irish Immigration, the Know-Nothings, and Political Violence in White Washington

Laws alone cannot explain the relative decline in Washington's black population in the 1850s. Another factor was immigration. Washington began attracting thousands of foreign-born white workers, thanks in large part to a federal building blitz intended to fortify the Union and show a renewed commitment to maintaining national unity in the wake of the Compromise of 1850. In addition to a long-awaited expansion of the Capitol, Congress funded several labor-intensive projects, including a new aqueduct and sewer system. With so much public building, there was heavy demand for laborers of all kinds, skilled and unskilled, immigrant and native alike. The nation overall experienced an immigration boom in the 1850s, but Washington's foreign-born population grew at one and a half times the national rate, reaching a peak of 16 percent of the city's white population in 1860.[48]

Many of the city's new arrivals were Irish. The blight that ravaged Ireland's potato fields in the mid-1840s pushed more than 1.2 million Irish immigrants, predominantly poor and Catholic, to American shores in the next decade. Most wound up in Boston, New York, and other northeastern cities, but thousands made their way south to Washington. The city's Irish population more than tripled in the 1850s to roughly 7,200, more than double the size of the next largest ethnic group, Germans (and more than double the size of the slave population). "There are, already, more Irish and German laborers and servants than *slaves*," wrote Frederick Law Olmsted in 1855, and "the proportion of white laborers is every year increasing."[49]

The immigrants came to a city with an established Irish community that boasted taverns, businesses, and churches — particularly St. Patrick's on F Street NW, which installed an Irish immigrant, Father Timothy O'Toole, as priest in 1854. Many Irish found housing in a marshy area along the edges of Tiber Creek about a half mile north of Capitol Hill, not far from the construction sites where they worked. Just a rough mingling of shanties at first, the neighborhood grew into Swampoodle, a linguistic combination of two prominent features of the area: "swamp" and "puddle." The lyrically named area became the heart of St. Aloysius parish and, eventually, Gonzaga College High School, a community fixture into the twenty-first century.[50]

Swampoodle was fiercely Irish and utterly poor, known for street violence, overcrowding, and clashes with the black community. Though legendary Irish leader Daniel O'Connell had condemned American slavery and likened the black struggle for freedom to Ireland's fight for independence, the Irish in Washington tended to adopt the mores of the local white population and developed a volatile relationship with the city's black residents. Unlike Germans and Scots, most Irish immigrants arrived in the city without marketable skills, so they competed directly with unskilled black workers, male and female alike. They faced a competitive disadvantage: black labor, enslaved or free, tended to be much cheaper.[51]

To combat what they perceived as unfair competition, Irish immigrants resorted to collective action, banding together with other white workers to force employers to choose between them and their black counterparts. In early 1852, for example, as the federal building boom was getting under way, more than 260 white workers petitioned Congress to ban the use of "free negroes, and Slaves in the public Buildings" and instead employ "Worthy White men," who were "the main support of the country in time of War or civil commotion." "The public office," the petition concluded, "was never designed for the people of that colour, but for the free white citizens of the united States."[52]

Collective action, combined with the legal framework of discrimination against free black workers, helped give the Irish a foothold in the low-skill economy. Irish women—stereotyped as "Bridgets" just as black domestics often were called "mammies"—gave employers an alternative to free black women, and they quickly came to dominate the domestic servant market. As demand slackened, fewer and fewer free black women migrated to the city. The same held true for black men. Famed black abolitionist Frederick Douglass observed in 1853: "Every hour sees us elbowed out of some employment to make room for some newly-arrived emigrant from the Emerald Isle, whose hunger and color entitle him to special favor. These white men are becoming houseservants, cooks, stewards, waiters, and flunkies"—the very kinds of jobs held by black men.[53]

Clustered at the foot of the economic ladder, many Irish fiercely resisted any implications that they belonged in the same class as black people, even though in 1860 Irish families owned but an eighth as much property as non-Irish white Washingtonians. Their economic circumstances forced them to do low-class work, and they sometimes proved to be prickly workers. Frederick Law Olmsted noticed differences between Irish and black servants during his stay in D.C. He found that the "aged negro" who helped him set his fire at his guesthouse was "more familiar and more indifferent to forms of subserviency than the Irish lads." The black "fireman" did not enjoy being subservient, but he seemed more resigned to his fate, Olmsted observed. He held "an expression of impotent anger in his face, and a look of weakness."[54]

Olmsted's observation illustrated a profound difference in outlook between free black people and Irish immigrants, which stemmed from the basic differences in their access to power. Though Washington offered black residents more economic opportunities than other Southern cities, most free black people could rarely expect much more than the low-income work in which they already were engaged—there was little upward mobility. Indeed, by being free, they had reached the pinnacle. Though they themselves were poor, many free black people had enslaved family members who looked to them for help. If the black fireman in Olmsted's room showed "an expression of impotent anger," it was because he had few economic, legal, or political opportunities through which he could change his situation.

The Irish "lads," by contrast, had higher expectations. They came to the city by choice and arrived to find an established Irish community that worked to connect them to jobs, homes, and social networks. If they ran into trouble, they could rely on a network of Catholic institutions built to aid the poor. They could become naturalized citizens and eventually vote, run for office, and participate fully in civic affairs. The Irish lads in Olmsted's room may have appeared less "familiar and indifferent" to subservience because they could more easily envision a future in which they would not have to be subservient.

Washington's Irish considered themselves white, claimed privileges associated with being white, and often proved sensitive to perceived slights about their social status. "They are unwilling to associate with the blacks," wrote one Irish observer, and "their constant effort is to free themselves from the shackles of servitude." Yet by taking the low-status work typically associated with black workers, the fair-skinned Irish faced significant class and religious bigotry. White ethnic boundaries have blurred in twenty-first-century America, but in the mid-1800s they stood out in sharp relief. The District's Irish were "a wild-looking, undisciplined and turbulent people . . . both men and women being much given to fighting and drinking," one white Washingtonian of Scottish descent generalized, reflecting typical prejudice. "It was believed, and was probably true, that no one could control them except their priests." One slave owner told journalist Olmsted that Irish workers were "dishonest, would not obey explicit directions about their work, and required more personal supervision than negroes."[55]

Before the annual St. Patrick's Day parade, it was not unusual for residents in Irish neighborhoods to find "stuffed paddies" hanging from nearby trees. Filled with straw, empty liquor bottles protruding from the pockets, these effigies played on stereotypes of Irish drunkenness and stupidity. Irish workers also had to confront the stereotype of "dumb Paddies," which Olmsted defined as "Irishmen who do not readily understand the English language, and who are still weak and stiff from the effects of the emigrating voyage."[56]

Irish immigration helped reinvigorate "nativist" sentiment among white Americans nationwide. Nativist critics accused the Irish of being heavy drinkers prone to crime and violence, and they worried that Irish involvement in politics would lead to voter fraud, bloc voting, and control of local government by the pope in Rome. Washington had experienced a short-lived nativist movement in the 1830s, but that movement had rejected religious bigotry, in part because its leadership included many Catholics. The nativism of the 1850s, however, was profoundly anti-Irish and anti-Catholic, and it spawned an enigmatic, nationwide political movement officially called the American Party but that came to be known as the Know-Nothings. Originally meeting in secret—when asked about the party's doings, members would respond, "I know nothing"—the movement took hold across the Northeast. The Know-Nothing party rejected both major political parties, offering a third way that appealed to many economically anxious working- and middle-class white voters.

In Washington, Know-Nothings tapped into both ethnic prejudice and class resentment. With the liberalization of the city's voting rules, poor white men now had access to the polls. Many native-born white laborers flocked to the Know-Nothings because they viewed it as antiestablishment; a vote for the new party was a vote against both the arrogant, wealthy class and the foreign Catholics in their midst. For decades, Washington's local elections had been staid affairs dominated by men such as W. W. Seaton, the respected editor of the *National Intelligencer* who served as mayor throughout the 1840s. But with the rise of the Know-Nothings, Washington's municipal elections became confrontational and tinged with xenophobia.[57]

For three tense years, the Know-Nothings infused local politics with drama and violence, much of it targeting the Irish community. The party roared to power in 1854, winning a majority on the Common Council and the Board of Aldermen and capturing the mayor's seat despite being opposed by what one observer called "a large majority of the reflecting portion of this community." In a brazen incident that same year, a gang allegedly linked to the Know-Nothings broke into the Washington Monument construction site, absconded with an enormous stone that Pope Pius IX had donated to the project, and dropped it into the Potomac. During the 1856 elections, the *Evening Star* reported, a line-breaking incident at a polling station grew into a massive melee in which the "Irish were pursued, and beaten, and pelted with stones and brickbats, with little resistance on their part." Local police, filled with Know-Nothing appointees, did little to stop the violence.[58]

The Know-Nothing movement helped bind the city's Catholic community together. The early Catholics in Washington descended from old Maryland slaveholding families. Patrician Catholic leaders worked assiduously to assimilate into the broader white community and tended to view poor Catholic immigrants as a nuisance and a burden. But faced with an existential threat from the Know-Nothing party, not just locally but in Congress, too, the Catholic community came together in unprecedented ways. "We all live upon persecution and we are now well supplied with food," wrote the Washington correspondent to the *Catholic Mirror* in 1854. Immigrants such as Father Timothy O'Toole of St. Patrick's Church responded by rejecting assimilation and building strong, self-sufficient Catholic institutions. St. Aloysius, built in Swampoodle in 1857, was a proudly immigrant and overwhelmingly Irish church that ministered to the needs of its laboring congregants and developed a wide range of social services, including an orphanage and benevolent society to care for the poor, sick, and aged.[59]

As Washington Catholics united across class lines, they found allies in the city's elite leadership. Blindsided by the Know-Nothings, establishment leaders attacked the movement as, in the words of one letter writer to the *Evening Star*, "anti-American and anti-Christian." The editors and readers of the *Evening Star* and the *National Intelligencer* excoriated the movement and defended Washington's Catholics. "Of all places this city should be the very last to entertain narrow-minded and proscriptive prejudice against Catholic and naturalized citizens," wrote "A Native Protestant" in the *National Intelligencer*, noting that Catholics such as Notley Young, Daniel Carroll, and James Hoban had been instrumental in the building of the city.[60]

The city's white elite sought to undercut the Know-Nothings by lumping them together with the city's most reviled political group: abolitionists. For two decades, abolitionists had earned the enmity of much of white Washington. By the early 1850s, as the Whig Party disintegrated over slavery, many prominent abolitionists, including Pennsylvania congressman Thaddeus Stevens and Massachusetts senator Henry Wilson, saw the Know-Nothing movement as an opportunity to break the national stalemate on slavery. Led by Wilson—who later became the author of the bill that emancipated Washington's slaves—Northern Know-Nothings pushed for the party to oppose slavery. Know-Nothings in D.C., including Vespasian Ellis, the slaveholding editor of the city's Know-Nothing paper, the *Daily American Organ*, insisted that slavery was none of the federal government's business. The issue came to a well-publicized head at the party's national convention in 1855, when Southern Know-Nothings beat back Wilson's effort to get the party to officially embrace abolition. Though the proslavery forces had won, the political damage had been done—the Know-Nothings and abolition were linked in many minds.[61]

During the 1856 elections, the *Evening Star* denounced "the fanaticism of Abolitionism and Know Nothingism" and blamed political violence on "the treasonable sentiments of Abolition and Know Nothing orators and presses."[62] That year proved to be the high-water mark for Know-Nothings in the city as they lost the mayor's race and most of their seats on the Board of Aldermen and Common Council.

But the political violence continued, reaching its climax in 1857 with an Election Day riot at the Northern Liberties Market on Seventh Street NW (site of today's Mount Vernon Square). Abetted by local police, a Know-Nothing-inspired mob of more than twelve hundred, armed with guns, knives, clubs, and a six-pound miniature cannon, commandeered the streets, forcing Washington's mayor to appeal for help from President James Buchanan, himself the son of Irish immigrants. Buchanan sent one hundred marines to quell the violence, which they did after a bloody confrontation that left eight people dead and two dozen more wounded. It was the first time since the Jefferson administration that federal troops had fired on American citizens, and many Washingtonians condemned the killings as "military executions." The Know-Nothings lost badly in the election that day, and they were never again a serious political force in the city.[63]

By the late 1850s, the nativist movement had petered out, yet slaveholding Washington remained a politically volatile city. After abolitionist John Brown attempted to inspire a slave revolt in Harpers Ferry, Virginia, in October 1859, nervous Washington officials requisitioned arms from the federal War Department, posted guards on all entry points into the city, and ordered police to break up meetings of black people, public or private. During the city's mayoral contest the following spring, Democrat James Berret won reelection with the help of a paramilitary force that disrupted Republican Party gatherings and intimidated voters. After Republican Abraham Lincoln won election to the presidency in November 1860, nearly three hundred enraged members of the National Volunteers, a Democratic militia, ransacked the Republican Party's headquarters in Washington. Political violence, politically motivated arson, and vigilantism plagued the nation's capital as one Southern state after another seceded from the Union in late 1860 and early 1861. The country and its capital tumbled toward a civil war that would, in the words of one white Washingtonian, "turn everything and everybody topsy turvy."[64]

"Yankee City": The Civil War Comes to Washington

On the eve of the Civil War, D.C. remained a largely Southern city, geographically, culturally, and politically—more than 75 percent of the population not from the city itself was from the South. Most white residents shared the Southern inclination to defend slavery, condemn abolitionists, and fear the rise of the antislavery Republicans. William Owner, a cantankerous and voluble white resident whose diary captured the anger and frustration of many white Washingtonians, wrote that the North simply wanted to "subjugate the South and Steal Niggers." Democrats had controlled the presidency for eight years and filled federal offices with Southerners and "doughfaces" (Northerners who supported the South). Many Southern sympathizers held "important civil, military, and naval positions," reporter Ben Perley Poore noted, and they "remained, truculent and defiant, to place every obstacle in the way of coercion by the Federal Government."[65]

The District's lack of political rights colored many white Washingtonians' perceptions of the conflict between North and South. As residents of the federal city, they had experienced the frustration of having the national government impose its will on the city's elected representatives, such as when Congress banned the slave trade. They understood the feelings of impotence when government officials failed to safeguard their interests. They shared the Southern fear of an aggressive national government meddling in states' internal affairs. To add to the indignity of it all, they did not even have a say in the election that made Lincoln president—it would be another hundred years before Washingtonians could vote in presidential elections.

Yet even after Lincoln's victory in November 1860, few white Washingtonians waved the banner of secession. "The idea of secession or disunion is terrific and *appalling*," wrote Elizabeth Lindsay Lomax, a white mother and army widow with Southern roots but Union sympathies. "*God defend us from such a calamity.*"[66] Secession and war posed a mortal threat to the city. If both Maryland and Virginia were to secede, the home of the federal government would be surrounded by enemies, an island adrift in a hostile sea. The government would have to flee to the North, leaving behind a city without a purpose. Without the federal government, without the Union, Washington would wither.

In an angry editorial, the *Star* denounced local secessionists for supporting the South even though "they know that their own property and that of their friends and neighbors depends on the preservation" of the Union. Washington's "destiny is that of the Union," wrote a correspondent in the *Atlantic* in January 1861. General Winfield Scott, the hulking Virginian who (unlike his protégé Robert E. Lee) chose to stay loyal to the Union even after his home state seceded, told President Lincoln: "Sir, the capital can't be taken; the capital can't be taken." It would be an unimaginable, perhaps even fatal, blow to the Union.[67]

For many local white people, preserving the Union remained the top priority, and they worried that too much emphasis on the abolition of slavery could undermine that goal. The prominent Blair family exemplified this perspective. Originally from Kentucky, Francis Preston Blair (called Preston) came to Washington in 1830 to become part of Andrew Jackson's informal "Kitchen Cabinet" and stayed to publish the *Globe* newspaper. Blair and his politically active family lived in a two-story brick house directly across from the White House (now the official presidential guesthouse) and spent their summers at a country Maryland outpost along a small creek sparkling with mica, which they named Silver Spring.[68]

Though the family owned slaves, they considered themselves political moderates on the issue. They helped launch the antislavery Republican Party and opposed the extension of slavery into the Western territories, but they rejected abolition as impractical and antagonistic toward the South, unless it was accompanied by a plan to "provid[e] homes for the blacks elsewhere." Most important for the Blairs, as Francis Jr. wrote, was "to support the Constitution & Union—about which we care more than we do the niggers." Like the Blairs, many of the city's new immigrants, particularly the Irish, felt strong ties to the Union even as they opposed abolition and rejected the Republicans (where many Know-Nothings had found a home).[69]

Lincoln sought to reassure white Southerners, Northern Democrats, and moderates in his own party that he had no intention of abolishing slavery anywhere that it already existed, including Washington. During the campaign, he had talked about limiting the expansion of slavery, but he never broached abolition. Had he done so, he never could have won his party's nomination, let alone the election. After his aborted legislative attempt to outlaw slavery in the District in 1849, he avoided the issue of emancipation in Washington. "I have no thought of recommending the abolition of slavery in the District of Columbia, nor the slave trade among the slave states," he assured one worried Southerner in December 1860. Even after secession and the beginning of hostilities, Lincoln argued repeatedly that the goal of the war was not to end slavery—he sought first and foremost to maintain the physical and political integrity of the Union.[70]

Despite Lincoln's assurances, few white people in the South trusted him. They looked at his record and concluded that he was, at best, a closet abolitionist. As the Southern states seceded, Southern political leaders and bureaucrats, including many of the city's oldest, most powerful families, packed up and left Washington, often taking their slaves with them. About four hundred white men from the District joined the Confederate army. Former mayor Walter Lenox fled to Richmond to work for the Confederate government. Wealthy banker and local philanthropist W. W. Corcoran, who later created a renowned art museum, did not hide his Southern sympathies, though he lacked the courage to act on them—he sat out the war years in Europe. Some white residents stayed in the city and secretly worked to aid the South. In the months between the election and Lincoln's inauguration, rumors about Southern conspiracies to take the city abounded, and Republicans questioned the loyalty of local residents. Mayor James Berret was arrested for refusing to swear an oath of loyalty to the Union.[71]

Lincoln's March 1861 inauguration passed without major incident, but the simmering tensions boiled over barely a month later. On April 12, South Carolina troops fired the first shots of the war at Fort Sumter, a federal fort in Charleston Harbor. Many Washingtonians worried that the Confederacy would target the capital, particularly after Virginia seceded on April 17. With the enemy in sight across the Potomac and without significant military installations for protection, the city was terribly vulnerable. Lincoln himself told his cabinet that if "I were [Confederate general Pierre G. T.] Beauregard I would take Washington." Residents' fears only grew when a civilian mob in Baltimore attacked soldiers from Massachusetts sent to defend the city, and the bloodied troops arrived in D.C. on April 19 with four dead. Local militias hastily mustered in the streets, and residents nervously awaited reinforcements, fearing that an invading Confederate army might arrive first.[72]

Jacob Dodson did not simply wait for saviors to arrive. A free black Washingtonian whose family had worked for Missouri senator Thomas Hart Benton, Dodson had spent many rugged years traveling through the West with famed explorer (and presidential candidate) John C. Frémont. Now thirty-five years old, Dodson was an expert marksman with military experience, and he offered to mobilize the free black community to defend the Union capital. On April 23, he wrote Secretary of War Simon Cameron promising the services of "three hundred reliable colored free citizens of this City, who desire to enter the service for the defense of the City." But Cameron refused. "I have to say that this Department has no intention at present to call into the service of the Government any colored soldiers," he wrote a week later. Cameron apparently was willing to risk the capital's safety rather than set a politically perilous precedent of allowing black men to fight on behalf of the Union.[73]

Two days after Dodson wrote his letter, the beleaguered city welcomed several thousand troops from New York. (Among them was Robert Gould Shaw, who later would gain fame as the white commander of an all-black regiment and whose name graces a prominent neighborhood.) The siege of Washington was lifted.[74]

The city soon crackled with life as tens of thousands of migrants of all sorts came to town—soldiers and officers preparing for combat, government clerks administering the war, entrepreneurs seeking to profit from wartime contracts, runaway slaves seeking freedom in the Union capital. Now the headquarters of the Union army, D.C. became "a military camp, a city of barracks and hospitals," visiting journalist Noah Brooks wrote. "Long lines of army wagons and artillery were continually rumbling through the streets; at all hours of the day and night the air was troubled by the clatter of galloping squads of cavalry; and the clank of sabers, and the measured beat of marching infantry, were ever present to the ear." Military barracks sprang up in empty lots, and the streets thrummed with drilling soldiers on parade. "The city is like a beehive on swarming day, all bustle, activity and apparent confusion," wrote reporter Lois Adams. The city's population exploded. The Metropolitan Police estimated that D.C.'s population nearly doubled between 1860 and 1864, growing from barely 75,000 to roughly 140,000 people.[75]

Northern Republicans streamed into Washington. In an era before civil service protections, Lincoln administration officials such as abolitionist Treasury secretary Salmon P. Chase systematically replaced proslavery government clerks with antislavery ones. The character of the District shifted dramatically as ideas once considered radical and taboo a year or two earlier now enjoyed official sanction. Republicans, for instance, invited abolitionist speakers to participate in the Smithsonian Institution's lecture series. Sayles J. Bowen, an ambitious white abolitionist from New York who had worked with Myrtilla Miner in the 1850s, attended the lectures and was amazed: "Every man who lectured there would have lost his head if he had dared utter the same sentiments in Washington only one year before."[76]

As in other cities, D.C.'s press was partisan, and leading newspapers in the city were unabashedly pro-Union. The *National Intelligencer* represented the Lincoln administration, the *National Republican* spoke for conservative members of the party, and the *Daily Chronicle* was the voice of the radicals. Even the *Evening Star*, which had opposed Lincoln, shifted to the Republicans. Southern sympathizers—"Secesh," as they were called by Unionists—may have remained in town, but their voices were drowned in a chorus of pro-Union sentiment. Washington, crowed the *National Republican* in December 1861, was becoming a "Yankee city."[77]

"A Social and Political Revolution in Our Midst": Washington's Slaves Win Their Freedom

Elizabeth Keckly witnessed Washington's wartime transformation from her perch in the White House, where she served as a seamstress.[78] The daughter of a prominent Virginia plantation owner and his house slave, Keckly had endured emotional, physical, and sexual abuse during the thirty-seven years she was enslaved—her only son was born after she had been raped repeatedly by one of her owners. Taught to sew by her mother, the resilient and resourceful Keckly became an expert seamstress while still enslaved in St. Louis, and she used her skills to earn money and win friends among the well-connected white women who were her clients. With their help, she purchased freedom for herself and her son in 1855, and five years later she launched a new life in Washington.

As a free black woman moving into the city, she needed a license from the mayor to stay, and she used one of her client's connections to secure one. She enjoyed a meteoric rise, earning local renown for designing dresses for the wives of such prominent figures as Robert E. Lee and Jefferson Davis. Just a day after President Lincoln's inauguration, Keckly became the primary dressmaker for the new first lady, Mary Todd Lincoln. The two women grew extraordinarily close — Lincoln called Keckly her "one true friend" — and Keckly became an influential part of D.C.'s free black community.[79]

Keckly, like other black Washingtonians, strongly supported the Union army. Her son, George, passing as a white man, volunteered for the First Missouri Volunteers in 1861 and was killed at the Battle of Wilson's Creek that August. Despite the president's protestations otherwise, black people across the South viewed the war very much as a war about freedom. They saw the Union army as an army of liberation, and almost immediately enslaved people began fleeing their plantations wherever Union soldiers appeared. The slaves' initiative in running for their own freedom forced Lincoln's hand and pushed him eventually to support emancipation.[80]

For the first year and a half of the war, Lincoln sought to maintain a delicate political balance. On the one hand, he could not allow the seceding states to destroy the Union, so he had to act swiftly and harshly to put down the rebellion. On the other hand, he did not want to alienate the slave states of the Border South, whose support was necessary to winning the war. Maryland, in particular, was crucial. If Maryland were to secede, then the federal government and Union army would have to decamp for safer territory farther north, a crushing blow both symbolically and substantively. Maryland, which had voted for the Southern Democratic ticket in the presidential election, had a Know-Nothing governor who sought to keep the state neutral in the war, and Lincoln worked to assuage his concerns.

Lincoln's desire to maintain the support of Maryland and other border states led him to craft a slaveholder-friendly policy on fugitive slaves. He initially ordered Union soldiers to imprison all fugitive slaves and give them up to their owners. In the first full month of the war, soldiers in D.C. captured seventy-three runaways, threw them in the Blue Jug, and then returned them to slavery. But that policy defied strategic sense. Enslaved workers, after all, were essential to the South's war machine. Why should Union soldiers act as slave catchers for traitors who had seceded from the nation?[81]

Union general Benjamin Butler, a Massachusetts Democrat who had supported Jefferson Davis's failed presidential bid in 1860, defied Lincoln's orders. Operating out of federally held Fort Monroe, Virginia (about 180 miles south of D.C.) in June 1861, Butler encountered three runaway slaves in his camp and refused to send the men back into slavery, even after the owners came to fetch them. Instead, he kept them with his soldiers, calling them "contraband of war." The legally questionable term stuck—soon, fugitive slaves as a group were called "contrabands."[82]

Other Union officers followed Butler's lead, angering slave owners in Southern states that had not seceded. Maryland congressman Charles Calvert denounced the army for allowing enslaved people to settle in camps around Washington, claiming that the camps served as "receptacles for our slaves." Desperate to maintain their support, that July, Lincoln reasserted his position: generals had to allow slaveholders to get their slaves back. Confusion reigned until early August, when Congress passed the first Confiscation Act, which allowed federal forces to seize and emancipate those enslaved people whose owners were found to have used them to assist Confederate armies. It did not apply, however, to slaves held by owners in loyal slave states (such as Maryland) or in the District. If any of those slaves tried to escape, they were subject to capture and return by force of the Fugitive Slave Act, which remained in effect.[83]

In the months that followed the Confiscation Act, hundreds of enslaved people—including many Maryland fugitives, who had no legal protection—flooded into the District, where they found shelter and safety in the homes of local black residents. Their presence in the city raised another important question: How did one know whether a runaway slave's owner was loyal to the Union or not? One man determined the answer to that question, the District's federal marshal, Ward H. Lamon.[84]

A Virginian with a Herculean frame and proslavery instincts, Lamon had been the president's law partner and later became his self-appointed bodyguard. As marshal, Lamon ran the Blue Jug, which quickly became overcrowded with captured fugitives. Believing that most of the runaways came from Maryland and thus had fled "loyal" owners, Lamon refused to consider them "contraband" and instead enforced the letter of the Fugitive Slave Act. He crowded them into the old jail, where they endured wretched conditions in what one government report had described in summer 1861 as "a badly ventilated, unwholesome building."[85]

The Blue Jug became a lightning rod for antislavery criticism—abolitionists dubbed it the "Washington Slave Pen." Senator Henry Wilson of Massachusetts and his antislavery allies in Congress hired pioneering private detective Allan Pinkerton to investigate Lamon and conditions at the Blue Jug. Pinkerton found sixty alleged runaway slaves held without charge, some of whom were actually free, and he charged that unclaimed runaways were still being sold to recoup jail costs. A sensational two-page set of illustrations appeared in *Frank Leslie's Illustrated Newspaper* depicting horrific scenes at the jail, sparking outrage nationwide. Criticism became so intense that Lincoln himself had to intervene,

Senator Morton's Washerwoman, Gateway of Corridor.

SECRETS OF THE PRISON-HOUSE—THE BLACK HOLE OF WASHINGTON.

"*Secrets of the Prison-House — Washington's Black Hole.*" *Even after the Civil War began, more than three thousand people remained enslaved in the nation's capital. Arthur Lumley's engraving, published in the December 28, 1861, edition of Frank Leslie's Illustrated Newspaper, helped encourage Congress to ban slavery in D.C. Library of Congress.*

AL

IIGTON D.C.

IN JAIL

The Witness and Criminal,
Corridor of Jail.

ordering Lamon to stop imprisoning runaway slaves unless they were accused of committing an actual crime.[86]

The controversy surrounding the Blue Jug helped fuel the movement to outlaw slavery in Washington. By late 1861, secessionist representatives had cleared out of the Capitol, giving Republicans relatively free rein to pursue their legislative agenda. Senator Wilson took the lead in drafting a bill that effectively would emancipate the District's slaves, and he earned the support of not just abolitionists but many moderate Republicans, including the editors of the *National Republican*.

Wilson's bill infuriated most white Washingtonians. The editors of the *National Intelligencer* railed against the "sudden, forcible, and total act of emancipation," while the *Evening Star* listed "Twenty Reasons Why the Bill to Emancipate the Slaves in the District of Columbia Should Not Pass." Though pro-Union, the *Evening Star* remained proslavery, hoping to find a balance between the preservation of the city—which required supporting the Union—and the preservation of white power, which required supporting slavery. Reflecting the prevailing sentiment of white elites, the editors warned that the bill was "but the beginning of a social and political revolution in our midst." If Congress could free "our negroes against our will," they reasoned, then it "can and perhaps will confer upon them equality in civil and political privileges with the whites."[87]

The members of the city's Board of Aldermen and Common Council also sought to dissuade Congress from passing the emancipation bill. In a "Joint Resolution of Instruction" that they sent to Congress in early April, the members warned that the bill would end up "converting this city . . . into an asylum for free negroes—a population undesirable in every American community." Alderman William Moore went further. "If this spirit of fanaticism will prevail, we will be in the midst of horrors we never dreamt of," he said. "It will be a question of equality or extermination. The races can never exist together as equals."[88]

The editors of the *Evening Star* and other local white people were right on one point: Congress was indeed imposing its will on D.C. residents. But local democracy had never been a congressional priority. Republican members of Congress saw D.C. as a place to test their racial policies. Ohio senator John Sherman, whose older brother William would win glory as a Union general, argued that Washington was the perfect location for "the experiment in emancipation." Washington "is a paradise for free negroes," where black people "enjoy more social equality than they do anywhere else," Sherman argued, so it made sense to emancipate Washington's slaves first.[89]

Although most Southern representatives were no longer present, the emancipation bill met resistance in Congress. Northern Democrats and some Republicans thought that it would hurt the Union's war efforts and argued that Congress did not have the authority to outlaw slavery anywhere. Border state representatives worried that it would set a precedent for outlawing slavery in their home states, with Maryland representatives fearing (presciently, as it turned out) that their slaves would flee to Washington. In the Senate, a battle erupted over colonization after Senator Garrett Davis of Kentucky introduced an amendment that would require emancipated Washingtonians to leave the country. The vote on the amendment stalemated at 19–19, forcing Vice President Hannibal Hamlin to cast the tie-breaking "nay." Instead of forced colonization, the final bill included a clause encouraging voluntary emigration.[90]

The bill passed easily: 29–14 in the Senate on April 3, 1862, and 92–38 in the House on April 11. Lincoln signed it on April 16, which became known as Emancipation Day in Washington.

From Lincoln's perspective, the bill was not ideal. It ordered immediate emancipation, rather than the gradual emancipation he had long advocated, and it certainly had not gotten support from local residents, as he had wanted. But, as the president wrote following his approval of the bill, "I am gratified the two principles of compensation and colonization are both recognised and practically applied in the act."[91]

Titled "An Act for the Release of Certain Persons Held to Service or Labor in the District of Columbia," the bill did not even use the words "slave," "slavery," or "emancipation." It allowed "loyal" slave owners to make claims for compensation for their newly freed slaves. It established a three-man commission to assess claims and make payments of up to $300 per enslaved person, and it created a $1 million fund for those payments. In a remarkable step, commissioners were required to accept testimony "without the exclusion of any witness on the account of color." The law also set up a $100,000 fund to help black people "to emigrate to the Republics of Hayti or Liberia."[92]

The emancipation bill was just the beginning of what was indeed, as the Star had feared, "a social and political revolution in our midst." Not content simply to free the District's enslaved people, Republicans in Congress sought to eliminate the legal vestiges of slavery in the city. In a burst of legislation in late spring and early summer 1862, Congress dismantled the city's black codes, established a public school system for black students, and required "that in all judicial proceedings in the District of Columbia there shall be no exclusion of any witness on account of color." Black people now could pursue any economic activities without legal restrictions, they could assemble peaceably without official permission, and they no longer faced a racially discriminatory curfew.[93]

It was a legislative revolution of stunning speed and magnitude, and it sparked celebrations in black communities across the North. Yet among black Washingtonians the response was relatively restrained. Not wanting to antagonize their white neighbors or goad them into violence, black church leaders discouraged parades or raucous public festivities in favor of private celebrations and "a day of thanksgiving and prayer." Days before the bill passed, Daniel Payne, presiding bishop of the African Methodist Episcopal Church, offered a sermon of advice to the "ransomed," the enslaved people who would soon be freed: "Welcome not to indolence, to vice, licentiousness, and crime, but to a well-regulated liberty" that demanded faith, education, and "work, work, work!" Within a week of emancipation, members of the Fifteenth Street Presbyterian Church resolved that "by our industry, energy, moral deportment and character, we will prove ourselves worthy of the confidence reposed in us in making us free men."[94]

Though black Washingtonians universally embraced emancipation, they were split on the bill's provision for colonization. President Lincoln remained committed to colonization—one reporter called it his "favorite panacea for the national troubles"—and hoped to organize a party of free black people and newly emancipated slaves to launch a settlement in Chiriquí, in present-day Panama. Several well-known black leaders in the city, including the magnetic Henry McNeal Turner of Israel Bethel Church, endorsed Lincoln's plan and petitioned Congress to fund it. Through the summer of 1862, recruiting agents found a receptive audience among formerly enslaved Washingtonians, who saw colonization as a chance to start afresh in a new place far away from white racists.[95]

But other black leaders, including John F. Cook Jr., were angered by the renewed push for colonization. An educator as his father had been, the twenty-seven-year-old Cook helped launch the Social, Civil, and Statistical Association (SCSA), a civic group composed of well-educated, relatively well off black Washingtonians. Many SCSA members harbored suspicions about the colonization movement and pounded colonization agents—verbally and physically—for taking "heartless and unprincipled advantage" of former slaves.[96]

Cook and other SCSA members were part of a delegation of black leaders who met with President Lincoln that August to discuss the Chiriquí plan. Before arriving, the delegation issued a sharply worded resolution condemning the idea as "inexpedient, inauspicious, and impolite." Lincoln called their opposition "extremely selfish" and insisted that it was "better for us both . . . to be separated." Despite significant high-level support, however, the Chiriquí plan ultimately dissolved in the face of logistical difficulties, continued black resistance, and diplomatic opposition from Central American governments. The issue faded after the Emancipation Proclamation, which took effect on January 1, 1863 and essentially made freedom—not colonization—official federal policy.[97]

The D.C. emancipation bill established a three-man Federal Emancipation Claims Commission to adjudicate claims. The commissioners hired a former slave trader from Baltimore, B. M. Campbell, to help them assess the value of enslaved people. Campbell, one observer later noted, did his job "with great particularity, making [slaves] dance about to show their suppleness of limb, and open their mouths to prove that they had sound teeth." Though some Washington slave owners had either sold their slaves or sent them to live elsewhere, within three months of the bill's passage the commissioners had approved 909 claims for 2,981 enslaved people from more than a thousand owners. Another 111 slaves, deemed too young, too old, or too sick to warrant compensation, were freed without remuneration at all. The city's largest slave owner, George Washington Young (descendant of Notley Young), received $17,771.85 for the 69 slaves that he claimed—about $430,000 in twenty-first-century dollars. Even the pious Sisters of the Visitation asked for, and received, compensation for the 12 enslaved people the Georgetown convent owned. In all, the government spent $993,406 to compensate the former slave owners.[98]

Some of the compensated claimants were black. Throughout the South, free black people periodically purchased family members, but they sometimes did not file the proper paperwork or pay the necessary fees to get them legally freed. One free black man, Gabriel Coakley, purchased the freedom of his wife and family in the late 1850s, but he never submitted their paperwork. Hence, they legally "belonged" to him. So, with an affidavit from a leading white attorney, he applied for compensation and received $1,489.20.[99]

Not all slave owners complied with the provisions of the law. Alexander McCormick owned five people on a plantation that straddled the border between Maryland and Northeast Washington. Most of his land, as well as the slave quarters, fell on the District side of the border. In early 1862, as Congress debated the emancipation bill, McCormick hastily built new homes for his enslaved workers on the Maryland side. Because they no longer lived in the District, he argued, they were not subject to the emancipation bill, and he refused to submit a compensation claim for them. Without such a claim, the slaves could not be freed. Realizing that as many as 150 slave owners had avoided the law by failing to submit claims, Congress amended the emancipation bill to allow enslaved people to file claims on their own—a revolutionary step. McCormick's slaves, Emeline Wedge and her two children, her sister, Alice, and her mother, Mary, filed a petition and testified before the commissioners that they actually lived and worked in the District. On December 30, 1862, they finally gained their freedom.[100]

So, too, did Philip Reed, a skilled metalworker who was helping to cast the bronze Statue of Freedom that soon would be placed atop a new Capitol dome. And Eleanora and Caroline Bell, two fugitives from the *Pearl* who had remained enslaved in Washington. And one-year-old Abraham Lincoln Hawkins, named for the newly elected president. Nearly 3,100 men, women, and children held in bondage in the nation's capital became free. With District emancipation coming nearly nine months before the Emancipation Proclamation took effect, they were the nation's "first freed," a distinction they would hold with pride for generations to come.[101]

It had taken more than sixty years of relentless resistance, desperate escapes, political agitation, and, finally, the outbreak of war, but slavery in Washington was dead at last. Already a top destination for escaping slaves and free black people, Washington now became even more powerfully associated with black opportunity. What had been a steady stream of black migrants became a torrent. The city was about to enter a time of unprecedented transformation.

FIVE

Emancipate, Enfranchise, Educate

Freedom and the Hope of Interracial Democracy, 1862–1869

This District has been *experimented upon* in various forms of legislation, odious to the citizens ... and now the most tyrannic blow of all is threatened by the rude power of Radicalism in Congress. The attempt is to be made to *force negro equality upon the unwilling people of the District of Columbia, who have just protested, almost with unanimity, against such equality.* — National Intelligencer, January 1866

Franklin Square today is a patch of green between Thirteenth, Fourteenth, I, and K Streets NW. Named for Benjamin Franklin, the square does not feature a statue or marker of its portly namesake, but it does offer shade trees, a mesmerizing fountain, and a measure of quiet in a canyon of the city. The square's edges sparkle with glassy towers built for the lobbying elite, with one exception: the red-brick Franklin School, designed by renowned German architect Adolf Cluss in 1868. A marvel of sophisticated architecture when it opened, by the late twentieth century it had been turned into a homeless shelter. In 2008, city leaders decided to close the shelter, sparking raucous protests that raised questions of race, class, and equity in a rapidly gentrifying city.

Franklin Square has long been a site of controversy and celebration. Indeed, two years before the Franklin School opened, the square hosted one of the most memorable events in the city's history: the first post–Civil War Emancipation Day celebration. Held on April 16, 1866, the fourth anniversary of D.C. emancipation, the celebration began with a lengthy parade that traversed miles of rutted streets from Georgetown to the Capitol, making sure to stop by the home of dedicated abolitionist Charles Sumner, as well as the Executive Mansion, where marchers called out for President Andrew Johnson. The crowd cheered when Johnson appeared, though its demands for equal rights directly challenged the president's policies.[1]

The train of five thousand marchers representing every form of organized black activity in the city—military battalions, fraternal organizations, church

"Celebration of the Abolition of Slavery in the District of Columbia by the Colored People, in Washington." More than ten thousand people celebrated Emancipation Day at Franklin Square in 1866. The annual celebration on April 16 was among the most important days on the calendar of black Washingtonians for much of the late nineteenth century. Library of Congress.

groups, Freemasons, political parties—was so long, recalled General O. O. Howard, the white leader of the Freedmen's Bureau, that "there was no point from which one could see the entire length." The procession wended its way to Franklin Square, where upwards of ten thousand spectators, a "dense mass of colored faces, relieved here and there by a few white ones," according to *Harper's Weekly*, joined the marchers in celebration, song, and prayers of thanksgiving. The air was alive with music and energy. "Bands were playing, drums beating, men hurrahing in all directions, while the crowd . . . moved to and fro," wrote one reporter.[2]

Festooned with banners and flags, the speaker's platform held more than a hundred people, a veritable "Who's Who" of abolitionists and Radical Republicans, including General Howard, Connecticut senator Lyman Trumbull, who coauthored the Thirteenth Amendment banning slavery, and Massachusetts senator Henry Wilson, sponsor of the D.C. emancipation bill. The keynote speech was delivered by Henry Highland Garnet, the black pastor of Fifteenth

Street Presbyterian Church, whose renown among orators was matched perhaps only by Frederick Douglass. Six feet tall with a stately bearing despite an amputated leg, the former Maryland slave captured the celebratory mood with an emotional speech. "To-day the principles of liberty are triumphant," Garnet told the crowd. "God is with us and we must be free."[3]

The event was not simply a time to celebrate abolition, emancipation, and the Union victory of a year before. It also was an opportunity to flex the black community's newfound political muscle and galvanize supporters for future political battles. Emancipation was but the first step toward first-class citizenship; freedom alone would be insufficient to protect the interests of black residents. With the slaves freed and the war won, black people now sought to secure the most fundamental right in a democracy: suffrage. "We have received our civil rights," read a banner hanging above the speaker's platform. "Give us the right of suffrage, and the work is done."[4]

The Franklin Square Emancipation Day celebration was a powerful, public manifestation of the almost unimaginable change Washington had experienced since the beginning of the war. Not even half a decade before, Washington was a slave city ruled by black codes that barred "tumultuous" meetings of black people; now thousands of organized black Washingtonians commandeered much of downtown for a day of festivities. Just a few years earlier, individual black people faced legal barriers to owning firearms and no black man could serve in the military; now entire regiments of armed black militiamen marched openly in the streets. Before the war, politics was the realm of white men alone; now, with support from white Radicals in Congress, black people in Washington organized politically and pushed publicly for the right to vote. It was a stunning transformation that infused black people across the region with hope that they would be able to participate fully in an interracial democracy unlike anything the nation, indeed the world, had ever seen.

Conservative white Washingtonians, however, watched the spectacle with dread. "The day and night closed with whiskey drinking and all manner of nig devillry," grumbled William Owner in his diary. So many black revelers converged on the area that white people "had to take refuge on steps & in stores, as was my case until the nigs passed." As he peered out at the masses of black people taking over the city's streets, Owner's mind raced to the future political implications of the event: "What an army of nigs for white mens taxes to feed!"[5] Owner feared that he was witnessing a fundamental political shift, one that would force him and other white supremacists to the side as black Washingtonians and their white allies assumed control not just of the streets but of politics as well.

For Washington, perhaps even more so than the rest of the nation, the war and Reconstruction were a time of upheaval. Because Congress wielded exclusive authority over the city, Washington was the one place where congressional Radicals could implement their policies without interference from state and local authorities. Even as the war raged, Radical Republicans sought to turn Washington into what Charles Sumner would call "an example for all the land," the prototype of an integrated America where black people enjoyed political and civic (though not social) equality.[6]

Each major piece of Reconstruction legislation, from freedmen's relief to black men's suffrage to education, was "field tested" in the District before being implemented across a resistant South. The transformation was rarely smooth or uncontested. Critics complained that Washington was being used as "an experimental garden for Radical plants," and white conservatives fought to prevent the seeds of equality from taking root. But no one could deny that the nation's capital, once a Southern bastion of slavery and the slave trade, was at the forefront of racial and political change.[7]

"With All Their Worldly Goods on Their Backs": Black Migrants Pour into Washington

In spring 1862, with the outcome of the war still very much in doubt, John Washington had freedom on his mind. Twenty-four years old, enslaved since birth, Washington knew that the Union army was approaching his home in Fredericksburg, Virginia, and he wanted to join it. Light-skinned and raised as a house slave on a country plantation, he learned to read and write—skills that helped him woo a free black woman named Annie (whom he had wed in early 1862) and later write a memoir of his escape from slavery.

By April 18, 1862, just two days after President Lincoln signed the D.C. emancipation bill, Yankee soldiers were within a mile of the Fredericksburg hotel where Washington worked as an enslaved barkeeper. His bosses closed the hotel and demanded that he follow them to the Confederate army lines, but he "secretly resolved not to go." Bursting with excitement, he watched from atop the hotel as the Yankees approached: "I could not begin to Express my new born hopes for I felt already like I was certain of My freedom Now." That night, listening for the sounds of Union bands playing the "Star-Spangled Banner," he and a cousin sneaked up the Rappahannock River, crossed through the Union lines, and left slavery behind forever.[8]

Washington worked for the Union army for several months until he learned that there was a $300 bounty on his head. Leaving his pregnant wife in Fredericksburg, he and six family members headed north to D.C. They had to sleep out on Fourteenth Street NW the night they arrived before finding lodging in Georgetown the next day. Washington "had no trade then and knew not what to do," but he soon found work bottling liquor for $1.25 a day. Annie Washington and their newborn son joined him soon thereafter, and they began a new life in the nation's capital.[9]

The Washingtons were among several hundred black Fredericksburg residents who migrated to D.C. beginning that summer. Many of them, including the Washington family, were members of Fredericksburg's Shiloh Baptist Church. Once in D.C., they worked quickly to reestablish the church in a "little shanty" on L Street between Sixteenth and Seventeenth Streets. The Washingtons remained faithful congregants as the church expanded to more than eight hundred members and built a two-story brick sanctuary before moving in 1924 to its present location at Ninth and P Streets NW.[10]

The Washington family was part of a torrent of black migration to the city in the wake of the emancipation bill. Fugitives fled from across the South, but especially from the neighboring states of Maryland and Virginia. They arrived as individuals and as families, and sometimes in massive groups, and they kept coming for the duration of the war. By 1870, Washington's black population had more than tripled to forty-three thousand, jumping from 19 percent of the city's total population to 33 percent. "Washington seems to be a kind of a Mecca for sable gentlemen," wrote a thrilled William J. Wilson, a black educator from New York who first visited the city in May 1863. "It is blacks, blacks, blacks everywhere. Blacks on the government wagons—blacks on the drays—blacks on the hacks—blacks on the dirt-carts—blacks in the hotels, in the barbers shops, in all the houses, on all the streets." The flood of migrants seemed to confirm white Washingtonians' worst fears about emancipation.[11]

Combined with the influx of white soldiers, bureaucrats, and wartime entrepreneurs, the black migration pushed the city to its limits. The incoming migrants—called "contrabands" or "freedmen"—were overwhelmingly poor, unskilled, and uneducated. Unlike John Washington, the vast majority were illiterate, compared to just a 30 percent illiteracy rate among free black people in the District. They came to Washington, White House tailor Elizabeth Keckly recalled, "with all their worldly goods on their backs." Wartime demand for unskilled labor was relatively high, so most of the former slaves could find work, but the cost of living in the city was exorbitant due to shortages in housing, food, and basic supplies. They lived in excruciating conditions in often the least desirable locations, erecting shanties along the city canal, crowding into alleys, piling into leaky hovels, and boarding in stable lofts.[12]

Black Washingtonians opened their doors and institutions to the new arrivals. In Washington, the *Weekly Anglo-African's* correspondent wrote, "we rejoice more over one poor downtrodden soul escaped from chains, than over the taking of ninety and nine cities." Henry McNeal Turner of Israel Bethel Church praised the black community for having "thrown open their finest parlors, given up their kitchens, garrets and even closets to shelter these escaping sons of humanity." Elizabeth Keckly, herself not far removed from slavery, spearheaded the formation of the Contraband Relief Association with fellow members of the Fifteenth Street Presbyterian Church, and other churches formed similar organizations. The National Freedmen's Relief Association (NFRA) commended black Washingtonians "for the interest and zeal which they have manifested in behalf of their less fortunate brethren."[13]

Middle-class black residents wanted to absorb the migrants and help them establish themselves—"uplift" them, in nineteenth-century parlance—but the magnitude of the challenges that former slaves faced at times overwhelmed the capacity of private efforts. Former slave and abolitionist Harriet Jacobs, whose autobiography, *Incidents in the Life of a Slave Girl*, had made her a legend in antislavery circles, visited Washington in the summer of 1862 and was appalled by the living conditions she witnessed among the formerly enslaved. "I found men, women and children all huddled together, without any distinction or regard to age or sex. Some of them were in the most pitiable condition. Many were sick with measles, diphtheria, scarlet and typhoid fever. Some had a few filthy rags to lie on; others had nothing but the bare floor for a couch." A smallpox epidemic ravaged the city's black community in 1862, spreading rapidly as cold and desperate former slaves huddled together in cramped, dirty conditions.[14]

The scale of the migration forced the federal government to step in to help the formerly enslaved adjust to their new lives—the city government refused to offer any assistance. Through a newly created "Contraband Department" (a precursor to the Freedmen's Bureau) within the Quartermaster Department, the army put freedmen to work building the ring of forts that were to protect the city from a Confederate invasion. Workers and their families tended to settle near the forts, establishing the roots of black communities that would flourish near Fort Reno, Fort Dupont, and other military installations into the twentieth century.

Freedmen and women also labored in local hospitals and did a variety of jobs, including digging ditches, cleaning, sawing wood, making fires, gardening, cooking, and "scavenging" through garbage. Compared to white laborers, one military official claimed, "the negroes are much superior workers, more attentive to their duties, less inclined to dissipation and readily controlled." So-called contraband workers had economic leverage in wartime Washington. Able to sell their labor and choose their employers for the first time, former slaves maneuvered to secure the best deals possible. With demand high, even manual laborers could earn between $20 and $25 a month with rations—significantly more than other Northern workers, though still not enough to keep up with Washington's rising cost of living.[15]

Many of the formerly enslaved, however, were not able to work—they were too old, too young, or too sick. To aid the sick and elderly, the army created a Contraband Fund, financed by a deduction of $5 a month from the wages of black workers in the Quartermaster Department. This "contraband tax" rankled some free black laborers, who objected to having to pay for formerly enslaved families. One group complained to Secretary of War Edwin Stanton that they should no more "pay a tax for the benefit of the contrabands" than should "white labor[er]s of our class," but it remained in place.[16]

The Contraband Fund helped finance the "contraband camps" that the government had established in the city. Like modern refugee camps, contraband camps were intended to be safe, temporary residences where people could get shelter, food, and employment assistance. Once established, however, they attracted long-term residents and became breeding grounds for disease as well as attacks, verbal and physical, from local white people who resented the fugitives' presence. As many as ten thousand former slaves passed through such camps in the District area during the war.[17]

The District's military governor, James S. Wadsworth, a wealthy New York abolitionist, struggled to create a humane system for dealing with the large numbers of migrants pouring into the city. Overwhelmed military officials initially threw homeless former slaves into the Old Capitol Prison, where they shared space with Confederate prisoners. Fears of a smallpox outbreak in early 1862 led Wadsworth to requisition housing along Duff Green's Row, the famed set of boardinghouses across from the Capitol that included Abolition House, where Abraham Lincoln had lived while a congressman in the 1840s. The row houses quickly filled up, with some four hundred people cramming into space intended for fifty.[18]

The camps were becoming a humanitarian crisis, and Wadsworth tapped into what had been the prewar antislavery movement to help address the situation. With emancipation, abolitionists' focus shifted from helping fugitive slaves escape to helping former slaves adjust to freedom. Both because it was the nation's capital and because of the massive number of refugees there, Washington became a magnet for Northern missionaries, particularly white women who arrived to work with an alphabet soup of relief organizations such as the

National Freedmen's Relief Association and the American Missionary Association (AMA).

They saw their work as a divine calling. The Washington chapter of the NFRA, launched by federal employees just weeks after the D.C. emancipation bill passed in April 1862, aimed "to teach [former slaves] Christianity and civilization; to imbue them with notions of order, industry, economy, and self-reliance; [and] to elevate them in the scale of humanity, by inspiring them with self-respect." These private organizations not only provided much of the staff who worked in the contraband camps but also raised funds and solicited in-kind donations from Northern donors as well as local black churches to supplement the scant rations and clothing provided by the government.[19]

The AMA's Danforth Nichols, a Methodist minister from Boston with an unblemished abolitionist record, became superintendent of contraband camps in June 1862. One of his first initiatives was to relieve overcrowding by building Camp Barker on Twelfth Street and Vermont Avenue NW. Located on what had been a cemetery and a brickyard before the war, Camp Barker (or the "Washington Contraband Depot," as Nichols called it) opened in July 1862 with four hundred residents, but it expanded rapidly. By April 1863, it housed a thousand residents squeezed into ten-by-twelve-foot cabins, each of which bulged with more than a dozen people. Residents lacked adequate privies, water, and sanitation, and diseases spread like wildfire—a smallpox epidemic in summer 1863 ravaged the camp, killing more than two dozen residents a week.[20]

Camp Barker festered barely a mile north of the White House, and President Lincoln passed by each day that summer on his way to and from his seasonal cottage near the Soldiers' Home in Northwest. In May 1863 Superintendent Nichols worked with military officials to move the camp inhabitants across the Potomac to a "Freedmen's Village" to be built on the Arlington estate of Confederate general Robert E. Lee—a delightful irony not lost on the camp's planners or its residents. Officially dedicated that December, Freedmen's Village symbolized the missionary zeal that Nichols and other white abolitionists brought to their relief work. On paper, it resembled a modern planned community, featuring an orderly set of fifty two-family homes arranged along a country road that wound around a central pond, with a hospital, a school, a chapel, and a "Home for Aged and Infirm Freedmen." Camp planners hoped that the "pure country air" would improve residents' health, and they expected the work program to encourage Yankee virtues of self-reliance, hard work, and thrift.[21]

Camp Barker, Freedmen's Village, and other contraband camps in the Washington area provided essential help to newly freed black people, but they also helped transform and ultimately destroy the interracial reform community that had existed in the antebellum era. In part, reformers simply were overwhelmed by circumstances—emancipation and war had triggered a migration of such size and speed that even those genuinely committed to helping the former slaves struggled to find adequate solutions, particularly given the meager resources available from a war-strapped federal government. But issues of class, culture, and control also tore the community apart, largely along racial lines.

Before the war, white and black antislavery reformers tended to share middle-class values and tastes—a respect for fine manners, an appreciation of social distinctions, an emphasis on discretion and prudence. The black people who got involved in interracial organizing often were among the city's elite, including relatively wealthy, well-educated, and often mixed-race African Americans who worked closely and interdependently (and at times deferentially) with white abolitionists. When Danforth Nichols arrived in Washington, he toured the city with one black minister and ate dinner with another, noting approvingly that "Washington has good tea and the blacks know how to make it and serve it up too according to the rules of etiquette."[22]

During the war, however, reformers encountered a very different class of black people. The masses of fugitive and freed slaves who poured into the city tended to come directly from plantation life, and they did not share the tea-drinking refinement of either white reformers or elite black Washingtonians. Penniless, jobless, and unschooled, they encountered educated white Northerners who were sympathetic to their plight but often looked down on them. Camp staff and relief workers developed a sense of paternalistic duty in their relationships with the former slaves, an attitude that often manifested itself by controlling black behavior and decisions. "To reason with them is out of the question," Nichols explained. "You must tell them what to do."[23]

In an earlier era of slavery, the paternalism of sympathetic white abolitionists may have been grudgingly tolerated or even welcomed. No more. Emancipation had broken the grip of deference, and many black Washingtonians challenged any hint of condescension. Throughout the war, they bristled at some of the decisions benevolent white reformers made, they chafed at the restrictions imposed on them, and they challenged the limitations they encountered. They claimed their rights as full citizens, not simply as former slaves. "I give up my child upon the word and honor of the government to go and tote his musket and he had gone and lost his life," testified Freedmen's Village resident Betsy Brown in a complaint against camp superintendent Nichols. "I think Sir that is enough."[24]

Superintendent Nichols was a particular target for black critics. He made peremptory decisions without consulting either camp residents or local black leaders, earning a reputation for condescension and mistreatment. When he decided to move Camp Barker residents to Freedmen's Village, residents balked—80 percent of them simply refused to go, telling one missionary "they would rather starve in Washington than go to Arlington to be under Nichols." Where Nichols and other white reformers saw an opportunity to live and work in a healthy environment, the formerly enslaved saw a return to Southern slavery. They viewed Nichols as "better suited to an overseer of a Southern Plantation." Black correspondent and military recruiter Thomas Hinton called him a "perfect tyrant" and a "brute" for evicting aged residents from the community. After opening Freedmen's Village, military officials destroyed Camp Barker, yet more than five hundred former residents remained in the area.[25]

As Nichols and other white reformers discovered, many black people did not want to be passive recipients of white benevolence—they wanted to control their own destinies in a postemancipation world. William J. Wilson personified this demand. Wilson served as a teacher at the Camp Barker school, the only black teacher employed in an American Missionary Association school in the area. Born enslaved, Wilson managed to secure his freedom and headed to Brooklyn, where for twenty years he was a teacher and principal. He earned a reputation for both educational excellence and public activism. He wrote under the pen name "Ethiop" in Frederick Douglass's antislavery paper and sometimes ran afoul of local white opinion.[26]

Impressed with Washington when he first visited in 1863, Wilson moved to the city the next year to run the Camp Barker school. The building had no privy and only a few broken chairs for furniture, but Wilson and his wife, Mary, turned it into a bustling school averaging about 250 students, including many adults. They needed more help, badly, yet William insisted on one thing: the teachers in the school had to be black. "Colored people must be taught to do our own work, being assisted only by the dominant class. This is as essential as the work to be done," he told his bosses. "As long as the dominant class are to fill among us the first places, even when it can be avoided & we to be regarded as minors and recipients of favors we shall be but the same helpless & dependent people, slaves." The Wilsons may have shared the same goals as Danforth and other white reformers—they all wanted to help former slaves become productive, self-reliant, and independent citizens—but they and other black activists placed a high priority on autonomy. The whole point of being free was to be able to do for oneself.[27]

Conflicts over class, culture, and control not only divided white and black reformers but also erupted within Washington's black community. Many leading black Washingtonians, such as educator John F. Cook Jr., had been born free, were educated, and lived relatively stable lives before the war. They had worked alongside middle- and upper-class white people in the battle for black freedom, and they aspired to middle-class ideals. Before the war, the predominating mores of educated black D.C. absorbed and acculturated the small numbers of migrants from the rural South. That changed with the sudden influx of tens of thousands of former plantation slaves during the war.

Elated when emancipation finally came, black leaders nonetheless harbored fears that the rural migrants could undermine their hard-fought gains in the city. These new Washingtonians seemed so different, so country, so boisterous, and, to some middle-class black people, so ill-prepared for freedom. "The transition from slavery to freedom was too sudden," Elizabeth Keckly wrote, and former slaves "were not prepared for the new life that opened before [them]."[28]

Despite black leaders' efforts to emphasize the middle-class virtues of work, temperance, and education, some former slaves struggled to find employment and got into trouble with the law. Concerns about former slaves circulated within the black community. Black correspondent Thomas Hinton complained of overdressed freedmen "who have made up their minds not to hurt themselves a[t] working." The divisions were not lost on white observers. Journalist Lois Adams witnessed conflicts between native black Washingtonians and the newcomers, noting that "some of the tinctured natives of Washington affect great disgust towards their more pure blooded, but less aristocratic contraband brethren and sisters." Military official William Doster wrote, "The free colored negroes at Washington hated [former slaves] as rivals. The slaves despised them for being runaways."[29]

Former slaves appreciated the generosity shown to them, but they sometimes resented the air of superiority and condescension they sensed from native Washingtonians. One anonymous letter writer to the *Weekly Anglo-African* in 1864 had had enough of the "unkind" criticism and "prejudice" against Southern migrants, particularly from Northern visitors. "We are a sensitive people, who have been unjustly treated and criticized by persons who think when coming to Washington that they are coming South among a lot of slow ninnyheads," the writer cautioned. "Do not come among us with your hastily-formed opinions, backed up by hearsay, but bring us light, example, and wisdom, and not so much faultfinding."[30]

Despite periodic intrarace squabbling, the black community generally remained united in embracing and advocating for expansive definitions of freedom, equality, and citizenship that moved far beyond simply not being a slave. The rapid growth of Washington's black community certainly posed challenges, but it also offered opportunities for redefining race relations in the city. Black

Washingtonians, whether native or of more recent vintage, joined together to assert themselves in the face of wartime efforts to restrict the revolutionary reach of emancipation.

"Freedom, Freedom, Freedom Everywhere!":
Black Washingtonians Push for Revolutionary Changes

Emboldened by their swelling numbers and empowered by the sense that they had the backing of the federal government, black Washingtonians challenged authorities in unprecedented ways. Among their first targets was the Fugitive Slave Act, which technically remained in force for slaves escaping from the Border South even after the passage of the D.C. emancipation bill in April 1862 and the Emancipation Proclamation in January 1863. The D.C. federal court created a fugitive slave commission in 1862 to help slave owners reclaim their runaway property, but the commissioners found that they simply could not enforce the law. They struggled with federal officials, notably the District's military governor, James Wadsworth, and they encountered almost insurmountable resistance from black Washingtonians.

Crowds of black residents harassed would-be slave catchers and packed the courthouse to testify before the commissioners. By late May 1862, the *National Republican* reported, there were "constant brawls and fighting in our streets [and] daily spectacles harrowing to the feelings of the humane." The Fugitive Slave Act, the editors argued, "cannot be enforced here without excitements and collisions, which will be lamentable, and may even be dangerous to the public peace." Though the law would remain on the books until 1864, by mid-1862 it was rendered all but dead in the nation's capital.[31]

One Virginia slave owner discovered the futility of trying to reassert claims to formerly enslaved people now residing in Washington. Accompanied by his Episcopal minister, he journeyed to D.C. to reclaim several enslaved women who had run away from his plantation and found work in Washington as laundresses for the Union army. During a meeting with Superintendent Danforth Nichols and the former slaves, the owner pleaded for their return, but the women refused. Furnishing Nichols with a butcher knife, one of them instructed him to "let the wicked blood out of that man who has come to take my daughters." The slave owner left empty-handed.[32]

Black residents also laid claim to the city's public spaces. Beginning soon after emancipation, the streets of Washington became a staging ground for black celebrations of all sorts. Black organizations such as the Grand United Order of Odd Fellows took their meetings and conventions into public areas, marching in the streets with what journalist Lois Adams described as "their showy regalia, with bands of music playing as they march, bearing wreaths and decorated mottoes, with the Stars and Stripes floating over them along the whole line of their advance."[33]

The rhetoric at these public events—bold, emphatic, even confrontational—reflected the striking new sense of power and equality that black Washingtonians felt. At an 1863 Emancipation Day celebration, Thomas Hinton praised a black soldier who had bayoneted a white soldier for insubordination and excoriated the continued discrimination he witnessed in the city.

After thousands of students and teachers from the Sabbath School Union marched from Fifteenth Street Presbyterian Church through downtown to Israel Bethel Church, one participant marveled, "The proslavery citizens could hardly believe their own eyes." By 1863, black people had transformed the streets of Washington, trod by slave coffles just a few years before, into the proving grounds of emancipation.[34]

Black Washingtonians also pushed for full access to education. "Keep your children in the schools," Bishop Payne had urged the newly freed slaves upon emancipation, "even if you have to eat less, drink less and wear coarser raiments." And they did. "Their great desire is to learn to read," wrote Harriet Jacobs of the newly freed Washingtonians she met. Eager for the education that had been denied them, former slaves flocked to the private schools established by local churches, freedmen's aid societies, and the newly freed themselves. These schools often were housed in makeshift buildings with few resources, but by 1864 the city boasted more than two dozen day schools and eighteen night schools educating more than 4,600 black students.[35]

There had been antebellum black private schools. Now, however, black leaders pushed for access to public education as well. Before the war, city law set aside 10 percent of tax revenue for a public school fund, but that money supported only white schools. After emancipation, Congress required that 10 percent of tax revenue collected from black taxpayers be set aside for "a system of primary schools" for black students to be run by a federally appointed Board of Trustees of Colored Schools. For two years, however, the city council simply refused to send the money to the schools. Mayor Richard Wallach made his opposition to black public education a winning issue during the June 1862 elections, so D.C.'s first official black public school did not open until March 1864.[36]

Even with this delay, black Washingtonians established public schools earlier than elsewhere in the South. The schools were segregated, but teaching and running them was an interracial effort. Emma V. Brown, a mixed-race woman who had been a student at Myrtilla Miner's school, returned to the city after attending Oberlin College and started a school for black children in her home on P Street in Georgetown. Working closely with white school commissioner Daniel Breed and a white assistant from the New England Freedmen's Aid Society, Frances Perkins, Brown began teaching at one of the first black public schools in the city. She later became principal of the Sumner School at Seventeenth and M Streets NW.[37]

Black Washingtonians not only pushed for their rights as free citizens but also sought to shoulder one of the foremost responsibilities of citizenship: serving as soldiers to defend the nation. Since Jacob Dodson's unaccepted offer to supply black men to defend the city during the tense days in April 1861, black leaders and their white allies had pushed the Lincoln administration to enlist black soldiers in the Union army. They saw fighting in the military as an indisputable claim to full equality and manhood. "When you get the gun," said District resident Samuel Wilson, "you will be a man."[38]

The Emancipation Proclamation opened the door to black military service in January 1863, and a biracial effort led by educator John F. Cook Jr., Underground Railroad conductor Anthony Bowen, and the Reverend Henry McNeal Turner soon emerged to recruit a black regiment in Washington: the First United States Colored Troops. Some volunteers came from prominent black families, but the bulk of the 3,265 black people in Washington who served in the Union army were former slaves who had migrated to the city. Some better-off black men, like their white peers, chose to pay for substitutes to serve in their place—a practice that incensed Bowen. The war offered "a golden opportunity for the colored man to fight for [our] own freedom," he told a crowd at Wesley A.M.E. Zion Church in 1864. We "ought to prove [ourselves] worthy of the freedom [we] enjoy."[39]

By the end of June 1863, the city's first black soldiers assembled for duty and began training on Mason's (now Roosevelt) Island in the Potomac. The sight of black men in crisp blue Union uniforms drilling confidently on Washington's streets captured the vast changes in black status engendered by the war. Where once black people had occupied a clearly subordinate role and depended on white magnanimity, they now asserted themselves as full citizens in a democracy—holding events in public spaces, educating their children at public expense, organizing for political action, and taking up arms to fight for the Union.

White supremacists in Washington reeled in response to the massive changes that were transforming the city. Whereas black people saw emancipation as just the first step toward becoming full citizens, most white Washingtonians viewed emancipation as the final destination, a ceiling for black aspiration. Many white Unionists in Washington may have grudgingly accepted the reality of emancipation, but they rejected anything beyond that. Black people could be legally free,

Company E of the Fourth Colored Infantry, stationed at Fort Lincoln in Northeast Washington. More than 3,200 black Washingtonians served in the Union army. Their service and contribution to the Union victory helped propel postwar efforts to win the right to vote. Library of Congress.

but they could not be equal to white people. City leaders such as Mayor Richard Wallach sought to limit the impact of emancipation through political maneuvering and obstruction. Their intransigence led white journalist Lois Adams to decry "the timid, truckling spirit of office holders of the District," whose "truly Southern horror of such words as abolitionism, radicalism, progress, etc.," has shown that "if slavery is dead, its spirit is not."[40]

Businesses, particularly the city's new streetcar companies, struggled to find a balance between rising expectations among black customers and the reactionary anger of many white customers. Chartered in 1862, the District's first streetcar company (the Washington and Georgetown Railroad) followed the general custom established by the city's omnibuses—black people were not allowed to sit inside the cars but could stand along the outer platform, where they would be exposed to the elements. Black riders now objected to the practice. Military recruiter and journalist Thomas Hinton called such segregation "one of the features of slavery as it exists in our midst." Black soldiers in particular refused to stand on the outer platform. As one reporter noted, "The soldiers all ride the street cars or any other cars they want to ride in; and you might just as well declare war against them as to declare that they can't ride there because they are colored."[41]

White conductors firmly resisted any change in custom. One highly publicized incident involved Major Alexander Augusta, a black surgeon in the Union army who was tossed off a Fourteenth Street line streetcar into the rain. The streetcar company sought to avoid trouble by opening separate cars for black riders, but in postemancipation Washington that simply was not enough. Protests continued, and in 1864 Congress, led by Republican senator Charles Sumner of Massachusetts, used its power to grant charters to force the Metropolitan Railway Company to offer equal service to white and black passengers.[42]

Some white residents reacted to the revolutionary changes with violence. Black soldiers became a prime target. The *Constitutional Union*, a newspaper started during the war by white Unionists who opposed emancipation, fumed about "the swagger and air of hauteurs" displayed by black soldiers. White violence in the face of such arrogance was understandable, the editors argued, because black men in uniform "are puffed up with vanity on account of their new profession as soldiers, and . . . thinking themselves better than white men, are insolent and overbearing."[43]

Bands of white thugs also attacked the city's most visible black institutions — churches and schools — and sought to intimidate preachers and teachers. White vigilantes used violence to send a clear message that black people should still expect to be treated as second-class citizens. White policemen rarely intervened to stop such violence, and too often there was little redress for black victims. "The law," seethed Thomas Hinton in the *Liberator*, "is simply for the white man, not the black."[44]

White violence, however, could not prevent black Washingtonians from laying claim in 1865 to the two most symbolic public buildings of American democracy. In February, the pastor of Fifteenth Street Presbyterian, Henry Highland Garnet, became the first black person to speak in the Capitol when he addressed Congress on the passage of the Thirteenth Amendment banning slavery. The event carried tremendous symbolic importance. Enslaved people had helped build the Capitol, slave coffles had passed in its shadow, and black people had once been barred from the grounds. Now one of the city's foremost black leaders stood in the speaker's well.

Described by Lois Adams as "an educated, well-read man, an earnest, pleasing speaker, and a fervent pleader for the rights of his oppressed and suffering people," Garnet spoke before galleries that were "thronged on all sides," mostly with eager black visitors. Not only did Garnet praise Congress for ending what he considered a sin against both God and the founders of the country, but he also laid out a postemancipation agenda for black America: "Emancipate, Enfranchise, Educate, and give the blessings of the gospel to every American citizen."[45]

The assassination of Abraham Lincoln and the end of the Civil War in April 1865 inspired black Washingtonians and their Republican allies to mourn, celebrate, and rally in front of the second prominent symbol of democracy: the Executive Mansion. To maximize its symbolic import, planners chose to host the event on the Fourth of July. Before emancipation, the Fourth of July had grated on black nerves, a cruel reminder of American hypocrisy on race and freedom. But with the end of the war and the passage of the Thirteenth Amendment by Congress (it had yet to be ratified by three-quarters of the states), the holiday became yet another chance for black people to claim their rightful status as full citizens of the country. They prepared a massive celebration on what is now called the Ellipse, south of the President's House. Sponsors claimed that it was "the first time that the colored people have attempted any celebration of a national character," and thousands turned out with banners, flags, and food. With John F. Cook Jr. presiding and abolitionist Senator Henry Wilson as the keynote, a series of speakers made the case for black rights in a postemancipation world as President Lincoln's successor, Andrew Johnson, looked on from afar.[46]

By 1865, it was clear that Washington had changed in irrevocable ways. Comparing the city to its antebellum counterpart, white abolitionist James McKim wrote to a friend, "Now, what do I see today? Freedom, Freedom, Freedom everywhere! In the Presidential mansion, in both houses of Congress, in the Supreme Court, . . . in the hotels, in the public parks, on the streets, everywhere is freedom and everybody free! Not nominally and abstractly, but really and actually." McKim captured the excitement that many people felt about the stunning transformation of the city, but he exaggerated the extent of actual freedom enjoyed on the streets of Washington. How much freedom "everybody" would get to enjoy in Washington would depend in large part on the political battles that loomed in the years immediately after the war.[47]

"An Opportunity to Support Themselves":
The Freedmen's Bureau and the Transition to Postwar Freedom

The stunning new dome atop the Capitol, completed in December 1863, overlooked a city transformed by war from what one observer called a "quiet, retired place" housing a seasonal government into the administrative nerve center of a burgeoning federal state. Wartime exigencies had forced Congress to begin modernizing and improving the city's roads, sewer system, and waterworks, including the $3.3 million Washington Aqueduct that opened in 1863. For four years, the city pulsed with the energy of newcomers, and Congress's wartime appropriations fueled an economic boom that employed thousands of workers in government offices, army stockyards, military forts, and hospitals. The city's population swelled to nearly 127,000 in 1865, the majority of whom had arrived since the war began—about half of white residents and two-thirds of black residents were newcomers to Washington.[48]

The transformation within Congress was no less remarkable. No longer the dominion of slaveholding Southern scions, Congress now was ruled by the upstart Republican Party, emboldened and embittered by four years of war and the assassination of the party's first president. Led by Radicals such as Senator Charles Sumner of Massachusetts and Representative Thaddeus Stevens of Pennsylvania, Republicans in Congress saw the postwar period as an opportunity to expand federal power and remake the nation along more egalitarian lines—and a chance to punish their enemies. They pursued an ambitious set of policies that established a firm foundation for black rights and opportunities in housing, work, education, and politics.

The best place to begin implementing these policies was Washington, where Congress had exclusive legislative authority. Though the city had never been occupied by the Confederacy, Radical Republicans viewed the local white population as "rebels at heart" and treated Washington as a laboratory for what became known as congressional, or Radical, Reconstruction.

One of the first experiments in that laboratory was the Bureau of Refugees, Freedmen, and Abandoned Lands (known as the Freedmen's Bureau), a new federal agency focused on helping former slaves adjust to a life of freedom. After two years of wrangling—in part because many black leaders, including Frederick Douglass, feared the paternalism inherent in such an agency—in March 1865, Congress established the Freedmen's Bureau within the War Department. With pious Union general O. O. Howard at the helm, it quickly became among the most visible postwar government agencies. Until it was dissolved in 1872, the bureau pursued creative and controversial programs that would shape race relations in the city for years to come.[49]

The bureau was responsible for "all subjects relating to refugees and freedmen from rebel states," a sweeping mission that encompassed housing, education, family reunification, and employment assistance—a striking expansion of federal power at a time when no federal agency had ever dispensed aid directly to individuals. This aid came with a set of expectations, however. An unstated but driving part of the bureau's mission was to "civilize" the formerly enslaved by teaching them to be self-sufficient and encouraging them to embrace middle-class virtues of work, thrift, prudence, and faith. Because of its status as the capital, its proximity to lawmakers and the North, and the migration of nearly thirty thousand former slaves to the city, Washington became a focal point for Freedmen's Bureau activity.[50]

The Freedmen's Bureau faced daunting challenges. The city was in shambles at the end of the war. The Union army had turned the National Mall into a stockyard, nearly all the trees within the city limits had been felled, many city parks had become open-air hospitals, and the roads were rutted almost beyond repair. The rapid demobilization of the military devastated the local economy as army-dependent business dried up. "Washington is a seething, steaming, groaning maelstrom of used-up humanity just now," wrote Lois Adams in June 1865.[51]

The community of freedpeople was in dire straits. Still labeled "contrabands" by many local white people—William Owner groused that "it is perfect non-sense to call a Stolen Southern nigger a Freedman"—they struggled when the manual labor jobs on which they depended disappeared with the army. With unemployment upwards of 80 percent, they congregated in squalid camps and festering slums, stalked by disease and hunger. One desperate group of former slaves in Northwest collected bones from dead horses and sought to peddle them as fertilizer to farmers; fearing the spread of disease, bureau health officials ordered the operation closed. A city councilman estimated in 1866 that half the migrants who arrived in Washington since the war began had already died.[52]

To address this humanitarian crisis, the Freedmen's Bureau worked with both the military and private aid organizations to coordinate relief efforts, providing food, fuel, blankets, and clothing to destitute Washingtonians. Such direct charity was intended to be temporary. Bureau officials worried that freedmen and women might become too dependent on federal aid, and white critics such as Mayor Richard Wallach claimed that "thousands of contrabands" were being "allured to this 'paradise of freedmen' by the temptations to indolence offered by the gratuities of the Freedmen's Bureau."[53] Yet the need was so great that the bureau continued to dispense direct aid throughout the life of the agency.

With the military gone, bureau officials struggled to find work for freedpeople within the District. Washington during peacetime simply did not offer enough economic opportunities for unskilled workers. So the bureau became a labor placement office, with agents connecting Northern employers with black laborers. The bureau even paid transportation costs for black people to leave the city, leading to charges that it was "trafficking in negroes." Within three years, bureau officials claimed, they had helped more than 7,600 former slaves find employment outside D.C. Such work, the bureau's John Eaton said, gave freed black people "an opportunity to support themselves, free from the vices and diseases which are likely to arise from inhabiting abodes of filth and spending their time in idleness, a sanitary and social peril and an expense to the Government."[54]

Many former slaves, however, refused to leave Washington, where they had established themselves and where they believed that they could count on federal protection. By the thousands they squatted on unoccupied land, particularly near Union forts, or lived in squalid, privately owned barracks, often incurring the wrath of white neighbors. Determined to remain in the city, they pushed not only for temporary aid but also for land of their own.[55]

Freedpeople's desire for land, combined with the bureau's own interest in developing black self-sufficiency, pushed officials to create programs that encouraged black land and home ownership. Sensitive to white criticism, bureau officials looked to create "Negro colonies" in areas that were either already black or were uninhabited and thus far from white neighbors. In this way, the bureau encouraged the process of racial segregation in housing that would mark the late nineteenth century.[56]

Perhaps the most successful home ownership program was the Barry's Farm community in Southeast Washington. Barry's Farm had its roots in white landowners' attempts to evict black squatters living on their lots in the Meridian Hill area of Northwest. General Howard met with black families in the area to discuss the issue, and several of them told him what they wanted: land. Howard proposed creating a black colony on the eastern side of the Anacostia River, just south of the small white community of Uniontown, an area that remained almost entirely rural at war's end.[57]

In 1867, Howard used Freedmen's Bureau funds to purchase 375 acres from the family of a deceased slave owner, James Barry. Given local hostility to black landownership, a white intermediary purchased the land, and the family had no idea that it was to be turned into a black settlement. The bureau divided the area into roughly one-acre plots and sold them to former slaves for $125 to $300 per acre, including enough lumber to construct a two-room house. Residents had two years to pay. One early resident was Emily Edmonson, the famed former slave who had attempted to escape on the *Pearl* in 1848. Within two years, 266 families had moved to Barry's Farm, and residents soon built a school, a church, and other community institutions. Officially renamed Hillsdale in 1874, the area formed the nucleus of what would become the city's largest black community.[58]

Another Freedmen's Bureau success was education, where the agency's priorities dovetailed with the black community's interests. The bureau built dozens of schools for black children, often by incorporating existing private black schools into the public system. Indeed, the line between public and private blurred as the public bureau worked closely with teachers and staff members supplied by private freedmen's relief organizations. In January 1866, there were 5,600 black students enrolled in more than fifty day schools; by June, more than 10,000 students were attending school. When city superintendent of education Henry Barnard conducted a survey of black education in 1867, he found that a higher percentage of black children were in school than white children. Black students displayed a remarkable "avidity for learning," Barnard wrote. "In no case has a colored school ever failed for the want of scholars." [59]

The drive for learning extended to higher education as well. Immediately after the war, the National Lincoln Monument Association proposed building a college for freed black people to honor the slain president. Though that idea faltered, in March 1867 Congress chartered a new, coeducational, racially integrated university to be built near the site of a former contraband camp on Seventh Street NW. Originally financed by the Freedmen's Bureau, the campus featured a three-story, granite-foundation academic building with thirty-two classrooms, a dormitory for female boarding students (named for antebellum educator Myrtilla Miner), and a hospital. The trustees named the university in honor of bureau head O. O. Howard, who later became its third president. [60]

From its inception, Howard University was open to all races (the three daughters of Danforth Nichols, the white former superintendent of contraband camps, attended), but it focused primarily on black students, who were the vast majority of the student population. Under General Howard's leadership, the university, like other colleges for black students founded across the South during this time, sought to instill the virtues of piety, discipline, and work. But it also emphasized intellectual pursuits, offering a comprehensive curriculum with mandatory Greek and Latin courses as well as professional education in law and medicine. By the late nineteenth century, Howard had earned a reputation as the nation's premier black institution of higher education.

For all its successes, however, the Freedmen's Bureau faced serious challenges. The bureau staff was a combustible mix of people with conflicting approaches to providing relief. Veterans of the antislavery movement, attracted by the organizational mission, put a priority on compassion, equality, and racial justice. They often clashed with the bureau's military men, who emphasized self-sufficiency and efficiency, and political superiors, who feared possible electoral consequences. Josephine Griffing, a white Connecticut abolitionist and women's rights advocate, lasted just a year on the bureau's D.C. staff as she fought repeatedly with her supervisors. After being fired, she complained to a friend: "I do not mean to say there is a *direct conspiracy* and *intent to kill off these*

Blacks, but I do assert that in this city thousands have died who only needed the aid that could have been secured if the President and the Freedmen's Bureau had been disposed to acknowledge the just claims of these emancipated people."[61]

Whether military or civilian, bureau officials generally shared a commitment to reshaping black behavior to conform to the standards of white society, a paternalistic approach that ignored freedpeople's desire for autonomy. One troubling example of how the bureau interacted with the local black community came in 1866 during the cleanup of Murder Bay. Located south of Pennsylvania Avenue in what is now called Federal Triangle, Murder Bay was overcrowded, disease-ridden, and desperately poor. In a report to Congress, police commissioner A. C. Richards described extended families crowded into "stifling and sickening" eight-foot-square hovels "without light or ventilation."[62]

Bureau officials feared that such squalid living conditions fostered moral as well as physical decay, so they secured wagonloads of lime and forced residents to disinfect their homes and then whitewash both the outside and inside walls. No one in the community was consulted, no permission was granted, and no one could refuse to participate. Though bureau officials boasted that the homes were "in as good a sanitary condition as was possible," the experience revealed a lack of respect for black autonomy. After a life of slavery, freed black people treasured autonomy above all else, and they often resisted the paternalistic attitudes and policies of bureau officials.[63]

The bureau's mission also ran afoul of many local white leaders, conservative members of Congress, and other opponents of black equality. Local officials such as Mayor Wallach viewed the contraband community as a serious problem and complained that it was "impossible" to fund the bureau's efforts. City councilman Samuel Peugh worried that the "oppressive duty Congress has imposed upon us" would force the city to cut services to white people.[64]

Other white residents accused the Freedmen's Bureau of racial favoritism. From his window on F Street NW, William Owner fumed as he watched bureau agents deliver wagons of firewood to black neighbors, with "not a stick delivered to the 'poor white trash.'" In his characteristically blunt language, Owner complained in his diary: "The Nigs get all—white men pay for it."[65] Such criticism helped force changes in bureau policy, and it began distributing aid to destitute white people as well. Of the 9,264 people who received aid in 1866, about 45 percent were white.[66]

Despite relentless opposition, internal dissension, and a tendency to control black behavior, the Freedmen's Bureau made significant progress in a remarkably short time. By the time it closed its doors in 1872, it had helped countless people survive a difficult period, found employment (both in D.C. and elsewhere) for thousands more, helped lay the foundation for black public education, and created a self-sufficient black community in Anacostia. The first federal agency committed to improving social welfare, the bureau helped drive the tremendous transformation of the city in the years after the Civil War ended.

"Without the Rights of Suffrage, We Are without Protection": The Fight for Black Men's Right to Vote

George Hatton embodied the promise of the new era that dawned with the end of the war. Born enslaved in Prince George's County, Hatton gained his freedom in an unusual way—from Henry Hatton, his own free black father. After George's original owner died, Henry Hatton purchased George, his mother, and his siblings, and the family moved to Washington. Henry never filed the official paperwork to legally free George and two other children, so when the D.C. emancipation bill passed in April 1862 he filed a compensation claim for his three "slaves." He was paid $1,839.60.[67]

Described as a "dark mulatto," George Hatton stood a stocky five foot six, "brim full of wit and good sense" in the words of a contemporary, with a powerful voice, a winsome speaking style, and a combative personality. At an 1863 Emancipation Day celebration, the twenty-year-old Hatton adamantly insisted that "he would not ride in the [street] cars until he had his rights and could sit inside." Two months later, he was among the first black men to sign up for military service with the U.S. Colored Troops. As he and other black men stood in line at the enlistment station, a crowd of angry white people and policemen accosted them. Hatton refused to budge, daring them to fire. None did.[68]

Fighting in the war convinced Hatton that black men had earned their freedom—"The fetters have fallen—our bondage is over," he wrote—but lingering racism within the Union army made him skeptical that black people would be treated as full citizens in America. Hobbled by a gunshot wound to his left knee suffered at the Battle of Petersburg, Hatton returned to Washington in 1864 ready to assert his rights as a combat veteran and full citizen. He joined the Republican Party and waded into political battles over suffrage, integrated schools, and labor rights. Within five years, the twenty-seven-year old former slave was elected to the city's Common Council.[69]

George Hatton's meteoric rise from slave to councilman shows just how much had changed in Washington since the 1850s. He and other black office holders were the fruit of perhaps the most controversial seed in the "experimental garden for Radical plants": suffrage.

The push for black male suffrage began during the Civil War. The D.C. emancipation bill and the Emancipation Proclamation made no mention of suffrage because the issue was so explosive—only the most radical of white Republicans supported the idea in 1862 or 1863. President Lincoln and other moderate Republicans argued that civil equality—emancipation—did not necessarily involve political equality—the right to vote. But black advocates and their Radical white supporters insisted that the two could not be separated. To be full Americans, they argued, black men had to be able to vote; there simply was no in-between, nonvoting status between slave and citizen.

During the war, black men began to organize politically through the Union League. Founded in 1863, the Union League in D.C. initially advocated racial separation, but within a year it had become interracial, filled with many of the men who had been involved with recruiting black soldiers. The Union League was an early foray into the realm of interracial politics, giving black leaders a chance to work with white counterparts and learn the ways of political organizing.[70]

The war itself, and the crucial role that black soldiers played in helping to win it, pushed more and more white Republicans to embrace black men's suffrage. By 1864, when Congress began debating the renewal of the city charter, Charles Sumner and other Radicals sought to require black men's suffrage. "To withhold the franchise from any human being solely on account of his color, is unmanly, unchristian, and un-American," wrote the editors of the National Republican in December 1864. By April 1865, even President Lincoln began to bend to the call, stating that he preferred that the franchise "were now conferred on the very intelligent, and on those who serve our cause as soldiers"—an utterance that moved John Wilkes Booth to scuttle his plans to kidnap the president and instead settle on murder. Yet resistance from conservative Republicans and local white leaders stymied the wartime push.[71]

After the war, black Washingtonians placed suffrage at the top of their agenda. During the massive Fourth of July memorial to President Lincoln held in front of the White House, speaker after speaker insisted that the right to vote was essential. Senator Henry Wilson, author of the D.C. emancipation bill, pointed out that Mayor Wallach had declined the invitation to attend the event, but "I have a sort of dim idea that if you held the right of suffrage, Mayor Wallach and perhaps the whole city government would be here." Soon thereafter, black church leaders organized a United Franchise League to coordinate a suffrage campaign. In the heavily black First Ward, which covered much of downtown Washington from the canal to Rock Creek, black professionals spearheaded the First Ward Civil Rights Association, which promoted voting rights and organized boycotts of businesses that opposed suffrage.[72]

One of the First Ward's most prominent leaders, educator John F. Cook Jr., helped lead a petition drive to encourage Congress to support black men's suffrage. The petition emphasized that black men had earned the right, noting the sacrifices of black troops, the success of D.C.'s black entrepreneurs, and the black commitment to constructive community institutions. "We are intelligent enough to be industrious, to have accumulated property, to build and sustain churches and institutions of learning," the petition read. "Without the rights of suffrage, we are without protection, and liable to combinations of outrage." It attracted more than 2,500 signatures before it was sent to Congress in fall 1865.[73]

The petition found a receptive audience among Radical Republicans. Though a minority within their own party, Radicals set the postwar legislative agenda, and they made the D.C. suffrage bill a top priority—it was H.R. 1, the very first piece of legislation that the House considered when the new Thirty-Ninth Congress convened in December 1865. As with emancipation, Radical Republicans hoped to use Washington as a testing ground for black men's suffrage, which they planned to implement across the South. In extending the franchise to black men, Congress was "inaugurating a policy not only strictly for the District of Columbia, but in some sense the country at large," argued Senator Lot Morrill of Maine. The bill "completes Emancipation by Enfranchisement" and would "set an example to the whole country," Senator Sumner agreed. "It becomes a pillar of fire to illumine the footsteps of millions."[74]

Yet black men's suffrage remained intensely controversial, even among Republicans. The *Evening Star*, a moderate Republican newspaper that grew increasingly conservative as the decade wore on, considered the suffrage bill to be "the opening of a war on the rights of the white laboring men of the whole Union." Giving the franchise to the "most ignorant and incapable contraband negroes," the *Star*'s editors warned, would "africanize the city" and turn it into a "negro Utopia." Only one local paper, the *Chronicle*, supported suffrage, and then only with restrictions against giving the ballot to former slaves and men without property. The Radicals stood alone in advocating "universal" manhood suffrage, without exclusions.[75]

Opponents of black men's suffrage also recognized that the District could set a precedent for the nation. "The fight over suffrage in Washington is but an experiment, a skirmish, an entering wedge to prepare the way for a similar movement in Congress to confer the right of suffrage on all negroes of the United States," warned Senator Garrett Davis of Kentucky. "It is following up the tactics of the party four years ago, when the assault upon slavery in this District heralded the general movement that was to be made against it."[76] As Washington went, so would go the nation.

Fear of black political power fused with fears of "social equality" in the minds of many opponents of black men's suffrage. Few public figures, black or white, claimed to support social equality, which implied no social distinctions or restrictions on interracial relationships in private life. Knowing the power of the "social equality" bogeyman, even supporters of black men's suffrage took pains to argue that they supported *civic* equality (equal protection of the laws) and *political* equality (suffrage and office holding), but *not* social equality.[77]

Opponents, however, insisted that one would lead to the other. The editors of the *National Intelligencer*, who fairly represented the views of white Democrats, explained how granting the right to vote to black men would lead inexorably to race mixing. Black voters would, "by the hocus-pocus of caucus, out-wit and out-vote whites for a nomination" and then help elect black officials, who would work closely and start spending time with their white colleagues. They would "mingle in the levees and in fashionable gatherings of 'that set;' send their children to the same schools; and finally . . . have and hold all the relations in business and other associations as if they were of the same race, blood, stock, or lineage."[78]

Most white Washingtonians reacted to the postwar push for black men's suffrage with alarm bordering on hysteria. In late 1865, local leaders hastily implemented a referendum on black suffrage. Restricted to white voters and boycotted by white Republicans, the referendum yielded predictable results. In Washington City, only 35 voters supported extending suffrage to black men, while 6,591 opposed the idea; in Georgetown, the vote was 712–1 against. Given what Mayor Wallach deemed the "unparalleled unanimity of sentiment," white leaders used the referendum results to argue that the principles of democracy itself demanded that Congress reject the suffrage bill.[79]

"Negro equality against self-government," blared the headline of a *National Intelligencer* editorial, one of several illuminating articles in early January 1866 that outlined the white community's case against black men's suffrage. "The people of the District of Columbia are not the slaves of Congress," the editors insisted. "This District has been *experimented upon* in various forms of legislation, odious to the citizens," and now Radicals sought "to *force negro equality upon the unwilling people of the District of Columbia, who have just protested, almost with unanimity, against such equality.*" As the District's representatives, the editors continued, Congress should abide by the democratically expressed wishes of local white voters, particularly given the fact that only five of twenty-four Northern states allowed black men to vote at the time. "*The issue will be between the right of self-government, as vested in fully qualified citizens, and the Radical attempt to force negro equality over the dearest privilege of Americans.*"[80]

The Union may have won the war, but the battle over black men's suffrage stiffened the rebellious spine of many white Washingtonians. They brazenly displayed "a spirit which was supposed to have collapsed with the rebellion," wrote an astonished Ohio journalist, Emily Edson Briggs, in early 1866. "Great flaunting pictures of General Lee appear at conspicuous places to attract the attention of passers-by. He has taken Washington at last."[81]

A select committee of the city council, led by Councilman Samuel Peugh, flatly rejected any notion of black equality. "The white man, being of the superior race, must, and ever will, rule the black," Peugh declared. "This is a white man's country and Government, not a colored one's." A report from the House Committee on the District of Columbia called it "degrading" to allow "poor weak-minded negroes who have no idea of government, any number of whom have just emerged from a state of slavery, to exercise the highest political privilege given to man upon earth." Pushing the suffrage bill, warned the editors of the *National Intelligencer*, could lead to a "war of races."[82]

Believing that black people, particularly the former "contrabands," had little capacity for or interest in politics, many white Washingtonians blamed the controversy on scheming, power-hungry Northern Republicans. At an 1866 meeting in Washington, the Central Executive Committee of Irish Citizens condemned Radicals in Congress for attempting "to convert the negro slave at once into the negro voter, and thus virtually give the government of the Slave States over to whatever body of sharp white men who could wheedle or control the negro." An irate William Owner wrote that "Nig suffrage" would "place the majority of the whites under the rule of the minority and give the whole political power to the ignorant negroes who will be under the rule of northern emissaries and by whom their votes will be controlled."[83]

Suffrage did indeed appeal to a growing number of Republicans, for both egalitarian and political reasons. Many Radicals, including Charles Sumner, Henry Wilson, and Thaddeus Stevens, genuinely believed in black political equality and saw suffrage as an essential element of full citizenship. Only with the ballot could black people hold political leaders accountable and protect their community's interests. More strategically minded Republicans recognized the political benefit of building a broader base for the party—once granted suffrage, black voters could be expected to vote almost uniformly for the party of Lincoln, the party that had freed the slaves. Black voting thus was key to maintaining political power and implementing the Republican vision of postwar Reconstruction.

The issue also touched an emotional chord. Radical and moderate Republicans alike remained bitter about the war and particularly resented the pervasive pro-South sentiment in Washington during the conflict. Some did not hide their hostility toward local white people. Indiana representative George Julian argued that black men should be granted the right to vote not just "as a matter of justice to them" but also "as a matter of retributive justice to the slaveholders and rebels." In D.C., Congress "has the power to punish by ballot, and there will be a beautiful poetic justice in the exercise of this power." It did not matter, Julian continued, whether black men were qualified to vote: "As between [black men] and white rebels, who deserve to be hung, [black men] are eminently fit."[84]

The House passed the black men's suffrage bill in January 1866. Black spectators and white supporters in the House galleries whooped with excitement when votes were counted.

Throughout 1866 black Washingtonians pressured the Senate to pass the voting rights bill. At the Franklin Square Emancipation Day celebration in April, in letters to local newspapers, during speeches and sermons—they made it clear that they could not be fully free without the ballot. "Our right of franchise," wrote one black Washingtonian, is something "which we will never cease contending for until obtained."[85]

Their support helped bolster the strength of the Radical Republicans, who grew increasingly influential within their party as they clashed with President Andrew Johnson, a Southern Democrat and former slaveholder who appeared more sympathetic to former Confederates than to former slaves. Johnson's leniency toward the South and Southern states' refusal to ratify the Fourteenth Amendment angered many Northern voters, who propelled Republicans to massive victories in the 1866 congressional elections. Conservative and moderate Republicans edged toward the Radicals' camp, particularly on black men's suffrage in D.C. In December 1866, even before the newly elected members took office, the Senate passed the suffrage bill.

President Johnson promptly vetoed it, arguing that it was "imposed upon an unwilling people" and "would engender a feeling of opposition and hatred between the races" by allowing black voters to have "the supreme control of the white race."[86] Congress overrode the veto on January 8, 1867, however, and the bill went into immediate effect. What had been unthinkable a half decade before had become the law of the nation's capital and soon would become the law of the land.

"Quite a Revolution": The End of the White Monopoly on Political Power

Black men in Georgetown had the first chance to show the power of the franchise. In February 1867, they voted to oust incumbent mayor Henry Addison, who had complained about "nigger voting" and had long been a scourge of the black community. Black voters, the *Evening Star* reported, "exercised their new privilege with becoming modesty," and their success inspired Republican leaders in Washington City, where citywide elections would be held in June. Black leaders hurriedly organized their own political clubs and joined the interracial Central Republican Association to mobilize and register new black voters.[87]

To the chagrin of white conservatives, the black elite—educated, prosperous, native to the city—joined forces with the maligned former "contrabands" in supporting the Republican Party. Through the ward Republican clubs, established black leaders such as John F. Cook Jr. worked alongside young black Civil War veterans like George Hatton, former slaves such as Michael Shiner, and new Southern migrants, including the Reverend William J. Walker of Shiloh Baptist Church. These clubs not only registered voters but also gave black men a chance to exercise collective power on behalf of black Washingtonians. The Seventh Ward Republican Club, for example, challenged advocates of colonization and organized a citywide campaign against the Potomac Ferry Company for discriminating against black customers. The political organizing efforts were remarkably successful: despite being only 30 percent of the population, by election time black men were nearly 50 percent of registered voters.[88]

This unprecedented exercise of black power triggered a counterresponse from white supremacists. Fearing that lingering resentment might depress white voter turnout, the *National Intelligencer* and other white leaders called for a vigorous registration drive. At "white voters" meetings in the spring of 1867, they sought to shake white residents out of their political apathy. "There's only one way whites can beat blacks," argued one white voter. "That's by out-registering them." And register they did—70 percent more white voters registered for the 1867 elections compared to the year before. By Election Day, about 9,800 white men and 8,200 black men had registered, but white anti-Radicals knew that the black vote would go almost entirely to Republicans while the white vote would be split. If the Republicans won, warned one speaker at a raucous preelection rally, they would "extend the right of suffrage all over the Southern States to the cornfield negroes" and thereby trigger "a war of races, and the result must inevitably be the annihilation of the black race."[89]

A new political day was dawning. Starting at 2:00 a.m. on Election Day, June 4, 1867, black buglers and horn players marched through the streets reminding folks to vote. Black Washingtonians came out in force, lining up as the polls opened and waiting patiently with umbrellas to protect against the sun. Though no black candidates were on the ballot that day because the city charter still barred black officeholders, black voters wrought significant change. Republicans, who had played only a marginal role in local politics before 1867, won a majority of seats on both the Board of Aldermen and the Common Council. Black people celebrated with bonfires and singing in the streets. The outgoing president of the council, William W. Moore, criticized the "better informed portion of the African race residing in the city" for having allied themselves with lower-class black people "for the purpose of overshadowing the white race, and wresting from them all political power."[90]

District Republicans were creating an interracial, cross-class coalition that promised to be a political juggernaut. Racial discrimination remained, however, particularly in employment. In early 1868, nearly five thousand black workers petitioned Congress to address racially biased hiring for public jobs. "There is still such prejudice against our color, and especially against our condition as freed people of color, that we are excluded from almost every sphere of employment, except those which are most burdensome, temporary and menial in their character," they wrote. White laborers often refused to work with their black peers, making it difficult for black workers to secure decent jobs.[91]

Lingering discrimination not only undermined black economic prospects but jeopardized the Republican political project. Even as party leaders stressed equality, racial tensions undermined the party. As D.C. Republicans mobilized for 1868 municipal elections, they split on the question whether to put black candidates on the ticket. Black Republicans petitioned Congress to remove color and property qualifications for office holding. "The Black man has shown his valor, his patriotism and his worth in the field, and his ability, his integrity and his fidelity in civil life," read one petition from George Hatton and other Fourth Ward Republicans. The test for public office "should be the Jeffersonian criterion. Is he Capable? Is he honest? Is he just?"[92]

Congressional Republicans did indeed change the city charter to allow for black candidates, but some white Republicans offered pragmatic political objections, fearing that "defeat was certain" if black candidates were on the ticket. During one tumultuous meeting of the First Ward Republicans, the argument became heated and someone yelled, "Monkeys!" as black members spoke. A disgusted black Republican, Alfred Day, explained why he supported black candidates for office: "The white man did nothing for the colored man, and we want nothing more to do with them."[93]

Despite such tensions, Republicans came together in the mayoral election of 1868, which pitted abolitionist and Radical Republican Sayles J. Bowen against Democrat John T. Given, who ran on an "Anti-Radical" or "Conservative" ticket. A tall, bearded New Yorker who had moved to Washington in the 1840s, Bowen had an abrasive personality but earned strong support within the black commu-

"Significant Election Scene at Washington, June 3, 1867." Black voters first cast their ballots during 1867 municipal elections in Georgetown (February) and Washington City (June). Black men voted and served as election officials, as depicted in this sketch from Harper's Weekly. Library of Congress.

nity for his long-standing support of black public schools, his vociferous defense of black men's suffrage, and his efforts to help former slaves get relief. He ran on a platform of economic progress, promising to modernize the city and undercut a nascent effort to relocate the national capital to St. Louis.[94]

Bowen's appeals to black voters unnerved his opponents, who attacked him as a "falsifying and fraudulent office-beggar" and an "ultra demagogue." On

Election Day, the *National Intelligencer* ran an anti-Bowen editorial under the headline "The Negro War upon Whites" and claimed that the Republicans were "import[ing]" black men from the countryside and paying them $3 to vote.[95]

The contest ended in controversy—Bowen won by fewer than a hundred votes, but incumbent Mayor Wallach refused to allow him access to the mayor's office. The conservative *Georgetown Courier* warned: "The races are now pitted against each other in deadly animosity, and but very little added excitement is required to drench the streets of the national capital in human blood." It took several weeks of political chaos before the new mayor could take office, joined by the city's first black elected officials: the black-majority First Ward chose educator John F. Cook Jr. as alderman and barber Carter A. Stewart for the Common Council.[96]

Bowen's administration brought remarkable change to the city and its politics. Determined to reward his supporters, the new mayor appointed black people to about 30 percent of the positions in his administration. He named two black men to the all-white fire department, installed black men as ward commissioners, and tapped a black doctor as public health physician. In June 1869, two black police officers integrated the city's police force.[97]

Bowen inaugurated an era of massive public works projects as city workers planted trees along K Street, built four miles of sewers and fifteen miles of sidewalks, and smoothed and graded the notoriously rutted roads. These projects not only put thousands of unemployed laborers to work but also strengthened Bowen's political support among working-class black voters—because Washington lacked an industrial base, black workers relied heavily on public works projects for employment. Black people "shared in and enjoyed the general prosperity of that time," recalled Perry Carson, Mayor Bowen's bodyguard, who later became a prominent black political leader in Southwest. "Many a modest little home ha[d] been erected and maintained from the 'nest egg' started during Bowen's regime."[98]

By 1869, the movement for biracial democracy in Washington seemed to be on the verge of making revolutionary changes. Newly elected Republican president Ulysses S. Grant took office with a vision of transforming Washington into a powerful symbol of federal supremacy, a goal that meshed well with Mayor Bowen's plans to modernize the city. Grant immediately signed bills vetoed by his predecessor that struck the word "white" from the charters and laws of Washington and Georgetown, and gave black men the right to serve on juries.[99]

In May, after a group of black and white city councilmen were denied service at two city eateries, the city council banned racial discrimination in places of public entertainment—and a majority of the white city council members voted for the bill. The next year, the council strengthened the law by extending the ban to include eateries, hotels, and other private establishments. These laws later provided the legal foundation for D.C.'s post–World War II civil rights movement.[100]

Washington's reputation as a haven for black advancement attracted some of the nation's top black intellectuals and political personalities, including Ohio lawyer John Mercer Langston, who led the new Howard University Law School, and Frederick Douglass, who became owner and editor of the *New National Era*. The June 1869 elections brought a new crop of black elected officials to power as John F. Cook won the citywide Office of the Register and black men from each of the city's seven wards—including George Hatton from the Fourth Ward—won election to the Common Council.[101]

It was "quite a revolution," the *Evening Star* conceded. No longer governed by an all-white, proslavery elite, Washington instead embraced biracial democracy. The white monopoly on political power was over. Or so it seemed.[102]

Incapable of Self-Government

The Retreat from Democracy, 1869–1890

The old fogies are opposed to negro suffrage; and as they cannot withdraw it, they seek to diminish if not destroy, the opportunities for its exercise. Here is the whole secret of the recently inaugurated movement to take away our municipal government.
— *New National Era*, January 1870

A small, grassy triangle is all that marks the junction of Virginia Avenue, Sixth Street, and D Street in Southwest Washington today. Across Virginia Avenue lay the railroad tracks; down the block rises a nondescript, 1950s concrete box of an office building. Noisy and drab, the intersection attracts few pedestrians. There are no historical markers in the vicinity, nothing to indicate that anything of note has ever happened there. More than a century ago, however, on this forlorn spot that was once part of Notley Young's sprawling plantation, stood a grand, three-story brick building called Island Hall, which served as a staging ground for the drama of race and democracy in post–Civil War Washington.

Island Hall got its name from the surrounding Southwest neighborhood. Sandwiched between the Potomac to its south and west and the notorious City Canal to its north and east, Southwest was a rural backwater cut off from the rest of the city. It was an island, literally and figuratively, and it retained its moniker and its distinctive culture for generations, even after the canal was filled in during the 1870s. Part port city with a thriving wharf, part suburban en-clave with large residential plots featuring gardens and chickens, the Island was perhaps the postwar city's most diverse area. Home to a large Irish community, it boasted several Catholic churches, and its richest resident was an Irish con-tractor named Patrick Cullinane. A thriving community of German Jews lived near Island Hall, its Talmud Torah Synagogue later rising along E Street. Along the Potomac were fishing families living a river-oriented lifestyle that seemed quite foreign to the government clerks a mile to their north.[1]

In the decades after the Civil War, the fastest-growing population on the Island was black. The area east of Four-and-a-Half Street SW had long been home to a small community of free and enslaved black people, including Underground Railroad conductor Anthony Bowen. After the war, freedpeople in search of inexpensive housing were drawn to this enclave. The area thickened into a bustling, densely populated neighborhood that was nearly 80 percent black and almost all working-class. Many of the poorest residents crowded into burgeoning alley communities, where families piled into unsanitary hovels without indoor plumbing. By 1880, almost 10 percent of the city's black population lived on the Island.[2]

Island Hall was a common meeting ground for this diverse set of Southwest communities, serving protean purposes that reflected the varied nature of neighborhood life. Its cavernous ballroom hosted church services, community fairs, and political meetings, while its smaller rooms welcomed students, lodge members, politicians, and entrepreneurs. During the war, the Union army requisitioned it to serve as a hospital for wounded soldiers. When the armed conflict ended, Island Hall became a venue for democracy in all its participatory, contentious glory. It played host to a wide range of groups discussing the issues of the day—the Hope Division advocating temperance, the Fenian Brotherhood talking about Irish independence, the Workingmen's Convention calling for an eight-hour day.[3]

But the most vexing issue on the floor of Island Hall was District politics. The wartime growth of the black community on the Island ushered in a tumultuous period in the area's political history, as it had elsewhere in the city. Island Hall served as the central arena and polling site for the surrounding political precinct, which was evenly balanced between black and white—during the 1871 election, there were 940 registered white voters and 930 registered black voters. As battles over black suffrage and interracial democracy escalated in the late 1860s and early 1870s, the hall became an explosive venue that hosted competing groups under its roof.[4]

Island Hall was the regular stomping ground of the Seventh Ward Republicans, a boisterous bunch whose raucous meetings often featured heated internecine disputes and challenges to party authority. Shortly before the 1869 elections, the group assembled there to select representatives for the D.C. Republican Party's nominating convention. The party's central committee had determined that fifteen men would be chosen, ten black and five white—but the Seventh Ward Republicans would have none of it. After much debate, they rejected the color requirements, insisting that "there were no such words in the Republican party as white or colored." Instead, they would choose on merit alone, and they selected an interracial slate that included Anthony Bowen, Irishman Patrick Cullinane, and Perry Carson, Mayor Bowen's burly black bodyguard.[5]

That same week, conservative white Democrats convened in Island Hall, their angry voices filling the air as they denounced the course of postwar events. At the Republican meeting, a cacophony of voices had overwhelmed the chair. The seething conservatives were more orderly, listening carefully to chairman Thomas Lloyd, a former city councilman, as he issued a powerful attack on the Radicals and their black allies, who had ousted him and other white Democrats from office. "The power of the Radical party is only temporary—deluding the negro to his own injury," Lloyd warned. "The handwriting [is] on the wall; the time [is] coming when the negro [will] find out who their true friends [are]." Having endured "reckless extravagance" in government, the "old citizens" were ready to reassert control. They would take their city back and "would not give the negro the right of suffrage but would give him food and employment."[6]

Lloyd and his conservative allies appeared to have lost the battle to prevent biracial democracy. Since the end of the Civil War, Washington had been the vanguard of a political revolution that swept the South. With the ratification of the Fifteenth Amendment in February 1870, the Constitution now enshrined the black man's right to vote, and across the South black voters changed the complexion of state legislatures and even Congress. Black Washingtonians voted in high numbers and grew more experienced in political organizing and mobilization with each passing year. The 1869 elections had solidified Republican control of the city, and black men now held posts at all levels of public life and in every ward. A retreat from suffrage and empowerment back to simply "food and employment" seemed unthinkable.

The long-term outcome of the experiment in racial equality and biracial democracy remained uncertain, however. For all the accomplishments of the immediate postwar period, biracial democracy in the District was fragile, a fledgling endeavor vulnerable to changes in economic conditions, national politics, and powerful personalities. As Thomas Lloyd warned, a counterrevolution percolated below the surface of D.C. politics as white supremacists organized in opposition to Radical rule. At places like Island Hall, they clashed with their Republican opponents and challenged the basic premise of self-government in the District. The outcome of these battles would determine the fate of democracy in the nation's capital for nearly a century to come.

"The Old Fogies Are Opposed to Negro Suffrage": The Counterrevolution against Interracial Democracy Begins

Alexander Shepherd did not embrace democracy, biracial or otherwise. Born in Southwest in 1835—just a few blocks from Island Hall—Shepherd was the son of a wealthy, slave-owning lumber and coal dealer. Any hope of inherited prosperity crumbled, however, after his father's death when Shepherd was just ten years old. He soon had to drop out of school to help support the family. He found his niche in the booming construction business of 1850s Washington, rising quickly to junior partner of a prospering plumbing and gas outfitting company. When the Civil War erupted, he enlisted and served honorably in the Unionist D.C. militia, the National Rifles.

Even before his militia term was up, Shepherd ran for political office, winning a seat on the city's Common Council in mid-1861. He immediately began promoting the cause that would define his political career: economic development and physical "improvements" that would, he emphasized in 1862, "make this metropolis worthy [of] the hallowed name it bears, and worthy to be the capital of the 'great Republic' of the world." After losing a bid for a spot on the Board of Aldermen in 1864, Shepherd—by now one of the city's wealthiest men—remained an active public promoter of economic development through both the city's largest newspaper, the Evening Star, of which he became a part owner, and the Washington Board of Trade, which he cofounded in October 1865. Square-jawed and powerfully built with abundant energy and a humorless intensity, Shepherd was a visionary leader who combined the sense of entitlement of an aristocrat with the restless ambition of a self-made man.[7]

During the war, Shepherd was strongly pro-Union but not antislavery—certainly not a Radical. Like most white Washingtonians, even those who supported the Union, he opposed emancipation, dismissed the idea of black equality, and rejected black suffrage. As a city councilman, he voted with a 14–4 majority opposing the District emancipation bill in 1862, and he helped at least one slave owner get compensation for her emancipated "property." Two weeks after the bill had passed, Shepherd argued that "agitation" on racial issues should cease and that he hoped "the discussion on the negro question in this city was at an end" so that city leaders could focus on more important issues. By 1864, he had come to accept emancipation, but he opposed efforts by "red-mouthed abolitionists" to put black men "on an equality with white men" and "was opposed to the principle of allowing negroes to vote, in toto."[8]

Shepherd did not simply seek to preserve white supremacy and whites-only politics. He also objected to the broad-based white democracy that had spread nationwide since Andrew Jackson's time. Embracing the founders' restricted definition of democracy, Shepherd believed that property owners alone should shoulder the responsibilities of leadership. Only the propertied had the long-term stake in the community necessary for thoughtful policy making, he argued. Allowing the poor to rule would give them license to tax and spend other people's money. Even as Radical Republicans in Congress and their local black allies pushed for a much more expansive definition of democracy that would include black men, Shepherd—and the businessmen, bankers, and real estate developers who supported him—began a countercampaign that ultimately would destroy democracy in the District altogether.

The city's journey from biracial democracy to universal disfranchisement (loss of voting rights) was a confusing one, with a variety of political twists and shifting alliances. It began with a movement to consolidate the District's three governments (Washington City, Georgetown, and Washington County) into a single administrative unit directly under the control of presidential appointees. Advocates of what became known as "consolidation" sought more than simply to dissolve administrative boundaries. They also aimed to revoke self-government in the District and replace it with an unelected board of commissioners appointed by the president. "The taxpayers of this city did not want elections of any kind, and had not wanted them for 20 years," Shepherd explained in early 1868. "We want an honest Board of Commissioners and no broken-down political demagogues."[9]

Supporters of consolidation and commission rule cast themselves as nonpartisan reformers interested in "efficient and harmonious" government and economic prosperity. Having three separate jurisdictions, they argued, bred confusion and complexity, delaying development and generating overlapping, often exorbitant expenses. A consolidated government ruled by commissioners would be more effective and efficient, Shepherd and his supporters believed, enabling the District to pursue citywide improvement projects. They insisted that Washington would blossom economically if Congress cleared away the underbrush of fractured self-government that choked off economic growth.[10]

Shepherd argued that consolidation and a commission government were a "business necessity, and should not be mixed up in any degree with politics, negro suffrage or anything else." Yet supporters and opponents alike understood that it was a direct response to the Radical push to extend voting rights to black men. The timing of the movement, the undemocratic solution it advocated, the conservative composition of its supporters—all indicated that consolidation aimed to offer a seemingly race-neutral solution to the problem of black political power and the excessive taxation, uncontrolled spending, and endemic corruption that white conservatives believed necessarily would follow black suffrage. To prevent such a calamity, they recommended eliminating democracy in the city.[11]

The consolidation movement began to gain traction in late 1865, just as Radicals started agitating for black suffrage, and it accelerated in direct proportion to the extent of black political power. It attracted support from a wide range of white conservatives, uniting self-described "old citizens" (native white Washingtonians with antebellum city roots) and Democrats who vehemently opposed black suffrage with the businessmen of the newly formed Washington Board of Trade. A nonpartisan organization that included both Democrats and wealthy Republicans, the Board of Trade promoted economic growth above all else. Its founding members—including Shepherd, banker George W. Riggs, and financier W. W. Corcoran—mobilized "taxpayers" and "intelligent citizens" in support of consolidation and commission rule.

In 1868, when the city's charter was up for renewal, Shepherd and his allies on the Board of Trade pushed to amend the charter by replacing the elected municipal government with a federally appointed commission government. The *Evening Star*, which had supported consolidation but had been skeptical of rule by commissioners, began to soften its stance—perhaps because it was now partly owned by Alexander Shepherd. Its editorials began arguing against self-government. The right to vote "has proved a delusion and a snare, causing us to grasp at the shadow of representation and power, and to lose the substantial benefits that might have been gained by a system of rule for which the National Government would be responsible." The privilege of voting, the *Star*'s editors argued, is perhaps "a bauble that we had better exchange for more substantial benefits"—namely, federal funding for "a system of improvement and adornment for the national metropolis commensurate with the grand scale upon which it was planned."[12]

The idea of trading the right to vote for increased federal funding touched off a furor among District Radicals, black and white, who responded with a full-throated defense of democracy. The Radical-dominated city council issued a blistering resolution condemning the effort as an "anti-republican scheme" and "an attempt to deprive the people of this city from Exercising the common prerogatives of freemen, and to govern them by means of a moneyed aristocracy." Incensed District residents sent petitions to Congress attacking the movement and its supporters. One petition dismissed consolidation advocates as "speculators in real estate and adventurers" and "all those who sympathized with or assisted the rebellion, and who are determined at all hazards to deprive the colored man of his vote." Congress, still under Radical sway, voted in May 1868 to renew the city's charter without changing the structure of government.[13]

Despite its wealth, influence, and newspaper power, the consolidation movement floundered initially because it ran counter to the democratic spirit of the times. Too many people were too invested in the political system to consider abandoning self-government. Stymied, Shepherd and his business allies abruptly shifted strategies. Rather than push directly for a consolidation bill that would disfranchise District residents, they sought to pursue their economic goals by co-opting the Radical movement.

As it became clear in early 1868 that Congress had no intention of amending the charter to his liking, Shepherd and his *Evening Star*—which for years had aggressively opposed black suffrage and the Radicals' racial agenda—suddenly embraced mayoral candidate Sayles Bowen, hoping that having a Radical in office would make Congress more willing to fund city improvement projects. Shepherd's new direction alienated old-line conservative Democrats, but it revealed Shepherd to be a shrewd political opportunist. Temporarily bowing to political realities, he laid aside his concerns about race and democracy in order to pursue the economic development he championed.

The alliance did not last long. Bowen was elected mayor, but his political coalition began to crumble early in his term as many erstwhile supporters turned against him. Bowen angered many black voters when he pushed a plan to combine the separate white and black school boards into a single city-run board but rejected calls to integrate the schools themselves. The issue split the black community, with many prominent black leaders such as John F. Cook openly opposing the mayor and questioning his motives. Many black voters also questioned the mayor's attempts to build an interracial coalition of Republican laborers, complaining that the "Radical Irish" were getting jobs at the expense of black workers.[14]

More crippling, however, were the financial problems that undermined his administration. Bowen's ambitious agenda to remake the city with massive public works projects appealed to both workers who wanted jobs and businessmen who sought city contracts. But the projects required significant sums of money that the city simply did not have. Bowen turned to Congress in the summer of 1869 yet came away empty-handed. He reassessed property values and issued bonds, which only swelled the city's debt and raised the local tax burden, antagonizing moderate Republicans and energizing the administration's opponents. Hobbled by debt and chronically cash-strapped, the city could not afford to pay its workers, alienating a core constituency. "A man that works and is not paid is still a slave," read one sign at an anti-Bowen rally. As the city debt ballooned, the mayor became the target of corruption allegations.[15]

D.C.'s Republican Party began to splinter. A new group, the Independent Reform Republicans, broke from Bowen and created an interracial coalition of the mayor's critics. It was a testament to the extent of voters' alienation that the new party attracted both former-slave-turned-councilman George Hatton and businessman Alexander Shepherd. A vocal supporter of school integration and an advocate for black workers, Hatton objected to the mayor's mishandling of the schools and his inability to get the city's fiscal house in enough order to pay its workers. Shepherd saw the Bowen administration as too incompetent to carry out the public works projects needed to transform the city.[16]

Shepherd and Hatton agreed on one thing: Bowen had manipulated black voters. To cheers and laughter at one meeting, Hatton insisted that "the time is passed for the corrupt individuals who desire to ride into office on the backs of the black man, to crack the party whip and say, 'Niggers, wheel into line.'" The *Evening Star* accused Bowen and his "ring" of having "a thorough contempt for the great mass of the colored people, treating them as so much merchantable voting material, to be bought by a little gutter-work." Just a few years later, Shepherd himself faced similar accusations.[17]

In the 1870 mayoral elections, the Reformers nominated Matthew Emery, a successful stonemason and architect who embodied the pragmatic, economically minded Republicanism that many Bowen critics craved. Abandoned by national Republican leaders as well as many of his local black allies, Bowen was crushed in the June elections and never again played a significant role in District politics. Though Emery was not a Radical, he publicly acknowledged black voters as an important constituency to be courted. "The great questions of universal freedom and universal suffrage have been settled by the voice of the nation," Emery emphasized in his first message as mayor. "We feel that these questions no longer concern us, and we are glad to be permitted to dismiss them and turn our attention to matters of more immediate local interest."[18]

But Emery was premature (or perhaps disingenuous) in declaring suffrage a closed question. Conservative leaders in the District refused to concede that black voting and biracial democracy were irreversible, and during the next four years they waged a successful battle to eliminate suffrage altogether.

Even as they supported Emery's mayoral campaign in early 1870, Shepherd and other Reform Republicans joined with conservative Democrats to push a new strategy to consolidate and revamp the District's governing structure. The Bowen administration had been such a disaster, Shepherd contended, that it raised questions about the capacity of black voters to rule responsibly. "Here the experiment of universal suffrage was first made, and ... (unfortunately) Sayles J. Bowen was placed in his present position as a representative man, to demonstrate that our colored citizens were capable of choosing proper men as rulers."[19]

Shepherd's point was clear: the experiment had failed. Black voters had had their chance and had chosen poorly. Now it was time not simply to change mayors but to alter the structure of voting to ensure that such mistakes could not happen again.

Instead of trying to get everything they wanted all at once—consolidation plus rule by unelected commissioners—the Reformers chose a new path: a consolidated "territorial" government modeled on the governments established in the Western territories. Shepherd and his allies wined and dined members of Congress, taking some on a Potomac River cruise complete with champagne and music. Their intensive lobbying worked. In February 1871, Congress created a single territorial government for a consolidated District of Columbia. The new government was a democratic hybrid, consisting of a presidentially appointed governor, upper Legislative Council, and Board of Public Works alongside a popularly elected lower House of Delegates and nonvoting representative in the U.S. House.[20]

Though District voters could still elect some officials, most of the power in the new territorial government was vested in the presidential appointees, particularly the Board of Public Works, which controlled the distribution of contracts and patronage. President Grant shared Shepherd's vision of using public works to transform the city physically into a grand capital appropriate for a powerful national government, and he appointed Shepherd to the five-man board. Shepherd immediately asserted control, turning it into the most powerful arm of city government. Shepherd's nominal boss, Governor Henry Cooke, served as a mere figurehead and rubber stamp. "Why is the Governor like a gentle lamb?" asked the Daily Patriot. "Because he is led by A. Shepherd."[21]

Shepherd claimed that 90 percent of the city's "bona fide taxpayers and property-holders" supported consolidation and the territorial government, but one significant bloc within the party was vociferously opposed: black voters. Though many black voters had abandoned Bowen for the Reform Republican Party, few supported consolidation because they saw it as a step toward disfranchisement. George Vashon, a black Freedmen's Bureau official who became Howard University's first professor, condemned the movement as "a base plot, designed to defraud the eight thousand freedmen therein of the elective franchise, and cheat them of their newborn freedom."[22]

As the reinvigorated consolidation movement began making calls for territorial government, black voices rose in opposition. The New Era, a weekly black newspaper launched in Washington in January 1870, made consolidation one of its early targets. "The old fogies are opposed to negro suffrage; and as they cannot withdraw it, they seek to diminish if not destroy, the opportunities for its exercise," editors J. Sella Martin and Frederick Douglass wrote. "Here is the whole secret of the recently inaugurated movement to take away our municipal government." That same month, the Board of Aldermen and the Common Council passed a resolution drafted by black alderman Carter Stewart condemning a commission form of government because it "impl[ied] that the people of this city are not qualified for the exercise of the right of suffrage and of self-government as allowed to every other people under our republican institutions."[23]

Black opposition to the new territorial government spanned all classes. While the black elite took to their lecterns and presses to express their discontent, black workers took to the streets. On June 1, 1871, the first day the territorial government took charge, public workers black and white walked off their jobs to protest the $1.25 a day wages that city contractors paid. Most white workers went back to work after a couple days, enticed in part by contractors who sought to exploit racial divisions by recruiting Irish workers for $1.50 a day. But black workers stayed on strike for nearly a week, demanding $2.00 for an eight-hour day. Condemned in the white press, the black strikers ultimately settled for a $1.50 compromise brokered by Alexander Shepherd. Their short-lived strike improved wages, but they soon discovered that they wielded far less influence in the new system than they had during the Bowen years.[24]

Though many black people distrusted him, Shepherd sought to cultivate their political support through patronage. About one-third of the territorial government's appointees were black, and Shepherd helped engineer (through Governor Cooke) several high-profile appointments: Frederick Douglass, who had recently moved to the city and edited the New Era, joined the Legislative Council; John Mercer Langston was appointed to the Board of Health; and John F. Cook was named the city's registrar.[25] Shepherd also hired black workers for public works projects and solicited black voters' support for a major loan referendum in late 1871.

Shepherd's efforts earned him significant support within the black community, though it was not universal—George Hatton, who had helped organize the strike, became an outspoken critic. Most black voters appreciated the economic opportunities that opened during the Shepherd era yet remained wary of Shepherd's tactics and any limits on the franchise. They were right to be skeptical.

"A Government City without a City Government": D.C. Loses the Right to Vote

Shepherd enthusiastically embraced his new power. Focused on promoting economic growth, Shepherd turned the Board of Public Works into an engine of taxpayer-funded development. When the new government took control in June 1871, the board proposed a $6.6 million ($864 million in twenty-first-century dollars) Comprehensive Plan of Improvements that promised to remake the city, by first refurbishing the downtown area and Pennsylvania Avenue and then moving north and west along Connecticut Avenue. The plan required a $4 mil-

"View of Washington City." Despite significant growth during the Civil War, Washington City in 1869 was still a relatively undeveloped urban area. As the controversial head of the Board of Public Works, Alexander Shepherd pushed for rapid economic development, particularly in Northwest Washington. Library of Congress.

lion loan, which District voters, white and black alike, approved overwhelmingly that November. Loan in hand, the Board of Public Works went on a building binge.

The results were extraordinary. With a brook-no-dissent style bolstered by unwavering support from President Grant, Shepherd hired laborers to build more than 150 miles of city streets, 120 miles of sewers, and 200 miles of sidewalks. City workers planted more than sixty thousand trees, filled in the disgusting city canal, illuminated Washington nights with some three thousand streetlamps, and razed the crumbling Northern Liberties Market. They improved streets and streetcar lines, spurring development in outlying areas and triggering a real estate boom. The area around Pacific Circle (now known as Dupont Circle) began to sprout Victorian mansions of the elite. Washington, wrote one admiring journalist, "has clothed itself anew, thrown away its staff, and achieved a transformation bewildering to its old residents."[26]

Shepherd's ambitious agenda and debt-fueled spending ran afoul of wealthy, white conservatives, particularly Democrats and longtime Washingtonians. They had supported consolidation and the shift to territorial government in the hopes of limiting black political power, but they quickly grew disenchanted when President Grant appointed only Republicans to the new government. "Not one old resident, nor a Democrat, nor a Catholic nor an Irishman," huffed the *Georgetown Courier*. Republicans dominated the April 1871 elections for the House of Delegates—though only two black men were among the twenty-two new legislators—and Democrats feared that the new government would continue to shut them out of power.[27]

Among the fiercest critics were two bankers whose names would resonate in D.C. for generations: W. W. Corcoran and George W. Riggs. Their jointly owned Riggs Bank was a city institution until it was bought out by PNC Bank in 2005. Corcoran, a Southern sympathizer, spent the Civil War in self-imposed exile in Europe, where he added to his world-class art collection. Returning home following the war, he became a leading voice in the business community and earned accolades with the opening of an art gallery in early 1871. His business partner, Riggs, also had deep roots in Washington and had been active in the Board of Trade after the war. Though they had supported consolidation, Corcoran and Riggs recoiled when the territorial government ran up the public debt. They helped lead an opposition movement by launching an anti-Shepherd newspaper, the *Daily Patriot*, organizing a petition calling for a federal investigation into the city's finances, and testifying against the government during congressional hearings.[28]

Organized as the Citizens Association of the District of Columbia, opponents of the territorial government charged the municipal government with wild spending and accused Shepherd of bribing and manipulating black voters. Ignorant black men, they argued, supported corrupt officials, who then raided the treasury. An 1872 *Daily Patriot* editorial titled "Our Black Rulers" charged that "venal adventurers" in the government used black people as "political puppets" to amass power. "These negroes bring nothing with them but empty hands and hungry mouths, and they produce nothing in the shape of subsistence," the editors claimed, yet they made up the machinery of the territorial government. To rid the city of corruption and restore economic sanity, they argued that Congress should abolish democracy in the District. "The majority of the voters here," Riggs testified in 1872, "are incapable of self-government."[29]

A Shepherd-friendly 1872 congressional investigation turned up little evidence of corruption and issued only a mild rebuke of the territorial government. But Shepherd continued to accumulate political enemies as rapidly as the government took on debt. He unabashedly linked public jobs to political support and rewarded his allies with hefty public contracts, leading critics to label him a "boss" in the mold of the infamous "Boss" Tweed of New York. Shepherd's government was a "little monarchy," wrote one observer. "Controlling the poor colored man's vote, and making his labor depend on it, and using it against the property and people of this city, is what these men are themselves doing." Shoddy work and bungled street-grading projects triggered lawsuits, while residents of Capitol Hill and other areas accused the administration of favoritism in its focus on developing the Connecticut Avenue corridor in Northwest. As the scandal-ridden President Grant stumbled in his second term and Congress continued its retreat from Reconstruction in the South, national reporters (particularly from Democratic papers) descended on the capital, eager to expose corruption in the Republican-run city.[30]

The territorial government might have been able to outlast its critics had it not been for its financial difficulties. The public projects that transformed the city came with a hefty price tag, and like Mayor Bowen, Shepherd had no money to pay for them. By early 1873, the government was nearly broke, and it stopped paying teachers, laborers, and other city employees. Shepherd sought to issue more bonds, levy higher taxes, and win further federal support to finance planned improvements, but his political support was eroding. Yet he still had the confidence of President Grant, who appointed him governor in September 1873 after Henry Cooke resigned.[31]

Just a few days after Shepherd assumed the governorship, the bottom fell out of the national economy. The Panic of 1873, triggered by the financial fall of Henry Cooke's brother, megafinancier Jay Cooke, hit the District particularly hard because as governor Henry Cooke had invested city funds heavily in his brother's enterprises. When Jay Cooke went bankrupt, so did the city. Shepherd's government essentially collapsed. "Washington is certainly a beautiful city" thanks to Shepherd, wrote the *Nation*, but "the territorial government has broken down, its debt is enormous, and its accounts in such confusion that the amount is unknown. Taxes are onerous and discriminating, contracts are unperformed, and school teachers unpaid."[32]

As the city collapsed, so did the Freedman's Savings Bank, a particularly crushing blow for the black community. Founded in Washington in 1865 by abolitionist financiers, the bank aimed to encourage former slaves to save money, accumulate property, and establish themselves as productive citizens. It grew tremendously. By 1873, there were members in all thirty-seven states with millions of dollars in deposits, and the bank became a source of tremendous pride for black Washingtonians.

During the Shepherd era, however, white bank officials began to loan money to themselves and their friends at below-market rates, and Governor Cooke used bank funds to bail out his brother's failing Northern Pacific Railway. When the city went bankrupt in 1873, they allowed the Board of Public Works to "repay" outstanding loans with IOUs rather than cash. Within a year, the bank had folded, and thousands of small depositors and black organizations lost their savings. Furious, black leaders in D.C. who had been involved with the bank, including Frederick Douglass, denounced the "grand rascals" who had caused the collapse and called on the federal government to repay depositors. It never paid a cent. The Freedman's Savings Bank, founded to promote thrift and saving, ultimately encouraged black cynicism about financial institutions, the Republican Party, and even America itself.[33]

The economic mess prompted a new bipartisan congressional investigation of the city government. This time, investigators turned up evidence of serious graft. Though nothing suggested that Shepherd personally profited, the investigation highlighted the extent to which his relentless, ends-justify-the-means push to "improve" the city led to conflicts of interests, influence peddling, no-bid contracts, and cost overruns. The bill for his public works projects reached nearly $21 million (nearly $3 billion in twenty-first century dollars), about $14 million more than originally projected and more than double what Congress had allowed.[34]

The investigating committee's report excoriated Shepherd and the Board of Public Works for excessive spending, but it also laid blame on District voters for allowing the legislature and the board to spend so freely. Given the inability of voters and their elected representatives to restrain themselves, the committee recommended returning the city to rule by unelected commissioners, as it had been governed in its founding era in the late eighteenth century.[35]

Congress, not a body accustomed to moving quickly, rendered a swift and painful judgment not only on the excesses of the Shepherd administration but also on democracy in the District. In June 1874, just two days after the committee's report came out, Congress voted 216–22 to end the territorial government and revert to a presidentially appointed board of three commissioners to manage the city and pay its debts. By law, one commissioner had to be a member of the U.S. Army Corps of Engineers; by custom, the other two commissioner spots were split between Democrats and Republicans. In response to local pressure, Congress pledged to cover 50 percent of the city's annual budget, acknowledging that the federal presence in Washington added expense (by requiring upkeep for public buildings) and curtailed revenue (because federal property was not taxed). Though this new system of commissioner rule initially was intended as a temporary measure, Congress made it permanent in 1878.[36]

District men, white and black, rich and poor, lost their right to vote. They would not cast another meaningful ballot for nearly a century.[37]

The scope of disfranchisement was remarkable. "Under this bill," wrote the editors of the Nation, "not a vestige is left of popular municipal government: aldermen, common councilmen, mayors, boards of works, school boards, police boards, primaries, conventions, all are swept away, and the entire government is handed over to three men, appointed by a foreign authority, responsible not to their fellow citizens, but to the President and Senate." With the new law, explained District commissioner Thomas Bryan, Congress hoped that it could "be forever free from the disturbing influence of elections in its immediate neighborhood." Washington had become "a government city without a city government," white writer Mary Logan later observed.[38]

Losing the franchise stunned District voters and elected officials. Members of the House of Delegates—now unemployed and powerless—responded with a symbolic protest in which they temporarily looted their chamber, taking everything from desks and chairs down to soap and a feather duster. Though the items were all returned the next day, reformers seized on the prank as evidence of the inherent corruption of D.C. democracy. For decades, mere mention of the "feather duster legislature" elicited guffaws from elite Washington and became a pithy shorthand for the excesses of biracial democracy.[39]

The racial implications of the shift to commissioner rule were not lost on contemporary observers. "In this District, the experiment was first made of giving the black man the suffrage," wrote the National Republican in 1874. "Has it come to this, that the Republican party admits and acknowledges its failure? And is it ready to try the further experiment of taking the suffrage away from white and black alike?"[40] For many Republicans weary of the Radical focus on civil rights, the answer was yes.

Only two of the maligned House of Delegates' twenty-two members and none of Shepherd's close advisers were black, yet critics blamed black voters for the scandals and spending of the "feather duster legislature," as well as the Shepherd administration. Put in place by "ignorant negro voters," Shepherd's government had exercised "irresponsible power," concluded the Nation. The city "should be controlled by the responsible and not by the irresponsible portion of the people who chance to dwell there." Harper's Weekly, a Republican publication that had generally supported the Radicals' racial agenda, nonetheless supported the return to commissioner rule as a matter of "expediency" and administrative efficiency. "It is not negro suffrage, it is ignorant suffrage, which is dangerous," the editors argued. By moving to an appointed city government, Washington could set an example for other municipalities.[41]

Alexander Shepherd, the man who had done so much to undermine democracy in the District, struggled to find his place within the new government. President Grant nominated him to be one of the District's three new commissioners in 1874, but the Senate overwhelmingly rejected him. Within two years, Shepherd was bankrupt. In 1880, he abandoned the city to seek his fortune in Batopilas, Mexico, where he built a prosperous silver-mining operation that he ran for more than twenty years before his death in 1902.[42]

In his absence, Shepherd's reputation grew. Elite white Washingtonians, many of whom had fought him while he was in office, now celebrated his accomplishments. "Washington owes him an inextinguishable debt," editorialized the city's new Democratic paper, the *Washington Post*, in 1885. "To his talent, his courage, his indomitable purpose, this city is indebted for its beauty, its attractiveness, its prosperity." In 1909, white city leaders commissioned a statue of the man they hailed as the "father of modern Washington" to be placed in front of the Municipal Building. As black scholar W. E. B. DuBois reflected ruefully decades later, "the harm and dishonesty of the Shepherd regime was charged to the colored voter, while the beauty and accomplishment of the reborn city was put to the credit of white civilization."[43]

Although Shepherd was lionized, other leading figures of the Reconstruction era did not fare so well. Former mayor Sayles Bowen remained in the city, a shell of his former self. Wealthy when he was elected, he made a series of bad investments, lost his fortune, and wound up working as a night watchman in a federal building. Cantankerous to the end, he died with little fanfare and few friends; he was buried in an undistinguished grave in Congressional Cemetery. Few, then or now, recalled his advocacy of black education and suffrage.[44]

George Hatton, who had catapulted from slavery to the city council and helped organize black opposition to both the Bowen administration and the territorial government, also struggled. After his political career ended with the imposition of commissioner rule, he turned his rhetorical skills to the ministry, leaving Washington for Kentucky in the 1870s. Bedeviled by alcohol, he attempted suicide in 1894 and later returned with his wife to the Washington area, where he died in 1904.[45] Like Bowen, Hatton's extraordinary life and contributions to the city largely have been forgotten.

Congress's two-step retreat from democracy in the District—first by limiting voter influence in the territorial government, then by abolishing elected offices altogether—was a precursor to the national Republican retreat from Reconstruction across the South. Three years after Congress passed the D.C. disfranchisement bill, the Compromise of 1877 ended Reconstruction by removing federal troops from the South. Within a generation, bills limiting voting rights had passed every Southern state legislature. It also set an undemocratic precedent for how to deal with nonwhite peoples abroad. More than two decades later, after the Spanish-American War left the American military in charge of the Philippines, the army general responsible for drafting Manila's city charter cited D.C. as a reason for denying the Filipinos self-government.[46]

The Republican Party, no longer interested in defending its civil rights agenda, instead followed Alexander Shepherd's model of promoting economic development for the benefit of white elites. In Washington, this meant downplaying or ignoring the interests of the black community and focusing on economic growth to build a grand capital "worthy of the name." Development had triumphed over democracy. The era of biracial elected government in the District was over. It would take nearly a century for a new one to begin.

"Mecca of the Colored Pilgrim": D.C.'s Educated Black Community Flourishes

Orindatus Simon Bolivar (O. S. B.) Wall witnessed firsthand the retreat from democracy. Serving as one of the city's justices of the peace, Wall held out hope that the setback was temporary, a slight detour on the long march to freedom that his own life exemplified. Born in 1825 to an enslaved mother and her white owner, he was sent at age twelve to be raised in a Quaker community in Ohio. Wall became a shoemaker in Oberlin, a center of abolitionism, and in 1858, he and other antislavery vigilantes defied the Fugitive Slave Act to rescue a runaway slave threatened with recapture.[47]

During the war, he joined with his brother-in-law, John Mercer Langston, to recruit black volunteer soldiers for the celebrated Massachusetts Fifty-Fourth Regiment and other black units. He himself became among the first black men to reach the rank of captain. At war's end, Wall joined the Freedmen's Bureau and was sent to protect freedpeople in South Carolina. Broad shouldered and thickly built, the light-skinned Wall approached middle age with high hopes for the postwar era.[48]

Wall arrived in D.C. in 1867, just as interracial democracy began to flourish in the city. He took full advantage of the city's opportunities for black political power and economic advancement. When Langston launched Howard University Law School, Wall was among the first students. He bought a luxurious home on the outskirts of the city, near Howard — his $3,500 property was worth more than any other in his integrated neighborhood. He opened a law office while his wife, Amanda, taught in a local black school, and the couple integrated the First Congregational Church.[49]

In the next decade, Wall held a variety of public posts, including city tax assessor, representative in the territorial government legislature, and magistrate of a police precinct. Even after disfranchisement, he stayed active in public life. He founded the Howard Hill Aid Society to help poor people living in his neighborhood, and he served as master of ceremonies for the twentieth anniversary of Emancipation Day in 1882.[50]

The Walls, the Langstons, and other highly visible black families helped solidify Washington's reputation as a haven for black opportunity. Despite disfranchisement, D.C. remained a magnet for black migrants in the 1870s and 1880s. As biracial Reconstruction governments were overthrown across the South and lynching became a gruesome feature of the Southern landscape, a steady stream of black men and women made their way to Washington. The city's black population grew by 74 percent between 1870 and 1890, staying roughly one-third of the total population and reaching more than seventy-five thousand. With the largest black population of any city in the country, Washington was "the capital of the African race," wrote one white reporter for *Harper's*.[51]

Though political life had shriveled, Washington still offered unparalleled educational, economic, and social opportunities for the small slice of black residents who could take advantage of them. Black intellectuals, activists, and educators poured into the city, attracted by Howard University and civic institutions such as the Bethel Literary and Historical Society, a private club founded in 1882 that featured debates among the leading black thinkers of the time. One regular speaker at the society was black educator Mary Ann Shadd Cary, who claimed that D.C. was "the Mecca of the colored pilgrim seeking civil religious social and business enlightenment, and preferment or protection."[52]

Shadd Cary herself was among these pilgrims. Born free in Delaware, the outspoken and often combative Shadd Cary launched an abolitionist newspaper in Canada, becoming the first black woman in North America to be a newspaper editor. She recruited black soldiers for the Union army before moving to Washington in September 1869 to teach school. Her brother, two sisters, and a niece followed her to the city soon thereafter. (She had family connections to Washington—her brother-in-law, Isaac Cary, had won a suit against D.C.'s restrictive black code back in 1836.) Shadd Cary graduated from Howard University Law School in 1883, the second black woman in the nation to earn a law degree, and at age sixty she began practicing law. A prolific journalist who wrote for the *New National Era* and the *People's Advocate*, she also promoted women's suffrage and founded the Colored Women's Progressive Franchise Association. She and other educated, active, and ambitious newcomers helped the city's elite black community thrive in the late nineteenth century.[53]

As Shadd Cary's example attests, the city's black public schools were a na-

TABLE 3 Washington's population, 1870–1900

Year	Total	Black (% of pop.)	White (% of pop.)
1870	131,700	43,404 (33.0)	88,278 (67.0)
1880	177,624	59,596 (33.6)	118,006 (66.4)
1890	230,392	75,572 (32.8)	154,695 (67.1)
1900	278,718	86,702 (31.1)	191,532 (68.7)

Source: U.S. Census Bureau, "Historical Census Statistics on Population Totals by Race"

tional draw for teachers and students alike. By the 1880s, the haphazard postwar collection of semiprivate black schools had solidified into a stable system of black public schools run by an integrated city Board of Trustees, which also oversaw the white school system. By congressional mandate, the board provided relatively equal resources to the two school systems, paid black and white teachers roughly the same amount, and gave black school officials significant autonomy in running the schools.[54]

Under the leadership of Francis Cardozo, a South Carolina transplant who had been the first black person in the country to hold statewide office, Colored Preparatory (known as M Street) High School developed into the nation's top black high school, and perhaps the best school in the city, black or white. Established in 1870, two years before a white high school opened in Washington, M Street was America's first black public high school and offered a college preparatory curriculum. Its teachers boasted degrees from prestigious institutions such as Harvard and Oberlin. Often limited by racial prejudice from pursuing other, more lucrative careers, these highly qualified faculty members devoted themselves to preparing future generations of black leaders. M Street graduates went on to Amherst, Williams, and other top colleges.[55]

Along with educators, federal workers formed the core of Washington's growing black middle class, a feature of black life that made the city unusual, particularly for the South. Other Southern cities, notably New Orleans and Charleston, boasted a well-connected black elite alongside the poor masses, but Washington had a sizable and important middle class composed largely of people holding relatively well paid and secure jobs within or connected to the federal government. During Reconstruction, black people parlayed their newfound political power and access to Republican lawmakers into increased public employment through patronage. After disfranchisement, they relied on their connections to powerful Republicans to maintain their federal positions. Frederick Douglass, for example, served as U.S. marshal and later became the federal Register of Deeds, a lucrative post that was held for two decades by black men.

Despite their lack of voting power, black Washingtonians often found their loyalty to the Republican Party rewarded in the form of government jobs, helping to counterbalance the increasingly restrictive private job market.[56]

The creation of the nonpartisan system of federal civil service in 1883 helped give less well connected black applicants the chance to compete for a burgeoning number of clerkships and other midlevel positions. By 1891, 10 percent of the federal workforce was black. With steady work and decent pay, federal agencies such as the Treasury Department, Government Printing Office, and Freedmen's Hospital gave ambitious black Washingtonians a chance to buy homes and provide stable lives for their families. Federal jobs, appointed or merit based, attracted black migrants to the city and sustained the black middle and upper classes.[57]

Because of federal jobs, opportunities for black teachers and other professionals, and impressive educational opportunities, the city became renowned as the capital of the black elite. The District, an 1887 tour book claimed, had "more intelligent, cultured, well-to-do colored people than any other American city." Washington was home to top black intellectuals such as Alexander Crummell, a New Yorker and one-time colonization advocate who became the prominent pastor of St. Luke's Episcopal Church; wealthy entrepreneurs like James Wormley, whose prestigious hotel hosted the negotiations leading to the Compromise of 1877 that ended Reconstruction; scions of old-line Washington families, such as city tax collector and businessman John F. Cook Jr.; political activists such as W. Calvin Chase, the pugnacious editor of the city's foremost black newspaper, the *Bee*; and high-ranking black officials and former officeholders, including Blanche K. Bruce, a U.S. senator from Mississippi who remained in the District after his Senate term ended in 1881. "The Washington Negroes are probably the wealthiest group [of black people] in the country," wrote black scholar W. E. B. Du Bois.[58]

The dean of the black elite was Frederick Douglass, the former fugitive slave, abolitionist, and indefatigable champion of human rights, whose "high personal character and great abilities," wrote *Harper's Weekly*, "have won universal recognition and esteem." Though he had helped launch the *New Era* in 1870, Douglass did not move to the city permanently until two years later. He eventually settled in Anacostia and bought a majestic, fifteen-acre hilltop estate with sweeping views of the Anacostia River and downtown Washington, not far from the black community of Barry's Farm, where his three sons lived. His sons helped run the *New Era* and threw themselves into community activism.[59]

Being "elite" in black Washington was not simply a function of money. Indeed, some elite families struggled financially as they sought to keep up the appearance of wealth. A variety of factors played into whether an individual or a family could be considered part of what the *Bee* dubbed "The Four Hundred," the wealthiest, most accomplished families in the city (though the number of upper-class families was likely fewer than one hundred). Being employed in a white-collar federal position conferred higher social status, as did how long a family had been in Washington, though many prominent figures within the elite black community were newcomers with high-level positions, including Mississippian Blanche K. Bruce and P. B. S. Pinchback, a Louisiana native who had been the first black governor in the nation.[60]

Skin color also mattered. Because many of the city's most successful black families had tangled racial roots, prominent black leaders including O. S. B. Wall, John Mercer Langston, and Blanche K. Bruce were "mulattos" (having one black parent), "quadroons" (having one black grandparent), or "octoroons" (having one black great-grandparent). Evidence of white ancestry was a source of status and pride, and "mulattos" were twice as likely to work in professional positions. Black newspapers ran ads for face bleach that promised to "turn the skin of a black or brown person five shades lighter, and a mulatto person perfectly white." At the tony Fifteenth Street Presbyterian Church, light-skinned parishioners in the late 1880s objected to the appointment of a dark-skinned pastor (even though the church's founder, John F. Cook Sr., himself was dark skinned). Given the vast differences in education, ambition, and opportunities, social equality within the black community was "absolutely *impossible*," wrote the editors of the black *People's Advocate*.[61]

In the years after disfranchisement in 1874, Washington's black leadership was composed primarily of people who had cut their teeth during the abolitionist movement, the Civil War, and Reconstruction. Having fought for and witnessed the tremendous progress that black Americans had made during their lifetimes, they generally believed in the possibility and ultimate wisdom of assimilating into the larger American society. "Assimilation, not isolation, is our true policy and natural destiny," Douglass told one Emancipation Day crowd. Wherever possible, they sought to gain membership in existing white organizations, rather than create their own. Still committed to integration as an ideal, this cohort sought to win recognition of its own elite status from white "society" and shared the Victorian tastes of their white counterparts, from dress to leisure activities to the lavish homes where they could entertain in the manner of the day.[62]

Crucial to winning full respect and being treated as equal citizens was regaining the right to vote. As the *Bee*'s Calvin Chase wrote in 1884, "We can do what we want when we have suffrage, but not before."[63] When Congress passed the

1878 bill to strip Washington of democratic self-government, it claimed that it was making a "permanent" change to the structure of the city's government. But black Washingtonians refused to accept disfranchisement as a final verdict. Losing the ballot rankled, particularly after it had taken so long for black people to win the right in the first place. Unwilling to give up the gains of Reconstruction, they fought to restore voting rights in the city where they had been able to wield unprecedented political power just a few years before.

A "Sacred Right" or a "Meaningless Bauble"? Washingtonians Debate the Right to Vote

Disfranchisement hurt both black and white voters, but it had a devastating impact on black Washingtonians because it crippled their ability to defend and advance their interests. Suffrage, Frederick Douglass told the *Star*, was "the greatest protection of my race." Without the ballot, black leaders struggled to hold city officials accountable or secure access to public jobs. The commissioners who ran the city—all three of whom were white men, as all commissioners would be until 1961—routinely ignored black concerns. Black laborers complained that they were denied city contracts, which were an important source of jobs in a city without major industries. The commissioners also turned a blind eye to black poverty, which persisted at distressingly high rates. By 1890, nearly 40 percent of the black population was illiterate, 80 percent of patients at Freedmen's Hospital were considered too poor to pay for health care, and the black infant mortality rate was a stunning 338.5 per 1,000 births.[64]

Appointments to city positions vanished. During Reconstruction, black men could expect to land roughly a third of city appointments, but in 1879 only one black officer was among the fifty appointments to the police force, and no black men at all received positions in the fire department. Not surprisingly, perhaps, antiblack police brutality increased, becoming a source of bitterness in the black community and a regular feature in black newspapers. "Negroes are not respected" by police, charged Perry Carson, a leader of working-class black people in Southwest. After a white officer killed a young black man in Hillsdale, Carson called D.C. police "assassins" and led an "indignation movement" to get city officials to prosecute the officer.[65]

As during the abolitionist movement and Reconstruction, black leaders sought white allies to win back the right to vote. After the permanent disfranchisement bill passed in 1878, O. S. B. Wall joined with John F. Cook, white former mayor Sayles Bowen, and white former police commissioner A. C. Richards in organizing an interracial movement to press the case for "unlimited suffrage" before Congress and the American public. Richards was an Ohio abolitionist who came to Washington in the 1850s, and he was one of four city councilmen who had voted to support emancipation in 1862. Within months, the local Republican Central Committee had a full-fledged suffrage operation headed by Charles Purvis, a black doctor at Freedmen's Hospital. "The interests of the District will never be protected until the people have a voice in selecting their rulers," Purvis argued. Throughout the 1880s, the suffrage movement remained an interracial endeavor.[66]

Suffrage supporters appealed primarily to the idea that voting was an essential element of citizenship. The argument was simple: as American citizens, Washingtonians were entitled to the ballot. Like their abolitionist forebears, they freely used the language of the Declaration of Independence and the Constitution to advance their cause, insisting that suffrage was a "sacred right" of all Americans and could not be denied on any basis. "This is a republican form of government, where each and every citizen ought to have equal political rights, no taxation without representation," read an 1883 Emancipation Day proclamation calling for the restoration of suffrage.[67]

Not only was suffrage a basic right of citizenship, supporters argued, but it also was necessary because the commissioners did not represent the people of the District. In the early years of commissioner rule, the appointees were men with few ties to the city or its residents. Many Washingtonians, even some who supported the new government, considered them to be out of touch and insufficiently knowledgeable about the city or its needs. "Men are selected to rule over us who are strangers to our people," complained A. C. Richards. The commissioners, the *Bee* charged, were "an aristocratic coterie"; the *National Republican* dismissed the District government as "arbitrary, oppressive, and to some extent lawless, and has excited wide dissatisfaction bordering on disgust." The only way to improve it, suffrage advocates argued, was to abolish rule by commission and reestablish democratic self-government.[68]

The interracial push for suffrage won strong support from an increasingly vociferous labor movement. Beginning in 1892, the Knights of Labor and the American Federation of Labor, claiming to represent about twenty thousand Washington workers, joined forces to initiate a class-based push for local self-government. With suffrage, labor leaders argued, workingmen of both races would be able to hold city officials accountable and secure beneficial city contracts. An aggressive new labor newspaper, the *Washington Times*, committed itself to a self-described "crusade" for voting rights, arguing that no issue was "of more vital, all-pervading interest to the people of the District of Columbia than this question of suffrage, of self-government." Labor leaders held mass meetings, led petition drives, passed resolutions in support of universal suffrage (for male and female, black and white), and testified before Congress repeatedly in favor of an 1896 bill introduced by Senator Jacob Gallinger of New Hampshire that called for a referendum on suffrage in the District.[69]

Despite a flurry of activity, however, the Gallinger bill failed and the suffrage movement fizzled. Supporters simply could not convince Congress to reconsider its blanket ban on District voting, in large part because they confronted widespread and well-organized opposition from the local white press and the white business community. Once the commissioner government had been established in 1874, it quickly gained the favor of the city's white elites, who "soon ceased even to regret the loss of the right to vote," wrote the Nation. Instead of having government in the hands of black Republicans and their untrustworthy white allies, the city now was safely in the hands of three esteemed white men, all appointed by a Congress that had abandoned its Radical agenda and was growing far more attuned to elite concerns.[70]

Former U.S. postmaster general and longtime Washington resident Horatio King voiced the sentiments of many white property owners when he wrote that "a wise and merciful act of Congress" had "happily" eliminated suffrage. Under democratic government, "the taxable [that is, propertied] citizens had not only 'but a partial voice' in the matter—they were utterly powerless, as they will be again, if unqualified suffrage is restored." For King and other white elites, it was far better to keep power in the hands of the few rather than the many.[71]

Part of the opposition was economic. Many of Washington's most influential white leaders believed that self-government would jeopardize the federal government's 50 percent contribution to the city budget. They feared that Congress would not be willing to foot the bill for a city run by locally elected officials. "The maintenance of streets and avenues, and the proper administration of its government, far beyond any local need, are necessarily so great that they cannot be met" without federal funding, argued the Board of Trade. Budgetary stability and administrative efficiency simply were more important than political rights, and the city's taxpayers willingly gave up suffrage to promote economic development. When weighed against the tangible benefits of federal money, the Star concluded, "The ballot is a meaningless bauble in this District."[72]

But beneath these economic arguments lay a core of racism, manifested by the distorted, racialized memory of biracial democracy that had become the commonsense consensus among many white Washingtonians. As elsewhere in the South, white people came to remember Reconstruction in Washington as a tragic, turbulent era when the excesses of interracial democracy overwhelmed the forces of moderation and responsibility. "The tax-payers were completely swamped" by newly arrived former slaves, wrote the *Star*, and scheming "Murder Bay politicians"—shorthand for Radical Republicans—took advantage of them and "controlled the whole elective machinery." Facing excessive spending, widespread corruption, and racial animosity, "a conservative Northern element felt obliged to interpose in order to save the common property and respectability of all," wrote journalist George Townsend in *Harper's*.[73]

This dubious interpretation of Reconstruction quickly hardened into incontrovertible truth among most white Washingtonians—even though the infamous territorial legislature had only two black members and white appointees on the Board of Public Works had committed the worst abuses. "An experiment had been tried in negro suffrage and it had failed," concluded one influential academic study in 1893. "Men fresh from the plantation, where they had had absolutely no schooling in the duties of citizenship, men without any interest of associations or property in the welfare of the District beyond the fact that they expected to make a living there, had been at one stroke clothed with powers equal … to those of the white race," which was "best qualified" to lead the community.[74]

A blunter encapsulation came from Senator John Morgan of Alabama, a former Confederate general, during an 1890 debate on restoring D.C. suffrage. The black-supported local government had been "abominable and disgraceful," Morgan claimed, and Congress "found it necessary to disfranchise every man in the District of Columbia, no matter what his reputation or character might have been or his holdings in property, in order thereby to get rid of this load of negro suffrage that was flooded in upon them." It was akin, Morgan claimed, "to burn[ing] down the barn to get rid of the rats, … the rats being the negro population and the barn being the government of the District of Columbia, 'the feather-duster legislature.'"[75]

Suffrage would lead once again to "negro domination," wrote the *Star*, and that explains "why tax-payers are almost unanimously opposed to the restoration of suffrage here." Even though "the present form of alien government is about as bad as can be devised," declared the *Post*, "a system which gives the control of the District to ignorant and depraved negroes, is still worse." According to Mary Logan, an astute observer of elite Washington who came to the city with her war hero husband, John, white people in D.C. "decline[d] to subject themselves to the dangers of the vote of so large a colored element in municipal elections. It does not take long for the Northerner who settles here to become used to this way of thinking."[76]

The best way to restore democracy in the District, some suffrage opponents argued, was to encourage black migration out of the city. Washington, an 1878

Post editorial argued, had "surplus negroes"—it was a white-collar town without many farming or industrial jobs, so unskilled black workers who migrated from surrounding plantations had no economic role to play. The city would be "wealthier, healthier and happier for an immediate exodus of 15,000 or 20,000 of her negro population," the *Post* surmised. In the absence of mass emigration, the only solution was "a firm, but benevolent movement on the part of the white race as a whole to disabuse the negro of the delusions which have been instilled into him during the last dozen years," including suffrage. One *Star* reader reiterated the point some seventeen years later: "If you get rid of the 90,000 negroes residing in this city I am in favor of suffrage. As long as they are here I am opposed to it."[77]

In the face of such racially charged opposition, white supporters of suffrage felt compelled to confront the issue of color. The fear that "the colored vote would control ... is the old, stale bug-bear, worn threadbare," lamented Joseph Potter, the secretary of the American Federation of Labor. Former Union general Charles Hovey challenged the notion that black voting caused corruption during Reconstruction, pointing out that "the officers who participated in [the corruption] were appointive ones." Simon Wolf, a well-respected diplomat and Jewish leader, told the *Post*, "The negro is as much entitled to vote—and his vote would be more intelligently cast—as the ignorant Irishman, the ignorant German, or the ignorant white American."[78]

Suffrage advocates rejected the argument that black voters were necessarily "ignorant and depraved," as opponents charged. With the advance of black education, they argued, more and more young black men were becoming fit for citizenship. "If popular government were now restored, a considerable percentage of the colored voters would be found to possess fair educational qualifications" and would vote responsibly, the *Daily Critic* noted in 1883. Black people had changed with the times, said one white suffrage supporter. "When suffrage in the District was abolished, the population was largely made up of colored persons from the south. Then they were ignorant and there was trouble, but now that they have become educated they are good citizens, and suffrage now would not be what suffrage was shortly after the close of the war." The *Bee*'s Calvin Chase agreed. "There is a young educated element in this city" that would exercise its right to vote intelligently.[79]

But suffrage opponents remained unconvinced. The problem was not that a few educated, thoughtful black men such as Frederick Douglass or John Mercer Langston might vote. It was the black masses, and their ability to wield power through their numbers, that they feared. "The difficulty with suffrage here is in the slum element," explained former governor Alexander Shepherd when he visited Washington in 1895. "I do not mean that to insult the negroes, for there are many intelligent colored people in the capital, who are fully competent to have a voice in affairs, but in recent years there has grown up a large population who would dominate affairs if there were suffrage."[80] When white critics envisioned a world of universal suffrage, they imagined contraband supporters looting the city treasury under the direction of the imposing leader of working-class Washington: Perry H. Carson.

"Respectability and Rowdyism": Class and Color Divide D.C.'s Black Community

Perry Carson and his constituents—poor, numerous, loud, and uninterested in deference—embodied what white people feared in black voting. Carson was a Southwest political maestro, a former whitewasher who rose to become a bailiff, saloonkeeper, and government appointee. Born free in Princess Anne County, Maryland, in 1842, Carson had been arrested as a teen for helping abolitionists find safe houses for escaping slaves. He volunteered with the Union army during the war and afterward came to Washington, where he found work as Mayor Sayles Bowen's bodyguard and later Alexander Shepherd's messenger. During Reconstruction he organized an informal black regiment called the "Boys in Blue," which earned respect within the black community by defending residents against attacks from Irish hooligans in Swampoodle. The regiment served as a useful vehicle for political mobilization and gave him the title he carried thereafter: "Colonel."[81]

Though unschooled, Colonel Carson was literate and had a magnetic presence and a powerful speaking style. In the 1870s, he became the most prominent leader of working-class black Washington. Carson "practically controlled the great colored vote of the District for years," the Evening Star claimed. His personal story inspired supporters. "Twenty years ago this man came to Washington poor, despised, with his whitewash brush on his shoulder; today he teaches what can be done for he takes his place in the foremost ranks," one supporter told a crowd of Republicans in 1884. Six foot, six inches tall, nearly 250 pounds, with dark skin and prematurely silver hair, he cut an unforgettable figure as he sat in his bright yellow regalia atop an impressive gray horse at the front of each year's Emancipation Day parade.[82]

Carson drew his support from black workers, who were the vast majority of black Washingtonians. In the 1870s, only 3 percent of black workers were classified as government workers, clerks, or professionals; nearly 75 percent were unskilled laborers or domestic workers.[83] Pushed by economic necessity and the hardening of the color line, low-income black workers lived in increasingly black neighborhoods throughout the city. Some of these black neighborhoods, such as the U Street corridor, Hell's Bottom near today's Logan Circle, and Fort Reno in upper Northwest, grew from contraband camps that had been located nearby. As freedpeople put down roots in the city, they branched out to nearby areas. Other black neighborhoods, including the growing enclave on the Island, east of Four-and-a-Half Street SW, had long been home to free and enslaved black people.

Many working-class black residents lived in alley communities that became a notorious feature of Washington's urban landscape. The city's grid layout created massive blocks with narrow alleys that extended deep into the extensive block interiors. Along the street front stood large homes or row houses generally occupied by middle- and upper-class residents. Within the alleys, one- and two-room shacks were home to the working class. The residents of the two communities often never met and had little to do with one another.

Relatively rare in antebellum Washington, alley communities flourished during and after the Civil War as residents scrambled to find homes in the increasingly populous and crowded neighborhoods of the old city. Real estate developers eager to meet increasing demand for housing maximized the earning potential of large city blocks by lining the alleys with dozens of dwellings. Many homes were built in "blind" alleys that were accessible only by way of another alley, thereby creating communities completely hidden from street view. Early alley communities were segregated by class but not necessarily race—one Union soldier patrolling Tin Cup Alley on the Island in 1863 commented that the alley was "occupied by white and black, all mixed up together." [84]

But as the number and size of alley communities grew, they became increasingly segregated and absorbed much of the large black migration during and after the war. By 1880, there were about 231 named alleys in the city, housing 10,614 people, 87 percent of whom were black; by 1897, a police department special census found 18,978 alley residents, 93 percent of whom were black. Nearly a quarter of the city's black population lived in alleys. [85]

Alley communities generally were poor, crime ridden, and unhealthy. With no indoor plumbing and little ventilation, alley dwellings spawned and spread diseases that ravaged residents already suffering from insufficient diets. Alleys had an exceedingly high mortality rate, particularly among newborns. An 1873 Board of Health report, written under the direction of John Mercer Langston, decried the "miserable dilapidated shanties" that characterized many alleys and insisted that they were "unfit for human habitation." [86]

Alley life was hard, but the alleys also fostered a resilient sense of community. Like a modern suburban cul-de-sac, alleys offered a quiet haven far from the bustling street, a place where everyone knew everyone else and adults could pass time visiting on the stoop as the children played in the street. United by poverty and isolation, hostile to outsiders and "street people," self-described "alley people" relied on one another for childcare, emotional support, emergency assistance, and camaraderie. Cooperation helped them survive the brutal living conditions and sustain their communities. Indeed, though few residents owned their homes, alley communities endured, often through generations.[87]

Alley residents and other working-class black Washingtonians played an active role in local politics. During the Reconstruction era, they voted, planned rallies, attended conventions, and made their voices heard in the public sphere. After disfranchisement, they remained involved in Republican Party politics (stories periodically surfaced of black Democrats, a rare breed within a party that was committed to white supremacy), and they threw their support behind Perry Carson.

Carson exerted his influence through the Republican National Convention (RNC), at which state delegations gathered to nominate a presidential candidate, hammer out the party platform, and set the national party's agenda. Although D.C. was not a state and had no electoral votes, the national party allowed local Republicans to select delegates to participate in the conventions. The local party took this selection process very seriously because it represented the only chance for city residents, black or white, to register their political desires within a national party. Working-class black men turned out in force for the meetings, giving Carson their overwhelming support.

Carson served as Washington's black delegate to the RNC for every election between 1880 and 1900. Often raucous affairs full of theatrical oratory, intense lobbying, and the occasional physical flare-up, these meetings repulsed the *Post* and other suffrage opponents, who described them in graphic, racially tinged terms. "It is scarcely possible to form an adequate conception of the brutality and diabolism, the beastly ruffianism, the unrelieved and loathsome animalism of the gangs that yelled, shrieked and fought in the primaries," the *Post* told readers in 1888. This wild behavior, "with all its Senegambian features and worse than Senegambian methods," underscored the importance of keeping control of the District government safely in the hands of the unelected white commissioners. "Property-holders and order-loving citizens may well be pardoned for their dread of being governed by such mobs." Never again should black voters control the city, the *Post* vowed. "There is a law that is higher than any human enactment—a law of nature—that forbids negro rule in white communities."[88]

Carson and his supporters not only attracted criticism from white suffrage opponents. They also antagonized many elite black leaders, who rejected the *Post*'s racism but nonetheless viewed Carson as an embarrassment. To men such as Calvin Chase, Carson and his rough-hewn constituents were an obstacle to the restoration of suffrage because they reinforced the negative stereotypes that white people held about black politics.

Chase was the sharp-witted, passionately political editor of the city's most prominent black newspaper, the *Bee*. Born free into an aristocratic, light-skinned black family in Washington in 1854, Chase wrote provocative editorials attacking white racial prejudice and challenging black people to stand up for their rights. The paper's masthead promised "Honey for Our Friends, Stings for Our Enemies." After disfranchisement, when many black elites abandoned politics, he dove headlong into the political fracas, hoping to lead a movement of educated black people—the community's "best men"—who could assert themselves as the city's proper leaders. Few could match Perry Carson's physical presence, but Chase came close. Standing six foot three with broad shoulders and a booming voice, he did not cower during convention showdowns with Carson and his followers. For nearly three decades, the two men personified the political split in the black community.[89]

Chase believed that Congress would never reconsider suffrage unless and until black voters proved themselves worthy of the ballot. The best way to do so was by electing honorable men to serve as leaders. "As long as rowdyism reigns in this District," he wrote, "so long are we to be denied of self-government." Winning back the ballot would be a "dangerous thing and a disgrace to the intelligence of this community, so long as the mob reigns." The key to earning suffrage, he believed, was to defeat the Carson machine, and he used the *Bee* to attack Carson personally and politically. "If the city of Washington was searched, there could not have been a more ignorant man found to represent this community than P. H. Carson," he wrote.[90]

Despite his near-monopoly on the black press and his widespread support in elite circles, Chase struggled to match Carson's popular appeal. Every four years, Chase mounted a challenge to Carson's control of delegate selection to the RNC; every four years, Carson emerged the clear winner. Frustrated by his inability to win over the masses of black voters, Chase attributed his opponent's success to whiskey and other bribes. After a defeat in 1884, he fumed (in a line that echoed the rhetoric of white suffrage opponents), "Negroes who would sell themselves out are incapable of self government." The solution, he came to believe, was to place qualifications on who could vote. "If we are to have suffrage, let it be restricted. Let us convince all that we, as young men represent the sentiment of respectability and that this cause of ours is a just one."[91]

In his embrace of qualified, rather than universal, suffrage, Chase typified the view among elites, black and white, in Washington and across the country, who lived very different lives than the masses of laborers. Reconstruction had helped unite the black community behind the Radical push for biracial, cross-class democracy, but in the wake of disfranchisement, the expanding reach of Jim Crow forced black Washingtonians out of politics and the public sphere. Mirroring the divisions emerging nationwide, black life in D.C. became more stratified as the color-conscious elite pursued educational and economic opportunities that largely were unavailable to their poorer, less-educated, darker-skinned neighbors. As business owners, teachers, federal clerks, and other professionals, they lived in nicer homes, enjoyed different leisure activities, and aspired to "respectability." These differences in lifestyle and outlook manifested themselves politically.

Many elites considered themselves (and were officially classified as) "mulatto" rather than "black," and they chafed when white observers lumped them together with the rest of the black population. Alice Parke Shadd, whose husband was a doctor at Freedmen's Hospital, voiced this elite frustration in an 1890 *Post* feature on black "aristocrats." Described as "a white woman" with "no appearance of the African blood in her," Shadd complained of the "humiliation" she felt because "the white race refuses to consider this mixture of blood, or our education and abilities. It persists in classing such men as my husband with the lowest of the race."[92]

Black workers, in turn, resented elite condescension. John E. Bruce, a satirist whose parents had been enslaved and whose mother was a domestic in Washington, mocked wealthy black people who "wouldn't be caught dead with an ordinary Negro." Elite black society, he wrote, was "all tinsel, shadow and show." Writer Charles W. Chestnutt, who later gained fame for his novels exploring the complexity of racial identity, wrote that "the colored people of Wash. are very extravagant and spend all their earnings, great and small, in a vain attempt to keep up 'style' and a high-toned society."[93]

Often accused by Calvin Chase of pandering to "the lowest of the race," Carson adroitly tapped the deep currents of class conflict, at times questioning the commitment of black elites to the community. "There are plenty of mulatto men in this District who, like myself, have never tried to get rid of their race; who have never tried to play white, and who have always been found working to build up that downtrodden race which Sumner, Lincoln and Grant brought out from servitude," he told one applauding audience. "But there are some in this town who want to be white men, who have advertised for white ladies [to] act as servants in their homes." One leader he singled out in particular was John

Mercer Langston, whom he labeled "a white man's man" who had never been "in his taste, habits, or association, a negro at all."[94]

The percolating anger between well-to-do black people and the black working class—and between Chase and Carson—erupted publicly over Emancipation Day celebrations. During the Reconstruction era, Emancipation Day was the most important day on the calendar of black Washingtonians. The annual parade brought all classes of the black community together and galvanized them for political action. By the 1880s, however, Emancipation Day began to lose its unifying appeal, becoming instead a stage for internecine black conflict, a public airing of class tensions within the black community.[95]

Chase and other elites grew increasingly distressed by the celebrations that Carson led and, more broadly, the behavior of the working-class black people he represented. Emancipation Day had become increasingly dominated by "ruffians" whose outlandish outfits and rowdy behavior mortified "the most thrifty and self-respecting among us," Chase charged. "We are not to be governed by the rabble and mob that has been a disgrace to this community. What the people desire is a respectable gathering."[96]

Like Chase, Frederick Douglass feared that the disorganized event gave ammunition to white critics intent on belittling the black community. Emancipation Day should "help us shorten the distance between ourselves and the more highly advanced and highly favored people among who we are," Douglass argued. Instead, it had become a wild mélange of "tinsel show, gaudy display, and straggling processions, which empty the alleys and dark places of our city into the broad daylight of our thronged streets and avenues, thus thrusting upon public view a vastly undue proportion of the most unfortunate, unimproved, and unprogressive class of the colored people, and thereby inviting public disgust and contempt."[97]

For many years after disfranchisement, Chase sought to wrest control of the event from Carson, who served as grand marshal. He used his editorial platform to promote a different kind of Emancipation Day, one that would project an image of refinement, decorum, and education—the image that he and other elites hoped would help win respect among white people and lead to the resurrection of rights lost after Reconstruction. By 1886, a frustrated Chase proposed a competing celebration, a subdued parade that would culminate at Israel Bethel Church, where a series of dignified speakers would be united in their message of uplift and responsibility. Urging all "respectable people" to attend his event, Chase argued that the black community had to choose between "respectability and rowdyism."

But the colonel's grip on Emancipation Day only strengthened. His supporters had no interest in moving off the streets to sit quietly in church pews, and both groups went ahead with their plans that year. In subsequent years, the dispiriting factionalism only worsened. "Are the colored people of Washington, D.C.—as a mass—retrograding?" wondered one reporter for the black *Cleveland Gazette* in 1888. Chase dismissed the 1888 parade as "void of dignity, uniformity and respectability, . . . a disgrace," and called on black people to raise money for charities rather than spend it on showy parades.[98]

The event lingered on for another decade, though fewer and fewer of the black elite or middle class participated. Marred by outbreaks of violence in the late 1890s, the annual parade lost its official imprimatur as local school officials no longer gave black public school students the day off to attend. The last large-scale parade was held in 1901. By then, even Carson called on the black community to stop the parades in favor of indoor celebrations at schools and churches. Small neighborhood celebrations continued into the 1950s, but it would be another century before Emancipation Day returned as an official holiday in the District.[99]

By the time the last Emancipation Day band stopped its march, it was clear that Washington was a very different place for black people from what they had hoped it would be a generation earlier. During the Civil War and Reconstruction, Washington was a "Yankee City" on the leading edge of racial change in America. Thousands of former slaves migrated to D.C., joining white Radicals and educated black leaders to drive an ambitious experiment in biracial democracy. They made remarkable progress in a short period of time. Black men won the right to vote, black leaders won elected office citywide, black workers gained access to public and private sector jobs, black schools became national models, and city officials passed sweeping antidiscrimination laws.

Yet that very success triggered a backlash from white conservatives and business leaders who persuaded Congress to retreat from the promise of biracial democracy, first by limiting electoral power in a territorial government in 1871 and then by eliminating self-government altogether in 1874. In the decades that followed, Washington rolled back Reconstruction-era racial progress, part of a regionwide effort to enforce white supremacy. When city commissioners compiled the District Code in 1901, they quietly dropped the local antidiscrimination laws from the books (though they did not repeal them). The city continued to boast a diverse and growing black middle class, but black political power and aspirations withered. The door to biracial, cross-class democracy seemed to have been slammed shut.

SEVEN

National Show Town

Building a Modern, Prosperous, and Segregated Capital, 1890–1912

A city without factories, without tenement houses, without many foreign-born citizens; a city without a mayor or aldermen, and in which no one votes; a government city without a city government; ... a city in which the servants, coachmen, driver, and many of the business men, even policemen, are Afro-Americans; ... —a city unique in all these respects, and many others, is Washington. — MARY LOGAN, 1901

LeDroit Park in the early twenty-first century can feel a bit like a different city from a different era. Going north from downtown Washington across Florida Avenue (what used to be called Boundary Street), the streets suddenly break free from the rigidity of L'Enfant's city grid, thrusting at odd angles as if to defy the haughty French-born engineer and his antiquated plan. Gothic-inspired cottages and elegant Italianate villas with expansive porches sit majestically back from narrow roads. Many of the original nineteenth-century homes survive and were rehabilitated in the early twenty-first century as well-heeled investors and residents rediscovered the area. Though the city has imposed its numeric system on LeDroit Park, residents today resolutely retain the tree-inspired names that marked the roads when the neighborhood was first developed in the late nineteenth century.

Now enveloped by the city, LeDroit Park was Washington's first post–Civil War residential suburb, a bucolic area that attracted wealthy city residents looking for a touch of rural tranquillity. It was the vision of Amzi Barber, a white Ohioan who came to the city shortly after the Civil War to run Howard University's Education Department and later became the school's acting president. A minister's son, Barber had studied for the ministry at Oberlin but found more earthly rewards in Washington real estate. In 1873, he and his brother-in-law persuaded the university to sell them fifty-five acres less than half a mile south of campus, and they began developing LeDroit Park, which they named in honor of their father-in-law. Barber's success with LeDroit Park, combined with acrimony over his abortive, scandal-ridden tenure as Howard's president, led him to abandon education and devote himself to business.[1]

From its inception, LeDroit Park was exclusive. Early advertisements promised "no poor buildings" and "protection from all nuisances and undesirable features." It offered a full range of city amenities in a country setting, all within a couple miles of the Capitol. Famed architect James McGill designed dozens of homes. By 1880, there were sixty-four unique country mansions that sold for up to $12,000 at a time when government clerks might earn $1,000 a year. Like a modern gated community, the neighborhood had its own private trash service and hired watchmen to "keep out intruders and undesirables," one early observer wrote. "It was as exclusive a settlement as one might want or imagine, and its residents were of the very highest type." For the first two decades of its existence, LeDroit Park was entirely white.[2]

But Barber worried that his vision of an exclusive enclave was being shadowed by the looming presence on the hill to its north: Howard University. By the 1880s, Howard boasted some of the nation's top black scholars and was gaining a reputation as the nation's top black university. The area surrounding the university, known as Howardtown, attracted growing numbers of black residents of all classes. The presence of an expanding black community on LeDroit Park's northern border jeopardized the very exclusivity that Barber wanted to promote, so he sought to cordon off the development with a fence. On the southern end, facing downtown, he built an elaborate iron and wood structure with an ornate gate; on the northern end, facing Howardtown, there was just "a high board fence, unpainted and unsightly," the Post reported."[3]

As both LeDroit Park and Howardtown grew in the 1880s, the fence became a lightning rod for controversy. Howardtown residents complained that the fence blocked the most direct route between the university and downtown, forcing people to take a circuitous detour around LeDroit Park anytime they wanted to shop or go to work. Some LeDroit Park property owners also complained that the fence depressed property values by limiting access to their neighborhood and preventing residents from enjoying city services such as fire protection.

By 1886, many Howardtown residents had begun sneaking through the fence, which prompted LeDroit Park leaders to enforce a neighborhood ban on outsiders. Tensions escalated in August 1888 when a group of disgruntled LeDroit Park property owners, aided by black workers, tore down the fence. Incensed fence supporters quickly rebuilt it, added barbed wire, and hired a black police officer to guard it. The ragged barrier was torn down and rebuilt several times in the next three years as a "fence war" raged, to the delight of reporters who covered the controversy with undisguised amusement.[4]

Most observers understood that race and class were the underlying causes of the tension. Howardtown, the *Post* wrote, was a "more or less odorous locality" featuring "a picturesque collection of tumble-down shanties inhabited by colored people." Without the fence, one LeDroit Park resident explained, "the most objectionable element in our population will crowd through here at all hours of the day and night and the object that made us build our homes here will be entirely defeated." At one point, fence supporters asked city commissioners to buy Howardtown, level it, and turn it into a park. Doing so, they claimed, "would remove all grounds for [our] objections to the removal of the fence." One incredulous commissioner wondered if they "desired to drive the colored people off the earth." [5]

After a series of lawsuits brought by white homeowners, the fence came down for good in 1891. Black pedestrians walked freely through LeDroit Park's streets, and black buyers began seeking homes in the area. In 1893, a Capitol Hill barber named Octavius Williams became the neighborhood's first black home-owner—his daughter lived in the neighborhood into the 1970s. The Williams family endured shots fired into their home and other indignities, but black residents continued to trickle in and white owners began to trickle out. The complexion of the neighborhood slowly changed. By the early 1900s, LeDroit Park featured a substantial "colored colony" of black homeowners; by World War I, it was almost exclusively black and would remain so for the rest of the twentieth century. It became home to the city's best-known black leaders, including activist Mary Church Terrell and her husband, Robert, educator Anna Julia Cooper, and poet Paul Laurence Dunbar. LeDroit Park addresses became a coveted sign of success, a marker that one had made it into the black elite. [6]

The development of LeDroit Park as a rural retreat for wealthy white residents and its transformation into the prime neighborhood for the black upper class exemplified the massive demographic and spatial changes that reordered the racial geography of the city in the decades between disfranchisement in 1878 and the election of Woodrow Wilson to the presidency in 1912. Through Reconstruction, Washington featured racially and economically diverse neighborhoods in every quadrant of the city, and downtown Washington remained a vibrant residential and commercial area. By the second decade of the twentieth century, however, the city looked vastly different.

As the federal government expanded and real estate boomed, the city burst its bounds and extended far beyond the central core. Driven by real estate developers, urban planners, and congressional leaders who could act without local democratic accountability, the city became a "national show town" featuring a monumental core of federal buildings and monuments. Its residents spread out into surrounding neighborhoods that were increasingly segregated by race and class, as exclusive suburban enclaves put physical and psychological distance between wealthy white Washingtonians and the masses of poor residents, black and white. Without the pull of integrated politics to promote interracial interaction, life in Washington became more segregated than ever before.

"The Rim of Washington Is Knocked Off": D.C. Grows Racially and Economically Segregated

From his experience to his profession to the handlebar mustache that graced his face, Myron M. Parker epitomized the white businessman of Gilded Age Washington. A Vermont veteran who served under Union general George Armstrong Custer during the Civil War, Parker came to Washington in 1865 to become a clerk in the War Department. He studied law at night and earned a degree from Columbian College (precursor to today's George Washington University), but like LeDroit Park founder Amzi Barber he was lured by the city's biggest private industry: real estate. He launched his own real estate company and grew fabulously wealthy as the city expanded. By the 1880s, he had established himself as a major player within D.C.'s business community.

Like most Vermonters at the time, Parker was a lifelong Republican but not a Radical. As a young man busy with education and work, he did not get involved in the political struggles of Reconstruction, but he soon discovered that being a wealthy businessman opened many political doors, particularly after disfranchisement in 1874. In an age when businessmen were heavily involved in public affairs, he stood out as an ambitious civic leader who earned lavish praise from the press. Parker, the Post gushed, was a "public-spirited, go-ahead citizen" who is "thoroughly imbued with modern ideas of progress and improvement."[7]

Parker was well positioned to take advantage of the tremendous changes that were sweeping Washington in the last decades of the nineteenth century. Despite the political and financial scandals of the Shepherd era, the city boomed, with the population more than doubling from 131,700 in 1870 to nearly 280,000 by 1900 (making D.C. the third largest city in the South, after Baltimore and New Orleans). The expanding power and prestige of the federal government, as always the engine of the Washington economy, drove that growth. Having assumed unprecedented authority during the Civil War, the federal government continued to play an ever-larger role in American life, and its bureaucracy grew apace. The number of federal employees in Washington rose from a mere 2,200 at the start of the war to more than 28,000 by the turn of the century.[8]

Although the majority of migrants to Washington in the immediate postwar period were black, after 1870 more white people arrived in the city. Many of the newcomers resembled Myron Parker—young, relatively well educated Northerners in search of white-collar economic opportunity. Because Washington "is a government city and nothing else," as Massachusetts senator Henry Cabot Lodge noted, it lacked a strong industrial base to attract the masses of immigrant laborers who packed the factories of other Eastern seaboard cities.[9]

The city also attracted a new breed of spectacularly wealthy Western mining magnates and other nouveaux riches who were interested in Washington not only because it was the center of national power but because it was easier to break into high society in D.C. than elsewhere. These new Washingtonians changed the composition and character of the city as old-line Southern families faded in importance and new families emerged on the scene. The city was so awash in new people and new money that Mark Twain used Washington as the setting for his satiric 1873 novel *The Gilded Age*, which eventually became a shorthand moniker for the excesses of the time.[10]

The city itself expanded, due in large part to a transportation revolution. Before the Civil War, Washington was a "walking city"—residents generally could walk to their jobs, the markets, entertainment venues, and other places. Nearly all city residents, white and black, rich and poor, lived within the confines of downtown Washington or Georgetown. The hilly areas beyond Boundary Street remained sparsely inhabited and rural. Horse-drawn streetcars first appeared during the war, an early form of public transport that gave Washingtonians a slightly larger range of distance they could travel. Technological innovations by the 1880s led to electric streetcars, which allowed people with means to live atop the escarpment north of Boundary Street. The improved transportation, combined with the growing population and accompanying housing shortage, helped drive the development of land far from the city center. "The rim of Washington is knocked off," noted the newly formed Board of Trade in 1890. Washington was now reaching far beyond the original city laid out by Peter L'Enfant.[11]

As the city grew larger, more prosperous, and more modern, it also grew more segregated. Antebellum D.C. neighborhoods were racially and economically diverse because there simply was not enough room for people to isolate themselves to any significant degree by class or race. In 1860, the city's wealthiest man, banker W. W. Corcoran, lived on the same H Street block as a low-income black widow, Letha Turner, and successful black hotelier James Wormley.[12] But the new neighborhoods that emerged in the late nineteenth century were far more likely to be racially and economically homogenous, creating a segregated geography for the city that would last throughout the twentieth century.

Among the first areas to become segregated was the West End, just east of

Georgetown. The transformation of the West End was due in large part to a particularly conspicuous and influential newcomer named William Stewart, who arrived in Washington in 1865 as the first senator from the new state of Nevada. A New Yorker with a Yale pedigree, Stewart went west and made a fortune in mining. His wealth paved his way into the U.S. Senate, and he came to Washington, cowboy hat perched atop his head, ready to make even more money. He immediately turned his entrepreneurial vision and risk-taking temperament to the city's real estate market. Betting that the city would develop toward the northwest, he joined with two of his mining buddies to spend $600,000 at ten cents per square foot (more than $10 million in twenty-first century dollars) on land out in the city's West End, then a fringe area inhabited largely by low-income workers. He staked a claim to Pacific (now Dupont) Circle, building a massive five-story, red-brick mansion in an area dotted with worker shanties and little else.[13]

Initially dubbed "Stewart's Folly" by skeptics, the house helped pioneer the transformation of the area. Under Alexander Shepherd—a friend of Stewart's—city improvements such as street grading, water mains, and sidewalks flowed primarily to the northwest along the arteries of Connecticut, New Hampshire, and Massachusetts Avenues, which converged at Pacific Circle. By the time the mansion opened in 1873, land was selling for $5 a square foot and Stewart looked like a real estate genius. During the next three decades, the city's wealthiest residents and foreign delegations built ever-larger, more elaborate homes and embassies that dwarfed "Stewart's Castle" and sent land values soaring.[14]

For a time, the area remained racially and economically mixed. Black residents of the area, noted a *Harper's* reporter in 1875, were particularly resolute in remaining on the land. "The tenacity with which they cling to property is one of the most remarkable manifestations in human development, and although graded, underpinned, taxed, and tempted, they hold to their lots and shanties in the fashionable West End of the city with a prescience and resolution." Mary Logan noted, "On many streets the mansion and the shanty yet stand side by side."[15]

Some black families managed to sell their land at a handsome profit, but as the assessed value of their land grew, so did property taxes. It became increasingly difficult for low- and middle-income people to afford to live in the West End unless they were live-in servants. Poor people remained in neighborhood alleys, including "Chinch Row" between Eighteenth, Nineteenth Streets, L, and M Streets. Chinch Row featured outdoor box toilets without water, sewer connections, or sometimes even doors. But on the streets of the West End, what was once an integrated, lower-income neighborhood hosting small farms, slaughterhouses, and other small businesses changed into an exclusive, upper-class white neighborhood. By the turn of the twentieth century, the West End had become a fashionable district inhabited primarily by the wealthy.[16]

Senator Stewart's friend and fellow Nevada mining millionaire Francis Newlands had even grander ambitions. Not content simply to make money, he wanted to build an ideal community: Chevy Chase, named for a Scottish hunting ground. Using a series of straw agents and front companies to conceal his plans, Newlands spent millions of dollars in the 1880s buying seventeen hundred acres of land in the far reaches of Northwest Washington, on both sides of the city's border with Montgomery County, Maryland. He financed a streetcar line that stretched from downtown eight miles out to Chevy Chase Lake, and he devoted more than three decades to developing a model community that featured large country homes and luxurious amenities.[17]

Early boosters did not specifically reject black residents, but Senator Newlands was well known for his antipathy to black people—he once proposed a "white plank" to the Democratic Party platform that would disenfranchise black voters and bar Asian immigrants because "this should be a white man's country." All prospective homebuyers were carefully screened. As one brochure promised: "The only restrictions imposed are those which experience has proven necessary in any residential section to maintain or increase values and protect values and protect property builders against the encroachment of undesirable elements." In the context of turn-of-the-century Washington, it was clear what lessons "experience" had taught and who might be considered "undesirable."[18]

The Chevy Chase Land Company actively protected its segregated exclusivity. In 1909, the company sued a developer who had sold homes to black families in a subdivision called Belmont near the intersection of Western and Wisconsin Avenues. It reacquired the land and chose to let it remain undeveloped for decades rather than allow black residents to live there. Even in the twenty-first century, relatively few black or poor people live in Chevy Chase. The area that would have become Belmont now houses Saks Fifth Avenue and other luxury stores.[19]

Where real estate developers and wealthy politicians were not involved, diverse communities grew organically. One such community was Tennallytown (now spelled "Tenleytown"), a hilly area in upper Northwest just a bit west of Senator Newlands's Chevy Chase. Still relatively rural in the late nineteenth century, Tennallytown was a sprawling neighborhood with about a thousand residents, roughly one-third of whom were black. Some free black families had owned land in the area before emancipation, including the prominent Wormleys—patriarch James T. Wormley had owned perhaps the finest hotel in the city in the 1870s and 1880s, and his extended family owned hundreds of acres in Tennallytown. Most black residents, however, arrived as refugees during and after the war. They squatted in the area around Fort Reno, the highest point in the city, and bought land there when the army sold off its property following the war. They lived on large lots and tended spacious gardens alongside white neighbors. Though black and white residents attended separate churches and schools, they lived in close proximity and built an interdependent, integrated community that thrived for decades.[20]

But Tennallytown was exceptional. LeDroit Park, the West End, and Chevy Chase were more emblematic of an era that witnessed the rise of racially and economically segregated communities throughout the city, sometimes displacing older communities that had been mixed. In the decades after disfranchisement, developers cashed in on the real estate frenzy by building suburban residential areas for white homebuyers along what would later become the Red Line of the Metro. Some developments, such as Kalorama and Washington Heights, were intended for the upper class; others, such as Brookland and Petworth, aimed for the middle class. None were created for the poor or black. As a rule, suburban subdivisions were racially and economically segregated.[21]

"Representative Aristocracy": White Washingtonians Embrace and Control Government by Commission

This new pattern of residential segregation found support not only among city leaders who controlled the new commissioner form of government but also among white residents who organized themselves into citizens associations to protect their neighborhoods. Made up of white male property holders, citizens associations proliferated in the 1880s and 1890s. They had a mission to maintain property values, keep taxes low, and lobby for city services in their neighborhoods. The earliest one, the East Washington Citizens Association based in Capitol Hill, had its roots in Reconstruction and had charged the Shepherd regime with unfairly channeling city projects to favored wealthy constituents in Northwest. After disfranchisement in 1874, citizens associations mushroomed across the city as people struggled to make their voteless voices heard.[22]

By the turn of the century, there were twenty white neighborhood groups that regularly petitioned the commissioners to voice their concerns. "The great success of this peculiar city government," observed a scholar in 1897, "is due in no small degree to the jealous watchfulness of these citizens associations." The associations, wrote another, "furnish a substitute for representative self-government" and helped insure that the city government, though "autocratic in nature," was nonetheless "democratic in operation." The "democracy" claimed by the citizens associations excluded black citizens, who comprised nearly one-third of the population. Black Washingtonians responded by organizing their own neighborhood groups, which they differentiated as *civic* associations (into the twenty-first century, neighborhood citizens associations remained primarily white, while civic associations were primarily black). When white groups formed an umbrella Federation of Citizens Associations (FCA) in 1910, leaders explicitly rejected including the black civic associations.[23]

The citizens associations helped to justify and enforce residential segregation with their emphasis on defending "property values," a protean idea that encompassed everything from beautifying the neighborhood to securing city services to policing potential residents. For many white homeowners, the presence of even a single black family in a neighborhood meant a decline in property values. Black families, they feared, would inevitably bring crime, poverty, and ugliness to their streets. White property owners used the citizens associations to "improve" their neighborhoods by keeping black and poor people out of them. As the Columbia Heights Citizens Association boasted in a brochure, "Nowhere within the District of Columbia can be found a community freer from the objectionable classes than on the 'Heights.'" By focusing on maintaining "property values," citizens associations helped drive the shift to a segregated city.[24]

Citizens associations generally shared the same goals of improving their neighborhoods, but they often bickered with one another and regularly accused the commissioners of favoring one of their rivals. Some of the most active associations were in East and South Washington, where residents complained that the commissioners ignored their needs and allowed railroad tracks, industrial sites, and poor infrastructure to disrupt their communities. With so many aggressive neighborhood groups competing for the commissioners' attention and funding, some local leaders feared that too much parochial "sectionalism" hurt the city and made Washingtonians seem like small-minded people narrowly interested only in their own neighborhoods. In December 1886, these leaders coalesced to form the Committee of One Hundred dedicated to "the improvement of our local government through a ... reliable expression of local opinion."[25]

The Committee of One Hundred did not survive long. Though its founders pledged to avoid politics, the committee could not avoid the fractious issues of suffrage, governance, and race. Many members from East and South Washington, led by Michael Weller of the East Washington Citizens Association, objected to the three-man commission that ruled the city and argued that the committee should push for the restoration of full suffrage and representation. An Englishman whose grandfather was among the Redcoat troops who burned the city in 1814, Weller immigrated to America shortly after the Civil War, married a Capitol Hill woman, and went into real estate, becoming a passionate advocate for eastern Washington. Though a Democrat, he became perhaps the city's most aggressive white advocate for suffrage, defending the ballot and home rule as a simple matter of principle: "The present form of government is undemocratic."[26]

Weller's insistence on self-government ultimately split the Committee of One Hundred. Conservative members worried that any change in the structure of government could jeopardize the federal government's 50 percent contribution to the city's budget, and they feared that tinkering with the commissioners could lead once again to black voting. They abandoned the organization in the fall of 1889 to form the Washington Board of Trade, a new group that accepted disfranchisement as an unchangeable reality and focused instead on economic growth and preserving the federal government's financial support of the city.[27] The Board of Trade soon became the most important political organization in the city, often more powerful than the commissioners themselves. More than any other local organization, it helped create and perpetuate a modern segregated Washington.[28]

The Board of Trade portrayed itself as an unbiased, nonpartisan group of respected, civic-minded leaders who put the city's interests above their own personal or neighborhood interests. Because of the city's peculiar relationship with Congress and its lack of self-government, board founders considered it essential to have an organization that could represent the city's interests "in a public, impartial, unsectional way." In a city dependent on government more than the private sector, the board focused less on "trade" than on economic development and city beautification. From its inception it sought to win congressional approval and funding to "carry out the great plan conceived and inaugurated by the projectors and founders of our city."[29]

Composed primarily of men born in the Northeast and Ohio, rather than the District or the South, the board attracted lawyers, realtors, and merchants from across the city, though most lived in increasingly prosperous Northwest. Among the board's twenty-seven charter members were Beriah Wilkins and Crosby Noyes, the editors of the Post and Star; grocer John H. Magruder and retailer Samuel W. Woodward of Woodward & Lothrop, whose businesses would become long-standing Washington institutions; and James T. Wormley, the black owner of the Wormley House hotel. (Throughout the 1890s, the all-male board was lightly integrated—of the more than four hundred members, four were black.) For president, board members chose realtor Myron Parker.[30]

The board flourished under Parker's leadership, quickly becoming the most influential voice in city affairs. Stepping into the void that disfranchisement left, it offered elite Washingtonians an outlet to express their political desires and gave them an organized presence within the commission form of government. The board worked to position itself as the most knowledgeable source of local information, the experts on whom the commissioners and congressional policy makers could rely. It set up more than twenty committees to study everything from public buildings and transportation to water supply and public health. Revealingly, there were no committees on poverty or suffrage.

Board members regularly wrote reports, testified at hearings, and lobbied the commissioners and members of Congress, and they worked to cultivate personal relationships with the city's masters. "The board knows the strength of social influence," wrote one observer. Its annual dinner attracted dozens of congressmen, and it regularly took policy makers out for dinner cruises along the waterfront. The Board of Trade was "practically a state legislature, city council and chamber of commerce combined into one," Parker claimed in the board's second annual report.[31]

In 1892, just three years after the board's founding, its influence became much more direct when Parker stepped off the board and became a commissioner. Parker helped solidify the relationship between the commission and the board, and his tenure began a long period in which Board of Trade membership became almost a prerequisite for local leaders to be considered for a commissioner's post. Board members and commissioners collaborated closely to advance their shared interests. By the turn of the century, "there was comparatively little of the old wrangling before Congress of contending delegations of citizens," boasted board president Theodore Noyes. "What has been accomplished through the cooperation of the District Commissioners, the Board of Trade, and the Congressional committees dealing with District affairs has been an object lesson in the value of harmony."[32]

Board members had little interest or incentive to return to self-government. Indeed, they vigorously opposed efforts to restore the ballot because suffrage would disrupt the board's cozy relationship with the commissioners. Government by commission, Parker wrote in 1891, was "economical and better" because it was "free from political entanglements." When the issue of suffrage arose in Congress in 1896, commissioners referred the matter to the board, which squelched it.[33]

An appointed government running the capital of a democracy seemed paradoxical, and political scientist C. Meriwether pithily captured its contradictions. "By law, the system is a benevolent despotism; in practice, it is a representative aristocracy," he wrote in 1897. But elite white Washingtonians touted the virtues of what the *Star* labeled "the best-governed municipality not only in this country but even in the world." The absence of popular voting, the *Star* argued, gave commissioners the freedom to offer "honest government because they have no obligations which conflict with their sense of public duty." Disfranchisement, in effect, had created good government. "Although many good citizens have regretted that in the National Capital taxation without representation is the principle of government," argued city commissioner Henry B. F. MacFarland in 1900, "it is generally admitted that for the District of Columbia the present form of government is the best possible." Washington's government excelled, MacFarland insisted, because it was "a government by the best citizens."[34]

Government by the "best citizens"—appointed commissioners who worked in close cooperation with the businessmen of the Board of Trade—may have been effective and "harmonious," but it was fundamentally undemocratic. It was essentially a government of, by, and for the elite. Scholar Delos Wilcox warned that the long-term impact of this kind of government corroded democracy, and he insisted that the city ultimately should govern itself. "Otherwise even the most beautiful city and the most perfect administration would only go to demonstrate the failure of democracy as a means of working out our great national problem of municipal government." Wilcox and other dissenters, however, were lonely voices as a chorus of city and national leaders at the turn of the century called for Washington to be remade into a sparkling, segregated "city beautiful."[35]

"White City and Capital City": The McMillan Plan and the Rise of the Monumental Capital

When Charles Moore arrived in Washington in 1889, few could have predicted the extraordinary role he would play in reshaping the physical layout of downtown Washington. Born in New Hampshire shortly before the Civil War, Moore graduated from Harvard and settled in Michigan to become a journalist. He befriended a Detroit businessman and Republican Party leader named James McMillan, who was making a fortune manufacturing railroad cars and promoting utilities. McMillan used his millions to win a seat in the U.S. Senate in 1888, and he asked Moore to join him in Washington as his aide.

At thirty-four years of age, the earnest, bespectacled, and well-connected

Moore arrived in town with little knowledge of or interest in local affairs. When Senator McMillan became chair of the Senate Committee on the District of Columbia in 1891, Moore assumed the role of committee clerk, a position that placed him at the center of intense debates over the future of the city during the next dozen years. Because of D.C.'s unique political structure, Moore—neither a native Washingtonian nor an elected official, neither an urban planner nor an architect—wielded extraordinary influence over the shape and structure of the city.[36]

Soon after Moore began his work with the Senate District Committee, the Panic of 1893 triggered the deepest economic downturn in the nation's history to that point. Washington became a theater for social unrest when an integrated group of several hundred unemployed men dubbed "Coxey's Army" marched from Ohio to the Capitol to demand a massive public works program to put people back to work—the first such protest to come to D.C. Though the presence of the federal government sheltered Washington from the harshest effects of the depression, the city struggled. As wealthy and middle-class residents moved out to the leafy suburbs touted by the Board of Trade and real estate developers, older neighborhoods within downtown Washington deteriorated and alley communities burgeoned.[37]

Moore viewed these troubles through the lens of a powerful social movement that came to be called Progressivism. The Progressive movement arose in response to the social ills associated with urban life—disease, crime, overcrowding, unsanitary living conditions—that had resulted from the tremendous growth of the nation's cities in the last decades of the nineteenth century. Worried that economic turmoil could lead to social tumult, middle-class reformers sought to create order, stability, and cleanliness out of the chaos of the urban environment. The movement took many forms: temperance advocates sought to limit liquor, good government reformers pushed for the secret ballot, and social workers built settlement houses to improve living conditions in poor neighborhoods.

In Washington, perhaps the most influential Progressive effort was the "City Beautiful" movement, which aimed to shape and improve the character of urban residents by beautifying the physical structures of the cities in which they lived. Reformers believed that if they could improve how cities looked and functioned, then they would improve how city residents behaved. Beautiful buildings, parks, and common areas would inspire people to show moral and civic virtue. Landscapers, architects, and engineers revolutionized civic design, emphasizing grand, monumental civic buildings that dominated cityscapes and evoked pride and awe in residents.[38]

The ideal envisioned by City Beautiful enthusiasts was the "White City" of the 1893 World's Fair in Chicago—a unified, gleaming expanse of shimmering, Neoclassical buildings that captured international attention and inspired a generation of city planners. Progressive planners such as Daniel Burnham, the architectural mastermind behind the World's Fair exhibition, saw a potential White City in Washington. A planned city from the outset, Washington appealed to planners' sense of order and possibility, offering them an opportunity to show the world how the City Beautiful movement could reshape a city. In an article titled "White City and Capital City," Burnham wrote, "Here, in the nation's capital, the American people have declared shall be the theater for an exhibition of what plan, single and comprehensive, can do to develop and correlate the diversified parts of the urban and rural landscape of an already beautiful city."[39]

Unlike other Eastern cities, Washington did not have an extensive industrial sector that polluted the water and air, and it lacked a large population of immigrants who crowded into filthy slums elsewhere. "No other city seems to have made beauty its first thought, and relegated the harder and coarser things of life to a secondary place, as Washington has," wrote one observer in *Scribner's Magazine*. With thoughtful planning, the national capital could be the embodiment of national ideals, a unique expression of American beauty and a model for cities across the country.[40]

A second feature of Washington that appealed to city planners was what made it unique among American cities: disfranchisement and government by commission. In the minds of men such as Daniel Burnham and Charles Moore, Washington was simply a creature of the federal government, a national city that should be ruled by the nation, not locals. "The nation's capital is governed by the citizens of the United States, who choose its aldermen and the members of its legislature when they elect senators and representatives; and that Congress deals with the District of Columbia in an enlightened spirit," Moore wrote. Indeed, concurred Montgomery Schuyler in the *New York Times*, the power to determine what is "beautiful and harmonious" was "more safely lodged with the authorities of the District of Columbia than with those of any city dependent for its government on the suffrages of all its adult male inhabitants." Without having to be concerned about local democratic accountability, planners could work with a relatively small group of local and national leaders to implement their vision. District residents who might object to the planners' efforts—including the black community and the poor—had little opportunity to shape the conversation.[41]

Local leaders on the Board of Trade and in the press strongly supported the Progressive effort to beautify the city and make it a national showpiece. Since its inception, the board had consistently sought to strengthen the relationship between the federal government and its capital, and it had long advocated for the federal government to establish a new comprehensive plan for the city. In the 1890s, economic difficulties and complaints from thrifty congressmen led Congress to back away from its pledge to pay 50 percent of the District's budget. Fearing an erosion of federal support, city leaders sought to reinvigorate the relationship by supporting efforts to revitalize downtown Washington and "make the national capital the most beautiful in the world." Using the city's centennial in 1900 as an opportunity to make their case to the nation, city leaders urged Congress to "improve the District of Columbia in a manner and to an extent commensurate with the dignity and resources of the American nation."[42]

They found a willing ally in Charles Moore's boss, Senator James McMillan. Unlike William Stewart, Francis Newlands, and other businessmen-turned-senators, McMillan did not seek to enrich himself in the D.C. real estate market. Instead, as chair of the Senate's District Committee he became an effective advocate for the beautification of the capital. Working closely with the Board of Trade, he pursued an ambitious agenda to remake Washington and challenged his colleagues in Congress to live up to their fiduciary commitment to the city. At his behest, in early 1901 the Senate created the Senate Park Improvement Commission of the District of Columbia, with McMillan himself as chairman and Moore as secretary. They assembled a team of prominent architects who had been responsible for the White City, including Daniel Burnham, Charles McKim of Boston, and Frederick Law Olmsted Jr. The trio, with Moore in tow, spent seven weeks visiting European cities as they began imagining how to transform America's capital into a monumental city with the grandeur and gravitas of its Old World counterparts.[43]

In January 1902, less than six months after they returned from Europe, the commissioners produced a plan that would dramatically reshape the city. Though many of its ideas had been proposed in various forms at one point or another, the McMillan Plan (as it became known) combined them into a unified whole. Launched with a sophisticated public relations effort that included glossy brochures, a stunning model of the future city, and a gala event at the Corcoran Museum of Art—President Theodore Roosevelt and his wife, Edith, attended—the McMillan Plan earned widespread praise for the breathtaking scope of its vision and the elegant beauty of its design.[44]

Enamored with Peter L'Enfant's original plan for the city, the McMillan Commission members believed that the city should be treated as "a work of civic art." Deviations from L'Enfant plan—including the railroad tracks across the Mall, the Smithsonian Castle that stood incongruously in the middle of it, and the Victorian architecture along its sides—were to be "regretted and, wherever possible, remedied" by removal. The McMillan Plan proposed turning the Mall into a civic park, a wide expanse of grass stretching between the Capitol and a proposed memorial to Abraham Lincoln, bounded on the sides by trees and Neoclassical government buildings. The plan also called for a unified system of parks along Rock Creek and the Potomac and Anacostia Rivers, connected by aesthetic bridges and tree-lined parkways.[45]

Despite strong support from President Roosevelt, city leaders, and many members of Congress, the plan faced several formidable challenges, including the untimely death of Senator McMillan in August 1902, powerful opposition from the territorial and parsimonious Speaker of the House Joseph Cannon, and controversies about the placement of the Department of Agriculture and the Lincoln Memorial. But over time the McMillan Plan proved remarkably resilient and withstood most challenges, particularly after the creation in 1910 of the Commission of Fine Arts, which served as a permanent protector of the plan's principles. Charles Moore served on the commission for nearly three decades and helped insure the implementation of his boss's vision. Even with the interruption of World War I, the plan proceeded apace with the construction of the Lincoln Memorial in the 1920s and Federal Triangle in the 1930s. Its principles have guided planners ever since. The McMillan Plan helped turn downtown Washington into a city of marble and monuments, the closest physical expression of the White City the nation would ever see.[46]

With the implementation of the McMillan Plan, yet another "new Washington" was born, wrote awestruck architectural critic Montgomery Schuyler. Isaac Marcosson in *Munsey's Magazine* claimed that to see the transformed D.C. "is to behold the realized dream of a triumphant democracy, clad in beauty and power." It was a triumph for Charles Moore and other boosters who saw Washington primarily as a capital city that would serve as a national monument, rather than a living city for local residents. It was a triumph of buildings over people, of the "capital" over the "city."[47]

"The Negro Shanties in the Heart of the City Will Disappear": Reformers Target Alley Communities

Like the reforms pursued by Alexander Shepherd thirty years before, the McMillan Plan paid little attention to Washington's poor. In their quest to beautify the city, planners emphasized landscape design, building architecture, and conceptual unity. They barely paused to consider the effects that their plans might have on poor residents. Despite a call from the Associated Charities of

Washington to "give especial consideration to [the city's] poorer neighborhoods," the 171-page plan mentioned low-income people only once—as an impediment to the construction of a parkway.[48]

The McMillan Plan, boasted Daniel Burnham, embodied Americans' desire for their leaders "to remove and forever keep from view the ugly, the unsightly, and even the commonplace." Indeed, much of the plan hinged on the removal of many slums and alleys surrounding the Capitol and the Mall to make way for new public monuments and government buildings. In the gleaming vision of the new White City, the poor had no place. One writer in *Washington Life* put it bluntly in 1904: "The greatest drawback to the civic beauty of Washington is its negro population, whose poor dwellings are found on every hand, and constitute the greatest menace to real estate values in the city." The McMillan Plan helped make good on a prediction by a *Harper's Weekly* reporter several years earlier: "It will not be many years before the negro shanties in the heart of the city will disappear. They are already giving way to the march of wealth and splendor."[49]

The construction of Union Station, one of the early projects implemented after the approval of the McMillan Plan, exemplified how the creation of something beautiful came at the expense of the poor. The railroad tracks that crisscrossed the National Mall had long been a source of dismay among city leaders and City Beautiful planners. The unsightly tracks marred the view, the pollution and noise spoiled the ambiance of the setting, and trains sometimes hit animals and people. Removing the tracks was key to realizing the larger vision of the plan, so it was an early priority. With personal lobbying from Daniel Burnham and $3 million in financial incentives offered by Congress, the Pennsylvania Railroad and the Baltimore & Ohio Railroad agreed to abandon their stations near the Mall and unite to build a majestic Burnham masterpiece of Neoclassical design. Union Station—named not for the Union of the Civil War but for the union of the two major railroad companies serving the city—was planned for just north of the Capitol, on the southern edges of Swampoodle. Teams of mules helped lay the foundation, and hundreds of Italian stoneworkers were imported to work on the project, which lasted from 1903 to 1907.[50]

More than fifteen hundred of Swampoodle's poor Irish residents, along with their black neighbors who lived primarily in the alleys, were forced to leave as the construction leveled hundreds of homes. Homeowners were paid for their property, and some moved to more spacious homes up North Capitol Street, but renters had to find new homes in already-crowded alleys elsewhere. Hardscrabble Swampoodle transformed into a gleaming gateway to the nation's capital. As its residents moved away, the neighborhood slowly vanished. By the 1940s, it ceased to exist and few even remembered its whimsical name.[51]

Although the destruction of Swampoodle was perhaps an unintended consequence of building Union Station, the "ugly" and "unsightly" alley neighborhoods of downtown D.C. were directly targeted for destruction. In the decades after the Civil War, the city's alleys had attracted the intermittent attention of government officials, and during the 1870s the Board of Health condemned nearly a thousand alley dwellings. After disfranchisement, however, alley construction boomed as health officials lost the power to condemn buildings. The growth of alley communities and the deterioration of alley dwellings, particularly in older neighborhoods, inspired a new generation of Progressive reformers to fight for an outright end to all alley housing in the city.

Clearing out the alleys became a compelling priority that united white city planners and business leaders interested in making downtown a beautiful, monumental city with white social reformers intent on improving the lives and character of the poor. To build public support for their efforts and inspire lawmakers to act, reformers published vivid reports, shocking photographs, and sensational news articles that exposed the deplorable living conditions of D.C. alleys. With funding from local community groups, Labor Department investigator Mary Clare de Graffenreid surveyed life in fifty D.C. alley dwellings in 1896. The overcrowded dwellings she studied lacked sewer connections and drainage, relied on pumped water from dirty wells, and often had outdoor privies that created a "smothering" stench. The "disgusting surroundings" had a debilitating effect on alley residents. "These unfortunates are beyond the pale of decency and morality," de Graffenreid wrote, and only an exceptional few could lead "wholesome, though laborious, lives" in such an environment.[52]

De Graffenreid's report helped inspire local housing reformers to launch a philanthropic housing movement to attract private investment and apply business principles to build abundant low-cost housing. Driven primarily by concerns about public health, the city's reputation, and the debilitating effect of inadequate housing on the character of the poor, reformers such as George Kober, a professor of hygiene at Georgetown, promised "philanthropy that pays dividends." But they struggled to raise significant capital to fund their plans, and their business orientation led them to focus not on the poorest alley residents but on the upwardly mobile "deserving" poor. "Preference should be given to the industrious and respectable applicants," housing officials insisted, on the theory that providing solid housing for "the better class of wage earners" would encourage this ambitious class to vacate decent homes that the poor could then occupy. Despite modest successes—by 1904, housing reformers had built homes for 140 low-income families (30 of which were black)—the movement failed to make a significant dent in the housing problem.[53]

Washington's centennial in 1900 and the McMillan Plan only attracted more scrutiny to the alleys of the nation's capital. Famed photographer Jacob Riis, whose 1890 book *How the Other Half Lives* inspired legions of muckraking journalists, declared Washington's alleys among the worst in the world. Riis shot photos that juxtaposed the dispiriting alleys with the majestic Capitol and other impressive government buildings. The alleys were "a festering mass of corruption" that "kill the home life and kill the home spirit," Riis told a packed audience at First Congregational Church in December 1903. He urged Congress and his friend President Roosevelt to act immediately to eliminate alley housing.[54]

Reporters wrote breathless stories in the manner of anthropologists visiting foreign cultures, invariably highlighting the most dysfunctional aspects of alley life. Willow Tree Alley in Southwest, hidden within a block adjacent to the U.S. Botanic Garden just a few hundred yards from the Capitol, was among the largest alleys and attracted significant attention from the media and reformers. Home to more than five hundred low-income residents, including many poor Irish families whose homes in Swampoodle had been destroyed, Willow Tree was, according to the *Post*, "a foul slum in which the criminal and degraded classes congregate, dwelling together under every circumstance of physical and moral depravity." During one raid in Willow Tree, police found fifteen men in a ten-by-fifteen-foot room, sleeping on straw covered with vermin. One reporter found "no water whatever; sanitary drainage practically non-existent; disease stimulated by uncleanliness of every sort; shacks without cellars, without any drainage; swarming with child life."[55]

White alley reformers, city leaders, and the local press all agreed: a capital city that hoped to be the beautiful representative of a nation with global ambitions certainly could not tolerate the danger, dirtiness, and dysfunction of the alleys. Alley clearance was a matter of enlightened self-interest. As de Graffenreid wrote, improving alley conditions was both "the selfish interest" and the "highest moral obligation" because alleys were "urban health destroyers" that can introduce "filth, diseases, and epidemics" into an "otherwise healthy community." The Monday Evening Club was more graphic, producing a map of an alley under a blaring headline: "The Blind Alley of Washington, D.C. Seclusion Breeding Crime and Disease to Kill the Alley Inmates and Infect the Street Residents."[56]

With their emphasis on orderly middle-class virtues, their fear of "contagion" from alley dwellers, and their presumption that they had all the answers, the Progressive alley reformers are easy to condemn as arrogant busybodies who sought to impose their worldview on the poor. Indeed, their language can seem hopelessly patronizing to modern ears. However, unlike planners and city leaders who generally ignored the poor or fantasized about simply removing poor people from the city, alley reformers such as Charles Frederick Weller of Associated Charities put the lives of poor people front and center in discussions of D.C. life.

A Chicago Progressive and leader of the national playground movement, Charles Weller (no relation to suffrage advocate Michael Weller) came to Washington at the turn of the century to open a settlement house in Southwest. On his arrival, he lived for several weeks at a time in Willow Tree Alley, Swampoodle, Howardtown, and other notoriously poor areas to get firsthand experience in the lives of the poor. He then spent nearly a decade giving lectures, writing reports, testifying in Congress, and advocating for alley clearance in a city where too many people, he complained, were blinded by "a self-confident complacency."[57]

Appointed to the President's Homes Commission by President Theodore Roosevelt, Weller wrote a powerful plea for alley reform titled *Neglected Neighbors*, in which he detailed stories of alley dwellers from across the city. He called for something akin to a McMillan Plan for the poor, a "*Comprehensive Plan* for the steady, progressive, uncompromising elimination of all the evils represented by the alleys, tenements and shanties of the National Capital." He envisioned alleys being replaced by "garden cities" abounding with parks and playgrounds and common areas, all of which he believed would encourage alley dwellers to live more "wholesome" lives.[58]

Though Weller shared some of the same goals as local leaders who sought to turn Washington into a "city beautiful," he differed significantly by linking the city's future to suffrage and self-rule. Weller saw disfranchisement as being at the root of much of Washington's dysfunction and concluded *Neglected Neighbors* with an impassioned appeal for democracy in the District. In Washington, he wrote, "a comparatively small number of resourceful citizens" wielded influence on the appointed government, but the "less resourceful masses" had little opportunity to be involved. Without the franchise, most Washingtonians either did not know about public issues or did not care about what was going on because they could not do anything about it. Suffrage is "an important, and even an indispensable" step to improving the city because it would help develop "a more adequate social consciousness," he argued.

Weller recognized that race was a major impediment to democratic reform, but he urged leaders to move beyond it. "The local bugbear, the presence of a large colored population, should not be deemed a conclusive argument against popular suffrage in Washington, for in any democratic government it is not safe in the long run to exclude any group of citizens from this educational relationship to the community's life."[59]

Weller did not make much headway on disfranchisement, but the alley reform movement earned some symbolic victories in the early twentieth century. The infamous Willow Tree Alley was among the first targets of congressional action. With funding from Congress, the city bought the alley from individual landowners and turned it into a park with a baseball diamond, wading pools, and sandboxes to inspire "the moral improvement and well-being of the community," according to the *Star*. Alley reformers won powerful allies, including the District's commissioners and the local press as well as First Lady Ellen Wilson, who led high-society matrons and others on "grand tours" of local alleys to bring attention to the issue. Wilson was a particularly effective advocate. As she lay dying from a terminal kidney disease, she continued to pressure Congress to act on alleys. On the day she died, August 6, 1914, Congress passed a bill to end alley housing in Washington by 1918.[60]

The Alley Dwelling Act was a striking triumph for alley reformers, but it did not actually eliminate alley housing. World War I intervened, creating an acute housing shortage that led Congress to delay implementation of the ban, and the delays continued through the 1920s. As of 1925, despite three decades of agitation, more than thirteen thousand poor people still lived in alleys.[61]

Even when successful, alley clearance had unintended consequences because it magnified the shortage of low-cost housing, particularly for black residents. As Charles Weller explained, "In some places, for example, an alley inhabited by colored people will be changed into a minor street where only white families will be accommodated. In other cases, land values will be increased by the opening of an alley; more costly houses will be erected and the supply of places available at low rentals will be diminished." Intended to improve the lives of poor people, alley reform often uprooted them from their neighborhoods and pushed them out of the city center. For black residents barred from moving to the new, segregated suburbs, finding housing became exceedingly difficult.[62]

The Progressive reforms of the late nineteenth and early twentieth centuries dramatically reshaped the physical layout of the nation's capital. As City Beautiful planners sought to build a capital city worthy of the name Washington and alley reformers worked to rid the city of its slums, the city came to look quite different, slowly taking the shape that is familiar to modern-day residents and visitors: a core of federal buildings and public monuments downtown, with increasingly segregated neighborhoods radiating outward from the city center. The process of transformation was uneven and contested, as different visions for the city clashed in often-vociferous debates. But one important element missing from many conversations about planning the city were the voices of the people who would be among the most affected by the changes that reform wrought: the city's black residents.

"What It Means to Be Colored in the Capital of the United States": Jim Crow Settles in the District

Mary Church Terrell never lived in an alley. Born in Memphis in 1863, Terrell was the daughter of former slaves who became successful business owners and were among the wealthiest black people in America. She excelled in school, earning both a bachelor's degree and a master's degree in classics from Oberlin. After college, she spent more than two years in Europe studying foreign languages, a highly unusual experience for a black woman of her time. She came to Washington in 1890 to teach at the Preparatory School for Colored Youth (known as M Street High School), where she met Robert H. Terrell, the Harvard-educated scion of an elite black family from Virginia. They married in 1891 and became one of the city's most highly respected black couples.

Encouraged by Frederick Douglass to continue her career even after marriage—D.C. school regulations forbade married women from teaching—Terrell founded the National Association of Colored Women in 1896 and was appointed to the city's Board of Education, the first black woman in the nation to serve on a school board. She wrote frequently for popular publications across the country and became well known for her outspoken views on race relations, women's suffrage, and education. Tall and slim with fair skin, Terrell embodied upper-class black refinement.[63]

Washington offered Terrell and other black people significant opportunities unavailable anywhere else in the South. As the national capital, Washington held out a promise of freedom and opportunity, a hope that the federal government would enforce the Constitution. "Washington wasn't South," insisted Velma Davis, a black domestic who migrated to the city in the early twentieth century. "It's the capital, and you had more chances for things. Jim Crow [segregation] was there, but it was still not the South to us." A black South Carolina tailor explained in 1906 that he planned to move to D.C. because "I want to be as near the flag as I can."[64]

As the rest of the South sank into an abyss of lynching, debt peonage, and codified segregation in the late nineteenth century, black migration to Washington remained strong. The city's black population increased by more than 45 percent between 1880 and 1900, and it had the nation's largest black community—

nearly eighty-seven thousand people—accounting for more than 31 percent of the city's population. Though schools were segregated, many public institutions were not. Black residents could freely read in the majestic Carnegie Library at Mount Vernon Square (newly opened in 1903), ride the city's streetcars, dine in federal cafeterias, and stroll along the Mall without restriction. They enjoyed a wide range of public leisure activities, from gardening to biking, and they devoured the *Washington Bee*, the *Colored American*, and other black-run newspapers. Some prominent black writers even contributed to white newspapers such as the *Evening Star*.[65]

The federal government remained a major employer of black people, and through Republican Party patronage, African Americans won both federal and local government appointments. President Theodore Roosevelt appointed Robert Terrell as D.C.'s justice of the peace in 1901 and later elevated him to become the nation's first black federal judge. Black Washingtonians even could challenge white authorities in court and win. In one celebrated incident, police arrested a Census Bureau clerk named Robert Pelham Jr. for interfering with a white police officer who was beating a black woman. In court, Republican senator William Alden Smith of Michigan represented Pelham. The jury acquitted him, and the policeman was later fined for "conduct unbecoming an officer."[66]

The opportunities for employment and advancement in Washington stemmed in part from the city's undemocratic political structure. As Progressive journalist Isaac K. Friedman explained in *Collier's* magazine, because all Washingtonians, black and white, lacked the ballot, "the numerical majority, and hence the political superiority, of the African is not feared by the Caucasian." Despite periodic complaints about living in a republic but lacking the fundamental right to vote, "the conservative men of business, dreading 'nigger rule,' are quite content to leave this paradox well-enough alone."[67]

The city's black residents had more leeway than their peers in the region, but that was not to be confused with power. Instead of being respected and even feared for their political potential, as they had been during Reconstruction, black Washingtonians were at times patronized as an amusing feature of the capital city. *Harper's Weekly* reporter Henry Loomis Nelson wrote, "Whether the black of Washington was free or slave, or the offspring of bondmen or freemen, he is kindly treated at the capital, treated as we treat irresponsible children, and with that feeling, too, of friendliness that one cannot help entertaining for those that afford amusement and add to the pleasures of life." Mary Logan observed, "The negro does not lack encouragement so long as he makes no effort to 'run things.'"[68]

Despite Washington's reputation as a "colored man's paradise," many black

Washingtonians struggled to make ends meet. Although the federal government offered middle-class salaries and opportunities for educated black clerks and professionals, it gave black manual laborers little pay and few benefits. More than 80 percent of black federal workers made less than $840 a year (roughly $21,000 in twenty-first-century dollars). The municipal District government, meanwhile, was even less hospitable to black employees—only 9 of 450 city clerks were black, as were just 9 of 398 firefighters. Outside of government, black workers endured harsh working conditions and minimal pay, and black migrants to the city found few job opportunities.[69]

Women, who made up a majority of black residents, often had little opportunity for advancement, even if they were educated. Roughly 90 percent of employed black women at the turn of the century worked in domestic service. "A kitchen was where a colored woman got work," lamented Geneva Wilson, who had arrived in the city with a teacher's certificate from Tuskegee Institute. "There's not a thing else for you to do. Just clean, cook, and hope for a change." For Mary Johnson Sprow, the daughter of former slaves in Virginia, life in D.C. meant "to clean and scrub, days in and days out. . . . Work is all for a poor girl like me." Women who could not find work as domestics took in washing and sewing or sold the flowers, vegetables, and eggs that they grew on tiny plots around their houses.[70]

Black Washingtonians of all classes suffered as Jim Crow spread across the region in the late nineteenth and early twentieth centuries. Disfranchisement in D.C. had proved to be the beginning of a regionwide movement to remove black people from politics across the South through literacy requirements, poll taxes, and grandfather clauses. After 1901, not a single black man remained in the U.S. Congress. By the turn of the century, the federal government had abandoned any effort to enforce Reconstruction-era laws protecting Southern black rights, and the Supreme Court's 1896 ruling in *Plessy v. Ferguson* legitimized "separate but equal" treatment in public institutions. The Court cited Congress's support of separate schools in Washington as evidence of the constitutionality of segregation.

Jim Crow laws passed in neighboring states impinged on the rights of black Washingtonians. After Maryland passed a law segregating its trains in 1903, Perry Carson boarded a train in D.C. and immediately was ordered to the "colored" section. "I'm certainly in the District of Columbia, conductor," Carson protested. "There is no 'Jim Crow' law in this place." To which the conductor replied, "I don't know about that, nor care, but you colored folks will have to take the 'Jim Crow' car when we start from Washington." In a hurry and unwilling to make a scene, Carson retreated.[71]

Within Washington itself, the racial climate chilled considerably. Public the-aters, restaurants, and other venues that once had been integrated now began to set color restrictions as emboldened Southern Democrats in Congress and their local allies sought to impose Southern-style segregation more firmly across the city. At the behest of Senator Ben Tillman of South Carolina, Congress passed an antivagrancy bill that broadened the definition of "vagrant" to include the unemployed and threatened to throw all such people "living in idleness" into the workhouse for up to a year. The target of the bill, Tillman explained, was the city's large black population, which he blamed for "criminality" caused by "the overeducation of some negroes who are made to have higher aspiration[s] than it is possible for them to attain."[72]

Representative Thomas Heflin of Alabama not only sponsored a bill to segre-gate the city's streetcars but also took vigilante action. In March 1908, he shot and wounded a black man whom he claimed had been using foul language on a streetcar (a wayward bullet hit a white bystander as well). Though roundly criti-cized, Heflin spent not a minute in jail and returned to Congress determined to push his streetcar segregation bill through. Former D.C. schools superinten-dent William Chancellor praised Heflin and criticized "timid whites" for letting "thousands of brutal negroes" run amok in the city. He called on Congress to "give the District prohibition, separate cars, ordinances calculated to encourage industrialism, practical schooling, and laws against vagrancy" to help the "dis-franchised and helpless" city answer its "negro question."[73]

Mary Church Terrell, like other black elites, was sheltered from the harsh-est effects of Jim Crow, but she burned with resentment at the myriad ways in which skin color limited opportunities for black people in the city. In a widely read address she delivered in 1906, she detailed "what it means to be colored in the Capital of the United States." It meant a daily dose of humiliation as black Americans—in contrast to dark-skinned foreigners as well as white people of any class—were "thrust out" of restaurants, hotels, and other public institu-tions "like leper[s]." It meant limited economic prospects as black workers were barred from unions and relegated to menial occupations. It meant facing "intol-erable" discrimination in stores, streetcars, housing, and elsewhere. The result, she warned, was that "early in life many a colored youth is so appalled by the helplessness and the hopelessness of the situation in this country that in a sort of stoical despair he resigns himself to his fate."[74]

Compared to the rest of the South, Washington at the turn of the century still offered relatively more opportunities for employment, education, and economic advancement, and it did not suffer the brutal racial violence ravaging the South. But despite all the opportunities and accomplishments, particularly among the black elite, "negro life in Washington is a promise rather than a fulfillment," wrote poet (and LeDroit Park resident) Paul Laurence Dunbar in 1900.[75] Compared to life in the city a generation before—and compared to black aspirations—the decades bracketing the turn of the twentieth century witnessed a frustrating decline in political power, social standing, and economic opportunity for black residents. Jim Crow was settling in Washington, and a new generation of black Washingtonians struggled to stake their claim to the city.

"We Want Our Own": Black Washingtonians Demand Autonomy Despite Jim Crow

In the face of an increasingly hostile white community, the internal divisions that had wounded the black community in the latter part of the nineteenth century slowly began to heal. Class distinctions remained, particularly in social life, but by the early twentieth century, the black elite had shifted its approach away from assimilation toward "uplifting the race" as a whole. Where once they had sought entry into white clubs and organizations, often excluding the black poor, now black leaders created their own parallel groups. Where once they sought to win white approval by strenuously accentuating the differences between themselves and the black working class, they now created cross-class alliances to strengthen the entire community. Where once their wealth depended primarily on white benefactors, now their fortunes increasingly were linked to the black working class through business and community institutions. The black members of the Washington Board of Trade resigned, tacitly acknowledging their lack of influence in the group. The city became more visibly segregated. "In Washington, the separation of the races is more nearly complete than in any other city of the union," wrote black social worker Osceola Madden in 1908. "The better class of white and colored people know absolutely nothing of each other."[76]

Mary Church Terrell exemplified this new approach among black elites. She was part of a younger generation of black leaders in Washington who had come of age in the wake of disfranchisement and segregation. Unlike Frederick Douglass, John Mercer Langston, and others of the Civil War era, this generation had not tasted the victories of abolition and the war; they knew only the bitter fruits of Reconstruction's demise. Educated and ambitious, yet convinced that white Washington had little interest in racial equality, they urged racial solidarity rather than assimilation, black self-sufficiency rather than dependence on white patronage, black institutions rather than interracial politics. Faced with growing local and national hostility to equality, these new leaders advocated a strong sense of racial pride and channeled their energies into developing and sustaining their own businesses, schools, and institutions to survive and thrive in a city that seemed to have lurched off the track to freedom.

Terrell and other black leaders called for racial solidarity across lines of class and skin color. "Negroes as white as the Executive Mansion, or as black as the subcellar of the Capitol, are lumped together and discriminated against alike," noted the *Colored American*. Hence, it made pragmatic sense for the black community to make common cause. Frederick Douglass's son, Charles, urged fellow black Washingtonians to close ranks in the face of white hostility. A veteran, civil servant, and former president of the Bethel Literary and Historical Society, Douglass seethed at the ways in which white supremacists were rolling back the gains of Reconstruction. After the Grand Opera House decided in November 1899 to reestablish the color line and force black customers to the balcony, he called for a boycott and criticized the "lack of self-respect" of black patrons who paid for a Jim Crow seat. "Build your own theaters as you do your churches," he advised, adding, "Are we forever to be dependent upon the whites for theaters, hotels, cafes, and stores of all descriptions?"[77]

In advocating for the creation of black businesses, Douglass echoed the calls of Andrew F. Hilyer, a leading advocate of "the new business movement." Born enslaved in Georgia shortly before the war, Hilyer grew up in the Midwest and came to Washington to attend Howard University Law School in 1882. He became an accountant for the Treasury Department, dabbled in real estate, and devised two profit-generating inventions. But his passion was cultivating black business. Seeking to build a sense of camaraderie and shared mission among black entrepreneurs, in 1892 he began publishing the *Union Directory*, a compendium of black business achievement, and he spoke frequently about the need for black people to embrace business as the means to social progress.[78]

Black businesses benefited from the rise of segregated black neighborhoods such as on the Island in Southwest and along U Street between Seventh and Fourteenth Streets NW (later known as Shaw). White businessmen often refused to work in black neighborhoods, leaving the market open for black businesses such as the Capital Savings Bank, in which Robert Terrell was an officer. Whereas black businessmen of earlier generations made their mark by catering to wealthy white patrons—recall Beverly Snow and his fine Epicurean restaurant and James Wormley's upscale hotel—black entrepreneurs in the late nineteenth century focused on serving black customers. Black-owned funeral parlors, barbershops, restaurants, and retail stores proliferated across the city. By 1901, Hilyer's *Union Directory* cataloged more than 1,000 black-owned businesses in Washington. Seven years earlier there had been just 120.[79]

Perhaps the most vigorous and effective promoter of self-help and racial

"Students of the National Training School for Women and Girls, Washington, D.C." Nannie Helen Burroughs founded the National Training School for Women and Girls in Northeast Washington in 1909. Imbued with Burroughs's spirit of self-reliance, the school encouraged students to "Work, Support Thyself, to Thine Own Powers Appeal." Library of Congress.

pride was Nannie Helen Burroughs. The dark-skinned daughter of former slaves, Burroughs excelled at M Street High School (where she had both Mary Church Terrell and Anna Julia Cooper as mentors) but struggled to get a job in the D.C. school system after her graduation in 1896, which she attributed to "politics" that gave advantages to better-connected, lighter-skinned peers. The snub became a burr in her saddle, driving her on a life's mission to open educational and employment opportunities for low-income black women. A powerful orator, she became head of the National Baptist Women's Convention and spoke out often against lynching, employment discrimination, voting restrictions, and other impediments to black progress. She also took aim at class divisions and colorism within the black community. Her 1904 essay, "Not Color but Character," brimmed with indignation at the "wholesale bleaching of faces and straightening of hair" by black people suffering from "colorphobia." "Color is no badge of superiority of mind nor soul," she wrote.[80]

Among Burroughs's lasting achievements was the National Training School for Women and Girls, which she founded in 1909. The school opened with thirty-five students on a six-acre site atop a hill on Fiftieth and Grant Streets NE (now home to the private Nannie Helen Burroughs School). Burroughs called it the "school of the three B's"—the Bible, bath, and broom—and its motto captured its spirit of self-reliance: "Work, Support Thyself, to Thine Own Powers Appeal." Though it offered classes in classics and Burroughs insisted on proper grammar, the school focused primarily on Christian education and preparing its students to work, even as domestic laborers. "Two-thirds of the Colored women must work with their hands for a living, and it is indeed an oversight not to prepare this army of breadwinners to do their work well," Burroughs said.[81]

The emphasis on self-help and building black institutions did not preclude politics and collective organizing against segregation and racial discrimination. Although all Washingtonians, black and white, were denied the opportunity to exercise political power in traditional electoral ways, white community leaders wielded considerable influence with the commissioners and Congress through the Board of Trade and neighborhood associations. By contrast, black community leaders often felt that their concerns were routinely ignored. This imbalance of influence did not inspire black people to slink away from the public sphere to the confines of a "secret city," the term used by many turn-of-the-century observers to describe the life of black Washington that was "hidden" from white view. Instead, they remained politically active and routinely registered their collective demands before the city's congressional rulers.

Mass meetings were one way in which black people sought to organize the community, attract media attention, and press their case in the court of public opinion. Usually hosted by churches, mass meetings often were held in response to particular incidents—a lynching in the South, a racially motivated attack such as Rep. Heflin's streetcar shooting, or a racist comment from a local official. In early 1900, for example, an outraged black community held multiple mass meetings to protest Commissioner John Wight likening D.C.'s black residents to "safecrackers" and criminals. "Washington people can't vote, you know," black federal worker Swan Kendrick wrote his fiancée, "and the mass meeting is the only means we have of letting public men, congressmen, etc. know what we think about things." Kendrick's assertion notwithstanding, black Washingtonians expressed their grievances in a variety of public ways, from signing petitions to staging protests. Mary Church Terrell and other outspoken leaders regularly testified before congressional committees, the black press powerfully articulated the community's concerns to a broad readership, and black residents organized their own neighborhood associations.[82]

Perhaps most important, many black Washingtonians channeled their political energy into the public school system. At the turn of the century, the city's black public schools were the pride of the black community, and black leaders viewed education as an essential precondition for racial uplift. They argued that by becoming educated, productive members of society, black people would "prove" themselves worthy of being treated as full citizens. Yet black schools were not simply a vehicle for accommodating the next generation to the realities of segregation. They also undermined the mindset of white supremacy by instilling pride and offering opportunities for black power and leadership.

Although they resented the inferiority implied by segregated schools, black Washingtonians actively defended D.C.'s black school system and fought tenaciously for Congress to uphold the latter part of "separate but equal." Compared to their counterparts in the rest of the South, they were able to exert significant influence within the schools. For more than three decades after the creation of the segregated school system in 1868, the black schools had been run by a black assistant superintendent, George F. T. Cook (the Oberlin-educated brother of John F. Cook Jr.). Cook reported directly to the school district's board of trustees, which by custom was integrated, and white trustees generally deferred to black board members on matters concerning black schools.

Denied the ballot, black citizens petitioned Congress directly and testified in support of schools at congressional hearings. They pushed for equal funding for facilities and equal pay for teachers, which were mandated by law but rarely followed in practice. Despite continued discrimination, the per pupil expenditures for black students in Washington were double the amount spent for students of either race in neighboring Virginia. Black school advocates also insisted on hiring black people to work in black schools. White women had taught extensively in black public schools for decades, but by 1901 no white teachers remained. From the central office administrators to the manual laborers who maintained the facilities, the schools were black. Though they were never fully autonomous—they still had to report to white authorities and seek funding from congressional appropriators—black administrators had wide latitude to run their schools.[83]

Black control of the schools came under direct attack in 1900, as Jim Crow was hardening across the city and region. Accusing Assistant Superintendent Cook of nepotism and negligence, white school officials encouraged Congress to assume control over the black schools. "I do not think [black Washingtonians] are fit to be let alone" to run their schools, argued white school trustee General George Harries at a congressional hearing. "We have our heredity, and we have a little more civilization than they have, and I think we have a keener sense of what is right and what is wrong than they have." As Congress considered a bill proposing to abolish the position of black assistant superintendent altogether, the city's black community mobilized to defend their schools' administrative autonomy.[84]

Black opponents of the plan emphasized the symbolic importance of having a black official serving in such a prominent role and thus being a proper role model for the black community. "Abolish this system and you strike a death blow to the pride, incentive, and esprit du corps of the colored citizens of Washington," warned black resident N. B. Marshall. They also staked a claim to their rights as citizens to run their own schools. "We want our own," wrote Calvin Chase in the *Bee*, rejecting white leadership of black schools as reminiscent of "the old antebellum idea, that the colored people are unfit for self government." If white people were intent on enforcing segregation, then black people had the right to run their own schools, and they would exercise whatever political muscle they had to demand it. Through letters to members of Congress, congressional testimony, newspaper editorials, and mass meetings, black Washingtonians argued forcefully and effectively that black schools should remain in the hands of black school officials.[85]

Black pressure forced a modest retreat. Congress adopted a reorganization plan that preserved black autonomy, but in diminished form. Instead of abolishing the black Assistant Superintendent post, Congress created a new (white) superintendent position to supervise two Assistant Superintendents, one white and one black. The plan also created a new director of high schools, meaning that the black community lost direct control over M Street High School and Miner Normal School, which trained teachers. Unsatisfied with the new system, black community members refused to accept the reorganization as a final verdict. Their simmering concerns boiled over in 1904 in response to a controversy at M Street High School, where principal Anna Julia Cooper sought to assert her administrative independence from the white director of high schools, Percy Hughes.

A former slave, Oberlin graduate, and celebrated author who was in many ways the doppelgänger (and at times a rival) of Mary Church Terrell, Cooper pursued an ambitious agenda of strengthening the school's classic curriculum, raising the number of graduating students, and helping graduates win scholarships to prestigious colleges. Hughes considered her to be insubordinate and sought to discredit her by publicly accusing her of neglecting discipline and relaxing academic standards. Incensed by the attack on a beloved school leader, much of the black community rose to her defense. The ensuing controversy prompted several investigations and helped precipitate another congressional reorganization of the schools in 1906. Driven in part by black complaints, Congress abolished the director of high schools position and placed M Street High, Miner Normal School, and the Armstrong Manual Training School (built in 1902) under the direction of the black assistant superintendent. Once again, black political pressure had protected black autonomy in the schools.[86]

The reorganization battles united the black community. Though class divisions remained, black Washingtonians almost unanimously fought for black autonomy and equated educational excellence with their ability to run their schools relatively free from white interference. Their political mobilization solidified the city's black school system's reputation as a model for the nation. Whereas many of their Southern peers languished in ill-equipped schools that reinforced their subordinate role in society, black students in D.C. enjoyed relatively well maintained schools with top-notch faculty members who taught courses in African American history and encouraged them to attend colleges of all kinds. The District's black schools stayed up-to-date with such Progressive educational reforms as improved teacher training and the introduction of kindergarten, and they offered a variety of enrichment programs, including a lecture series featuring prominent black leaders and field trips to the area's cultural and historical sites. M Street High School (renamed in honor of poet Paul Laurence Dunbar in 1917) became the flagship high school for all of black America, graduating more students than any other black high school in the country.[87]

The success of D.C.'s black schools—and the local community's successful defense of autonomy in the schools—inspired black people nationwide. In the early twentieth century, D.C. was more than just the seat of the national government; it also embodied the hopes of black America. "The influence of a man of our race who resides in the District of Columbia is far from local—it is national," said Booker T. Washington at M Street High School's graduation in 1905. "Failure here is not local but national, and success here is not local but national."[88]

But the city also symbolized the frustrating disconnect between the nation's egalitarian ideals and its reality of racism. "Surely nowhere in the world do oppression and persecution based solely on the color of the skin appear more hateful and hideous than in the capital of the United States," wrote Mary Church Terrell in 1906, "because the chasm between the principles upon which this Government was founded, in which it still professes to believe, and those which are daily practiced under the protection of the flag, yawns so wide and deep." A new president taking office in 1913 would widen that chasm even more.[89]

EIGHT

There Is a New Negro to Be Reckoned With

Segregation, War, and a New Spirit of Black Militancy, 1912–1932

Injustice to the colored community of the Nation's Capital has in the past and in the future always will arouse resentment throughout the land.
—ARCHIBALD GRIMKÉ, 1918

The main building of the Bureau of Engraving and Printing sits on the southern edge of the National Mall, just across Fifteenth Street from the groves of cherry trees that festoon the Tidal Basin. A massive Neoclassical building of Indiana limestone and granite trim with columns soaring nearly one hundred feet along its facade, it occupies more than an entire city block, with a 224,000-square-foot vault and nearly ten acres of floor space for its thirteen hundred employees. The bureau's imposing size does not deter tourists. Each year, about a quarter-million people take a peek at the presses rolling out fresh greenbacks. The bureau's D.C. facility prints more than 3.4 billion notes a year.[1]

The bureau's main building opened to great fanfare in March 1914. Dubbed "the last word in factory construction," it cost $2.8 million (roughly $300 million in twenty-first-century dollars) and incorporated the most modern features of its time, including a state-of-the art cooling system that kept drinking water at a chilled 45 degrees and 32,700 panes of glass that filled the floors with abundant natural light. Spacious lunchrooms led to a rooftop promenade with panoramic views of the Potomac. Though not part of the original 1901 McMillan Plan, the bureau's new building followed the plan's call for architectural coherence and was part of the transformation of downtown Washington in the early decades of the twentieth century. Gone were dingy, poorly lit Italianate structures as well as modest row houses and alley tenements. In their place rose Neoclassical behemoths, marble testaments to the growth and power of the federal government. The bureau's new home spoke to the solidity and stability of the federal government and the seriousness of the work that its employees conducted.[2]

The bureau epitomized the tremendous growth of the federal government in the decades following the outbreak of the Civil War. The agency did not even exist when the war began. Federal officials quickly realized that the nation's money supply was inadequate to meet the financial exigencies of the war, so in 1862 Congress gave the Department of Treasury authority to begin engraving, printing, trimming, and inspecting paper money. With five employees, Treasury official Spencer Clark launched what eventually would become the Bureau of Engraving and Printing (it got its permanent name in 1874). The bureau expanded rapidly as the federal government embraced an ever-larger role in national life. By century's end, it employed more than 2,300 people in its cramped plant on the corner of Fourteenth and B Streets SW. By World War I, employment topped 8,400.[3]

Much of the bureau's work was hard, noisy, and dirty—more akin to an industrial factory than a white-collar federal agency. It attracted hundreds of both Irish immigrants and black workers from nearby neighborhoods. Male printers and their female assistants endured low pay and notoriously poor working conditions. Women at the bureau were among the first federal employees to organize a union. Bureau work may have been difficult, but like other federal jobs it offered black workers a measure of employment security, social mobility, and prestige, as well as insulation from the racism of the private labor market.[4]

Despite periodic complaints about subtle racism within the federal hiring process, the government remained relatively meritocratic and accessible. An ambitious, educated black worker could take the civil service exams and earn a white-collar clerkship that could lead to a middle-class future. Because most upper-level positions were closed to blacks, the Post observed in 1909, "the most capable of the negroes" competed for mid- and low-level clerkships. "Naturally the colored man often comes out ahead in the examinations, and when that happens there is nothing to prevent his getting the appointment."[5]

In addition, political patronage through the Republican Party remained a vital source of opportunity for black office seekers. The number of black federal workers in Washington more than quadrupled in the decades after the Civil Service Commission was established in 1883, reaching nearly 2,800 by 1907. More than 400 black professionals and clerks worked in Washington's federal offices, including James Napier, the register of the Treasury, whose signature appeared on every dollar bill printed by the U.S. government from 1911 until March 1913.[6]

Black employment at the bureau followed a similar pattern. The agency hired its first black female employee, Frances Flood, as a printer's assistant in 1890. When two white printers balked at working with her, the Republican chief of the bureau fired them, earning widespread praise from the black community. Black applicants thereafter flocked to the agency. By 1893, about a third of the bureau's examination applicants were black and nearly one hundred black women worked as printer's assistants.[7]

But the federal government could be a fickle friend. Even after the civil service reforms of the 1880s, the fortunes of black employees in federal government jobs remained vulnerable to shifts in the political winds and changes in leadership. At the bureau, the doors of opportunity closed soon after the appointment of Kentucky Democrat Claude Johnson to head the agency in 1893. Described as a "negro hater" by the *Bee*, Johnson led a systematic purge of skilled black employees. Within a year, fewer than ten black printer's assistants remained. A Civil Service Commission investigation condemned the firings, yet Johnson remained on the post. Only with the return of Republican rule in 1897 did the bureau reopen to skilled black employees. By 1908, the number of black women printer's assistants had climbed past two hundred.[8]

Racial problems within the bureau flared again after Democrat Woodrow Wilson was elected president in 1912, mirroring tensions within the federal bureaucracy and the city at large. During Wilson's two terms in office, race relations within the federal government became perhaps the most important issue facing the city's black residents. It was a time of "New Freedom"—Wilson's Progressive vision of an orderly society—and "New Slavery"—black Washingtonians' description of the imposition of Jim Crow across the city. It was a time when calls for self-determination, both for black people and for the city itself, rang with renewed resonance as the city became the administrative command center for a war to "make the world safe for democracy." It was a time when the federal government itself became a battleground as a new spirit of militancy infused racial struggles throughout the nation.

These were decades of racial conflict and contestation, of resentment and resignation, both within the columned cocoons of agencies such as the Bureau of Engraving and Printing and outside on D.C.'s streets. The bureau's sparkling new building, like the other beautiful federal monuments dotting downtown Washington, conveyed a sense of grandeur and modernity, but they could not ameliorate the racial inequality and rage that roiled the nation's capital in the 1910s and 1920s.

"The New Slavery": Black Washingtonians Challenge
Segregation in the Federal Government

Rosebud Murraye had been working as a printer's assistant at the Bureau of Engraving and Printing for nine years when Democrat Woodrow Wilson took office in March 1913. A native Washingtonian officially classified as "mulatto" by the census, she was born in 1885 and graduated at age nineteen from Scotia Seminary in North Carolina. Shortly after graduation, she took the civil service examination and earned an entry-level position in the bureau. She worked her way up through several promotions and by 1913 had reached, she wrote, "as far as I could go." Active in her community and her church, Murraye lived near the burgeoning black cultural and commercial strip along the U Street corridor in Northwest.[9]

Murraye and her coworkers at the bureau found themselves on the front lines of a renewed battle over segregation in federal departments that gained intensity after Wilson's arrival in the White House. Virginian by birth, academic by training, Progressive by politics, Wilson catapulted from the presidency of Princeton to the governorship of New Jersey to the White House in less than three years. The first Southerner elected to the presidency since before the Civil War, Wilson embodied the regional reconciliation among American whites that had taken place since Reconstruction. He campaigned on a promise of "New Freedom," and he brought to Washington an administration of Democrats committed to Progressive ideals of governmental efficiency and experimentation.

Many of Wilson's appointees also embraced Southern ideals of white supremacy. Like the new president, they did not see a contradiction between Progressivism and segregation. Soon after his inauguration, Wilson replaced all but two of his predecessor's black appointees with white men, and his administrative appointees quietly encouraged the racial segregation of federal workers, building on sporadic efforts that had begun under Presidents Roosevelt and Taft. With Wilson's blessing if not his direct orders, administration officials isolated black workers in "Negro corners," forced them to use "colored" toilets, and even erected a few "Whites Only" signs in federal buildings. When challenged by activists to explain the growing segregation in his government, Wilson argued that physical separation of the races was necessary to avoid racial "friction ... discontent and uneasiness," and thereby both promote efficiency and protect black workers from further discrimination.[10]

Emboldened Southern Democrats in Congress attacked the city's residual integrated customs, reintroducing bills to segregate streetcars and prohibit interracial marriage in D.C. Senator Francis Newlands of Nevada (the founder of Chevy Chase) proposed sending all black people out of the United States, while the National Democratic Fair Play Association lobbied hard against the appointment of black people to federal positions. The persistent attacks on black federal workers undermined black morale in the city. "I have never seen the colored people [of Washington] so discouraged and so bitter as they are at the present time," wrote Booker T. Washington in August 1913.[11]

Federal employees wait for treatment at a Public Health Service dispensary. President Woodrow Wilson solidified racial segregation throughout the federal government, demoralizing black Washingtonians and stunting black economic ambitions. Although most federal buildings in Washington did not have explicit segregation signs, they sometimes appeared, as in this Public Health Service dispensary. Library of Congress.

The Bureau of Engraving and Printing was among the first agencies to feel the brunt of the new emphasis on segregation. One evening in early April 1913, not even a month after Wilson's inauguration, Acting Secretary of the Treasury John Skelton Williams, a native Virginian, dropped by the bureau and was horrified to see that "young white women and colored women were working together side by side and opposite each other." Williams put the bureau's director, Joseph Ralph, on notice that the new administration would no longer tolerate such laxity.[12]

Though initially worried that segregation within the bureau would be "unpracticable," Ralph and other agency officials hurriedly complied with Williams's request. They established separate toilets and lockers, and they set aside tables in the back of the lunchroom for black employees. Encouraged by the new, more militant spirit of segregation, some white employees initiated complaints about their black coworkers. In July, a white woman named Rose Miller complained about a black supervisor, Louise Nutt, in the Wetting Division; within a week, Director Ralph had replaced Nutt with a white man.[13]

Like antebellum slaveholders who insisted that their slaves were happy with their condition, Williams, Ralph, and other administration officials claimed that not only did their black employees benefit from segregated treatment but they actually preferred it. Responding to criticism from Belle La Follette, the rabble-rousing wife of Progressive senator Robert La Follette of Wisconsin, Williams reported that there was no "general order" to segregate the bureau at all. The lunchroom tables for black workers were set aside simply because "it is believed that it would be better for them to associate together when eating their lunches." Most black workers, Director Ralph said, complied without complaint. "Colored employees have expressed themselves as believing that arrangements of this kind, including separate toilet conveniences, were very satisfactory and proper," explained Ralph, "and it would seem that the claim of discrimination is made only by colored persons who do not desire to associate with members of their own race."[14]

Not everyone at the bureau was willing to go along with the new system. Not long after Williams's initial visit in April, Rosebud Murraye and two other black printer's assistants, Bertha Saunders and Maggie Keys, deliberately challenged him by repeatedly sitting at tables with their white coworkers, even after two employees, one white and one black, suggested that they move. Ralph called them into his office. With him was Charlotte Hopkins, a prominent white housing reformer, who lectured the women about accepting the way things were. When the women pushed back, noting that there actually was no separate lunchroom, just a waiting room next to the toilets, Hopkins responded, according to the *Bee*, "Why will you go where you are not wanted? Do you know that the Democrats are in power? If you people will go along and behave yourselves, and stay away from places where you are not wanted, we may let you hold your places."[15]

Murraye, apparently, was unwilling to "behave." According to Ralph, she was "impertinent" and "insolent" at the meeting. She and her coworkers decided to boycott the lunchroom entirely because they felt "our food choked us." Not all the black employees supported them, however. According to an anonymous black employee, an "old time Negro Mammy" upbraided the young women for complaining and told them that they should be grateful that they still had jobs."[16]

Stymied internally, Murraye and her partners in protest brought their complaints to a new organization that had first appeared on the local scene a year earlier: the National Association for the Advancement of Colored People

(NAACP). Founded in 1909 by an interracial collection of liberals, the NAACP sought to create a nationwide network of civil rights organizations that would fight the spread of Jim Crow and push for full political and civil equality. Though black Washingtonians had participated in a variety of short-lived political groups in the early 1900s such as the National Negro Suffrage League and the Negro Personal Liberty Party, none proved to have the staying power or political clout of the NAACP.

With scholar-activist W. E. B. Du Bois as its intellectual driving force, the NAACP represented a direct challenge to the most prominent black leader of the time: Booker T. Washington. Washington, a politically savvy Southerner popular among white people, encouraged black self-sufficiency and economic sustainability within the reality of segregation. He adroitly used patronage and his connections to white politicians to build a powerful political machine based out of the Tuskegee Institute he founded in Alabama. The bristly, Northern-born Du Bois dismissed Washington's "accommodationism" and urged black Americans to reject segregation in all forms. Equally brilliant, ambitious, and headstrong, Washington and Du Bois had a complicated relationship and grew to resent one another, each encouraging his supporters to disassociate with the other's ideas and initiatives.[17]

The "Bookerites" and the "Radicals" clashed periodically in the District, but many black Washingtonians refused to choose sides, borrowing liberally from the ideas of both camps. Mary Church Terrell, for example, worked closely with W. E. B. Du Bois and championed "Radical" ideas; yet she nonetheless declined to speak ill of Booker T. Washington and as a member of the Board of Education she supported the vocational training that the Bookerites championed. "I appreciated Dr. Washington's effort to train the masses to earn a living because I knew that no race can hope to stand on a firm financial basis without a well-trained laboring class," she later wrote. Her husband, Robert, was an avowed Bookerite who owed his judgeship to the Tuskegee machine and claimed that "99 percent" of D.C.'s black residents supported Washington.[18]

Howard University's Kelly Miller also sympathized with both approaches. A math professor whose passion for racial equality drew him into sociology, Miller became one of the most prolific black political writers and speakers of his time, but he was accused of "straddling" rather than taking a clear side in the struggle. Miller defended himself by responding, "Effective horsemanship is accomplished by straddling"—in a treacherous, ever-shifting political arena, Miller and many other black Washingtonians preferred deft maneuvering to rigid dogmatism.[19]

The D.C. branch of the NAACP, launched in March 1912, was a "big tent" that encompassed the full range of opinion within the city's black leadership. With its large base of middle-class supporters and its proximity to federal lawmakers, it soon became the largest and most influential NAACP branch in the nation. Unlike the national organization, it was predominantly black—the local D.C. branch had but few white members, some of whom, like Belle La Follette, were neither native Washingtonians nor longtime residents. White Washingtonians generally were unaware of or uninvolved in the increasing activism within the black community.[20]

When Rosebud Murraye and her colleagues arrived at the NAACP in spring 1913, however, they received little help from the branch's founding president, J. Milton Waldron. (They eventually took their story to Belle La Follette, who published an interview with the three women in La Follette's Magazine; Murraye later was fired for "insubordination," and La Follette helped her find a new job.) Waldron was embroiled in a draining leadership crisis of his own making. The headstrong pastor of Shiloh Baptist Church, Waldron had grown increasingly disenchanted with the Republican Party and campaigned for Democrat Woodrow Wilson in 1912. After Wilson was elected, Waldron told a Richmond audience that white Southerners were "our best friends in everything except politics," and effectively blamed black people for their own disfranchisement with their slavish loyalty to the Republican Party.[21]

Waldron's speech ignited a firestorm of criticism within the D.C. branch. Local critics, led by educator and activist Nannie Burroughs, joined with national NAACP officials who hoped to rein in the growing power of the D.C. branch, and they ousted Waldron in the summer of 1913. In his place they appointed Archibald Grimké, who took over as interim president in September before being selected officially in January 1914.[22]

Grimké was a man who defied stereotype. Born enslaved in 1849, one of three mixed-race sons fathered by a prominent South Carolina planter, he was the nephew of Angelina and Sarah Grimké, perhaps the most important white Southern abolitionists in the antebellum era. After the Civil War, he moved north, attended Lincoln University in Pennsylvania, and became the second black graduate of Harvard Law School. He worked as a lawyer, editor, and author before earning an appointment from Democratic president Grover Cleveland to serve as U.S. consul to Santo Domingo from 1894 to 1898.

Shortly after returning to the United States, Grimké moved to D.C. to live with his brother Francis, the pastor of Fifteenth Street Presbyterian Church. As a columnist for the widely read New York Daily Age and president of the American Negro Academy, Grimké was, in Kelly Miller's words, "a radical among radicals" who forcefully rejected white supremacy. Fiercely independent and provocatively iconoclastic, he at times supported and criticized both Du Bois and Booker T. Washington. With snow-white hair and a trim moustache to match, Grimké became the city's most recognizable and effective black leader in the 1910s.[23]

Grimké seized on the issue of segregation within the federal government, viewing it as an opportunity to unite the city's fractious black community behind the fledgling D.C. NAACP and build a national interracial movement for racial equality akin to the antebellum abolitionist movement. Within months, he brought focus and energy to the D.C. branch, and it grew from 143 to 700 members. The branch coordinated a series of protests and mass meetings, including one October 1913 rally that attracted an overflow crowd of nearly ten thousand to the Metropolitan A.M.E. Church just five blocks from Wilson's White House. Wilson had delivered "the unkindest blow ever dealt us by a President since emancipation," Grimké charged, and efforts to segregate black employees in the federal government aimed "to insult, to humiliate, to degrade, and to reduce [black people] to a new slavery."[24]

The campaign against federal segregation built on Washington's rising stature in the national consciousness. With the United States asserting itself as a global power in foreign affairs, Washington assumed added significance as the center of an expanding national government. No longer dismissed as a dusty country town, the city received national adulation as the gleaming federal city envisioned by the McMillan Plan took shape. Grimké and other local black leaders sought to capitalize on the city's new cachet to draw attention to its racial injustice. Seizing on Wilson's penchant for sweeping, idealistic statements, they pointed out just how far the nation's capital fell short of those ideals. Race discrimination in Washington, wrote the editors of the black weekly *Independent*, "is not patriotic, it is not democratic."[25]

The NAACP's efforts helped thwart passage of many antiblack measures in Congress, but it failed to prevent the spread of segregation within the federal government. Throughout Wilson's two terms in office, white administrators refused to hire or appoint qualified black applicants, wrote negative personnel reports about black employees, and denied promotions to veteran black workers. A 1914 executive order required photographs to accompany federal job applications, and many agencies began requiring personal interviews, making it easier for administrators to discriminate against black applicants.[26]

The Wilson administration's uneven but ultimately successful effort to segregate the federal workforce did more than simply demoralize black federal workers in Washington. It also placed a ceiling on their ambitions and effectively narrowed one of the few avenues for economic advancement and job security still available to educated black people.[27]

TABLE 4 Washington's population, 1910–1930

Year	Total	Black (% of pop.)	White (% of pop.)
1910	331,069	94,446 (28.5)	236,128 (71.3)
1920	437,571	109,966 (25.1)	326,860 (74.7)
1930	486,869	132,068 (27.1)	353,981 (72.7)

Source: U.S. Census Bureau, "Historical Census Statistics on Population Totals by Race"

The case of John Abraham Davis shows the impact that Wilson's policies had on black federal workers. A native Washingtonian born to a white lawyer and his black housekeeper, Davis graduated as the valedictorian of M Street High School and began his career at the Government Printing Office in 1882. He started as a low-level laborer earning twenty-five cents an hour. Three decades later, he had risen to a white-collar clerk position. Described by one supervisor as "thorough, energetic, and conscientious in his work, which is of the highest order," Davis earned a $1,400 salary and supervised a staff of ten, including nine white workers. His family enjoyed a middle-class lifestyle with a fine home on S Street NW and an eighty-five-acre farm in rural Virginia.

But the Wilson administration put a halt to Davis's upward mobility. A month after Wilson's inauguration in March 1913, Davis's GPO supervisors demoted him and cut his salary 15 percent. The next year, they pushed him all the way down to laborer, where he earned $500 annually in the position in which he had begun his career thirty years before. Davis protested vehemently but could not undo the damage. Dependent on his federal salary, his family's fragile middle-class existence crumbled, and they descended into poverty.[28]

As the federal government became less and less hospitable to black employment, the city's appeal as a beacon of black advancement dimmed. Black migration to Washington slowed. By 1920, barely 25 percent of the city's population was black, the lowest level since before the Civil War.[29]

"The Disgrace of Democracy": Racial Discrimination in Wartime Washington

In their battle to contain the spread of segregation, black Washingtonians gained rhetorical ammunition from America's involvement in a European conflict that erupted in 1914 and came to be known as the Great War (and, later, World War I). Like the Civil War before it, the Great War had a transformative effect on the nation's capital. Washington was, in one journalist's estimation, "the war-time capital of the civilized world," the command center of an extraordinary bureaucratic war effort as the Wilson administration asserted unprecedented control over the nation's economy and industries. In addition to the expanding armed forces, the government raised an army of white-collar workers—clerks, bookkeepers, stenographers, and other low-level employees, most of them women—for a host of new federal agencies that would oversee the war effort. "The town has jumped in population like a bonanza mining-camp," marveled a *Harper's* correspondent. Within four months of the U.S. entry into the war in April 1917, an estimated 60,000 to 75,000 new workers had arrived in the city. By war's end, D.C.'s population had swelled to 526,000, an increase of about 50 percent since the war began.[30]

Unlike the Civil War, however, the vast majority of the Great War–era migrants to Washington were white, and many of them were from the Deep South. While Northern industrial cities such as Chicago and Detroit experienced massive influxes of rural black people fleeing the South to work in booming defense factories, black migration to Washington was but a trickle by comparison. Given the barriers to federal employment erected earlier by the Wilson administration, few black migrants could expect more than a menial position in the burgeoning bureaucracy.[31]

White newcomers quickly absorbed the racial customs of the city, but wartime exigencies often made it difficult to enforce rigid segregation, particularly in residential areas. The crush of war workers strained the city's meager housing resources, and rents spiked, more than tripling in the first year of the war. Housing officials abandoned the plan to eliminate alley housing by 1918 and instead scrambled to create more space. The federal government built dozens of temporary dormitories near Union Station, and officials sometimes seized unoccupied homes and pressured homeowners to open their doors to boarders. "Our homes are no longer our castles," groused one Washington woman. "If you leave your house overnight you are likely to find it full of gum-chewing young women in the morning."[32]

Despite the difficulties of finding housing, many white migrants refused to seek rooms in black neighborhoods. One estimate claimed that even at the height of the housing crisis, four thousand rooms remained vacant because they were not located in Northwest and were thus "outside the pale." At times, however, the desperate need for rooms led white workers to board in black homes. White war worker Josephine Lehmann helped friends from Michigan find a place to stay, "but," she lamented, "it was kept by a woman of too dark a complexion to suit us, and was in a neighborhood settled entirely by others whose skin was of the same shade." They took the room, but Lehmann resolved to find them a better place.[33]

The war not only undermined the practicality of racial segregation, it also gave black Washingtonians, and African Americans across the country, a powerful weapon to attack the intellectual foundation of Jim Crow. By donning the uniform and fighting for their country, black soldiers could prove their manhood and stake a strong claim to full citizenship. If the nation could trust black soldiers to make the world safe for democracy, the argument went, then surely it could not deny them their basic rights as citizens. Though local NAACP head Archibald Grimké and others harbored grave doubts about the wisdom of the war, most black leaders in Washington calculated that support would do more than dissent to advance their cause. Touting what one local church official called "the Negro's high sense of patriotism and faithful sense of duty," they organized rallies to urge black men to register for the draft. Nearly 26,500 did so.[34]

Black Washingtonians were among the first soldiers called into service—the 50 officers and 929 enlisted men of the First Separate Battalion of the D.C. National Guard mustered in late March 1917, a week before President Wilson officially declared war. They took up posts to protect the White House and other strategic points around the city. Nearly 600 black Washingtonians served in the 372nd Infantry Regiment of the segregated Ninety-Third Division, which was organized by Frederick Douglass's son Charles Remond Douglass and won the respect of French and American military officials alike.[35]

Service during the Great War—and the racial discrimination within the military that they often endured—catalyzed many black veterans who returned to Washington eager to fight for racial equality. Rayford Logan, an M Street High School alumnus and Williams College graduate who later gained fame as a pioneering historian at Howard University, was an officer in the 372nd. After his combat service ended he remained in France for several years rather than return to face continued discrimination in Washington. Negative wartime experiences spurred another M Street graduate (and Amherst College alumnus), Charles Hamilton Houston, to become a civil rights litigator.[36]

Back home, black leaders linked the war to the ongoing battle against disfranchisement, segregation, and racial violence in America, seizing on the wartime rhetoric of democracy and self-determination to call for greater racial justice. Howard professor Kelly Miller made the connection clear on the pages of the Evening Star just days after Congress declared war on Germany. "There need not be the slightest apprehension concerning [the black man's] loyalty, soldierly efficiency or willingness to serve his country," Miller assured his readers. But black loyalty should be rewarded. "Those who fight for the honor and glory of the flag are worthy of a full measure of freedom and privilege under that flag."[37]

Persistent racial discrimination, however, threatened to undermine black support for the war. Soon after the mobilization began, it became clear that the military did not intend to train black recruits for combat; instead, they would be relegated to serving white soldiers in subordinate roles as cooks, custodians, and other manual laborers. Aware that exclusion from combat would perpetuate black soldiers' second-class citizenship rather than bolster their claims for equality, Miller joined with Archibald Grimké and other black Washingtonians to push for integrated military training camps at a meeting with Secretary of War Newton Baker in early May. Baker refused but later agreed to establish segregated training camps to prepare black officers for command. "Jim Crow camps" were not ideal, Grimké and Miller knew, but black soldiers at least would get the chance to prove their mettle in battle.[38]

Black Washingtonians used the rhetoric of the war to challenge racism on the home front as well. When the Red Cross refused to register black nurses, the College Alumnae Club, a local group of educated black women (and a precursor to the National Association of University Women), wrote a public letter to President Wilson to register their frustration. "The Irish, the German, even, is treated as any other citizen," they wrote. "We, alone, are in this, as in everything else, segregated." They challenged Wilson to "show your belief in democracy by striking a blow at its enemy in America"—racial discrimination. After black guests were excluded from the Ladies' Gallery and the restaurant in the U.S. Capitol, Grimké and the NAACP questioned their mistreatment in terms of Wilsonian idealism: "Is our country at war to make the world safe for democracy, irrespective of the race or color of its multitudinous peoples, or has our country declared war against Germany merely to make the world safe for white peoples?"[39]

Within the war bureaucracy, black workers also encountered discrimination, as Mary Church Terrell discovered. Terrell took the civil service examination and filled out a questionnaire detailing her abilities, including her fluency in both German and French. Impressed with her qualifications, a supervisor called her into his office but was taken aback to see that she was not the white woman he had expected. He refused to hire her. Instead, she found an entry-level clerk position in the War Risk Insurance Bureau. Her supervisor there mistakenly assigned the fair-skinned Terrell to an all-white room, where she worked for two months before officials realized the error and dismissed her on trumped-up charges of incompetence. "It was one of the most galling experiences of my life," she later wrote. She found a new position in the "colored women's section" at the Census Bureau, but objected when agency officials barred black women from using the bathroom they had been using for years. She challenged the official who issued the order and resigned in protest when he refused to rescind it.

"The work was enjoyable and I needed the money, to be sure," she recalled. "But the idea of remaining in a section over which were placed men who had no regard for the feelings of colored women was abhorrent to me."[40]

Even as black Washingtonians experienced and fought government-sanctioned bigotry in the military and bureaucracy, they also reacted angrily as racial violence erupted across the country in summer 1917. In East St. Louis, Illinois, sensationalistic press reports of a black crime wave fanned smoldering political and economic resentment among white men toward black migrants newly arrived from the South. After two white people, including a policeman, were killed in a black neighborhood, angry white mobs spent three days rampaging through the black part of town burning homes and brutalizing anyone they saw. Unchecked by local authorities, the mobs murdered more than a hundred black people, yet no one was brought to justice. A month later, black soldiers in Houston retaliated against ill treatment at their segregated base by marching into town in assault formation and killing more than a dozen white people. Unlike in East St. Louis, however, authorities moved quickly to punish the perpetrators—thirteen of the soldiers were executed immediately and another sixteen were sentenced to death.[41]

The East St. Louis "race riot" and the execution of the black soldiers in Houston, along with a series of gruesome lynchings that year, outraged black Washingtonians. Dunbar High School teachers defied school board policy by wearing symbols of mourning in protest. At a public meeting at Howard Theater, two black veterans warned, "We owe no special allegiance to a government that discriminates, segregates, and permits lynching and burning at the stake." Black leaders such as Kelly Miller and Archibald Grimké sharpened their criticism of President Wilson. In an August 1917 open letter to the president titled "The Disgrace of Democracy," Miller called the president's domestic efforts to support freedom a "lamentable failure" and challenged him to do more to protect black rights and prevent racial violence. "Why democratize the nations of the earth if it leads them to delight in the burning of human beings?" Grimké grew increasingly frustrated as the war progressed, angered not only by the persistence of racial discrimination but also by what he perceived as the national NAACP's morally compromised strategy of supporting the war effort.[42]

Black dissent drew the attention of military officials, who feared that black residents of the nation's capital were turning against the war. The Military Intelligence Division (MID) had an office dedicated to "Negro Subversion," and its agents kept tabs on Kelly Miller and other outspoken black leaders and regularly reported on what it considered evidence of German propaganda among black Washingtonians. "It is remarkable how many negroes in Washington are Pro-

German," one German shopkeeper in the black neighborhood of Uptown (now called Shaw) told a military investigator. One nervous military official asked that the black D.C. National Guard troops protecting the White House be removed due to "the unsettled condition of the country at large, and of Washington in particular, especially in connection with the negro question."[43]

In June 1918, the MID dispatched its only black agent, Major Walter Loving, to investigate the "feeling of unrest among the colored people of this city." An M Street High School graduate who had spent his military career as an Army musician and band director before the war, Loving found that there could not be a "more trying time in this city." He defended the loyalty of the black community but acknowledged that some black workers were capitalizing on the war to earn a better living. With so many new war workers in town, Loving wrote, "servants know that the demand for help is much greater than the supply and they are taking advantage of the opportunity" to demand higher wages, more schedule flexibility, and greater autonomy in the workplace. One cook whom he interviewed insisted that "she would not cook for any white person for less than seventy-five dollars a month" because she knew that "cooks were hard to get and she could get a job anywhere." This "air of independence," even "arrogance on the part of the servants," Major Loving noted, "greatly alarm[ed] the white people of the District." It should not, however, "be taken as German propaganda, but as a feeling of their own importance to the household."[44]

The self-assertion that Loving found among Washington servants was part of a larger shift among many black Americans during the Great War and afterward. The rhetoric of freedom and democracy that permeated the war effort and the strong record of black troops abroad encouraged black people nationwide to think differently about themselves and their country. Having fought for freedom overseas, many black veterans returned to America unwilling to conform to custom, unwilling to submit once again to an inferior status. The black soldier "has come back not as he went but a New Negro," declared Archibald Grimké. "He has come back to challenge injustice in his own land and to fight wrong with a courage that will not fail him in the bitter and perhaps bloody years to come."[45]

"Race War in Washington": The 1919 Race Riot and Its Consequences

A new spirit of militancy, embodied by national figures such as union leader A. Philip Randolph and black nationalist Marcus Garvey, infused black life in postwar Washington as black veterans and nonveterans alike pushed to make sure that the war would lead to significant changes in the city's racial climate. "By his demonstrated loyalty, valor, and efficiency in practically every branch of military service ... [the Negro] *has proved his right to be granted a fuller measure of justice, respect, opportunity, and fair play in time of peace!,*" wrote Emmett Jay Scott, a Howard University administrator who had been the highest-ranking black official in the Wilson administration during the war. Local NAACP member J. R. Hawkins issued a black "14 Points" manifesto to parallel President Wilson's postwar plans. It called for political rights, economic opportunity, and the abolition of segregation, lynching, and discrimination.[46]

The confidence and swagger of the "New Negro" frightened and angered white people in Washington and elsewhere who hoped to reinforce the segregated status quo after the war ended. Their resentment of black progress and perceived militancy only grew after the November 1918 armistice, which ended the war overseas but triggered economic and social upheaval at home as millions of soldiers returned home to recession, unemployment, and labor strikes. Racial violence swept across the country during the "Red Summer" of 1919, leaving hundreds dead and wounded in places from Philadelphia to Elaine, Arkansas. Washington would not be able to escape the violence.[47]

The city faced significant challenges as it transitioned to peacetime. Its population leveled off at 455,000, about 100,000 more than when the war started. The bureaucracy shrank, the military demobilized rapidly, and the economy withered, leaving few jobs for the many servicemen and war workers who decided to stay in the Washington area. Many demobilized soldiers skirted the line between federal and local authority by remaining in uniform, though they no longer were active in the military. Hundreds joined the Home Defense League, a quasi-military community vigilance group. Young, restless, and often idle, these trained military men regularly caroused in the streets.[48]

To this volatile mix was added a final spark: a series of sexual assaults by a black man in June and July 1919. As police rounded up black suspects and white posses scoured the city for the perpetrator, the local press tapped into deep-seated white fears of interracial sex by printing sensationalized stories about the "attacks on white women" (even though the first victim was a black teacher). Fully aware of how the press had inflamed racial tensions in East St. Louis in 1917, the D.C. NAACP wrote a letter in early July to the editors of the city's four major newspapers warning that they were "sowing the seeds of a race riot by their inflammatory headlines." Those seeds bore fruit less than two weeks later.[49]

At about 10:00 p.m. on Friday, July 18, a young white woman, Elsie Williams, was walking home from her job at the Bureau of Engraving and Printing when two black men reportedly accosted her and tried to steal her umbrella. Though Williams was unharmed, the incident triggered what the *New York Times* dubbed the "Race War in Washington." Williams's husband worked at the Naval Aviation Service, and word of the incident spread quickly through the city's military community. The next night, a mob of several hundred white men, mostly soldiers and some in uniform, descended on the black neighborhood of Bloodfield in Southwest and attacked several black residents. The mob, wrote the *Baltimore Sun* approvingly, was "bent upon showing the negro population of Washington that this is a white man's town and that white men not only propose to run it but to make safe their homes." The police intervened, but no arrests were made—the officers simply asked members of the mob to disperse, and they did so without further incident.[50]

The NAACP immediately wrote to Navy Secretary Josephus Daniels demanding that he "restrain the sailors and marines who . . . were responsible for the disturbances." But Daniels and other federal officials did little after the first night of attacks. City authorities, too, failed to take adequate measures to prevent further violence. Encouraged by the lack of police enforcement, the mob grew larger and bolder on Sunday night. The *Post* estimated that it reached between one thousand and two thousand men and "surged through the downtown district, seeking negroes" along Pennsylvania Avenue. Wielding knives, guns, clubs, and rock-filled handkerchiefs, white men in the mob attacked two black men in front of the White House, savagely beat black passengers they dragged off of streetcars, and drove through black neighborhoods firing shots.[51]

As the violence escalated, black leaders met with city officials and called on local and federal officials to act to quell the "extreme lawlessness" in the city. But the violence continued, in part egged on by the press. On Monday, July 21, a front-page *Post* story informed readers that "a mobilization of every available service man stationed in or near Washington or on leave here has been ordered" for a "'clean-up' that will cause the events of the last two evenings to pale into insignificance."[52]

Black Washingtonians, particularly war veterans, interpreted the notice as a clear warning of imminent attack. Unwilling to let D.C. become "a new East St. Louis," they organized to protect their community from both white mobs and the authorities. Critics accused the police of abetting the violence by giving "the impression both to Negroes and white men that they were the allies of the white men." Because local gun dealers refused to sell firearms to black customers, some black men drove to Baltimore to secure weapons and ammunitions to distribute in D.C. Snipers positioned themselves atop row houses, and armed black patrols walked U Street between Sixth and Fourteenth Streets NW. At Howard University, ROTC officers prepared to deliver weapons and ammunition, while light-skinned veterans infiltrated the white mobs. The black community was "calm and determined, unterrified and unafraid," wrote NAACP investigator James Weldon Johnson. "They had reached the determination that they would defend and protect themselves and their homes at the cost of their lives."[53]

With the black community now retaliating against white attacks, Monday night witnessed the deadliest violence. Secretary of War Newton Baker ordered cavalry to the city, and Police Chief Raymond Pullman called up a provost guard of four hundred men to cordon off the downtown areas, but the fighting spilled out across the black areas of Uptown and Southwest. "Bands of whites and blacks hunted each other like clansmen through the night," reported the Washington Times. "There is no precedent in Washington's history for such a race riot as this."[54]

On Tuesday, after three nights of escalating violence, Secretary Baker asserted control of the situation (President Wilson, who had been on a Potomac River cruise when the violence erupted, was too sick and preoccupied to pay the riot much attention). Baker dispatched hundreds of federal troops, and within hours, the Post reported, "the National Capital was practically an armed camp." Aided by torrential rains that fell that night, the federal troops kept the streets relatively clear, and the violence ebbed. After four days of chaos, six people lay dead, scores were injured, and hundreds were in jail—about ten black people were arrested for every white one during the course of the riot. For all the bloodshed, there was remarkably little property damage, as rioters focused on attacking one another rather than destroying buildings.[55]

As city residents swept up the broken glass and patched up the wounded, a surge of pride coursed through the black community. Rather than allowing the white mob to rampage with impunity, they had stood up and defended their neighborhoods, prepared to "die for their race, and defy the white mob," wrote a thrilled Neval Thomas, an NAACP member and Dunbar history teacher. "We are dealing with a new negro and not a slave," preached the Reverend J. Milton Waldron of Shiloh Baptist Church on the Sunday after the riot. "The Negroes saved themselves and saved Washington by their determination not to run but to fight—fight in defense of their lives and their homes" an admiring James Weldon Johnson wrote in the magazine Crisis. "If the white mob had gone on unchecked—and it was only the determined effort of black men that checked it—Washington would have been another and worse East St. Louis."[56]

The riot revealed not only the physical power of the black community but also its legal, political, and media strength. As violence raged, black leaders held public rallies, spoke to the press, and conducted back channel diplomacy with white authorities. After the riot, black lawyers fought to exonerate those arrested during the melee. With black spectators jamming the courtrooms, they were able to overturn most of the convictions and fines. Even Carrie Johnson, a black seventeen-year-old convicted of manslaughter for killing a white detective during the riot, eventually was freed.[57]

Black leaders and their allies went on a national media offensive to set the record straight about the causes of the riot. In *Survey* magazine, George E. Haynes, a black economist at the U.S. Department of Labor, blasted the sensational press coverage in the weeks before the riot and blamed the violence on "unpunished lawless acts of white persons against Negroes" as well as mutual "misunderstandings, fears, and suspicions." The NAACP's Herbert Seligmann, writing in the *New Republic*, argued that black crime was simply a public cover for the real reason for white violence — "a determination to put the Negro back where he was before the war" because white men feared that "Negroes were getting too high wages and were becoming 'independent,' i.e., were no longer as servile as southern white men wished."[58]

The "race war in Washington," coupled a week later by an outbreak of racial violence in Chicago, frightened many white observers in the District and around the country. Shocked by the scope of the violence and the willingness of black residents to retaliate, they laid much of the blame on the black community's new spirit of militancy. "The majority of the negroes in Washington, before the great war, were well behaved, with a half-Northern and half-Southern viewpoint," wrote the editors of the *New York Times*. "Most of them admitted the superiority of the white race, and troubles between the two races were undreamed of."[59]

Major J. E. Cutler of the MID, a white sociologist who specialized in race relations, identified several reasons for the riot, none of which implicated the white soldiers who had formed the mob. The root cause, he argued, was "the long continued propaganda that has been carried on here urging the colored people to insist upon equality in all respects with white people and to resort to force, if necessary, in order to establish their rights." Having fought back, "many of the negroes are convinced that they won out against the whites in the riots, that they showed their superiority over white rioters and over the police, that even the troops were unable to do much against them." This attitude could produce "some very serious race clashes in the near future," Cutler warned. "Beyond a doubt, there is a new negro to be reckoned with in our political and social life."[60]

Major Walter Loving, Cutler's black colleague in the "Negro Subversion" unit of the MID, offered a more sympathetic perspective on this "new negro." Praised (or damned) by his military superiors as "the best type of 'white man's negro,'" the conservative, circumspect Loving had grown increasingly frustrated by the mistreatment of black soldiers and the targeting of black civilians during the war. As he analyzed the riots in Washington and elsewhere, Loving saw a people pushed to their breaking point. "The Negro has decided that he has endured all that he can endure," he wrote in his final report before leaving the MID. "He has decided to strike back."[61]

The defiance of Washington's black community inspired black observers nationwide, highlighting once again the city's strategic and symbolic role in black America. Commenting on the effects of the riot in Washington, the editors of the *Chicago Defender*, the nation's largest black newspaper, wrote, "The younger generation of black men are not content to move along the line of least resistance as did their sires."[62] Unlike the civil disturbances that would ravage D.C. after the assassination of Martin Luther King in April 1968, the 1919 riot caused little long-term damage to the city's black neighborhoods. Resentment over official inaction during the riot lingered, but many black Washingtonians felt justifiably proud of their community's courage in the face of white violence. Riot participants were "patriots in the cause of democracy," one writer in the *Bee* proclaimed, hailing "the dawn of a new democracy." The riot helped forge a more confident, assertive black culture in Washington and elsewhere that would flourish even as segregation hardened in the decade to come.[63]

"This Suffering, yet Beautiful Little World of Striving": D.C.'s Assertive Black Culture in the 1920s

Neval Thomas was not a young man in the 1920s, but he certainly was one of the "new Negroes" who frightened Major Cutler. Born in Ohio in 1874, he came to Washington at the turn of the century and worked at the Library of Congress while earning two degrees at Howard. Like Mary Church Terrell, he loved traveling and developed a global perspective on race and democracy that he taught to his history students at Dunbar High School, where he spent nearly three decades. A bachelor who dedicated his life to the struggle for racial equality, he was among the founding members of the D.C. branch of the NAACP and developed a reputation for uncompromising militancy. When Archibald Grimké stepped down as the head of the local branch of the NAACP in 1925, the dapper, determined Thomas was the unanimous choice to be his successor.[64]

Thomas exemplified the assertive spirit that suffused D.C.'s black community in the 1920s. Like many of his black neighbors, he felt a keen sense of pressure to challenge racism in the city. As Howard professor Kelly Miller explained in 1925, "a heavier weight of responsibility rests upon the colored citizens of the national capital to insist in and out of season on the full rights of the race" because "what is done here is taken as a pattern for other communities to copy."

Resisting "racial insult and humiliation" was "a duty that [the black man in D.C.] owes himself, his race and the nation." Throughout the decade, black Washingtonians openly and vigorously challenged the city's resilient racism and built strong community institutions that instilled black pride and undermined the intellectual basis of white supremacy.[65]

In the year or two after the riot, black Washingtonians had reason to be cautiously optimistic about the possibility of racial progress. Local white newspapers, though not apologetic about their role in fomenting the crisis, nonetheless offered more positive coverage of the black community. The city honored black veterans at a December 1919 rally at which a variety of white dignitaries, including former president Theodore Roosevelt, praised their efforts during the war. The presidential election of 1920 also offered a measure of hope, as the despised Woodrow Wilson left office after eight racially tumultuous years. During the campaign, Republican senator Warren Harding of Ohio, who was rumored to have black ancestry, unequivocally endorsed racial equality and insisted that African Americans had "earned the full measure of citizenship bestowed."[66]

But cautious optimism soon gave way to frustration and anger at what the black-run *Washington Tribune* called "the growing Southern sentiment that has pervaded the Capital." The *Tribune*, the local NAACP, and other black organizations vociferously objected as President Harding and subsequent Republican administrations severed the party's historical connection to black voters by solidifying rather than dismantling the Wilson administration's segregationist policies. Harding barely cracked the door of black federal employment, appointing only three African Americans to federal positions in his first year. When Harding's supervisor of public buildings and grounds brazenly blanketed picnic areas in Rock Creek Park with "For White Only" and "For Colored Only" signs on Easter Sunday in 1922, the NAACP mobilized its allies and quickly got the signs removed.[67]

Black voices also condemned the disgraceful treatment of black visitors at the May 1922 dedication of the Lincoln Memorial, a massive, Greek-inspired shrine on reclaimed land at the western edge of the National Mall. In time, the memorial would become a potent symbol of freedom, a marble monument to the egalitarian ideals of the man known as "The Great Emancipator" and the Union that he had preserved. On this brilliant spring day, however, the memorial marked just how far the nation had regressed on race. Event organizers forced black ticket-holders to sit in a segregated area far from the stage. Many angry guests walked out before the event began.[68]

During the dedication itself, the assembled dignitaries studiously avoided Lincoln's legacy of emancipation and instead celebrated the regional reconciliation among whites that had taken place since the Civil War. The day's sole black speaker was Robert Russa Moton, who had succeeded Booker T. Washington as president of Tuskegee Institute. Moton originally drafted an incisive, angry speech highlighting how America had failed to achieve Lincoln's expansive vision of freedom. After Lincoln Memorial Commission censors objected, he delivered a tame paean to the nation's racial progress, a speech that "consisted only of platitudes," lamented the *Washington Tribune*. "He failed to measure up to the opportunity that was his, to truly represent the race." [69]

Neval Thomas compared Moton's timid, acquiescent remarks to the bracing rhetoric of Henry Highland Garnet, whose speech before Congress in April 1865 had urged the United States to "emancipate, educate, enfranchise" black Americans. At the dawn of emancipation, the emboldened Garnet spoke with unbridled moral force in challenging the nation to do right by its black citizens in the promising era to come. After a half-century of racial violence and growing segregation, the chastened Moton could but mouth soothing bromides to salve the consciences of white listeners. Much had changed since Garnet stood before Congress, and not for the better.[70]

The dedication of the Lincoln Memorial took place at a time when the Ku Klux Klan had reemerged as a national political force. Defunct since the 1870s, the Klan was reborn in Georgia in 1915 and quickly grew into a powerful organization with chapters across the nation, including the District. The D.C. chapter, founded in 1921, claimed several hundred members and sought to present a benign image—it even fielded a baseball team. According to the "grand goblin of the Capital Domain," the local Klan chapter was merely a volunteer "auxiliary to the police department." Its newsletter, however, railed against "insolent and presumptuous" black Washingtonians who "feel that once they cross the Potomac and come under the federal government, they may indulge in liberties and even license." Though the local chapter was never very active, the national Klan dramatically displayed its strength when more than thirty thousand Klan members from across the nation paraded along Pennsylvania Avenue in full regalia in 1925 and again in 1926, despite protests from the NAACP as well as local Jewish and Catholic organizations.[71]

The resilience and visibility of segregation in the nation's capital frustrated Neval Thomas and other black Washingtonians. In a 1923 essay for the *Messenger*, a monthly that actively promoted the goals of the New Negro, Thomas articulated the anger that many of his educated black peers felt. "Except for a few years of the Reconstruction, the national capital has been to the Negro a scene of sorrow," Thomas wrote. "The more cultured and ambitious the Negro, the greater is the delight in humiliating him, and in forestalling his progress, and since the World War for democracy the greater is that determination."

And yet, Thomas refused to give in to despair. "The white man keeps the full weight of his superior numbers, oppressive spirit, and unjust monopoly of political power, hard pressed against this suffering, yet beautiful little world of striving, but we grow to fuller stature in spite of it all." Many successful black Washingtonians responded to national insults and local inequality with a defiant sense of pride. "I have not been to a white play house in Washington for more than a quarter century," wrote Kelly Miller in the *Afro-American*. "I know that I have missed much. But some values are better missed than gained at so great a sacrifice of self respect. Manly ignorance is preferable to servile intelligence."[72]

Despite—and in part because of—the strictures of segregation, much of black Washington thrived as the city's economy boomed in the 1920s. Shut out from pursuing opportunities in the larger white society, black entrepreneurs and community leaders channeled their energies into developing self-sufficient neighborhoods and institutions where black enterprise and culture flourished. The locus of D.C.'s middle- and upper-class black culture was U Street. Anchored by Howard University to the east, the U Street corridor stretched for a dozen blocks to Sixteenth Street on the west. The greater U Street area boasted more than three hundred black-owned businesses and organizations, including the Whitelaw Hotel and the Industrial Savings Bank, both established by a remarkable, unschooled black entrepreneur named John Whitelaw Lewis. Home to Howard professors, federal employees, teachers, and other successful black professionals, the area epitomized black striving and economic achievement. It also was known as "black Broadway," featuring numerous theaters and music clubs where native son Edward Kennedy "Duke" Ellington rose to jazz prominence. U Street, one resident remembered, was the place "where you put your finery on."[73]

Black intellectual life flourished along U Street as well. Howard philosophy professor Alain Locke, the first black Rhodes Scholar, was a driving force behind the nationwide cultural movement that came to be known as the "New Negro Renaissance." Though the movement was associated most commonly with Harlem in New York, black Washingtonians played an active role. Locke's *New Negro*, published in 1925, contained works by thirty-five authors, poets, and playwrights, nearly half of whom had lived in or were from Washington. Many were women, including Angelina Grimké, daughter of NAACP head Archibald Grimké, who taught at Armstrong and Dunbar High Schools while writing poetry on the side. Grimké and other black intellectuals gathered on Saturday night at the "S Street Salon" hosted by Georgia Douglas Johnson, a Department of Labor bureaucrat by day and a poet and activist by night. The "Saturday Nighters," along with the Howard Players and a bevy of black literary societies, encouraged a sense of camaraderie among D.C.'s black intellectuals.[74]

The intellectual ferment along U Street challenged prevailing notions about race, class, gender, and sexuality. Novelist Jean Toomer, who had skin so light and hair so straight that he often was mistaken for a white man, even by black neighbors, questioned the very idea of race. The grandson of P. B. S. Pinchback, who served briefly as the first black governor in the nation, Toomer lived in LeDroit Park and was a product of elite black Washington. A graduate of M Street High School and Howard University, he regularly joined the Saturday night gatherings at Georgia Douglas Johnson's house as he worked on what became his breakthrough novel, Cane, published in 1923. He identified as black but chafed at America's rigid racial duality. After Cane won critical acclaim, Toomer rejected being labeled a "great Negro writer" and articulated a vision of racial hybridity that was more than a half-century ahead of its time.[75]

Toomer never "passed" for white, but some light-skinned African Americans did, capitalizing on their fair skin—and white obliviousness to gradations in skin color within the black community—to enjoy the benefits of whiteness. Passing could be a form of subterranean resistance to the culture of white supremacy, an individual challenge to an unjust system of racial categorization. Stories abounded of black Washingtonians who worked in "white" jobs by day, then returned home to their black families and neighborhoods at night. Light-skinned black patrons often took seats in white sections of local theaters, prompting the white owners to hire black "spotters" who could identify and remove black customers seated in the "wrong" section. The cultural fascination with passing—and the threat that such racial fluidity could pose to America's dual racial structure—peaked in the 1920s, as popular literature and even movies explored the topic.[76]

Passing was a risky, fraught phenomenon. It was a strategy accessible only to those with the fairest skin, a group already privileged within black Washington. Though it highlighted the absurdity of Jim Crow and the arbitrariness of racial categorization, passing also challenged black self-identity and undermined the elite black community. Many prominent, mixed-race black Washingtonians of the late nineteenth century—including O. S. B. Wall, Richard Greener, and Blanche K. Bruce—had children or grandchildren who eventually chose to live their lives as white people. Passing may have offered tangible benefits such as access to better jobs, housing, and education, but it also came with a heavy price, as those who "passed" often felt disconnected from their communities and lost their sense of self.[77]

Another "Saturday Nighter," writer Marita Bonner, gave voice to the particular rage percolating within many black women of the New Negro era. A Boston native with a degree from Radcliffe College, Bonner arrived in D.C. in 1924 to teach at Armstrong High School and soon penned an essay that catapulted her to prominence within black intellectual circles: "On Being Young—a Woman—and Colored." Published in the *Crisis* in 1925, the essay explored the depths of Bonner's anger at being "entangled—enmeshed—pinioned in the seaweed of a Black Ghetto." At a time when white flappers were breaking cultural taboos with their short hair, smoking, and frivolity, Bonner offered a serious critique of racism and sexism. "Every part of you becomes bitter," Bonner wrote. "You long to explode and hurt everything white." Black women were expected to sit quietly and simply endure abuse, but Bonner offered a subversive twist. "You must sit quietly . . . [l]ike Buddha—who brown like I am—sat entirely at ease, entirely sure of himself; motionless and knowing. . . . And then you can, when Time is ripe, swoop to your feet—at your full height—at a single gesture."[78]

Bonner, Toomer, and other black intellectuals also challenged the pomposity, materialism, and "smug self-satisfaction" they saw within elite black Washington. Langston Hughes, an aspiring poet who was the grandnephew of Reconstruction-era leader John Mercer Langston, spent a year living with his mother and other relatives in Washington. He came away unimpressed by the stuffy strivers of U Street: "Never before, anywhere, had I seen persons of influence,—men with some money, women with some beauty, teachers with some education,—quite so audibly sure of their own importance and their high places in the community." Just a few blocks away, he found a more vibrant, exciting culture in the working-class communities along Seventh Street NW. "Seventh Street was always teemingly alive with dark working people who hadn't yet acquired 'culture' and the manners of stage ambassadors, and pinks and blacks and yellows were still friends without apologies," Hughes wrote. Disenchanted with the conformity of the city's "cultured" class, Hughes, Toomer, and other black thinkers fled the city for Harlem.[79]

Divisions of class, color, and culture undermined the short-lived sense of shared purpose among black Washingtonians that marked the 1919 riot. Even as black pride surged with the New Negro movement, elite black Washingtonians took pains to distinguish themselves from the working class, and light skin remained a marker of social status. Wealthier black Washingtonians attended different schools—usually the college preparatory Dunbar High School, rather than Armstrong, which focused on industrial training. They prayed at different churches—refined congregations such as Fifteenth Street Presbyterian rather than the boisterous Baptists. And they resided in different areas—LeDroit Park and U Street, rather than Southwest, Seventh Street, or in alleys (even in 1925, more than 10 percent of the black population lived in alleys).[80]

Refined and sober in their tastes, members of the black middle class and elite looked with disdain on what they perceived as the exuberant religiosity and frivolous spending habits of lower-class black Washingtonians. "There was as much prejudice between blacks themselves as there was between blacks and whites," recalled Edward Feggans, a dark-skinned, middle-class black resident. "If you were light and bright, and almost white, you could fit into the social realm of the city without meeting the economic criteria." Anna Murray, an elderly, light-skinned black woman, acknowledged such discrimination to an interviewer, explaining, "I think most of us do it in order to protect our children" from the negative influences of the lower class. "The social breach between the masses and the classes of Negroes in Washington is more pronounced than in any other city of the country," Howard's Kelly Miller claimed.[81]

The lower-income black community that many elites scorned also flourished in the 1920s. It grew significantly as Southern migration to Washington increased during the decade. By 1930, the city was more than 27 percent black, and the vast majority of black residents were poor or working class. Many migrants were women who came not to pursue their own dreams but instead to fulfill family obligations. They boarded with their kin and took over household responsibilities—caring for children and the elderly, cooking and cleaning, taking in laundry—to allow other family members to work outside the home. Over time, they, too, found paid work, often as servants in the homes of white families. The newcomers struggled with homesickness, relentless work schedules, and occasional condescension from native black Washingtonians, and they felt significant financial pressure to support their families back home. "Once you started work you knew people in Tennessee was dependin' on those pennies you earned," recalled domestic worker Dolethia Otis. "You dared not quit!"[82]

Despite the pressures of work and family, black domestic workers asserted themselves to preserve their dignity and protect their interests. They used their records of "faithful service" to push their white employers for greater benefits, such as annual visits back to their Southern homes, and they seized opportunities to catch a show at Howard Theater or a club on Seventh Street. They scrimped and saved to escape "live-in" work, where they resided in the home of their employer, donned starchy uniforms that made them feel servile, and were isolated from their community and church. Despite the economic security of such work, they yearned for the autonomy of "live-out" work, which gave them more flexible working hours and a chance to live on their own.[83]

Working-class migrants built critical community institutions to help themselves survive and thrive in their new home. Often through local churches with ties to communities across the South, they formed "pennysavers clubs" that offered microloans and gifts to help members in need; they established "home groups" and sponsored dinners for newcomers; and they maintained their Southern cultural and culinary traditions. "Having family and church and being around people from home," recalled domestic worker Fannie King, "that's what helped you get set and straightened out, and let you [give] help . . . to others." Many of the community institutions founded to help migrants adjust to city life during this era, including the Georgetown Club of South Carolina, endured into the twenty-first century.[84]

"Drive the Colored Folk out of Washington": Restrictive Covenants and the Push for Segregated Neighborhoods

No matter their social or economic class, black Washingtonians struggled to find decent housing. Shut out from new suburban housing developments, black residents in the 1920s increasingly sought homes in older, predominantly white neighborhoods, often along trade and transportation routes such as U Street, Eleventh Street, Georgia Avenue, and Florida Avenue in Northwest. What followed was an uneven, tense, and often confrontational process of neighborhood transition that would be repeated across the city in the decades to come.

In a seminal 1929 study commissioned by the Washington Interracial Council, Howard University sociologist William Henry Jones analyzed how neighborhoods shifted from "white" to "black." At the root of neighborhood change, Jones argued, was the reluctance of wealthy white people to live in racially integrated areas. "White people with considerable social and economic status—the class that is capable of maintaining racial solidarity of the community by prejudice and public opinion—do not prefer to live in culturally heterogeneous communities," he wrote. Once black people began moving into predominantly white areas, white residents with means took advantage of improving transportation to move farther from downtown, into Chevy Chase, Takoma Park, or other segregated suburbs. Their departure signaled to their less privileged white neighbors that the neighborhood was in "decline."

Conditioned by real estate agents, developers, and policy makers with an interest in preserving segregated neighborhoods, many white residents assumed that black neighbors would bring crime and blight, thereby depreciating property values. In a survey of white attitudes, Jones found that white people left racially changing neighborhoods for a variety of reasons, including the sense that black people were "too gregarious" and would be "bad for the community." A handful believed that blacks were inferior, though an almost equal number worried that they might "grow to like the Negroes." By far the most common and powerful explanation for leaving was social pressure, "the fear of public opinion and the attitudes of other whites." They left their homes primarily because they thought their white neighbors would think less of them if they didn't. Those who remained in the increasingly black neighborhoods tended to be poor, elderly, and foreign-born.[85]

Some white residents, however, refused to move. Instead, they hoped to stem the tide of black encroachment by enforcing racial solidarity through racial restrictive covenants that were written into housing deeds. Enforced by the courts, these covenants were private contracts in which white property holders agreed to restrict the sale, rent, or transfer of their properties to racial and religious minorities. Racial restrictions on housing had existed in Washington since 1854, when the city's first suburb, Uniontown (located across the Anacostia River from the Navy Yard), was developed exclusively for white residents. But restrictive covenants proliferated in the wake of a 1917 Supreme Court decision that prohibited state and local governments from mandating segregation through zoning ordinances but did not address exclusionary agreements among private individuals. As the black population in D.C. and other cities grew and spilled over into traditionally white areas in the 1920s, more and more white residents turned to racial restrictive covenants as a tool to protect the racial character of their neighborhoods. These covenants not only barred black residents but also often specifically excluded Jews, Arabs, "Persians," and other groups.[86]

Restrictive covenants raised many legal questions, and the test case on their constitutionality arose in D.C., triggered by a black Washingtonian named Helen Curtis. The wife of a well-known black ophthalmologist, Curtis had the resources to buy a home anywhere in the city. Like many other black homebuyers, she looked at homes in white neighborhoods because they tended to be more modern and in better condition. She hired a white real estate agent— otherwise, she likely would have been shown only homes in well-defined black areas—and chose a well-kept, three-story row house at 1727 S Street NW, about equidistant between the fashionable white areas near Dupont Circle and the burgeoning black cultural mecca of U Street.[87]

Curtis was hardly alone. For years, black homeowners had been moving steadily westward along S Street, and by 1920 few white families remained on the 1400 and 1500 blocks. West of Sixteenth Street, however, S Street remained predominantly (though not exclusively) white—and a determined group of thirty white homeowners on the 1700 block sought to keep it that way. The group, which included lawyers, government officials, and businessmen, signed a pact pledging that they would never let their properties "be used or occupied by, or sold conveyed, leased, rented, or given to Negroes or any person or persons of the Negro race or blood." Filed in August 1921 and solidified by a $5 fee, the agreement was intended to remain in force for twenty-one years.[88]

Just a few months later, however, the covenant was broken when one of the signers, Irene Hand Corrigan, accepted Helen Curtis's offer to buy her home. Confronted by her angry white neighbors, Corrigan claimed that she did not know that Curtis was black and tried to renege on the deal. Curtis pressed forward with the sale; Corrigan, desperate to sell the property, complied. A white neighbor and a cosigner of the covenant, Jack Buckley, sued Corrigan for violating the covenant. Another neighbor and cosigner, James S. Easby Smith, became lead attorney in the case.

The trial court and the D.C. Court of Appeals supported Buckley and upheld the constitutionality of restrictive covenants, citing the city's widespread use of segregation laws as precedents. Backed by a coalition of local black groups, NAACP lawyers appealed to the U.S. Supreme Court, arguing that restrictive covenants would "drive colored folk out of Washington." But the Court refused to hear the case, declaring in *Corrigan v. Buckley* (1926) that it lacked jurisdiction to intervene because the restrictive covenant was a valid contract among private individuals.[89]

This devastating precedent gave white homeowners legal sanction to bar black buyers from their neighborhoods. Restrictive covenants flourished in D.C. and throughout the nation in the decades that followed. In Washington, citizens associations took the lead in organizing homeowners to sign covenants on their property. In the months after the decision, the North Capitol Citizens Association, which represented the Bloomingdale area, convinced nearly all neighborhood homeowners to sign covenants. Prospective black home buyers were threatened with lawsuits, and if a covenant was broken the association assumed the expenses of the ensuing legal challenge. The Mount Pleasant Citizens Association created a committee devoted to restrictive covenants and hired a full-time worker to gather signatures and monitor property sales in the area. Within three years, covenants covered about 90 percent of the neighborhood. Mount Pleasant remained virtually all white until after World War II.[90]

Ironically, however, the restrictive covenant that sought to keep the 1700 block of S Street segregated proved ineffective. Though Curtis and her husband eventually gave up on the S Street property (they bought a place a few blocks away), other black people moved in elsewhere on the block. A few months after the initial hubbub erupted over Curtis, Howard administrator Emmett Jay Scott purchased a home just three doors down. Infuriated white neighbors quickly sought an injunction against allowing him to move in, but the wily Scott surreptitiously moved his furniture in under the cover of darkness and promptly ensconced himself in the property, thereby establishing a fait accompli that could not be undone. As the Curtis case wound its way through the courts, Scott remained on the block and other black residents followed. White people, including Jack Buckley, the instigator of the case, moved away. By the time the Supreme Court ruled on the case in 1926, the block was mostly black.[91]

What happened to the 1700 block of S Street confirmed the fears of many white Washingtonians who worried that once the wall of segregation was breached, there would be no stopping a rising tide of black people. They foresaw for the entire city what happened in LeDroit Park, which in one generation had turned from an exclusive enclave for wealthy white residents into an all-black neighborhood.

But the reality of life in Washington was never quite as clear-cut as a "wall" metaphor suggests. Segregation in Washington was uneven and quirky, a confusing array of unwritten customs rather than formal laws. Black people could sit on streetcars, read in the public library, and watch the Washington Senators play at Griffith Stadium, but they could not go to concerts, sit next to white people at the movies, or watch the Fourth of July fireworks from the Capitol steps. Black shoppers could shop at Garfinckel's and other department stores downtown, but they could not try anything on. Black people lived all over the city, and even in supposedly "white" or "black" neighborhoods, white and black families lived side by side or on the same block, often for many years. Even U Street, the signature street of black Washington, included white-run cafés, ice cream parlors, and stores that operated on a segregated basis. The "rules" were never fixed and were constantly challenged and redefined.[92]

Within segregation, interracial relationships could and did develop, particularly in low-income areas where white immigrants lived alongside black neighbors. Though many immigrants quickly absorbed the larger culture's racist view of African Americans, their poverty and physical proximity meant that they had far more regular and relatively egalitarian interaction with black people than their higher-income peers. They also shared a sense of being outsiders. In the context of early twentieth-century racial classification, Jewish, Greek, and other eastern European immigrants were not considered fully "white" and experienced racial and religious discrimination. In the small Greek community that developed around Saint Sophia Greek Orthodox Church at Eighth and L Streets NW, Greek business owners employed black workers and served black customers in "Mavriko" (black) restaurants that were open to black and Greek patrons alike.[93]

Southwest Washington was an area where segregation particularly struggled to take root. In the 1920s, much of Southwest remained a land of low rents, dilapidated housing, and outdoor plumbing, a world away from the stately row houses of U Street or the comfortable country manors of Chevy Chase. Four-and-a-Half Street was the major commercial thoroughfare, running north from Greenleaf Point all the way to B Street (now Constitution Avenue) on the Mall. The area, one observer wrote, had "a reputation of being one of the toughest sections of the city," and was home to three distinct communities that clustered in different sections—black residents generally to the east of Four-and-a-Half Street, native-born white residents to the west, and Jewish immigrants in between.[94]

Within each group residents re-created the communal institutions and kinship networks that had sustained their people in the far-flung areas from which they originated. Native-born white residents were often the children or grandchildren of Irish, German, and English immigrants, and they lived in tightly knit neighborhoods that resembled the small towns of the old country. Jews built two synagogues in Southwest and created a family and community-oriented life reminiscent of an eastern European shtetl. African Americans lived in a communal culture of extended family and church that harked back to their roots in the rural South.

Though there may have been little social interaction among the three groups, there was no strict segregation, and many blocks had a multicultural mix. U Street was considered "black" and Connecticut Avenue was "white," but Four-and-a-Half Street was both as Jewish, German, and Irish shopkeepers developed long-term relationships with their black customers, and black businesses catered to an integrated clientele. United by class, Southwest residents shared many common experiences and developed interracial relationships that were increasingly rare in the more prosperous areas in the north of the city.[95]

The personal relationships that individual Jews or Greeks developed with their black neighbors did not counterbalance the pervasive system of segregation that relegated black Washingtonians to second-class citizenship. Though never as rigid as many white Washingtonians might have hoped, segregation proved remarkably effective at undermining black progress and stifling black ambition in the early decades of the twentieth century. Democrat Woodrow Wilson institutionalized racial subordination within the federal government, a policy solidified during a decade of Republican control of Congress and the White House in the 1920s. Racial violence targeting D.C.'s black community, highly visible demonstrations of white power at the Lincoln Memorial and in Klan parades along Pennsylvania Avenue, and the spread of racial restrictive covenants all revealed the strength and resilience of white supremacy in the nation's capital.

And yet, despite the suffocating climate of segregation, black Washingtonians built self-sustaining neighborhoods and community institutions that affirmed black self-worth, cultivated black pride, and challenged the culture of white supremacy. Black self-assertion—by middle-class NAACP members fighting segregation in the federal bureaucracy; by cooks demanding higher wages during the war; by veterans insisting that their military service entitled them to full citizenship; by residents posting themselves on rooftops to protect their neighborhoods from white mobs; by intellectuals challenging hierarchical ideas about race and class; by domestic workers carving out their own niche within a harsh work environment—defended black dignity in a city that black residents claimed as their own. For all its flaws, wrote Kelly Miller in 1926, "Washington is still the Negroes' Heaven," and black residents refused to relinquish control of it.[96]

NINE

Washington Is a Giant Awakened

Community Organizing in a Booming City, 1932–1945

The Negro of Washington has no voice in government, is economically proscribed, and segregated nearly as rigidly as in the southern cities he contemns. He may blind himself with pleasure seeking, with a specious self-sufficiency, he may point with pride to the record of achievement over grave odds. But just as the past was not without its honor, so the present is not without bitterness.
—STERLING A. BROWN, Works Progress Administration's 1937 *Guide to Washington*

Langston Terrace Dwellings is a public housing project with architecture re-markable enough to earn a spot on the National Register of Historic Places. Located near the intersection of Benning Road and Twenty-First Street NE, the project became known as "Little Vietnam" for its drug-related violence in the late twentieth century. In 2001, the D.C. Preservation League listed Langston Terrace Dwellings as one of the city's ten "most endangered sites," and residents today continue to struggle with violence and drugs.[1]

When it opened in 1938, however, Langston Terrace embodied the optimism of the New Deal. Named for black Reconstruction-era hero John Mercer Langs-ton, the 274-unit complex was the first federally funded public housing project in the city (and second in the nation). It was a model of federal-local collabora-tion, with funding provided by the federal Public Works Administration (PWA) and implementation in the hands of the Washington Committee on Housing, a coalition of local housing groups. Intended for black renters, the project em-ployed black laborers, skilled tradesmen, and construction engineers. The prin-cipal architect was Hilyard Robinson, a native black Washingtonian, graduate of M Street High School, and World War I veteran who took leave from Howard University to design the project.[2]

Robinson and his team created a modern, neighborly landscape with large swaths of open space, accessible playgrounds, and celebratory sculptures sprinkled throughout the thirteen-acre campus. Adorning the buildings of the central courtyard was *The Progress of the Negro Race*, a *terra cotta* frieze by sculptor

Daniel Olney portraying inspirational scenes of African Americans on their historical journey from slavery to freedom. Designed in the International Style, the utopian community promised spacious units with central heating and electricity at below-market rates, a place "where a family of moderate means can live in modern comfort," claimed the *Afro-American*. With a government-subsidized rent of $6 a month (including utilities), "private enterprise cannot even hope to compete," the *Star* wrote.[3]

Langston Terrace attracted more than 2,700 inquiries from interested black renters, most of them working people with modest incomes who sought a way out of deteriorating neighborhoods. PWA officials screened applicants in search of model citizens who would ensure the success of the project. Competition for spots in the complex was fierce. One hopeful even included a letter of recommendation from First Lady Eleanor Roosevelt—and was rejected. Applicants stressed their wholesome respectability and their desire to lead a better life. "We are very anxious to get settled in a nice home in a decent neighborhood where we can bring up our child successfully and make desirable friends," wrote applicant Myrtle Middleton. After its opening in 1938, Langston Terrace won plaudits from observers and residents alike as "one of the most attractive low-cost housing projects of the federal government."[4]

Langston Terrace is an enduring legacy of the Great Depression in Washington. Contrary to some observers' notions that D.C. was "depression-proof," Washingtonians suffered along with the rest of the nation. More than 18 percent of the city's residents were on emergency relief, compared to 10 percent in New York and 12.5 percent in Baltimore. Panhandlers dotted city streets—"even outside the gates of the White House they ply their trade," wrote one reporter. Federal workers also felt squeezed as Congress slashed civil service salaries by more than 8 percent in 1932 and another 15 percent the next year.[5]

The Depression hit the black community particularly hard. More than 75 percent of the city's unemployed were black, and more than half of the city's 132,000 black residents received federal relief. Domestic workers, the vast majority of whom were black women, saw their wages drop from $40–$50 to $30–$35 a month. Washington had the nation's worst black infant mortality rate, with more than 115 black children under age one dying for every 1,000 live births. "Transient camps" sprang up across the city, housing hundreds of homeless black people in squalid conditions reminiscent of Civil War–era "contraband" camps. Even in the middle-class black community of LeDroit Park, homeowners struggling to make ends meet converted their Victorian homes into apartments. "I detect an air of dank and crumbling decay" in the once-glamorous neighborhood, lamented a *Washington Tribune* reporter.[6]

Washington became the site of national protests as the unemployed sought to make their voices heard. In early June 1932, a ragged but resolute band of World War I veterans, black and white, converged on Washington to demand an early distribution of a promised federal payment (dubbed a "bonus"). The destitute "Bonus Army" swelled to nearly 20,000 and established a massive, interracial tent colony on the Anacostia Flats within sight of the Capitol, as well as more than two dozen smaller camps throughout the city. After the Senate killed the bonus bill, about 6,000 veterans remained in D.C. for more than a month and a half, living in deteriorating conditions before President Herbert Hoover ordered the group's removal in late July. More than 500 soldiers led by General Douglas MacArthur (and assisted by Major Dwight D. Eisenhower) used tanks, tear gas, and armed battalions to clear the camps and burn them down.[7]

Hoover's rough treatment of the Bonus Army helped propel New York's Democratic governor Franklin Roosevelt to the White House in 1932. With a winsome smile and unflagging optimism, the charismatic Roosevelt campaigned on a promise to cut federal spending and balance the budget. On taking office, however, he launched the New Deal, an unprecedented peacetime expansion of federal power in which the government embraced a much larger role in the American economy. The federal bureaucracy blossomed with dozens of new federal agencies. Between 1933 and 1935, the number of federal workers in Washington jumped from 63,000 to 93,000; by 1940, it reached 166,000. While other urban areas contracted, D.C. grew by more than a third, topping 663,000 people by 1940—larger than twelve states. Much of the increase came from the city's black population, which grew by more than 40 percent during the 1930s.[8]

The capital thrived with new people and new energy. "The New Deal has made the capital a boom town," wrote journalist David Cohn in the *Atlantic*. Massive public works projects run by the Works Progress Administration employed thousands of workers and altered the city's downtown landscape as a host of new federal buildings appeared, including the Supreme Court building, the Federal Trade Commission building, and the enormous Department of Agriculture headquarters.[9]

As the city boomed during the New Deal and World War II, a new generation of black activists and their allies arose to challenge Jim Crow, find decent housing, and fight for economic survival. "The Negro," wrote NAACP attorney Charles Hamilton Houston, "sought to occupy his rightful place as an American citizen without adjective, hyphen or qualification." They used new forms of protest, including boycotts, union organizing, and sit-ins, and they formed interracial alliances with a growing number of white people, in Washington and around the country, who saw racial inequality in the nation's capital as a stain on America's reputation. "Washington today is the center of the new push for Negro equality," wrote a *New York Times* reporter in 1943, "a sort of laboratory in which some of the specific means for advancing the Negro are being tried." This experimentation produced mixed results at the time, but the community activism and interracial organizing of the 1930s and 1940s helped lay the foundation for the postwar civil rights movement.[10]

"A Public Danger and a Nuisance": Alley Clearance and the Push for Affordable Low-Income Housing

John Ihlder considered himself an ally of the black community. Born aboard a German ship anchored in Baltimore in 1876, Ihlder was a proud descendant of abolitionists and came of age at the height of the Progressive era. After graduating from Cornell, he began his career as a reporter in the mold of muckraker Jacob Riis. Drawn to the housing issues that he covered, he left journalism to become a housing activist, though he retained a reporter's zeal for conflict and controversy.[11]

Ihlder moved to Washington in 1920 to work at the U.S. Chamber of Commerce. After a brief stint in Pittsburgh, he returned in 1933 to help establish the Washington Housing Association, an organization devoted to developing low-income housing. By that time, the lifelong Progressive Republican had come to believe that private housing initiatives alone could not meet the desperate needs of the poor, and he looked to incoming Democratic president Franklin Roosevelt to bring public resources to his life's work. With almond-shaped blue eyes and an impish smirk, the combative but optimistic Ihlder became the face of housing reform in Washington for the next two decades.[12]

Ihlder represented a new spirit of reform in Washington in the 1930s as middle- and upper-class reformers created interracial social service organizations to address public problems. They established a local Community Chest, which organized charitable giving. By 1931, it was raising more than $2 million annually to distribute to local organizations. Like Ihlder, Community Chest head Elwood Street believed that any social service work should embrace the entire city, and before he took the job he insisted that the organization's efforts include outreach to the black community. With black Howard professor Kelly Miller serving as vice president, the Community Chest funded a variety of groups that worked exclusively in black neighborhoods, including settlement houses with biracial governing boards.[13]

Housing was perhaps the city's most intractable problem, an issue that intertwined race, poverty, and the city's political impotence. Newcomers and longtime residents alike struggled to find decent housing in a city with high rents and few vacancies. Entire swaths of residential development—an arc beginning along the Potomac in Georgetown and extending across the northern tier of the city through Tennallytown, Chevy Chase, Takoma Park, and Brookland—were essentially off-limits to black residents. Even in black neighborhoods, black renters had to pay higher rents than their white counterparts. Incomes fell during the Depression, but rents remained high because of strong demand, often consuming well more than half a family's income. Forced to find housing wherever they could, many newcomers crowded into alley dwellings and boarded with kin, placing ever-increasing strains on neighborhoods, schools, and social services. One survey of an area along North Capitol Street found that most homes had "leaky roofs, warped floors, broken windows, [and] doors which wouldn't close." A "large percentage of the buildings . . . were old, dilapidated, and in such a state of disrepair, in many cases, as to be almost unfit for human habitation."[14]

For John Ihlder and other housing reformers, the persistence of alley dwellings was particularly galling. Two decades after the passage of the Alley Dwelling Act of 1914, the resilient alley communities remained, growing ever more impoverished and segregated. Many middle-class housing reformers linked material shortcomings with moral deficiency. "The alleys represent the poorest and least resourceful sections of Washington and foster a large percentage of its crime, poverty, disease, immorality, and high rate of infant mortality," wrote black sociologist William Henry Jones in a 1929 study. Alleys, Jones continued, were "the nuclei of a certain retrograde kind of Negro culture" and had become "the habitats of a class of people who are unable, or who do not wish, to measure up to white cultural standards." Jones's emphasis on the cultural deficiencies of the black lower class—so jarring to modern ears—underlay much of the reform efforts in the 1930s. Housing reformers believed fervently that, in Ihlder's words, "with dwellings of a different type, the character of the people will be altered."[15]

Jones's study helped to reignite the fight to end alley housing. Shortly after it was published, Ihlder called for a new federal ban on alley dwellings, and during the next several years the effort gained support from civic organizations, city planners, and newspaper editors. The New Deal accelerated the movement. Eleanor Roosevelt, though she declined to participate in the first lady ritual of touring Washington slums, encouraged housing reformers to push for a new bill. Written largely by Ihlder himself, the Alley Dwelling Act passed in 1934.[16]

The act promised to transform low-income housing in the city. It aimed not only to eliminate alley housing but also to fund public homes for former alley

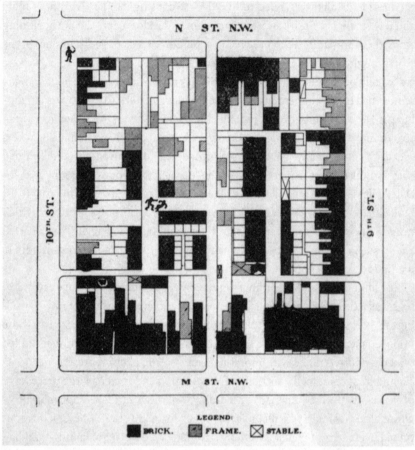

N ST. N.W.

10ᵀᴴ ST.

9ᵀᴴ ST.

M ST. N.W.

LEGEND:
BRICK.   FRAME.   STABLE.

"The Blind Alley of Washington, D.C." Housing reformers sought to eradicate alley communities, which they considered to be breeding grounds of vice and immorality. Despite decades of reform efforts beginning in the 1890s, alley communities remained a distinctive part of D.C.'s urban landscape through the mid-twentieth century. Monday Evening Club, Directory of Inhabited Alleys of Washington, D.C.

residents—a radical departure for the federal government, which (apart from temporary World War I–era efforts to build dorms for war workers) had never ventured into the housing market. The bill created the Alley Dwelling Authority (ADA), a federal agency that had the local power to condemn structures, remove tenants, and build new units. Congress appointed Ihlder to head the new agency. Though Congress gave the ADA only $500,000 in funding—the original bill had asked for $3 million—the ever-ebullient Ihlder confidently believed that the agency would meet its ambitious goal of eliminating all of D.C.'s alley housing in just ten years.[17]

The goal of clearing alleys had widespread appeal, but there was no consensus about what to do with alley residents once the slums were demolished. For Ihlder and other reformers, the answer was public housing. Noting that private industry had failed to meet the demands of low-income residents, Ihlder argued that the ADA should embrace an expansive agenda of housing construction. He refused to demolish any homes until alternative housing could be secured for displaced residents, and he pushed Congress—ultimately, without success—to appropriate sufficient money to provide public housing for all former alley residents.[18]

But public housing was exceedingly controversial in an increasingly segregated city. The ADA's 1937 plan to replace a notorious alley in the Foggy Bottom neighborhood in Northwest, for example, generated significant opposition. The ADA leveled more than ninety alley homes and built a modern two-story, twenty-four-unit apartment complex in St. Mary's Court on Twenty-Fourth Street. Ihlder and the ADA originally planned for black residents to occupy the new homes, but white developers and residents objected. "Negro occupancy would hinder development," they complained. "Opening of the new apartments to colored tenants will tend to make permanent the Negro population" in the area and would lead, they feared, to decreased property values and a white exodus to other neighborhoods. Black residents from the Lincoln Civic Association countered with protests of their own, enlisting support from citywide white organizations such as the Washington Housing Association. Their protests helped convince the ADA to allow black residents to occupy the new apartments.[19]

Ihlder's commitment to public housing and his sincere efforts to rehouse displaced residents drew withering criticism in Congress, particularly from Southern members of the District committees in the House and Senate. Long among the least desirable assignments for a member of Congress, the District committees became, by the 1930s, a haven for Southern segregationists concerned about creeping integration in the nation's capital. Coming from the one-party South where black voters were disfranchised, these Democrats were a key part of the New Deal coalition, and they used their positions to derail reforms that they feared would undermine segregation in Washington.

The chairman of the House Subcommittee on District Appropriations was Ross Collins, a Mississippi lawyer who lavished money on military weaponry but choked off funds for reform efforts in the District. After the Community Chest released an exposé of Washington slums titled "First City—Worst City," city officials called on Congress to spend $3.2 million on programs to help the poor. Collins coolly trimmed it to $900,000. When Elwood Street, then in charge of the city's Department of Public Welfare, asked him to increase funding for poor black girls at Nannie Helen Burroughs's National Training School for Girls, Collins refused. "My constituents wouldn't stand for spending all that money on niggers," he explained. Congressional opposition ensured that housing reformers never had enough money to achieve Ihlder's goal of housing displaced residents in public units.[20]

The ADA also provoked opposition from private homebuilders and business groups, which charged that "socialistic" government interference in the housing market created unfair competition with private interests. Determined to prove that market forces could better address the city's housing crisis, private companies such as the Washington Sanitary Improvement Company and the Washington Sanitary Housing Company undertook new low-income housing projects. Unwilling to assume the financial risk of renting to less desirable tenants, these private housing companies instead focused on low-income white people and what they called "colored tenants of the better class." With significant fanfare, the two companies built 1,034 units for low-income residents between 1934 and 1939. In a city where tens of thousands of low-income residents needed housing, the inability of private housing developers to meet demand only underscored the magnitude of the problem.[21]

The ADA attracted critics within the black community as well. Too often, the black people whose lives were most affected by housing reforms were left out of policy-making decisions. The black community's views on alley clearance were not monolithic—many middle-class black leaders considered alleys embarrassing and harmful to the fight for racial equality, whereas alley residents themselves often defended the close-knit communities in which they lived. Yet there was a universal fear that the elimination of alleys would lead to displacement.

Few black Washingtonians had faith that white housing reformers had their best interests at heart. Ihlder may have been committed to finding decent homes for former alley residents, but other city planners wanted to convert alleys into usable space for commercial development. Ulysses S. Grant III, grandson of the former president and head of the National Capital Parks and Planning Commission, considered alleys "a public danger and a nuisance." He envisioned one alley near Union Station being replaced with "tea gardens catering to the guests of [nearby] hotels, and garage space for their cars." Despite Ihlder's promises, Grant's ideas were closer to reality. As the *Star* reported in late 1937, most ADA alley clearance projects did not result in new homes for displaced residents. Instead officials generally used the land for parks or garages.[22]

One persistent thorn in the ADA's side was Lincoln Civic Association head Edward Harris, who had helped preserve St. Mary's Court for black residents. Harris gave voice to growing concerns about displacement resulting from alley clearance efforts. For several years after the St. Mary's Court fight, he challenged Ihlder and the ADA to live up to their promises. Slum clearance, Harris insisted, should not involve "routing, colonizing, and depriving Negro people of homes." He and his allies accused the ADA of having "disregarded human habitation by removing dwellings, scattering and not rehousing former tenants," and undermining "the faith and confidence of colored citizens."[23]

Harris also worried about displacement caused by federal development because the government was gobbling up residential neighborhoods as part of its New Deal expansion. In Harris's Foggy Bottom neighborhood, the government planned to build new headquarters for the War and Navy Departments, displacing three hundred families. City projects had similarly disruptive effects on low-income and minority communities. In 1929, city commissioners uprooted the District's largest concentration of Chinese residents to build a new municipal center, only to abandon the project and transform the area into a park when tax receipts shriveled and Congress cut the federal contribution. Despite objections from the white business community, roughly six hundred Chinese residents moved to H Street NW, between Sixth and Seventh Streets, where they established what is known in the twenty-first century as Chinatown (see Chapter 14).[24]

In public meetings, congressional testimony, and letters to Franklin and Eleanor Roosevelt, Harris consistently pointed out the uncomfortable truth that the ADA never had either enough money or power to build public housing units on the scale necessary to meet the challenge of displacement. Such concerns only grew as black residents—stymied by restrictive covenants, pressured by local white leadership and government officials, and discouraged by lending institutions—slowly abandoned long-standing communities in Fort Reno, Georgetown, and other now predominantly white areas.[25]

"We Will Condemn Your Property": Fort Reno, Georgetown, and the Disappearance of Black Communities

Fort Reno in upper Northwest offered a prime example of how federally supported local development displaced poor people and exacerbated the city's housing problem. Built by Union troops during the Civil War, Fort Reno attracted "contrabands" who formed the nucleus of a small but thriving postwar black community. Enveloped within the sparsely inhabited, mostly white area of Tennallytown, Reno's black residents lived far from the crowded alleys and enjoyed abundant open space, land for vegetables and chickens, and a bustling school. Elite Washingtonians long considered the area too hilly and remote from downtown, but white developers in the early twentieth century, inspired by the successful development of Chevy Chase, Takoma Park, and other remote suburbs, coveted Tennallytown for its hilltop views and "country air."[26]

As farmland turned into single-family homes, white developers and compliant local officials eyed the land around Fort Reno, envisioning parks and schools for white children to increase property values. The only obstacle was Reno's black community. So white developers, with support from local and federal officials, began an effort to purge black residents. First, they bought up land adjacent to the fort "for the purpose of preventing further building for colored occupancy," developer Harold E. Doyle explained years later. The next step was to dislodge the longtime landowners. Although the Chevy Chase Land Company "tried every way possible to get these colored out," according to one white observer, black homeowners refused to sell. The real estate companies and local citizens associations then pressured the federal government to purchase the property through the newly created National Capital Parks and Planning Commission.[27]

The commission exercised the power of eminent domain and offered minimal compensation to landowners as it bought land around Reno to build Alice Deal Junior High School (opened in 1930) and Woodrow Wilson High School (opened in 1935). The two schools today sit within a forty-five-acre gem of greenery in a neighborhood studded with million-dollar homes. "It was a matter of offering little, what was a little bit of money" for their property, recalled Mary Daniel, a black resident of Reno. "Either that or we will condemn your property." Developers razed dozens of homes and three churches during the removal process, ripping the social fabric of Fort Reno's black community irreparably. By 1940, few black families remained in the area. Forced to abandon the only homes that they had known, the uprooted families, some of whom had lived in Reno for more than half a century, sought rental housing elsewhere, often in areas where they had no family ties or connection to their neighbors.[28]

What happened in Fort Reno was not an isolated experience. It was part of a larger pattern of displacement that took root in the 1920s and flourished as housing segregation solidified in the 1930s and 1940s. A similar result happened in Georgetown, where local development combined with private neighborhood "revitalization" efforts to put significant pressure on low-income residents to leave areas in which they had lived for decades.

By the early twentieth century, Georgetown was in decline. The silting of the Potomac had ruined the port. The C&O Canal, never the economic engine that its boosters had promised, closed for good in 1924 following a devastating flood. Grimy dwellings and crumbling buildings pockmarked the area. Beginning in the 1920s, a group of white residents—led by John Ihlder, who lived at 2811 P Street—started an influential Home Owners Committee of the Citizens Association of Georgetown that launched a rehabilitation effort to restore the neighborhood's Federal-style homes. Ambitious white residents, sometimes with speculative interests, refurbished old homes, created a historical society, and placed revitalization at the top of their agendas.[29]

During the 1930s, Georgetown became a hip locale for young New Dealers and members of the federal elite. By the 1940s, one observer noted, Georgetown had become "a quaint, historic, desirable place for white people to live." The low-income, mostly black residents who clustered south of the C&O Canal between the Potomac and Rock Creek could not afford to rehabilitate their dilapidated homes or pay the rapidly rising rents, and they were denied loans from local lending institutions. Over time they fled to other parts of the city. In the twenty-first century, Georgetown remains one of Washington's whitest and wealthiest areas.[30]

Housing developments, whether public or private, tended to displace low-income residents and exacerbate residential segregation because they were built within a larger context of codified segregation that was growing stronger. By the 1930s, racial restrictive covenants were the norm in white communities across the city and increasingly in the surrounding suburbs of Montgomery County, Maryland, and Fairfax and Arlington Counties, Virginia, where long-standing rural black communities slowly receded in the face of white in-migration. As neighborhoods such as Tennallytown–Fort Reno, Georgetown, and Foggy Bottom became wealthier and whiter, black residents were hemmed in to areas where they already predominated, even as thousands of Southern migrants continued to arrive. With fewer and fewer outlets for the black population, black neighborhoods grew increasingly poor and crowded. Washington took on the pattern that would characterize it for the rest of the twentieth century: an increasingly poor, black inner city ringed by almost exclusively white neighborhoods and suburbs.[31]

Middle-class white reformers of the 1930s, though sincerely committed to ameliorating the horrible living conditions of the District's poor, generally did not address the city's fundamental racial or economic inequalities. They did not fight restrictive covenants, push for integrated public housing developments, or work to end segregation in the government and unions. Instead, they found ways to work within the system of segregation rather than challenge it, often tolerating or even encouraging practices that many black Washingtonians found unacceptable.

At the ADA, Ihlder hired a black housing assistant, Charles Flagg, but he sometimes scheduled ADA staff retreats at segregated venues and simply did not allow Flagg to attend. Community Chest director Elwood Street hired no black employees and regularly held events in segregated facilities. "There are too many difficulties that would arise" if black employees were hired, explained a white official who served on the organization's budget committee in the late 1930s. "The niggers [do] not measure up to the whites," he went on. "They are dull and lack intelligence."[32]

With such attitudes ingrained in many white elites, it would have been exceedingly difficult for Ihlder, Street, or other white reformers to challenge segregation even if they had been so inclined. Their success at raising money to build low-income housing, provide recreational opportunities, or otherwise improve living conditions for the black poor rested on their ability to convince people with money—wealthy Washingtonians and District Committee members in Congress—that their reforms were reasonable but not radical. They had to assure their financial masters that their efforts would not upset the segregated balance of life. Hence, the ADA refused to support housing projects that defied the predominant racial demographics.

Ihlder believed that he was doing as much as he could in a frustrating and constrained political context, and he bristled at criticism from the black community. Black critics, he argued, simply asked for too much when they demanded that he and the ADA fight for integrated public housing. "In the District of Columbia and in Congress the preponderant opinion is so strongly against this that such a policy adopted by the ADA would kill it." Instead, he proposed "to build for Negroes in areas now occupied by Negroes," but his critics "say it were better to leave conditions as they are." The humanitarian in Ihlder rebelled against simply "leav[ing] these people ... until white opinion will accept Negroes as next door neighbors."[33]

But what Ihlder saw (to his chagrin) was that more and more black Washingtonians—with an increasing number of radical white allies—were no longer satisfied with the charitable crumbs that fell from a segregated table. They had "only one desire," Ihlder acknowledged, "full racial equality." And they were not going to wait for white reformers to give it to them.[34]

"Don't Buy Where You Can't Work": The New Negro Alliance and the Challenges of Interracial Grassroots Organizing

John Aubrey Davis was a child of Woodrow Wilson's Washington. Davis was born in 1912, the year Wilson was first elected, and grew up among D.C.'s ambitious black middle class in "Striver's Row," an area between Sixteenth and Nineteenth Streets just northeast of Dupont Circle that was home to black Howard professors, business owners, and federal clerks. Davis's father had worked in the Government Printing Office, but his promising career had been stunted by President Wilson's segregationist practices (see Chapter 8). Embittered by the experience, the elder Davis nurtured a sense of outrage in his children and took them along to NAACP rallies, including an anti-lynching march when John was just nine years old.[35]

At Dunbar High School, John Davis learned history and protest from NAACP head Neval Thomas, and he studied writing at Williams College in Massachusetts, where he earned Phi Beta Kappa honors and graduated summa cum laude. So light-skinned and fair-eyed that he once was thrown out of a "colored only" train in Virginia because the conductor thought he was white, Davis later would earn a Ph.D. in political science and serve on the NAACP's research team for *Brown v. Board of Education*. Davis was among the new generation of local activists who would use new tactics and tap new allies to fight for equality in the nation's capital.[36]

In 1933, driven by what he later called "the double assertiveness of youth and race revolt," Davis returned home from college determined to improve the economic prospects of black workers. He approached the District branch of the NAACP with an idea to conduct systematic boycotts of discriminatory businesses in black neighborhoods, but branch leaders rebuffed his plan, fearing that confrontational tactics could lead to white economic retaliation. After Neval Thomas's death in 1930, the group had grown conservative and complacent; internal bickering and turf battles led the national office to revoke the District branch's charter in 1937, an embarrassing reprimand for what had been perhaps the NAACP's most powerful local branch in the 1910s and 1920s. Though the charter was restored two years later, it would be another decade before the NAACP played a significant role in District civil rights struggles.[37]

Undeterred, Davis implemented the idea on his own. On August 28, 1933, he led a small march of pickets in front of the Hamburger Grill at 1211 U Street NW to protest the firing of three black employees. The protest sparked the creation of the New Negro Alliance, which sought to leverage black purchasing power into expanded economic opportunities for black workers. Davis enlisted other young college graduates as well as what he recalled as "young guys from the street corner" in what he hoped would be a cross-class organization. Like other "Don't Buy Where You Can't Work" efforts in Northern cities, the alliance used private negotiations, public protests, and economic boycotts to pressure business owners to hire black employees in nonmenial positions. They targeted businesses in black neighborhoods that catered to a black clientele and thus were more vulnerable to consumer pressure.[38]

The Hamburger Grill protest was an immediate success—within two days, the black employees were back at work. The alliance quickly scored two more important victories in late 1933 by persuading the *Evening Star* and the A&P grocery store chain to hire more black employees. The group's early success earned praise and publicity from the black press and black pastors, and by early 1934 it counted about a thousand members from across the black community, including Walter Washington, who later would become the city's first black mayor. Its picket lines featured educator Mary Church Terrell, Roosevelt administration official Mary McLeod Bethune, and other high-profile black Washingtonians. The nation's top black legal talent, including the NAACP's Charles Hamilton Houston and his protégé Thurgood Marshall, offered pro bono assistance to alliance attorneys. By 1938, the group claimed to have secured more than five thousand nonmenial jobs for black workers.[39]

The alliance inspired a backlash from white employers and customers who resented the group's picket lines, which disrupted foot traffic outside targeted stores. "If they want colored clerks, why don't they start a store of their own?" groused one white employee of Peoples Drug store, which refused to acquiesce to alliance demands. White customers sometimes rallied around targeted stores. As one researcher noted about a protest at the Peoples on Fourteenth and U Streets NW, "Since the colored have been standing out in front the white trade has increased."[40]

The alliance's aggressive tactics landed it in court. The group spent much of 1934 and 1935 attempting unsuccessfully to fight two separate injunctions against the boycotts. But a third case made its way to the Supreme Court and would prove to be the alliance's most lasting legacy. The case involved the Sanitary Grocery Company, a Delaware chain with dozens of stores in Washington. In April 1936, Sanitary opened a store near Eleventh and U Streets NW, just a couple blocks from the alliance's headquarters. It refused to hire black clerks, prompting the alliance to station a lone picketer who patrolled the area with a sandwich board reading, "Do Your Part! Buy Where You Can Work! No Negroes Employed Here!" After Sanitary sued, alliance attorneys argued that nonviolent pickets and boycotts were a form of protected free speech. By a 6–2 margin, the Supreme Court decided in favor of the alliance, ruling that the "peaceful and orderly dissemination of information" about a labor dispute was lawful, even by people or groups not directly involved in the dispute.[41]

Though little known today, the Court's March 1938 decision in *New Negro Alli-*

ance v. Sanitary Grocery had a profound impact on the course of social movements nationwide. In the short run, it encouraged the spread of "Don't Buy Where You Can't Work" efforts around the country and gave the alliance a powerful weapon to use in its battles with local companies. Within a year, nearly all the businesses along the U Street and Seventh Street NW commercial corridors had agreed to Alliance demands. In part due to bad publicity stemming from the case, Sanitary Grocery changed its name to "Safeway," but it remained steadfastly discriminatory in its hiring practices for years to come despite continued alliance demonstrations.[42]

In the long run, the *New Negro Alliance* ruling was a watershed victory for protesters of all types. It protected the use of boycotts and pickets as a protest tactic, giving the Court's imprimatur to labor unions, civil rights groups, and other activists seeking to use consumer power as leverage against corporations.

The alliance's efforts to protect black workers met ideological opposition from within the black intelligentsia and the labor movement. For some radical black thinkers, such as Howard professor Abram Harris, the alliance's strategy of promoting black hiring threatened to undermine class-based interracial alliances among workers. They argued that all "Jobs for Negroes" efforts only provoked white retaliation and divided the working class at a time when workers needed to unite across racial lines.[43]

Radical labor organizers, often affiliated with the Communist or Socialist Parties, also rejected race-specific tactics and focused instead on building interracial alliances of workers. The parties were small and controversial, but the terms "Communist" and "Socialist" were not the career-ending epithets that they later would become during the Cold War. The parties challenged racial discrimination at a time when both Republicans and Democrats wooed white supremacists. Many of the District's radical activists worked with or within the Congress of Industrial Organizations (CIO), founded in 1935 as a challenge to the racially segregated American Federation of Labor (AFL). Committed to organizing all workers within a particular industry, the CIO embraced interracial unionism and created unprecedented opportunities for black workers to bargain collectively and exercise leadership roles. Though Washington did not have a large industrial base, the CIO was active in the city, attempting to organize workers across racial lines in private industries and the federal government.

Interracial organizing was exceedingly difficult, in part because manual labor remained unofficially segregated into "white" and "black" jobs. Black workers generally were relegated to the dirtiest, most menial, and least paid work; white employers often justified the job discrimination by claiming that black workers were simply unsuited for skilled work. Asked why the Cafritz Construction

Company hired no black carpenters, the company's bookkeeper explained, "To be a carpenter one must be intelligent, have a certain amount of training and imagination. Everyone can't do carpentry."[44]

As the Depression deepened, more and more white workers were willing to accept whatever jobs they could find, often displacing their black counterparts. In 1938, ten thousand women (90 percent of whom were black) lined up to get job applications for two thousand janitorial positions available in the federal government. A melee erupted when police helped white women at the back of line get applications first, ahead of black women who had waited in line all night. White women could move down the economic ladder to take a janitorial job; black workers, however, could not do the reverse. White workers retained a virtual monopoly on the better-paying, skilled jobs. By the end of the decade, more than 98 percent of the city's boilermakers, motormen, conductors, machinists, and telephone linemen were white men, and more than 97 percent of the stenographers, telephone operators, and clerical workers were white women.[45]

White workers jealously guarded their benefits, consistently objecting to working alongside African Americans. District unions affiliated with the AFL almost uniformly excluded black workers, making it difficult for them to find work or bargain for better working conditions. Race also became a handy way for business owners to sabotage unionizing efforts. "It seems the employer would tell the niggers what was the use of joining for as soon as they could the whites would kick them out," explained a white official with the Bakery Salesmen union. "And to the whites they would say why deal with those niggers, if you just wait a while we will kick them all out and get whites."[46]

It was not simply white workers or owners who feared interracial unions. Black workers, too, were skeptical, worrying that joining forces with white counterparts would jeopardize their own jobs. Annie Stein, a white organizer with the Restaurant Alliance of the AFL, encountered significant resistance to unions among black workers. Not only did they worry about discrimination from their white colleagues, but they also "fear that their jobs will be filled with whites if they are paid the same wages," Stein said. "The colored know that the only reason they have the jobs is because they are willing to accept less pay."[47]

Despite such obstacles, union organizers made headway in the District during the 1930s by applying simple economic logic. As the Bakery Salesmen union official put it, "A white bricklayer gets $12.00 a day and a nigger only $6.00 a day. The result is the niggers are undercutting the whites and being in competition with one another they both lose." White workers only hurt themselves by excluding their black counterparts, he believed. "It's no use trying to keep the nigger down as it only keeps the rest of us down."[48]

The CIO-affiliated United Federal Workers of America (UFWA) made interracial organizing an explicit goal when it launched a campaign to organize federal workers in 1937. Unlike the other two unions that represented federal workers, the UFWA eagerly recruited black workers and challenged segregated conventions within the federal government. President Roosevelt made several high-profile black appointments such as Mary McLeod Bethune, who became director of the National Youth Administration, and Robert C. Weaver, who was the Department of Interior's adviser on Negro Affairs, but his administration did not undo the segregated hiring practices within executive agencies. With the New Deal came a burst of new hiring, but aspiring black employees often did not benefit. The new Civil Works Administration, for example, received 4,500 applications from white job seekers and hired 2,000 (a 44 percent hiring rate); it received 2,600 applications from black people but hired only 115 (a 4 percent hiring rate).[49]

At the UFWA's helm was Eleanor Nelson, the white, slightly built daughter of a U.S. representative from Maine. Radicalized by the treatment of the Bonus Army marchers in 1932, Nelson became a member of the Communist Party. Under Nelson's leadership, the union fought for collective bargaining rights for all workers, and it refused to hold meetings or social events in segregated facilities. African Americans served as UFWA officials, represented the union at public events, and ran many union affiliates. The city's biggest black union was the UFWA-affiliated United Cafeteria Workers' Local Industrial Union Number 471, run by Oliver Palmer, a soft-spoken black South Carolinian who bused dishes for twenty-five cents an hour in the Treasury Department. The UFWA's communist leanings limited its appeal and ultimately led to its downfall in the 1940s, but for a brief period the union made modest gains to establish collective bargaining rights for federal workers.[50]

Outside of the federal government, labor activists sought to improve working conditions for manual laborers, particularly in the laundry industry. Laundry was big business in D.C. — "A white-collar town is a good place for a laundryman" went the local joke. The CIO established a local laundry workers' union to help laundry workers fight for shorter hours, better pay, and more breaks from their sweltering jobs.[51]

Inez Robertson, a part-time organizer for the local union, began working in a laundry at age fourteen and joined the union in 1937, when she was in her twenties. Despised by management as "one of those CIO niggers," she sought to organize the lowest-paid workers, most of whom were black, at Arcade Laundry at 1010 Vermont Avenue NW, where she had worked for seven years. Arcade's owner, Harry Viner, paid the company's 150 workers the standard industry wage of twenty to twenty-five cents an hour, but he often punched them out at 4:30 p.m. regardless of whether they actually left work. "If any of the girls should kick, they would be fired," Robertson explained. "They were all too afraid to do anything." The union launched a series of strikes at Arcade beginning in 1937 and culminating in 1941. Despite Viner's full-page appeals for public support in the Star and other newspapers, the workers won—their pay increased to twenty-five to thirty cents an hour for a forty-eight-hour week.[52]

The laundry workers' union, the UFWA, and other CIO-affiliated unions may not have revolutionized working conditions in Washington, but they showed the potential for interracial organizing even during a time of seemingly rigid segregation. The union movement broadened the pool of white allies willing to work for racial equality and established nationwide interracial networks among activists. White union organizers defied the notion that all white people supported segregation, and many of them—most prominently Annie Stein—became active in Washington's post–World War II civil rights movement.

The unions allied themselves with radical civil rights organizations at work in Washington, particularly the National Negro Congress (NNC). Founded at Howard University in 1935—Howard was experiencing a renaissance in activism under the leadership of its first black president, Mordecai Johnson—the NNC was a national organization dedicated to building a coalition of radical labor, religious, and civic organizations to fight racial discrimination, particularly in the workplace. The outspoken socialist head of the Brotherhood of Sleeping Car Porters, A. Philip Randolph, served as president. Though much of the NNC's work focused on Chicago, New York, and other industrial cities, its leaders saw the Washington Council as vitally important because they believed that race relations in the nation's capital set the tone for racial struggles throughout the United States. Like the UFWA and other left-wing organizations, the NNC ultimately foundered on the shoals of Cold War politics, but for a decade after its founding it was among the most visible and effective civil rights organizations in the city.[53]

The NNC's top priority in Washington was police brutality, an issue that resonated deeply in the black community. Aside from the 1919 riot, the District had little experience with the white mob violence that plagued other Southern communities, but black Washingtonians suffered disproportionately from "legal" violence at the hands of law enforcement officials. During Reconstruction, Washington's police force had been filled with black recruits. After disfranchisement in 1878, however, it had become an almost all-white force. In 1933, there was one white police officer or firefighter for every 153 white D.C. residents, but only one black officer or firefighter for every 2,047 black residents.[54]

District police were notorious for their rough treatment of black residents, particularly the poor. Black Washingtonians often endured abusive language, unwarranted searches, and physical force, even during routine investigations. "Niggers have no constitutional rights," growled one police officer during a raid in which he verbally abused a black woman, knocked her mother to the ground, and rummaged through her home without a warrant. "The Constitution was made by and for white men." An NNC study found that local police had killed an average of four black men every year during the late 1920s and early 1930s. The black press regularly reported cases of D.C. officers using excessive force against black women as well, often displaying photos of bruised and battered victims.[55]

The wanton use of violence by D.C. police had an effect akin to lynching elsewhere in the South: it reinforced the system of racial subordination and discouraged black people from challenging their "place" in society. Black residents, especially in low-income areas, came to fear "John Law" almost as much as "Jim Crow." Despite vehement objections from black witnesses, reporters, and civic groups, perpetrators rarely faced official sanction, and the abuse continued. As one frustrated NNC activist wrote, "If you are a colored woman enthroned in your house at five o'clock in the morning and a police sergeant weighing some three hundred pounds pushes his night stick onto your stomach and calls you a God Damn Nigger, there is NOTHING you can do about it."[56]

The NNC launched a vigorous, coordinated campaign to end police violence in the nation's capital. Led by national secretary John P. Davis, in 1936 local NNC activists began investigating the police and publicizing egregious examples of police mistreatment of black residents. They worked with churches, unions, civic groups, and civil rights organizations such as the New Negro Alliance to mobilize community members and put grassroots pressure on political leaders and city officials. Recognizing the political impotence of the District, they also cultivated supporters in Congress and pushed them to investigate the District police department.[57]

The NNC's efforts came together in the summer of 1938 after the police killed a mentally ill black World War I veteran named Leroy Keys. Seizing on community outrage in the wake of Keys's death, the NNC organized a broad coalition of organizations, from the Communist Party to the moderate Inter-Racial Committee, to protest the killing. At one July march, two thousand protesters, about four hundred of whom were white, planned to carry caskets for each victim of police brutality in the previous decade. The police prohibited the caskets, but sign-toting marchers chanted "Stop legal lynching!" as a crowd of ten thousand lined the streets. "A crisis of violence is impending," wrote the Reverend Robert W. Brooks, the black pastor of Lincoln Congregational Church. "How long will the law-abiding citizens of the District tolerate these assassins in uniform to continue to tyrannize the public?"[58]

The NNC gathered twenty-four thousand signatures on a petition calling on President Roosevelt to fire the police chief, suspend five officers, fund pensions for victims' families, and create a civilian review board. "Our lives, our homes, our liberties each day are made less secure because of unrestrained and unpunished police brutality," the petition read. The anti-police-brutality campaign proved remarkably successful, at least in the short term. At a mass meeting in June 1939, the Washington Council of the NNC "celebrated one year of blustering city life in which no policeman found it necessary to defend himself by cutting down harmless citizens," reported activist John Lovell in the *Crisis*. Keeping the pressure on with more parades, mass meetings, and media campaigns, activists scored an important victory two years later when the hated police chief, Ernest Brown, stepped down. His successor, Edward Kelly, proved much more amenable to the demands of the black community, and within four years he had tripled the number of black officers on the force.[59]

Like the New Negro Alliance's boycotts and the CIO's interracial unionizing, the National Negro Congress's campaign against police violence showed that new kinds of community organizing could produce important results. But pickets and protests were no substitute for political power. Black Washingtonians still struggled to protect their interests because they lacked the power to hold public officials accountable and ensure that they address black grievances. "When Washingtonians are granted suffrage the Negro will get his civil rights the next day," wrote Victor Daly, a black official in the U.S. Department of Labor, in the *Crisis*. "That is one reason why the people in the capital do not vote now." The movement to win D.C. voting rights, however, faced struggles all its own.[60]

"The Alley Will Dominate the Avenue":
Race and the Struggle to Win Suffrage in D.C.

In the early decades of the twentieth century, a new suffrage movement grew increasingly militant in its calls for District voting rights, paralleling the nationwide push for women's suffrage. After disfranchisement in 1878, efforts to restore the ballot had united black activists with a host of white Republicans and labor leaders who remained committed to the egalitarian goals of Radical Reconstruction. By the 1920s and 1930s, however, the struggle for voting rights, like so much of life in Washington, had become polarized along racial and economic lines.

Support for suffrage grew in part because the federal government had failed to live up to its fiscal obligations. The disfranchisement bargain struck in the 1870s was simple: in exchange for giving up their claims to suffrage, District residents gained the security of having the federal government pay for half of the city's annual budget. The "half-and-half" plan became sacrosanct among local leaders. Fear of losing the federal contribution helped doom previous efforts to restore the franchise.

Frugal members of Congress, however, soon began reconsidering the half-and-half plan, and in 1921, Congress abandoned it altogether. By 1937, the federal government contributed less than 15 percent of the city's budget, angering local leaders and triggering a fiscal crisis that threatened the city's solvency. In a seven-part exposé of the District government, *Washington Post* reporter Merlo Pusey described a "hamstrung democracy" burdened by "divided authority, congressional indifference and fiscal uncertainty." As a result, local officials struggled to meet basic public health standards, provide adequate schools, or keep the city safe. Suffrage supporters argued that if D.C. had representatives in Congress, then the city could secure stable funding and prevent undue meddling in District affairs.[61]

A prime mover in the suffrage movement was Theodore Noyes, the white editor of the *Evening Star*. A native Washingtonian with undergraduate and law degrees from Columbian College (which later became George Washington University), Noyes inherited the editorship of the *Star* from his father, Crosby Noyes, in 1908 and spent decades advocating for the development and beautification of the District. Noyes was convinced that the best way to protect the District's economic and political interests was to have a voting representative in Congress. District residents were "defective and delinquent Americans," he believed, and until they could vote for their own representative, the city could expect only meager congressional support. In 1917, he helped form the Citizens' Joint Committee on National Representation for the District of Columbia, which drove the suffrage movement for the next two decades.[62]

With positive coverage in the *Star* and other white newspapers, the suffrage movement gained support from leading white organizations, including the Board of Trade, the "Voteless" League of Women Voters, and the Federation of Citizens Associations. An unofficial referendum held in April 1938 drew nearly one hundred thousand voters and showed overwhelming support for both local suffrage (88 percent) and national representation (93 percent). Black Washingtonians were even more supportive—one *Washington Post* poll showed that 95 percent of black respondents supported suffrage compared to 80 percent of whites.[63]

The racial split grew wider on the question of self-government (known locally as "home rule") for District residents. Black Washingtonians generally supported both national representation and home rule but placed a higher priority on the latter. Walter A. Pinchback of the black Bloomingdale Civic Association testified in 1938 that "every fair-minded citizen of the District would like to have the privilege" of national representation, but "would it not be better for Congress to establish some form of local government, whereby the citizens could choose their own officials who would be directly responsible to them?"[64]

Most white voters also supported home rule, but Theodore Noyes, the Board of Trade, and other white elites adamantly opposed it. Home rule, they believed, would lead to black control, as they believed it had during Reconstruction. Black voters would support huge spending increases, rack up debt, and levy higher taxes, all of which would hurt business, lower property values, and encourage wealthy people to leave Washington. The city has "a color problem," wrote Grover Ayers of the Ten Miles Square Club in the *Post* in 1938. "In the past, politicians used the colored vote as they intend to do should Congress grant the District any kind of suffrage today." John Turner of the Sixteenth Street Highlands Citizens Association told Congress that "Negro domination" would ruin the city, so "national representation is the safest course to pursue with the mixed population in the District."[65]

Ongoing racial concerns led the *Post*'s Merlo Pusey to dismiss suffrage as inherently impractical and undesirable. With so many white residents choosing to vote by mail in their home states, the balance of power would be held by black voters, Pusey argued. "Stimulation of racial politics in the Nation's Capital is not a pleasant prospect." A more apocalyptic assessment came from white resident and community gadfly Clinton Howard, the grandnephew of Civil War general O. O. Howard. At a 1943 congressional hearing, Howard warned that if D.C. were granted suffrage, the city would be ruled by "the under-privileged, illiterate, proletarian class. . . . The alley will dominate the avenue."[66]

The specter of black political power, Theodore Noyes acknowledged, undercut the elite effort to win D.C. representatives in Congress: "We have had a hard time getting this Congress to discriminate between national representation and the Negro dominating in local suffrage." No suffrage bill passed Congress before World War II. The city's continued disfranchisement undermined the ability of its activist community—whether suffrage supporters, union organizers, advocates for racial equality, or others—to make decision makers pay attention to their concerns. Living in the nation's capital put their local struggles tantalizingly close to the halls of power, but they usually failed to generate much national attention or sympathy. For civil rights activists, that began to change in early 1939, when a controversy surrounding black opera singer Marian Anderson trained the media spotlight on racial segregation in the nation's capital.[67]

"Blight on Democracy": Racial Discrimination in D.C. Attracts National Attention

Anderson, perhaps the foremost black artist of her time, was invited to perform in Washington as part of an annual concert series sponsored by Howard University. Concert organizers hoped to have her sing at Constitution Hall, a spectacular four-thousand-seat auditorium on D Street NW just off the Ellipse in front of the White House. Owned by the Daughters of the American Revolution (DAR), Constitution Hall opened in 1929 and was the city's largest performance space. It also was segregated. Black patrons could attend events, provided they sat in "colored-only" areas, but the DAR banned black performers.[68]

The Anderson concert planners knew of the "white artists only" policy but hoped that the singer's fame and accomplishments (and the prospect of a sold-out venue) would convince the DAR to reconsider. The women who ran the DAR were neither impressed nor interested; they rejected the request. Anderson's team then asked the city's school board for permission to perform at white Central High School, home to a two-thousand-seat auditorium. Following the recommendation of school superintendent Frank Ballou, the board refused.

The DAR's decision, coupled with the school board's rejection, triggered an extraordinary, biracial backlash. "The barring of Marian Anderson ... was a note heard 'round the nation," wrote Victor Daly in the Crisis. "It was like a spark that ignited the whole city."[69] Though ordinary black Washingtonians had long been mistreated by police, packed into overcrowded neighborhoods and schools, and humiliated by the city's Southern customs, the Anderson snub touched a raw nerve, particularly among the black elite. It seemed to serve notice, once again, that no matter how accomplished a black person could become, she or he still would be treated as a second-class citizen in the nation's capital.

Local black leaders, with visible and vocal white allies, seized on l'affaire Anderson as an opportunity to bring national attention to the state of race relations in the city. They formed the Marian Anderson Citizens Committee (MACC), chaired by NAACP lawyer and former school board member Charles Hamilton Houston. With support from a network of ninety local groups, MACC coordinated an effective grassroots campaign involving petitions, letters to the editors of local newspapers, telegrams to local and federal officials, and interracial mass meetings that attracted up to fifteen hundred people (about a third of whom were white). Citizen pressure forced the school board to reconsider its decision, but the board reasserted its policy of segregation and agreed to allow Anderson to perform only if "the concession will not be taken as a precedent." Concert organizers and the MACC refused to accept such conditions.[70]

The grassroots work paralleled a behind-the-scenes effort to win support from sympathetic members of Congress and federal government officials, including Interior Secretary Harold Ickes, who had served as the president of the Chicago NAACP, and First Lady Eleanor Roosevelt, a token member of the DAR. Ickes embraced the movement immediately. Roosevelt initially was reluctant to get involved publicly for fear it might hurt the cause—by 1939, she had become a lightning rod for criticism from white conservatives owing to her consistent support of integration. But in late February she publicly resigned from the DAR, spurring the effort to find a place for Anderson to perform in Washington.[71]

As Easter Sunday approached, MACC members coalesced around an audacious idea: to host a concert on the steps of the Lincoln Memorial. Secretary Ickes loved the plan and secured President Roosevelt's approval. Less than two weeks later, an interracial crowd of seventy-five thousand braved a blustery wind to hear Anderson sing a stunning rendition of "My Country 'Tis of Thee" as well as several spirituals. The event helped recast the meaning of the Lincoln Memorial and the legacy of Lincoln himself, transforming the site into a space for black protest; it became a monument not only to the man who preserved the Union but also to the Great Emancipator, the racial conscience of the nation.[72]

MACC members felt almost giddy with the sense of possibility. "Washington is a giant awakened," wrote an excited John Lovell. Mary McLeod Bethune believed the concert was a breakthrough moment: "Through the Marian Anderson protest concert we made our triumphant entry into the democratic spirit of American life." After a decade of growing activism among black Washingtonians, Bethune, Lovell, and other local leaders hoped that the Anderson concert would help force institutional changes and break down barriers to black employment, housing, and education.[73]

Some observers hailed the Anderson concert as a turning point in the long struggle for racial equality in the nation's capital, but substantive, enduring long-term change required more than a high-profile concert on the Mall. The image of the interracial crowd united on behalf of American ideals faded quickly. After the concert, "Negroes were still unable to attend theaters, use Central High School or Constitution Hall, or to exercise their rights as American Citizens," wrote the editors of New Negro Opinion. "The pent-up emotions of thousands of Negroes were discharged quietly over the Reflecting Pool and then the straight-jacket of social policy and racial prejudice was quickly made secure and operative again."[74] The concert had been a remarkable moment of interracial unity, a symbolic victory that lifted the spirits of black Washingtonians and their allies, but it produced little substantive change.

Despite efforts by the local MACC to capitalize on the media attention by pushing for an end to all segregation in the nation's capital, the momentum dissipated as the nation's attention quickly shifted to the brewing war in Europe. With Adolf Hitler's German army marching across the continent, President Franklin Roosevelt called on America to become "the arsenal of democracy." The federal government and federally funded defense industries began hiring at a frenetic pace, and the nation's capital grew dramatically. Even before the United States officially entered the war in December 1941, there were upwards of two hundred thousand federal workers in D.C., roughly double the peak number during World War I. The metropolitan area's population soon soared to more than a million. With this "new Army of the Potomac" on its streets, Washington became "the wartime capital of the Western World, an eager, scurrying overcrowded metropolis," wrote James Reston in the *New York Times Magazine* in June 1941.[75]

Black newcomers were among the masses who flooded into the city, part of what would become the greatest internal migration in American history. Pushed by agricultural woes and racial violence and pulled by the promise of economic opportunity, hundreds of thousands of people, black and white, left the rural South in the 1940s. Most of them wound up in industrial cities such as Chicago and New York, but many black migrants, particularly from Virginia and the Carolinas, headed for Washington. The city's black population surged by nearly 50 percent during the 1940s, reaching more than 280,000. By 1950, black people made up 35 percent of the population, the highest percentage in the city's history.[76]

When they arrived in Washington, black workers often struggled to find work. The city government often shut black jobseekers out—not a single black person, for example, could be found among more than five hundred workers at the municipal jail, the workhouse, or the National Training School for Boys—and black workers also faced significant hurdles to federal employment. Despite race-neutral hiring protocols, some agency heads and federal contractors, particularly in defense industries, found ways to discriminate against black applicants and employees. Brotherhood of Sleeping Car Porters leader A. Philip Randolph and other black labor and civil rights organizers met with Roosevelt administration officials to protest such employment discrimination, to no avail. So, "as a last resort of a desperate people who had failed to get decisive results,"

Randolph wrote, he and his allies launched the March on Washington Movement to bring tens of thousands of black people for a march along Constitution Avenue to the Lincoln Memorial in July 1941.[77]

Fearing racial violence and negative publicity, President Roosevelt hurriedly issued Executive Order 8802 barring discrimination in defense industries based on "race, creed, color, or national origin." The order also created the Fair Employment Practices Committee (FEPC) to adjudicate claims of workplace discrimination. Randolph called off the march and claimed a stunning victory that proved the power of pressure politics. The episode showed that Roosevelt, like many other politicians, "will remain aloof from the Negro question until there is an organized resentment and pressure as to make it a national embarrassment if he does not act," wrote Howard University law student and activist Pauli Murray.[78]

With federal protections in place, black federal employment increased significantly. By 1944, the Urban League reported, there were 41,566 black federal workers in Washington, up from fewer than 10,000 before the war. Roughly 9 percent of federal workers were black. Yet black workers still were confined to the lowest-paying jobs—a 1942 survey showed that more than 60 percent of black federal workers did custodial work while only 2.3 percent were in upper-level positions.[79]

Though Randolph's threatened masses never descended on D.C., the looming war thrust the nation's capital into an uncomfortable spotlight. Washington was "a blight on democracy," wrote Alden Stevens in a blistering *Harper's Magazine* article that hit newsstands in December 1941. "Washington the capital is a symbol of democracy and America. Washington the city is a symbol of almost everything that sincere and thoughtful men know is wrong with democracy and America." Writing for a national audience, Stevens exposed how inadequately prepared the city was to handle the extraordinary influx of war workers, but he reserved his sharpest critiques for Washington's racial practices. "Here in the Capital of a nation dedicated to the proposition that all men are created equal, one-third of the residents are forbidden the theaters and the restaurants of the principal business area, are effectively blocked in their search for employment, are commonly charged two to three times as much rent as the other two-thirds are charged for equivalent accommodations, and are hated and feared because they do not like it," Stevens wrote. "Washington combines the worst features of North and South."[80]

Soon after Stevens's article appeared, Japanese warplanes attacked a U.S. naval installation in Pearl Harbor, Hawaii, and the United States immediately joined what came to be known as World War II. It was a war, President Roosevelt had said during his 1941 State of the Union speech, to defend the "Four Freedoms" on which a peaceful world rested: freedom of speech and religion and freedom from want and fear. As the Great War had a generation earlier, this second world war would open opportunities for racial activism in the nation's capital.

"Are You for 'HITLER'S Way' or the 'AMERICAN Way'?":
Wartime Activism in the Nation's Capital

Jewell Crawford Mazique was a face of black patriotism during the war. A Georgia native with mixed Creek, Cherokee, and black heritage, Mazique graduated from Spelman College in 1935 and moved to Washington to attend graduate school at Howard University. She married a Howard medical student and, after earning her master's degree, worked two jobs to put her new husband through school. She also helped raise three of her nieces in their home on 1861 California Street NW, just north of the Striver's Row neighborhood where the New Negro Alliance's John Aubrey Davis grew up.

Mazique briefly was a "government girl" during World War II, working as a file clerk in the Library of Congress. An intense woman who combined radical political ideas with conservative personal habits, Mazique left her government position in 1943 to become a union organizer, community activist, and feminist pioneer. She had little interest in the social life of elite black Washington to which her education, income, and marriage entitled her. Instead, she devoted herself to political action and was a frequent presence on picket lines, at mass meetings, and in congressional hearings.[81]

Svelte and attractive with a photogenic smile, Mazique was chosen in 1942 to be the subject of an extensive "day in the life" photo collection by the Office of War Information (OWI), which highlighted the wartime contributions of black Americans as part of its mission to boost support for the war. Aware of the political implications of the project, she agreed to be photographed because she hoped the exposure would help improve black employment prospects in the federal government. In the propaganda photos, which were distributed to press organizations nationwide in 1943 (one appeared in an OWI booklet, Negroes and the War), the smartly dressed Mazique chats with white colleagues, works diligently in the library stacks, passes out flyers at a union rally, donates plasma at a Red Cross blood drive, sits quietly next to a white woman on a crowded streetcar, speaks to church members about black efforts for the war, and reads to her adoring nieces. She appears as the model of patriotic, middle-class black America.[82]

"Jewal Mazique, worker at the Library of Congress." The Office of War Information followed Jewell Mazique for a "Day in the Life" portrayal of black patriotism during World War II. Here, Mazique rides home next to a white woman on a Washington streetcar. Library of Congress.

As Mazique knew, her experience was not typical of black Washington or even black federal workers. Another OWI photo project, this one by black photographer Gordon Parks, offered a starker portrayal of black life in D.C. The Kansas-born Parks arrived in Washington shortly after Pearl Harbor to begin a fellowship with the Farm Security Administration. Angered and disillusioned by the discrimination he encountered in his new home, Parks determined to use his camera "to show the rest of the world what [the] great city of Washington, D.C., is really like."[83]

Parks trained his lens on Ella Watson, a janitor for the federal government. The daughter of a man murdered by a Southern lynch mob, Watson never earned a high school diploma and struggled to support her family on her meager salary. If Mazique represented the achievement of black Washington, Watson symbolized its despair and persistent lack of opportunity—illustrated dramatically by Parks's haunting *American Gothic, Washington D.C.*, picture of Watson standing plaintively, mop and broom in hand, before an illuminated American flag. The OWI, perhaps not surprisingly, did not widely distribute the Watson pictures.[84]

The contrasting images of Mazique and Watson revealed the sensitive and often controversial representation of race in Washington as the nation prepared for and fought another world war. Recognizing that racial prejudice in the capital city was a public relations nightmare, federal officials and propagandists touted the loyalty, prosperity, and integrated life that Mazique and other successful black people led, while downplaying the poverty and prejudice that Watson and her low-income peers faced. When the second edition of the Work Progress Administration's guide to Washington appeared in 1942, censors carefully edited the chapter on "The Negro in Washington" by Sterling Brown, a black poet and English professor at Howard. Gone were Brown's incisive critiques of the city's race relations and his discussion of contemporary struggles against racial discrimination that had appeared in the 1937 edition; all that remained was a triumphal story of black progress.[85]

But officials could not contain the revolutionary potential of the war. Even more than the Great War, the struggle against the Axis powers offered racial egalitarians the opportunity to sharpen the contrast between American ideals of freedom and the reality of racism. The nation's "race problem is a war issue," wrote activist Pauli Murray. With the German and Japanese enemies openly pursuing regimes of racial superiority, activists argued that racial equality was the American way. White supremacy was not just morally wrong, it was un-American. Activists had powerful champions within the federal government, as well as support from a generation of scholars who were chipping away at the intellectual foundations of racism.[86]

As black soldiers fought overseas, black workers built airplanes, and black clerks staffed the federal war bureaucracy, civil rights activists nationwide pursued a "Double V" campaign aimed at defeating fascism abroad and Jim Crow at home. "Negroes, like other American citizens, helped build America, love America, want to defend America," wrote black War Manpower Commission employee Lucia Pitts in the *Washington Post*. "They must have their rightful share not only of woe and tribulation and sacrifice, but of economic opportunity and faith in America."[87]

Despite pressure to mute protests during the war, Jewell Mazique and other local activists staked a claim to that "rightful share" by challenging the hiring practices of the Capital Transit Company, a private corporation that owned a public monopoly to operate Washington's only bus and streetcar lines. Unlike in other Southern cities, public transportation in Washington had remained integrated since Reconstruction, when the city's streetcars had been a flashpoint for racial conflicts. None of Capital Transit's well-paid drivers or streetcar operators, however, were black. All its black employees toiled in the maintenance division or as custodians. Even as it faced a desperate wartime labor shortage that forced 30–50 percent of its buses to be idled, the company refused to hire black motormen, instead recruiting white women and government workers to moonlight as part-time drivers.[88]

Activists saw Washington's streetcars as a highly visible place to make a wartime statement about American values and show, as one *Post* letter writer put it, "that the 'four freedoms' are more than just mere words." With support from a broad array of allies including the national NAACP and the federal Office of Defense Transportation, the newly organized Committee on Jobs for Negroes in Public Utilities sponsored a "Late to Work?" ad campaign highlighting the impact that Capital's "petty racial prejudices" had on the war effort. It flooded the Fair Employment Practices Committee with petitions signed by nearly six thousand Washingtonians of both races and urged the FEPC to stop Capital Transit's "anti-social and unpatriotic" discrimination. The black community, the FEPC chairman acknowledged, saw "the promotion of its race to trolley platforms as the test of government sincerity in promising equal opportunity to all Americans."[89]

Capital Transit's management refused to budge. Washington "has always been considered a southern city," company officials argued, and many Southern white war workers harbored prejudice that could lead to strikes, "physical violence," and "bloodshed" if black operators were hired. Furthermore, company president E. D. Merrill claimed, black people simply were not qualified to be drivers, in part because they did not have "years of cultural experience behind them."[90]

After a series of hearings in November 1942, the FEPC ordered the company to stop discriminating. Grudgingly, the company hired Bernard Simmons, a college graduate employed as a private chauffeur, as its first black streetcar operator apprentice. When Simmons reported for work in February 1943, however, sixteen white union members refused to train him and sat with their buses idle until he was ordered off the premises. Offered a job as a custodian instead, he rejected it. He then was fired.[91]

In response, Mazique and other activists set up pickets at busy intersections — her sign read, "Negroes drive Tanks in Tunisia, why not buses and street cars in Washington?" — and staged a "Capital Transit Week" of protests in May that culminated with an eight-hundred-person march to Franklin Square, site of the spirited Emancipation Day celebration back in 1866. Despite the organized protests and repeated orders from the FEPC, however, the transit company did not comply. Its platforms remained lily-white until it went bankrupt in 1956. The FEPC proved toothless in the face of implacable white resistance.[92]

The Capital Transit fight paralleled an effort by Howard University students to break the day-to-day habits of segregation in Washington's public spaces. Wartime rhetoric about freedom, combined with a military draft that compelled young men to serve in a segregated army, spurred the students to act. "The city epitomized the great gap between official United States war propaganda and racial practices within our own borders," recalled Pauli Murray, one of two women in her Howard Law School class. "Segregation in the nation's capital was an especially galling indignity."[93]

A North Carolina native with a degree from Hunter College, Murray already was a veteran of civil rights protest. She gained national attention during her unsuccessful attempt to integrate the University of North Carolina in 1938 and spent time in a Virginia jail for refusing to sit at the back of a segregated bus. She had the ear of First Lady Eleanor Roosevelt, whom she had befriended a decade earlier and with whom she corresponded regularly. Several years older and more experienced, the fiery, focused Murray became a leader and mentor for protesting Howard undergraduates such as Ruth Powell.[94]

Powell arrived at Howard from Massachusetts in 1942. Like photographer Gordon Parks and other non-Southern black newcomers, she reacted angrily to segregation in Washington. She spent many afternoons sitting alone at whites-only counters, seething in silence as she waited in vain for service. In January 1943, she took two Howard classmates with her for some hot chocolate at the United Cigar Store on Pennsylvania Avenue NW. Initially refused service, they remained at the counter until the police arrived and ordered the managers to give them their drinks. But after the women objected to being charged more than twice the usual price, the police escorted them to jail.[95]

The women's "stool-sitting" technique (the term "sit-in" had yet to be coined) won widespread support on campus. One survey found that more than 97 percent of Howard students believed that black students should actively fight for equal rights, even during wartime. Through the campus chapter of the NAACP, Pauli Murray and other Howard students raised money, sponsored speakers, and lobbied Congress to pass a D.C. civil rights bill. They also planned a series of direct action protests modeled on Mohandas Gandhi's nonviolent campaign against British rule in India. "Are you for 'HITLER'S way' (Race Supremacy) or the 'AMERICAN way' (Equality)?" read flyers that activists distributed.[96]

Like the New Negro Alliance, the student protesters targeted stores in black areas, such as the Greek-owned Little Palace near Fourteenth and U Streets NW. Students picketed the Little Palace for four days in April 1943, forcing the owner to change the store's service policies. The next year, fifty-six students spent a day sitting on stools at Thompson's Restaurant at Eleventh Street and Pennsylvania Avenue downtown. By the end of the day, management had buckled, and the students were served.[97]

The victory was short-lived, however. Like the Capital Transit Company, Thompson's did not change its official policy on segregation, and before students could start a renewed campaign, nervous Howard administrators intervened. Shortly before the students' demonstration in April 1944, Mississippi senator Theodore Bilbo had taken charge of the Senate District Committee. An irascible segregationist who called for the deportation of black soldiers to Liberia, Bilbo eagerly used his position to derail any civil rights initiatives. Howard was a federally chartered institution whose budget depended heavily on federal funding, and Howard president Mordecai Johnson and the board of trustees felt that they could ill afford to antagonize Bilbo and other congressional appropriators. They forced the students to call off further protests. When direct action protests resumed after the war ended, Howard students largely were uninvolved.[98]

The Howard sit-ins and Capital Transit protests sparked concerns about the potential for violence in a city where racial tensions were "near to the boiling point" in summer 1943. After a devastating race riot erupted in Detroit that June, middle-class civic leaders of both races created the Citizens' Committee on Race Relations, which sought to conduct a systematic "inventory" of racial problems and propose peaceful policy solutions. Like other such groups across the South, the Citizens' Committee sought primarily to harmonize race relations and ameliorate tensions rather than challenge white supremacy or economic inequality.[99]

For the Citizens' Committee and other middle-class reformers, housing loomed as the city's "No. 1 social problem." As during previous wars, Washington could not keep pace with the rapid influx of so many new people. Newcomers crammed into overcrowded neighborhoods, pushing rents up even as housing conditions for poor black residents deteriorated. The overwhelming demand for housing put an end to slum clearance. Alley properties were more lucrative than ever, and housing authorities could not justify demolishing even the most dilapidated of homes when it was virtually impossible to find alternative places for former residents to live. "Bad as most of these slum pigsties may be," wrote Agnes Ernst Meyer, the philanthropic wife of the new editor of the *Post*, "they cannot be condemned until there is some place for the Negro to go."[100]

One social worker investigating a public housing unit found "three families living in a four-room frame shack with a yard toilet, an outside water supply, a leaky roof, cardboard partitions between some of the rooms, an unsafe stairway, and walls from which much of the plaster had fallen." Wartime priorities once again had trumped housing concerns. Alley housing, which was supposed to have been eliminated by 1944 (and 1918, before that), endured long after the war's end in 1945.[101]

The federal government's wartime expansion compounded the housing crisis, as officials exercised the power of eminent domain to buy up residential property for new government facilities, often in predominantly black areas. Hundreds of low-income black families in downtown D.C. had to leave their homes to make way for new Social Security, Railroad Retirement, and Census buildings. Across the Potomac in Virginia, federal authorities uprooted more than a thousand black residents of East Arlington to expand Arlington National Cemetery and create a network of roads leading to what would become the Pentagon.[102]

In a free housing market, pent-up black demand would inspire developers to increase supply by building more units. But the D.C. market was never free: restrictive covenants limited black mobility, lending practices restricted black access to loans, and white resistance to integrated housing artificially shrank black housing options. White developers, busy building homes for thousands of new white war workers, simply ignored growing black demand. They did not build a single private development for black families during the war. Black Washingtonians, the Citizens' Committee noted, were "squeezed tighter and tighter into a few little 'islands' within the District."[103]

Into the breach stepped a black preacher, Elder Lightfoot Michaux. The colorful and controversial head of the Church of God, Michaux came to the District in the early 1930s and established a storefront church on Georgia Avenue NW that quickly blossomed into an evangelical empire with a popular radio show, a bustling "Happy News Café," and mass baptisms in the Potomac. With donations from white supporters as well as black congregants, Michaux built Mayfair Mansions, a 596-unit complex on Benning Road NE, far from existing white neighborhoods. Mayfair Mansions was the largest single development for black families built during the war, but Michaux aimed to attract black professionals, not the poor.[104]

Low-income black residents and war workers looked to public housing to re-lieve the housing pressure. They found that federal and local housing authorities abided by white demands for segregated housing. The federal Defense Homes Corporation followed the lead of John Ihlder and the local Alley Dwelling Au-thority (which was rechristened the "National Capital Housing Authority" in 1943). Although he claimed that housing black war workers was a top priority, Ihlder insisted that authorities "should not mix races in a housing project" and should seek only "to provide housing for each race on sites already occupied by that race."[105] When the war began, the federal government hurriedly built dozens of two-story barracks for war workers downtown—for whites only.

Despite Ihlder's assurances, however, white citizens associations and private homebuilders almost uniformly opposed black public housing developments, particularly after Eleanor Roosevelt called for desegregated public housing in the District in late 1943.[106] The white Federation of Citizens Associations de-manded the abolition of the National Capital Housing Authority altogether, and it worked with the local Home Builders' Association to scuttle wartime housing developments. Though public housing opponents often couched their criticism in race-neutral language about costs and local control, much of their objec-tion stemmed from racial fears, as the FCA's president, Harry Wender, acknowl-edged during testimony before a Senate subcommittee in June 1944.

A Jewish attorney who prided himself on his biracial community work in Southwest, Wender saw himself as a moderate, mediating force between white segregationists and advocates of immediate racial equality. He supported pub-lic housing, even as the organization he led opposed it. Wender told the sena-tors that race was the "very highly inflammable" reason for white opposition to public housing. White residents wanted to protect "the present pattern of the community," and without ironclad guarantees to protect segregation in pub-lic housing, the "people of Washington are going to, by a very vast majority, oppose it."[107]

In the face of vociferous white opposition to integrated housing, wartime housing advocates did not attack segregation itself but challenged housing au-thorities to provide more and better housing options for black residents. One important new activist was Dorothy Height, the black leader of the Phyllis Wheatley YWCA at Ninth Street and Rhode Island Avenue NW. A Richmond native with a master's degree from New York University, Height arrived in Wash-ington in 1939 at age twenty-seven at the beginning of what would be a seven-decade civil rights career. The Wheatley Y offered affordable housing to low-income women at its four-story headquarters, but Height recognized that city and local officials needed to take aggressive measures to meet the demand of thousands of war workers.[108]

When Height confronted federal housing officials about why so few housing projects were being built for black workers, she was told, "The blacks always look after their own." Even black housing official Robert Taylor proved unsympathetic. Black Washingtonians did indeed "look out for their own"—many opened their homes to boarders or relatives coming up from the South—but Taylor's indifference incensed the inimitable Height. She promptly sent volunteers to survey residents about conditions in their neighborhoods and reported their findings to Taylor at a meeting attended by more than three hundred women. Pressure from Height and other black activists helped insure that the federal Defense Homes Corporation built "hotels" for black war workers, including Lucy Diggs Slowe Hall, a 322-bed dormitory at 1919 Third Street NW named for the late black tennis champion and Howard University dean.[109]

Even as they worked with white officials to win access to better housing, many black Washingtonians feared that housing planners, public and private, shared a desire to push black residents away from desirable downtown areas. Nearly every black resident interviewed in a mid-1940s study believed that "there is a plan afoot to gradually segregate the entire colored population" across the Anacostia River. Black activist Geneva Valentine worried that the government would simply buy up land and "tak[e] over whole Negro communities" and "wipe them out in the District of Columbia, rebuilding and changing its occupancy altogether." Fears of displacement or removal even led some black residents to support white citizens associations in their opposition to public housing. Echoes of such concerns would be heard in coming decades as black Washingtonians struggled to cope with postwar urban renewal and gentrification.[110]

Despite wartime pressure, determined white resistance at the local and federal levels largely preserved segregation in the nation's capital during the war years. In fights against employment discrimination, segregated public spaces, and inadequate housing, racial egalitarians often achieved symbolic or small-scale victories but ultimately failed to defeat Jim Crow. At war's end, Capital Transit Company still had no black operators, Thompson's Restaurants still refused to serve black customers, and black residents still could not find housing in much of the city. Despite the sweeping rhetoric about freedom, democracy, and the "American Way" that accompanied the U.S. war effort, World War II stalled racial progress in D.C.

But the ground underneath white segregationists was shifting rapidly. During the 1930s, advocates for racial equality pioneered new strategies, built extensive interracial alliances, and tapped broader networks of allies nationwide. Though their efforts produced only modest, short-term results, they helped lay a foundation for a remarkable postwar movement that would transform Washington. As the nation celebrated the end of the war in 1945, the nation's capital was about to begin a period of profound racial change unseen in the city since the days of Reconstruction.

TEN

Segregation Does Not Die Gradually of Itself

Jim Crow's Collapse, 1945–1956

We, the citizens of Washington, D.C., are sick of segregation. It is wrong and indefensible. It makes us vulnerable to national and world-wide criticism.
—Petition to President and D.C. Board of Commissioners, 1953

John Philip Sousa Middle School on Ely Place in Southeast Washington sits across from the pristine ballfields of the Washington Nationals Youth Baseball Academy and the lush hills of Fort Dupont, the District's second largest park. Named for the famed U.S. Marine Band leader from Southeast who composed "The Stars and Stripes Forever," the school attracted international attention as a civil rights battleground in the early 1950s and is now a National Historic Landmark. A $34.5 million renovation in 2008 rehabilitated the building's fading brick and glass exterior, modernized the interior, and added a civil rights museum for a student body that is almost entirely African American.[1]

When it opened in 1950, Sousa Junior High was intended solely for white students from the burgeoning middle-class communities of Fort Dupont and Benning Heights. Though twenty-first-century Washingtonians often assume that neighborhoods east of the Anacostia River have always been predominantly black, "Far Southeast" was roughly 83 percent white at midcentury. White developers plotted the Fort Dupont and Benning Heights areas in 1907, rejecting L'Enfant's grid system in favor of meandering roads that traced the hills and valleys of the natural landscape. The neighborhoods originally housed exclusive communities protected from black encroachment by racial restrictive covenants.[2]

As the city's population surged in the early 1940s, the Alley Dwelling Authority rapidly erected apartment complexes in the area, and white federal workers poured in. With its dead-end streets and cul-de-sacs that deterred traffic, the area attracted so many families that local schools soon were overwhelmed. Kimball Elementary School, just a third of a mile from Sousa, was so crowded that students had to go on half shifts. The *Post* reported in 1949 that "children entering the sixth grade this fall never had a full day of schooling." To relieve the congestion, school officials went on a postwar construction binge in Southeast. Sousa Junior High was the crown jewel, a palatial thirty-eight-room facility with two gymnasiums.[3]

Sousa's sparkling campus caught the attention of black families in Hillcrest and other black neighborhoods nearby. They had to send their children to over-crowded, poorly equipped junior high schools across the Anacostia River.[4] Impatient with the increasing disparities between the white and black school systems, black activists decided to challenge segregated schools directly, rather than fight the school system to abide by the latter part of "separate but equal." When Sousa opened on September 6, 1950, they marched to the school's front door seeking admission for eleven impeccably dressed black schoolchildren. Denied entry, they sued D.C. school board president Melvin Sharpe; eleven-year-old Spottswood Bolling, the son of a widowed bookbinder for the General Services Administration, became the face of the case. *Bolling v. Sharpe* eventually wound its way to the U.S. Supreme Court, where it became a companion case to the momentous *Brown v. Board of Education* decision in 1954.

Spottswood Bolling's simple request for admission struck at the heart of seg-regated life in Far Southeast and across Washington. For the white families who moved there in the 1940s, the neighborhoods of Far Southeast offered many attractions—low-density development, minimal crime, moderately priced housing, and beautiful vistas of downtown. Life in these neighborhoods, as in other white areas across D.C., was largely segregated at the end of World War II, protected by the laws and customs of a city that remained officially dedicated to preserving racial separation. Three decades after the rise of the New Negro brought a burgeoning spirit of militancy to the struggle for racial equality, Washington remained a Southern city whose white leaders defended racial re-strictive covenants, upheld the dual school system, and supported Jim Crow practices. Confident white conservatives believed that they could parry any post-war attack on their segregated way of life, just as they had after World War I.

Yet the world of segregated Washington, seemingly so resilient, proved to be remarkably fragile. Within a decade, the pillars of that world had crumbled under the pressure of ceaseless community agitation, powerful interracial alli-ances, key Supreme Court decisions, and strategic support from federal authori-ties, including Presidents Harry Truman and Dwight Eisenhower. Despite their lack of voting power, black Washingtonians and their white allies across the nation used a variety of political and legal strategies to rouse public opinion and force Congress and the courts to dismantle the legal framework of Jim Crow. The end of official segregation coincided with—and helped spur—massive demographic shifts that by 1957 had turned Washington into the nation's first major city with a black majority. In Far Southeast, the transformation was dramatic: between 1950 and 1970, the area went from 83 percent white to more than 85 percent black.[5]

The years between the end of World War II in 1945 and the Supreme Court's 1954 decision in Bolling v. Sharpe were the most decisive period in the city's history since the 1860s. Only the heady days of the Civil War and Reconstruction saw so much racial change happen so quickly in Washington. Suddenly, it seemed, segregation in the nation's capital collapsed, half a decade or more before similar changes happened elsewhere in the South. By the end of the 1950s, the institutions of public life in Washington—schools, hotels, restaurants, theaters, recreation facilities, government agencies, unions, professional associations—were no longer racially segregated.

For civil rights supporters, the transformation was breathtaking, a stunning achievement after many decades of struggle. Yet the new Washington also was bewildering for white conservatives who now felt alienated and powerless, victimized by forces beyond their control. Both could agree with the assessment from a 1959 report on race relations in the capital: "A major social revolution has taken place in Washington."[6]

"Intolerable": Racial Discrimination in the Capital of the Free World

Charles Hamilton Houston was as responsible as any individual for the postwar revolution that toppled Jim Crow in D.C. He was well prepared for the struggle. Born in 1895, Houston was the grandson of enslaved Kentuckians but the son of an ambitious, educated, middle-class Washington couple. A quiet, serious only child, Houston finished M Street High School at age fifteen and graduated magna cum laude from Amherst four years later. When the United States joined the Great War in 1917, he volunteered to become an officer and witnessed blatant racial discrimination both during training and in France. "I was damned glad I didn't give my life for my country," a bitter Houston recalled. "I was determined that if I lived I was going to have something to say about how this country should be run." On returning to Washington, he witnessed the July 1919 riot that exploded not far from his parents' house at Tenth and R Streets NW.[7]

The riot, coupled with his wartime experience, fueled Houston's determination to use the law to fight racial discrimination. He headed to Harvard Law School, where he was the first black editor of the Harvard Law Review. At age thirty-four, he became vice dean of Howard University Law School, which then offered only night classes and had little prestige. The relentless, no-nonsense

Houston transformed Howard into an accredited institution with a demanding curriculum and a star-studded faculty focused on a racial justice mission. "He was hard-crust," remembered his most prominent student, future Supreme Court justice Thurgood Marshall. "He made it clear to us that when we were done with law school we were expected to go out and do something with our lives."[8]

Impatient with injustice but disciplined in temperament, Houston became special counsel to the NAACP in the 1930s and engineered the organization's strategy that gradually dismantled the legal framework of segregation, both in Washington and across the South. In the two decades before his untimely death in 1950 at age fifty-four, Houston was involved in nearly every major legal case involving segregation, including *Missouri ex rel. Gaines v. Canada* (1938), in which the U.S. Supreme Court ruled that states that maintained a graduate school for white students also had to provide in-state graduate education to black students. He also was active in local racial struggles, from the New Negro Alliance to the Marian Anderson concert to the Capital Transit protests. A strapping six feet tall with copper skin, prominent cheekbones, and an austere, unflappable demeanor, Houston earned a reputation as a dogged, sharp-minded litigator.

Given his experience during and after the Great War, Houston knew that whatever gains had been achieved during World War II could easily be lost in the aftermath. Indeed, even before troops began returning home in late 1945, the forces of segregation began reasserting themselves in Washington. The backlash against racial equality could be felt in downtown businesses such as Lansburgh's department store on Seventh and E Streets NW, which had begun serving black customers at its soda fountain during the war but quietly returned to segregated service after white customers complained.[9]

It was visible in the actions of local officials, including the city's Board of Recreation, which voted in June 1945 to reinforce rather than repeal its segregation policy for public recreational facilities.

It manifested itself in the postwar demise of the Fair Employment Practices Committee, which closed its doors permanently in 1946 after segregationists in Congress led a successful campaign against it.[10]

And the backlash reverberated in the thundering rhetoric of Senator Theodore Bilbo of Mississippi, the chair of the Senate District Committee, who told one cheering crowd back home, "I wanted this position so I could keep [Washington] a segregated city." When Bilbo was reelected in 1946, the *Post* lamented that "the Confederacy, which was never able to capture Washington during the course of [the Civil War], now holds it as a helpless pawn."[11]

Senator Bilbo was indeed a serious impediment. All appropriations for the

Charles Hamilton Houston was the architect of the NAACP's strategy to dismantle the legal structure of segregation. A community activist as well as a dogged litigator, Houston was involved in nearly every civil rights effort in D.C. in the 1930s and 1940s. Photograph by Addison N. Scurlock, Scurlock Studio Records, Archives Center, National Museum of American History, Smithsonian Institution.

city went through his committee, so city leaders avoided antagonizing him. But his blatant bigotry and blustery broadsides about "Negro inferiority" did not represent the way racism in D.C. generally worked. Washington's conservative white leadership—the appointed commissioners, the businessmen of the Board of Trade, the city planners, the leaders of the Federation of Citizens Associations—tended to be recalcitrant but refined, neither as explosive nor as extreme as Bilbo or his segregationist colleagues in Congress. Though they were no less committed to keeping Washington segregated, they usually couched their racism in soothing rhetoric about promoting "harmony" and avoiding "unnecessary dangerous friction," rather than in threats of violence or base appeals to racial hatred.[12]

Racial segregation was simply "a natural state" preferred by white and black people alike, according to Clifford Newell, the head of the FCA. He and other "well-meaning white people" who believed in segregation had no "feeling of animosity" toward racial minorities. "The provision of equal opportunities . . . for all citizens does not necessarily imply that they must be enjoyed in common," argued the Rhode Island Avenue Citizens Association. To segregate was not necessarily to discriminate, in their view. As FCA official John Connaughton told the *Washington Daily News*, "There is no discrimination in Washington."[13]

Ulysses S. Grant III epitomized Washington's powerful but low-key segregationists. The grandson of the famed Union general, Grant was a West Point graduate who came to Washington in the 1920s and spent four decades leading various city planning organizations. Though raised in the North and abroad, he approached race relations from the South. While running the National Capital Parks and Planning Commission from 1942 to 1949, Grant used federal money to clear out downtown slums, build modern housing complexes for white federal workers, and move low-income black residents elsewhere. Black activists accused him of attempting to create a "Hitler-like ghetto in the far northeast section of the District . . . and in the rear of Anacostia," a charge Grant vehemently denied. He called himself "a very sincere friend of the colored people," but he spent a career embedding segregated housing patterns into D.C.'s residential geography.[14]

Those patterns hardened even as Washington changed dramatically during and after the war. Like other urban areas, the District was fast becoming the center of an expanding metropolitan area, a region more than just a city. Even after the war ended and demobilized soldiers returned home, the federal government, and particularly the peacetime military bureaucracy, continued to expand with the Cold War. The Washington region grew apace, but all the growth took place in the suburbs. The city's population peaked above nine hundred thousand in 1943, then began a steady, six-decade decline. Washington's share of the region's population shrank from 68.5 percent in 1940 to 36.9 percent two decades later.[15]

Suburbanization exacerbated the area's racial and economic segregation, due in part to federal policies. The Federal Housing Administration (FHA), a New Deal agency designed to increase home ownership, produced maps that categorized neighborhoods according to their risk level for mortgage loans. Most black neighborhoods in the central city, as well as neighborhoods in racial transition, were outlined in red ink and labeled "Type D," the riskiest designation. New homeowners, including returning veterans using money from the G.I. Bill, generally avoided such neighborhoods and headed instead for the blue-lined "Type A" areas, most of which were in the suburbs. Because selling a home to even one black homebuyer could jeopardize an entire neighborhood's credit

TABLE 5 Washington's population, 1940–1960

Year	Total	Black (% of pop.)	White (% of pop.)
1940	663,091	187,266 (28.2)	474,326 (71.5)
1950	802,178	280,803 (35.0)	517,865 (64.6)
1960	763,956	411,737 (53.9)	345,263 (45.2)

Source: U.S. Census Bureau, "Historical Census Statistics on Population Totals by Race"

rating, many suburban communities and real estate brokers used the FHA's "redlining" to justify restrictive covenants that barred selling homes to racial minorities.[16]

Redlining effectively shut black homeowners out of the suburbs during this unprecedented period of federally financed suburbanization. Black people were 34 percent of the suburban D.C. population in 1900 but only 6 percent in 1960. The few black suburbanites lived primarily in racially isolated rural enclaves such as Sandy Spring, Maryland, that dated to the nineteenth century. Red-lined neighborhoods, meanwhile, deteriorated as access to capital for investment dried up and relatively poor Southern migrants arrived. More than 12 percent of black homes in the city lacked running water; more than 16 percent lacked electricity.[17]

Essentially all of the Southern black migrants who poured into the Washington area during and after the war settled in the city, while nearly all the white newcomers went to the suburbs. Whereas the District's black population more than doubled in twenty years, from 187,266 in 1940 to 411,737 in 1960, its white population declined by nearly one-third. The suburban population, meanwhile, jumped nearly 330 percent, reaching more than 1.3 million in 1960. In 1939, FHA officials had predicted that "eventually the District will be populated by Negroes and the suburban areas in Maryland and Virginia by white families." Thanks partly to FHA policies, by the late 1940s this process was well under way.[18]

Washington was not only changing demographically and spatially but also becoming more cosmopolitan and influential. The United States emerged from the war as the world's sole atomic superpower, raising the capital's international profile and magnifying its importance in global affairs. With the growing Cold War rivalry between the United States and the Soviet Union, Washington became the "capital of the free world," the showcase of American values. During the world war, racial issues could be ignored by a nation focused on winning battles; during the Cold War, however, civil rights itself became a battleground as Soviet propagandists delighted in bringing the world's attention to American racial hypocrisy, particularly in the nation's capital. "Every incident of racial discrimination [in D.C.] is avidly seized upon for propaganda by our enemies," wrote Phineas Indritz in the *Nation*.[19]

Houston and other civil rights activists seized on the rhetoric and reality of the Cold War to argue that racism in Washington threatened national security by undermining America's moral authority and hindering its efforts to sway other countries to its side in the Cold War. "The United States has assumed a leadership role among the member nations of the United Nations—members who represent all races, creeds, and colors," noted Francis McPeek, a white pastor who later cochaired the Committee for Racial Democracy in the Nation's Capital. "It will become increasingly embarrassing to high government officials, as well as to our citizenry, to extend the hospitality of our land to visiting personages who must see and often suffer the racial restrictions placed upon one-third of our own Washington citizenry."[20]

Harry Truman, the diminutive World War I veteran and former haberdasher who assumed the presidency on Franklin Roosevelt's death in 1945, was surprisingly receptive to this line of argument. Despite his roots in segregated Missouri, Truman came to see civil rights as both a moral and a strategic issue. He, along with a number of high-ranking State Department officials, recognized how racism hampered American foreign policy (and how important black votes were to the Democratic Party). He proved more willing than his predecessor to embrace civil rights. "We shall not . . . finally achieve the ideals for which this Nation was founded so long as any American suffers discrimination as a result of his race, or religion, or color, or the land of origin of his forefathers," he declared in a remarkable 1948 civil rights address to Congress.[21]

Truman issued executive orders to end racial discrimination in the federal government (Executive Order 9980) and ban segregation in the military (Executive Order 9981), and his administration offered critical support to the growing bipartisan coalition of racial liberals and foreign policy realists who believed that national security interests demanded an end to racism in Washington. He appointed the President's Committee on Civil Rights to study race relations and recommend appropriate changes in civil rights law. The committee's watershed 1947 report, *To Secure These Rights*, called Washington "a graphic illustration of a failure of democracy." The city's racial situation was "*intolerable*," the committee concluded, and it recommended ending all codified racial discrimination in the District. Truman supported the committee's recommendations, though he did not appoint commissioners who wanted to implement such radical ideas.[22]

The local civil rights community enthusiastically embraced the *To Secure These Rights* report. Having witnessed the power and effectiveness of the Marian

Anderson Citizens Committee, a growing, interracial core of local activists—including black and white lawyers, labor organizers, veterans, scholars, and clergy—established action committees to do research, promote awareness, coordinate strategy, raise funds, and conduct protests. They employed a variety of judicial, political, and educational strategies: detailed studies to reveal the extent of discrimination, lawsuits aimed at undermining the legal foundation of segregation, public relations campaigns designed to win sympathy from a national audience, direct action protests targeting local businesses, and lobbying efforts attempting to sway key members of Congress.[23]

There were committees for everything. The Citizens Committee on Race Relations monitored acts of discrimination throughout the city; the Committee for Racial Democracy in the Nation's Capital sought to create a coalition of like-minded civic, social, and labor organizations to push for civil rights legislation; the Veterans Citizens Committee to Oust Bilbo pledged to picket until the Mississippi senator left office.[24]

Among the more active groups was the Committee against Segregation in Recreation (CASR), which challenged the District Board of Recreation's segregation policy. Recreation was a serious issue in an increasingly crowded city without adequate play space. Images of black children banned from playing on empty white playgrounds stoked anger within the black community and helped humanize the callousness of segregation. With support from some eighty community groups, the CASR bombarded the recreation board with letters and petitions, publicized examples of positive interracial recreation, and championed the board's lone black member, Alice Hunter.

A graduate of Miner Teachers College and president of the D.C. Federation of Parent-Teacher Associations, the soft-spoken Hunter became a vocal critic of the board's policies, a woman whose personal warmth and charm masked her unshakable determination to end discrimination. But Hunter and the CASR struggled to win over the board's white members, including chair Harry Wender, who claimed to abhor racial discrimination personally but insisted that the board had to maintain segregation to comply with District law. The committee found more success in fighting discrimination in private recreational entities such as the Uline Arena on Third Street NE, which proved vulnerable to economic pressure.[25]

Civil rights committees tied their campaigns to larger national themes and struggles. They tapped the expertise, prestige, and financial resources of the increasingly broad array of sympathetic white supporters across the nation, particularly in the courts. Such powerful allies and the changing local and global context help explain why black Washingtonians could make so much more progress in the decade after World War II than they had in the previous seventy-five years. Calvin Chase, Nannie Helen Burroughs, Archibald Grimké, and other local black leaders in earlier decades were no less aggressive, creative, or hard-working than the activists of the 1940s and 1950s; they simply operated in a much more constrained context in which their claims to racial justice did not resonate beyond the circles of black Washington or serve the needs of political elites.

The reliance on influential white allies, Cold War rhetoric, and the courts came with a price, however. Aware of the need to appeal to a broad national audience, local activists focused on press-friendly issues that could attract widespread support and provide winnable court cases, such as housing, youth recreation, or public accommodations, rather than on economic matters such as unionization, income inequality, or employment discrimination that could trigger accusations of communism.

Despite such limitations, the postwar movement for racial equality slowly eroded the confidence that Washington's white conservatives had in their ability to resist changes to their way of life. White segregationists felt as if their city was slowly slipping from their grasp, and they hoped to strengthen their hold on housing by reinforcing the restrictive covenants that blanketed Washington's white neighborhoods.

"Our Hard-Earned and Much-Loved Homes": The Battle over Racial Restrictive Covenants in Housing

White use of racial restrictive covenants grew in the immediate postwar period, particularly in areas such as Bloomingdale, Brookland, and Columbia Heights that bordered expanding black communities. Fearing that the high black demand for housing—and the higher prices black buyers had to pay—would tempt white residents into selling out, white homeowners, real estate firms, and lending agencies collaborated to prevent a black "invasion" that they assumed would destabilize white neighborhoods and lower property values.[26]

The Washington Real Estate Board's code of ethics clearly stated that "no property in a white section should ever be sold, rented, advertised, or offered to colored people," and it barred agents who did so. It also policed the advertising pages of local newspapers to ensure that property listings were appropriately segregated by race. Commercial lenders refused to offer loans to black customers who sought financial support to buy homes in white neighborhoods. Citizens associations rallied white homeowners to support and expand the use of covenants. They often helped homeowners set up "ghetto funds" to support legal action against people who broke covenants. White organizations defended the use of restrictive covenants, wrote the Congress Heights Citizens Association, "because we feel abolition of covenants would deteriorate the value of our hard-earned and much-loved homes."[27]

Many white Washingtonians did not blame black people for buying homes as much as they blamed outsiders for fomenting racial tension—Communists, the media, civil rights agitators, the Supreme Court, even Eleanor Roosevelt. Real estate agents were a favorite target. "Unscrupulous real estate agents—white and colored—are using unfortunate and frequently innocent colored people to amass fortunes for themselves and [to destroy] white communities," fumed one white attorney. At a 1947 community meeting, a white homeowner in Northeast mused about taking "a nice healthy club or a crowbar" to the heads of real estate agents seeking to undermine his neighborhood but, he lamented, "our only redress is in courts."[28]

One man who inspired the wrath of white homeowners was Raphael Urciolo, a rogue agent who had been barred from the Washington Real Estate Board for selling white properties to black people. An Italian immigrant and Central High School alumnus with degrees from Catholic University, the University of Maryland, and the University of Rome, Urciolo was a lawyer, teacher, author, and linguist who spoke ten languages. As a member of the Catholic Interracial Council, Urciolo didn't "believe in covenants at all" and testified in court that he "would prefer to sell to the colored man because he has so much harder time getting a home." He also conceded that he liked selling to black buyers because they paid 30 percent to 40 percent more for their homes.[29]

Urciolo sold the home that ultimately destroyed the legal underpinnings of restrictive covenants in D.C. and established Charles Hamilton Houston as the foremost black lawyer in the nation. In June 1944, a black couple, James and Mary Hurd, bought a home through Urciolo at 116 Bryant Street NW, across from McMillan Park and just a few blocks east of Howard University. Noticing that there were black-owned homes throughout the neighborhood, including several on that block, the Hurds assumed that there would be no problem with their arrival. They were wrong.[30]

The Hurdses' home was one of twenty on the block still covered by restrictive covenants, and news of the sale reached white attorney Henry Gilligan, who was on retainer with the North Capitol Citizens Association to pursue "continuous litigation." A former school board member who lived around the corner, Gilligan had spent two decades enforcing restrictive covenants without having lost a case. He threatened the Hurds with legal action if they did not move immediately. When the Hurds were unable to sell the house quickly enough to satisfy the white neighbors, Gilligan hauled them—and, in a separate case, Urciolo as well—into court on behalf of several neighbors, including Lena Hodge. In their complaint, the plaintiffs claimed that having black residents on Bryant Street would be "harmful, detrimental and subversive" of their "peace of mind, comfort and property rights," and would make the area "undesirable as a neighborhood wherein white people may live." It already seemed to be less attractive to white residents—by the time the case went to trial, three other houses on the block had been sold to black buyers.[31]

Gilligan had reason to be confident that his unbeaten streak would continue in the case against the Hurds. Courts, after all, had been quite friendly to white homeowners in their battle to preserve segregated neighborhoods. In the two decades since the U.S. Supreme Court in *Corrigan v. Buckley* (1926) had determined that restrictive covenants were private contracts not subject to constitutional scrutiny, the federal appeals court had turned back repeated challenges. In one celebrated wartime case, *Mays v. Burgess* (1945), a black government employee was forced from her home on the 2200 block of First Street NW, not far from the Hurdses' house.[32]

But federal appeals court Judge Henry Edgerton, a well-respected Kansan appointed by President Roosevelt, dissented from the *Mays* ruling. Noting that "our *Corrigan* decision was probably unsound when it was rendered," Edgerton argued that the court should consider not only the changing housing situation throughout the city but also the effect of restrictive covenants on the black population.[33] Edgerton's dissent encouraged Charles Hamilton Houston and his liberal allies in the legal community to view restrictive covenants as potentially vulnerable to a constitutional challenge in the postwar world.

Houston served as the Hurdses' defense attorney, joined by a brilliant young Howard Law graduate, Spottswood Robinson III (who later was appointed as the first black judge on the D.C. circuit). They were among more than a dozen civil rights lawyers around the country who were challenging covenants in court. The District Court and U.S. Court of Appeals both bowed to precedent and ruled against the Hurds, but Judge Edgerton issued another stinging dissent in the appellate decision. He forcefully articulated the case against what he considered inequitable and indefensible racial restrictive covenants, arguing that they had helped create a "ghetto system." "The question is whether law should affirmatively support and enforce racial discrimination." The answer, he insisted, was no.[34]

Houston, Robinson, Urciolo, and a white government attorney named Phineas Indritz, who volunteered to help after he read Judge Edgerton's dissent, appealed *Hurd v. Hodge* to the U.S. Supreme Court. In 1948, the Court heard the case along with a companion suit, *Shelley v. Kraemer*, arising out of St. Louis. Two justices recused themselves because restrictive covenants covered their own homes, including Justice Wiley Rutledge's wooded manor on Indian Lane near American University. In his argument before the Court, Houston emphasized one essential question: "Shall we in the United States have ghettoes for racial, religious and other minorities, or even exclude such minorities entirely from white areas of our country, by a system of judicially enforced restrictions based on private prejudices and made effective through the use of government authority and power?" The judicial enforcement of prejudice was "plainly incompatible with [the] reasons why the United States fought in the war," Houston argued. "Racism must go."[35]

The Court decided unanimously in May 1948 to overturn the lower courts' rulings in *Hurd v. Hodge*, finding that judicial enforcement of race-based restrictive covenants violated the Civil Rights Act of 1866 by limiting black Washingtonians' equal right to own and use property. The covenants no longer were legally enforceable, and the Hurds could keep their home.[36]

Racial restrictions did not end overnight. Indeed, many homes, particularly in wealthy neighborhoods west of Rock Creek Park, maintained restrictive covenants for years afterward, protected by peer pressure among white homeowners and enforced by developers rather than the courts. But *Hurd v. Hodge* was a turning point. White real estate agents and property owners remained committed to preserving white neighborhoods, using violence at times, but black homebuyers had the weight of the law behind them for the first time. Within a few years, most of the city's neighborhoods had opened to black settlement. The decision encouraged housing activists nationwide to push for integrated public housing, which was soon incorporated into the Housing Act of 1949.[37]

The *Hurd* decision also showed that the Supreme Court was willing to overturn its precedents in race cases. Barely two decades after the *Corrigan* decision had solidified restrictive covenants as a legal means of preserving residential segregation, the Court saw fit to change its mind. What else might the justices reconsider?

The "Lost Laws": Annie Stein, Mary Church Terrell, and the Collapse of D.C.'s Discriminatory Legal Structure

Annie Stein spent her life challenging authority. The daughter of poor Ukrainian Jewish immigrants in Brooklyn, Stein embraced radical politics as a student at Hunter College in the early 1930s. She proudly joined the Communist Party, telling one crowd, "If fighting for lower tuition fees, for the rights of the Negro, for higher wages for student workers, for lower prices for the lunch room—if that be a Red then let's be Reds." That comment earned her the attention of the Federal Bureau of Investigation, which would track her for the rest of her life. A lithe five foot, seven inches with a thin face and prominent features, Stein personified the menace that unnerved Washington's white conservatives: a radical agitator bent on destroying cherished customs.[38]

Stein first came to D.C. as part of a student protest in 1933, and she saw firsthand not only the city's segregated patterns but also their fragility. When she joined a large, interracial group of students to demand service at a whites-only restaurant, they were not tossed out because "there were too many of us," she noted. "It struck some of us that a sizable group could make jim-crow restaurants tremble." She returned to Washington after graduation and worked briefly in the Works Progress Administration before leaving to focus on labor organizing. As chair of the Women's Trade Union League in D.C., she helped organize low-wage laundrywomen and restaurant workers. During the war she led a citywide strike to protest wartime inflation.

By the late 1940s, Stein was the primary caregiver for two young children and lived with her husband in a crammed two-bedroom apartment in Trenton Terrace, a predominantly Jewish complex on Trenton Place SE that was filled with aging New Dealers and liberal activists. Dubbed a "leftist nest" by the House Committee on Un-American Activities, Trenton Terrace attracted flocks of FBI agents who monitored the Steins and their neighbors and rummaged through their trash. As secretary of the local chapter of the Progressive Party, she learned to mute her Communist affiliations but never renounced them.[39]

Stein played an outsized role in the local civil rights struggle after the publication of *Segregation in Washington*, an incendiary ninety-one-page booklet that appeared in December 1948, seven months after the *Hurd* decision. The culmination of more than eighteen months of research, the report featured compelling anecdotes, pictures, and statistics that dissected Washington's racial practices and revealed the full extent of discrimination. It was produced by the National Committee on Segregation in the Nation's Capital, an interracial Chicago-based group backed by the Julius Rosenwald Fund. The organization's membership boasted an impressive lineup of prominent liberals, including former first lady Eleanor Roosevelt, Walter Reuther of the United Auto Workers, and then-Minneapolis mayor Hubert Humphrey. Fourteen of the committee's ninety-one members were from Washington, including Howard University president Mordecai Johnson, sociologist E. Franklin Frazier, and the ubiquitous Charles Hamilton Houston.

Written for a national audience, the report emphasized Washington's role as a "symbol of democracy" in the Cold War battle of ideas. Its unsparing analysis showcased racial discrimination in education, employment, health care, and housing, blaming primarily the Board of Trade, real estate companies, and other business interests whom the committee accused of profiting from discrimination by pandering to "the least tolerant white people." It also condemned the District commissioners, housing officials, and other public authorities who tolerated discrimination and helped the city become "the capital of white supremacy." Only the federal government, the report concluded, "has the power to break the chains that bar a quarter of a million Negroes in Washington from their equal rights as Americans."[40]

Segregation in Washington confirmed what local white conservatives had long feared: the momentum of elite public opinion had shifted significantly in favor of civil rights, at least at the national level. Yet segregationists, both in Congress and locally, continued to resist changes to a way of life they considered natural and harmonious. After the publication of *Segregation in Washington*, the Federation of Citizens Associations responded with an indignant, eight-page statement attacking the report for its "viciously distorted" picture of race relations in Washington. Tracing the roots of racial antagonism back to Reconstruction, the group warned that the "dangerous overnight repeal" of segregation "will bring about chaos, further inflame both races, and add fuel to the fires of racial misunderstandings." Rather than trying to impose integration "by legislation or administrative fiat," it argued, black Washingtonians instead "must appeal to the fairness and open-mindedness of members of the majority who, in the last analysis, will determine the issue."[41]

But racial reformers had appealed to the "fairness and open-mindedness" of white people for decades, with little success. Moral suasion alone was not enough to destroy Jim Crow—it required direct action, both on the streets and in the courts. The publication of *Segregation in Washington* in late 1948, coming so soon after the *Hurd* decision, accelerated racial progress. In the next year, Washington hosted an integrated presidential inauguration, local white parochial schools lifted racial exclusions, and the National Zoo and Washington National Airport eliminated their segregation policies. The National Capital Parks and Planning Commission added a black architect and removed all racial designations from its planning maps. "Before too long, at the present rate of progress, Washington may stop being a national disgrace," wrote one observer.[42]

Yet more struggles remained, particularly in combating segregated private businesses. *Segregation in Washington* inspired activists to challenge private racial discrimination by publicizing the discovery of what became known as the "lost laws." Amid the student sit-in movement of 1943–44, Howard Law School librarian A. Mercer Daniel was conducting background research when he discovered that an 1872 law banning racial discrimination in District businesses had never been repealed. The law required restaurants, barbershops, "ice cream saloons," and other establishments to serve "any respectable, well-behaved person, without regard to race, color, or previous condition of servitude." By the late nineteenth century, the customs and laws of segregation had settled across Washington, and city officials no longer enforced Reconstruction-era antidiscrimination statutes. When officials wrote D.C.'s legal code in 1901, they simply did not include such laws. "Since there is no record of [the law's] repeal," *Segregation in Washington* noted, "some lawyers speculate that it may still be technically in full force and effect."[43]

Charles Hamilton Houston joined a legal team headed by Joseph Forer and David Rein, two Jewish lawyers affiliated with the National Lawyers Guild, to end the speculation; black attorney and future judge Margaret Haywood also served on the team. The legal research took little time. Forer recalled that the team spent barely an afternoon to determine that the 1872 law, along with another from 1873, was indeed still valid. The court challenge, however, would take four years, and Houston would not live to see its conclusion—he died of a heart attack in June 1950, a victim of his own relentless work ethic.[44]

In May 1949, the attorneys presented their findings to the District commissioners and called on them to enforce the antidiscrimination laws. The commissioners passed the legal issue off to the city's counsel, who dallied for months without action. To pressure officials to act, Annie Stein and other local activists decided to buttress the legal case for the antidiscrimination laws with direct action to dramatize the issue. They created perhaps the most effective civil rights committee to date: the Coordinating Committee for the Enforcement of the D.C. Anti-Discrimination Laws. Despite its unwieldy name, the group proved quite nimble in battling recalcitrant businesses that segregated patrons, served black customers at rear windows, or otherwise discriminated against black people.[45]

The Coordinating Committee was led by Stein and Mary Church Terrell, two women of different races, religions, styles, and generations who shared a feisty determination to end Jim Crow. Terrell, at age eighty-six the grand dame of Washington's civil rights movement, remained a vociferous advocate for racial equality. She embraced her role as chair of the Coordinating Committee, willing to walk a picket line, testify before public officials, or pigeonhole a reporter to give a piece of her mind.

While Terrell was the elegant face of the campaign, Stein was the adrenaline. The scrappy, indefatigable thirty-six-year-old was a swirling force of nature. Her husky voice, salty language, and frenetic energy struck a sharp contrast to the stately, dignified Terrell, whom she adored. She melded an idealist's commitment to racial justice with a commander's mastery of strategy and logistics. Stein ran the committee's operations out of her apartment. Committee members fondly recalled how she "usually had the handle of a mimeograph machine in her hands and stood in her bedroom cranking out leaflets or letters or press releases far, far into the night." It was Stein who convinced Terrell to serve as the organization's leader. For nearly four years, the two were the heart and soul of the movement.[46]

"Segregation does not die gradually of itself," Stein wrote in a December 1949 memo to committee members. To destroy it, she plotted a methodical attack on multiple fronts. Reviving the "lost laws" might seem "limited in scope," she acknowledged, but it would have "a powerful effect on the whole segregation pattern by exposing more sharply the present inequities in schools, recreation, movies, etc." With dozens of local civic organizations offering support, the committee could pursue several lines of attack at once. It educated the public about the "lost laws" and the extent of discrimination in D.C.; negotiated with local businesses to encourage them to desegregate; planned and coordinated pickets and boycotts of uncooperative stores; lobbied city commissioners, Congress, and the president for legislative action; and pursued litigation to win the judicial imprimatur for desegregation.[47]

The committee's opening salvo was to create a test case by directly challenging segregation at a local restaurant. The choice was not coincidental. The committee selected Thompson's Restaurant, which had been the target of the Howard sit-ins half a decade before. On January 27, 1950, Terrell led an interracial group of four "respectable, well-behaved" committee members to Thompson's for a meal. The manager refused to serve them. "I asked if Washington was in the United States and if the United States Constitution applied here," Terrell recalled, to which the manager replied, "We don't vote here." The group left without eating, but it had accomplished its larger goal: to create a documented case of discrimination that violated the Reconstruction-era laws.[48]

The incident triggered a response from city officials. Within weeks, the city commissioners agreed that the antidiscrimination laws indeed were still in effect, a remarkable turnaround for a body that had resisted racial equality since its inception. With the city itself now officially in support of the lost laws, Terrell led another interracial group back to Thompson's. Once again, they were rebuffed. The city then sued.

The Washington Restaurant Association encouraged its members to maintain their segregated policies. One businessman feared "economic suicide" if black patrons were served. "Why the place would be overrun with them in a week," he claimed. "It would be broke in a month." The Board of Trade offered legal help and submitted a friend of the court brief on behalf of Thompson's.[49]

As the litigation wound its way through the courts, the committee sought to use the pressure of negative publicity to encourage businesses to drop their segregation policies voluntarily. It sent out interracial testing teams to determine which white-owned businesses would serve all customers—the State Department and foreign embassies were particularly interested to know where diplomats could expect service without discrimination. As the list grew, Terrell and Stein used it as leverage in negotiations with reluctant managers. Quiet negotiations often were effective, but when management proved particularly stubborn, the committee pulled out the pickets. Its first target was Kresge's five-and-ten-cent store in the heart of the Seventh Street NW commercial district. In December 1950, Terrell, dressed in an ankle-length fur coat and stylish scarf, took her cane and braved a snowstorm to lead the first picket. After eight weeks in which a hundred volunteers distributed more than forty thousand leaflets, Kresge's changed its policy.[50]

Once Kresge's surrendered, the other discount stores on Seventh Street quickly followed suit. The committee hoped to repeat that pattern with department stores by targeting Hecht's, a grand establishment on Seventh Street that got about 25 percent of its business from black customers. In February 1951, Hecht's sponsored an ad campaign in support of "Brotherhood Week" in which the store called for equal treatment of all people. When the ad appeared, Stein and Terrell pounced, questioning management about why the store refused to serve black customers at its basement lunch counter; the manager claimed that the ad was just a "gesture." Three months of negotiations failed, and in May the committee called for a boycott. Supporters sat in at the lunch counter, sent eight thousand postcards to management, and manned a well-dressed picket line for two hours daily throughout the summer and fall. Hecht's finally began serving everyone in January 1952. Terrell led the first interracial luncheon.[51]

Private negotiations, the potential for negative publicity, and the threat of boycotts opened up individual stores, but the legal case for the enforcement of the "lost laws" followed a tortuous path. The Municipal Court initially dismissed the suit in July 1950, claiming that the antidiscrimination laws had been "repealed by implication" when Congress created the District's new commissioner form of government in 1878 and with the 1901 rewriting of the District's legal code. The Municipal Court of Appeals then reversed that decision in May 1951 and ruled that the antidiscrimination laws were indeed still valid—but city officials decided to delay enforcement until all appeals had been exhausted. In January 1953, the U.S. Court of Appeals overturned the lower court's decision, ruling 5–4 that the laws "are presently unenforceable." The Coordinating Committee turned to the Supreme Court.[52]

At each stop along its exasperating journey through the legal thicket, the Coordinating Committee benefited from the guidance and support of the Department of Justice. In a powerfully worded brief to the U.S. Court of Appeals, Truman's attorney general Philip Perlman made an unequivocal case for dismantling segregation in the nation's capital, which he considered a "serious flaw in our democracy." Not only did the city's segregation defy the federal government's ban on racial discrimination against federal employees, but it undermined the nation's foreign policy.[53]

This clear federal support for desegregation continued under Republican Dwight Eisenhower, who took office shortly after the appeals court's decision. In his first message to Congress, delivered in early February 1953, he endorsed home rule for D.C. and declared that he would "use whatever authority exists in the office of the President to end segregation in the District of Columbia." Eisenhower's attorney general, Herbert Brownell, encouraged civil rights attorneys and filed a supportive brief in the *Thompson* case.[54]

The Supreme Court decided the case quickly. On June 8, 1953—not even six months after the appeals court's decision—the Court ruled unanimously in *District of Columbia v. John R. Thompson Co.* that the antidiscrimination laws "survived ... all subsequent changes in the government of the District of Columbia and remain today a part of the governing body of laws applicable to the District." With stunning clarity, the Court swept away the remaining legal justifications for segregation in District businesses.[55]

After more than six decades of struggling against the racial prejudice she saw around her, Mary Church Terrell had achieved her sweetest victory. The eighty-nine-year-old met up with some friends from the committee, and the interracial bunch went for a celebratory luncheon at Thompson's. The manager himself served them. "I will die happy to know that the children of my group will not grow up thinking they are inferior because they are deprived of rights which children of other racial groups enjoy," Terrell exulted. She died just a year later. Annie Stein mourned her dear friend from New York City, where she had moved just after the *Thompson* decision. She spent the next three decades fighting for integrated education. She died in 1981.[56]

After nearly a decade of concerted protest, most of the major legal barriers to equal access in Washington had fallen. Race-based restrictive covenants lost their legal force; businesses, restaurants, and theaters now offered service to customers of all races; local colleges and private secondary schools integrated their student bodies; the first integrated public housing development, Stanton

Dwellings, opened to great fanfare; and public recreation areas were open to everyone. "The people of the District have been taking sure strides away from the old injustice of segregation," the editors of the *Evening Star* wrote in an approving 1952 editorial.[57]

But one long-standing obstacle remained, what one activist called "the stronghold of Washington's segregation": the public schools. The dual school system did not have long to live either, but its story deserves special consideration. And that story begins with a black barber who had the temerity to challenge the city's postwar political establishment, both white and black.[58]

"It Would Not Happen to White Children":
Parent Activists Challenge Separate and Unequal Schools

Gardner Bishop was a talker. The son of a barber, he earned prizes as a high school debater in Rocky Mount, North Carolina, but never went to college. He moved to Washington in 1930 and found work cutting hair at a local barbershop, where his mouth proved to be a liability. Unable to resist challenging his white customers' racist comments, he eventually got fired. He then opened his own shop for a black clientele, the B&D Barber Shop at 1515 U Street NW, which he ran until he retired in 1985. For thirty-five cents, customers could get a haircut and an earful from the gruff, unrefined, tell-it-like-it-is owner.

The brawny, mustachioed "barber of U Street" generally steered clear of white Washington, but he was not one to abide quietly by the city's segregated customs. When his eldest daughter, Judine, was four years old, he let her play on an empty playground near their home. A white District police officer pulled up and pointed to the "Whites Only" sign at the playground entrance; Bishop replied, "She can't read." The comment earned him a trip to the police station and a $10 fine, but he had the satisfaction of standing up to a demeaning system.[59]

Bishop had no love for the ways of white folks, though he also scorned the habits of what he called "highfalutin blacks," the wealthier, well-educated black elites who dominated activist circles in the mid-1940s. In his mind, the local NAACP was a snobby "social group" whose members looked down on the poor and working-class people who were his customers, his neighbors, and his friends. The black poor faced "double Jim Crow," he believed. "I'm black and I'm poor so I'm segregated against twice." He resented how black school officials controlled the black schools—called "Division 2" (the white schools were "Division 1")—and protected their own at the expense of the poor black majority.[60]

Bishop's anger boiled over in 1947, when overcrowding forced Judine (by then a teenager) to attend Browne Junior High School part-time. He and other working-class parents tried to get their children placed in another school, but black administrators refused transfers "unless you were a big nigger," he recalled. "If you didn't have the right pull your children stayed right there in the swamp." Bishop became an outspoken advocate for the Browne parents. "I had more mouth than anyone else, and I worked for myself so there wasn't much chance of being punished by the whites," he said. Their initial protests against black school officials soon grew into an expansive and ultimately successful attack on the entire system of segregated schools in the District.[61]

The parents' anger can be traced to the deterioration of D.C.'s black schools in the decades following World War I. Though Dunbar High School remained the pride of elite black Washington, overall the city's black school system struggled to cope with the rapid growth of the black population, particularly as less-educated migrants from the rural South flooded into the city. The demographic changes spawned a funding crisis, due in part to the 1864 law that required the city to allocate school funds based on the number of black and white school-age children in the decennial census.[62]

The law originally aimed to ensure that black schools got their fair share of city revenues. But by the 1930s, it shortchanged the black system because white schools were shrinking as the black school population burgeoned. The white student population hit its peak in 1935 and declined steadily thereafter as more and more white families moved to the suburbs or chose to send their children to private schools. Between 1935 and 1947, the number of white students dropped by 15 percent, while the number of black students increased by more than 28 percent. By 1950, black students were the majority in D.C. public schools. Because of the 1864 law, black schools received a decreasing amount of money per pupil compared to their white counterparts because in the years between the decennial census the black school population grew while the white population shrank. In 1946, white schools spent roughly 27 percent more per student ($160.21) than black schools ($126.52). By the late 1940s, the city's Division 2 school system was in crisis, suffering from overcrowded schools, overworked teachers, and overwhelmed administrators.[63]

The school that Judine Bishop attended exemplified the problems. A modern facility in 1932 when it opened, Browne Junior High served rapidly growing black neighborhoods throughout Northeast Washington. Browne was designed to educate 783 students, but by the time Judine Bishop enrolled in 1947 it was bursting with 1,727 students, more than double its capacity.[64]

To alleviate the overcrowding, the school board implemented a policy of staggered shifts in which students received only four and a half hours of instructional time—far below the board's own minimum standard of six hours.

Teachers taught both shifts, and class sizes ranged as high as fifty-eight students. There were no laboratories and just one small gymnasium for students to use. Only a mile away, white students knocked about in increasingly empty Eliot Junior High School, which had vacant classrooms, underused space, and room for another two hundred students. One white school official called it "a notable embarrassment" that "classrooms were vacant in schools past which Negro children had to walk to get to their overcrowded schools."[65]

Many black parents saw an obvious solution: alleviate the overcrowding in the short term by transferring black students to underused white schools. School officials, however, were in a bind. Committed to maintaining the segregated system, they worried that worsening racial disparities could trigger legal action or federal intervention, yet they feared that transferring modern, well-equipped schools built for white children would only encourage more white families to leave the system. Superintendent Hobart Corning insisted that any disparities between the white and black systems arose simply from circumstance, and with support from the school board, he began pumping money into the Division 2 schools in a belated attempt to equalize facilities. In 1947, 72 percent of the school district's construction funds went to black schools.[66]

Often over the protests of its black members—by law, the school board was composed of six white members and three black members, all appointed by federal judges—the board remained committed to policing racial lines in the city's schools. In 1944, former National Negro Congress head John P. Davis petitioned the board to admit his five-year-old son to a white school near his home in the Northeast neighborhood of Brookland. Anxious school officials quickly bought land across the street from Davis's house and displaced nine black families to build a temporary one-room "school" for the Davis boy until a larger building could be constructed (Mary McLeod Bethune Charter School sits on the site today).[67]

Three years later, a Mexican American student named Karla Galarza enrolled at a black vocational school to take dress designing classes with a skilled teacher who had studied in New York and Paris. Her choice defied conventional wisdom about the inferiority of black schools and threw racial identities into question. The school board deemed that Galarza and other Mexican Americans were white and thus had to attend white schools; it expelled her from her chosen school. Her father, a labor leader with a Ph.D. from Columbia University, condemned the decision and called for the resignation of the school district's leaders "to make way for educators in our Nation's Capital who can think of a Washington in terms of 1947 instead of 1867."[68]

The situation at Browne and other black schools attracted increasing criticism, particularly from activists in the Committee for Racial Democracy in the Nation's Capital. Established in May 1946, the interracial committee sought to raise national awareness about Washington's racial practices. "It is an undeniable fact that until segregated schools in Washington are brought to an end, the entire social pattern of racial segregation will remain unchanged," wrote the editors of the D.C. edition of the black *Pittsburgh Courier*, who helped launch the organization. Agnes Meyer of the *Post*, a member of the group's public information committee, published a lengthy exposé of conditions at Browne in March 1947. Meyer painted a sympathetic portrait of Browne's "well-mannered" students, "cultivated" teachers, and "poised" principal, while condemning school officials' indifference to the problems Browne and other black schools faced.[69]

The conditions at Browne prompted parents in the school's Parent Teacher Association to petition the school board in April 1947 to transfer black students to Eliot Junior High. Filed on behalf of Browne student Marguerite Carr, daughter of the PTA president, the petition and accompanying presentation before the board laid out in excruciating detail how the school's overcrowding deprived Carr and her classmates of an adequate education. Superintendent Corning acknowledged the deficiencies but refused to transfer any students. In response, the Carrs, the PTA, and their NAACP attorneys filed a class action lawsuit.[70]

As *Carr v. Corning* wound its way through the courts, dissatisfied parents rebelled against the black leadership. A court case would take years; meanwhile, enrollment at Browne had soared past eighteen hundred students with no signs of peaking. School officials decided to alleviate the overcrowding by transferring two old, poorly equipped white elementary schools to the black system for use by Browne students, a move black parents roundly condemned. "The average parent does not give a hoot about his child going to a white school, but he does not want the fact that his child must be segregated used as an excuse for his being given sub-standard, obsolete, hand-me-down school facilities abandoned by whites," argued parent Nellie V. Greene. The decision triggered the formation of a grassroots parent group that would take the dispute out of the boardrooms and courts and into the streets.[71]

At the first meeting of what would become the Browne Parent Group for Equality of Educational Opportunities, more than 160 parents signed a petition to the school board announcing a bold act of civil disobedience: they would not send their children to school until the school board provided "adequate relief from part-time schooling." Gardner Bishop became the eminently quotable, highly visible spokesman for the group, but he certainly was not the only driving force in the movement. More than half of the petition signers were housewives or retired women, and the two cochairs were particularly active women with previous experience in political activism: Nellie Greene and Capitol View Civic Association leader Joy P. Davis. They were a proudly grassroots group, but from the beginning its membership spanned the full range of classes within the black community.[72]

The strike began on December 3, 1947. Parents picketed Browne and the majestic Franklin School downtown, where the Board of Education had its offices. They also visited local and federal officials to press their case in person (though White House guards prevented them from dropping in on President Truman). As the strike continued into January 1948, pressure from school officials, criticism from Browne's principal and other black leaders, and the hardships imposed by the strike itself took a toll on parents. Picket lines thinned, and Bishop and other leaders of the Browne Parent Group turned to the man at the center of the NAACP's multipronged assault on District segregation: Charles Hamilton Houston.[73]

Despite Bishop's mistrust of elite black leaders, he and Houston bonded immediately, and the two became strong allies and close friends during the next year. Houston promised to file a series of lawsuits aimed at equalizing school facilities. His first salvo was a lawsuit that held members of the Board of Education personally liable for "willfully refusing to equalize education and knowingly perpetuating inequality." Pointing out the burdens borne by Browne students, Houston argued simply, "It would not happen to white children." With the lawsuit filed and a strategy in place, Houston and the Browne Parent Group stopped the strike on February 2. The next day, officials adopted a revised plan that incorporated five buildings to ensure that all Browne students received a full day of classes.[74]

The two-month strike signaled that a new phase of school protest had begun. Unafraid to use civil disobedience if necessary, parents organized themselves to challenge school authorities and demand a say in school decision-making. With unassailable credibility as parents, strike leaders helped dramatize school inequality and forced officials to address their concerns. Although the parents did not achieve their immediate goal—school officials did not transfer Eliot Junior High to black students—the impact of the strike would reverberate far beyond Browne.

The strike catalyzed Gardner Bishop, Joy Davis, and other Browne Parent Group leaders to form the Consolidated Parent Group in September 1948 to fight school discrimination citywide. Bishop became president of the group. With three barbers now working for him, he had the flexibility to meet with Houston, arrange pickets, talk with the media, gather petition signatures, and take depositions to buttress the various lawsuits that Houston was pursuing.

The group provided Houston and his legal team with a strong grassroots presence and helped maintain momentum as the lawsuits proceeded.[75]

The Browne strike also jolted Congress into action. Disturbed by the issues raised by striking parents, Representative Everett Dirksen, a pro–civil rights Republican from Illinois and the new chairman of the House District Committee, called for a thorough investigation into the city's schools. The committee hired George D. Strayer, an eminent professor emeritus of education from the Teachers College of Columbia University, to lead a team of twenty-two researchers. Strayer's blistering, 980-page report relentlessly criticized the school district's "unresponsive" administration, "complicated, inflexible, and cumbersome" financial system, and "inadequate" facilities, funding, and academic programs, particularly in the black schools.[76]

Released in February 1949, the Strayer report confirmed what black parents and activists had been saying about woefully underfunded, inadequately staffed, and poorly housed black schools. His criticisms could not be dismissed as the carping of Communist-inspired parents or the work of rabble-rousing lawyers. Widely read in policy-making circles, the Strayer report became Exhibit A as black parents, community activists, and NAACP lawyers made their final, decisive case against legally segregated schools in the nation's capital.[77]

"Degrading, Demoralizing, Undemocratic, and Detrimental to This Country as a Whole": The End of Legally Segregated Schools in D.C.

In the wake of the Strayer report, school officials faced increasing pressure to deal with severe overcrowding. The problem was particularly acute at the secondary level: black high schools were more than 50 percent over capacity, while white high schools were nearly 25 percent under capacity. Black Cardozo High School, located in a decrepit building at Ninth Street and Rhode Island Avenue NW that the white system had abandoned two decades before, had more than seventeen hundred students—double its capacity—and had no playgrounds or recreation areas. Classes were held in corridors, basement rooms, and even outside.[78]

The Strayer report recommended closing Cardozo completely, but where would the students go? Given the curricular and programmatic needs of high school students, school officials could not simply transfer underused white elementary schools, as they had in previous cases. Instead, by mid-1949, black parents and activists began pushing the board to embrace a simple, but politically perilous, solution that even Strayer had not dared to recommend: move Central High School to the black system.

School officials had transferred nearly a dozen white schools to black pupils since the end of the war in 1945. But Central High School was no ordinary facility. Founded in 1882, Central moved in 1916 to a nine-acre site at the corner of Thirteenth and Clifton Streets NW, where the school district built a "castle on the hill" to match the gleaming monuments envisioned in the McMillan Plan. Sitting majestically on a steep rise with panoramic views of downtown, Central was an architectural marvel, a community landmark, and the pride and joy of white Washington. The school's 47,000 alumni included some of Washington's most prominent leaders. Central resembled a small college, boasting an oak-paneled library, multiple laboratories, several gymnasiums, an indoor track, even an armory and rifle range. Designed to educate 1,950 students, Central had seen its enrollment dwindle to 1,437 by 1948. Black parents and activists eyed the spacious building to alleviate overcrowding and give black students access to a first-class facility.[79]

The idea to transfer Central to the black school division had begun percolating among activists after the Browne parent strike in 1948, and the stunning statistics outlined in the Strayer report helped catalyze a citywide "Central for Cardozo" movement. The effort united the parent activists mobilized by the Browne strike with the city's broader civil rights community. One early and effective advocate was Paul Cooke, a professor at Miner Teachers College and head of the local black teachers' union. A graduate of Dunbar High School with a Ph.D. in education from Columbia University, Cooke synthesized the Strayer report into a compelling case for transferring Cardozo students to a different school.[80]

Gardner Bishop and the Consolidated Parent Group backed Cooke by gathering ten thousand signatures on a mammoth mid-1949 petition to the school board demanding "immediate relief" from overcrowding. Activists pounded school board members with letters and waged a high-profile media campaign. Their full-page advertisements and frequent letters to the editors of local newspapers quoted the Strayer report and touted the support of an interracial coalition of civic organizations, including the NAACP, the American Veterans Committee, and the D.C. League of Women Voters (headed by a Central alumna). "This is no fight by or for Negroes," read one ad, "but a fight by and for Americans."[81]

Transferring Central appealed to some white conservatives as a way to forestall full integration—one Federation of Citizens Association member warned, "If you don't give them equal opportunities, you will find equal opportunities forced upon you." But the prospect of losing the cherished institution horrified most white Washingtonians. "Central is not merely a tradition," wrote one aggrieved alum to the school board president. "It is a living force for good." Outraged white parents and alumni assailed the school board at public hearings in September 1949 and spent months mobilizing opposition to the idea.[82]

Despite protests from white alumni, the school board voted 5–2 in March 1950 to transfer Central. Two white members joined all three black members in supporting the transfer. Angry Central alumni insisted that the school no longer bear the name etched in stone above the arched Gothic entryway. School officials complied and erased Central High School from the educational landscape. The building became home to Cardozo High School, which still stands on its hilltop overlooking downtown (though the etched "Central" remains visible above the entrance).[83]

Perhaps as much as any court decision or event, the loss of Central convinced conservative white Washingtonians that the city was no longer theirs. Even the full-throated opposition of Central's powerful alumni had not swayed the decisions of federally appointed officials grappling with a multitude of conflicting interests, including a vocal, growing interracial network of local and national activists. Losing Central helped break the back of white resistance to desegregation efforts. Though the white citizens associations remained active, their efforts grew more shrill and less effective. A sense of gloom pervaded conservative white Washington, a feeling that the war had been lost even if they could still win a battle here or there.[84]

Central High became Cardozo, but the city's school system remained segregated and the school board had no plans to integrate. It had support from the federal Court of Appeals. In February 1950, just a month before the school board's decision to transfer Central High School, the federal appeals court dealt civil rights forces a dispiriting defeat in *Carr v. Corning*, the class action suit filed shortly before the Browne parent strike two years earlier. The court majority found no evidence of discrimination against black students and ruled that school segregation was both constitutional and supported by Congress.[85]

But racial egalitarians took heart in the spirited rebuttal from Henry Edgerton, the judge whose prescient dissents in the restrictive covenant cases anticipated the Supreme Court's precedent-reversing 1948 decision in *Hurd v. Hodge*. Once again on the losing end of a 2–1 vote, Edgerton wrote another devastating dissent in *Carr v. Corning*. The contrarian judge condemned the majority for ignoring the Strayer report, which he cited extensively to show that there was unequivocal evidence of "great inequalities between white and colored schools." "The District of Columbia is not a provincial community but the cosmopolitan capital of a nation that professes democracy," Edgerton concluded, and the courts need not wait on Congress to rectify this glaring injustice.[86]

The *Carr* decision, combined with Charles Hamilton Houston's death two months later, prompted a significant shift in legal strategy. Under Houston's direction, the Consolidated Parent Group had pursued several cases aimed at equalizing resources among segregated schools. As he lay dying, Houston had encouraged the group to reach out to his Howard Law colleague James Nabrit. The brilliant son of a Georgia minister who graduated at the top of his class at Northwestern Law School, Nabrit was not interested in the cases—he thought that the equalization strategy had run its course. He proposed to become the group's lawyer only if they launched a direct assault on segregation itself. Bishop and the Consolidated Parent Group agreed. They hired Nabrit and began searching for a test case.

They found one in Sousa Junior High School in Southeast. After school officials announced that they would open Sousa in fall 1950, the Consolidated Parent Group demanded black students have full access. School officials, led by black assistant superintendent Garnet Wilkinson, suggested turning the old Birney School over to black students, prompting howls of protest from black parents. That September, they pressed their case before the Board of Education, arguing, in Bishop's words, that "dual systems have never produced equality and the general rule is that the colored child always bears the brunt of inequities."[87] Segregated schooling, the parents wrote on a cardboard petition, was "degrading, demoralizing, undemocratic, and detrimental to this country as a whole."[88] When the school board refused to budge, they sued board president Melvin C. Sharpe on behalf of eleven-year-old Spottswood Bolling.

Bolling v. Sharpe was decided alongside four companion cases that comprised *Brown v. Board of Education of Topeka*. Attorneys James Nabrit and George E. C. Hayes (who as a school board member in 1947 had condemned the Browne parent strike) presented their arguments to the Supreme Court on December 10, 1952; the justices reheard the case a year later.

Like the attorneys in *Brown*, Nabrit and Hayes emphasized the international context in which the case was being heard, charging that segregated schools violated the United Nations charter and undermined America's leadership in the world. But *Bolling* was distinct because of the District's unique political status. Nabrit and Hayes could not use the Fourteenth Amendment to argue that black students had been denied equal protection of the laws because the amendment did not apply to the District, only to states. Instead, they used the Fifth Amendment's due process clause to challenge Congress's power to impose dual schools on the city. Unlike the attorneys in the *Brown* cases, they never raised the issue of equal facilities or disparities between the black and white school systems, and they did not argue that separate was inherently unequal. Rather, they focused solely on whether school officials had the power to deny students entry to Sousa on the basis of race. "We submit that in this case, in the heart of the nation's capital, in the capital of democracy, in the capital of the free world, there is no place for a segregated school system," Nabrit concluded. "This country cannot afford it, and the Constitution does not permit it, and the statutes of Congress do not authorize it."[89]

The attorney for the school board, Milton D. Korman, captured the dismay that many white Washingtonians felt about losing the dual school system and their entire segregated way of life. A lifelong Washingtonian and alumnus of Central High School, Korman emphasized the good intentions with which white people established segregated schools. "The dual system was not set up to stamp these [black] people with a badge of inferiority," he argued. Instead, it emerged from a "kindly feeling"—school officials simply wanted black children to be educated "in a place where they are wanted, in a place where they will not be looked upon with hostility." He speculated that in time, perhaps, schools could be integrated once there was "a general acceptance of the proposition that these two races can live side by side without friction, without hostility, without any occurrences." Until then, however, he urged the Court to leave the issue to Congress. Korman's plaintive appeal swayed no one on the Court.[90]

As the Supreme Court deliberated on Bolling, the school board struggled with how to prepare for the impending decision. When the board solicited input from community members about how best to desegregate schools, angry segregationists in Congress and in local citizens associations condemned the action as "presumptuous." After adopting a wait-and-see attitude, the board found itself under attack from its newest member, Margaret Just Butcher, who had joined the body in June 1953. A Dunbar graduate with a Ph.D. from Boston University, the petite forty-one-year-old English professor was proper in etiquette, charming in manner, and stylish in dress. But Butcher was a fierce critic of inequities in the schools and perceived foot-dragging by school officials. At every board meeting, in every newspaper, at every opportunity, Butcher pushed administrators to seize the initiative on desegregation in advance of any Supreme Court ruling. They preferred to wait for the Court.[91]

The Court's decision came on May 17, 1954. "We hold that racial segregation in the public schools of the District of Columbia is a denial of the due process of law guaranteed by the Fifth Amendment to the Constitution," wrote newly confirmed Chief Justice Earl Warren in a short, 550-word opinion in Bolling v. Sharpe. The city's ninety-two-year experiment with segregated schools was over. "I think it's a wonderful thing for this country," said Sarah Bolling, mother of plaintiff Spottswood Bolling, now fifteen years old. "Now we can hold up our heads before the world."[92]

Federal and local officials responded swiftly to the *Bolling* decision. President Eisenhower immediately told city commissioners that he wanted Washington to serve as a model for the nation, and within eight days the school board had approved a nondiscrimination resolution in teacher and student placement. Superintendent Corning then proposed a gradual desegregation process involving a limited number of schools in fall 1954, with the rest waiting until fall 1955 to be desegregated. The plan also gave students the option of completing their studies at their original schools if they chose.[93]

Corning's plan struck Margaret Just Butcher and parent advocates as unnecessarily slow and complicated. Butcher accused the superintendent of creating "a checkerboard scheme in which a stipulated number of Negro students were being sent to a stipulated number of white schools, thereby burdening the Negro student as an interloper and actually solving only the problem of overcrowded schools." The plan passed over her objections.[94]

That September, school officials transferred about 2,700 black students to formerly all-white schools, and white schools opened to black students who lived in adjacent neighborhoods. About half of the school district's students went to at least nominally integrated schools. (Ironically, Spottswood Bolling himself attended an all-black school.) The first weeks passed without incident, a remarkable accomplishment considering the violence and chaos that erupted when desegregation came to other Southern cities.[95]

Newspapers cheered and school administrators breathed a sigh of relief, but simmering tensions boiled over in early October after officials transferred more black students to white schools. In protest, as many as 2,900 white students from Anacostia, Eastern, and McKinley High Schools, as well as several junior high schools, staged a three-day walkout. The striking students held demonstrations with their parents and pastors, including a march down Nichols Avenue (now Martin Luther King Avenue) with sign-toting mothers pushing strollers. One group of about 50 Anacostia students protested in front of the Supreme Court. "We've been pounded and drilled all our lives that Negroes are inferior and it's just not easy to change when you've been taught something all your life," explained one student. The protests quickly fizzled after Superintendent Corning threatened to revoke the students' extracurricular activities if they did not return to class. There were no more organized protests against desegregation.[96]

By fall 1955, the local and national press celebrated "a remarkably smooth year" in the city's schools. A five-part *Evening Star* series portrayed earnest students, teachers, and administrators collaborating to make desegregation work

After the Supreme Court ruled school segregation unconstitutional in Bolling v. Sharpe (1954), D.C.'s public schools desegregated relatively rapidly. Sporadic protests erupted, including this October 1954 march by white families in Anacostia. Reprinted with permission of the DC Public Library, Star Collection, © Washington Post.

despite "exaggerated" fears and rumors. The relatively easy transition to racially mixed schools was seen as evidence that the city had come to accept desegregation. "Washingtonians believe integration in the Nation's Capital is 'going well,'" claimed one survey published in the *Post*. Supporters lauded the school district and heralded a new era of race relations.[97]

Such rosy assessments overestimated white Washingtonians' acceptance of desegregation. By 1954, after nearly a decade of losing battles against an increasingly powerful opposition, white conservatives felt besieged and battered, overwhelmed by the civil rights movement, federal power, demographic shifts, a changing international context, and other forces beyond their control. The lack of violence accompanying school integration reflected white conservatives' resignation, perceived impotence, and grudging respect for the rule of law, rather than an embrace of racially mixed schools.

The Federation of Citizens Associations challenged pupil and teacher assign-

ments and filed suit to block the implementation of the school board's desegregation plan, but the case quickly was dismissed. When the Supreme Court refused to consider the FCA's appeal in January 1955, the organization essentially
gave up. "I'd say that we're through," conceded the group's attorney. Frustrated
white conservatives channeled their rage into a successful campaign to block
the reappointment of Margaret Just Butcher to the Board of Education in 1956,
but their influence on school affairs was waning.[98]

Unable to block desegregation, many white families expressed their opposition to desegregation in a quiet, law-abiding, but ultimately devastating way: by
taking their children out of D.C.'s public schools. What came to be called "white
flight" from the inner city did not begin with the *Bolling* decision, but school desegregation accelerated the trend of suburban migration. In the two years after
Bolling, the number of white public school students dropped by 29 percent, from
49,106 to 34,758. Many all-white schools, including Eastern High School, became entirely black within five years. By 1965, there were 15,364 white students
left in D.C. public schools, barely 10 percent of the student population, and
those students were clustered in overwhelmingly white schools in relatively well
off neighborhoods west of Rock Creek Park. Those figures changed little in the
following half-century.[99]

Even liberal white supporters of school desegregation often took their children out of the public schools. White school administrator (and future superintendent) Carl Hansen dubbed it "the White Dilemma" as white liberals grappled
with how to respond to what they feared would be the disciplinary problems,
lower academic standards, and potential interracial dating in desegregated
schools. Most concluded that they wanted none of it. Hansen himself confessed
that he, too, preferred for his children to attend schools where they would be
the dominant racial group.[100]

Though by 1956 organized local resistance to school desegregation was
flagging, Southern segregationists were just beginning a powerful campaign
of "massive resistance" that would maintain segregated schools across much
of the region for more than another decade. Key to this offensive was a series of
hearings in September 1956 orchestrated by Representative John McMillan of
South Carolina to embarrass D.C. school officials and smear desegregation
as unwise, even dangerous. A University of South Carolina football star who
vigorously defended the tobacco farmers in the northeastern part of his state,
McMillan rose to the helm of the House District Committee after Democrats regained the House in the 1954 elections. "Johnny Mac" was an avowed segregationist who spent the next two decades sabotaging civil rights in D.C.[101]

McMillan created a special House Subcommittee to Investigate Public School

Standards and Conditions and Juvenile Delinquency in the District of Columbia, headed by Democratic representative James Davis of Georgia. Four of the subcommittee's six members had recently signed the Southern Manifesto, in which they pledged to "use all lawful means to bring about a reversal" of desegregation. With a $75,000 budget and an ax to grind, the subcommittee hired a zealous investigator and spent nine days grilling more than fifty school officials, administrators, teachers, and community members about how integration had created chaos, dumbed down the curriculum, and exposed white students to tuberculosis, venereal disease, and other health risks.[102]

The hearings depicted school integration in D.C. as an unmitigated disaster and a warning to the nation. It may be too late to save Washington, the segregationist subcommittee majority implied, but with resistance white people could prevent such horrors of integration from happening elsewhere. Congressman Davis assembled the most lurid and alarmist testimony from the hearings into a forty-eight-page pamphlet and distributed fifty thousand copies across the South. Chock-full of tales of oversexed, undereducated black "delinquents" preying on white students and teachers, the pamphlet emphasized the "wide disparity in mental ability between white and Negro students" and insisted that integration in Washington was "not a model to be copied by other communities." It helped galvanize white opposition to school desegregation efforts nationwide.[103]

Before, during, and after the Davis subcommittee hearings, desegregation supporters rallied to defend the record of the city's integrated schools. The press panned the hearings—the Post deemed them a "hatchet job"—and local religious and community leaders created the Washington Committee for Public Schools to mobilize support for integration. Under intense questioning from the subcommittee, assistant superintendent Carl Hansen defiantly insisted that school integration in Washington was "a miracle of social adjustment"; several months later, he wrote a booklet by that title extolling the efforts of teachers and students in integrated schools. Howard professor of education Ellis Knox published a study refuting the committee's findings. District schools, Knox wrote, "are providing a higher level of education than ever before."[104]

Even the most committed desegregation supporters did not deny that serious problems abounded in the schools. The subcommittee deliberately exaggerated the disciplinary problems in integrated schools, but the low achievement of black students compared to their white counterparts was not a figment of the segregationist imagination. Margaret Just Butcher and other stalwart activists recognized the serious educational deficiencies of many black students. "I would have been amazed if the Negro child, moving from a segregated school to a desegregated school, had performed more ably—after contending with inferior schools, overcrowded classes and a lack of teachers," Butcher argued. Yet she did not blame integration or innate black inferiority, as segregationists did. "It is segregation that has perpetuated the Negro educational lag," she maintained.[105]

The schools reflected serious problems within the city itself. By late 1957, Superintendent Corning declared, school desegregation was "complete," but this did not mean that D.C. schools were integrated. "Desegregation is merely the moving about of people and things," Corning noted. "Integration is a much longer process. Its success will depend on creation in the community of the social climate necessary for the progress of education." Full integration proved elusive, however, because it was connected to larger troubles facing Washington. "Integration is uncovering problems of health and welfare as well as those of direct educational shortages which were long half-concealed behind the curtain of segregation," wrote Douglass Cater, a sympathetic white journalist who investigated D.C. schools for the *Reporter* in late 1954. Cater found that Washington was "a true model for the nation" with people in the school system working hard to make integration work, but city leaders needed to address serious problems in housing, urban development, and the economy if D.C. hoped to avoid becoming a place "where only the very poor and the very rich continue to live in the heart of the city."[106]

The trouble was that Washingtonians lacked the power to do anything about these problems. Without self-government, they remained at the mercy of the District Committees in Congress, which were dominated by segregationist Southern Democrats who sought to punish the District for its civil rights advances. "Unless the people of Washington win their long-sought home rule, the very success [of integration] could bring on a gradual debasement of education, a general decline in civic conditions, and perhaps a form of continued segregation within the schools because of the further spreading of slum areas in the center of the city," Cater wrote. "It would be tragic indeed if this major forward step in democracy should be frustrated by Federal restraints that prevent Washington's citizens from governing themselves democratically."[107]

The decade following the end of World War II witnessed remarkable racial reforms in Washington, which by 1957 had become the first major city in the country to have a black majority. Segregation in the city had not died gradually of itself—it was killed by the concerted efforts of an interracial group of activists, parents, lawyers, writers, federal workers, and others committed to an egalitarian capital. These civil rights advocates seized on Washington's changing political, economic, and demographic context to push federal authorities to support racial change. With desegregated schools, restaurants, theaters, transportation, public housing, and recreation areas, "the Capital is as thoroughly integrated in all phases of its community life as any other city in the country," claimed a *New York Times* reporter in 1956.[108]

But the end of legal segregation did not end racial inequality in Washington, nor did it address D.C.'s serious economic and political dysfunction. In the 1960s, Washingtonians seeking to create a democratic, equitable city would find that their struggle was just beginning.

ELEVEN

How Long? How Long?

Mounting Frustration within the Black Majority, 1956–1968

Direct action has called attention to problems and gotten token changes but it has made no real basic changes. Political and economic force will bring about permanent change. —JULIUS HOBSON, 1964

Southwest is Washington's "stepchild area," wrote urban critic Jane Jacobs in 1956, a place "blackballed by geography" and "buffeted by official whims." The smallest of Washington's quadrants in both size and population, Southwest does not feature distinct neighborhoods with historic names that reach back into the city's past; the entire area is known simply as "Southwest." Dubbed "the Island" in the mid-nineteenth century, it historically has been isolated physically and culturally from the rest of the city, separated first by the infamous City Canal, then by a set of unsightly railroad tracks, and now by a confusing network of highways and exit ramps. These concrete ribbons slice Southwest into several pieces and render it relatively inaccessible to outsiders. Though tourists and many Washingtonians overlook Southwest, its history is central to the racial turmoil and activism that marked the city in the 1950s and 1960s.[1]

The Southwest we see in the early twenty-first century did not develop organically through two centuries of urban growth. Instead, it emerged suddenly in the decades after World War II. In the late 1940s, city officials, urban planners, and their allies in the local press and business community grew increasingly worried about "the flight to the suburbs." The loss of city residents, wrote the *Post*'s Chalmers Roberts in a 1952 series ominously titled "Progress or Decay?," was "the central civic problem in Washington today." City leaders feared that inner city "blight"—a term borrowed from agriculture to depict a seemingly natural process of disease and decay—was "infecting" the older neighborhoods in downtown Washington, including Southwest.[2]

At midcentury, Southwest was home to twenty-three thousand residents, more than 70 percent of whom were black and about 90 percent of whom were poor. "Inside bathrooms, kitchen sinks, central heating and electric lights are

Southwest Washington in the early 1950s was home to twenty-three thousand people, most of whom were black and poor. Nearly all the buildings in the foreground of this picture were destroyed as part of "urban renewal" in the 1950s and 1960s. Library of Congress.

luxuries of extreme rarity," noted a 1942 survey; a decade later, another study found that 80 percent of the housing units were substandard. Journalists and photographers regularly juxtaposed ramshackle homes and plywood privies with the majestic Capitol and elegant federal buildings located just blocks away. But Southwest also featured fine row houses of brick or wood with carefully tended front and back lawns. Indeed, the Homebuilders' Association of Metropolitan Washington found that many homes were "as sound and in many cases as large as fashionable homes in Georgetown."[3]

Ignoring this complexity, urban planners and city boosters made Southwest ground zero in a national movement for "urban renewal," a federally supported effort to use modern planning to revitalize and redevelop crumbling residential areas. Without concerted action, advocates warned, cities would wither as they lost jobs, shoppers, and taxpayers to the suburbs. In Washington, the driving force behind urban renewal was the Redevelopment Land Agency (RLA), created by Congress in 1945 to buy up unsightly city lots, clear them out, and then offer them at reduced prices to private contractors for redevelopment. Under the leadership of local department store magnate Mark Lansburgh, the RLA prioritized projects that lured middle-class residents and shoppers back to the city. The agency received its first major funding through the National Housing Act of 1949.[4]

The bill launched the era of federal urban renewal in American cities. As it was during the City Beautiful movement, Washington became an early testing ground for urban renewal both because of its symbolic importance and because planners could work directly with city commissioners and business interests without any democratic accountability. One optimistic 1955 report proclaimed that with concerted planning, the liberal use of "fight blight funds," and rigorous code enforcement, in a decade "Washington could become the country's first major slumless city."[5]

Many within the black community opposed urban renewal from the beginning. When planners in 1949 considered redeveloping Marshall Heights, a low-income, semirural black neighborhood in Southeast, they ran into opposition from the well-organized homeowners in the area. The black *Pittsburgh-Washington Courier* articulated black residents' frustration and fear of displacement: "The plea that 'thousands of Negroes will lose their life savings and become renters or objects of charity; hundreds of Negro business enterprises will be wiped out; hundreds of Negro churches will be destroyed and their membership scattered; Negro professional men will lose their clientele' is seen as a poor excuse for not making Washington the most beautiful city in the world."[6]

Hoping to avoid such concerted opposition, the RLA in June 1951 selected for its first major project a 550-acre site in Southwest that encompassed nearly the entire quadrant. Most area residents were renters, who had less incentive and power to fight such projects. Initial plans drawn up by architect Elbert Peets called for gradual redevelopment by rehabilitating the older housing stock, building low-income housing units, and working carefully to maintain the character of the neighborhood and ensure that current residents would not be displaced.[7]

Peets's plan did not impress RLA officials, however. They commissioned an alternative produced by the renowned architect team of Louis Justement and Chloethiel Woodard Smith. The pair offered a bold plan to level the entire area and replace it with gleaming modern developments featuring luxury apartments and townhomes, a massive shopping center, a renovated waterfront with high-rise commercial buildings, and an elegant promenade connecting the neighborhood to downtown. The plan envisioned an entirely new Southwest with high real estate values, abundant open space, and modern amenities to appeal to

wealthier residents. It also would require displacing nearly the entire population of Southwest.[8]

The competing proposals went before the National Capital Parks and Planning Commission, which had insisted in its 1950 comprehensive plan that any
redevelopment should offer displaced residents "substitute housing of a 'decent,
safe, and sanitary character,' at prices they can afford."[9] The Planning Commission proposed a compromise that promised to maintain the area's character (as
Peets had advocated) and included a provision requiring that at least one-third
of the new units be set aside for low-income housing.

In practice, however, urban renewal in Southwest followed the clear-and-
rebuild approach of the Justement-Smith plan. Powerful backers, including the
Metropolitan Board of Trade and the *Washington Post*, pushed for wholesale redevelopment, and federal officials with the Housing and Home Finance Agency
refused to fund projects that emphasized rehabilitation.[10]

The first bulldozers began clearing the area in April 1954, but legal and financial problems delayed initial construction for more than two years. Two business owners in the targeted area challenged the constitutionality of the entire
process, arguing that it was illegal for the RLA to take their land because their
properties were neither housing nor dilapidated; the land was going to be used
for private development rather than public use; they were not receiving just
compensation; and they had not been given due process under the Fifth Amendment. The lawsuit threatened urban renewal projects across the country, and the
case quickly landed on the Supreme Court's docket.

In December 1954, the Court ruled unanimously in *Berman v. Parker* that city
officials did indeed have the right to take the land. "If those who govern the
District of Columbia decide that the Nation's Capital should be beautiful as well
as sanitary, there is nothing in the Fifth Amendment that stands in the way,"
wrote Justice William O. Douglas, who framed the matter as a moral impera-
tive. "The misery of housing may despoil a community as an open sewer may
ruin a river."[11]

Despite such stirring rhetoric, the largely forgotten decision in *Berman v.
Parker* had a devastating impact on low-income and black communities in the
District and elsewhere. The same Court that had laid a legal foundation for
racial equality in Washington in its decisions on segregation in housing (*Hurd v.
Hodge*), businesses (*D.C. v. Thompson*), and schools (*Bolling v. Sharpe*) now gave its
approval for what became the wholesale destruction of a poor, predominantly
black community.

During the next two decades, at a cost of about $500 million (about $4.6 billion in twenty-first-century dollars), the neighborhoods of old Southwest dis-

appeared from the landscape. In their place rose modern projects such as Capitol Park, built atop the notorious Dixon Court alley. Completed in 1965, Capitol Park featured five high-rise residential buildings set amid a reflecting pool, public art, and other amenities. Its design earned a prestigious merit award from the American Institute of Architects. Urban renewal in Southwest won widespread praise from planners, city officials, the Metropolitan Board of Trade, and the press for combining "suburban wholesomeness with urban stimulation," as the *Post*'s architectural critic Wolf Von Eckardt wrote.[12]

Modernization came at tremendous cost. In his 1959 "church-eye view of urban renewal" for the National Conference of Catholic Charities, Father Robert G. Howes—an urban renewal advocate—warned that developments in Southwest "show tendencies to place the City Beautiful and the City Prosperous ahead of the City Human." Despite early promises that no families would be evicted and that new housing would be built to meet the needs of current residents, urban renewal destroyed 99 percent of Southwest's buildings, forced fifteen hundred businesses to move, and displaced twenty-three thousand residents. In their place came 5,800 new housing units for a population half its original size.[13]

As early as 1956, the RLA shifted away from providing affordable housing, citing rising costs and a change in priorities. Ultimately, only one housing complex, with just 310 units, was built for low-income residents in Southwest. By 1960, the average rent in Southwest was more than double the District average. The award-winning new developments attracted wealthier, mostly white residents to the area, but at the expense of low-income, mostly black inhabitants. The racial demographics of Southwest flipped—in 1950, the area had been almost 70 percent black, but in 1970 it was nearly 70 percent white, at a time when the rest of D.C. was growing more heavily black. Ezekiah Cunningham, the eighty-four-year-old owner of a small grocery store in Southwest since 1907, summed it up: "Well, it seems like they're handin' out a passel o' joy and a passel o' sorrow."[14]

Most residents had no choice but to leave. "Relocation isn't such an unhappy experience," insisted RLA director John Searles, though residents believed otherwise. Of more than 4,500 relocated families, only 12.5 percent remained in Southwest; 46.5 percent went to Southeast, 25.1 percent went to Northeast, and 15.8 percent went to Northwest (the largest, whitest, and wealthiest quadrant). In his 1966 study *Where Are They Now?*, Daniel Thursz interviewed nearly a hundred families uprooted by urban renewal in Southwest. Though most of the displaced residents said that their new homes were in better condition than their old homes, a significant majority remained in poverty, felt socially isolated in their new neighborhoods, and suffered a profound sense of loss. "No matter how dirty, inadequate, and unsanitary the old Southwest was, it was also *home* for families that had been there for a long time," Thursz concluded. The new Southwest "has risen over the ashes of what was a *community* of well-established, though poor, inhabitants."[15]

As residents dispersed, they flowed into already-crowded black areas, often worsening conditions in those neighborhoods. "All the Southwest did was to move the slums over here," complained one black homeowner in Northwest. Thousands also found relatively cheap public housing in Far Southeast, helping to turn many neighborhoods from white to black within a decade. Concerned that the spread of poor Southwest residents would turn the nation's capital into "a city of monuments and indigents," the white Federation of Citizens Associations called for a "Nationwide resettlement program" to remove them from the city entirely.[16]

While nervous homeowners feared the effects of displacement, the strongest criticism of urban renewal came from civil rights activists. Urban renewal, charged the Reverend Walter Fauntroy of New Bethel Baptist Church, "is urban removal—the removal of Negroes from choice sections of town." By the early 1960s, the phrase "urban renewal" had become an epithet within the civil rights community, a shorthand description of how policy makers and planners routinely overlooked the needs of low-income residents.[17]

The catastrophic impact of urban renewal helped catalyze an era of grassroots citizen activism throughout Washington in the decade after the legal barriers to racial segregation had tumbled. From the late 1950s to the late 1960s, black and white activists fought back against the business interests and unelected officials who ran Washington, challenging embedded economic inequalities in the black-majority city. Mobilizing citizen power, they struggled to stem white flight, open economic opportunities, build affordable housing, end police brutality, and win home rule. It was a time of extraordinary social ferment, escalating tensions, and explosive confrontation as Washingtonians questioned the basic relationship between the city and the nation.

"When the School Gets to Be All Negro It's a Problem": White Flight from the City

Marvin Caplan stood on the front lines of racial change in Washington. A Jewish Philadelphian by birth, Caplan descended from a long line of kosher butchers, but his love of literature and language landed him in the Army Specialized Training Program during World War II. He studied Japanese with Japanese American teachers who also taught him about internment camps and other humiliations

Japanese Americans endured. The experience stirred his political conscience, and Caplan returned to the United States after the war committed to a racially egalitarian vision of American democracy. He moved to Washington in 1952 to take a reporting job, and within weeks he was sweating on a picket line outside Hecht's department store, taking orders from his neighbor Annie Stein. Warm and genial with a toothy grin and sparkling eyes, he quickly endeared himself within Washington's community of radical secular Jews.[18]

Caplan, his wife, Naomi, and their three children moved in 1957 to Manor Park, a leafy, middle-income area east of Georgia Avenue NW near the Maryland border. As they soon learned, their new neighborhood was a "battlefield" of white flight to the suburbs, and "we came to recognize every For Sale sign as a banner posted by an advancing army," he later wrote. The enemies, Caplan and his white neighbors believed, were profit-seeking real estate agents who hoped to encourage jittery white homeowners to sell at reduced prices. The agents then would inflate the prices and sell to black buyers. They used a variety of "block-busting" and "panic selling" techniques to stoke white fears, often bombarding white homeowners with repeated phone calls and blanketing blocks with fear-inducing flyers warning them to sell before it was too late. Once a single black person or family moved into an area, agents considered it in "transition," and the city's three daily newspapers allowed them to advertise properties in the area as "for sale to colored."[19]

Predatory realtors made a nice scapegoat, but the reasons for white migration to the suburbs were more complex. As unseemly as their tactics may have been, the agents were responding to a real need. Black homebuyers desperately sought decent housing, and they had little access to the suburbs of Maryland and Virginia. The suburbs, observed the U.S. Commission on Civil Rights, formed a "white ring around the District"—or "a white noose," as many black Washingtonians called it. White migration to the suburbs began in earnest after World War II, as city dwellers lured by the prospect of spacious new homes and easy financing left urban areas nationwide. As suburbs grew, employers soon followed. Even the federal government, concerned in part about a potentially catastrophic atomic attack on downtown Washington, began to decentralize its operations by moving agencies to the suburbs.[20]

Suburban migration was well under way before the key civil rights victories of the early 1950s, but desegregation in housing and schools accelerated the process significantly. The statistics were stunning. Between 1950 and 1960, D.C.'s white population dropped by a third; the city swung from being nearly 65 percent white to being roughly 54 percent black. Many neighborhoods went from being predominantly white to almost exclusively black.[21]

White people who left racially changing neighborhoods often feared declining real estate values, deteriorating schools, and a loss of status. Having black neighbors, they felt, inherently made a neighborhood less desirable. "There is often a belief that once the first Negro family moves into a block many others are bound to follow and the block will change completely," demographer George Grier explained in 1962. White residents worried about the "tipping point," the point at which a neighborhood turns irreversibly black and then, the *Post's* John Maffre wrote, "the whites panic and scatter, the way the Arctic lemmings rush mindlessly into the sea."[22]

Even liberal white supporters of integration, including the Caplans, struggled with the decision about whether to leave the city. In an introspective July 1960 article for the *Atlantic*, Marvin Caplan articulated the ambivalence with which he, his wife, and other white liberals viewed the racial transformation of their Manor Park neighborhood. Initially, the Caplans welcomed the first black families in the area and "with a feeling of pride and rightness we saw our eldest child go off to a recently integrated public elementary school." The black neighbors were unfailingly polite and often quite accomplished, but white fears multiplied as schools that had been majority white soon became more than 80 percent black. Rumors spread, and nervous white residents huddled closer, yearning for other white families to move in.[23]

What did they fear? On the surface, Caplan wrote, he and his white neighbors shared a vague, unsettling sense that things would somehow be different, less manageable, less familiar. There might be "Negro turbulence" that could bring "overcrowding . . . and profanity and violence on our quiet streets." But "behind the appearance of middle-class respectability," Caplan wrote, lay sex. "Intermarriage is the abruptly blurted fear."[24]

The Caplans supported integration, but they did not want to become "the last white family on the block." And yet they chose to stay in the District, throwing themselves into organizing their neighborhood to prevent further white flight. In summer 1958, after a failed attempt to integrate the Manor Park Citizens Association, the Caplans recruited black pharmacist Warren Van Hook and an interracial group of like-minded friends to launch Neighbors, Inc., a private organization dedicated to creating stable, integrated, middle-class communities in four neighborhoods of single-family, owner-occupied homes along Sixteenth Street and Georgia Avenue in upper Northwest: Manor Park, Brightwood, Shepherd Park, and Takoma. It was, Caplan said later, "an act of resolution and despair."[25]

United by shared class backgrounds, the early members of Neighbors, Inc., sought to protect what they considered the middle-class virtues of the area—quiet streets, well-kept homes, good schools, vibrant churches and synagogues—in an integrated atmosphere. The organization received key institutional support from Tifereth Israel, a Conservative Jewish synagogue on Sixteenth Street that chose to stay in the Shepherd Park neighborhood rather than follow many of its congregants to the suburbs. Like the Caplans, many of the most active white members were Jews animated by their faith's history of persecution and sense of solidarity with the black struggle. "You shouldn't have to tell a Jew what's wrong with ghettos," explained Marvin Caplan.[26]

Neighbors, Inc., stressed the economic and practical benefits of integrated life, self-consciously embracing interracial living as a positive good, a dynamic part of urban life that contrasted sharply with the sterile segregation of the suburbs. In spring 1959, with 175 dues-paying households, the group began helping residents research housing laws, recruit new families, organize interracial community events, and publicize the benefits of integration. It produced photo-laden brochures showing integrated groups of children playing happily together, established a popular art and book fair, hosted community teas and block meetings, and published a monthly newsletter. Members hoped to entice federal officials and other professionals to the area, offering Georgetown-style home and garden tours to showcase the beauty and middle-class tastes of the integrated neighborhoods.[27]

The group also challenged racial practices and policies that undermined their effort to maintain an integrated neighborhood. In one of its first initiatives, Neighbors demanded that local newspapers stop allowing real estate agents to list properties by race. It gathered 2,500 petition signatures and helped build a coalition of more than forty organizations to protest the practice. By mid-1960, the chastened newspapers had changed their ways. It fought Federal Housing Administration policies that denied federal loans to homebuyers seeking homes in "transitional" neighborhoods, pressured real estate agents to stop their "blockbusting" techniques, and questioned "inaccurate" and "misleading" crime statistics, charging that they spawned unwarranted fears of city life.[28]

Neighbors, Inc., attracted abundant media attention and won lavish praise from policy makers and foundation funders. By 1965, the fourteen-hundred-member organization claimed that it had successfully checked white "panic selling" and "stabilized" the neighborhood, allowing members to focus on more mundane community issues such as streetlights and garbage collection. "They have become, whether they wanted to or not, a model," wrote *Star* reporter Haynes Johnson in 1965. By that time, however, the organization had retreated to the northernmost neighborhoods of Shepherd Park and Takoma, where white people remained a solid 77 percent majority. The southern areas of Brightwood

Two girls play at the Neighbors, Inc., 1964 Art and Book Festival at Coolidge High School in Northwest Washington. Neighbors, Inc., sponsored dinners, festivals, and other community events to encourage interracial interaction and to stem the flow of white flight from the city. Reprinted with permission of the DC Public Library, Star Collection, © Washington Post.

and Manor Park had lost most of their white residents as lower-income black people from Southwest and elsewhere found housing in the area.[29]

For all its successes, the group struggled with internal divisions, particularly over new resident recruitment. From its inception, Neighbors' biracial board of directors acknowledged that to maintain a stable white presence it would have to focus its recruitment efforts on wooing white families who shared the group's values. Though it did not actively discourage black homebuyers, it measured its success by the number of new white families that had moved into the area. This emphasis led it to choose a white woman, Margery Ware, to serve as its first executive director over a black candidate with more experience, and over time the incessant push to attract white families increasingly irritated black supporters. "You have to have a very tough skin to be a Negro in Neighbors," confessed one black member.[30]

The organization's biggest challenge was the shifting racial composition of the schools, particularly Paul Junior High School, located on Eighth and Ogle-thorpe Streets NW at the far southern edge of the Neighbors neighborhoods. Paul had become 75 percent black by 1963, a ratio "too steep for most white persons," group leaders warned in an internal memo. "It is now almost certain that the success or failure of the NI [Neighbors, Inc.] demonstration in residential integration turns on the junior high question." Behind the scenes, they pressed school officials to build a new junior high school in the predominantly white areas farther north. In public, they offered studies, statistics, and personal testimonials from Paul staff and parents to counter the perception that increasing black enrollment necessarily meant decreasing academic standards.[31]

Despite its efforts, Neighbors could not stem white flight from the schools. "For many [white] parents," observed Haynes Johnson in the Star, "the ultimate question is the percentage of Negroes in the schools." By 1960, Roosevelt High School in Brightwood had become almost exclusively black. By the mid-1960s Coolidge High School in Takoma was 90 percent black, and the Shepherd Park and Takoma elementary schools were majority black and faced rapidly declining numbers of white students. Even white supporters of integrated schools nervously eyed the growing black population in schools. "When the school gets to be all Negro it's a problem," acknowledged one white member with two preschool children. "There's no denying it."[32]

The Caplans' daughter Freya was among a handful of white graduates from Coolidge High in 1968, and she bluntly told her parents that they should not allow her younger siblings to "go through what I've gone through"—racial bullying, social isolation, and fear of physical violence. After much agonizing and family therapy, Marvin and Naomi Caplan decided to pull their younger children out of Paul Junior High and arranged to have them enrolled in predominantly white Alice Deal Junior High on the west side of Rock Creek Park. Marvin Caplan described the experience in biblical terms, likening himself to Abraham and "every father who finds himself stubbornly and blindly ready to sacrifice a child for his beliefs." Though he did not regret temporarily "consigning our children to neighborhood schools," Caplan felt guilty about it for the rest of his life. By the 1970s, Coolidge, Paul, and other Neighbors, Inc., neighborhood schools were virtually all black.[33]

Not all white people could avoid "consigning" their children to local schools by simply arranging for them to attend an out-of-boundary school or by sending them to one of the area's burgeoning private schools. For blue-collar white residents, particularly in Anacostia, Congress Heights, and other parts of Far Southeast, the end of segregation spelled the end of life in the city entirely.

Congress Heights, a neighborhood of red-brick bungalows with rolling hills and commanding views of downtown, was a working-class white community tied by kin and culture to the South. Even into the 1950s, Congress Heights remained relatively rural, with low population density, long stretches of undeveloped land, and a hog farm that reached to the Maryland border. The home of D.C.'s hillbilly music scene—Jimmy Dean and other country music notables performed in local bars—Congress Heights was for whites only. If a black person crossed into the area, recalled one black resident from nearby Barry Farm, "you might get a beer bottle thrown at you, and next thing you know, you're getting your ass whupped." As white teens in prosperous Northwest grew their hair long and embraced the hippie look of the 1960s, the sons of cabdrivers, pipefitters, mechanics, and other blue-collar workers in Congress Heights kept their hair slicked back into ducktails and wore tight T-shirts with a cigarette pack rolled up on the shoulder.[34]

White flight from public schools happened slowly in Far Southeast. With few other options, white families continued to send their children to local schools long after they were desegregated. Far Southeast remained two-thirds white in 1960, and Anacostia High School, site of white student strikes in fall 1954, was roughly 50 percent white into the mid-1960s. The new Ballou High School in Congress Heights, built in 1961 to relieve overcrowding at Anacostia High, had a white majority until the mid-1960s. One white teacher in 1963 called it a "model school" with "no racial conflict, no violence, no disrespect for teachers."[35]

Racial change came swiftly in the mid-1960s, a full decade after school and housing desegregation began. Local employment dried up when the nearby naval gun factory closed and Bolling Air Force Base slashed its workforce. Many white workers with ties to the military installations no longer had an economic reason to stay in Far Southeast, and they felt culturally alienated as the area began to fill up with lower-income black residents.

Public policies also helped drive neighborhood change. Beginning in the 1950s, zoning changes reserved up to 75 percent of the residential land in Far Southeast for rental apartment housing, attracting renters displaced by urban renewal in Southwest. The city built public housing units throughout the area and purchased private complexes to convert into public housing. By the end of the 1960s, 85 percent of housing units in Far Southeast were multifamily apartments and three-fourths of the city's public housing residents lived there.[36]

As the area's population surged, local schools suffered significant overcrowding, and essential city services such as garbage removal, street cleaning, and police protection failed to keep up. "Serious deficiencies in public services have resulted from concentrating so many apartment developments in this neighborhood," noted a 1970 D.C. government report.[37]

By the end of the 1960s, barely 5 percent of the area was white, and the few remaining white residents were bitter. "It's like little Africa," complained one white mother who had moved to D.C. from West Virginia. "This whole place is infested." A local minister empathized with their plight. "They have this feeling of, 'What's happening to my world?'" Too poor, too old, or too stubborn to move out to the suburbs, the white residents who remained felt isolated from the rest of the city. "They see apartment units that 10 years ago housed small, white families fall apart as poor Negro families with six and seven children move into one- and two-bedroom units," wrote Carl Bernstein in the *Post*. They often resented white Washingtonians on the other side of the river. "It's nice to live in Spring Valley [a wealthy white neighborhood in Northwest] and not be a racist," commented one white resident. "But it's different if you have to live out here."[38]

Two decades of white flight after World War II left Washington's white community with a new racial geography and class orientation. It was not just smaller but also older, wealthier, more geographically concentrated, and more politically and culturally liberal. The loss of the white working class meant that race and class were more closely correlated in late twentieth-century Washington than ever before. Whereas once white people of all classes lived in every quadrant, often in residentially integrated areas, by the end of the 1960s few white people lived in the eastern two-thirds of the city. Andrew Kopkind and James Ridgeway of the *New Republic* called Washington's residential pattern "a kind of *apartheid*": "Like the Belgians in old Leopoldville, the whites live mainly in one large colony of their own; in Washington it is called Northwest."[39]

Wealthy white people primarily nestled into neighborhoods west of Rock Creek Park or in the redeveloped complexes of Southwest, areas protected by high real estate prices. They sent their children to lightly integrated schools, public and private, and lived a life largely segregated by race and class. Few blue-collar white people remained in the city. They abandoned Far Southeast and decamped for Prince George's and Calvert Counties in Maryland, leaving Washington for good. Traces of D.C.'s white working class vanished as surely as had the neighborhood of Swampoodle decades before.

"Angry, but Not Filled with Rage": Julius Hobson's Fight for Good Housing, Jobs, and Schools

Julius Hobson did not fit the image of a 1960s civil rights leader. He was an atheist, not a minister; a statistician, not a student; a man more comfortable in a suit and tie than jeans or a dashiki. Born in Birmingham, Alabama, in 1919, Hobson grew up the son of an elementary school principal and a small busi-

The outspoken Julius Hobson became D.C.'s most visible civil rights leader in the early 1960s. As the head of the Congress of Racial Equality and later the Association of Community Teams, Hobson challenged white authorities in creatively confrontational ways. Reprinted with permission of the DC Public Library, Star Collection, © Washington Post.

ness owner, in a home where education was prized. As an artillery spotter during World War II, he earned two Bronze Stars, and during his time abroad he read Marx, Rousseau, and other European thinkers. Intellectually invigorated, he returned to the United States as what he called a "Marxist Socialist, but not a Communist," a label he never renounced. After earning an engineering degree from Tuskegee, he enrolled in graduate school in economics at Howard, but a dispute with his white adviser led to his expulsion. Hobson found work as a federal civil servant, first as a researcher with the Library of Congress and later as a statistical analyst for the Social Security Administration.[40]

Dressed in his trademark fedora and white shirtsleeves, a pipe protruding from the corner of his mouth, the trim Hobson looked every bit the cerebral government statistician that he was, but for a pair of smoldering eyes. Dubbed "D.C.'s angriest man," he seethed at the racism and economic inequalities embedded in American life. "I'm angry, but not filled with rage," he told one reporter. "Rage is born out of frustration and the failure to deal with problems. Anger carries direction, planning and determination." Hobson's anger found direction in the early 1950s when he had to drive his son, Julius Jr., past white

Woodridge Elementary to attend overcrowded black Slowe Elementary a mile away. He joined the Parent Teacher Association, became a vice president in the Federation of Civic Associations, then got involved in the NAACP, "each organization theoretically becoming more radical as I went along," he recalled.[41]

Hobson's work attracted the attention of the Congress of Racial Equality (CORE), which hired him in April 1961 to run its struggling D.C. chapter. Founded in 1942, CORE was a pacifist organization dedicated to using nonviolent direct action to challenge racial inequality. It joined two new national civil rights organizations that were engaging in high-profile protests across the South: Martin Luther King's Southern Christian Leadership Conference (SCLC), formed in 1957 after a successful bus boycott in Montgomery, Alabama, had thrust the twenty-six-year-old preacher into the national spotlight; and the Student Nonviolent Coordinating Committee (SNCC, pronounced "snick"), founded in 1960 after a wave of student sit-ins.

With SNCC, SCLC, and CORE planning peaceful protests that triggered violent reactions from white opponents, the national civil rights movement entered a dramatic new phase of confrontational politics. Hobson helped bring that growing militancy to the nation's capital. He expanded CORE from a mere fifteen members to several hundred, and it became among the city's most visible and active civil rights organizations of the early 1960s. Blunt, profane, and unpredictable, Hobson combined righteous indignation with rigorous research, using statistics and showmanship to wage war against Washington's racist practices.[42]

Hobson was the most strident of a new generation of young black leaders in town. One steady, studied voice for equality was Sterling Tucker, a wiry, energetic Ohioan who was thirty-two when he came to D.C. in 1956 to run the Washington Urban League. A prolific writer and a favorite source for the white media, Tucker articulated the Urban League's statistics-rich studies as well as the gut-level emotional toll that racism exacted on black Washingtonians.[43]

Representing a new generation of ministers was Walter Fauntroy, a colleague and protégé of Martin Luther King who headed the local chapter of SCLC. A graduate of Dunbar High School, the cherubic Fauntroy went to Yale Divinity School and returned in 1959 at age twenty-six to become pastor of his home church, New Bethel Baptist, on Ninth and S Streets NW.[44]

A new voice in the black press belonged to C. Sumner "Chuck" Stone, a thirty-six-year-old firebrand who became editor of the *Washington Afro-American* in early 1961. Stone was a former Tuskegee Airman and Wesleyan University graduate who immediately generated controversy for his biting condemnations of the "lethargic" black middle class and "militant Uncle Toms."[45]

For these civil rights leaders, Washington in the early 1960s presented a unique set of challenges. By many measures, the nation's capital was a black success story. It boasted America's wealthiest, most educated black community. The city's post–World War II civil rights movement already had dismantled the kinds of Jim Crow laws that their counterparts across the South still were protesting. Most of official white Washington spoke the rhetoric of tolerance rather than exclusion. In 1961 President John Kennedy tapped lawyer John B. Duncan, an active civic leader who had been heavily involved in the "Central for Cardozo" movement a decade earlier, to become the city's first black commissioner. Political pressure even had forced the integration of the Washington Redskins, which in 1962 became the last team in the National Football League to add black players to its roster.[46]

Such progress encouraged black leaders to seek more than mere desegregation. They expected all black Washingtonians to reap the full fruits of freedom, including good jobs, decent homes, and high-quality schools. Yet mounting expectations met frustrating reality as D.C. struggled, as did Northern cities, with an amorphous set of problems linked to entrenched racial inequalities—rising unemployment, stagnant wages, deteriorating neighborhoods, and overcrowded schools. Two issues topped the list of black grievances: discrimination in employment and housing.

Black median income in 1960 was 70 percent of white income, the same level as two decades before. Though both the federal and District governments had official nondiscrimination policies, unwritten barriers remained. In some federal agencies, the Urban League found, black workers earned 35 percent less than their white counterparts. Within the D.C. government, black employees made up more than half of the workforce but less than 10 percent of its highest-paying positions. The private sector was worse, Hobson charged. "In private industry, for all practical purposes there is no place for Negroes."[47]

There also was no place for black people to go for decent, affordable housing. Housing discrimination was a bottleneck on black aspiration, an issue that cut across all classes of black Washington. Restrictive covenants had been legally unenforceable since 1948, but 1960 census figures showed that D.C.'s neighborhoods were more segregated than ever before. Black residents paid up to 50 percent more than white residents did for comparable housing, and black housing units were roughly five times more crowded than white units. As more people crammed into older black neighborhoods, public services could not keep up, schools expanded beyond capacity, and living conditions deteriorated. By 1963, D.C. led the nation in tuberculosis, venereal disease, and infant mortality. "When whites remind the Washington Negro how far he has come in the past decade," wrote the *Post*'s Robert E. Baker, "the Negro points to slums and ghettos as evidence of how far he has to go."[48]

Washington's lack of representative government compounded the problems. More than half of the ninety-one public boards and commissions dealing with city affairs had no black members at all, a remarkable sign of black political invisibility. City officials routinely ignored black concerns, particularly on employment and housing. In 1963, for example, a group of fed-up tenants in a dilapidated apartment house on Girard Street NW signed a petition detailing numerous violations of the city's housing code, including unlit hallways, a malfunctioning furnace, and inadequate plumbing. City officials simply forwarded the petition to the landlord, who promptly evicted the petitioners.[49]

Black Washingtonians could not expect support from federal lawmakers either. Angered by civil rights advances, Southern segregationists in Congress tightened their grip on the committees that ruled Washington. The Southerner-dominated House District Committee, led throughout the 1960s by John McMillan of South Carolina, responded only to white residents, wrote political scientist Martha Derthick, and in general played "an obstructionist role in District government, willfully and maliciously frustrating the best interests of the District."[50]

Another impediment was the Senate appropriations subcommittee responsible for the District budget, headed by a former Ku Klux Klan member with a flair for theatrical oratory: Democrat Robert Byrd of West Virginia. McMillan, Byrd, and their Southern colleagues reworked city budgets, eviscerating welfare, education, and housing programs while beefing up the police force. Frustrated Washingtonians grumbled that the segregationists acted as saboteurs. "These men are dedicated to the proposition that the District cannot work as an integrated, progressive city, and they have it within their power to make it fail," wrote Andrew Kopkind and James Ridgeway in the *New Republic*.[51]

Segregationists in Congress pounced on news stories that cast the District in a negative light, including a racially charged incident at the annual City Schoolboy Championship football game on Thanksgiving in 1962. A major charity event held at newly built D.C. Stadium (later renamed for Robert F. Kennedy), the game attracted a record crowd of more than fifty thousand. The public school champions, predominantly black Eastern High, battled the private school champions, predominantly white St. Johns College High School. With the game winding down and St. Johns leading 20–7, an on-field skirmish among the players helped trigger a postgame brawl as upwards of two thousand black teenagers and young adults stormed the field and attacked white St. Johns fans with fists, bottles, and bricks. More than five hundred people were injured as the fracas spilled out into adjacent neighborhoods, where black residents opened their doors to shelter fleeing white fans. City officials, student leaders, and the media initially sought to downplay the racial dynamics of the riot, but few television viewers, spectators, or observers could ignore the racial divisions. "The explosion of hate stemmed mostly from my own people," wrote black reporter Simeon Booker, who attended the game.[52]

White Southerners in Congress trumpeted news of what they called "a race riot of the most vicious kind," pinning the blame on "integrated education" and linking it to what Democrat John Bell Williams of Mississippi called "the sky-rocketing rate of Negro crimes of violence against white people." Williams articulated the anxieties of many white Washingtonians, who attributed the city's rising crime rates (which were increasing significantly, as they were across the nation) almost entirely to the black community, particularly the masses of less-educated, low-income black migrants from the rural South. "Fear of Racial Violence Haunts Capital" blared one *New York Times* headline in 1963. Reporter Russell Baker described a series of black attacks on white victims as evidence of the "casual savagery that occurs regularly behind the noble postcard facade that Washington shows the American tourist."[53]

Civil rights supporters sought to place the Thanksgiving Day violence and the city's crime problems in a larger context of inequality. An interracial citizens committee led by a former Eisenhower aide investigated the melee and in January 1963 issued a blistering report that assigned blame to the event's sponsors, school officials, police, and Eastern's white football coach, among others. The report also traced the deeper roots of the violence. "What happened on Thanksgiving Day was but a serious symptom of a larger problem," it concluded, pointing to the city's lack of self-government, overcrowded schools, and discrimination in employment and housing as reasons for the anger that spilled out after the game.[54]

Fears of more racial violence gave new urgency to local civil rights initiatives, including CORE's "merit hiring" campaign, which Hobson had launched the year before. Like the New Negro Alliance's "Don't Buy Where You Can't Work" protests thirty years earlier, CORE's campaign used pickets, negotiations, and boycotts to pressure businesses to hire black employees at all job levels. Hobson also compiled a "Selective Buying Guide," akin to Annie Stein's famous list of desegregated restaurants a decade earlier, to publicize cooperative businesses. "In every establishment we went into we raised hell and got blacks into token positions," Hobson recalled. After leading more than eighty pickets, he claimed credit for helping some five thousand black people get hired in about two hundred companies.[55]

The success of the merit hiring campaign encouraged activists to use direct action protests to challenge racist rental practices and push for an "open" or "fair" housing law that would require all housing to be accessible to residents of any race. CORE investigated housing discrimination, helped residents file complaints, and pioneered a "dwell-in" program in which white people rented apartments in white complexes and then allowed black people to occupy the homes as "guests." CORE launched a series of protests in May 1963 against developer Morris Cafritz for renting units in his apartment complexes solely to one race or the other. A lifelong Washingtonian who had lived in an integrated alley in Georgetown as a child, Cafritz had married the city's most prominent social hostess. By targeting him, CORE attracted widespread attention within official Washington and the media. Within two months Cafritz came out in support of CORE's call for a citywide open housing law.[56]

To raise the visibility of the housing and employment campaigns, CORE joined the NAACP and SCLC for a march downtown on June 14, 1963. Held weeks after police dogs had savaged civil rights protesters in Alabama and just days after a white supremacist murdered NAACP leader Medgar Evers in Mississippi, the "March for Freedom Now" attracted a peaceful, integrated crowd of more than three thousand, about three-fourths of whom were black. They marched first to the District Building, where Bishop Smallwood Williams of the SCLC concluded a lengthy prayer by asking, "How long will the Negro people suffer shame, indignities, inhumanities, degradation, . . . and brutality?"[57]

Chants of "How long? How long?" echoed through the crowd. Not long, answered Commissioner Walter Tobriner, who promised that the city would issue a fair housing ordinance before the end of the year. The protesters then moved on to the Department of Justice, where Attorney General Robert Kennedy stood with a bullhorn atop a rickety platform. Questioned about persistent job discrimination within the federal government, Kennedy grew "defensive and angry," according to the *Afro-American*'s Chuck Stone, but he vowed, "We can and will do better."[58]

Two months later, the national "March on Washington for Jobs and Freedom" brought 250,000 protesters to the steps of the Lincoln Memorial. Despite widespread fears of racial violence, the event was smooth and orderly, thanks in no small part to local activists on the Washington Coordinating Committee. Chaired by the SCLC's Walter Fauntroy and the D.C. NAACP's Edward A. Hailes, the committee included Julius Hobson, Sterling Tucker, and the heads of other local civil rights groups. They helped recruit between 25,000 and 35,000 marchers from the Washington area, arranged for local lodging, and organized hundreds of volunteers to help with security and crowd control. Hobson, the *Post* revealed two decades later, also kept the FBI informed of the plans.[59]

Yet the March on Washington, so resonant in historical memory, had little impact on the local movement. Rather, it may have marked a high point in collaboration within Washington's notoriously fractious civil rights leadership. Hobson, in particular, often alienated other black leaders, many of whom he dismissed as "mild-mannered, soft-spoken, pasteurized Negroes." He also gradually lost support within CORE. He grew impatient with the organization's dedication to nonviolence as a way of life, and his authoritarian administrative style and abrasive personality clashed with its consensus-oriented culture. "You can't run a revolution with Roberts Rules of Order," he grumbled. In June 1964, a dissident faction in the D.C. chapter worked with CORE's national leadership to expel him from the group.[60]

Cast adrift from CORE, without a donor base to appease, Hobson became free to pursue a more radical course. He shifted his strategy away from protests toward building power. "Direct action has called attention to problems and gotten token changes but it has made no real basic changes," he observed in April 1964. "Political and economic force will bring about permanent change." He formed a local chapter of a new militant organization called Associated Community Teams, whose objectives were to "isolate Uncle Tom," "reject white liberals," and promote "Black Unity." The group refused white help. "We don't hate [white people]," one internal memo read. "WE JUST DON'T NEED THEM."[61]

Hobson worked best as a community gadfly, a one-man thorn in the side of establishment leaders of both races. He enjoyed engaging in what he called "guerrilla tactics" and "psychological warfare" — high-profile stunts designed to bring attention to poor living conditions in black neighborhoods. Shortly after he left CORE, for example, he captured rats that scurried about in poor neighborhoods, put them in a cage atop his station wagon, and then held "Rat Relocation Rallies" in which he threatened to release the critters in Georgetown if the city did not establish eradication programs in black neighborhoods. Hobson never carried through on his threat — he drowned the rats at night — but the rallies spurred reluctant city officials to act. Hobson's headline-grabbing antics often exasperated Fauntroy, Tucker, and other established leaders, but he played a valuable role. "Washington needs a Julius Hobson," argued one white activist. "It's useful to have a lunatic fringe that keeps the community on edge and makes it possible for the moderates to move in."[62]

For all his creative protests, however, Hobson's most enduring legacy resulted from a more conventional tactic: a lawsuit against the school system.

Hobson believed that D.C.'s inadequate schools perpetuated racial inequality and had "failed the vast majority of students, consigning them to an economic, cultural and social junkheap." By the mid-1960s, after a decade of purported "desegregation," D.C. schools remained visibly and statistically separate and unequal. Most schools were more than 90 percent of one race or the other, and the school system spent 34 percent more per pupil on students in underenrolled schools in wealthier, white neighborhoods west of Rock Creek Park than it did on predominantly black and poor schools.[63]

Moreover, school officials instituted a four-tiered "tracking" system whereby students of similar abilities were grouped on the same "track," from "basic" for less able students to "honors" for the academically gifted. Hobson was among a host of critics who challenged tracking because in practice the tracks correlated very closely to race and class: the basic track filled with black and poor students, while white, middle-class students clustered in the higher tracks. When his daughter, Jean, was in middle school, Hobson discovered that she had been placed in "basic," effectively preventing her from taking college-preparatory courses. Incensed, Hobson filed a class action suit against Superintendent Carl Hansen, charging that tracking, though ostensibly race neutral, nonetheless prevented poor black students from receiving an equal education. It created, in Hobson's pungent phrase, "a system of programmed retardation."[64]

Federal circuit court judge J. Skelley Wright agreed. A crusading jurist ostracized in his native New Orleans for his support of civil rights, Wright ruled in June 1967 that school officials presided over a resegregated system that unconstitutionally deprived Washington's poor and black students of their "right to equal educational opportunity." In a scathing 118-page decision, he condemned the system's neighborhood school policy, which helped maintain racially and economically segregated schools that "damage the minds and spirit of all children who attend them." Superintendent Hansen's tracking program, Wright found, was based on racially and culturally biased tests that make it a "self-fulfilling prophecy" that poor and black students would be assigned to lower tracks "from which . . . the chance of escape is remote." Calling the D.C. school system "a monument to the cynicism of the power structure which governs the voteless capital," Wright ordered sweeping reforms, including an end to tracking and the special preferences that allowed white students to attend predominantly white schools.[65]

Hobson v. Hansen exposed the realities of what observers called "*de facto* segregation," forcing school officials to grapple with educational disparities within a "desegregated" system. After the school board chose not to appeal the decision, Superintendent Hansen resigned and filed his own appeal, which he lost. An ardent supporter of integration who had clashed with Southern segregationists a decade before, Hansen ended his career as a symbol of official intransigence on racial disparities. "Washington had changed during the past decade but Carl F. Hansen did not," wrote Susan Jacoby in the *Post*. As one community member put it, "Policies that seemed liberal during the 1950s in a city that basically had been a Southern town seem very conservative today."[66]

It was a bittersweet victory for Julius Hobson. His commitment to the case had drained his savings and dissolved his marriage, but the decision focused his energies by giving him a clear mission. He founded the Washington Institute for Quality Education and devoted himself to holding the school system accountable for implementing the decision. That Hobson—an ordinary civil servant and father possessed of neither political power nor financial wealth—could force such fundamental change was evidence of the extraordinary grassroots ferment that was percolating through the District in the mid-1960s. He was a pioneer, the first in a phalanx of aggressive community activists who challenged federal and local authorities. Like Hobson, "the new activists realized that without the vote, the policy makers would be influenced only by techniques and strategies that surprised, confounded, aggravated, delayed, or just plain scared them," wrote radical white journalist Sam Smith. And no one scared the establishment more than Marion Barry.[67]

"We Want to Free D.C. from Our Enemies": Marion Barry Takes on the D.C. Establishment

Born in 1936 into a sharecropping family in the Mississippi Delta town of Itta Bena, Barry moved to Memphis with his mother when he was five. After she remarried, Marion grew up in a crumbling tenement duplex, the only boy in a family with eight children. A focused, driven child with prodigious entrepreneurial energy, he became one of the first black Eagle Scouts in Memphis, then went on to excel at local LeMoyne College (now LeMoyne-Owen College). He earned a master's degree in chemistry from Fisk University and was just a thesis away from getting a Ph.D. when he dropped out to join the Nashville civil rights movement.

Somewhat older and more politically adept than his peers in the movement, he maneuvered to become the first chairman of the Student Nonviolent Coordinating Committee when it formed in April 1960. He held the position for just five months before drifting away as SNCC grew into the country's most dynamic civil rights organization. He returned in 1964, joining SNCC's New York office as a fund-raiser. Charismatic, ambitious, and adaptable, Barry spoke with a country accent and cultivated an image of a streetwise tough, but he also was skilled at chatting up wealthy white liberals on SNCC's Northern fund-raising circuit. SNCC's national leaders tagged him to revitalize its struggling D.C. chapter, hoping that his fund-raising prowess could turn the D.C. affiliate into a money machine for its Southern campaigns.[68]

Lean and muscular with a thin mustache, a straw hat, and a wardrobe of loose-fitting, African-inspired clothing, the twenty-nine-year-old Barry arrived in D.C. in June 1965 with a swagger that surprised the city's buttoned-down civil rights establishment; even the eccentric militant Julius Hobson wore suits and carried a briefcase. Barry's bold tactics, confrontational rhetoric, and proud defiance of authority quickly earned the admiration of poor black Washingtonians and the rapt attention of the white press. At the same time, he annoyed, angered, and often frightened many leaders within the city's middle- and upper-class communities, black and white.[69]

Barry arrived in Washington just as the national civil rights movement shifted gears. Successive waves of sit-ins, Freedom Rides, and demonstrations had pounded the Southern political establishment and forced a reluctant federal government to intervene on behalf of civil rights protesters. The movement achieved its greatest legislative victories with the Civil Rights Act of 1964 and the Voting Rights Act of 1965, which together used federal force and funding to protect black voters and end segregation in public places.

Now the movement faced what aging labor leader A. Philip Randolph called "a crisis of victory." As the framework of legal discrimination collapsed, movement activists struggled to find solutions to stubborn racial inequalities. Mounting rage in black ghettoes erupted in riots in New York, Los Angeles, and other cities in the summers of 1964 and 1965. Martin Luther King, fresh from his triumphant Selma, Alabama, campaign that led to the Voting Rights Act, shifted his focus to the urban North. He eyed Washington as a potential site for a mass movement and visited the city in August 1965, but he ultimately chose to focus on Chicago for his first urban campaign. Simmering ideological and generational tensions exploded within the movement as many younger radicals, disenchanted with King and disillusioned with the political process, rejected nonviolence as a strategy, abandoned integration as a goal, and embraced the rhetoric of revolution. SNCC expelled its white members and selected Stokely Carmichael as its new chairman in 1966.[70]

Already a grizzled veteran of the struggle at age twenty-four, the lanky Carmichael personified and articulated the movement's emergent radicalism. A native of Trinidad who grew up in the Bronx, he was a star student who enrolled at Howard in 1960 and immediately reinvigorated the university's dormant tradition of activism. He spent more time in Southern cotton fields than in the class-room, organizing black voters, challenging segregation laws, and often getting thrown in jail. During a June 1966 speech in Greenwood, Mississippi, he captured the growing radicalism of the age when he thundered, "We want black power!"[71]

Many black Washingtonians straddled the line between "civil rights" and "black power," as they had half a century earlier when there was a similar split between Booker T. Washington and W. E. B. Du Bois. They often embraced black power rhetoric even as they sought to work within the system to effect change in their communities. Marion Barry exemplified this approach. With his roots in SNCC, he had the experience, language, and attire of a militant, but he harbored long-term political ambitions and never renounced working with white people.

When he arrived to run SNCC's Washington office, Barry immediately began laying plans to make SNCC a player in local politics. Not content to simply raise money for other SNCC projects, he wanted to harness the collective strength of D.C.'s black majority to build economic and political power. He dismissed Washington's black leadership as "undemocratic and self-seeking" and proposed that SNCC pursue a D.C. "action project." As the nation's capital, the city was "a key pressure point for us," and despite SNCC's Southern campaigns the organization was "still generally unknown to governmental people in Washington." A massive local movement would force federal officials to pay attention.[72]

Barry hoped to use the tactics that SNCC had honed in its Southern campaigns, but his approach to organizing D.C. was fundamentally different than that of other activists in the organization. In the rural South, SNCC pursued what Barry called a "base-action" strategy. SNCC organizers invested tremendous amounts of time and energy building a base of community support before launching a direct action campaign. But in a large urban area with more than half a million black people living in dozens of neighborhoods, Barry thought that such a painstaking approach would take far too long. Ever impatient, he preferred an "action-base" strategy whereby SNCC would act as "a catalytic agent in which a few of us think of the programs and actions which will catalyze the community to begin to build a base."[73]

Once the base was built, the key to long-term power was the ballot. "The problems of the Negro community cannot be solved without the vote," Barry argued, and "this will never happen unless there is massive demand for the vote." He wanted to use the energy and momentum of civil rights to jump-start the struggling local home rule movement, which for two decades had been driven by the Washington Home Rule Committee. The committee's interracial board of directors included Julius Hobson and other black leaders, and by 1963 it explicitly linked the issue to civil rights. Yet it was an unwieldy and largely ineffective group composed of busy people whose top priorities lay elsewhere.[74]

The home rule movement stagnated even as District residents scored an important victory in 1961 with the ratification of the Twenty-Third Amendment, which allowed them to vote for president for the first time since 1800. The amendment initially called for D.C. residents to get voting representation in the House of Representatives proportional to the city's population (which in 1961 would have been three seats) as well as in the Electoral College, but the House stripped it of congressional representation and capped D.C.'s electoral vote at three. Passed by Congress in June 1960, the amendment quickly gained ratification by the requisite thirty-eight states and became law in March 1961.[75]

Though it passed quickly, supporters noticed an undercurrent of racial opposition. Only one Southern state voted to ratify the amendment, and in the Midwest and New England, the Star's Haynes Johnson observed, state legislators "wondered if the right to vote wouldn't be thrown away by giving it to a city where more than half the people are colored." Despite such concerns, President Lyndon Johnson became the first president since Thomas Jefferson to win office with actual D.C. votes after 90 percent of the city's two hundred thousand eligible voters cast their ballots in 1964. Yet D.C. voters still had neither representation in Congress nor self-government.[76]

President Johnson saw home rule as a vital part of his overall civil rights strategy and threw his weight behind a 1965 bill that would have created an elected city council. As Congress deliberated on the bill, the Metropolitan Board of Trade launched a nationwide effort to kill it. The board (two-thirds of whose members lived in the suburbs) lobbied members of Congress and sent letters to dozens of newspapers claiming that "a great many Washingtonians—including the overwhelming majority of local civic, professional and business leaders—are opposed to home rule legislation." Like so many before it, the bill passed the Senate but died in the House. Congressional Quarterly attributed the bill's defeat in part to fears of "Southerners and some Northerners of both parties that the Negro majority would dominate the city elections and consequently the city government"; it also noted that local organizations "had little real capacity to influence the votes," while national supporters did not put "muscle" into the effort.[77]

Congressional Quarterly's damning analysis and the Board of Trade's brazen lobbying angered local civil rights activists. After the bill's defeat, grumblings of protest arose from the D.C. Coalition of Conscience, a biracial confederation of about forty local religious, civic, and civil rights groups formed in early 1965 to "give visibility to the unmet needs" of the city's poor. Chaired by SCLC's Walter Fauntroy and Paul Moore, the white Episcopal suffragan bishop of Washington, the coalition planned to picket outside the Board of Trade's offices on K Street NW to mobilize support for home rule. The coalition, however, suffered from "too many leaders, not enough troops," according to one critic, and it soon found itself outmaneuvered by the nimble upstart from Memphis.[78]

As coalition members prepared their pickets, Marion Barry mobilized Washington's black community around a mundane but fundamental issue: bus fare. In fall 1965, the D.C. Transit Company, headed by an ostentatiously wealthy New York entrepreneur named O. Roy Chalk, announced plans to raise bus fares by a nickel to thirty cents—double the cost of a bus or subway ride in Manhattan. SNCC and other civil rights groups protested immediately with petitions, rallies, and testimony before the Metropolitan Area Transit Commission, to no avail. Chalk's intransigence, however, gave SNCC a clear enemy and a chance to cultivate what Barry dubbed "believability," the sense that people could effect change in their own lives. SNCC called for a citywide bus boycott to protest "this proposed economic rape."[79]

The boycott coordinator was Willie J. Hardy, a no-nonsense, forty-three-year-old Democratic Party activist who ran a local antipoverty organization. Hardy focused her organizing energies on the Benning Road bus line that traveled through the heart of several black neighborhoods in Northeast. She established forty-five "ride-in stations" at churches, barbershops, and other locales where commuters could catch a free ride, and she arranged for volunteers to pass out a hundred thousand leaflets showing a beefy Chalk stealing bread from starving kids.[80]

The day of the boycott, January 24, 1966, dawned blustery and cold, but the sight of empty buses barreling down Benning Road brought warm smiles to SNCC faces. Barry boasted that the boycott was 90 percent effective and cost D.C. Transit 150,000 fares; the company dropped the planned fare increase. It was "a staggering success," according to the *New Republic*. The protest "gave the people of Washington some faith in their own power," Barry told SNCC's national leaders. And, after barely half a year in the city, he had his first clear organizing victory.[81]

Buoyed by the boycott, Barry seized the initiative on home rule by launching the Free D.C. movement. He intended to bring SNCC methods—"education and mobilization of the people, economic pressure on businessmen by withholding our buying power from those who did not support the right to vote and, when necessary, demonstration"—to a movement marked by timidity and failure. He unabashedly linked home rule to the other problems that plagued black Washingtonians. "We want to free D.C. from our enemies, the people who make it impossible for us to do anything about lousy schools, brutal cops, slumlords, welfare investigators who go on midnight raids, employers who discriminate in hiring, and a host of other ills that run rampant through our city," Barry announced at the organization's first press conference in February. He called for a boycott targeting business owners who opposed home rule.[82]

Armed with two hundred thousand leaflets proclaiming, "In Chains 400 Years . . . and Still in Chains in D.C.!," Free D.C. volunteers asked merchants to take action in favor of home rule by signing a petition, writing telegrams to Congress and the president, and displaying six-by-nine-inch, orange-and-black "Free D.C." stickers in their store windows. Though the Coalition of Conscience already had been picketing on the issue, its members recognized that they had been upstaged and chose to support Free D.C.[83]

Free D.C. struggled almost from the minute Barry announced the effort. As part of the original plan, movement leaders demanded that storeowners contribute to a political action fund, a controversial tactic denounced as "blackmail" by members of Congress, the Board of Trade, and even home rule supporters. Some early allies, including the NAACP, backed out of the movement.[84]

Barry quickly abandoned the demands for money, and Free D.C. forged on with the boycott, focusing initially (as the New Negro Alliance did a generation earlier) on merchants in commercial areas along H Street NE and Fourteenth Street NW, where black consumer power was strongest. That approach, however, generated criticism among consumers and business owners alike who complained that it aimed at the wrong target. When Barry attempted to pressure the larger businesses run by the leaders of the Board of Trade, the movement sputtered. By summer, Free D.C. had gone mostly dormant. That fall, the home rule bill in Congress failed once again.[85]

Despite its short, turbulent life, Free D.C. left a lasting legacy. It generated significant media attention, and with more than seven hundred businesses posting supportive stickers, it punctured the myth that the business community stood united against self-government. The movement's pressure frightened the Board of Trade and spurred it in April to name the first black member to its board of directors—George E. C. Hayes, one of the lawyers who argued *Bolling v. Sharpe* a decade before. The effort also helped SNCC pioneer its wildly successful block parties, which introduced the organization to the community and generated enthusiasm for the movement, particularly among young people.[86]

Perhaps most important, Free D.C. profoundly affected the course of Marion Barry's career. Along with the successful bus boycott, Free D.C. established his reputation as an innovative and daring, if controversial, leader willing to challenge powerful interests on behalf of the poor black community. The movement's failure forced him to rethink his priorities and reflect on how to create change in a city he was only beginning to understand. Besieged by critics—members of Congress and white conservatives denounced his "immoral, un-American and unjust" tactics, established black leaders questioned his rhetoric and strategy, and militant activists condemned his use of white volunteers—a frustrated Barry blamed black fear and apathy. He complained that black Washingtonians "have psychologically grown accustomed to people who come in and do things and go out," and were "not accustomed to doing things for themselves."[87]

Barry also acknowledged his own miscalculations. The biggest lesson he learned from Free D.C. was to focus on issues that are more tangible for people. "It's very difficult to talk to a man about his right to vote when the plaster is falling off his wall, or he doesn't have any food, or his kids are hungry," Barry conceded. "It's a hard issue to mobilize people around." Fighting the good fight on home rule was simply not enough. People needed to see direct, immediate changes in their lives, he told his fellow SNCC organizers. "The people have to believe that we have strength, that we have power, . . . [and] can get things done."[88]

"The New Militancy of the Urban Poor": Organizing the Community to Demand Federal Resources

One way to get things done was to work within the system, which suddenly had become more open to community input. In his January 1964 State of the Union speech, President Johnson launched the War on Poverty, an ambitious array of federal programs from Head Start to Job Corps that aimed to lift millions of poor Americans into the middle class. The federal Office of Economic Opportunity (OEO), run by the indefatigable Sargent Shriver, channeled antipoverty funds into the local United Planning Organization (UPO), a nonprofit agency established by city commissioners in 1962 to combat juvenile delinquency. The UPO had a $35,000 budget and one full-time employee when James G. Banks took over in 1963; two years later, it had a $21 million budget and eleven hundred employees.[89]

The new antipoverty programs did more than turn on a spigot of federal cash; they also transformed how the programs were administered by requiring that poor people have the opportunity for "maximum feasible participation" in the programs that benefited them. Pushed by Julius Hobson and other activists, James Banks, UPO's pipe-smoking leader, aggressively used his large budget to hire community people to run programs on behalf of the poor. A native of Barry Farms and a graduate of Dunbar High School and Howard University,

Banks had supervised the relocation of displaced Southwest residents during urban renewal, an experience that initially discredited him within the activist community. But he proved open to creative ways to involve local people in anti-poverty programs and found room on the payroll for civil rights activists, including Marion Barry, who left SNCC under duress in early 1967.[90]

Though some activists grumbled that UPO money distorted the movement by "buying off" community members, UPO gave poor people both resources and a measure of administrative control, encouraging them to develop their own sense of power. By 1968, more than fifteen hundred low-income residents, many of them women, served in administrative and advisory positions through the UPO and other community action programs in D.C. "No longer meek recipients of handouts," the Post's William Raspberry wrote in 1967, "they become vocal, insistent and demanding."[91]

Perhaps no place better exemplified what Raspberry called the "new militancy of the urban poor" than the Southeast Settlement House. Founded in 1929 by pioneering black physician Dorothy Boulding Ferebee, Southeast House offered a variety of social services, from recreation programs for children to health clinics for senior citizens. With an infusion of $133,000 from UPO in 1965, Southeast House became a locus of radical organizing activity, as local residents became paid community organizers who hosted meetings, held rallies, and confronted city officials about rat infestations, overcrowded schools, and inadequate recreational facilities.[92]

Southeast House organizers helped form a creative tenants' group called the Barry Farm Band of Angels in response to the National Capital Housing Authority's 1966 plans to refurbish the Barry Farm public housing complex. The Band of Angels demanded that their views be considered in the planning process and pressured housing authority director Walter Washington into conducting a tour of the complex. Their tactics worked. Washington quadrupled the funding for the renovations and allocated the money toward the interior improvements that were the focus of residents' complaints, rather than the exterior repairs that planners had prioritized.[93]

Etta Mae Horn was among the local residents inspired by Southeast House organizers to challenge local authorities. A single mother of seven, Horn had an eighth-grade education and physical disabilities that forced her to depend on welfare payments and subsidized housing to support her family. After persistent organizers banged on her door, Horn joined the Barry Farm Band of Angels and embarked on a career of welfare activism in which she attacked the patronizing attitudes, offensive procedures, and opaque policies of city welfare officials. In 1966, she helped found the Washington Welfare Alliance, which later became affiliated with the National Welfare Rights Organization, to help bring the views of welfare recipients into the national debate over welfare reform. With her booming voice, stubborn independent streak, and flair for attention-grabbing tactics—she once disrupted a welfare department office celebration by sticking a picket sign in the middle of a cake—Horn became one Washington's most recognizable and controversial welfare advocates, one of hundreds of black women who became politically engaged through antipoverty activism.[94]

As Etta Horn and the Barry Farm Band of Angels challenged city planners and welfare officials in Southeast, residents in the Northwest neighborhood of Mid-City banded together after the National Capital Planning Commission targeted the area for urban renewal in 1966 and renamed it "Shaw." The commission took the name from the area's junior high school, which honored Robert Gould Shaw, the white Civil War officer who commanded one of the Union army's first black regiments. By the early 1960s, school officials and area residents alike labeled the dilapidated, overcrowded school "Shameful Shaw," a mirror of the deterioration in the surrounding neighborhood.

From his perch behind the pulpit of New Bethel Baptist Church, just two blocks from the school, Walter Fauntroy could see the corrosion of the area. But he and other local activists feared that urban renewal would level the neighborhood's quaint townhomes, displace the residents, and turn the area into "another Southwest" of soulless high-rise condominiums. Fauntroy helped organize the Model Inner City Community Organization (MICCO), a coalition of about 150 churches, civic groups, and businesses that aimed to give Shaw residents "a voice and a hand in the rebuilding of their community." Chastened by the Southwest experience and concerned about rising urban anger, federal officials in the new Department of Housing and Urban Development granted MICCO $1.8 million to help planners solicit input from local residents and incorporate their ideas into the renewal plans.[95]

The money—a stunning amount that reflected the newfound power of grass-roots organizations—gave MICCO an opportunity "to give the Nation an instructive example of how a depressed slum area can be renewed with, for and by the people who live there," said Fauntroy, who took leave from his church to work with MICCO full time. The organization hosted countless community meetings and rallies to overcome residents' apathy and skepticism of urban renewal. It sponsored an extraordinary March 1967 parade led by Fauntroy's mentor, Martin Luther King, who called MICCO's work in Shaw "the most massive and comprehensive assault on slums ever initiated in this country." The group even developed a theme song, sung to the tune of "Michael Row Your Boat Ashore":

Old Southwest, it lost its fight, Hallelujah!
But our Shaw's gonna turn out right, Hallelujah!
Old Southwest did one thing wrong, Hallelujah!
Stayed unorganized too long, Hallelujah!"[96]

Though MICCO attracted criticism from city officials and militant activists alike, it successfully preserved the aesthetic character of the neighborhood and prevented mass displacement of low-income residents.[97]

MICCO showed how community activists could use federal resources to protect the interests of the poor, a lesson not lost on Marion Barry. Barry wanted to capitalize on the fear that coursed through white officialdom as riots burned through Detroit, Newark, and other Northern cities in the summer of 1967. Jittery federal officials, including Labor Secretary Willard Wirtz, worried that Washington might explode next. A Midwesterner known as a vigorous champion of workers' rights, Wirtz collaborated with Barry on a new community program to address youth unemployment.[98]

Ignoring the customary red tape for such projects, Wirtz quickly approved a $300,000 grant to help Barry launch Pride, Inc., which used the federal money to hire, train, and supervise young black men—often called "dudes" even in media and official reports—on civic improvement projects. In dark green, military-style denim uniforms, Pride workers fanned out across the city that August, cleaning up garbage, killing rats, and beautifying dilapidated areas. Initially funded as a temporary summer program, Pride earned plaudits from the press, and after Barry pushed for year-round funding, Wirtz delivered a $2 million grant.[99]

Pride, Inc., built a modest record of success, but like MICCO, it attracted a diverse array of critics, some of whom charged that it was "nothing more than a blatant attempt to buy summer peace, and at a fairly cheap price." White conservatives attacked it as a "junior black power movement" and questioned the selection of a mercurial twenty-year-old with an arrest record, Rufus "Catfish" Mayfield, to run the multimillion-dollar program. Pride also raised eyebrows among black nationalists such as Stokely Carmichael, who were skeptical about taking government money and working with white federal officials. Yet Pride gave Barry and his coterie of supporters the opportunity to make a tangible difference in the lives of the poor, and it helped him build a base of community support. After he ousted Mayfield in an internal power struggle, Barry took full command of the program.[100]

Pride, MICCO, the United Planning Organization, and other local organizations encouraged poor Washingtonians to claim their share of public resources.

Instead of protesting to get federal and local officials to act on their behalf, they demanded resources to allow community members to implement their own programs. They mobilized local people and pressured officials to fulfill the promise of "maximum feasible participation." By pushing for adequate resources and insisting on having control of the money being spent in their communities, these antipoverty organizations helped remake the relationship between the federal government and its capital city.

"Act as If You Were Elected": The Newly Appointed
City Council Confronts Police Brutality

No president had as positive an impact on Washington as Lyndon Johnson. Every president since Harry Truman had offered rhetorical support for home rule, but Johnson took substantive steps to make it happen, even without congressional support. Driven by a fear of urban riots, the mounting pressure for action on home rule, and a desire to cement his civil rights legacy, Johnson reshaped the landscape of D.C. politics by abandoning the three-man commissioner form of government that had ruled the city since 1874. His unilateral action put the city on an irreversible path to self-government.

Johnson's plan, which went into effect in August 1967, created a nine-person city council headed by a single mayor/commissioner. He framed the measure as a way to create "a better organized and more efficient government" that could combat growing crime, but he also saw it as a step toward full home rule even though all members of the council were appointed by the president and Congress retained veto power over its budget and legislation. Conservatives on the congressional District Committees recognized it as an attack on their power, while the local Board of Trade feared the reorganization would lead to full home rule. Both vigorously opposed the reorganization, but Johnson prevailed.[101]

Johnson's initial appointments to the council reflected how much Washington had changed in just six years since activists had hailed the nomination of the first black city commissioner. Tokenism no longer would suffice, and Johnson recognized it. He avoided controversial militants such as Julius Hobson and Marion Barry, but he appointed a black majority to the council, including Walter Fauntroy and Sterling Tucker, as well as strong white civil rights supporters such as Democratic National Committee (DNC) delegate Polly Shackleton. Most important, he named a black man, Walter Washington, as commissioner, the unelected mayor of the District.[102]

Washington had deep roots in the city. A native of Jamestown, New York, he came to D.C. in 1934 to attend Howard University, joined the New Negro Alliance, and married Bennetta Bullock, the daughter of the prominent pastor of Third Baptist Church. He burrowed himself in the municipal housing bureau-cracy—his first job was as a junior housing assistant for John Ihlder in the Alley Dwelling Authority—and rose to become the first black head of the National Capital Housing Authority in 1961. A consummate bureaucrat well versed in the intricacies of municipal government, he also was active in a variety of commu-nity organizations, including the Urban League and the United Planning Orga-nization. But he was no radical, in either temperament or ideology. Congenial and self-effacing, Washington seemed a safe choice for Johnson at a time when fears of racial violence flared within Congress and federal agencies. "Act as if you were elected," Johnson advised Washington on his taking office in November.[103]

One of the first tests for the new city council was addressing police brutality, a long-standing source of frustration and anger that cut across class lines and united the city's fractious black leadership. Police mistreatment of black citi-zens became an explosive social issue in the 1960s as crime spiked in Wash-ington and other urban areas. The annual number of murders in D.C. jumped from 81 to 278 between 1960 and 1969, while the violent crime rate nearly qua-drupled, according to the FBI.[104]

The crime surge in the nation's capital attracted breathless media coverage and bubbling indignation from federal authorities. President Johnson worked with Congress to pour money into the Metropolitan Police Department, im-prove coordination between federal and local law enforcement officials, and pass legislation to expand local police powers. One controversial antiloiter-ing law allowed police officers to arrest people for "failure to move on," even if they were committing no crime. Marion Barry was arrested on the charge in May 1966.

These new laws were enforced by a police department that remained more than 80 percent white and largely nonresident in a city that, by the mid-1960s, was more than 60 percent black. In the ghetto, police officers were perceived as "the symbol of white supremacy and suppression," wrote the Council on Human Relations, a municipal agency that, under the leadership of tenacious Ruth Bates Harris, made police reform a top priority.[105]

Swedish anthropologist Ulf Hannerz, who spent much of 1967 and 1968 conducting research in a D.C. ghetto for his pioneering book Soulside, noted the tense, fraught relationship between poor black residents and the police. "The use of disliked epithets—'boy,' 'nigger,' and so forth—shows that many policemen do not bother to hide their prejudice, and some excessive use of force cannot be understood as anything but police brutality," Hannerz observed. As crime rates rose, police resorted to force more often, but ghetto residents complained that they focused less on helping people than on protecting property. "The police say, 'Let the niggers cut each other up,'" local residents told Hannerz. "They don't care as long as it is not in a white neighborhood. They're just watching out for the stores."[106]

Clashes between police and black residents erupted frequently, including an incident at the Southeast House in August 1966 that nearly escalated into a full-scale riot. City officials routinely ignored citizen complaints about police brutality. In nearly two decades since the police department created a Complaint Review Board in 1948, only once had it reprimanded an officer for misconduct. Aware of the department's worsening relationship with the public, Police Chief John Layton worked with the Council on Human Relations to mediate disputes and created a civilian committee to serve as a liaison between citizens and police. The department changed its training procedures and began to promote more black officers, but frustration continued to mount. After spending a year on the chief's committee, Julius Hobson angrily resigned, fuming that the group was concerned primarily with improving the department's image and "acted as a buffer to soften the blows and impact of continued police harassment of the helpless poor."[107]

When the new city council took office in November 1967, it immediately faced a police crisis in the Southeast neighborhood of Congress Heights. According to residents, a rogue officer routinely used racial slurs and mistreated black residents. At the behest of Ruth Bates Harris, the new city council investigated the officer and held hearings at which residents, including antipoverty activists and uniformed Pride, Inc., workers, testified about a range of abuses. The hearings provoked a furor, and pressure from police officials and their allies in Congress forced Mayor Washington to intervene and declare that the council had no authority to review police conduct. It was a humbling reminder that, President Johnson's rhetoric notwithstanding, the new government had little actual power to respond substantively to citizens' complaints.[108]

The city council's impotence in curbing police abuses only fueled anger in the black community. In late 1967, Black Power activist Stokely Carmichael returned to D.C. hoping to channel that anger into unified action. Fresh from a five-month world tour in which he was feted as a hero by Guinea's Ahmed Sékou Touré, Cuba's Fidel Castro, and other world leaders, the former SNCC chairman aimed to establish his base of operations in the nation's capital. In January 1968, he convened a hundred leaders to form the Black United Front (BUF), a coalition that sought to unify disparate black groups and speak with one voice for "a rightful and proportionate share in the decision making councils of the District, and rightful and proportionate control of the economic institutions in the Black community." The BUF spanned the center-left ideological range within the black community, from moderates such as Sterling Tucker and Walter Fauntroy to radicals such as Julius Hobson, Willie J. Hardy, and Marion Barry. More conservative organizations, including the local NAACP, business groups, and the Committee of 100 Ministers, declined to participate, but the coalition quickly asserted itself as a strident advocate for racial justice. With a majority of the city's black leadership pledging to work with the nation's foremost advocate of Black Power, Washington appeared primed for even more radical protest in the years to come.[109]

By early 1968, the legislative victories of the national civil rights movement and years of growing grassroots activism had fueled what SNCC workers called a "revolution of rising expectations" as civil rights leaders, antipoverty activists, and residents embraced an increasingly ambitious agenda to build black political and economic power. Progress, however, did not keep up with expectations. Despite two decades of protests, negotiations, hearings, and reports about racial inequality, Washington remained separate and unequal, the divide between black and white only seemed to grow wider, and frustration within the low-income black community intensified. Some federal officials, reporters, and business owners hoped that the presence of the federal government and a strong black middle class made D.C. "riot-proof," while weary activists lamented the difficulty of mobilizing the city's black community to fight for racial justice. "You could take a little black girl, dress her in organdy, take her downtown, pour gas over her, burn her, and it wouldn't move the community," groused Julius Hobson in 1967.[110]

But others who lived and worked among poor Washingtonians saw the potential for serious violence. "There is legitimate fear among many that one or more of the area's pockets of despair may simply explode if something isn't done soon to relieve conditions," Walter Fauntroy warned in 1966. Anger, frustration, and resentment, particularly in the ghettos of black Washington, mounted against the forces that controlled the city: Congress, the police, the Board of Trade—"the Man" and the "white power structure," in the parlance of the time. In a chapter titled "Waiting for the Burning to Begin," anthropologist Ulf Hannerz wrote that "the foundations for rebellion against these outside powers exist long before the eruption comes."[111]

The eruption came on April 4, 1968.

TWELVE

There's Gonna Be Flames, There's Gonna Be Fighting, There's Gonna Be Rebellion!

The Tumult and Promise of Chocolate City, 1968–1978

More and more Washingtonians are unwilling to accept that being the seat of government should deny them the right to enjoy the supposed fruit of that government, freedom. —SAM SMITH, 1974

The intersection of Fourteenth and U Streets NW occupies a special place in the heart of black Washington. For much of the twentieth century, Fourteenth and U was the bustling transit hub of a black commercial district that offered block upon block of stores, restaurants, theaters, and clubs that catered to black customers and featured black artists such as Duke Ellington, who grew up nearby. It was here that SNCC, SCLC, Pride, and other civil rights organizations established their headquarters in the 1960s. And it was here that black Washingtonians congregated when news of Martin Luther King's assassination reached the nation's capital a little after 7:00 p.m. on Thursday, April 4, 1968.

King had been in Washington often in early 1968 as he prepared to launch the Poor People's Campaign, an ambitious effort to bring thousands of impoverished people of all races to the nation's capital to raise awareness of persistent poverty across America. The Sunday before his assassination, he preached at the Washington National Cathedral to explain the campaign. "We are not coming to tear up Washington," he told the four thousand members of the audience. "We are coming to demand that the government address itself to the problem of poverty."[1]

As the devastating reality of King's death began to sink in, SNCC staffers met with the group's erstwhile leader, Stokely Carmichael, at SNCC's headquarters at Fourteenth and W Streets. A seething Carmichael, who viewed King as a mentor even though the two differed significantly on many issues, burst out of the office with about two dozen followers in tow. They marched south along Fourteenth Street, stopping at stores along the way and demanding that they close in King's honor; nervous managers complied. Walter Fauntroy had been updating the White House on the situation all evening, and he hurried out to intercept the group near T Street. "This is not the way to do it, Stokely," Fauntroy pleaded. Towering over the diminutive councilman, Carmichael assured him that the group only wanted to shut businesses down. Indeed, he and SNCC staffers at times physically intervened to prevent the crowds from damaging property. At one point, Carmichael brandished a gun and admonished anyone interested in violence to go home.[2]

But at about 9:30 p.m., someone shattered the plate glass window of the Peoples Drug store on U Street, site of many New Negro Alliance protests three decades before. It was as if a dam had been broken, releasing pent-up anger that coursed through the area around Fourteenth and U and spread to the black commercial strips along Seventh Street NW and H Street NE, as well as black neighborhoods in Far Southeast. Realizing that he was unable to control the crowds, Carmichael retreated from the scene.[3]

The situation quickly spiraled out of control. Police officers, who initially had stood by as the crowds gathered, now scrambled to restore order as thousands of people, almost all of them black, roamed largely unimpeded through the streets, smashing windows and looting. Police used tear gas in a vain attempt to disperse the crowds (they also teargassed the SNCC office, with about twenty members inside). Fires erupted, and when firefighters arrived on the scene they were met with stones and bottles.[4]

The chaos continued for hours even as Fauntroy, Ruth Bates Harris, and other black leaders walked the streets encouraging people to go home. "We were outnumbered," one police officer later recounted. "It must have been hundreds to one, children of all ages, women, everybody." An appalled Mayor Walter Washington toured Fourteenth Street by car that evening and watched dumbfounded as looters happily clambered through broken store windows to steal clothes, electronics, and other goods. "There was a sort of holiday gaiety about it all, people laughing and talking," wrote black *Star* reporter Paul Delaney, who accompanied Washington. Only a rainstorm that hit about midnight dampened spirits.[5]

When Washingtonians awoke on Friday, they found police officers lining the streets of downtown as tear gas and smoke wafted across the city. The glass-strewn streets of the black commercial districts were largely clear. Mayor Washington kept the schools and government offices open and ordered an immediate cleanup. The mayor and the press condemned the violence, but many activists made no effort to soothe the raw emotions of the night before. "You just can't expect people not to react this way," said Edward J. MacClane, president of the largely middle-class Federation of Civic Associations. "The city has been

The riots following Martin Luther King's assassination in April 1968 devastated whole swaths of black D.C., including this stretch of Seventh Street NW. Despite the devastation, many black Washingtonians saw the riots as cathartic and were hopeful for a post-riot renaissance. © Matthew Lewis / Washington Post.

heading this way for a long time." At a morning press conference, Stokely Carmichael defiantly called on black residents to arm themselves in preparation for a war of liberation. That afternoon, he went to Howard University, just up the hill from where rioters had torched Seventh Street businesses. "We will go out tonight," he told a crowd of several hundred. Waving a gun, he added, "Don't loot—shoot."[6]

Even as Carmichael spoke, looting and arson had begun anew, and city officials quickly realized that they could not stop the growing violence. The specter of rioters spreading through downtown Washington compelled President Johnson to step in. He ordered the National Guard, the Eighty-Second Airborne Division, and the 503rd Military Police Battalion into the city. The troops initially struggled to reach the riot areas—thousands of suburb-bound workers clogged the streets attempting to flee the city—and the violence continued long into the night with "fires raging unattended, sidewalks heaped with soggy mashed loot, smoke covering all," the Star reported. By dawn on Saturday, the 13,600 federal troops had D.C. under control. It was the largest deployment for any riot in the nation's history, and images of troops patrolling the streets of the smoldering nation's capital unnerved people nationwide.[7]

The violence was not completely random. Police and media reports, as well as anecdotal evidence, confirmed that some rioters often avoided black-owned businesses, which identified themselves with "Soul Brother" signs in their storefront windows. Ben's Chili Bowl on U Street remained open throughout the riots, serving as a strategic center for community activists. Safeway—a grocery chain reviled in the black community since it fiercely fought the New Negro Alliance decades earlier—found its stores "particularly hard hit," the *New York Times* reported, while its rival, Giant, suffered relatively little damage. Giant's owner, Joseph Danzansky, supported Marion Barry's work with Pride; as the violence escalated, he and Barry established food distribution centers in the riot areas, and Barry sent Pride workers to protect Giant stores. Yet raging fires engulfed businesses owned by civil rights supporters alongside those run by racists. Mortimer Lebowitz, a former Urban League president who had marched with Martin Luther King in Selma, watched helplessly as three of his four clothing stores burned.[8]

Mayor Washington banned the sale of alcohol, flammable liquids, and firearms, and imposed a nightly 5:30 p.m. curfew that remained in effect for a week. Sporadic violence forced the cancellation of the annual Cherry Blossom Festival Parade, but by Sunday the city largely was calm. Thirteen people had died, most by fire and smoke inhalation; two were killed by police. Entire blocks along the black commercial corridors of Fourteenth Street NW, Seventh Street NW, and H Street NE had been reduced to rubble, with charred hulks standing in place of thriving businesses. More than nine hundred businesses were damaged or destroyed, roughly 5,000 people lost their jobs, and 2,000 were left homeless. According to the *Post*, about 20,000 people had been involved in the rioting and the police had arrested more than 7,600 people (90 percent of whom were black men), primarily for violating the curfew.[9]

The riots had exposed the powerlessness of the local government, but Walter Washington earned praise for his calm, firm action during the chaos. With support from Attorney General Ramsey Clark, Washington repeatedly resisted calls by Senator Robert Byrd and others to give police "shoot to kill" orders. The National Capital Area Civil Liberties Union, normally a fierce critic of police, praised officers' "restraint and coolness." White business owners and community groups, however, condemned Clark and accused Police Chief John Layton of being too timid with looters. "We were sacrificial lambs," one white businesswoman told Senator Byrd.[10]

Black Washingtonians surveyed the damage with a mix of anger, sadness, defiance, and determination. Many agreed with Lucie Kusen, a self-described "black power advocate," who called the looting in her Northeast neighborhood "senseless and irresponsible." Yet nearly half of black Washingtonians in one survey believed that the riots had served "a useful purpose." Calvin Rolark, the black publisher of the *Washington Informer*, called them a "consumer's rebellion" against businesses that had "victimized ghetto residents." The riots offered "instant urban renewal," many black residents joked, destroying predatory businesses and dilapidated housing that should have been condemned long before.[11]

There also was a sense of exhilaration. "White people . . . tell you to go to school and get educated and then they give you some penny-ante job and expect you to feel like the world has been so gracious," wrote one anonymous black government employee in the *Post*. She had been arrested during the rioting but expressed little guilt about her involvement. "The black people in this city were really happy for three days. They have been kicked so long and this is the one high spot in their life."[12]

The riots were both catastrophic and cathartic, a crisis that captured the nation's attention and gave the city's problems widespread visibility. "Washington now has the opportunity to rebuild politically, socially, as well as physically," argued the Reverend Channing Phillips of the Black United Front. Perhaps out of the chaos could come some good—so long as local residents planned the rebuilding effort and did the work themselves. "If things are rebuilt the same way, they are going to be burned down again," Marion Barry warned a week after the riots. "We (the community) must insist that if white merchants want to come back into our community, they will have to come as partners."[13]

The appointed council, in office barely six months when the disturbances occurred, held a series of public hearings at which nearly one hundred local residents testified. Its report, released in May, strongly condemned the violence and rejected calls to exclude all white people from the rebuilding process. The report, written by its white chairman, John Hechinger, owner of a dominant hardware store chain and scion of a prominent Washington family, also acknowledged the deep roots of community anger. "The black community of Washington should have a central and powerful role in the planning and implementation of policies for rebuilding and recovery," the council emphasized. "What came through was the universal demand for the right of self-determination for the neighborhoods that need rebuilding."[14]

The decade following the April 1968 riots was a clamorous, unpredictable period of citizen-driven politics, cultural and political experimentation, and swift change. It was a tumultuous but hopeful time for a city lovingly dubbed the original "Chocolate City" by funk band Parliament in 1975. The District gained a measure of local power for the first time in nearly a century, and Washingtonians of all races—including a growing Hispanic community in the Adams Morgan and Mount Pleasant neighborhoods—pushed for self-determination, community control, and participatory democracy.

On the evening of King's assassination, Sammie Abdullah Abbott was in the streets doing what he did best: protesting. To the consternation of police, he and an interracial band of picketers staged a demonstration at the LeDroit Park home of Mayor Walter Washington. Abbott was the gravelly voiced grandson of Syrian Christian immigrants, a tiny white man with a prominent nose, black-rimmed spectacles, and a rim of trim, white hair around a bald crown. Born in 1908, he grew up in Ithaca, New York, and attended Cornell University briefly before dropping out to organize workers. He moved in 1940 with his wife, Ruth, to Takoma Park, Maryland, just over the District line—he refused to live in D.C. itself because he wanted to be able to vote. He earned a Bronze Star in the U.S. Air Force during World War II, then threw himself into the postwar peace and civil rights movements, catching the attention of the FBI and the House Un-American Activities Committee; after being blacklisted for two years, he started a career as a freelance artist.[15]

Accustomed to defying authority, Abbott was a bundle of angry energy—"I'm a perpetually mad person," he once said. Like Julius Hobson, he channeled his anger into organized protest. In 1964, he found the cause that would consume the next decade of his life and cement his legacy as a social activist: freeways. Ruth told him that their home stood in the path of a planned freeway that would travel through Northeast Washington and Takoma Park to connect with the newly opened Beltway in suburban Montgomery County. With eight other distressed homeowners along the route, the Abbotts launched the Emergency Committee on the Transportation Crisis (ECTC) and became leaders in what would prove to be one of Washington's most significant and successful protest movements.

Freeway construction had been a pillar of city planning since the 1930s. The passage of the National Interstate and Defense Highways Act of 1956 made freeways a national security priority, and Congress pledged to pay 90 percent of the costs of building them. With billions in federal funding at stake, a broad array of powerful interests in the D.C. area united behind freeways: business owners in the Metropolitan Board of Trade seeking to lure suburban shoppers back to the city, construction companies eager for lucrative contracts, city planners hoping to implement visionary projects, newspaper editors and local boosters encouraging growth and development, local officials searching for a larger tax base and solutions to "urban blight," and members of Congress looking to reward friends with patronage and pork. In the 1950s, construction began on I-395 through Southwest Washington and I-295 (the Anacostia Freeway), which sliced through Far Southeast. Planners, politicians, and pundits debated the details of various plans, but until the early 1960s few people questioned the overall wisdom of building so many highways in the first place.

That began to change after the National Capital Planning Commission released its 1959 *Transportation Plan*, which outlined a 329-mile network of highways that would crisscross the metropolitan area, including 29 miles of interstates through the city itself. Planners envisioned three concentric circles of multilane freeways: an Outer Loop (later called the Beltway) that ringed the city; an Intermediate Loop of parkways; and an Inner Loop that traversed downtown. A series of radial highways branched out from the Inner Loop and sliced through city neighborhoods to connect to the Outer Loop.[16]

The plan looked clean and coherent on paper, but it did not account for the disruption and displacement that would occur in the neighborhoods where the freeways were to be built. By some estimates, 5,400 homes in D.C. would be destroyed, displacing up to twenty thousand residents. Thinking about traffic efficiency more than politics, planners also failed to anticipate the outrage that would accompany their proposed Northwest Freeway, which cut through the tony neighborhood of Cleveland Park, home to many white professionals as well as members of Congress and other federal officials.[17]

One incensed Macomb Street NW homeowner was Peter Stebbins Craig, a graduate of Oberlin and Yale Law School who worked for a prominent downtown law firm, Covington & Burling. Craig helped launch the Northwest Committee for Transportation Planning to organize opposition to the plan. With their legal savvy, careful research, and extensive connections on Capitol Hill, Craig and his allies pilloried the proposed freeway at public hearings and in the courts. As *Post* columnist George Lardner put it, "protectors of the status quo use[d] phone calls, first names, and chats at the country club" to derail the Northwest Freeway. Within a year, a sympathetic Congress imposed a five-year moratorium on freeway construction west of Twelfth Street NW and north of the Inner Loop, thus sparing the city's wealthiest, whitest neighborhoods.[18]

Residents in predominantly black and poor neighborhoods did not win such protections, though black organizations from the radical SNCC to the middle-class Federation of Civic Associations opposed freeway construction. After Congress nixed the Northwest Freeway, a headline in the *Afro-American* blared, "Plan to Destroy Homes: Thousands of Colored People to Be Driven Out of D.C.; White Homes Saved." In 1963, Bishop Smallwood Williams, activist pastor of Bible Way Temple on New Jersey Avenue NW, called on Senator Hubert Humphrey of Minnesota to protect his church from being demolished by the construction of I-395, but he succeeded only in rerouting the road behind the church building. It leveled the rest of the neighborhood. "Something must be done to stop the senseless destruction of colored people's homes for the sole benefit of white motorists from Maryland and Virginia," Smallwood said.[19]

Having been stymied trying to plow through Northwest, freeway advocates sought a less direct but politically more palatable way to link the proposed downtown Inner Loop to the Beltway. In late 1964, city planners proposed building a ten-lane North-Central Freeway that would cut through Brookland and other predominantly black neighborhoods of Northeast, as well as the moderate-income, mostly white suburbs of Takoma Park and Silver Spring, Maryland. Officials estimated that the freeway would displace about thirteen hundred families, more than half of them in the District.[20]

The North-Central Freeway catalyzed Sammie Abbott and his allies into action. Abbott and the Emergency Committee on the Transportation Crisis wanted to kill new highway construction altogether in a city that already, by 1964, had the most freeway mileage per capita in the nation. Any solution to the transportation crisis, the ECTC insisted, "must proceed from the basis that all, not some, communities must be preserved, that all communities, not some, must be served, that all, not some men are entitled to the protection of the law in the defence of their rights." Instead of freeways, the ECTC called for an extensive system of public transportation, including a subway that would connect poor neighborhoods to downtown.[21]

Driven by economic self-interest, political pragmatism, and moral idealism, Abbott and the ECTC deliberately created an interracial, cross-class coalition that could wage a sustained, multifront campaign to defeat the highway lobby. Launched at a time when the national civil rights movement was splintering over questions of racial separatism, ECTC from its inception united "rich and poor, black and white, behind militant leadership."[22]

Abbott wanted to bring white homeowners in Northwest into ECTC's coalition. Among his first recruits was Peter Craig, who was then leading the opposition to a proposed eight-lane bridge across the Potomac River at Three Sisters Islands near Georgetown University. Though the two differed markedly in style—Abbott was a rabble-rousing agitator, Craig a cool-headed insider—they shared a passionate disdain for freeways and the havoc they threatened to wreak on city neighborhoods. Abbott called Craig up and challenged him, "All you care about is the rich white folks west of [Rock Creek] park." Recalling the conversation years later, Craig laughed, "He guilt-tripped me, and being a good Quaker I fell for it." Working with a local citizens' group called the Committee of 100 on the Federal City, Craig lobbied on Capitol Hill, testified at hearings, and, most important, pursued antifreeway litigation.[23]

But Abbott was neither ideologically nor temperamentally suited to lead a respectable reform effort that navigated comfortably within established political channels. He and other ECTC cofounders believed that the people most endangered by highways should drive the antifreeway movement: the city's black poor. Abbott recruited Reginald Booker, a black General Services Administration worker whom he heard speak at a neighborhood meeting. When he was a child, Booker and his family fled their home in Southwest during urban renewal, and after graduating from Roosevelt High School he became active in various civil rights protests. Often clad in Black Power attire—a dashiki and dark sunglasses—the tall, lean, twenty-six-year-old Booker struck a sharp physical contrast to the short, suit-and-tie clad Abbott, but the two were kindred spirits who developed a close relationship that lasted more than two decades. Booker became chair of the ECTC in February 1968, while Abbott worked as publicity director. They brought in Marion Barry of Pride and Charles Cassell of the Black United Front to serve as vice chairmen.[24]

The ECTC cast the freeway fight in explicitly racial terms. "No white man's road through black man's home!" became the battle cry as ECTC members testified at hearings, wrote letters to public officials and local newspapers, compiled reading lists for "Freeway Fighters," produced countless posters, pins, and pamphlets, and encouraged residents to resist developers, surveyors, and appraisers. Well aware of the media's power to advance the cause, Booker and Abbott were always willing to carry a controversial picket, create a compelling flyer, give an attention-grabbing quote, or cause a photoworthy confrontation. "Before another inch of these damn freeways gets laid down in the District," warned Abbott at one rally, "there's gonna be flames, there's gonna be fighting, there's gonna be rebellion!" "Reginald Booker and Sammie Abbott are ... crazy," wrote the Post's William Raspberry, "and that gives us our best chance to avoid being buried under freeway concrete."[25]

By 1968, ECTC and its antifreeway allies had begun to win significant victories on multiple fronts. Their interracial protests were growing larger, forcing the media and local officials to pay attention. They convinced a majority on the new city council to endorse a transportation plan that prioritized rapid transit over freeways. Within the federal government, a growing number of Johnson

"White Man's Road thru Black Man's Home." The interracial Emergency Committee on the Transportation Crisis fought freeway construction with grassroots protests, militant rhetoric, and relentless lawsuits. The committee's artwork often used racial imagery to highlight the social consequences of freeways. Emergency Committee on the Transportation Crisis Collection, Box 44, Washingtoniana Division, DC Public Library.

administration officials, including the nation's first secretary of transportation, Alan Boyd, questioned the economic impact and racial implications of massive freeway construction; Boyd even hired antifreeway lawyer Peter Craig. And the biggest victory came in the courts. In February 1968, a federal appeals court ruled that city officials had ignored an 1893 city law requiring public input on all planned highway construction, and it ordered an end to all planning and work on the freeways. The bulldozers ground to a halt.[26]

But citizen-driven activism ran into the harsh reality of D.C.'s political powerlessness. President Johnson's government reorganization notwithstanding, the city remained at the mercy of congressional committees and the pro-highway men who ran them. One particularly intransigent foe was Representative William Natcher, a Democrat from rural Kentucky who chaired the House Appropriations Subcommittee on D.C. A law-and-order segregationist wary of ceding any control to local officials in the black-majority city, Natcher had a thick drawl, a thin skin, and a deep determination to assert congressional authority over the nation's capital. He repeatedly threatened to withhold all funding for subway construction until the city committed itself to completing the entire system of highways.[27]

Freeway opponents refused to give in to what they considered blackmail.

With D.C. residents largely and loudly united against the freeways, in December 1968 the council approved a revised transportation plan that deleted the controversial North-Central Freeway and Three Sisters Bridge. Yet Natcher kept a tight hold on subway money, delaying the Metro's groundbreaking and adding millions of dollars to its cost. Pressure mounted on city officials to appease Natcher by approving a plan to complete the highway system.

The issue reached a raucous climax at a council meeting in early August 1969. Worried that council members would crumble under pro-highway pressure, more than two hundred ECTC members and other freeway foes packed the meeting room. Sammie Abbott stood on his chair to lead deafening chants of "No! No! No!" and then leaped on a police officer after council chair Gilbert Hahn ordered police to clear the room. "A fist-swinging, chair-throwing melee erupted," according to the *Post*. Abbott, Booker, Julius Hobson, and eleven other activists were arrested.[28]

The council reconvened behind barricaded doors and voted 6–2 to accept the Three Sisters Bridge and North-Central Freeway in exchange for getting funds to build a subway. "Congress showed us who was boss," lamented council member Polly Shackleton, who voted no. ECTC members condemned the council for having "sold out": "The D.C. 'Government' now stands naked as a sham." Even after the humiliating vote, Congressman Natcher refused to appropriate money for the subway until all freeway lawsuits were dropped or resolved.[29]

The council's capitulation only intensified the battle, triggering two years of intense protest and litigation that focused increasingly on the Three Sisters Bridge, which freeway advocates and opponents alike considered the key to the entire highway system. Once completed, the bridge would funnel tens of thousands of cars from northern Virginia into downtown Washington every day, necessitating the completion of the Inner Loop, the North-Central Freeway, and other projects. If they could stop the bridge, freeway foes believed, they could prevent all the other interstates from paving the District.

The ECTC worked with antifreeway activists from across the country, and they tapped the growing power of student protesters at area colleges to form the D.C. Student Committee on the Transportation Crisis. Students in the predominantly white committee embraced Black Power slogans and imagery, and they consistently articulated racial arguments against the building of the bridge. In October 1969, a few dozen students "occupied" the Three Sisters Islands in the middle of the Potomac, leading to 140 arrests. A month later, Abbott joined Marion Barry and Julius Hobson at a Georgetown University rally that ended with some two hundred protesters flooding neighborhood streets, setting fire to trashcans, and skirmishing with police.[30]

The street protests paralleled a prolonged court battle led by the Committee of 100's legal team, which successfully argued that Congress could not override the city law requiring public input on the Three Sisters Bridge. A series of federal court rulings beginning in April 1970 repeatedly affirmed District residents' right to comment on the design and planning of the bridge, and they ordered the city once again to halt construction. With support from the nascent national environmental movement and increasingly vocal prosubway activists in suburban Virginia and Maryland, the antifreeway movement broadened its coalition and gained allies in Congress. In December 1971, the House of Representatives finally ended Congressman Natcher's blockade of subway funding. By the time the first Metro trains began running on the Red Line in 1976, the Three Sisters Bridge, the North-Central Freeway, and other interstate projects were fading into memory.[31]

In the early 1960s, freeways crisscrossing the nation's capital seemed inevitable; ten years later, they were impossible; half a century on, they are unimaginable. Initially deemed quixotic, the antifreeway movement had a tremendous impact on the city. Much of what twenty-first-century residents and visitors love about Washington—bucolic neighborhoods, historic architecture, a walkable downtown—would have been destroyed by the vast network of freeways originally envisioned by city planners, Congress, local officials, and boosters in the press.

The legacy of the ECTC and the antifreeway movement extends beyond what was *not* built. It also points to what *was* built: a successful, interracial, cross-class coalition that united a variety of interests within the metropolitan area. Movement activists—from confrontational outsiders such as Sammie Abbott and Reginald Booker to court-savvy insiders such as Peter Craig—used a variety of strategies to outmaneuver opponents, persuade skeptics, and force reluctant local and federal officials to honor the wishes of D.C. voters. "In the most politically impotent city in the nation, black and white, poor and affluent, student 'crazies' and Covington and Burling lawyers had held out against the most powerful politicians in the country," wrote Sam Smith admiringly. It was a remarkable feat.[32]

"If We Can't Control It, Let's Kick It Out of Here":
Activists Push for Community Control of the Police

Washington crackled with protest energy in the late 1960s. Like antiwar, Black Power, feminist, and environmental protesters across the country, D.C.'s activists used increasingly forceful tactics to challenge local and federal authorities. One particular target was the police department, which many in the black community viewed as dangerous, corrupt, and filled with rogue, racist officers. After a series of police shootings of black citizens along Fourteenth Street during summer 1968, the Black United Front held neighborhood hearings on police behavior from which emerged a list of thirteen demands for "community control" of the police department. "We have always had community control [of police]," Ruth Bates Harris observed wryly. "The problem is that it has been white community control."[33]

Issued in September, the BUF's plan called for precinct-level and citywide citizens boards to recruit new officers, investigate charges of misconduct, and fire officers when appropriate; a ban on all-white police patrols in black neighborhoods; a requirement that all police officers live in the District; and the firing of Chief John Layton. The BUF presented its plan to council vice-chairman Walter Fauntroy, who sat on the coalition's steering committee. Fauntroy promptly endorsed it, as did the city's Democratic Central Committee as well as many of the city's white radicals. Indeed, some community control rallies featured majority-white crowds.[34]

Few law enforcement officials seriously considered ceding control over their officers to community members. With crime rates spiking—the number of robberies had increased more than eightfold since 1960—many traditionalists on the police force and their supporters, particularly among white residents, believed that "community control" would undermine officers' ability to do their jobs. During the 1968 presidential campaign, Republican Richard Nixon made the city a focal point of his "law-and-order" message, labeling D.C. a "crime capital." After he took office, Nixon proposed a sweeping D.C. crime bill that included several controversial provisions such as a "no knock" rule that allowed police officers to enter a suspect's home without warning.[35]

But some progressive-minded local and federal officials saw the need to reform the department. To improve the relationship between the police and the community, Robert Shellow, an owlish, thirty-eight-year-old white psychologist within the federal Office of Economic Opportunity, developed the Model Precinct Program. Shellow acknowledged that police were seen as "a coercive, adversary force, especially in Negro inner-city areas," so he proposed to establish twenty-four-hour storefront centers where neighborhood residents could have easy access to police as well as public health and welfare agencies. Shellow's plan also envisioned teenage "patrols" recruited to help police monitor suspicious activity, and it required officers to enroll in "sensitivity training" and black history courses. Thoughtfully prepared and reflecting the latest in social science research, the proposal quickly won approval from OEO, which pledged $1.4 million for eighteen months.[36]

It was a disaster.

From its inception, William Raspberry of the Post noted, the Model Precinct Program (also known as the Pilot Police Project) faced two serious problems: "First, the police are reluctant to relinquish any substantial control to the community. Second, the program gives the impression of trying to buy citizen informants in exchange for welfare services." At the first public announcement of the grant, the Star reported, Mayor Washington and other program supporters were "startled" to hear critics assail the idea as "a Nazi-like program" that will create "a neighborhood-based spy network."[37]

More than the specifics of the program, residents objected to the fact that none of the program's officials bothered to consult with anyone from the community that they hoped to reform. Even the OEO's own local antipoverty group, the United Planning Organization, had not been involved. At a time when Washingtonians were demanding more autonomy, the Model Precinct Program emerged, fully formed, from the brain of a white bureaucrat in a federal agency, and community members were expected simply to sign on. They refused. "All too often the mistake has been made of planning for the poor instead of with the poor," explained UPO head Wiley Branton after the UPO board, insulted at being asked to rubber stamp the plan, rejected it altogether.[38]

Office of Economic Opportunity officials forged ahead nonetheless. Shellow began hiring staff in August 1968, and Mayor Washington appointed thirty-nine community representatives to a committee that would hold neighborhood hearings and select a precinct to host the pilot project. Seeking to be representative of the whole city, the unwieldy board included black activists such as Marion Barry and Charles Cassell, as well as conservative white representatives from the Metropolitan Board of Trade and the Federation of Citizens Associations. Barry, Cassell, and other activists soon became disenchanted with the committee and quit. In their absence, the committee selected the Thirteenth Precinct to serve as the test site.[39]

It was an odd and ultimately doomed choice. Bounded by Rock Creek Park to the west, North Capitol Street to the east, Euclid and Calvert Streets to the north, and S Street to the south, the thirteenth precinct had the city's second highest crime rate and included much of the riot-torn areas along Fourteenth and Seventh Streets. But few of the area's seventy thousand residents expressed interest in the Model Precinct Project. Only forty had shown up to the public hearings on precinct selection, and most of them opposed the program entirely.[40]

The selection of the Thirteenth Precinct triggered a backlash from the Black United Front and Pride, Inc., both of which had their headquarters in the area. Marion Barry led the attack. As in the bus boycott two years earlier, Barry saw resistance to the Model Precinct Project as an opportunity to take a stand against a hated enemy and mobilize the community in support of radical change. With characteristic bravado, he threatened lawsuits, held mock "people's courts" to indict officials, and filibustered planning meetings—and then dared opponents to do anything about it. "This thing was forced on black people," he argued. "If we can't control it let's kick it out of here."[41]

Not all black residents supported Barry. He and his supporters often alienated older, middle- and upper-class black Washingtonians who were frightened both by the rising crime rate—which disproportionately affected black neighborhoods—and by the strong-arm tactics and radicalism of young activists. Off the record, worried black residents feared that if a person spoke in favor of the police program, "[he] might get his home burned down." Many came to support Sterling Tucker, the black leader of the Urban League who stressed both police reform and community responsibility.[42]

Yet Barry remained the most powerful voice in the debate over the pilot project. When it became clear that the OEO was going ahead with the program, he engineered a takeover of the elected citizen board. After Barry and a slate of his supporters won election to the board in February 1970, conservative members of Congress urged the OEO to kill the program. Office of Economic Opportunity officials stood firm and Barry became chair of the board. His combative but competent style earned both respect from board members and loathing from police—rank-and-file officers, one program trainer reported, considered him the "devil incarnate."[43]

The board never could wield authority over the police, but it did win control of the program's budget, procedures, and personnel. Among its first acts was to force Director Shellow to resign, leading to a rotating set of directors who did not provide consistent leadership. Hampered by incessant internal bickering, consistent community opposition, and dwindling official support, the program slowly faded into obscurity. After $2.7 million in federal funding (plus another $170,000 for an OEO-sponsored film about it), the project closed shop in early 1973.[44]

Had the Pilot Police Project been proposed ten or even five years earlier, it may have been welcomed. By 1968, however, Washingtonians were not willing to accept an officially approved, expert-designed program that ignored community input, no matter how much federal money came with it. "The people simply don't submit to arbitrary and harsh controls as we once did," explained the Black United Front's Charles Cassell. White people remained too "paternalistic," Sterling Tucker wrote. "They remain immobile in a time of change and upheaval, steadfast in their 'we-can-solve-their-problem-for-them' creed."[45]

The attempt to bring D.C. police under community control drew strength from national movements, but like the antifreeway protests, it was primarily a local fight for self-determination in a city long denied the power to govern itself. These battles sought to redefine the relationship between the federal government and the people of the capital city so that Congress and the unelected officials chosen to lead Washington could no longer simply dictate the terms by which D.C. residents had to live. Federal and local officials could still try to ram freeways through neighborhoods or foist unwanted programs on Washingtonians, but by the late 1960s such imperiousness met with increasingly vociferous and effective opposition. Citizen power was limited and often only negative—vocal, organized residents could stop some objectionable plans but lacked the power to implement new ideas—and their opposition was not always successful. Yet in the new era of confrontational politics, D.C. residents of all races demanded accountability, participation, and control. In short, they wanted democracy in the nation's capital.

"Between the White and the Black": Latino Immigrants Stake Their Claim to the City

Carlos Rosario helped bring Spanish speakers into the citywide calls for democracy. A native of San Juan, Puerto Rico, Rosario attended the University of Puerto Rico and served in a segregated Puerto Rican unit of the U.S. Army during World War II. He trained to become an X-ray technician and immigrated to the United States in 1950 to take a federal job with what soon became the Department of Health, Education, and Welfare. He and his wife, Carmin, moved to D.C. in 1952 and settled on Hobart Street NW in Mount Pleasant. Bilingual and educated with twinkling eyes and an easy smile, the charismatic Rosario channeled his abundant energy into building a sense of community out of the disparate group of Spanish speakers isolated in an English-speaking city accustomed to viewing itself solely in black and white.[46]

When he first came to Washington, Rosario recalled years later, "there was no Spanish community." At less than 1 percent of D.C. residents, the population of Spanish-speakers was small, unorganized, and politically invisible. It grew slowly after World War II as Latin American countries established embassies and international organizations such as the World Bank staffed offices, primarily along Sixteenth Street and Massachusetts Avenue NW. Professional staff and domestic workers clustered in the nearby neighborhoods of Mount Pleasant and Adams Morgan, which for decades had been bucolic streetcar suburbs for well-to-do white Washingtonians. The population expanded rapidly beginning in the late 1950s, spurred first by political turmoil in Cuba, Guatemala, El Salvador, and elsewhere, and later by the passage of the Immigration and Nationality Act of 1965, which allowed for greater immigration from Latin American countries. Though some of the new immigrants were professionals back in their home countries, the vast majority found low-wage work in domestic service, childcare, construction, and restaurants.[47]

Unlike in the American Southwest, where Latino immigrants primarily were male agricultural workers, women drove Latino immigration to Washington. Rosa Lopez was emblematic of D.C.'s nascent immigrant community. Born in El Salvador, Lopez worked as a housekeeper for an American family that was posted with the U.S. Agency for International Development in San Salvador in the 1960s. When the family returned to Washington, they brought Lopez with them, and she eventually became a permanent U.S. resident. She settled in Mount Pleasant, and her husband, Javier, joined her in 1968. In the ensuing decades, 35 Lopez family members made their way to the Washington area.[48]

Pioneering women like Lopez helped transform Mount Pleasant–Adams Morgan into the city's unofficial barrio, with "Se habla Español" signs and Latino restaurants, bodegas, barbershops, grocery stores, a churreria, and other businesses peppering the commercial strips near the intersection of Eighteenth Street and Columbia Road. Squeezed between mostly low-income black residents to the east and high-income white residents to the west, the community's heterogeneous population represented nearly two dozen countries and defied attempts at racial, economic, or political categorization. It boasted every shade of skin color from dark-skinned Panamanians to light-skinned Ecuadorians and every income level from working-class Guatemalan domestics to well-off Cuban entrepreneurs. Latino residents (called "Latins" or "Spanish speakers" at the time) simply did not fit into Washington's binary racial structure. "The Spanish-speaking are between the white and the black," explained Sister Maria Luisa of Mount Pleasant's Spanish Catholic Center.[49]

Rosario helped create communal threads to knit the city's Latino residents together. He began with social events—he started the Latin American Social Club to host dances, planned independence day celebrations for each of the nations represented in the area, and rented the Colony Theater on Georgia Avenue for Spanish-language movies. An English speaker with experience in the government, he positioned himself as a "fixer," a skilled problem solver who could help struggling Spanish speakers find jobs, secure housing, and deal with the city's bureaucracy. At movie screenings, "I always announced that any person who was looking for a job should call me, and I would help them," he remembered.[50]

The city's Spanish-speaking population boomed in the 1960s. According to the Census Bureau, between 1960 and 1970 the number of Hispanic people in Washington more than doubled to 15,671, though Rosario and other local leaders insisted the number was closer to 50,000. The community was always too diverse for a single leader to represent the variety of interests among Latino residents, but Rosario built a loyal following and gained a reputation as one of the few English-speaking spokesmen who could articulate Latino needs in the larger community.[51]

There were many immigrant success stories—Puerto Ricans finding solid government jobs, Cubans opening thriving small businesses—but Latino residents often struggled in Washington. They faced many of the challenges that confronted their low-income black neighbors, including discrimination in employment, housing, education, and law enforcement, but with the added barrier of language. One major concern was underemployment: language difficulties prevented many immigrants from taking jobs commensurate with their education and skills. "A carpenter cannot be a carpenter if he doesn't know the names of his tools, or understand what you want done," said Rudolfo Ramos of D.C.'s Latin American Alliance. "So to get by, he takes a job as a dishwasher." Underemployment was particularly galling for well-educated immigrants, who often had to take low-paying jobs outside their field because they could not get certified or meet the language expectations in their professions. Once on the job, workers often found themselves exploited by employers who refused to pay them adequate wages and threatened them with deportation.[52]

Not surprisingly, a high percentage of Latino immigrants lived in poverty. Manuel Gonzales, one of the few bilingual staffers at the United Planning Organization, estimated that the median income for Latino residents in Mount Pleasant was just $3,000, right at the poverty line; about 80 percent of Spanish-speaking students at the local Oyster Elementary School lived in poverty. Seeking to share the high cost of rent, many immigrants crowded into apartment buildings. Landlords happily took their rent but often refused to maintain the roach-infested buildings, claiming that the tenants violated their rental agreements by allowing too many people to live with them.[53]

For many Latino families, education was another barrier. They sometimes chose not to send their children to school at all, explained Franciscan priest

José Somoza, because "the children don't understand, they don't have a teacher who understands Spanish or they have to stay home to take care of younger brothers or sisters." Law enforcement presented another problem. The community struggled to communicate with local police officers—only 3 of 116 police officers in the Mount Pleasant–Adams Morgan precinct in 1967 spoke any Spanish—so minor incidents all too often blew up into serious altercations.[54]

"Add to this the problem of getting Social Security cards, employment, a reliable used car for $400 or $500, a driver's permit, license tags and so on in the cultural adjustment from adobe to cement, clay pots to aluminum, and unlocked doors to Washington-style fortress living," wrote Richard Critchfield in the Post. Despite the persistent belief in America as a land of prosperity, Cuban immigrant Martha Vidana acknowledged, "This can be a hard country to live in."[55]

Yet few Spanish-speaking residents spoke up or petitioned the local government for redress of their grievances. The reasons were largely economic: many residents worked long hours at grueling manual labor jobs, leaving little time or energy to devote to politics. Culture and experience also played a role. Many immigrants had fled countries where political activism could prompt deadly retaliation, so they feared speaking out; some came to the country without legal papers and avoided doing anything to attract attention from government officials; others simply did not want to complain about a country that had opened its doors to them. "Some of these people make a cross of the fact that they do not make demands," said one exasperated Latino leader.[56]

By the mid-1960s, Rosario and a handful of English-speaking Latino leaders such as the Reverend Antonio Welty of Good Shepherd United Presbyterian Church, a Colombian, began to organize the Spanish-speaking community. Adopting the strategies and rhetoric pioneered by civil rights activists, they confronted local and federal authorities to demand that government respond to the needs of the burgeoning Latino population. Rosario created the Committee for the Aid and Development of Spanish-Speaking Disadvantaged Minority in the District of Columbia and began to advocate for Latino interests within the English-speaking community. Welty organized 8:00 a.m. breakfasts at the Wilson Center on Irving Street NW, which by the late 1960s had become a hub of social activity for the growing immigrant population. The pair worked with public school officials to hire bilingual teachers and staff and offer adult English courses. They pushed police officials to start immersive Spanish-language training for officers, and they lobbied for money to pay for public health, recreation, and housing programs in Hispanic neighborhoods.[57]

Though many of the vocal leaders were men, the vast majority of people involved in these efforts were women—they staffed training programs, attended language classes, and helped orient new immigrants to the city. "Always it was the mothers, the wives," who sought help, said Casilda Luna, a Dominican janitor and community activist. "That's how the community began." Over time, these efforts to organize Spanish speakers helped forge a new "Latino" identity that crossed divisions of race, class, politics, and nation.[58]

As Latino residents grew more numerous and better organized, they sometimes clashed with their black neighbors. Despite periodic attempts to unite nonwhite minority groups into a class-based coalition, black and Latino residents in D.C. often approached one another warily. Like the Irish immigrants before them, Latino immigrants competed against black workers for low-income jobs, but they could not match black political strength. Many Latino residents referred to black and white people alike as "Anglos," a term that elsewhere meant "white people" or "boss." In late 1960s Washington, many Latino residents believed, "the black man is the boss man."[59]

Tensions flared on neighborhood streets, in crowded apartment buildings, and in the hallways of Lincoln Junior High School and other schools with significant Latino student populations. "The Spanish and the black live here together, but not integrated," worried Sister Maria Luisa. "They are not friends." Carlos Rosario, too, recognized the racial difficulties. "The two groups don't understand each other as well as they should, and haven't really begun to work together on common needs and interests," he said in 1970.[60]

Crime complicated the relationship between the black and Latino communities. As crime rates surged after the 1968 riots, many Latino residents saw themselves as easy targets for black criminals, and they urged more police protection in Mount Pleasant and Adams Morgan. Like their white and black peers, many better-educated, middle-class Latino residents left for the suburbs after the riots, spurring the growth of the Hispanic populations in Langley Park, Maryland, Arlington, Virginia, and other suburban communities. "Many would like to stay because of the [Latin] atmosphere" in Mount Pleasant, lamented the Reverend Welty, "but they're afraid."[61]

Those who remained in the District, wrote the Star's Philip Shandler, tended to be "those who need help the most: the newest, the most-under-employed, the least-prepared by background and experience to cope with the rising tensions." The riots refocused city officials' energies toward the needs of the black community, often at the expense of Latino concerns. An effort to train police officers in Spanish, for example, was scrapped after the riots. "Black has become the color of urgency," one Latino leader noted ruefully.[62]

Latino activists' efforts to organize their community often conflicted with the goals of black political leaders, as Carlos Rosario discovered. In 1965, Rosario helped found CHANGE (Cardozo Heights Association for Neighborhood Growth and Enrichment), an antipoverty nonprofit funded by the Office of Economic Opportunity. When the predominantly black organization faced internal struggles between moderate and militant members, the savvy Rosario maneuvered to become president by positioning himself as a "safe" candidate on whom everyone could agree. Many black members, however, complained that he focused too much on Latino needs. One board member remarked, "He's very conscientious, works very hard, but is simply unable to communicate effectively with people who don't speak Spanish—in this case, black people."[63]

As president, Rosario struggled with Executive Director Ruth Webster, a black mother of fourteen who embodied the civil rights goal of developing leadership within the poor black community. Webster believed that Latino residents and other ethnic minorities should learn "to adjust to the community they are living in." She wanted "racial and cultural integration" and did not believe that CHANGE should develop a "special program" for the Latino community. But Rosario and other Latino residents insisted that their community had specific needs, particularly for language training. When Webster refused help, they grew increasingly resentful.[64]

Latino political frustration manifested itself in complaints against Mayor Walter Washington. Like Ruth Webster, the mayor and many of his top officials believed that the Spanish-speaking community would best be served by universal, citywide programs, but Rosario and other leaders argued that their constituents needed targeted action. When Washington was first appointed in 1967, Rosario asked him to create a liaison office between the city and the Latino community. Washington agreed, but the person assigned to the position offered "zero service," Rosario complained, and quit without being replaced.

Lacking any electoral means to express their community's discontent, Rosario and other Spanish-speaking residents turned to Congress. In particular, they sought support from the Senate's sole Hispanic member, Democrat Joseph Montoya of New Mexico, who sat on the D.C. Appropriations Subcommittee. Montoya pressured the council to hold hearings on problems in the Latino community. Held in January 1970, the hearings gave Latino residents the opportunity to vent long-held grievances, including language barriers, exploitative landlords, difficulties with police, and struggles in the school system. The six black members of the council "recognized most of the complaints as the same ones that Negroes had been forced to deal with in earlier days," wrote William Raspberry in the Post. "The city has neglected its Spanish-speaking residents."[65]

Out of the hearings emerged the Spanish Community Advisory Committee, an appointed fifteen-member body that would make policy recommendations to city officials. Rosario became executive secretary and Antonio Welty served as chair, and Latino residents now had a direct point of contact within the city government. But efforts to build Latino political power suffered a serious setback with the publication of the 1970 census, which counted 15,671 Latino residents in D.C. (and another 55,000 in the Maryland and Virginia suburbs). Angry Latino leaders denounced the figures as wildly inaccurate, arguing that there was an undercount because Latino residents often refused to fill out census forms (particularly if they were undocumented immigrants) and census surveyors sometimes skipped or miscounted Hispanic households.[66]

Fearing that the low population totals could give city officials an excuse to ignore the community, Rosario joined with Marcela Davila, Casilda Luna, and other Latino leaders to amplify Latino residents' political voice through a Hispanic American Festival, an annual showcase of Latino culture. Like the Emancipation Day parades that black Washingtonians held in the post–Civil War era, the festival aimed not only to celebrate community heritage and achievements but also to offer visible evidence of the size and strength of the Latino community. "The festival was for us a demonstration to the American people that yes, we existed here," said Pedro Lujan, a Peruvian who helped found the celebration. First held in August 1971, the festival brought thousands of Latino residents to Columbia Road, attracting the attention of politicians and the media alike.[67]

The Hispanic American Festival and the Spanish Community Advisory Committee, along with other community organizations that sprouted in the early 1970s, did not immediately alleviate long-standing concerns in the Latino community. A one-day event and a small city office with a $40,000 budget could only do so much, and struggles with language, culture, and city bureaucracy persisted throughout the 1970s. But the years of political organizing and community mobilization that made Latino institutions possible helped transform the community into a visible political force. "We have come a long way in the last five years," noted a pleased Carlos Rosario in 1973. "The Spanish community is no longer a lonesome community." The timing of the Latino political awakening was auspicious, for it coincided with the culmination of the city's home rule movement. After nearly a century of appointed government, Washington was on the verge of winning the right to govern itself.[68]

"You Don't Need the Bullet When You Got the Ballot": D.C. Wins Home Rule

Anita Ford Allen was unapologetically old-fashioned in an era of upheaval. Born in 1925, she grew up in Anacostia surrounded by aunts, uncles, and cousins in a community she remembered as "close-knit, composed of generally hardworking families." Her roots were undeniably working class—her father worked nights at the Government Printing Office, her mother cleaned offices in the Library of Congress—but she had upwardly mobile ambitions. The valedictorian of Armstrong High School, she graduated summa cum laude from Howard and earned a master's degree from the University of Chicago, then returned to Washington to become a civil servant. She joined the federal Office of Education in 1965; two years later, she was appointed to serve on the D.C. school board. Light-skinned with a penetrating gaze, Allen stood five foot nine and often wore elaborate hats that made her seem even taller and more imposing. She developed a reputation for both her knowledge of educational policy and her blunt manner, a woman with little patience for either go-slow school administrators or gung-ho black separatists.[69]

Allen's passion for education led her to run in Washington's first election in nearly a century, the November 1968 school board election. The bill to establish an elected, eleven-member school board emerged on the heels of President Johnson's government reorganization plan in August 1967. It sailed through both chambers of Congress later that year with just three nay votes, becoming law shortly after the April 1968 riots. The election attracted sixty-four candidates with a variety of backgrounds, including federal workers, community activists, and nontraditional office seekers such as beautician Ilia Bullock, who paid her filing fee in small change jammed in brown paper bags. Activist Julius Hobson won the most votes; Allen survived a runoff to win an at-large seat.[70]

As local activists and community leaders shifted from protest to electoral politics, the school board—D.C.'s only elected body—became the focal point of political energy. The simmering tensions that had been kept in check by coalition building exploded into ugly fights for power and office. Allen, an avowed "liberal and an integrationist," rejected efforts to use schools to develop black political consciousness and clashed frequently with Hobson, Charles Cassell (who won election to the board in 1969), and other activists who pushed for community control of schools. "What most people want is better schools, not control," she argued. After she became president of the board in 1969, she presided over many fractious meetings that at times devolved into personal attacks. At one meeting, a group of black high school students taunted, "Hey, Mrs. Allen, are you black?"[71]

Allen, like Mary Church Terrell, Calvin Chase, and John Mercer Langston in eras past, embodied a middle-class, often light-skinned, within-the-system form of leadership that historically had exercised disproportionate influence within black Washington. That traditional leadership increasingly came under attack in the late 1960s. When Allen came up for reelection in 1971 she faced

Marion Barry, who represented a younger, militant form of leadership that appealed to a lower-income constituency. Turning his community organizing skills to politics, Barry ran a high-energy campaign for the part-time post and promised to bring radical change to a school board he labeled "the laughingstock of the nation." Though he had little experience with schools or education policy, Barry crushed Allen.[72]

By 1971, city residents had another outlet for their political energies: the office of the nonvoting delegate in Congress. Proposed by President Nixon as an interim step toward full representation, a bill creating the symbolic delegate post passed Congress in 1970. Though it had no voting power, the position attracted considerable interest, and the 1971 campaign pitted two civil rights heavyweights against each other: Julius Hobson and Walter Fauntroy. The two often had worked together, but they were very different men—the one, a profane, no-nonsense atheist who despised compromise, the other a gregarious preacher who enjoyed the give and take of deal-making. And they did not care for each other personally. During the campaign, Hobson mocked Fauntroy's self-important manner, calling him "little lord Fauntroy" and telling voters their choice was between "a man or a boy in Congress."[73]

The Hobson-Fauntroy campaign revived an old idea that would resonate in D.C. politics for decades: statehood. The idea to turn D.C. from a "federal city" into a state on equal footing with the rest of the Union dated back to the late nineteenth century when white labor leader A. E. Redstone called for the establishment of a new state of "Columbia." The idea languished until 1969, when the Reverend Douglas Moore, journalist Chuck Stone, and other black nationalists announced the creation of the D.C. Statehood Committee and vowed to use "whatever means necessary" to make Washington the fifty-first state. The committee never followed up on its dramatic announcement, but it inspired Sam Smith, the crusading editor of the alternative *Capital East Gazette* (later the *D.C. Gazette*), to take up the issue the following year. A native white Washingtonian who volunteered in the Free D.C. movement, Smith published "The Case for DC Statehood," in which he called on city residents to embrace "unfettered, uncompromised, self-determination": statehood.[74]

Needing a platform for his third-party run against Fauntroy, Hobson adopted Smith's idea and ran as the only candidate of the new Statehood Party. The name was deceptive—Statehood Party members were a diverse group of activists primarily interested in education, housing, and racial equality—but Hobson's campaign made statehood a serious, if divisive, topic of debate within the movement for D.C. self-determination. Hobson demanded immediate statehood even though there was little support for it in Congress, reasoning that a clear, uncompromising demand would bring the idea from the margins to the center. Fauntroy feared that pushing a statehood bill would lead to overwhelming defeat and undermine the self-determination cause in the long term. Even if Congress did approve statehood, Fauntroy believed, it surely would cancel the congressional payment, then roughly 20 percent of the city's budget—a scenario he likened to giving D.C. residents a "reservation ... after they kill off all of the buffalo." He advocated instead for a home rule bill and a subsequent constitutional amendment calling for full voting representation in Congress.[75]

Fauntroy handily defeated Hobson in the 1971 election. Once in Congress as nonvoting delegate, he built support for the city through a strategy he called "the arithmetic of our power politics." Black voters were in the minority nationwide, but Fauntroy noted that they held the balance of power in roughly 150 congressional districts, mostly in the South. If they stood united, they could sway elections and force the representatives in those districts to pay attention to their demands.[76]

Using this strategy, Fauntroy led a vigorous campaign to help unseat John McMillan, the notorious South Carolina segregationist who had opposed so many D.C. civil rights initiatives. Fauntroy sent dozens of organizers to McMillan's congressional district in 1972, rallying black voters (who made up 28 percent of the district) and highlighting McMillan's racist record. McMillan suffered a stunning defeat. Asked to explain his loss, he groused, "The colored people were bought out."[77]

McMillan's ouster cleared the way for home rule in D.C. His successor as chair of the House District Committee was Charles Diggs, a black congressman from Michigan with a long history of supporting greater D.C. autonomy. Diggs pushed the D.C. Home Rule Act through the House, and President Nixon signed it into law in December 1973—ninety-nine years after Congress stripped the city of self-government. The bill established an elected government with a mayor and a thirteen-member council empowered to levy taxes, determine spending, and pass legislation.[78]

Congress did not relinquish control entirely, however. To the dismay of self-determination advocates, all legislation passed by the council remained subject to congressional review and veto. "It's a joint partnership," Representative Diggs explained, but "Congress is the superior partner." The bill was a legislative remedy rather than a constitutional one, meaning Congress could revoke it in the future. Indeed, some members of Congress saw home rule as an experiment. As one influential representative told Diggs, "I'll give it five years, then we'll have to repeal it." The limited home rule bill was designed to "keep the natives happy and tranquil," grumbled the D.C. Gazette's Sam Smith.[79]

Despite its limitations, the home rule bill marked a significant milestone in D.C. politics and was justly celebrated as both a major achievement of the civil rights movement and an exciting opportunity to wield black power. The bill not only established the basic structure of elected self-government but also created a remarkable space for neighborhood autonomy. Tucked into the bill at the behest of Democrat Don Fraser of Minnesota was a provision creating Advisory Neighborhood Commissions (ANCs) that empowered residents to elect representatives within a two-thousand-person neighborhood district. With about 360 representatives elected to thirty-six neighborhood councils, the ANCs were a symbolic and substantive product of the times, an institutional form of participatory democracy that would flummox political leaders for years to come.[80]

The home rule bill set the stage for a new era in D.C. politics. The political energy generated by the school board and delegate races now flowed into the 1974 campaign for council. In a wide-open contest with no established slates and infant party organizations incapable of shaping the field, a veritable army of one hundred poverty officials, Black Power activists, federal appointees, and ministers crowded into the fourteen races for mayor and D.C. Council. It was a political free-for-all, with the exception of the race for council chairman— Urban League head Sterling Tucker ran unopposed, the only candidate to do so.[81]

The council that emerged reflected a remarkable shift from protest to politics. Walter Washington became mayor, and nine of the eleven elected black members were civil rights veterans, including Marion Barry and Julius Hobson. The council's two white members, Polly Shackleton and David Clarke, both had strong civil rights credentials. After years of challenging city officials and pushing for change from the outside, they now stood as elected leaders with official responsibilities. "In the early stages, some of the members were still damning the power structure and the system," Chairman Tucker recalled. "I had to remind them that they were the power structure and system."[82]

Having won (limited) home rule, self-determination activists planned a campaign for full voting representation in Congress to coincide with the nation's 1976 Bicentennial. It seemed a politically opportune time, as the Watergate scandal had knocked many conservative opponents of increased D.C. self-determination on their heels, and Democrats (who largely supported D.C. voting rights) held huge majorities in the House and Senate. Activists united behind a D.C. Voting Rights Amendment to the Constitution. Delegate Fauntroy introduced the amendment in Congress in 1975, imploring his colleagues to "mend a crack in the liberty bell." Self-Determination for D.C. (SDDC), a national advocacy group founded in 1971, coordinated an intense lobbying effort that inundated targeted members of Congress with phone calls, letters, and visits from professional lobbyists and citizen advocates.[83]

Their efforts bore impressive fruit. Both parties supported the amendment in their 1976 party platforms, and in March 1978 the House passed it 289–127. In the Senate, Fauntroy and SDDC won key support from Republican senator Strom Thurmond of South Carolina by promising not to rally black voters against him during his tough reelection campaign in 1978. The longtime civil rights foe lined up cosponsors among conservative Republicans and gave an extraordinary floor speech in which he declared that "human rights begins at home here in the nation's capital." The amendment passed 67 to 32 and headed to the states for ratification.[84]

The success of the D.C. Voting Rights Amendment symbolized D.C.'s rising national stature and the hope of the early home rule era. In 1975, funk band Parliament released an ode to D.C. titled "Chocolate City," a nickname popularized by local disc jockeys such as Nighthawk in the early 1970s and embraced by the city's black population. "You don't need the bullet when you got the ballot," cooed lead singer George Clinton. For many black residents, Chocolate City captured the pride and promise of home rule. The city enjoyed a flowering of black culture and consciousness expressed in go-go music (a style indigenous to the city), the DC Black Repertory Company (where SNCC veteran Bernice Johnson Reagon and others founded the a cappella group Sweet Honey in the Rock), and predominantly black Federal City College (folded into a new University of the District of Columbia in 1976). With an elected leadership that reflected the city's 71 percent black population, Washington reasserted itself as the capital of black America.

For some white residents, home rule only reinforced a deepening sense of insecurity and resignation. *Washingtonian* magazine captured white fears in a controversial October 1976 cover story featuring a provocative picture of an ice cream cone with one scoop of vanilla buried under four scoops of chocolate. The headline asked, "Can Whites Survive in D.C.?" with the subhead reading: "A 'Chocolate City' Mentality Is Taking Hold in the District. A New Kind of Racism Is Emerging." Writer John Sansing interviewed numerous white residents—many of whom professed to be political liberals—and found them nervous, alienated from the home rule government, and surprised at their own growing racial prejudice. One twenty-six-year-old teacher described herself as having changed from "lily white liberal to realistic racist" after having lived in Adams Morgan and fearing her black and Latino neighbors. Like many of her white peers, she saw Congress as the only check on the black majority. "I know it is terrible to feel, but when home rule really comes and we don't have Congress to protect us (whites), I would want to leave the District entirely," she said.[85]

For all the hope of the post-riot era, Washingtonians of all races recognized that D.C. faced serious demographic and economic problems. Like cities nationwide, Washington was hemorrhaging people. Between 1970 and 1980, its population shrank more than 15 percent to 638,333 as middle-class white families continued to leave for the suburbs, joined by an increasing number of middle-class black and Latino residents, as well as businesses that catered to them. The crime wave of the late 1960s and early 1970s appeared to have crested, but it had devastated huge sections of the center city. Boarded-up buildings, barricaded stores, and riot-charred hulks lined much of the commercial corridors along Fourteenth Street NW, Seventh Street NW, and H Street NE. Seeking ways to entice people back to the city and preserve the tax base, nervous policy makers focused on real estate development and worked closely with developers on massive projects such as a new convention center, the renewal of Pennsylvania Avenue, and the Metro.[86]

The emphasis on new development exacerbated a growing housing problem as developers eyed aging central city neighborhoods for revitalization projects. What came to be called "gentrification"—a word popularized in the 1970s to describe the process by which low-income residents of a neighborhood are gradually displaced by higher-income residents—already had reshaped several D.C. neighborhoods in preceding decades. The first wave of gentrification hit Georgetown in the 1920s and 1930s as white professionals moved into what had been a deteriorating working-class neighborhood and began to restore the area's old homes. By the 1950s, Georgetown had become among the city's most exclusive neighborhoods. Another wave of revitalization and displacement washed over Foggy Bottom and Capitol Hill in the 1950s and 1960s as developers refurbished "slum" houses and sold them to wealthier newcomers.[87]

But the displacement of the 1970s was much larger and more rapid than in the past. Attracted by rock-bottom housing prices and the success of restorationists in Georgetown and elsewhere, developers, speculators, and amateur flippers snapped up property in Adams Morgan, Mount Pleasant, Logan Circle, and other older neighborhoods. Young professionals followed fast on their heels, inspired in part by a back-to-the-city ethos rooted in the era's countercultural critique of the suburbs. "Low-income residents in these neighborhoods are forced

TABLE 6 Washington's population, 1970–1990

Year	Total	Black (% of pop.)	White (% of pop.)	Asian (% of pop.)	Hispanic (of any race)
1970	756,510	537,712 (71.1)	209,272 (27.7)	5,372 (0.7)	15,671
1980	638,333	448,906 (70.3)	171,768 (26.9)	6,636 (1.0)	17,679
1990	606,900	399,604 (65.8)	179,667 (29.6)	11,214 (1.8)	32,710

Source: U.S. Census Bureau, "Historical Census Statistics on Population Totals by Race"

out by escalating rents, an inability to come up with down payments to prevent their homes from being sold to new owners, and, in the case of homeowners, higher property taxes in their suddenly more expensive neighborhood," wrote the Post's Milton Coleman. "For the most part, the settlers staking out a new life in these once-neglected areas of glass-strewn sidewalks and rodent-infested alleys are white."[88]

Many developers focused on converting old apartment buildings or large tracts of townhouses into condominiums, displacing occupants in large and alarming chunks. Within just a few months in 1973, owners evicted tenants in eleven Adams Morgan apartment buildings and an entire block of Capitol Hill rooming houses. Condominium conversion accelerated as the decade wore on. A 1979 study found that about 12 percent of the city's apartment units had been or were in the process of being converted to condominiums. Real estate prices spiraled upward. In Adams Morgan, Mount Pleasant, and Capitol Hill, home prices doubled in less than five years, pushing them far beyond the reach of most of the black and Latino residents who called these neighborhoods home.[89]

Calling for "Neighbor Power," local activists mobilized to protect low-income renters and fight displacement by forming neighborhood-based tenants' rights groups such as the Capitol East Community Organization and the Adams Morgan Organization. The City-Wide Housing Coalition, founded in 1973, connected activists across neighborhoods. In the past, advocates for displaced renters found few friends in government. With the advent of home rule, however, they could leverage the might of activists-turned-politicians in their struggle against landlords and developers.[90]

Two such activists were Councilman David Clarke and Councilwoman Nadine Winter, who made antidisplacement legislation a priority. As one of its first moves in the home rule era, the council passed the D.C. Rent Control Act, which placed a cap on rent increases and gave tenants the first right to purchase their unit if a building was slated for condominium conversion. The following year, the council set benchmarks for developers who sought to convert apartments to condominiums. But Clarke and Winter's proposed penalty for developers who bought and quickly resold property—"flippers"—met stiff resistance from real estate interests, which worked with Revenue and Finance Committee chairman Marion Barry to block the bill.[91]

As city leaders debated antidisplacement legislation, renters on the 1700 block of Seaton Street NW in Adams Morgan fought back. In April 1976, Centre Properties of Bethesda, Maryland, bought several dilapidated row houses on the block. Planning to renovate the buildings and resell them for more than triple what they paid, Centre officials sent eviction notices to more than two dozen households. Most renters believed that they lacked the resources to fight Centre and decided to move, but nine families chose to challenge the developer. Seaton Street was no paradise—city inspectors found 959 health and safety code violations spread among the street's forty-four houses—but residents were deeply attached to their neighborhood and considered their ramshackle apartments "home." The nine defiant families contacted the Adams Morgan Organization, sued Centre Properties to halt the evictions, and began raising money to buy the homes themselves. "People are doing this all over—shoving people out," said resident Joseph Lewis Jr. "That isn't right." For more than a year, the Seaton Street tenants stayed put. Facing a rising tide of public disapproval, Centre Properties agreed to sell to the tenants just days before the case went to trial.[92]

Inspired by the Seaton Street protest and threatened by the accelerated pace of displacement, renters staged so many raucous and disruptive protests that the *Post* dubbed 1978 the "year of the renter's revolt." The protests pushed the council to pass a series of progressive measures to protect low-income residents and provide financial incentives to help them purchase their own homes. Although some of these laws were honored in the breach and others were allowed to lapse in the early 1980s, tenants and tenants' rights activists were nonetheless able to use them to slow displacement in some neighborhoods.[93]

"Our Last Chance to Solidify": The 1978 Mayoral Campaign

Gentrification and the growing income inequality that it reflected became major issues in the 1978 mayoral campaign. Incumbent mayor Walter Washington emphasized his experience and integrity and boasted of his role in the city's post-riot renaissance, but many voters had soured on his bland leadership. He faced a stiff challenge from council chairman Sterling Tucker, who won the support of Walter Fauntroy's formidable political network and emerged as the clear front-runner.[94]

The expected clash between two establishment titans, Tucker and Washington, was disrupted by the ambitions and political good fortune of hustling council member Marion Barry. On the council, Barry used his position as chair of the Revenue and Finance Committee to build relationships with the business community and establish a reputation as a canny politician capable of balancing the interests of D.C.'s diverse constituencies. Still relatively unknown or mistrusted in large parts of the city, particularly vote-rich, predominantly white Ward 3, Barry benefited, remarkably, from being shot.[95]

It happened on March 9, 1977. Armed groups of Hanafi Muslims, an off-shoot sect of the Nation of Islam that had established its headquarters in the Gold Coast area of upper Sixteenth Street NW, stormed the B'nai B'rith head-quarters on Rhode Island Avenue NW and the Islamic Center on Massachusetts Avenue NW, seizing more than a hundred hostages. A third, smaller contingent burst onto the fifth floor of the District Building, captured hostages near Sterling Tucker's office, and exchanged gunfire with police. A ricocheting shotgun pellet pierced Marion Barry in the chest as the councilman exited an elevator.[96]

Though the wound later would be dubbed superficial, initial coverage reported that Barry had been shot "near his heart," and pictures of the councilman, his chest wrapped in bandages, flashed across the evening news. Sitting in his hospital room, watching the cards and flowers pile up around him, Barry, ever the astute politician, believed that the shooting would give him the boost he needed to run for mayor. He summoned his fund-raiser to his bedside and directed him to open a campaign account. Though his odds were long, he threw his hat in the ring.[97]

Barry's decision to enter the 1978 mayoral election scuttled Walter Fauntroy's efforts to bring order out of the chaos that had characterized the early home-rule-era elections. Identifying Tucker as the more experienced and popular candidate, Fauntroy instructed Barry to "wait his turn" and run for council chairman. Instead, Barry cast himself as an outsider valiantly struggling against "political bosses" intent on anointing an administration "handpicked by a handful."[98]

The three-way Democratic contest divided the black electorate. Washington appealed to the older black elite, organized labor, and many working-class voters, particularly city employees; Tucker cultivated younger, middle-class black professionals, federal workers, and business owners; Barry received the smallest share of the black vote, mainly from young professionals and the poor. Black ministers supported either Washington or Tucker, while the Democratic State Committee split between Tucker and Barry.[99]

Though the candidates and their top aides were black, race remained a divisive factor in the election. "The fear of losing what limited black control there is in this city, a subject seldom raised publicly, is a constant backdrop to this year's election," wrote the *Post's* Milton Coleman. For many worried black residents, the fierce infighting among black politicians, the scandal-focused scrutiny of the media, and the return of white residents to gentrifying neighborhoods were signs of resurgent white political power. They pointed to comments by Metropolitan Board of Trade president Robert Linowes, who in April confidently predicted that the city soon would be racially balanced and solidly middle and upper class, with the poor commuting in from the suburbs. "There's a healthy sense of peril," commented one politically active black lawyer. "This is our last chance to solidify before whites will start demanding the top positions."[100]

With the black community divided, white voters held the balance of power in the election—and they broke for Barry. The former Black Power militant cultivated high-profile white supporters, including Nancy "Bitsy" Folger (the former chair of Proctor and Gamble) and young, ambitious developers Jeffrey Cohen and Conrad Cafritz, and he embraced socially liberal positions in favor of gay rights and marijuana legalization that angered black ministers but appealed to white liberals. He won support from white radicals, young white professionals who had moved into gentrifying neighborhoods, the politically potent white gay community centered near Logan and Dupont Circles, and even some established white voters in Ward 3.[101]

Fascinated by Barry's rise from sharecropper's son to councilman, many white voters viewed him as a break from the past, a man tough enough to deal with both the black poor and the white business interests. He gained the surprise endorsement of the *Washington Post*, whose editors were impressed with Barry's "quality of leadership" and lauded his "genuinely bold and alive commitment to make things happen." The *Post's* six pro-Barry editorials and the candidate's subsequent climb in the polls so unnerved Sterling Tucker that he desperately tried to coax Barry to drop out less than a week before the Democratic primary.[102]

The final tally was agonizingly close. Ahead by fewer than two thousand votes, Barry tentatively claimed victory on election night, but it would take two weeks of recounts and special pleading from Walter Fauntroy for Tucker to concede defeat.[103]

White voters and the *Post* had put Barry over the top, and as he approached the general election, he had to battle the impression that he was "the white folks' candidate," a poisonous label in the proudly black city. During the primary campaign, Barry aides had taken great pains to ensure that their candidate was not photographed too often with white supporters, and his press secretary had demanded that newspapers explicitly identify the candidate's new multi-

Newly elected Mayor Marion Barry receives the oath of office from Supreme Court Justice Thurgood
Marshall in January 1979. The son of sharecroppers and a civil rights activist who had arrived in D.C. in
1965, Barry embodied the hopes and promise of "Chocolate City." Reprinted with permission of the DC
Public Library, Star Collection, © Washington Post.

racial bride, Effie Barry, as a "light-skinned black woman" because her angular
facial features made her appear white in newspaper photos. But the role of white
voters in his victory—as well as the triumph of Betty Ann Kane, the first white
candidate to win an at-large council race—concerned some black observers.[104]

Soon after the primary, *Washington Afro-American* columnist Lillian Wiggins
voiced the whispered fears that "faceless and nameless people" had a "master plan" to undo black gains and reassert white control over the city. An outspoken member of the black middle class, Wiggins noted that African American
voters had split their vote while white voters had magnified their electoral clout
well beyond their numbers by coalescing behind particular candidates. Chastis-
ing black politicos for failing to guard against a united white voting bloc, Wiggins wrote that "the grab for power among black politicians struck a blow for
the master plan." She predicted that should Barry win the general election in

November "he too will feel the sting of the master plan" and counseled him to unify the black vote to protect himself. Wiggins's fears of a "master plan," later shortened to "The Plan," would echo through D.C. politics for the next three decades, cropping up whenever a corruption investigation or white political gains threatened black elected officials or gentrification displaced black residents.[105]

In the general election, Barry faced Republican Arthur Fletcher—a black Purple Heart recipient, former pro football player, and assistant secretary of labor under President Nixon. Though a formidable candidate, Fletcher could not compete in a 90 percent Democratic city, and Barry won 130 of the city's 137 precincts. Yet the results forecast the racial dynamics of city elections for the next two decades. Many of the white voters who supported Barry in the primary turned out for Fletcher in the general election. The seven precincts where Fletcher came out on top were in the wealthiest, whitest portions of Ward 3. Conversely, poor African Americans, who had backed Washington in September, gave the overwhelming majority of their votes to Barry. "So much for Barry being the 'white man's candidate,'" quipped one Barry campaign worker on viewing the returns.[106]

On January 2, 1979, Barry led an inaugural parade through the still riot-scarred Fourteenth Street corridor, past the Youth Pride office (which, in a take-off of a famous Virginia Slims cigarette ad, had hoisted a banner that read, "You've come a long way, Marion") to the District Building. Waiting to conduct the swearing-in ceremony was black civil rights veteran and Supreme Court Justice Thurgood Marshall, a student of the man who had devoted his life to make this day possible: Charles Hamilton Houston.[107]

The decade between the April 1968 riots and Marion Barry's victory in the 1978 mayoral election witnessed a remarkable political revolution in the nation's capital. When 1968 began, city residents remained politically impotent, ruled by Congress, unelected city commissioners, and a coterie of business interests as they had been since disfranchisement in the 1870s. Ten years later, Washingtonians enjoyed a measure of home rule and had elected a former civil rights agitator to serve as mayor alongside an elected council filled with community activists. Throughout the decade, D.C. residents exercised political muscles that had atrophied during a century of commissioner rule. The transformation was tumultuous, marked by devastating riots, surging crime, and middle-class flight from the city. Politics was often uncivil and chaotic as Washingtonians struggled to be heard in a clamorous era marked by attacks on authorities—Congress, the police, city planners, developers, and others. The District experienced "participatory democracy with all the frictions," as one black city official put it after a particularly bruising neighborhood meeting. But for city residents unused to local political power—and particularly for black Washingtonians—it was a thrilling, hopeful time.[108]

Marion Barry embodied those hopes when he took office in 1979. The new mayor recognized that his administration symbolized much more than his own individual success and that he bore a particular racial responsibility to run an effective government. "There's a feeling that blacks can't do anything right," he said. "We want to show blacks can be competent." The first civil rights veteran to run a major city, he represented the potential of black power. "There is a strong emphasis on the mayoralty of Barry and the people around him as role models," the *Post*'s Nicholas Lemann wrote. "Barry and his closest aides talk as if the eyes of the world are upon them." And indeed they would be in the decade to come.[109]

THIRTEEN

Perfect for Washington

Marion Barry and the Rise and Fall of Chocolate City, 1979–1994

Many blacks feel that a part of their own future is wrapped in Marion Barry's success as mayor. He is a symbol—the most visible symbol—of those blacks who grew up in the 60s, began to achieve affluence, status, and power in the 70s, and don't want to lose it in the 80s.—MILTON COLEMAN, *Washington Post*, 1980

Hidden behind lush trees, the four-story, rough-hewn gray stone town-house at 1345 Euclid Street NW is easy to miss. Though tall and imposing, the 4,335-square-foot structure fades into a row of four nearly identical neighbors. The building underwent modest renovations in 2010, and the massive home—it boasts eight bedrooms and four full bathrooms—looks clean but shabby, a relatively underpriced property in Columbia Heights's overheated twenty-first-century real estate market.[1]

A generation before, the building stood out as "Euclid House," the headquarters for the Community for Creative Nonviolence. The CCNV was founded in 1970 by Ed Guinan, a white stock trader who liquidated his assets and traveled to D.C. to study for the priesthood after being inspired by the Catholic Worker teachings of Dorothy Day. Rising to international prominence as a fiery anti–Vietnam War preacher, he envisioned the CCNV as a "boot camp" for like-minded activists, to quote one member. Yet as the decade wore on, he worried that the group's antiwar efforts ignored the poverty in their midst. "With all the intense international focus," Guinan recalled, "we were blindly stepping over the bodies here in D.C." In 1972, the CCNV refocused its energies on the poor and opened the Zacchaeus Community Kitchen in Shaw, where they fed upwards of four hundred people per day.[2]

Dedicated activists from across the country flocked to CCNV's "community," then located on N Street NW, just north of Thomas Circle. One charismatic but mercurial newcomer was Mitch Snyder, a Brooklyn Jew who had converted to radical antiwar Catholicism while in prison for fraud. With his passionate commitment and boundless energy, Snyder quickly emerged as a leading voice in the community, a man willing to confront injustice directly with strident rhetoric and brazen protests. His combative style clashed with Guinan, who by the mid-1970s had moved away from confrontational tactics toward living among and serving the poor. To avoid an internal rift, the community agreed in 1975 to open a second "house," ostensibly led by Snyder, dedicated to direct action protest. Euclid House was born.[3]

By the mid-1970s, the Columbia Heights neighborhood surrounding Euclid House was dangerous. Originally an elite subdivision, the area became a middle-class black enclave after the Supreme Court declared restrictive covenants un-enforceable in 1948. The neighborhood began to deteriorate in the 1960s. When black renters moved into the area, white apartment owners neglected upkeep, turning gorgeous buildings with commanding vistas into slums. The April 1968 riots left a trail of burned-out storefronts and wrecked apartment complexes along Fourteenth Street. After the fires cooled, drug dealers moved in, transforming the strip into one of the city's largest heroin markets. Desperate addicts resorted to burglary, prostitution, and mugging, compelling many middle-class homeowners to leave.[4]

The city accelerated the neighborhood's deterioration by using it as a dumping ground for exconvicts and the mentally ill. The property at 1345 Euclid became a home for men transitioning out of Lorton penitentiary, and D.C. officials sited six more group homes and halfway houses within a two-block radius. By the mid-1970s, many homeowners sold out to speculators who hoped that the gentrification under way in nearby Dupont Circle and Adams Morgan would make its way up to Columbia Heights. But the anticipated development boom never came, and investors simply boarded up their properties to ride out the economic storm.[5]

The same forces that transformed Columbia Heights into a slum attracted radical activists and community organizers. Many of the civil rights and Black Power organizations that had made the neighborhood their base in the 1960s remained in the 1970s. Pride, Inc., owned a gas station at the corner of Fourteenth and Euclid; the D.C. Alliance of Active Black Businessmen made its headquarters at the Pitts Motor Hotel on Belmont Street; and the Drum and Spear Bookstore, owned and operated by a coterie of SNCC alumni, was located at 1371 Fairmont Street. Several predominantly white New Left communities also took up residence, reinforcing and enriching the neighborhood's activist tradition: Sojourners, an antiwar Christian group dedicated to neighborhood organizing; the Columbia Heights Community Ownership Project, a collection of antigentrification advocates; and the Community for Creative Non-Violence.[6]

The move to Euclid Street had a powerful impact on Mitch Snyder and his fel-

low CCNV activists. All about them they saw abandoned houses held by speculators—Columbia Heights hosted a disproportionate share of the roughly four
thousand vacant homes spread across the city—while the working poor and
derelicts alike went homeless. The city provided no shelter for single homeless
adults, leaving the job to a network of faith-based nonprofit organizations that
provided a total of two hundred beds for men and fewer than two dozen for
women. The CCNV opened Euclid House to displaced neighborhood residents,
and by mid-1976, Snyder recalled, "Forty or more people per night were sleeping on our floor." The activists' energy, dedication, and refusal to judge those
in need endeared them to the poor people whom they served. "They didn't ask
for nothing," observed Robert Lewis, a recovering alcoholic who intermittently
stayed at Euclid House. They "just helped me back on my feet."[7]

Determined to address the systemic causes of the crisis, Snyder and the Euclid House community prodded Mayor Walter Washington's reluctant administration to create a shelter system for the city's growing homeless population.
City officials grudgingly complied, but the CCNV found that the city-run shelters were cruel places where homeless men sometimes were beaten by security
guards, forced to strip naked and shower before entering the premises, and
disgorged back onto the streets well before dawn. Many homeless refused to
submit themselves to such degradation and remained on the streets, sleeping
on steam grates or in abandoned cars. In the winter, they froze to death by the
dozens.[8]

Exasperated with Mayor Washington, Euclid House members found hope
in Marion Barry's 1978 mayoral victory. Though they did not participate in electoral politics, they had developed a working relationship with Barry—Snyder
even had visited Barry in the hospital after his 1977 shooting. On taking office,
Mayor Barry embraced the CCNV's reform agenda. "Shelter is a basic human
right," he declared in a February 1979 speech, and he insisted that his administration would ensure "adequate shelter for every person in need in the nation's
capital." He appointed a Mayor's Advisory Commission on Homelessness and
tasked it to come up with a plan for a comprehensive, decentralized small shelter and drop-in center system, precisely the type of system for which CCNV had
been fighting. It was an exhilarating moment for activists accustomed to being
ridiculed by officials and shut out of policy-making decisions.[9]

The excitement that Euclid House residents felt in early 1979 reflected the
sense of hope, optimism, and possibility that many D.C. residents embraced
in the early years of Mayor Barry's administration. Out of the ashes of the riot,
in the void created by white flight, against an inefficient and often indifferent
city bureaucracy, D.C. residents sought to shape a new, racially egalitarian, and

economically just city. Marion Barry became the vehicle for their lofty ambitions—his rise from sharecropper's son to street protester to chief executive of the nation's capital inspired many Washingtonians to think grandly about making D.C. a model Chocolate City.

"We're Going to Show Everyone That Black People Can Really Run Something": Marion Barry Takes Power

Ivanhoe Donaldson could not contain his excitement. The Student Nonviolent Coordinating Committee was about to run a city—and not just any city, but the nation's capital. Born in Harlem in 1941, Donaldson was the only son of a police officer and a homemaker, Jamaican immigrants who admired black nationalist Marcus Garvey and instilled in their boy a serene sense of self-confidence and pride. As a student at Michigan State University, he traveled on his own to North Carolina to attend SNCC's founding meeting, where he met Marion Barry. Though slight of build, almost delicate, Donaldson had a steely determination and volunteered for some of the most dangerous work in the South. He also was a voracious reader, an incisive thinker, and a brilliant tactician. In the mid-1960s, Donaldson helped Stokely Carmichael refine his ideas on Black Power, and as the movement turned from protest to politics, he bounced from state to state, leading some of the iconic campaigns that raised the first generation of post–Voting Rights Act black politicians to office.[10]

In between trips, Donaldson established his home base in D.C. "I wanted to live in a black city," he later recalled, and be "an organizer in national politics and the local community at the same time." Approximately three dozen of his SNCC comrades joined him in the District in the years after 1965 for many of the same reasons. They exercised a decisive influence on their adopted home, playing leading roles in everything from the formation of the black studies program at Federal City College to leading the campaign to pass the referendum approving the home rule charter. Donaldson reveled in their company. He shared an apartment with John Wilson, argued black politics with Charlie Cobb and Judy Richardson in their Drum and Spear Bookstore, and called on his movement allies to help elect their old friend Marion Barry to the D.C. Council in 1974.[11]

Donaldson managed Barry's improbable run for mayor in 1978 and, when the returns were in, again called on his movement colleagues to help the young mayor-elect. SNCC veterans filled Barry's administration, including Press Secretary Florence Tate, Minority Business Opportunity Commission Director Courtland Cox, Assistant City Administrator for Planning and Development James Gibson, Karen Spellman as director of Resident Services in the Housing

Department, and, of course, Donaldson, who served as general assistant. Nowhere else in the country had a black protest organization so thoroughly come to dominate a major city government. "We're going to show everyone that black people can really run something," a thrilled Donaldson remarked soon after moving into his District Building office in 1979.[12]

Mayor Barry shared Donaldson's desire to make D.C. a showcase for black political power. Only twelve years had passed since Carl Stokes of Cleveland won election as the first African American mayor of a major American city. In his wake had come an impressive group of black mayors, including Coleman Young (Detroit), Tom Bradley (Los Angeles), Maynard Jackson (Atlanta), and, of course, Walter Washington in D.C. Their results had been mixed. White flight, the disappearance of urban manufacturing jobs, and persistent poverty and crime had frustrated many of their efforts. Barry was sensitive to the criticisms of these administrations. "There are some white people who didn't think [black leadership] would work anyway and are saying, I told you so," he told the *Post* during his campaign.[13]

Barry bounded into the mayor's office in January 1979 determined to prove them wrong. Setting a frenetic pace, he worked thirteen-hour days, racing his secretaries into the District Building in the mornings and huddling with aides long after dinner. His was to be an "open, competent and compassionate" administration, one that was "responsive to the press . . . answered the phones and solved citizen problems." He hired a diverse team of energetic young city administrators who reflected the city's demographics. Though African American men predominated, Barry also brought a significant number of women, Latino officials, and gay people into the upper reaches of D.C. government for the first time.[14]

He also made the mayor's office unabashedly black. Barry festooned the walls outside his office with Senegalese tapestries, then revealed them to the public in an elaborate reception featuring the country's ambassador to the United States. In mid-1979, he embarked on a five-nation tour of Africa, culminating with a speech before a meeting of the Organization of African Unity in Liberia, a nation founded by black Americans resettled by the colonization movement a century and a half before.[15]

Barry aimed not simply to make local government more efficient and representative. He wanted it to work for people—particularly low-income black residents—who had been locked out of decision making since Reconstruction. He proposed a multimillion-dollar plan to "take the boards off" the city's estimated 4,500 abandoned homes. The flagship of the initiative was the Bates Street Project, a three-block rehabilitation effort in Shaw that had been stalled by bureaucratic red tape and funding problems. Barry jump-started construction by providing developers millions of dollars in interest-free loans. By the end of 1979, more than a hundred middle- and working-class families had moved into the newly renovated buildings, some with city subsidies to make them more af-fordable. Barry also nearly doubled the size of the summer youth employment program and created an initiative to reduce infant mortality.[16]

Though Barry worked hard to serve the needs of the poor, he was most suc-cessful in using city contracts to redistribute money and power to the black middle class. The city's population was roughly 70 percent black, but minority-owned businesses held only 7 percent of city contracts in 1978. Minority Busi-ness Opportunity Commission Director Courtland Cox intended to more than triple that number immediately, warning that city agency directors who failed to give 25 percent of their contracts to minorities "should seriously evaluate their positions in city government." Barry leaned hard on white contractors, telling them that they must hire black workers if they wanted city business, while Cox encouraged black entrepreneurs to create businesses specifically for city contracts and establish joint ventures with white-owned firms to increase their capacity.[17]

During Cox's tenure, the city rarely signed a contract that did not involve a minority company. By 1985, 35 percent of city contracts worth nearly $160 mil-lion were going to minority businesses. The initiative created a new crop of black millionaires, and some of the minority firms that got their start with the city, in-cluding Black Entertainment Television and the Peebles Corporation, eventually grew into industry heavyweights.[18]

Despite these successes, Barry almost immediately encountered systemic problems that undermined his administration's early promise. Foremost among them was the bureaucracy, a bloated workforce forty-four thousand strong that was woefully inefficient, terribly expensive, and at times astonishingly rude. Bureaucratic delays sabotaged the mayor's signature projects. Although the Housing Department had delivered the first one hundred units of the Bates Street Project in record time, by the summer of 1982 the rest of the houses were two years behind schedule and several million dollars over budget, due in large part to city workers failing to check contractors' work before issuing payments. Even Donaldson, who distinguished himself as an intimidating enforcer, found city workers so incompetent or recalcitrant that "what should have been a one-day project" could take "up to ten days of your time."[19]

Perhaps most damaging was the bureaucracy's failure to keep the books. The city's budget and reporting structure had changed little since before home rule, when municipal agencies were more closely tied to their federal counterparts than the District Building. In 1976, the Arthur Andersen accounting firm had judged the city's accounts "unauditable." Incoming city comptroller Alphonse Hill recalled that in 1979 each of the departments still acted as "little fiefdom[s]" with their own accounting, personnel, and payroll staffs and no central coordination, making it impossible to determine how much money the city was spending and on what. It would take the Barry administration two years and $6 million just to complete an audit—the first in the city's history.[20]

When administration officials finally figured out what was in the books, they discovered that the city had a deficit of $115 million, a long-term debt of more than $300 million, and an unfunded pension liability of nearly $740 million. Thus, rather than reforming the bureaucracy, Barry spent much of his first two years in office squeezing every extra penny out of the budget.[21]

To make up for the shortfall, Barry unveiled an austere 1981 budget that called for tax hikes, reduced city services, layoffs, and pay freezes. The cuts fell hardest on the poor, the elderly, and the homeless. For many who had gained substantive access to city services only when Barry entered office, including Mitch Snyder and the Community for Creative Non-Violence, the budget was particularly devastating. Just a year after he had promised a dramatic improvement of homeless services, Barry dissolved the Mayor's Commission on the Homeless and declared that the city would close two emergency shelters within seventy-two hours to save money. The CCNV scrambled to find a team of pro bono lawyers to fight the mayor's order and secured a judgment that required the city to keep the shelters open.[22]

The cuts splintered Barry's coalition. Labor leaders and youth groups condemned him for proposing to close community centers and lay off city workers but not make the business community pay "its fair share." A diverse group of city workers, housing advocates, and community activists booed him when he took the stage at a rally in front of the District Building. Accustomed to protesting authority figures rather than being the object of protest, Barry told them to "go to hell." "He cares more about the moneyed people," said one widow living on a fixed income. "He has turned his back on the poor and elderly."[23]

Just about the only constituency that grew closer to the mayor during the crisis were businessmen such as Robert Linowes, the white former president of the Greater Washington Board of Trade, who praised Barry for "making the hard choices." By December 1980, only 31 percent of African American residents approved of his performance in office. For the former activist, it was a rude awakening to the realities and constraints of political power.[24]

"Patronage Is Just Good Politics": Barry Builds a
Political Machine Amid Conservative Opposition

As an embattled Barry struggled to keep his coalition intact, the city landed in the crosshairs of a rising national conservative movement. Among conservatives' first targets was the D.C. Voting Rights Amendment (DCVRA), which traveled to the states for ratification in the months after Barry's election. Like the Equal Rights Amendment, which also was being considered for ratification, the DCVRA generated fierce opposition from a powerful array of grassroots organizations, think tanks, and pressure groups.

One particularly effective foe was the American Legislative Exchange Council (ALEC), a coalition of conservative state lawmakers and business interests founded in 1973. ALEC was part of a dense network of New Right organizations that used a series of overlapping issue campaigns — including taxes, affirmative action, the Equal Rights Amendment, gay rights, and the DCVRA — to mobilize supporters. In 1978, ALEC's new chairwoman, Arizona state representative Donna Carlson, put the fight against the DCVRA atop its agenda. Under Carlson's leadership, ALEC supplied research and talking points to dozens of conservative commentators who attacked the DCVRA as an effort to furnish "special privileges and power to Washington bureaucrats" and a scheme to elect "ultra liberal Democrats" who would support "federally financed abortions . . . gun control . . . labor law 'reform' and all other bills pushed by the union chieftains." ALEC incorporated criticisms of the amendment into beefy blue briefing books and sent one to every state legislator in the country. The group's lobbying efforts decisively blunted the amendment's early momentum.[25]

Conscious that overt racial hostility had become politically unpalatable, New Right activists walked a tightrope of playing down the race issue when opposing the amendment, while simultaneously appealing to white anxieties about black power. Patrick Buchanan found the balance. A pugnacious D.C. native who had grown up in Chevy Chase, Buchanan had helped craft President Nixon's strategy of painting the city as a "crime capital." Now he seamlessly weaved white anger at liberal policies into a potent argument against the DCVRA. Though he privately conceded that D.C. residents had a "legitimate grievance," publicly he labeled the amendment an "affirmative action program" and implored Americans not to set aside "two centuries of constitutional government . . . just so [civil rights activist] Julian Bond can have a Senate chair."[26]

Facing concerted conservative opposition, the drive to pass the DCVRA sputtered. By late summer 1980, only ten states had ratified the amendment. Nine states had rejected it by wide margins. The Republican Party, for only the second time since 1948, adopted a platform without a plank for D.C. voting rights. (The change endured—for the next thirty-two years the party would either remain silent on the issue or oppose any expansion of D.C. self-determination.) The federal elections in November 1980 sealed the amendment's fate by propelling to power conservative insurgents who had spearheaded opposition to the DCVRA, including newly elected president Ronald Reagan.[27]

The 1980 elections fundamentally altered the city's relationship with the Republican Party and the federal government. Since the advent of home rule in 1974, the liberals who controlled Congress had purposefully steered clear of fights over local legislation, seeking to give the new D.C. government the greatest degree of self-determination possible within the statutory confines of the Home Rule Act. Newly emboldened conservatives cast this convention aside, aggressively intervening in D.C. affairs and using the city as a marker in national policy debates. "Congress is the local government," argued Representative Philip Crane of Illinois after he and other Republicans successfully overturned the city's sexual assault legislation in fall 1981. "We have a responsibility to review everything the D.C. City Council does—everything."[28]

In the next five years, congressional Republicans introduced twelve disapproval resolutions—a congressional nullification of an act passed by the council—opposing everything from a 1981 city law decriminalizing consensual adult sodomy to a 1983 law divesting city funds from firms doing business with the white supremacist regimes of South Africa and Namibia. Representative Julian Dixon, a black California representative who was born in Washington and chaired the House Appropriations Subcommittee on D.C., lamented, "There is a plantation mentality among some of the members who believe they have to be the overlord because people in the District can't handle their own affairs."[29]

Conservative opposition mounted even as Marion Barry's political fortunes rebounded. After struggling through the budget crisis of his first year, Barry benefited from a downtown development boom sparked in part by the expansion of the city's Metro system. Throughout the old downtown, land prices spiked as developers leveled block after block of dilapidated row houses and built gleaming office towers in their stead, while the city's department stores spruced up their old buildings—Hecht's built a new facility, the first major department store built in a U.S. center city in decades. Barry accelerated the revitalization by cutting red tape for builders, working closely with the federal government to choreograph development, and moving forward with plans for a convention center above H Street between Ninth and Eleventh Streets NW. Beyond downtown, significant gentrification continued into mid-decade, and soaring real estate prices in the changing neighborhoods produced a windfall in property tax revenue.[30]

Barry used this new revenue to expand and improve city services, which helped him gain the support of a broad cross section of the black community. In Ward 7, a long thin slice of the city east of the Anacostia that contained both housing projects and a solid middle-class black community dubbed the "silver coast," the city improved trash pickup and public transportation, cleaned alleys and streets, named many residents to public boards, and refurbished libraries and playgrounds. This attention gave residents, long used to being ignored by the city government, the feeling that they were part of the governing coalition. "Marion brought us respect," said resident Kimi Gray, whom Barry appointed to head his Public Housing Advisory Board.[31]

The mayor also gave them jobs. Much like his Reconstruction–era predecessors, Barry faced the problem of finding employment for a large, low- and middle-skilled African American population in a city that lacked an industrial base. No longer pressed to cut the budget, Barry abandoned his efforts to shrink the bureaucracy and used the city government as an employment program. He gave public workers a 20 percent raise and went on a hiring binge that would last through his second term, adding four thousand workers to the already hefty payroll. The government grew dramatically, becoming the largest per capita in the country. Despite all those workers, the city bureaucracy could not shake its reputation for inefficiency and ineffectiveness, particularly in agencies that served the city's neediest people. But grateful city workers became the backbone of Barry's electoral coalition, raising charges of patronage from the press. "Patronage," replied Barry's reelection campaign manager Ivanhoe Donaldson, is "just good politics."[32]

Barry reaped the political rewards in his 1982 reelection campaign. In the Democratic primary (the only election of consequence in the heavily Democratic city), he faced Patricia Roberts Harris, an accomplished black lawyer who had served as secretary of health, education, and welfare in the Carter administration. Barry dodged Harris during the campaign, relying on his superior organization and last-minute improvements to city services to neutralize her criticisms and shore up his base. He also used race effectively to paint Harris — light-skinned, refined, with impeccable credentials — as not "black" enough. "There has always been a black candidate in D.C. elections," Donaldson told the *Post*. "Marion is that candidate." Harris angrily denounced the strategy, noting that she had participated in the 1943 Howard University sit-ins and "was involved in the civil rights movement long before Marion Barry."[33]

The mayor's strategy succeeded. Barry secured 59 percent of the vote, while Harris only managed to win predominantly white Ward 3. Barry won overwhelming black support in every ward, even among the black middle-class residents who had held out against him four years before. He had replaced his biracial coalition of 1978 with a cross-class black coalition.[34]

As Barry consolidated his hold over the African American electorate, white voters' ability to influence elections declined. White Democrats were a distinct minority within their party, while changes in the national GOP undermined local Republicans of all races. Since the home rule era began in 1974, D.C. Republicans had included a contingent of the city's socially conservative black middle class, liberal white Republican voters in Ward 3, and nationally known African American political appointees who swooped into town to run for office. The rise of the New Right within the national party, however, marginalized liberal black Republicans. Seeing its future in the white electorate, the party abandoned majority-black jurisdictions such as D.C., instead using them as straw men to score political points with white voters who lived elsewhere.[35]

With no serious opposition left in the city, Barry asserted his political dominance. Determined to preempt any future rivals and avoid repeating the budget battles of his first term, the mayor cowed the D.C. Council into political submission by dispensing or withholding city services depending on a council member's loyalty. Opposition to administration initiatives evaporated. In 1984, Barry instructed Ivanhoe Donaldson to run for Democratic State Committee chairman against Theodis Gay, a veteran activist who had kept the party relatively independent of the mayor. Donaldson trounced him.[36]

Barry even coopted most of the city's protest organizations by placing their leadership on the payroll or giving them city contracts. "We hire everybody who complains," grumbled Councilman John Wilson. "There are no independent advocacy groups in this city." The few activists whom he could not control, Barry defamed. When Mitch Snyder and the CCNV illegally converted a World War II–era temporary building at Second and E Streets NW into a homeless shelter, Barry dispatched trusted aide Lawrence Guyot, another SNCC veteran, to smear him as a "Jim Jones"–style "cult leader," a message echoed by the Reagan administration.[37]

With the Democratic Party firmly under his control and the Republican Party isolated in Ward 3, Barry stood alone as the most powerful political figure in local politics. "I may not be perfect," Barry crowed after he cruised to reelection in 1986, "but I'm perfect for Washington." Dubbing him "Boss Barry," the Post's Eugene Robinson surmised, tongue in cheek, that "the mayor's only real competition now is the U.S. Attorney." But his biggest enemy—and the city's—turned out to be much smaller and more powerful than the federal government. It was crack cocaine.[38]

"Everything Is Coming Unraveled": Crack Hits D.C.

While Marion Barry was busy building his political machine, Rayful Edmond III launched a local cocaine empire. Born in 1964, Edmond grew up the favored son of a large and loving extended family centered on his maternal grandmother's home at 407 M Street NE. His parents were part of D.C.'s solid black working class. Both were employed at the U.S. Department of Health and Human Services (DHHS), his father as a driver and his mother as a staffing specialist, and Edmond recalled being "spoiled to death" as a kid. Generous, athletic, and quick to flash a wide, disarming smile, Edmond proved popular with his peers at Dunbar High School, by then much diminished from its heyday as the crown jewel of black public education. They voted him "Mr. Sophomore," "Mr. Junior," and, as a senior, "Most Popular."[39]

Despite the accolades, Edmond struggled after graduating from Dunbar in 1983. He tried college and worked odd jobs, but he found himself drawn to the family business: drugs. Both of his parents dabbled in the drug trade to pad their incomes. His father, "Big Ray" Edmond Jr., earned extra money as a numbers runner and small-time drug dealer, while his mother, Constance "Bootsie" Perry, sold prescription diet pills to heroin dealers who used them to cut their product. The elder Edmonds did not hide their activities from young Rayful. "My mom and dad taught me the drug game," he recalled. "I was nine, ten years old."

After the Barry administration deprived Big Ray of his numbers hustle by creating a city-run lottery in 1982, he quit his job at DHHS and began importing cocaine from New York full time. Two years later, he offered his son a piece of the business. Rayful III picked up a kilo of cocaine from his father, broke it down, and headed to "the strip," the neighborhood open-air drug market that encompassed the 600 blocks of Morton and Orleans Place NE. It was the beginning of an extraordinarily lucrative and violent career.[40]

By the time Rayful Edmond became a dealer in the mid-1980s, D.C.'s illegal drug trade had been well established for more than half a century. The city's population of addicts, once confined to the back rooms of speakeasies and jazz clubs, exploded in size and spilled into the streets as the heroin trade flourished in the 1960s. By 1969, the city counted a population of approximately six thousand addicts, and despite President Nixon's "war" on the "dangerous and illegal drug traffic in the District of Columbia," the trade remained stubbornly persistent through the 1970s.[41]

In the 1980s, a growing number of District users turned to cocaine, a "rich man's drug" that appealed to white-collar workers who could afford its $100 a gram price tag. As a hub for young professionals, the D.C. region became a major market for cocaine. Lawyers and real estate developers snorted lines at Georgetown house parties; the maître d' and waitresses at the exclusive Palm Restaurant in Northwest dealt coke to lobbyists and socialites; even a few members of Congress dabbled until a 1983 investigation of drug use on Capitol Hill scared them into being more circumspect.[42]

Upscale drug dealers and addicts melded into the social landscape of majority-white suburbs and wealthy neighborhoods, but in the poor black communities of the center city they created large, disruptive open-air markets that sold to neighborhood junkies, lawyers on lunch breaks, and suburban commuters alike. Of D.C.'s sixteen open-air markets, the busiest was Hanover Place NW, a narrow, one-block lane about a mile and a half north of the Capitol. It became a twenty-four-hour operation with "long lines that lengthened on the weekends and around the first of the month, combined with a whole other mass of people and peddlers . . . boosters and hijackers," one resident recalled. In 1985, the market became a battleground as dealers fought for a piece of D.C.'s lucrative trade. Because of high demand and low supply, D.C. cocaine typically sold for double the price it fetched in New York.[43]

By the end of 1985, Washington surpassed all other U.S. cities in per capita drug arrests. The following year, as cocaine spread down the income scale to poor and working-class African American addicts, it topped heroin as D.C. users' drug of choice.

The city's growing drug epidemic became national news in June 1986 with the death of University of Maryland basketball star Len Bias. A hometown hero, Bias had grown up just across the city line in Hyattsville, Maryland. In the 1970s, middle-class black families like the Biases had begun to redraw the boundaries of Chocolate City. Seeking the good schools and green expanses of the suburbs, they poured across the Maryland line, buying midcentury tract homes on winding lanes in Prince George's County. White county residents fled before their advance, and by 1986 most of the communities along the District border had become majority black. Though determined to escape the city's ills, black residents who moved to Prince George's County often worked, worshiped, and socialized in the city. As one Hillcrest Heights resident put it, "Our affiliations are in D.C. We just live in Maryland."[44]

The Bias family was no exception. They attended Pilgrim A.M.E. Church on Seventeenth Street NE, and in his college years, Len frequented D.C. nightclubs such as Chapter III, just south of the Capitol. Thus, when the world champion

Residents protest an open-air drug market in Mount Pleasant. Open-air drug markets attracted dealers and users from across the city and suburbs. The markets flourished during the crack epidemic of the late 1980s. © 1989 Carol Guzy / The Washington Post.

Boston Celtics made Bias the second overall pick in the NBA draft, many black Washingtonians celebrated his good fortune as their own. But less than two days later, the graceful forward lay dead, victim of a cocaine overdose.[45]

Bias's death stunned Washingtonians as well as federal officials. Occurring amid growing national alarm over cocaine addiction, it generated a firestorm of media attention—magazines such as Sports Illustrated featured him on their covers, and the Post published hundreds of articles on the young forward in the months after his death. President Ronald Reagan delivered a prime-time television address exhorting Americans to join a "national crusade" against drugs, and Democrats in Congress hurriedly cobbled together the draconian Anti-Drug Abuse Act of 1986, which included mandatory minimum sentences for a host of drug crimes and a one-hundred-to-one disparity in sentences between crack and powder cocaine. The District featured prominently in the hearings on the bill, with some of the most dramatic testimony taken from a former dealer who sat behind a frosted glass panel to conceal his identity as he declared, "Cocaine is everywhere in Washington."[46]

With pressure from Capitol Hill and polls showing that District residents considered drugs the city's biggest problem, Barry launched his own drug war in August 1986 during his reelection campaign. "Operation Clean Sweep," which targeted the city's open-air markets, was the brainchild of Assistant Police Chief Isaac Fulwood, the officer whom Barry had promoted through the ranks following his heroics during the 1977 hostage crisis. Using a team of between one hundred and two hundred officers, the department saturated the drug markets, using "jump out squads" to apprehend dealers and "buy and bust" teams against users. Looking back, Fulwood marveled at the scale of the operation: "We were arresting, literally on the weekends, sometimes, 800 or 900 people." Residents of the affected neighborhoods cheered the program, thankful for a respite from the flocks of dealers chirping, "Are you looking?" and "I got it," and the ever-growing threat of violence.[47]

Operation Clean Sweep helped Barry cruise to reelection that November, but it offered only short-term relief for drug-ravaged neighborhoods. On Hanover Place, police set up a mobile command center in the middle of the block, boarded up forty-seven abandoned homes, and carted away three hundred tons of trash, including forty-one stolen cars—only to see the market return after they pulled out. With demand still high and dealers still plentiful, the drug trade thrived. By December 1988, Police Chief Maurice Turner declared the program a failure, despite spending $6 million and making nearly thirty thousand arrests. The mass arrests inflicted long-lasting damage by creating a generation of felons. Between 1985 and 1987, police arrested one of every four young men between the ages of eighteen and twenty-nine on drug-related charges. Because the program focused on the open-air markets, not the more discreet dealing in upscale neighborhoods, nearly all those arrested were African American.[48]

And Operation Clean Sweep failed to stop the spread of "crack."

Crack was a cheaper form of cocaine made from boiling the drug with baking soda or ammonia to create a hard, rocklike substance that could be smoked. It first appeared in major drug-importing cities such as New York and Miami, becoming widely available in D.C. in late 1986. Crack dramatically expanded the drug-using population, attracting the poor, teenagers, and casual users put off by the high price of cocaine—a small bag of "rocks" could be had for as little as $5.

More addictive than powder cocaine, crack packed a short, intense high that left users anxious for another hit. Desperate addicts took to selling whatever they could to buy the little white rocks. "I've seen mothers prostitute themselves and pimp their daughters for hits of crack," recalled Tony Lewis Jr., whose father ran an open-air market on First and Bates Street NW, in front of the houses Mayor Barry had hurriedly refurbished in 1979. To serve the expanded trade, dealers opened an additional three dozen drug markets, expanding the city total to nearly sixty by the end of 1987. Two years later, that number had more than doubled.[49]

No single individual did more to spread crack in Washington than Rayful Edmond III. After a brush with vice officers almost landed him jail in late 1984, Edmond decided to abandon street dealing and set himself up as a supplier. Using his large family and a group of neighborhood friends, he assembled an impressive smuggling, production, and retail operation that quickly came to dominate the strip. In 1987, he made a direct connection to Colombia's Cali Cartel and began importing massive amounts of high-quality cocaine, then selling it as crack at cut-rate prices. Along with his former Dunbar classmate Tony Lewis, Edmond imported perhaps seventeen hundred pounds of cocaine a month, roughly 20 percent of the District market.[50]

As addicts heard about Edmond's top-notch product, they flooded the strip and other markets where they could find it. On busy nights, Edmond's dealers carried out thirty sales a minute. Grossing roughly $2 million per week and lacking the contacts to launder it through legitimate businesses, Edmond spent lavishly on cars and jewelry (including a $45,000 diamond-encrusted Rolex), took his friends and family on outlandish shopping trips, and traveled frequently to New York, Las Vegas, and elsewhere. He also cultivated a public image of generosity and benevolence, buying people around the strip turkeys at Thanksgiving, paying overdue utility bills and rent, even handing out $100 bills to kids.[51]

With so much money to be made as crack expanded D.C.'s drug trade, well-armed Jamaican gangs from New York and Miami tried to muscle in on the business in 1986 and 1987, precipitating a bloodbath. Edmond and his D.C. counterparts traveled to Virginia to buy their own arsenals (the D.C. Council had passed strict gun-control legislation in the mid-1970s). Properly equipped, they repulsed the out-of-towners, then turned the guns on one another in a deadly struggle for turf, profits, and respect.[52]

Driven almost exclusively by a spike in drug-related killings, the number of murders in D.C. jumped from an average of 200 per year in the first half of the 1980s to 372 in 1988. Crunching the numbers in January 1989, a group of re-lieved Detroit journalists declared that D.C. had surpassed the Motor City to become the nation's "murder capital." Police proved powerless to stop the car-nage, in part because Mayor Barry had reduced their budgets and filled the de-partment's brass with political cronies.[53]

Barry tried to calm rattled Washingtonians, arguing that most of the killings were "targeted assassinations" among drug dealers, and hence the vast majority of the District was safe. The carnage was indeed confined almost exclusively to poor African American communities east of Rock Creek Park. In 1988, not one murder occurred in the affluent neighborhoods to its west. The mayor prom-ised "leadership, ideas, programs, and action" to address the problem, but the violence only increased. Each killing prompted retaliation from rival crews, and the police department's miserably low rate of solving murder cases left drug enforcers on the street. The notorious Wayne Perry alone slayed nearly three dozen people. Though federal authorities arrested Rayful Edmond in 1989, kill-ings rose unabated, peaking at 482 in 1991.[54]

Feeling abandoned by the city government, many communities took to bat-tling dealers and addicts on their own. In Mayfair Mansions, the sprawling apartment complex in Northeast built by Elder Michaux during World War II, residents invited the Nation of Islam to provide antidrug patrols in an open-air drug market so large and dangerous that police officers called it "little Beirut" and refused to respond to 911 calls until they could assemble overwhelming backup. The Muslim "Dope Busters" took up residence in the community, pro-viding a twenty-four-hour presence that commanded the respect of desperate residents.[55]

In Shaw, a brash, young Advisory Neighborhood Commissioner named Leroy Thorpe Jr. organized marches to shut down neighborhood crack houses. Like the Muslims, who sometimes assaulted suspected dealers, his actions veered close to vigilantism. "I was telling them I'd go get a bat, bust them upside the head," Thorpe recalled. "I was raw!" Another Shaw resident took to burning down crack houses. "Everything is coming unraveled," worried neighborhood activist Jeff Koenreich. "People are . . . taking matters into their own hands."[56]

"That Goddamn Bitch Set Me Up": The Fall of Marion Barry

As crack devastated the city, Marion Barry wrestled with his own addiction. The mayor had first tried cocaine in the late 1970s and developed a habit soon thereafter. By the mid-1980s, Barry could no longer hide the effects. His behavior grew erratic—long, unexplained trips, a diminished work schedule, slurring words in public—and even ardent supporters grew worried.

The U.S. attorney and local police had gotten wind of his drug use by 1982, but investigators struggled to build a reliable case. Barry continually outflanked them, covering up emergency room visits for overdoses and getting his contacts in the police department to quash inquiries. In 1984, U.S. Attorney Joseph diGenova uncovered evidence that a young District employee named Karen Johnson had carried on an affair with the mayor during which she sold him cocaine on more than two dozen occasions, but Barry lied to a grand jury and paid Johnson not to cooperate with investigators.[57]

Determined to catch the elusive mayor, the persistent diGenova broadened his investigation to seek evidence not just of drug use but also of corruption within the Barry administration. In 1984, Barry's ex-wife, Mary Treadwell, pleaded guilty to stealing hundreds of thousands of dollars from a public housing project owned by Pride, Inc. A year later, Barry's longtime confidant Ivanhoe Donaldson admitted to skimming $190,000 out of an unaudited Department of Employment Services account, while Deputy Mayor for Finance Al Hill confessed to steering city contracts to friends in return for kickbacks.[58]

Convinced that the mayor was complicit in such graft, diGenova in May 1987 staged a series of raids on five city agencies, minority-owned businesses with close ties to Barry, and the homes of Barry friends and employees. He found ample evidence that Barry and his top administrators used the contract system to ensure that black businessmen, many of them close to the mayor, secured millions of dollars in city contracts while making almost no effort to certify that the services they provided were adequate. One notorious offender was Cornelius Pitts, a Barry ally since the 1960s. Pitts charged the city exorbitant prices to house homeless people in his vermin-infested Pitts Motor Hotel—in 1986, a congressional committee condemned the shelter as the most expensive in the nation.[59]

By publicly announcing the raids and leaking information about what agents had seized, diGenova hoped to stir public outrage and generate pressure on

Mayor Barry and his allies to cooperate with federal authorities. Instead he triggered a racially tinged backlash. "Is diGenova investigating white contractors?" asked one black businesswoman who noted that two-thirds of the city's business was with white contractors, many of whom also had received preferential treatment and delivered poor services. He was not. Nor were many of his fellow U.S. attorneys around the country. Under President Reagan, federal investigators focused disproportionate attention on black elected officials and the minority contractors they worked to bring into government. The *Post*'s Gwen Ifill discovered that African American politicians, who were only 3 percent of all elected officials, were suspects in 14 percent of federal corruption investigations in the mid-1980s. Black observers nationwide grew alarmed by the probes, which they interpreted as attacks on black power, not corruption.[60]

Barry tapped into black anxiety over the federal government's disproportionate investigation of black elected officials. He denounced diGenova's raids as an effort by federal authorities to "run me out of office" and filed a lawsuit alleging that the U.S. attorney had violated the secrecy of the grand jury by leaking information about the investigations. Six national black political organizations filed friend-of-the-court briefs arguing that the Barry investigation was part of a national effort by federal prosecutors to "neutralize black political strength."[61]

Rumors of Barry's drug use, allegations of widespread corruption, and ongoing federal investigations eroded white support for the mayor. He had swept into office in 1978 with an interracial coalition and the backing of the liberal white establishment, including the *Post*, but in 1986 he won just 25 percent of the white vote and the *Post*'s editors had turned into fierce critics. As his addiction worsened and parts of the city government became thoroughly dysfunctional, their criticism turned into contempt. William Regardie, publisher of a monthly business magazine popular with wealthy white Washingtonians, caricatured Barry sniffing cocaine and handed out bumper stickers that read, "JUST SAY NO TO MARION BARRY." During a 1989 hearing on the city budget, Republican senator John Danforth of Missouri confronted the mayor: "This government is scandalously corrupt and hopelessly incompetent."[62]

President George H. W. Bush, elected in 1988, exploited the city's vulnerabilities by using it as a prop in his administration's war on drugs. In April 1989, the president's "drug czar," William Bennett, unveiled an $80 million plan to combat drug trafficking in D.C. by dramatically increasing arrests of street-level dealers and addicts—the same approach Police Chief Maurice Turner had deemed a failure just a few months before. The federal government was stepping in, Bennett claimed, because "the local government has not acted in as responsible a way as it should." Simultaneously, GOP strategists close to the president worked to soften the GOP's racial image by wooing Turner to run as a Republican against Barry in the 1990 mayoral election. Vice President Dan Quayle headlined a $500-a-plate fund-raiser and the president invited the lifelong Democrat to the White House to ceremonially change his party affiliation.[63]

The president's exploitation of the city's drug crisis reached its apogee in September with a prime-time television address in which he rolled out his $7.8 billion National Drug Control Strategy. To underscore his message that drugs were the "greatest domestic threat to the nation today," Bush held up a bag of crack cocaine that he claimed had been "seized" by federal agents "in a park just across the street from the White House." The prop suggested a capital city so unruly that drug dealers brazenly plied their trade outside the president's home. (White House aides had informed the president before the speech that drug dealers actually did *not* operate in Lafayette Park, but Bush was so enamored with the idea that Drug Enforcement Agency officials made it true. They selected an eighteen-year-old small-time dealer from Southeast, Timothy Jackson, drove him to the park, conducted the sale, then arrested him. Jackson's subsequent case ended in a mistrial because, the jury foreman said, "The jurors thought it was a setup.")[64]

For federal officials, the primary culprit for D.C.'s drug problem was the mayor himself. Despite five years of near constant investigation, Barry remained in office, charged with no crimes and widely popular with black voters. But investigators were closing in. In December 1988, Barry nearly walked into a local police buy-and-bust operation targeting his friend and fellow addict Charles Lewis. The son of a prominent Virgin Islands family, Lewis had fallen on hard times and, after he was apprehended, began cooperating with the police. He introduced U.S. Attorney Jay Stephens to a long list of friends, business partners, and former lovers who had done cocaine with the mayor. Stephens recognized that a jury likely would not convict Barry based simply on verbal testimony, however. He needed direct evidence of the mayor's drug use, and he sought to secure it by setting up a sting operation using one of the few people who had the increasingly cautious mayor's trust: Hazel Diana "Rasheeda" Moore.

Though a womanizer, Barry had a soft spot for Moore. Raised in a deeply religious, working-class Northeast home, the tall, sultry Moore became a top model whose face graced the covers of *Essence* and *W* magazines in 1975. Yet she struggled with drug use, and her career sputtered after a boyfriend was caught attempting to smuggle cocaine into the country. When she met Barry in 1986, Moore was penniless and living with her mother. The mayor gave her a $60,000 contract to teach young women "image consciousness" in the summer youth jobs program, and the two began a stormy, two-year affair in which they mixed sex, cocaine, or crack "at least 100" times, in Moore's telling. In 1989, she left the city to reunite with her three children in Los Angeles. That is where the FBI found her, living in a shelter, compelled to change by her revived religious convictions but unable to shake her cocaine addiction. She determined to atone for her sins by cooperating with federal investigators. "I prayed about my decision," Moore stated. "I wanted to cleanse myself." [65]

The plan was simple: Moore would lure Barry to Room 727 of the Vista International Hotel on M Street NW, where she would present him with the opportunity to buy and smoke crack as federal surveillance cameras rolled. When Barry arrived, he was more interested in sex than drugs and initially refused Moore's persistent suggestions that they smoke crack. After twenty minutes, he implied that he was open to buying drugs. Moore took Barry's money, purchased forty dollars' worth of crack from an undercover agent, and handed it to the mayor, who put the crack pipe to his lips, lit up, and inhaled. Federal agents and local police stormed the room and placed the mayor under arrest. An incredulous Barry sat on the bed muttering, "That goddamn bitch set me up." [66]

As news of the sting spread, black Washingtonians expressed both sadness and anger, seeing in Barry's fall a setback for the causes that many held as indistinguishable from the man. When the Los Angeles Times interviewed many Cardozo High School students, all of them voiced their outrage at what they perceived as the mayor's hypocrisy. "He was going around preaching [an anti-drug message]," stated seventeen-year-old Tracey Parker, "but he was doing it." Thirty-six percent of black D.C. residents polled by the Post said the sting was the mayor's fault alone. A slightly larger number, however—39 percent—blamed both a perfidious federal government and Barry equally. WOL-AM radio personality Cathy Hughes, who fielded thousands of calls in the days after the sting, noted that her listeners were struck by the mayor's carelessness, considering that he knew federal officials were targeting African American leaders. "Even if it was a setup," she argued, "You [Barry] knew they were trying to set you up." Another 20 percent of black residents polled believed that "law enforcement officials were out to get Marion Barry any way they could." [67]

Barry's embarrassingly public arrest turned him into a punch line for late-night comedians, but the mayor quickly gathered himself and organized a brilliant defense. He sought public sympathy by wrapping himself in a biblical tale of sin and redemption. Flanked by one hundred city pastors, he admitted to having an unspecified "problem" that had brought him "face to face with my deepest human frailties." He then checked himself into a drug and alcohol rehabilitation center and began attending church regularly. Behind the scenes he tried to arrange a deal with prosecutors, offering to plead guilty to a misdemeanor, a charge that would allow him to run again for office. With video evidence and ten witnesses who would testify to using cocaine with Barry, U.S. Attorney Stephens felt confident in his ability to secure several felony counts and rebuffed the mayor's entreaties.[68]

Barry, however, knew the city's black electorate better than Stephens. As he said before his 1990 trial, "All it takes is one juror saying, 'I'm not going to convict Marion Barry. I don't care what you say.'" He and his lawyers spent all their energy angling for that one juror by placing the government on trial. "Years ago the government made a determination that it would get Marion Barry," defense attorney R. Kenneth Mundy claimed in his opening statement, "and it would go to any lengths, any extremes to get him."[69]

The defense alleged a government conspiracy, knowing that D.C.'s black community was particularly sensitive to the idea that federal prosecutors were targeting black leadership for investigation. Since 1987, federal officials had brought charges against or leaked information from investigations of the most powerful black elected and appointed officials in seven states, including Maryland, New York, and Florida. Many of these officials traveled to Washington to make their case against the Justice Department, and they often appeared in local churches, on black radio programs, and at protest rallies. Many black Washingtonians—including those who opposed the mayor politically—feared, as did NAACP Executive Director Benjamin Hooks, that the Justice Department had placed an "undue emphasis on harassing black elected officials."[70]

The defense's claims resonated with roughly half of the jurors, and deliberations were deadlocked from the beginning. A group of five middle-aged, working-class black jurors blamed the government entirely. "They were out to get Marion Barry," said D.C. Corrections Department secretary Valerie Jackson-Warren. "I believe that with all my heart." Through eight exhausting days of debate, an opposing group of five younger African Americans and two white jurors failed to dislodge them from their position. Ultimately, they compromised: the jurors would convict Barry of one misdemeanor count, acquit him of another, and give up on the rest. When they announced the verdict on August 10, the mayor cracked a huge smile and his supporters outside the courthouse erupted into chants of "Ba-rry! Ba-rry!" He had dodged a bullet.[71]

Yet Barry's political future remained clouded. He had missed the filing deadline for the Democratic primary, but he registered as an independent and entered the crowded race for an at-large council seat. During the campaign, Judge Thomas Penfield Jackson, a jowly, patrician, Reagan appointee who had made little secret of his disapproval of the defense team's strategy, sentenced Barry to six months in prison. It was a stiff penalty for misdemeanor drug possession, one rooted in Jackson's belief that Barry had "given aid, comfort and encouragement to the drug culture at large." (Though Barry's defenders scoffed at Jackson's logic, Rayful Edmond made a similar argument from a federal prison in Marion, Illinois. "It's so many people that are out there talking about 'drugs is bad' that are using drugs themselves," he argued. "Just like Marion Barry.") Jackson's verdict also revealed his disdain for the older black jurors, who, he later claimed, "would not convict under any circumstances."[72]

Barry hoped that black voter resentment over the sentence would boost his campaign, but voters' sober-eyed understanding that the mayor suffered from a serious substance abuse problem counterbalanced their anger. In November, they handed him his only electoral defeat. Weeks later, Barry headed off to prison, seemingly finished in District politics.[73]

"A New Season": D.C. Struggles under a New Mayor

Sharon Pratt Dixon believed that she could renew the promise of Chocolate City. A third-generation Washingtonian, a child of the city's light-skinned elite, she had grown up along the edge of Washington's black belt, moving northward from LeDroit Park as the city opened up to African American homebuyers. In 1961, she graduated with honors from the newly desegregated Roosevelt High School, then headed to Howard University, where she studied political science. Pretty and petite—she stood only five feet, two inches tall—Dixon had hoped to become an actress, but her father, a distinguished jurist, convinced her to enroll in Howard Law School. There she met and married Arrington Dixon, who, with his wife's help, entered District politics in 1968 and rose to D.C. Council chairman within a decade.

Smart, self-assured, and driven—she once stated her intention of "going as far, doing and earning as much . . . as any man"—Dixon was not satisfied to serve as her husband's behind-the-scenes adviser. In 1976, she launched a political career of her own, winning the post of D.C. delegate to the Democratic National Committee. As part of Walter Fauntroy's organization, she officially was allied with Marion Barry, but like many upper-class black Washingtonians, she held the crude upstart in disdain. In 1982, she managed her friend Patricia Roberts Harris's ill-fated campaign to dethrone the vulnerable incumbent. Following Harris's defeat, Dixon focused on the national scene, becoming DNC treasurer in 1984.[74]

But as the city spun out of control Dixon returned to local politics with her own improbable campaign for mayor. Trumpeting her outsider status and promising to "clean house with a shovel, not a broom," Dixon tapped into many residents' desperate desire to break from the Barry years. A powerful endorsement from the *Post* helped Dixon win a majority of white voters and propelled her to a razor-thin victory in the 1990 Democratic primary. She then crushed her Republican opponent in the November general election to become the first African American woman to lead a major U.S. city.[75]

It was "a new season" in D.C. politics, Dixon declared at her inauguration in January 1991. An ambitious cohort of reformers had swept away a generation of elected officials, including both Marion Barry and Walter Fauntroy, who came in last in the Democratic mayoral primary. Replacing him as D.C.'s nonvoting delegate in the House of Representatives was Eleanor Holmes Norton, a respected attorney, civil rights activist, and Carter administration veteran who had never before held local office.[76]

Dixon capitalized on the sense of optimism to tackle the city's economic woes. When she took office, the country was in the midst of a real estate recession that devastated D.C.'s most important private industry. City tax receipts, largely reliant on real estate, shrank considerably. With the congressional payment frozen since 1985 in a silent protest against Barry, the city experienced a budget shortfall of $300 million. Dixon spent much of her first two months in office calling on her DNC contacts and charming lawmakers on Capitol Hill. Impressed with the polished and professional Dixon—a sharp contrast to her predecessor—Congress upped its annual payment by $200 million and appropriated an additional $100 million in emergency funding to close the budget gap. She received a similarly warm reception from the council, which approved more than $400 million in additional borrowing and granted Dixon the power to circumvent civil service rules to get rid of underperforming city employees.[77]

The first real test of her leadership came in May 1991, when riots erupted in an unexpected place: the diverse, eclectic Mount Pleasant–Adams Morgan neighborhood, widely regarded as the city's melting pot. In the 1980s, the neighborhood absorbed thousands of Salvadorans who had fled a murderous civil war and settled in the area, nearly doubling the city's Latino population. Mostly young, male, and poor, the new immigrants packed into dilapidated, overcrowded apartments, emerging each day to work as busboys, janitors, and construction workers—jobs that historically had gone to African American laborers. Fully half of the area's Latinos lived in households that contained four or more people and earned less that $20,000 per year. Because many immigrants had arrived without papers documenting their legal status, they could not vote and the Barry administration ignored them. It was as if Carlos Rosario, who passed away in 1987, had never existed. With little access to government services and concentrated in the most vulnerable segments of the economy, they were hit hard by the 1990 recession.[78]

As unemployed Salvadoran men filled neighborhood parks to wait for work and socialize, their more established neighbors, black and white, came to see them as alien and threatening. "Drunks regularly trash the neighborhood, use it as a latrine, harass women, break the area's saplings, scare the elderly and kids out of the parks, and pull knives or clubs on each other," complained a former ANC commissioner. Police officers, few of whom spoke Spanish, rousted loitering men from area parks, often becoming rough with the non-English speakers who could not understand. Tensions between the predominantly African American police and the Salvadoran community increased dramatically.[79]

Daniel Enrique Gomez knew these tensions well. Gomez arrived in D.C. from his native El Salvador in 1989 and secured a job washing dishes at the Georgetown Marriott. Once his shift was over, he would grab a bottle and catch up with friends at a small park at the corner of Seventeenth and Lamont Streets. On May 5, 1991, a balmy Sunday evening, Gomez and three friends were thoroughly drunk when officers Angela Jewel and Griselle Del Valle cited the men for public intoxication. The men resisted arrest, and during the ensuing scuffle Jewel shot Gomez in the chest, wounding him critically.[80]

Rumors that a black officer had shot and killed a Salvadoran man (some claimed he had been handcuffed when he was shot) coursed through the Latino community. Crowds of angry residents gathered along Mount Pleasant Street as hundreds of police reinforcements scrambled to the scene. By nightfall bystanders were throwing bottles and rocks at a wall of riot police. Groups of young men raged up and down the Mount Pleasant commercial strip, burning police cars, smashing windows, and looting. Though frightened by the violence, many residents could not help but sympathize. "They're standing up for their rights," insisted Mount Pleasant resident Bea Rodriguez. "If you live here you see a lot of abuse by police."[81]

Mayor Dixon inspired public confidence with her measured, compassionate response to the conflagration. She directed Police Chief Isaac Fulwood to contain rather than confront the rioters, a move later credited with saving lives and minimizing the reach of the riot. No one was seriously injured, and property damage was limited to the Mount Pleasant and Columbia Road commercial strips. Police made 230 arrests and contained the violence by the second night. For days, Dixon remained visible in the neighborhood, huddling with police, meeting with Latino leaders, and walking Mt. Pleasant Street to speak with residents. Her handling of the riot drew praise from residents of all backgrounds

In May 1991, a black police officer shot an unarmed Salvadoran man, triggering three days of riots in Mount Pleasant. Latino leaders charged that the city's black leadership routinely ignored the needs of Latino residents. Rick Reinhard.

and the D.C. Council. "Mayor Dixon grew immeasurably in my eyes during [the riot]," said Councilman Frank Smith, whose district included the riot area.[82]

Latino community activists were less impressed. The Mount Pleasant riot inspired a new generation of Latino leadership and kindled a new assertiveness that focused attention on the poor relationship between the city's black-run government and the fast-growing Latino community. Latinos made up more than 5 percent of District residents but less than 1 percent of municipal workers, and the city bureaucracy did a poor job of providing Spanish-language services. Latino leaders demanded their fair share of city resources. Longtime community leader Beatrice Otero pleaded for "equity and parity," while younger activists struck a more militant tone. Pedro Aviles, chairman of the D.C. Latino Civil Rights Task Force, an umbrella organization formed in the wake of the riot, sounded much like the young Black Power activists of a generation before when he warned, "Unless these problems are addressed in a comprehensive way, we will have the danger of having similar disturbances again."[83]

After the riot, Mayor Dixon promised to open the government to the Latino community, arguing that black Washingtonians must embrace an expansive vision of social justice that addressed all forms of exclusion and discrimination, not just those directed against the black community. She promised to revitalize the Office of Latino Affairs and pass reforms aimed at giving Hispanic residents a measure of power and influence in city affairs.

Yet in a recession economy, Dixon's initiatives received fierce opposition from within the black community. Some rejected Latino demands entirely. "If [Latinos] don't appreciate our country, get out," snapped Councilman H. R. Crawford. Others sought to protect their constituents' interests. "I believe the Latino community is entitled to their fair share of city contracts and services, but I won't allow that to happen at the expense of the African American community," asserted Councilman William Lightfoot. Dixon's initiatives stalled. By the end of her term, Latinos made up only 1.7 percent of city workers, many agencies still did not have translators, and Latino activists picketed the District Building as the cash-strapped council considered the elimination of the Office of Latino Affairs.[84]

Dixon's inability to produce meaningful reform for the Hispanic community mirrored the struggles of her administration overall. Her blunt manner and outsider status had been an asset on the campaign trail, but they proved a hindrance once in office. Alternately shy and abrasive, Dixon turned off voters who had become used to the glad-handing and deal-making at which Barry had excelled. Unaccustomed to being questioned, she demanded glowing media coverage and accused reporters of racism and sexism when they asked probing questions. Determined to rid the District Building of Barry cronies, she fired all the city's top administrators, wiping away years of institutional knowledge. In their stead she hired an unimpressive group of political neophytes and old law school buddies, few of whom possessed the expertise or experience to manage a government in crisis.[85]

Voters of all races soon soured on Mayor Dixon. She vowed to eliminate "bloat" by firing two thousand midlevel managers, a pledge that many black residents interpreted as an attack on their interests. *Post* columnist Courtland Milloy called Dixon's plan a brutal "chop at the heart of Washington's black middle class," designed to "impress some disinterested white men on Capitol Hill." Dixon hesitated to issue pink slips, angering her white supporters who expected her to clean out the bureaucracy. She eventually fulfilled her promise, but the process was haphazard and came almost entirely through retirements and buyouts rather than layoffs of low-performing workers. The controversy hurt morale, and city services, already dismal, deteriorated further. By the end of her first year in office, more than half of D.C.'s black residents disapproved of her performance.[86]

Mayor Kelly's—she had changed her name after marrying New York businessman James Kelly III in December 1991—fortunes continued to sink as Washington's economic situation worsened. By late 1992, she announced a projected billion-dollar shortfall for the next two years and warned of higher taxes, layoffs, and the "complete elimination of some services." Unable to balance the budget or even slow the growth of the deficit, she blamed D.C.'s tax and governance structure. The only long-term solution, she argued, was to "determine our own economic course" by becoming a state. Yet Kelly's embrace of statehood was not simply a desperate gambit to distract residents from her political problems. Despite D.C.'s violence, political turmoil, and economic struggles, the early 1990s appeared to be an opportune time to push for a state of "New Columbia."

"A Liberal Bastion of Corruption and Crime": The Push for D.C. Statehood

The statehood movement, which had its roots in Julius Hobson's 1970 campaign for nonvoting delegate, stalled following the irascible councilman's 1977 death from cancer. But the issue unexpectedly gained new life when Community for Creative Non-Violence founder Ed Guinan placed it on the 1980 ballot in the form of an initiative. Without consulting anyone in the self-determination movement, Guinan drafted a statehood proposal that required a four-step process: an up-or-down vote on the question of statehood, the election of forty-five delegates to a constitutional convention, the submission of a constitution to the voters for ratification, and, finally, an application to Congress for admission to the Union as the fifty-first state. The process was unorthodox and cumbersome, but Guinan believed that it could build a dense network of grassroots activists that would displace establishment leaders and empower citizens to address D.C.'s most pressing needs.[87]

Support for Guinan's initiative was lukewarm. The ballot question won, though by the underwhelming margin of 85,487 to 57,580—hardly a unanimous show of local support for statehood. Opposition was strongest in Ward 3, where D.C. Voting Rights Amendment supporters such as the League of Women Voters joined with white residents who feared a black government unencumbered by congressional oversight to oppose the measure.[88]

The statehood push displaced the well-connected elected officials, lobbyists, and civil rights activists who dominated the local movement for self-determination. Unconvinced by Guinan's strategy, these veteran activists stood aloof as what the *Post*'s Tom Sherwood described as "a potpourri of liberal community activists, a few elected or appointed officials and a sprinkling of political unknowns" declared for the forty-five delegate seats to the constitutional convention in January 1982. Mayor Barry did not even bother to run a slate of surrogates. Experienced elected officials such as Councilman David Clarke and former school board member Charles Cassell were rare in the sea of political unknowns who secured delegate seats. Despite a lack of interest from the community, the press, and city officials, the delegates assembled at Dunbar High School for the constitutional convention and produced, in just ninety days, a draft constitution for the state of New Columbia.[89]

The document staked out a host of political and social positions typically left to legislators. It guaranteed full employment, gay rights, and a living wage, protected public workers' right to strike, called for the public ownership of utilities, defended the legality of affirmative action, and expanded rights for those accused of a crime. The draft constitution was as much a "manifesto for social reform as an outline for a form of governmental structure," delegate Philip Schrag acknowledged. Convention president Charles Cassell called it "the most progressive official state document . . . in the history of this nation."[90]

Most local political elites, however, rejected the effort. The D.C. Republican Party and the Board of Trade denounced its economic provisions, while the Post and the Star claimed that its dense social clauses would doom it to failure before Congress. Even Sam Smith, the radical white editor of the Progressive Review who had outlined the case for statehood a decade before, wondered why delegates had not simply copied another state's constitution and "saved the new world order for later." Voters had similar misgivings, and only 53 percent voted to approve the constitution. In September 1983, Mayor Barry submitted the draft constitution to Congress, where D.C. delegate Walter Fauntroy gave it a "snowball's chance in July in Florida." Cassell chafed at Fauntroy's dismissal, but he admitted that the statehood forces could count just 3 supportive members of Congress out of 535. It never made it to the floor for a vote.[91]

The statehood idea might have remained buried in the bowels of Congress but for the intervention of Jesse Jackson, the nation's most prominent black politician. A Baptist preacher from South Carolina with a powerful presence and a national network of supporters, Jackson had first learned about D.C.'s lack of self-determination when he worked with Walter Fauntroy in the Southern Christian Leadership Conference. He helped Fauntroy on the D.C. Voting Rights Amendment campaign in 1978 and dominated the city's Democratic presidential primaries in 1984 and 1988. At the 1988 Democratic Convention he succeeded in inserting a pro-statehood plank in the party platform, the first time either major party had done so. Often in D.C. to lobby Congress or participate in national events, Jackson developed such an affinity for the city that he purchased a boarded-up house on the 400 block of T Street in LeDroit Park (next door to former mayor Water Washington).[92]

Following his unsuccessful 1988 presidential bid, Jackson mulled the idea of running for mayor of D.C. — Marion Barry famously scoffed, "Jesse don't wanna run nothin' but his mouth" — but he feared that leading a "city under occupation" would make him politically vulnerable and dilute his "national leverage." Instead, he sought an elected position that allowed him the freedom to maintain his role as a national civil rights leader. He believed that he found an answer in D.C.'s shadow senator, a nebulous post required as part of the 1980 statehood initiative for which the council had never scheduled elections. Hoping to use the office to lead a high-profile campaign for D.C. statehood, he pressured the council to hold elections, then dominated the ensuing contest in March 1990.[93]

Despite his popularity, Jackson found Democrats in Congress lukewarm and Republicans openly hostile as he pushed for statehood. After two years of lobbying, just thirty-one senators agreed to support a statehood bill sponsored by Massachusetts Democrat Edward Kennedy. Only one (Arlen Specter of Pennsylvania) was a Republican.[94]

The bill faced a robust, national grassroots campaign of opposition coordinated by Citizens United against D.C. Statehood, an offshoot of a conservative political action organization that later gained fame for its attack on campaign finance reform laws. Founded by Republican activist Floyd Brown, creator of the infamous Willie Horton ad in the 1988 presidential election, Citizens United linked D.C. statehood with support for Communist leader Fidel Castro, Arab terrorists, and "Black Muslim hatemongers." An emerging conservative media also fueled opposition to statehood. The *Washington Times*, an unabashedly right-wing newspaper founded in 1982 by the Reverend Sun Myung Moon of the Unification Church, published several thinly sourced articles portraying Jackson as petulant and self-important, while conservative talk show host Armstrong Williams made a name for himself as a black opponent of statehood on the local WOL radio station.[95]

Unlike with the Voting Rights Amendment in 1978, self-determination activists were poorly organized and had no reach outside of the city limits. Citizens for New Columbia, an independent group, hosted protests, hearings, commemorations, and informational events but failed to influence members of Congress. Despite clear signs that the statehood bill would not pass, Delegate Eleanor Holmes Norton pressed for a vote, and on November 21, 1993, the House defeated it 277–153. Not a single Republican supported the bill. "The District, a liberal bastion of corruption and crime, doesn't even come close to meeting statehood requirements," charged Republican Tom DeLay of Texas. "[Congress] ought to take back control of the city and clean it up."[96]

An angry Jackson blamed Democratic leadership for the legislation's defeat, while Norton and Citizens for a New Columbia tried desperately to put a positive gloss on the outcome by arguing that a vote on statehood—the first in the city's history—was a victory in and of itself. Following the bill's failure, Jackson withdrew from D.C. In December 1995, he announced that he would not seek reelection as shadow senator and would return to Chicago. After he left, the statehood forces fell into disarray. Always loosely organized and short of money, they had lost their one champion with a national profile and access to significant funding and support.[97]

In the fifteen years since the D.C. Voting Rights Amendment passed in 1978, opposition to D.C. statehood had become conservative dogma while national Democrats proved noncommittal. Recognizing that the struggle was all but hopeless, the experienced strategists and national figures who for a generation had led the movement for D.C. self-determination abandoned the cause, leaving the field to a motley crew of amateurs, dreamers, and demagogues.

"To Give the Powers That Be the Finger": Barry's Triumphant Return

As the battle for statehood raged, Marion Barry reemerged on D.C.'s political scene. The so-called Mayor for Life had never seriously entertained leaving politics despite his incarceration in a federal penitentiary in Loretto, Pennsylvania. From the day he arrived in prison, Barry worked the phones to check in with old campaign hands, measure his chances, and plan his comeback. With the help of supporters such as the Reverend Willie Wilson of Union Temple Baptist Church in Anacostia and former aide Sandra Allen, Barry had already choreographed his return to D.C. politics by the time he was released in April 1992. A caravan of six buses and a limousine met Barry at a motel not far from the prison. Some three hundred poster-waving supporters sang "Victory Is Ours" and cheered as Barry professed, "I've come out of prison better, not bitter." Three months later, he announced his candidacy for the council seat from Ward 8.[98]

Ward 8 was ideal for Barry's rebirth as a politician. Tucked between Prince George's County and the Anacostia River, it was D.C.'s southernmost jurisdiction, encompassing the area formerly known as Far Southeast. Residents were poor—22 percent fell below the poverty line, compared to 3 percent in predominantly white Ward 3—and amenities were few, with only one grocery store for the ward's nearly seventy thousand residents. The area led the city in infant mortality and claimed a disproportionate share of the carnage in one of the most violent urban areas in the nation. Ward 8 citizens, more than 80 percent of whom were black, felt isolated, neglected, frightened, and angry.[99]

Since 1976, Ward 8's representative on the D.C. Council was Wilhelmina Rolark, a combative lawyer and home rule activist who had helped coordinate Walter Fauntroy's successful effort to oust segregationist Representative John McMillan of South Carolina. Rolark and her husband, Calvin, publisher of the *Washington Informer* and founder of the United Black Fund, had long been Barry allies, but they broke with him following his 1990 arrest. Barry had not forgotten the insult, though he targeted Rolark primarily because he viewed her as politically weak.[100]

Barry also chose Ward 8 because it perfectly fit his redemption narrative and political style. Roughly half of Ward 8's black males were incarcerated or being processed through the criminal justice system, most for drug-related crimes, and Barry presented himself as a former addict and prisoner who knew their struggles. According to the Reverend Wilson, Barry was "a rare man that everyone in this community can identify with because they've been in the same places—in jail and in trouble and downtrodden, as he's been." Barry fed ward residents' desire for recognition and respect. Draped around his neck throughout the campaign was a piece of kente cloth stitched with the words "Ward 8. Second to None." Though he was, in effect, campaigning against policies of mass incarceration and neglect he himself had put in place, his message resonated. The city's political elites rushed across the river to support Rolark, but their efforts were futile. Barry trounced her by a three-to-one margin.[101]

With an eye on recapturing the mayor's office, Barry never stopped campaigning. Once on the D.C. Council he concentrated his energies on sometimes hopeless but politically popular citywide issues that gave him inroads with new constituencies. He also reshaped the electorate to his advantage by expanding the voter registration operation that had been crucial to his 1992 win. Week after week, a roving team of Barry campaign workers calling themselves the "Fighting 54th" (after the black Civil War regiment depicted in the movie *Glory*) combed housing projects and row houses in Wards 6, 7, and 8, cornering any unregistered voters that they could find and begging them to sign up. By election day, volunteers had added tens of thousands of new voters to the rolls, pushing the city's registration rate to 79 percent, an all-time high. Perhaps most important for Barry, the effort erased the huge advantage the wealthy western wards held over the poorer eastern wards.[102]

Meanwhile, Washington continued to descend into chaos. Murders topped 440 every year between 1990 and 1993. Fearful of revenge killings, most residents stopped speaking to a police force widely seen as incompetent and corrupt. In 1993, 113 officers were indicted for everything from working as paid security for drug dealers to abetting murder. The breakdown within the police department mirrored the overall deterioration in the city government.[103]

Terrified by the violence and tired of government dysfunction, those who could decamped to the suburbs—thirty-seven thousand residents, most of them black and middle or working class, left D.C. between 1990 and 1994, nearly double the number who had done so in the previous four-year period. Without their tax receipts, the city slipped deeper into debt. As 1994 came to a close, the projected deficit topped $700 million. Washington's sorry state and Mayor Kelly's inability to do anything about it earned her a whopping 67 percent disapproval rating, dooming her chances of reelection.[104]

Into the political vacuum stepped a resurgent Marion Barry, who used legions of newly registered voters to fuel his 1994 mayoral campaign. Alongside the uplifting themes of faith and redemption that propelled his D.C. Council campaign, he added a racial appeal: don't let the white folks pick your leader. He railed against the *Post*'s endorsement of his chief opponent, black councilman John Ray, and used Ray's heavy support in the western wards to paint him as the white folks' candidate. To the astonishment of political pundits nationwide, Barry easily won the Democratic primary. Even many middle-class black voters supported the incumbent. "I voted for Barry to give the powers that be the finger; to let them know that there is a palpable black rage even among the middle class," explained Leonard Knight, an African American lawyer.[105]

The vote split neatly along racial and geographical lines. In predominantly white Ward 3, support for Barry was near infinitesimal—just 586 of 17,333 votes cast—while in Ward 8, he won by a margin of four to one. Asked by a reporter what he had to say to the white voters who had opposed him, Barry snapped, "Get over it. Get over whatever personal hang ups you got." They would not. Soon after the primary election, one resident began a "Free Ward 3" movement, collecting signatures for an effort to retrocede the area back to Maryland. Most of his neighbors settled for crossing party lines and supporting Republican Carol Schwartz in the general election. These white Democrats (and a sizable number of middle-class black voters) swelled Schwartz's share of the vote to 42 percent, the largest received by a Republican since modern home rule began.[106]

As Barry returned to the mayor's office, the city found itself at the mercy of an increasingly hostile Congress. In November 1994, American voters delivered the House of Representatives to the Republican Party for the first time in forty years, elevating many legislators who opposed D.C. self-determination to positions of national leadership, including Speaker of the House Newt Gingrich and

Majority Whip Tom DeLay. Hoping to preempt a congressional takeover and set the terms of any government restructuring, within weeks of taking office Barry announced that the District was $722 million in debt. To stave off bankruptcy, he asked the federal government to assume control of essential city services, including courts and prisons, and give the city $250 million in aid to cover Medicaid overspending. In return, he promised to slash the budget and lay off city workers.[107]

Barry framed his plan in rebellious terms, arguing that the home rule system was broken from the start: "If we are going to be treated as a territory, half slave and half free, we ought not to pay the price that free people pay." Many black city residents cheered Barry's posture of defiance. "We talk a lot about how the District is like a plantation under the Republicans," stated Northeast resident Fred Cooper. "One thing we admire about Barry is he is refusing to be an overseer."[108]

Members of Congress, however, rejected these terms outright, demanding instead a loss of self-determination in return for federal help. Much as it had when it had disfranchised city residents in 1874, the normally lumbering legislature addressed the District's financial problems with head-snapping speed. In April 1995, Congress passed legislation establishing a Financial Control Board that would oversee the District budget, wield management authority over District agencies, and hold a veto over local legislation. After President Bill Clinton signed the legislation, Councilman Kevin Chavous remarked, "It is a sad day for the District."[109]

When black activists entered government in the late 1970s, recalled journalist Kojo Nnamdi, "We were not looking to run business or government the way white folks did. We were looking for the opportunity to run the government at a higher level of integrity." In some respects they succeeded. They changed the very nature of city government, decoupling it from the federal bureaucracy and making it more representative of the city's diverse population. They also redistributed wealth, building a large black working and middle class through public jobs and city contracts.[110]

Yet the man whom many District residents entrusted with their hopes ultimately let them down. The more time Mayor Barry spent in office, the more he adopted governing methods characteristic of big-city political machines. He cozied up to large developers and used public programs to buy political allegiance, while several of his aides and friends exploited the disorganized bureaucracy and city contracting system to pad their wallets. Other large cities experienced similar graft, but Barry's transgressions were magnified by a hostile national conservative movement that dominated the White House for most of his time in office and used the city as a symbol of black Democratic corruption and dysfunction.

Barry's failures made the very people that he had worked his entire political career to help more susceptible to the crack epidemic. As violence soared and city services deteriorated, the residents most in need suffered most of all, and D.C. teetered on the edge of bankruptcy. By the mid-1990s, Barry and his coterie of activists, now graying political veterans, struggled to maintain a much-diminished version of home rule. The expansive hopes and promise of Chocolate City were gone.

FOURTEEN

Go Home Rich White People

Washington Becomes Wealthier and Whiter, 1995–2010

Oh, white people! White people on my street. I don't believe it.
—SANDRA SEEGARS, 2009

Washington, D.C.'s Chinatown, centered on the 600 block of H Street NW, is like an Asian-themed Times Square—a head-spinning mix of Chinese culture and consumer capitalism. Emerging from the Metro at Seventh and H Street, visitors enter a crude re-creation of a pagoda festooned with huge video billboards flashing ads for everything from cell phones to cars. Just steps away, majestically spanning H Street is the Friendship Archway, a gilded, sixty-foot-high traditional Chinese gate erected in 1986. Chinese characters adorn every business, streetlamps resemble Chinese lanterns, and the twelve animals of the Chinese zodiac are embedded in the sidewalks. With its shopping, restaurants, and movie theater, the area has become something of a downtown mall. Street performers jockey with Black Israelites for space along sidewalks crowded with hungry office workers, gawking tourists, and meandering high school students. Amid the crush of humanity, however, one group is conspicuously rare: Chinese people.

Chinatown had once been a small but stable community located initially between Third and Four-and-a-Half Streets NW on the south side of Pennsylvania Avenue, where now sits the East Building of the National Gallery of Art. In the 1890s, Chinese merchants purchased half a dozen buildings in the area and opened restaurants and shops selling imported goods and curios. Small and dilapidated, crowded with boxes and thick with the smells of incense and tea, the shops were largely quiet during the day. In the evenings and on Sundays, however, the neighborhood came alive as Chinese laundrymen—only three or four women and no more than fifteen children were among the more than four hundred Chinese residents in D.C. in 1900—converged on the area to shop and socialize.[1]

Small in number and linked to a foreign nation represented in a local legation, the Chinese received different treatment from the white community than their black neighbors. City officials generally regarded the Chinese community as a harmless oddity that gave the nation's capital exotic flavor and vital labor. Local papers often remarked on Chinese residents' thrift and hard work while assuring readers that D.C. was free of the "notorious dens of vice" (opium dens) allegedly characteristic of other, larger Chinatowns.

The handful of Chinese children in D.C. enrolled not in black schools, as they did elsewhere in the South, but in white schools, where they often were the subject of bemused fascination. "Some of the [white] parents foolishly declar[ed] that they belonged in the colored schools," the *Post* reported when the first Chinese students enrolled in 1893. "But all . . . have been won over by their bright faces and attractive ways." With the precedent established, students of Asian descent attended white schools up through school desegregation in 1954. White Washingtonians generally did not fear negative consequences of such integration, perhaps because they believed, as the *Star*'s E. C. Kohn wrote in 1927, "The homogeneous character of the Chinese precludes any probability of their assimilation, and an oriental will likely always be an oriental wherever he is."[2]

Two decades before the destruction of Southwest during urban renewal, the Chinese experienced their own searing displacement. As federal lawmakers worked to remake the National Mall and Federal Triangle, the district commissioners laid plans to place a Municipal Center on the 300 block of Pennsylvania Avenue. They forced Chinatown merchants to sell the land, and demolition began in 1931. "Picturesque Chinatown, with its tea houses, quaint shops and air of eastern mystery, impervious for 40 years to western ways and customs, bowed at last to western progress," wrote the *Post*. The city made no provision for the merchants' relocation, and residents scattered as the bulldozers rolled in.[3]

But Chinese residents were organized into a dense web of family, mercantile, and benevolent associations, and led by the On Leong Merchants Association, they secretly purchased a series of storefronts on the 600 block of H Street NW. Despite attempts by nearby German Jewish merchants and homeowners to block what they dubbed the "Chinese invasion of H Street," nearly a dozen businesses relocated and established a new Chinatown. Reinforced by veterans who returned home with Chinese "war brides," the community reached its apex in the years following World War II, swelling to about fifteen hundred members and spreading east and west along H Street and north to Massachusetts Avenue. The community became a staple of city life. Residents of all backgrounds visited the neighborhood's six restaurants and, after 1950, craned their necks to catch a glimpse of the paper dragon undulating down H Street during the Chinese New Year parade.[4]

Yet just as the community had become established, suburbanization delivered a near death blow to Chinatown. Determined not to remain laundry operators, many D.C. Chinese pushed their children to enter the professions. By the 1950s, Chinese accountants, doctors, and government workers followed their white peers out to Bethesda and Wheaton, Maryland, and McLean, Virginia. As the center of Chinese life shifted to the suburbs, new immigrants bypassed Chinatown unless they were too poor to do so. By the mid-1960s, scarcely 10 percent of the D.C. area's Chinese population lived in Chinatown. Most of those who remained were senior citizens and bachelors who lived amid a deteriorating strip of stores and restaurants.[5]

The decline of Chinatown stimulated four major efforts to revitalize the neighborhood, each with diminishing participation from Chinese business owners and residents. In the early 1960s, a group of suburban-based Chinese business owners and professionals created the Oriental Commercial Center, a real estate syndicate designed to "save Chinatown," in the words of founding member Hamilton Moy. The commercial center organized white business owners into the Chi-Am Lions Club, an exclusive cross-cultural organization for interested investors. They were less concerned with maintaining the area as a home for Chinese than in building a commercial enclave set off by "oriental motifs." Despite a few early successes, the plan collapsed. The anticipated influx of investment never arrived, and the 1968 riots left a burned-out slum on Chinatown's northern border. "People got scared and stopped coming," said Jean Lee, whose parents owned a grocery store on H Street.[6]

Next, federal officials and the Metropolitan Board of Trade attempted to "rejuvenate" the neighborhood by siting a twenty-five-acre convention center on the north side of H St between Sixth and Tenth Streets. Residents, some of who remembered the 1931 displacement, argued that the project would destroy rather than revitalize their community and organized spirited protests. Though the demonstrations renewed community pride and forced officials to shelve the plans, they did not stop the area's decline. By 1980, only 302 Chinese lived in Chinatown, less than 2 percent of the metropolitan Chinese population.[7]

In the early 1980s, Mayor Marion Barry assembled a group of Chinese American business owners and professionals into the Chinatown Development Corporation for another attempt to redevelop the neighborhood. The corporation envisioned an economically diverse neighborhood anchored by a series of new commercial and mixed-use projects. Central to their plans was the Far East Trade Center, a $116 million, ten-story, glass-walled building that would house offices for international businesses, a Chinese-themed hotel, condominiums, and a ground-floor Asian marketplace. With its thirty-four Chinese American investors holding a 47 percent stake, the massive development promised to be the largest such deal involving Chinese Americans in the United States.[8]

The plans triggered a wave of land speculation, increasing pressure on Chinese residents and small business owners, but the promised development never came. The Far East Trade Center suffered from the same inexperience and lack of financing that plagued other minority contracting deals during the Barry years, and the project foundered. Hounded by crime, high taxes, and high rents, Chinese immigrants continued to shun the neighborhood. "All the Chinese people, the immigrants, leave Chinatown. Because no one wants to be here," explained Dai Tie-Sheng, a calligrapher who lived and worked at 803 H Street. By 1990, less than 25 percent of the property in Chinatown was Chinese-owned, and the community had thinned to a cluster of dingy restaurants and shops scattered amid parking lots and boarded-up buildings on Seventh and H Streets. Some derisively called it "Chinablock."[9]

Abe Pollin witnessed Chinatown's decline and the larger abandonment of downtown D.C., and he hoped to revitalize the area. The philanthropic owner of the Bullets basketball team and the Capitals hockey team, Pollin was dedicated to his hometown. He grew up in Brightwood, attended Roosevelt High School and George Washington University, and started his construction business in D.C. In December 1994, he brokered a deal with Mayor-Elect Barry to build an indoor sports arena on the southern edge of Chinatown.[10]

Chinese business owners on the Chinatown Steering Committee got involved only after the deal was struck, but they greeted the news with excitement. They haggled with Pollin about the location of a subway entrance and the architecture and design, but they did not negotiate about affordable housing even though the planned development threatened to displace the area's three hundred remaining Chinese residents and several small businesses. "No Chinese people will be able to afford to live in Chinatown," worried Wilson Lee, who ran a general store and herbal pharmacy on Seventh Street. "The Chinese people will be moved and you cannot have a Chinatown without people. There'll be nothing left but the arch." The merchants were sympathetic but saw their choices as between development and displacement or continued decline. "Sure, we want Chinese businesses," said Duane Wang, the one steering committee member who lived in Chinatown, "but if nobody comes, well . . . ."[11]

The twenty-thousand-seat MCI Center opened to great fanfare on December 2, 1997, and immediately became the centerpiece of the city's downtown redevelopment plan. During the following decade, Chinatown boomed. Land values and real estate taxes soared as sleek national chain restaurants and stores opened in newly remodeled storefronts. Though relentlessly promoted as a "Chinatown," only the Chinese merchants who owned their buildings and residents fortunate enough to secure Section 8 housing subsidies were able to stay—even the kitchen staff in the few remaining Chinese restaurants was largely Salvadoran. Washington's Chinatown had become less a community than, in the words of the District Government's 2009 Chinatown Cultural Development Strategy, a "premier destination for experiencing international Asian and Chinese American art and culture."[12]

The new Chinatown—bustling, multicultural, hip, but not Chinese—embodied the dramatic economic and demographic transformations that D.C. experienced in the early twenty-first century, as well as their costs. In the first decade of the new millennium, a similar process enveloped much of the city west of the Anacostia. Driven by a nationwide housing boom and post–9/11 government expansion, new development injected millions of dollars of capital into neighborhoods that had not seen significant investment since the 1950s. Young, affluent residents swarmed back into Washington, reversing the city's five-decade population slide, replenishing its tax base, and reshaping the landscape and the culture.

But as the city became younger, wealthier, and whiter, many established residents, particularly black Washingtonians, felt alienated from their new neighbors and unwelcome in their own city. Unable to afford homes as D.C. real estate prices skyrocketed, many lower-income residents sought affordable housing in the suburbs. Those who stayed used their dwindling political strength to fight back against displacement and the policy makers who supported unbridled development. As the pace of development and the in-migration of young professionals quickened, racial tensions in the city flared. On the verge of financial collapse in the mid-1990s, by 2010 the nation's capital was thriving economically but remained sharply divided along racial lines.

"Pawns of a Predominantly White and Callous Congress": The Financial Control Board Takes Control

Andrew Brimmer had watched the city slip toward insolvency in the early 1990s, and he hoped to bring it back from the brink. The third of five children born to black Louisiana sharecroppers in 1926, Brimmer had grown up picking cotton and slopping hogs until World War II offered him an escape. With the G.I. Bill, the diligent and driven former army sergeant moved swiftly though college, earned a Ph.D. in economics from Harvard University in 1957, and distinguished himself at the New York Federal Reserve Bank and the Commerce Department. President Lyndon Johnson nominated him to the Federal Reserve Board of Governors in 1966, the first black person to hold the prestigious post. With his close-cropped hair, business suits, and horn-rimmed glasses, Brimmer became, in the words of *Time* magazine, "the Federal Reserve Board's Jackie Robinson."[13]

Like Robinson, Brimmer was a determined integrationist, and he deemed as "misguided and not at all promising" the various economic and community control proposals advocated by Marion Barry and other Black Power activists. He was not, however, a racially obsequious "Uncle Tom," as some of his critics would later claim. From his perch on the country's most powerful financial body, Brimmer issued annual studies of black economic progress and forcefully advocated for federal spending to address black unemployment. He also maintained deep and fruitful connections with the black community, serving on the board of Tuskegee University and as president of the Association for the Study of Afro-American Life and History.[14]

Brimmer developed an affinity for and in-depth knowledge of his adopted home. Though he left the Federal Reserve in 1974, Brimmer remained in the District, basing his financial consulting firm on MacArthur Boulevard NW and commuting to his many academic and corporate board positions from his Northwest home. Between 1981 and 1992, the city government tapped the esteemed economist to conduct three separate studies of D.C.'s finances, which gave him a thorough understanding of the District's economy and its relation to the federal government. Brimmer's stature in the financial world, his connections to the black community, and his understanding of the city's finances made him a leading contender for the chairmanship of the Financial Control Board, which Congress established in April 1995 to oversee Washington's books.[15]

Though viewed by many D.C. residents as a hostile takeover by a punitive Congress, the initial creation of the Financial Control Board was a strategic retreat in which the city's elected leaders played an influential role. Originally suggested by Delegate Eleanor Holmes Norton to preempt Republican proposals to strip D.C. of self-government entirely, the idea won support from the new Speaker of the House Newt Gingrich of Georgia, a fiery partisan who regularly had attacked the District in his fifteen-year quest to win control of the House of Representatives. Gingrich hoped that working with Washington's black leadership could soften the Republican Party's antiblack image and provide an opportunity to showcase conservative antipoverty policies, including school vouchers and enterprise zones. The nation's capital could become an "urban jewel," he told Mayor Barry and Delegate Norton.[16]

With Gingrich determined to present the GOP as an enlightened partner in D.C.'s efforts to regain solvency, Congress crafted a bailout bill that left the home rule government largely intact. Drafted by a moderate Republican freshman from northern Virginia named Tom Davis, the legislation drew not from the undemocratic three-commissioner system of the pre-home-rule era but instead on a more cooperative model used in New York City, Philadelphia, and Cleveland. Under Davis's bill, a presidentially appointed Financial Control Board[17] could review and alter all budgets, financial plans, city leases, and contracts, but the mayor and the D.C. Council retained much of their executive and lawmaking functions. The board would stay in place until the District's credit rating had recovered and the city government posted four consecutive balanced budgets. Punitive enough to please Republican hardliners yet elastic enough to give D.C. continued home rule, the bill breezed through both chambers on a voice vote.[18]

Working through the Clinton administration, Norton set the tone for how the board would use its power. At her urging, President Clinton named Andrew Brimmer as chair of the board, along with four other D.C. residents with stated commitments to home rule, including Joyce Ladner, Marion Barry's old SNCC comrade who then was serving as the interim president of Howard University. Brimmer and his fellow board members embraced the limited role Norton envisioned for them.[19]

Despite the pivotal role city leaders had played in creating and staffing the Control Board, most African American residents did not trust the new body. Washingtonians of all races had grown weary of spiraling deficits, declining services, and devastating crime, and many resigned themselves to the idea that the city needed Congress's help to relieve the financial crisis. But a distinct racial split emerged on the issue. Where white residents overwhelmingly supported congressional intervention, many black Washingtonians viewed it skeptically. "No matter if the board is brown or black or white, they are going to be seen as pawns of a predominantly white and callous Congress," noted the Reverend Graylan Ellis-Hagler of Plymouth Congregational United Church of Christ in Manor Park.[20]

Attuned to black popular opinion, Mayor Barry cultivated African American residents' distrust of Congress and presented himself as their champion. After the board, in its first act, advised the mayor to cut spending and reduce the size of the bureaucracy by 5,600 workers, the mayor chastised members for their "insensitivity" to District residents. The following December, he supported more than 100 protesting city employees who used government vehicles to block the intersection outside the board's Thomas Circle offices during the morning rush hour. "I can understand the frustration many D.C. employees feel with regard to the powers and decisions of the control board," he said. For months Barry used the cooperative framework Norton had created to slow, if not sabotage, board initiatives.[21]

By early 1996, board members had given up on cooperating with Barry and the council. Calling the mayor "irrelevant," they announced that they would conduct their own reviews of the city budget and implement cuts without his input. "There is tremendous respect for home rule," said Control Board Executive Director John Hill. "But there comes a point in time when you just can't wait any longer."[22]

Barry initially pushed back. When the board called on him to fire Vernon Hawkins, a veteran bureaucrat and Barry loyalist who served as director of the Department of Human Services, the mayor objected, calling the board's request "absolutely anti-democratic, anti-American, un-American . . . totalitarian." Hawkins was a poor manager, but Barry viewed the issue as a test of his power and refused to back down. "The control board does not have the day-to-day responsibility of managing this government," he declared, "I do." Only when Speaker Gingrich informed him that his failure to cooperate "puts into doubt the whole issue of home rule" did Barry capitulate.[23]

As the battle for power between the board and the city's leaders escalated, Barry's personal problems reemerged. In April 1996, the mayor suddenly announced that he was suffering from "spiritual relapse and physical exhaustion" and would be leaving the city for an undisclosed period to recuperate. Though Barry was opaque about the reason for his abrupt departure, reporters soon heard rumors that he had made the announcement after a staffer caught him purchasing crack in the District Building. Boxing promoter Rock Newman, a principal backer of the mayor's 1994 campaign, encouraged Barry to "stop the maddening process towards relapse" and resign. Barry could not. His personal peccadillos continued that summer, further undermining the Control Board's faith in his ability to be a constructive force in the city's recovery.[24]

With Barry out of the way, the board undertook the difficult process of reforming the bureaucracy. Board members conducted in-depth studies of particularly troubled city agencies, assumed control, and replaced underperforming managers. Despite the board's decisive action, it was not enough for some conservative critics in Congress. Foremost among them were North Carolina Republicans senator Lauch Faircloth and representative Charles Taylor, respectively the chairmen of the Senate Appropriations Subcommittee on D.C. and the House District Appropriations Subcommittee. The two pilloried the board for being too sensitive to home rule. "It's time to stop worrying about stepping on toes," Faircloth insisted. They envisioned a much stronger board that would run the entire city directly.[25]

They found a vehicle for their ambitions in a 1997 bill to address the city's debt. Since the Home Rule Act took effect in 1974, city leaders had complained that Congress created insurmountable deficits by saddling the District with an unfunded pension liability and the financial obligations of a state but strictly limiting the city's taxing authority. Congressional leaders dismissed such complaints, blaming the city's financial problems on poor management alone. Now responsible for the city's finances, however, Congress realized that it had indeed created a massive structural deficit. It crafted legislation that assumed the city's $4 billion pension obligation and transferred control of a host of city services such as prisons and street maintenance to the federal government.[26]

The legislation had bipartisan support, with Speaker Gingrich and Delegate Norton as its most vocal advocates. But Senator Faircloth argued that the initial proposal was no more than a "multibillion-dollar bailout for a mismanaged city" and demanded direct federal control. He got support from an unlikely source: Financial Control Board chairman Andrew Brimmer. Furious at the mayor for failing to carry out his edicts, Brimmer urged Congress to place the District government under a city manager who would not be "constrained" by having to "look over his shoulder at either the mayor or the council."[27]

Delegate Norton succeeded in derailing the city manager idea, but what the District got instead essentially suspended home rule. The compromise National Capital Revitalization Act of 1997 provided the necessary bailout but required that the Control Board directly administer the city's nine largest agencies and appoint a chief management officer to run the government and report directly to the board. Barry was reduced to a ceremonial figure with direct oversight of only parks and recreation, libraries, and a few assorted commissions. The council fared even worse, as the legislation gave the board veto power over any law it passed or contract it brokered. Congressman Tom Davis, who managed the bill in the House, noted that out of respect for home rule, the board had been "reluctant to exercise their powers" between 1995 and 1997. "Now it's a congressional mandate."[28]

Barry decried the legislation as a "rape of democracy" and encouraged residents to "rise up in anger." A small group of activists took up his call, marching on Representative Davis's Falls Church, Virginia, home chanting, "Down with Davis! Up with Democracy!" and caravaning down to Clinton, North Carolina, to stage a raucous protest outside Senator Faircloth's hog farm. Others blamed the mayor. Sandra Seegars, once a Barry supporter, created the Committee to

Recall Mayor Barry, arguing, "After all the embarrassment, after all the hypocrisy, after all the corruption, and now that democracy has been stolen from the citizens . . . it's time to dump Barry."[29]

Most residents, however, appeared resigned to the congressional takeover. As the city crumbled around them, they believed that a loss of home rule was the price they had to pay for recovery. "Trash pickup is lousy, potholes, people moving out because crime is so bad," Brookland resident Vernon Ham groused. "Something had to change."[30]

Despite his tough rhetoric, Barry, too, came to accept the new order. Though polls showed him well ahead of possible opponents, he declined to run for re-election in 1998. Politically neutered by Congress, besieged by critics, and still battling his drug addiction, he reasoned that the struggle would not be worth the hollow prize of a ceremonial office. On May 22, in a self-serving speech in which he took credit for nearly every positive development in the city's recent history, the four-term mayor told residents, "There are areas I can better serve in outside of the government." Though Barry would come out of retirement to reclaim the Ward 8 council seat in 2004, he never again wielded significant power.[31]

It was the end of a remarkable era in D.C. politics. For three decades, Barry seemed to defy political gravity, rising from an unknown street protester to become the most dominant elected official in the city's history. He displayed an uncanny ability to take advantage of shifting political winds, moving deftly from Black Power militant in the 1960s to inclusive coalition builder in the 1970s to pinstriped power broker in the 1980s to reformed sinner in the 1990s. Despite his personal scandals and the city's struggles, he remained wildly popular among his core constituents—low-income black Washingtonians. "Marion Barry employed a lot of people, he made a lot of people middle class, he put a lot of people through college, he paid a lot of rent," said longtime ally Lawrence Guyot as he assessed Barry's legacy.[32]

Barry was Washington's tragic hero, a supremely talented politician who held the promise of leading the city beyond its historic divisions. But his personal flaws and managerial indifference, combined with the enormity of the city's problems, ultimately shattered that sense of hope.[33]

"Race Is Simmering Just beneath the Surface": The Uneasy Return to Home Rule

Barry's announcement upended the 1998 mayoral race. The three declared candidates—black Councilmen Harold Brazil and Kevin Chavous and white Councilman Jack Evans—scrambled to connect with voters in a suddenly wide-open contest. But all were blindsided by the arrival of an unexpected candidate in the race: Anthony Williams, the city's chief financial officer (CFO).

Thin and balding with a low, droning voice and a penchant for obscure analogies, the Yale- and Harvard-trained former Department of Agriculture CFO appeared to be little more than a quirky bureaucrat with shallow roots in D.C. The light-skinned Los Angeles native had moved to the city just three years before, rented a nondescript apartment in Southwest, and voted only once in local elections before entering the mayor's race. Described in the *Post* as a "numbers-crunching, bow-tie-wearing bookworm," Williams was shy and awkward in public—a sharp contrast to the glad-handing Barry. He was easy to underestimate.[34]

Williams's bureaucratic demeanor masked his driving ambition and keen political mind. The finance position he held was the second most powerful in District government, with authority over all the city's funds and the power to certify the mayor's budget numbers. Hired in part because Mayor Barry did not believe that he would use the job to become a political rival, Williams proved to be a cunning and capable strategist. He asserted his independence by publicly criticizing the mayor's budget decisions, developing a close relationship with Representative Taylor and other members of Congress, and cultivating his own constituency by attending more than a hundred community meetings. He gained a national reputation for his efforts to tame the District budget—*Governing* magazine named him "Public Official of the Year" in 1997. By the winter of 1998, he was seriously considering a run for mayor. A well-organized grassroots movement endeavored to draft him, and just ten days after Barry announced his retirement, Williams jumped into the race.[35]

In the ensuing campaign, Williams styled himself as a "new black leader" interested more in making the city run properly than in redistributing money and power. "I'm running because I believe District politics have changed from a politics based on political considerations and ideology to a politics based on a discussion of real needs and real results," he told voters.[36]

The various crises of the 1990s—the relentless violence, the crumbling schools, the inept public services, the congressional takeover of city government—had generated a desperate desire for good governance. The former finance chief promised competence, and his proposed reforms proved particularly popular among white and middle-class black voters, who helped him secure the Democratic nomination. Yet he struggled to win over poor and working-class voters, who still expected the racially targeted, redistributive policies characteristic of the Black Power era. With all the candidates pledging race-neutral delivery of city services, they stayed home. Turnout dropped from

52 percent of eligible voters in 1994 to just 30 percent in 1998. Despite the lack of African American enthusiasm for the Democratic standard bearer, Williams easily turned back a general election challenge by Republican Carol Schwartz.[37]

Williams's rise sped the transition back to local control. After Brimmer sided with conservative Republicans who advocated an end to home rule in 1997, an alarmed Delegate Norton asked President Clinton to select a new board chair when his three-year term expired. Clinton selected Alice Rivlin, a white Federal Reserve Board vice governor then serving as the director of the Office of Management and Budget. Like Brimmer, Rivlin was well versed in the District's finances. She headed two commissions that examined the city's books in the 1980s and early 1990s, and she helped select the initial Financial Control Board in 1995.

But unlike the hard-edged Brimmer, the diminutive, soft-voiced Rivlin believed that the board "should act more and more like a board of directors" to prepare local administrators so that the city could "run itself well without a board"—a position dictated as much by Barry's retirement as by her temperament. Following the general election, Rivlin and the board announced that they would return control of all District agencies to the mayor's office on Williams's inauguration in January 1999.[38]

For many black Washingtonians, however, the Williams administration appeared indistinguishable from the control board. As the new mayor and his team of young, aggressive white deputies set to work pursuing the reforms he had implemented as CFO—cutting costs, firing underperforming workers, closing or privatizing dysfunctional agencies—many already skeptical poor and working-class African American residents concluded that he did not care about their needs. "Race is . . . simmering just beneath the surface," stated Ward 8 activist JePhunneh Lawrence. "You can't just turn the administration of this city over to young white boys and expect people to say all is fine and dandy."[39]

Williams believed that the best way to show African American residents that he cared was by delivering top-notch public services to all residents in all parts of the city. "It's clear to me that . . . people want the services done in an equitable way," he argued. The tensions inherent in this ostensibly race-neutral approach were most apparent in the mayor's 2001 effort to close D.C. General, Washington's only public hospital.[40]

Founded by Congress as a hospital for the indigent in 1806, D.C. General had a troubled history. Underfunded and poorly managed from the outset, it boasted a miserable record of care stretching across two centuries. By the 1990s, it was in crisis, unable to make a dent in D.C.'s nation-leading rates of diabetes, infant mortality, and HIV/AIDS despite consuming tens of millions of dollars.

The Control Board recommended closing the hospital in 1995, but Barry had refused, considering the move politically perilous.[41]

In 2001, Williams decided that the day of reckoning had come. He planned to shutter the hospital and replace it with a network of private care providers who could feed patients into Greater Southeast Community Hospital. A diverse group of community activists, clergy, and unions protested, frightened at the impending loss of more than sixteen hundred jobs and doubtful that the mayor's plan would work. Many also loved the troubled institution. Generations had worked and received care at its sprawling campus on Nineteenth Street SE overlooking the west bank of the Anacostia. Though it provided poor service, it was the one place in the city that the poor and uninsured knew they would be admitted if the private care facilities farther west turned them away. "It's not just a hospital," insisted activist Sherry Brown. "A lot of people have an emotional attachment to it."

Williams plunged ahead nonetheless, using nearly a million dollars in city money to sell his plan to voters. Opponents adopted desperate tactics such as hunger strikes to stop him. Council members, nervously eyeing the 2002 elections and unconvinced that the mayor's plan would provide adequate care, unanimously rejected the initiative. In a show of overwhelming political force, however, the Control Board stepped in to thwart the popular will and help Williams close the failing hospital.[42]

Critics of the mayor's plan eventually were vindicated. In the years after D.C. General was shuttered, Greater Southeast performed so poorly that city inspectors recommended the revocation of its license; not long after, it went bankrupt. The African American communities in the eastern parts of the city were left with the same poor medical care that they had before privatization, but this time with fewer jobs and no control—just as they had feared.[43]

Despite Williams's political struggles, Washington's economic outlook improved. At the end of September 2001, the Control Board disbanded after six years of remarkable success. It had convinced Congress to correct much of the structural deficit, restored investor confidence, and put the city's books in order. Pulling D.C. back from the edge of bankruptcy in 1995, the board worked closely with the Williams administration to post four consecutive balanced budgets between 1998 and 2001. Even as the city braced itself for a dramatic decline in tourist revenue following the terrorist attacks on September 11, 2001, an optimistic board chair Alice Rivlin declared, "The fiscal situation is just light-years better."[44]

Many black Washingtonians, however, saw the Control Board's effects on the city very differently. While they, like all residents, appreciated the improved city services and economic condition, much of that progress was made by pushing them and their chosen leadership aside. The city's balanced budgets were achieved, in part, by firing hundreds of city workers, most of whom were black. Service improvements often came after privatization, which removed public services from the control of public employees, most of whom were black. And the city had temporarily lost home rule, in large measure to get rid of Marion Barry, black voters' chosen leader.

With the Financial Control Board gone, many frustrated black residents directed their anger at Mayor Williams, almost derailing his 2002 reelection campaign. With $1.4 million in the bank and facing four fringe candidates, Williams entered the contest as the overwhelming favorite. But his campaign struggled even to obtain signatures to get on the ballot in black neighborhoods. "Some black people don't want Anthony Williams to be mayor," observed Crystal Bishop, whose father had a contract to gather signatures. "They didn't really want to sign." As the filing deadline approached, Scott Bishop panicked, filling sheet after sheet with names such as United Nations head Kofi Annan and actor Kelsey Grammer, all in the same handwriting. For the infraction, the D.C. Board of Elections and Ethics fined Williams more than a quarter of a million dollars and removed his name from the September primary ballot, forcing the incumbent mayor to run as a write-in candidate.[45]

Seeing that the mayor was vulnerable among black voters, Barry confidant the Reverend Willie Wilson entered the race as a write-in candidate. Wilson charged that the mayor cared more about developers and new middle-class residents than the poor black residents of the eastern wards, whom he called "the voiceless, the hopeless, the disappointed, the disgusted." Though Williams won by a margin of three to one, the entire episode undermined the mayor's image as an effective, ethically upright technocrat. District resident and crisis management specialist Lanny Davis wondered, "How long are we going to let [Williams] ride on not being Marion Barry?"[46]

Williams had presided over a difficult transition from the instability and tumult of the mid-1990s to economic solvency and partial home rule in the early 2000s. Focused primarily on righting the economic ship, the wonky mayor and his allies placed a higher priority on bureaucratic competence and economic growth than on self-determination or equity. By 2002, Washington was positioned for an extraordinary economic boom that would fundamentally transform the city. But Williams and his allies ignored growing discontent, particularly within the low-income black community, about who benefited and who suffered from his administration's prodevelopment agenda. Black voters' anger with Williams intensified as a new wave of gentrification crashed across D.C. during the mayor's second term.

"We Are Headed for Some Bad Trouble":
Gentrification and Displacement in Turn-of-the-Century D.C.

Louise Thomas knew gentrification well—she had endured its effects nearly all her life. Born in Fayetteville, North Carolina, in 1924, she moved with her parents to Washington when she was five. Her father shoveled coal at a city-owned power plant to pay the rent on the family's shabby Georgetown apartment. Shortly before World War II, when Louise was still a teenager, the Alley Dwelling Authority condemned her family's home and evicted them. A developer bought the place, fixed it up, and sold it to a well-to-do white family. Such practices helped turn Thomas's racially mixed, economically diverse neighborhood almost uniformly wealthy and white within a decade.[47]

After leaving Georgetown, Thomas's family landed in the burgeoning black community of Columbia Heights, where she lived for the next six decades. Though another burst of gentrification threatened Thomas with displacement in the 1970s, it stalled in the 1980s when crack and crime scared developers out of the area. By the late 1990s, as the epidemic subsided, she was living in a twenty-eight-unit apartment building at 1418 W Street NW, where she and her neighbors developed a strong sense of community. Short, chocolate brown, with a plump, kind face, Thomas was a beloved figure. When one neighbor died of cancer, Thomas adopted two of the woman's eight children.[48]

Though Thomas and her neighbors invested time, money, and effort in their community, their landlords, Kenneth J. Welch and his son Patrick, did not. They neglected maintenance in 1418 W Street and racked up reams of housing code violations. Despite residents' complaints, the dysfunctional Department of Consumer and Regulatory Affairs did little to address the problems until 2000, when the Williams administration initiated a crackdown on "hot properties," rentals where slumlords flagrantly violated housing codes. To the delight of Thomas and her neighbors, city inspectors arrived at their building to look into their complaints. But rather than force the landlord to make improvements while residents remained in their apartments, the inspectors condemned the building and gave the residents twenty-four hours to evacuate. The city offered no moving or replacement housing assistance. For Thomas, the episode was a maddening replay of her family's displacement half a century before.

Rather than move, the W Street residents joined with Latino and Vietnamese renters from three other buildings that inspectors had condemned to sue the city, alleging racial discrimination. After months of "hot properties" enforcement, the Williams administration had issued eviction notices to dozens of tenants in Adams Morgan, Columbia Heights, and Shaw but had yet to sue a single landlord, leading many renters to fear that the city was working with white developers to displace the poor from gentrifying neighborhoods. The city was, in fact, negotiating with landlords to make repairs, but progress was slow and city officials did not inform tenants, thereby leaving them in the lurch. Pressured by the judge hearing the lawsuit to take tenants' concerns into consideration, the city increased pressure on the landlords, eventually securing a settlement for the W Street tenants stipulating that the owners fix up the building, sell it to the residents for a dollar, and refrain from owning rental property in the District in the future. After years of struggling to create community in the face of official neglect and landlord exploitation, Louise Thomas was a homeowner.[49]

Thomas's experience revealed the potential for displacement that could accompany Mayor Williams's ambitious citywide development strategy. During his second term, Williams worked closely with developers and financiers to clean up the city's housing stock to draw middle-class residents back to town in hopes of growing the tax base. Blind to the ways in which race and poverty limited residents' ability to take advantage of improving city services and increasing land values, Williams addressed the concerns of low-income residents only when their protests forced his administration to pay attention.

The mayor's interest in development grew out of his knowledge of the city's woeful financial outlook. Despite the 1997 bailout and Control Board–directed financial restructuring, the District still struggled to raise sufficient revenue. Suburban lawmakers in Congress vigorously protected the long-standing ban on a commuter tax, so 66 percent of the income generated in Washington was taxed in Maryland and Virginia, where the bulk of federal workers made their homes. In addition to churches, schools, and other institutions that do not pay taxes anywhere, D.C. officials also could not tax land owned by the federal government, embassies, and nonprofits. Fully 42 percent of District land thus did not contribute to city coffers.[50]

Before the 2002 election, the Williams administration commissioned an economic development study to figure out how to address the problem of limited revenue. The subsequent report concluded that D.C. needed to attract new middle-class residents to increase tax revenue. It urged city officials to "complement and extend Washington's tourist and city beautiful amenities" to shed its image as a home to "bureaucrats and poor people."[51]

Following the report almost to the letter, in January 2003 Williams announced a plan to attract 100,000 new middle- and upper-middle-class residents in ten years. The *Post* and other observers mocked what then seemed like a laughably ambitious goal—Washington had been losing population for more than half a century, reaching a new low of 572,059 in the 2000 census. But Williams forged ahead. He encouraged the Department of Housing to seize abandoned buildings and sell them to developers; auctioned off city-owned properties, including old schools and post offices; worked with Metro to spur development around transit centers; pushed the U.S. Small Business Administration to find ways to revitalize neighborhood commercial centers; and begged federal lawmakers to transfer huge parcels such as St. Elizabeths Hospital, Walter Reed Army Medical Center, and the Navy Yard to the city so that it could build entirely new communities, a process that the George W. Bush administration began in 2005.[52]

Though less ambitious than Williams, previous city leaders had implemented similar plans with marginal success. Mayor Marion Barry had built city offices to spur development along the riot-scarred H Street and U Street corridors in the 1980s, and he brokered the deal whereby the MCI Center became the anchor for a revitalized Chinatown. These earlier efforts had stalled by the late 1990s, but Williams's plans took off, largely because they coincided with several national developments that disproportionately affected the metropolitan area.[53]

First, with the ebbing of the crack epidemic, violent crime dropped in cities nationwide. The change in Washington was dramatic, with murders falling from a high of 482 in 1991 to 242 in 2000; by 2010, the number reached 132, the lowest total since 1964. Rates of burglary, armed robbery, and other crimes fell in tandem. As the city became safer, it grew more attractive to prospective residents and investors.[54]

The drop in crime accompanied a surge in Washington wealth stimulated by the expansion of lobbying in the 1990s and early 2000s. The terrorist attacks of 9/11 led to the creation of a mammoth new Department of Homeland Security and triggered extraordinary growth in the defense, intelligence, and information technology industries. Between 2000 and 2010, the amount spent on lobbying, defense, and federal contracting more than doubled, annually pumping hundreds of millions more dollars into the regional economy. All this money drew legions of young tech workers, lobbyists, office staffers, military bureaucrats, lawyers, and contractors into the Washington region.[55]

In an earlier era, nearly all these affluent newcomers would have gone straight to the suburbs. The majority still did. But driven by a "new urbanism" that rejected the energy-wasting car culture of the suburbs for compact, diverse, walkable communities, a significant portion of these new workers moved into older neighborhoods within the city. There they expanded on the centers of stalled gentrification in Capitol Hill, Logan Circle, Adams Morgan, Columbia Heights, LeDroit Park, and Shaw. The Williams administration's emphasis on revitalizing neighborhood commercial corridors and locating new development around public transportation hubs encouraged the migration.[56]

The promise of fabulous profits in the housing market also lured newcomers to the city. With interest rates at record lows and banks loosening credit requirements, buyers and investors poured into the housing market, pushing prices ever higher. Realtor David Hawkins recalled that potential buyers approached home sales like a competition, paying whatever it took to "win" a property. "There was almost no fear on the part of the buyers of overpaying for a house," he observed, "because they figured it would be worth more later."[57]

The market became so fevered and buyers so sure that prices would spiral ever upward that some bought properties sight unseen. In 2005, a group of Massachusetts investors purchased a house at 513 Florida Avenue NW, based solely on an Internet picture. This relatively common practice warranted notice only because, once inside, the owners discovered the mummified remains of the previous owner, an elderly African American man who had died in the bathtub five years before. Between 2002 and 2007, the median price of a house in Washington rose by an average of 75 percent, and often far more in the most desirable neighborhoods.[58]

With prices rising so quickly, developers and buyers soon ventured into areas outside of the L'Enfant city. By 2002, they were snapping up old crack houses in Trinidad and ripping tin sun shades and green AstroTurf off porches in Old City. Longtime residents were shocked to see young black professionals, and even some white ones, cramming into open houses in East of the River neighborhoods such as Congress Heights and Deanwood. During the filming of a documentary, Anacostia community activist Sandra Seegars interrupted an interview when she saw some white people walking through her neighborhood. "Oh, white people!" she exclaimed, chuckling to herself. "White people on my street. I don't believe it."[59]

Older residents found promise and peril in these developments. Some longtime residents profited from the changes sweeping over their neighborhoods. "Almost all of the families from my block cashed out," recalled Tania Jackson, an African American developer who had grown up in Columbia Heights. "People were getting offered ridiculous amounts of money for their houses." But 60 percent of D.C. residents were renters, most on low or fixed incomes. For them the burst of early twenty-first-century gentrification generated an affordable housing crisis. By 2004, the average rent on a two-bedroom apartment in downtown D.C. had risen to $1,187. For minimum-wage workers earning $6.60 per hour, an affordable rent constituting 30 percent of their income would have been just $343 per month.[60]

Many residents also got the impression that their new neighbors did not want them around. Kurt Ehrman, a white transplant from Kensington, Maryland, purchased one of the half-million-dollar row houses across the street from 1418 W Street, and he certainly hoped that Louise Thomas and her low-income neighbors would leave. "Change has been very slow," he complained. "The [Section 8 and cooperatively owned] buildings are an eyesore. How much are we willing to compromise to maintain affordable housing in the city?" He was not an outlier. When the *Washington City Paper* examined a Columbia Heights neighborhood listserv populated by 830 mostly new, well-to-do residents, it found a litany of complaints against "illegal immigrant[s]," "disgruntled, disrespectful, mean spirited, violently and criminally minded black youth," and "HOMIES, DERELICTS, DEGENERATES."[61]

The economic pressure and alienation from new residents moved many African American residents to assert their claims on the city. Some took to the streets to harass newcomers or paint pointed graffiti—"Go Home Rich White People" read one tag. Local activists engaged in a wave of cooperative organizing and called on the D.C. Council to strengthen rent control legislation. Others demanded that new residents defer to their rich history and long tenure in the neighborhood.[62]

Tensions flared, for example, between older African American residents of eastern Shaw and their Ethiopian neighbors over what to call a strip that once was home to flourishing jazz clubs. The Washington area had been a magnet for Ethiopian immigrants since a Soviet-backed coup overthrew Emperor Haile Selassie in 1974. By the early 2000s, Ethiopian and Eritrean merchants dominated the storefronts on Ninth Street between U and T Streets, and in 2005 they petitioned Councilman Jim Graham to rename the block "Little Ethiopia."

Theirs was a simple branding campaign designed to bring business to their cluster of storefronts, but many African American residents saw it as a threat to the neighborhood's history and identity. "They haven't paid their dues," argued neighborhood activist Clyde Howard. "Where were they during the riots? They're Johnny-come-lately. What gives them the right?" The local Advisory Neighborhood Commission, dominated by longtime black residents, urged the council to reject the Ethiopians' request. It did.[63]

As Washington natives and local activists grew increasingly apprehensive about the changes enveloping the city, they became more aggressive about challenging the Williams administration's relentless focus on development. Their anger erupted in 2004 over the mayor's plan to subsidize a new baseball stadium. Mayor Williams, an avid baseball fan and firm believer in the potential for sports stadiums to spark economic growth, made an aggressive bid for the Montreal Expos, a floundering team owned by Major League Baseball (MLB). By fall 2004, he had brokered a deal with the league that required the city to pay the entire $589 million cost of constructing a new stadium, slated for industrial land next to the old Navy Yard along the Anacostia.

Opposition to the deal was widespread and crossed socioeconomic and racial lines. After years of firings and budget cuts, most residents could not fathom spending more than half a billion dollars on a baseball stadium that would draw most of its fans from the suburbs. Ward 4 councilman Adrian Fenty, who represented the economically diverse black neighborhoods of upper Northwest, and At-Large Councilman David Catania, whose base of support lay with the gay community near Logan Circle and the Republicans of Ward 3, led the opposition.[64]

Determined to move forward, Williams campaigned hard for the deal among African American residents, holding public rallies where he noted that the owners had agreed to provide free tickets for low-income kids, sign contracts with minority businesses, and give priority to D.C. residents seeking jobs. The stadium, the mayor claimed, would be a "grand slam" for a long-neglected section of the city.[65]

Many black residents disagreed. Ward 7 resident Jauhar Abraham spoke for many East of the River residents when he told the mayor, "I'm concerned that you're fighting for baseball and we do not have a public hospital." In November 2004, amid the stadium negotiations, black voters replaced Williams supporters on the council with three stadium opponents: Kwame Brown, Vincent Gray, and the irrepressible Marion Barry. The three promised to focus their attention on the needs of the eastern wards and the poor, a rebuke to a government that had focused so much energy on development and drawing affluent residents back to the city.[66]

Williams scrambled to approve the deal before the new council took control in January, promising $70 million in funding for pet projects to seven council members. "Usually payoffs are more subtle than this," quipped Republican councilwoman Carol Schwartz. Outflanked by Williams and the probaseball faction on the council yet determined to address residents' concerns about cost, Chairwoman Linda Cropp slipped in a provision requiring that 50 percent of the construction cost for the stadium be privately financed. By a vote of 7–6, the council approved the deal. In April 2005, the renamed Washington Nationals played their first game at RFK Stadium, their temporary home while a gleaming Nationals Park rose in Southeast.[67]

After Williams won the stadium, he belatedly responded to lower-income residents' complaints about displacement by announcing a plan for housing the poor and working class called the New Communities Initiative. It sought to break up areas of concentrated poverty by building mixed-income neighborhoods and using the profits from the high- and middle-income units to subsidize those for lower-income residents. Hoping to avoid repeating the mistakes of alley reform, urban renewal, and other federal programs that displaced poor communities, city officials worked closely with public housing residents to craft the program. Residents of target areas demanded that New Communities require regular input from a representative tenant council, adopt a "build first" policy that obligated the city to produce new units before demolishing old ones, and create a plan for comprehensive social services to renew the neighborhood's "human capital" along with the infrastructure.[68]

The first designated site for the New Communities Initiative was the massive neighborhood of subsidized housing bounded by North Capitol Street, New York Avenue, K Street, and New Jersey Avenue NW, which planners called Northwest One. Just ten blocks from the Capitol, Northwest One was to be the initiative's showplace, a demonstration that the city had figured out how to revitalize a poor community without displacing residents. In an unexpected show of support for the program, Mayor Williams launched the project by invoking eminent domain against the owners of Temple Courts, a dilapidated ten-story, 520-unit building at the heart of the site, to prevent them from converting the building to market-rate units. His decisive action gained residents' trust. Excited by the initiative's promises and desperate to answer the pleas of the fifty-two thousand people on the housing assistance waiting list in 2006, the council pushed the District Housing Authority to create additional sites in the Anacostia, Deanwood, and Park View neighborhoods.[69]

Low-income black residents had made Williams respond to their concerns, but they still had to contend with the forces his administration had helped to set in motion. No sooner had Louise Thomas and her 1418 W Street neighbors become homeowners than developers began soliciting them to sell the building. It was a heady experience. People who had never had two pennies to rub together were being offered upwards of $110,000 per household. In 2003, Thomas found herself on the losing side of a tenant vote to sell the building. The buyers of 1418 W Street quickly flipped the property to another developer for a $1 million profit. The new owners remodeled the beat-up apartments into condominiums that sold for more than $200,000. Thomas now was back to renting in a neighborhood where prices were fast moving beyond her ability to pay.

Thomas remained anchored to the neighborhood through her daughter

Deborah, who led the fight to turn the nearby Capital Manor Apartments into a cooperative, but most of her old neighbors could not afford to stay in Columbia Heights. In 2005, perhaps the most frenzied year of D.C.'s housing boom, a reporter for *Crisis* magazine asked Thomas what she thought of the changes that had transformed her neighborhood. "Everything is being built for people who have money," she observed. "I was living in Georgetown when all the change happened, and you see Georgetown now. We are headed for some bad trouble."[70]

"Consensus Is the Absence of Leadership": Adrian Fenty and the Hope for a Post-racial D.C.

Adrian Fenty wanted to make Washington a "world class city." Born in 1970 to an Italian-American mother and African American father, Fenty grew up in the eclectic Mount Pleasant neighborhood and attended Woodrow Wilson, the city's most racially diverse high school. Athletic and academically driven, Fenty ran track and played basketball while studying English and economics at Oberlin College, the alma mater of many generations of middle-class leaders of black Washington. After earning a degree from Howard Law School, he settled with his wife in the predominantly black, upper-middle-class Crestwood neighborhood in Northwest. He took a job as counsel for the District of Columbia Committee on Education, Libraries, and Recreation and threw himself into neighborhood politics, becoming president of the Sixteenth Street Neighborhood Association and then commissioner on his local Advisory Neighborhood Commission.

Having come of age in a city that struggled simply to function, Fenty was obsessed with constituent services. He dug deeply into the minutiae of replacing damaged stop signs and cleaning alleys, and he grew frustrated with the sclerotic city bureaucracy. Competitive, energetic, and impatient, he determined that he could do a better job than his Ward 4 representative on the D.C. Council, Charlene Drew Jarvis. Emphasizing his youth (he was not yet thirty) and can-do spirit, Fenty ran a brilliant retail campaign, speaking with roughly half of the voters in his ward and sending the twenty-year incumbent down to defeat in 2000.[71]

On the council, Fenty maintained his focus on constituent services. He answered two hundred emails a day, kept up a steady stream of posts to six different neighborhood listservs, and regularly attended ANC, PTA, and civic association meetings. By the end of this first term, his Ward 4 constituents marveled at how his staff, often even the councilman himself, responded within minutes to requests for speed bumps, police patrols, or city-issued trash cans. His council colleagues, by contrast, complained that Fenty was better at campaigning than governing and quietly fumed as he constantly whispered with aides and typed away on his Blackberry during meetings. They resented how their brash young colleague talked to the media about the city's problems but failed to sit down with them and work out solutions. "He doesn't participate in the actual workings of government," groused Ward 2 councilman Jack Evans.[72]

In 2005, the relentlessly ambitious Fenty declared for mayor against Williams's presumptive successor, Council chairwoman Linda Cropp, a veteran lawmaker best known as a consensus builder. "We're much too satisfied that we're better than we were," Fenty insisted, promising that with "follow-through, responsiveness, and attention to detail" he could make Washington a model of efficient government for the rest of the country. And he personally delivered this message to tens of thousands of voters. Campaigning nonstop for more than a year, Fenty visited roughly half of the houses in D.C., earning many voters' support simply for showing up. "I was impressed that he knocked on my door," stated Woodridge resident Juanita Glover. "I don't remember someone doing that since Marion Barry."[73]

Fenty's intensive campaign and reputation for constituent services helped him win majority support from all racial and income groups. In the Democratic primary, Fenty won every precinct in the city, and he gobbled up 89 percent of the vote in the November 2006 general election. His astounding victories made him, in pollster Ron Lester's words, "the first [mayoral] candidate who has really transcended race, income and demographics." With his trim physique, shaved head, and multiracial heritage, the thirty-five-year-old Fenty embodied a hip cosmopolitanism that appealed particularly to the educated young migrants who flocked to Washington in the early twenty-first century.[74]

Fenty was on the leading edge of a new generation of black elected officials that journalists would dub "postracial." Like Newark mayor Cory Booker, Alabama congressman Artur Davis, and Illinois senator Barack Obama, this cohort had little experience with the racial oppression that had limited their parents' horizons. Highly educated and ambitious, they challenged an older generation of black politicians, confident that they could make government work better, particularly for the poor. And they were adamantly colorblind. "I certainly don't think about [race] a lot," Fenty responded when asked about the issue during his 2006 mayoral campaign. "I always heard politicians talk about race, but not the people. They were just talking about making sure every neighborhood gets the same attention."[75]

Fenty also was uninterested in the give and take of politics. Scorning consensus building and compromise, he believed that a strong leader "puts forward bold ideas and sticks to them," often quoting Margaret Thatcher's adage that "consensus is the absence of leadership." He pilloried his opponents as obstructionist members of a broken government or tools of special interests, touting himself as a representative of the popular will.[76]

The young mayor stocked his cabinet with young, forceful, Blackberry-wielding reformers and an odd assortment of loyalists and longtime personal friends—almost all of them white. Indeed, of the top ten appointments in the Fenty administration, only one was black, raising eyebrows in the African American community. "How can there be a scarcity of blacks for positions in the city with the most qualified black people in the world?" wondered Ward 4 resident Carlos M. O'Kieffe Sr. Fenty brushed off such criticism, believing that he knew the people's heart. "I feel like I'm doing what I was put in office to do," he stated. "When I talk to people in this city, the sense I get is that they want results, not process."[77]

Fenty delivered results. Using his newly created Capstat—a centralized database for measuring the productivity of each city program—Fenty took his legendary constituent services program citywide. Deputy Mayor for Economic Development Neil Albert expedited billions of dollars of development deals, accelerating the city's already overheated real estate market. Allen Lew and his newly created Office of Public Education Facilities Modernization began work on dozens of schools, community centers, and playgrounds. Police Chief Cathy Lanier implemented data-driven policing to reduce crime by swarming crime hot spots and placing "all hands on deck" on weekends.[78]

But Fenty believed that schools would be his legacy. "If we do not fix schools and challenge each child to reach their full potential," he told supporters shortly after his 2006 victory, "we'll never be the world-class city we want to be." On his first day in office, Fenty called for legislation to dissolve the school board and place D.C. Public Schools under direct mayoral control. Though many on the council distrusted Fenty, the system was in such poor shape that they were willing to try something new. That April the council granted the mayor the power to select a chancellor who would have full control over education policy, administration, and contracts.[79]

When Fenty assumed control of the city's public schools, the system was in free fall. Decades of white and then black middle-class flight, combined with leadership turnover and excessive bureaucracy, had crippled the schools. A decade of Republican efforts to create an education marketplace compounded the crisis by draining students and funding from traditional public schools. In 1996, Republicans in Congress, determined to implement market-based solutions to the problems of inner-city poverty, passed legislation establishing charter schools in the District. By 2006, the city had fifty-one charter schools serving more than seventeen thousand students and receiving $140 million in public money, numbers exceeded only by hurricane-ravaged New Orleans. In 2003, Republicans imposed vouchers on the city, establishing the D.C. Opportunity Scholarship Program over the objections of local elected officials. Each year thereafter, the program offered sixteen hundred public school students federal money to attend private schools.

As D.C. emerged as a national leader in the charter school and voucher movement, city schools hemorrhaged students. Between 1996 and 2006, the number of students in public schools dropped from eighty thousand to fifty-eight thousand, forcing the city to cut programs, fire teachers, and close schools. Voter confidence in the system dropped to 15 percent, the lowest on record.[80]

Fenty sought a transformational leader who could fundamentally reshape D.C.'s public schools in a short time. He found a kindred spirit in Michelle Rhee, a thirty-seven-year-old, Korean American education reformer who had never run a school system. It was a gutsy, unexpected choice. Rhee was a high-profile alumna of Teach For America (TFA), a nonprofit that placed recent graduates from elite universities in poor urban and rural schools to teach for two years. As a TFA corps member, she taught elementary school in Baltimore where she claimed (fraudulently, as it later turned out) to have made extraordinary achievement gains with her low-income students. She went on to launch the New Teacher Project (TNTP), a TFA spin-off that recruited and trained teachers for large school systems. At TNTP, Rhee made a name for herself as a fearless critic of teachers' unions that, she argued, protected poorly performing teachers.[81]

Rhee and TFA were the vanguard of a national education reform movement that united liberals and conservatives in pursuit of accountability in public education. The movement achieved its signature legislative accomplishment in 2001, when President George W. Bush partnered with liberal senator Ted Kennedy to pass the No Child Left Behind Act, which mandated annual standardized tests to all students beginning in third grade, then used those tests to measure school performance. Schools that showed "adequate yearly progress" earned increased federal support, while those that showed declines faced increased scrutiny, punishment, or, in the case of consistent poor performance, closure.[82]

Running D.C.'s troubled schools gave Rhee the opportunity to reform an entire urban school district in the backyard of the nation's lawmakers. Cocksure and tireless, Rhee was up to the task, but she initially demurred. She believed that effective school reform *required* conflict—with parents, with teachers, with elected officials—and she doubted that the mayor was willing to weather the

D.C. Public Schools chancellor Michelle Rhee became the national face of school reform but polarized Washingtonians. Her tumultuous tenure exacerbated racial tensions in the city. Mayor Adrian Fenty, standing behind Rhee to her right, gave his controversial chancellor unwavering support, contributing to his defeat in 2010. © Kevin Dietsch.

storm of "pushback and opposition." Fenty admired her aggressive approach and assured her that he would risk "everything" to turn the schools around. Rhee signed on.[83]

Rhee swept into the city determined to create a "culture of accountability" in a system where almost no one was fired for performance. Within days of coming to town, she blasted the system's central office staff as bloated and incompetent, making her point by walking a television crew through a school system warehouse where mounds of badly needed supplies sat forgotten and unused while students and teachers went without. "Teachers go out and spend their own money on this stuff," she seethed. The council stripped some of these workers of union protections, and Rhee immediately fired nearly a hundred of them.[84]

Leveraging the standardized testing required by No Child Left Behind, Rhee created a system for assessing administrators. She gathered scores for the D.C.

Comprehensive Assessment System and sat down with every principal in the city to deliver a simple message: if test scores do not go up, you will be fired. By the end of her first year she had fired twenty-four principals, including the head of the esteemed Oyster-Adams Bilingual School that her children attended.[85]

Rhee also sought to use test scores to measure teacher performance. She bypassed the teachers' union by using obscure credentialing rules already on the books to implement parts of her system and, she hoped, to fire hundreds of teachers she considered ineffective. She raised hundreds of millions of dollars in private money from foundations and wealthy individuals to pay bonuses to teachers whose students scored higher on standardized tests. Some teachers and principals grumbled about the relentless focus on testing and firing of personnel, but student scores jumped ten percentage points across the board in her first year, many teachers received bonuses, and Rhee earned lavish praise (though later investigations discovered that the jump in scores was attributable, in part, to cheating by teachers and administrators desperate not to be fired).[86]

By the end of 2008, Rhee had emerged as perhaps the national symbol of school reform. She traveled the "ideas" conference circuit, speaking to tech billionaires and philanthropists about how to save America's failing schools. Both presidential campaigns met with her to discuss education reform. Camera crews from *Frontline*, *60 Minutes*, and the 2010 documentary *Waiting for Superman* chronicled her every move. Nearly all of the coverage, and Rhee herself, related the same story of a relentless school reformer, driven by data and determination, whipping a dysfunctional urban system into shape. One enthusiastic journalist called her "D.C.'s Braveheart." [87]

Perhaps nowhere did this message come across more clearly than the December 8, 2008, issue of *Time* magazine that featured Rhee on the cover, holding a broom as she stood sternly in an empty classroom. "Teachers hate her. Principals are scared of her," wrote reporter Amanda Ripley. Rhee had become "the most revolutionary—and polarizing—force in American education." Rhee expressed her disdain not only for teachers but also for parents and politicians who opposed her reforms, calling their alleged excuses for poor student performance "crap." Though the story played well with her national constituency of education reformers, it alienated many D.C. parents, teachers, administrators, and even a few students. Cathy Reilly, head of the Senior High Alliance of Parents, Principals and Educators, an antiviolence organization focused on D.C. teenagers, called the cover story "disrespectful and denigrating." And these were the folks who voted in local elections.[88]

Much like his schools chancellor, Adrian Fenty, too, had become a media darling by late 2008. As he sped from meeting to meeting in his Smart Car, constituents treated him as a "combination of rock star and athlete," noted journalist Harry Jaffe in *Washingtonian* magazine. Young professionals jockeyed to get into his running group or formed their own, setting off an exercise boomlet within normally pudgy government circles. Pundits compared him to President Barack Obama, particularly after the pair appeared jointly at U Street's famed Ben's Chili Bowl in early 2009. But all the praise masked an explosive anger in the city's African American community with Fenty's autocratic style and his seeming disregard for the particular demands of black Washingtonians. Fenty steadfastly ignored it, convinced that results would supersede race. He was wrong.[89]

The first rumblings of black discontent with Fenty's reform agenda were apparent as early as 2007. In one of her first major moves as chancellor, Michelle Rhee unveiled a plan to close twenty-three underpopulated, underperforming schools, all of which were located in low-income black neighborhoods. Viewing parents and elected officials as enemies bent on scuttling the plan, she and Fenty presented the closings as a fait accompli and rushed to implement them before opponents could react. Unwilling, however, to acknowledge that they were ignoring constituents, Rhee held a series of meetings with affected communities where residents subjected her to withering criticism. Many expressed a love for their neighborhood schools, praised hardworking local teachers, and worried that the school closings would endanger their children or fail to improve their education. But the most prominent complaint was that the chancellor was not listening to them. "Nobody asked us what we thought of the plan," complained Cherita Whiting, president of the Ward 4 Education Council. "It was just handed to us and we were told, 'This is it.'"[90]

Rhee assumed that the anticipated results of her reforms—better-performing schools, higher-quality teachers, and higher-achieving students—would dispel any concerns about the means by which she produced them. But she was "deaf to the political realities of the city," wrote the *Post*'s Marc Fisher. Indeed, she pursued her agenda with an almost reckless disregard for the racial implications of her actions. She brought all-white teams of administrators with her to explain school closings to overwhelmingly black and Latino crowds. At the same time, she actively courted middle-class white parents. Though the percentage of the city's white population had topped 35 percent, white families typically moved to the suburbs or sent their children to private school after the elementary years, so only 6 percent of public school students were white. Determined to keep white students in the system (both to increase enrollment and to boost test scores), Rhee often personally solicited young professional parents in affluent and gentrifying neighborhoods, sending them emails and attending listening sessions in their living rooms. Like the Caplans and Neighbors, Inc., fifty years before, Rhee attempted to stop white flight by aggressively recruiting white families and catering to their interests.[91]

Many African American parents worried that Rhee's wooing of white parents ultimately would hurt their children. The schools in the gentrifying areas that Rhee targeted often were relatively well performing schools populated by the children of enterprising African American parents who had used the out-of-boundary system—a pupil assignment program in which students could apply to attend a school outside of their neighborhood district—to gain a better education for their children. If Rhee succeeded in convincing white parents in the neighborhood to send their children to these schools, out-of-boundary black children would be kicked back into their poorly performing neighborhood schools.[92]

Nowhere was this issue more combustible than at Rose L. Hardy Middle School in the affluent Glover Park neighborhood. Under the leadership of principal Patrick Pope, Hardy developed a well-regarded citywide arts and music magnet program that attracted largely middle-class black students from across the city. Only 10 percent of its students were white because few white students from the neighborhood attended. But after a $48 million renovation in 2008, white parents with children in Hardy's feeder elementary schools told Rhee that they would remain in the system if she could make Hardy more inviting. Rhee responded by transferring Pope, a white man popular with black students and parents but with a reputation for being prickly with neighborhood parents.

African American parents howled in protest. In their eyes, the chancellor was punishing a beloved principal who had served their children well to appease white parents who had a history of abandoning the system. Students stood by their principal. Hardy seventh-grader Claire Murphy Keller called Rhee "a real-life Dolores Umbridge," referring to a villain from the popular Harry Potter series. Rhee, however, refused to back down, again willfully blind to the racial effects of her reform agenda.[93]

Backed by Fenty, Rhee pushed on. During summer 2009, she hired 934 new teachers, including many young TFA-style recruits like herself. She then used the opportunity of a budget shortfall, precipitated by the economic recession of 2008, to justify the firing of 159 staff members and 229 teachers, the vast majority of whom were older and African American. Rhee claimed that the firings were necessitated by last-minute council budget cuts, but the council had instructed her to cut the money in question from the system's summer school offerings. She ignored the council, fully funded summer school, and then, faced with a shortfall, implemented an emergency reduction in force that, unlike regular layoffs, did not require her to follow union-negotiated seniority rules. Rhee rejected accusations that she had created the crisis to get rid of older black teachers, but that was the net effect of many of her reforms. By 2011, black teachers no longer were a majority in D.C. schools; just eight years before, they had comprised 77 percent of the teaching force.[94]

For many black Washingtonians, the teacher firings were the last straw. More than a thousand parents, teachers, students, and community activists held a "Rally for Respect" outside the Wilson Building. Waving signs that read "Sweep Her Out," and "This is not Rheezistan," the crowd cheered when Washington Teachers' Union president George Parker declared, "We are mobilizing to let Mayor Fenty and Chancellor Rhee know that we want respect, involvement, greater accountability and transparency." Rhee's approval rating plummeted in black neighborhoods. While 50 percent of African American voters believed that she was doing a good job in 2008, only 27 percent still asserted as much two years later. Despite this dwindling support, Fenty steadfastly stood behind his chancellor's decisions.[95]

Fenty's problems with the black community extended beyond Michelle Rhee and the city's schools into the field of real estate development. Unlike with schools, however, many African American voters complained that he was doing not too much, too fast, but too little, too slow.

In his first two years in office, Fenty supercharged the city's already booming real estate industry. He cut red tape for developers and rushed billions of dollars of deals through the permitting and approval process. When the 2008 economic recession halted construction in other cities, he pushed for the District to spend hundreds of millions to keep the boom going. "You kind of have to spend money to make money," he argued.[96]

The city actually benefited from the recession and housing crisis as high gas prices, terrible traffic, and an overbuilt housing market made the suburbs increasingly less attractive. After 2008, a growing percentage of migrants to the region chose the city over the suburbs. Between 2009 and 2011, D.C. gained nearly thirty thousand new residents, the vast majority of whom were educated white professionals. Entrepreneurs worked feverishly to capitalize on this demographic, opening a dizzying array of bars, restaurants, and gyms catering to young, white-collar workers with disposable income. Developers followed suit, accelerating the pace of high-end apartment and condominium construction.[97]

Fenty ensured that some of this development took place in the nearly all-black areas east of the Anacostia. Important new projects included the Department of Homeland Security on the former St. Elizabeths campus, a Giant super-market on Minnesota Avenue NE (the first supermarket in Ward 7 in twelve years), and an IHOP in Ward 8, which previously did not have a single sit-down restaurant.[98]

Many African American residents, however, believed that the mayor was not doing enough. Development in majority-black neighborhoods lagged behind that in gentrifying areas, and more important, market pressures threatened low-income black residents' ability to stay in the city. Much of the housing being created for new residents was not new construction. Instead, it was carved out of the low-income housing inventory. As the number of high-cost apartments tripled between 2000 and 2010, the number of low-cost units dropped by half. While the number of houses costing over $500,000 doubled, the inventory of low-cost homes shrank by two-thirds.[99]

As new homebuyers and developers gobbled up low-cost units in the private market, many poor residents and their representatives on the council pushed the Fenty administration to create more affordable housing. Yet Fenty did not make it a priority. Indeed, a mayor known for his impatient determination to make things happen immediately dragged his feet when it came to providing housing options for the poor.

The New Communities Initiative offered an instructive example of his ad-ministration's lackluster efforts. New Communities had been created in 2005 through a long year of difficult negotiations between the Williams administra-tion and the residents of the several public housing projects located in Northwest One. Many of the area's elderly residents had ended up in public housing after the federal government destroyed their Southwest homes in the 1950s, so they feared, in the words of community activist Alverta Munlyn, that any modern-day "urban renewal" would lead to "black people's removal." The Williams adminis-tration, however, convinced them that this time would be different.

With his autocratic style, Fenty violated that trust and undermined the initia-tive. After receiving complaints of rat and bedbug infestations in Temple Courts in March 2007, the mayor called a meeting with tenants. He told the 65 resi-dents in attendance that they could stay in the building as is or take Section 8 housing vouchers and leave. A majority elected to take the vouchers. Inclined to gather information directly from residents and distrust the organizations that claimed to represent them, Fenty disregarded the protests of the Northwest One Tenant Council and ordered all 211 families to vacate the building so that it could be demolished and replaced. Fenty's actions violated the "build first" agreement residents had brokered with the Williams administration, but the mayor prom-ised that all tenants would have a place in the new development once it was complete. "It's a lie," warned Diana Hunter, president of the Temple Courts Tenant Association. "When they tear down this building, we're not coming back."[100]

Events proved her right. Private funding for the planned development never materialized, and the Fenty Administration did not make New Communities a priority. Temple Courts became a parking lot. Its former residents scattered throughout the city's far eastern wards and Prince George's County, just as Southwest residents dispersed after urban renewal a half-century before. Similar problems existed at the other New Communities sites, and the affordable housing crisis worsened. Between 2008 and 2010, the low-income housing voucher and public housing wait lists grew by 47 percent and 61 percent, respectively.[101]

And yet, despite his controversial development policies and education reforms, Mayor Fenty appeared invulnerable going into his 2010 reelection campaign. Test scores were up, crime was down, the city was booming, and he had raised a whopping $4 million, scaring off most potential challengers. Polling showed that residents of all class and racial backgrounds favored the many improvements in city services under the dynamic young mayor. Highly popular among white voters, Fenty was assumed by many political observers to be rolling to an easy victory. "His reelection seems almost guaranteed," wrote Washingtonian's Harry Jaffe in March 2010.[102]

But Fenty had a major political problem. In a city where African Americans still constituted 63 percent of registered voters, most black residents viewed the mayor as arrogant and dishonest, and they believed that he cared more about upper-income white residents than themselves. "He's treated white folks with deference and black folks with diffidence," complained civic activist Lawrence Guyot.[103]

Many black residents seethed at what they perceived to be his deliberate insults of established black leaders. In 2009, Fenty had attempted to evict Cora Masters Barry (Marion Barry's ex-wife) and her nonprofit organization from the Southeast Washington Tennis and Learning Center, which she had worked to create and operate. Two of Barry's friends, Dorothy Height and Maya Angelou—among the most respected elder stateswomen in black America—requested a meeting to discuss the matter. Twice Fenty canceled on them, generating a firestorm of criticism from prominent black women across the country. A poll taken after the high-profile snub showed that three-quarters of D.C.'s black women, the city's most potent voting bloc, had a negative impression of Fenty.[104]

Other's noted that Fenty showed little urgency when faced with the serious problems that disproportionately affected the black community, including unemployment, which reached nearly 30 percent in Ward 8, and HIV/AIDS, which ballooned to a nation-leading 3 percent of the population (and was concentrated almost exclusively in low-income black neighborhoods). By 2010, 75 percent of all black voters disapproved of Fenty's performance in office. Many agreed with Antonio Robertson, owner of the Langston Bar and Grill on H Street, who argued that Fenty "has no special affinity for black folks."[105]

Desperate for a viable challenger to the mayor, several black activists and union leaders fixed on council chairman Vincent Gray, a former director of the Department of Human Services under Sharon Pratt Kelly who often had clashed with the mayor. A D.C. native and graduate of Dunbar High School, the light-skinned Gray was a bland politician nearly thirty years Fenty's senior. He entered the race in March, just five months before the Democratic primary, and campaigned on the slogan "One City," promising to unite a diverse city divided by race and class. Black voters' frustration with Fenty fueled Gray's campaign. Assisted by a broad coalition of African American political groups, unions, and churches, Gray quickly raised $2.8 million and focused on turning out the black vote.[106]

Confident that he knew the average voter's mind, Fenty ignored polls and rejected his advisers' frenzied pleas to pay attention to the black electorate. If there were problems with black voters, he reasoned, another round of door-knocking would win them over. Only in September, when polls showed that he had lost the black vote almost entirely, did Fenty concede his mistake and scramble to make amends. He cut a commercial apologizing for his "arrogance" — but then he skipped church services the Sunday before the election to run a triathlon.[107]

The same black voters who forgave Marion Barry for his many trespasses showed little tolerance for Fenty's transparently inauthentic attempt at humility. Eighty percent of them cast their ballots for Gray. An equal percentage of white voters supported the incumbent. Gray won easily, a sign that black votes still held the key to political power in the rapidly gentrifying city.[108]

In the end, Fenty's efforts to ignore race ultimately undid his political career. Like the Financial Control Board and Mayor Williams before him, Fenty had delivered his black constituents badly needed services, which many enjoyed, but he often did so in a manner that disempowered, denigrated, or even displaced them. "Fenty, his supporters raved, was making the trains run on time," wrote *Post* columnist Courtland Milloy in an incisive election postmortem. "That people were falling off the caboose and being railroaded out of town was just the price of progress." But, he continued, the people being left behind as Fenty charged into the future still could vote. "So people went to the polls and politely delivered a message: Most residents actually believe in representative democracy, thank you very much."[109]

That Must Not Be True of Tomorrow

History, Race, and Democracy in a New Moment of Racial Flux

The past has been a mint
Of blood and sorrow.
That must not be
True of tomorrow.
—LANGSTON HUGHES, "History," 1934

The original Busboys and Poets sits at the corner of Fourteenth and V Streets NW, just a block north of the epicenter of the 1968 riots. A combination restaurant, bookstore, lounge, and theater, Busboys took its name from Langston Hughes, the one-time busboy at D.C.'s Wardman Hotel who gained international renown as a poet (albeit one who denounced the snobbery of D.C.'s black upper class). After it opened in 2005, it became an immediate commercial and cultural success, attracting young, hip Washingtonians who swarmed the surrounding Shaw neighborhood in the twenty-first century.[1]

From its name to the expansive selection of black studies titles in its bookstore to the enormous mural depicting heroic figures of the civil rights movement that adorns one wall, Busboys consciously embraced a social justice mission and promoted African American history. Yet its clientele was predominantly nonblack, and it was owned and operated not by an African American entrepreneur but by Andy Shallal, an Iraqi immigrant who grew up in suburban Virginia. Busboys and Poets was just one of many D.C. establishments in the early twenty-first century, particularly in Shaw, that used themes, imagery, and people from black D.C. history to appeal to a new, affluent, multicultural clientele.[2]

Busboys and Poets epitomized the spirit of a growing, gentrifying city energized not only by new development but also by the election of Illinois senator Barack Obama as the nation's first black president in 2008. More than 92 percent of District residents cast their ballots for Obama—exceeding his highest vote total elsewhere by 25 percent—and thousands of D.C. residents traveled to the swing states of Virginia and Pennsylvania to knock doors on his behalf. When newscasters called the election late on the night of November 4, ecstatic interracial crowds gathered outside the White House and at the corner of Fourteenth and U Streets, just a stone's throw from Busboys and Poets, where they hugged, sang, cried, and danced into the wee hours.[3]

The following January, many Washingtonians joined the more than one million visitors who braved subfreezing temperatures to witness Obama's swearing in, their chilly frames packing the National Mall from the Capitol all the way to the Washington Monument. In an event thick with historical significance, Obama did not shy from the nation's and the District's racial past. He marveled that "a man whose father less than 60 years ago might not have been served at a local restaurant can now stand before you to take a most sacred oath."[4]

Yet once in office, Obama sometimes disappointed his ardent local supporters. Though many liberal Washingtonians relished seeing the country's first black first lady, Michelle Obama, visiting low-income students in public schools east of the Anacostia River, they lamented that she and her husband chose to send their two daughters to an expensive, mostly white private school. They also grew increasingly frustrated with Obama's failure to make D.C. self-determination a priority. It took him four years to place "Taxation without Representation" license plates on the presidential limousine, and he neglected to mention D.C. governance in any of his eight State of the Union addresses, despite intense lobbying from Delegate Eleanor Holmes Norton. In a series of contentious 2011 budget negotiations with conservative Republicans, Obama famously sacrificed the city. "John, I will give you D.C. abortion," he told Speaker of the House John Boehner, thereby acquiescing as congressional conservatives prohibited the District government from spending locally raised tax revenue to fund abortions for low-income women. "Let's be brutally honest," said black community activist Philip Pannell. "A Republican president would not have been worse" on D.C. self-determination.[5]

More ominously for many black Washingtonians, Obama's presidency accelerated the economic and demographic trends already under way in the early twenty-first century. Confronted with the nation's worst economic crisis since the Great Depression, the young president pursued universal legislation aimed at strengthening the middle class, studiously avoiding race-specific policies designed to address the needs of poor and black Americans. As the national economy stabilized, low-income black Americans continued to struggle, particularly in the nation's capital. Already gargantuan racial disparities in wealth and employment ballooned. An Urban Institute study found that in 2013 and 2014 white wealth in D.C. was eighty-one times greater than black wealth, and astronomical real estate values made it increasingly difficult for low-income residents to remain in the city.[6]

As thousands of white, Asian, and Latino millennials followed Obama into town and older, predominantly African American residents moved to the suburbs, the city lost its black majority. After cresting at nearly 538,000 (71.1 percent of the total population) in 1970, the number of black residents hit a low of barely 305,000 (50.7 percent of the total population) in 2010. By 2011, new census estimates revealed that black residents no longer were a majority of the population, "a swift and remarkable shift for a city that prides itself on being a hub of black culture and politics," wrote reporters Carol Morello and Dan Keating in the *Post*.[7]

From pulpits and parking lots to blogs and barbershops, these demographic changes rekindled questions of race and democracy that have marked Washington since its inception. For the hopeful, the shifting demographics hinted at a new, hip D.C. where young professionals of all colors populated flourishing, multicultural neighborhoods peppered with trendy establishments like Busboys and Poets. As millennials poured into the city, they upended the city's traditionally staid reputation. In 2014, *Forbes* magazine listed D.C. as the nation's "coolest" city, raving about its "abundant entertainment and recreational options" and "ethnically and culturally diverse population."[8]

For the political, the numbers raised questions of control, because a diminished black community likely would be forced to relinquish the political power it wielded for the previous half-century. "I'm wondering what the D.C. of tomorrow will look like, and whether I'll still have a seat at the table," worried black lawyer and neighborhood activist Charles Wilson. It was a matter of "who has the power to determine what this community is going to look like," explained the Reverend Cheryl J. Sanders, the black pastor of the Third Street Church of God near Mount Vernon Square in Northwest. "I want to have a voice in that. I don't want to be told to 'sit down and shut up while we cast the vision for the city.'"[9]

For the conspiratorial, the rising white population revealed the success of "The Plan"—an alleged multidecade plot by white business and political leaders to wrest control of the city back from black folks. "C'mon people, let's be honest," wrote one reader responding to a 2010 article on D.C.'s changing demographics in the *Washington City Paper*. "'The Plan' is working. White people are pushing black people out of the District—that's 'The Plan.'" Delivery truck driver Robert Adams recalled when the first white family moved into his Anacostia neighborhood in the mid-2000s. "It was like a buzz, like 'I told you they was coming back.'" With the median price of a home in Anacostia double or

TABLE 7 Washington's population, 1990–2015

Year	Total	Black (% of pop.)	White (% of pop.)	Asian (% of pop.)	Other (incl. mixed race) (% of pop.)	Hispanic (of any race) (% of pop.)
1990	606,900	399,604 (65.8)	179,667 (29.6)	11,214 (1.8)	16,415 (2.7)	32,710 (5.4)
2000	572,059	343,312 (60.0)	176,101 (30.8)	15,189 (2.7)	37,457 (6.5)	44,953 (7.9)
2010	601,723	305,125 (50.7)	231,471 (38.5)	21,056 (3.5)	44,071 (7.3)	54,749 (9.1)
2014*	658,893	322,858 (49.0)	287,277 (43.6)	26,356 (4.0)	22,402 (3.4)	68,525 (10.4)

Sources: Population figures for 1990: U.S. Census Bureau, "Historical Census Statistics on Population Totals by Race"; for 2000: U.S. Census Bureau, "Population by Race and Hispanic or Latino Origin, for All Ages and for 18 Years and Over, for the District of Columbia: 2000," https://www.census.gov/census2000/pdf/dc_tab_1.PDF; for 2010: http://factfinder.census.gov/faces/tableservices/jsf/pages/productview.xhtml?src=CF; for 2015: https://www.census.gov/quickfacts/table/PST045215/11.
*2014 figures are estimates.

triple what it had been in the 1990s, Adams no longer was able to afford his apartment. Bitter but resigned, he and his family moved to the more affordable Prince George's County.[10]

For the wistful, the changing census numbers meant the end of Chocolate City, the moniker immortalized by funk band Parliament and lovingly embraced by black residents after D.C. became a black-majority city in 1957. "Washington's makeover had created something of an identity crisis," wrote journalist Natalie Hopkinson in 2012. Decades of black control had "fostered a sense of black privilege, swagger and, yes, the hubris that comes with leadership." Many black Washingtonians now feared that the city would lose its soul. "Well, chocolate melts," lamented Howard University poet E. Ethelbert Miller. "We're seeing the eroding of a community. The city ain't gonna be black no more."[11]

The demographic revolution of the early twenty-first century was the latest chapter in the story of race and democracy in the nation's capital. For four centuries, race has been an ongoing source of conflict and division, the central fault line of D.C. political, economic, and social life. The democratic promises of this nation's founding documents have foundered repeatedly on the shoals of dispossession, slavery, segregation, violence, disinvestment, and our collective inability to grapple seriously with this country's racial sins.

But the history of the nation's capital is not simply what Langston Hughes called a "mint / Of blood and sorrow." Since the city's inception, men and women of conscience have struggled to dismantle the systems of racial inequality and mistrust that still haunt our nation. Theirs is a story not of blame and resignation but of action and resilience, of working to ensure that Washington's tortured racial past "must not be / True of tomorrow." We hope that this book will inspire Washingtonians to take up the challenge of black and white abolitionists, of former slaves and Radical Republicans, of civil rights and home rule activists, of freeway protesters and cooperative organizers, to build a more just, egalitarian, and democratic nation's capital.

ESSAY ON SOURCES

Chocolate City is built on mountains of primary and secondary research conducted by generations of historians who came before us, as well as by contemporary colleagues who work alongside us. This book is theirs as well as ours—it offers both our own original primary research as well as a synthesis of scholarly interpretations that have transformed the field of D.C. history during the past half-century. Indeed, the field has undergone changes as profound as those that have engulfed the city itself. Begun as a celebratory genealogical endeavor among well-to-do amateur historians, the history of the nation's capital has garnered increasing interest from serious scholars within the academy who have broadened the scope of the field and deepened our understanding of the dynamics of race, class, power, and gender in the city.

The first organized body to focus on D.C. history was the Association of Oldest Inhabitants of the District of Columbia, founded in 1865 to celebrate the city's "old" families at a time when Washington was awash in new residents. A more scholarly group convened in 1894 as the Columbia Historical Society. The thirty-six white men and women founders mainly were scientists and scholars working in the federal service and putting down roots in the city. They wrote and delivered papers, often reminiscences as well as research, that were bound and published as the *Records of the Columbia Historical Society*. In its early decades, the interests of the society reflected the composition of its white, professional, prosperous membership. Much of the history told in the earliest *Records* was theirs, though by the middle decades of the twentieth century the organization moved beyond its elite members' personal interests to publish research on city institutions, including both divisions of the segregated school system.[1]

In the early twentieth century, other city organizations began collecting a more diverse body of local histories. The D.C. Public Library's Washingtoniana Division, founded in 1905, collected materials covering a broad spectrum of local interests, reflecting its role as one of the city's few nonsegregated public centers. Though largely ignored by white historians, black Washington's social history was readily available in oral tradition, area churches, and the collections of Howard University's Moorland Foundation (now known as the Moorland-Spingarn Research Center). Howard scholars produced much of the most important early twentieth-century work on race in the city, including sociologist William Henry Jones's seminal studies on black recreation (*Recreation and Amusement among Negroes in Washington, D.C.*, in 1927) and housing (*The Housing of Negroes in Washington, D.C.*, in 1929). His colleague Sterling Brown's short essay on "The Negro in Washington" for the 1937 Works Progress Administration's *Guide to Washington* remains a powerful exploration of the critical role black Washingtonians have played in the city. E. Franklin Frazier conducted reams of fascinating interviews with D.C. residents for his celebrated *Negro Youth at the Crossways* (1940). Though still useful for their insights into black life, studies from this era often suffered from a preoccupation with the black elite and condescension for the black poor and working classes.

Like so much of U.S. historiography, interpretations of D.C. history were revolutionized by the mid-twentieth-century struggle for civil rights (and home rule). Many of the studies conducted in the decades following World War II sought to describe and detail the history of racial injustice in order to dismantle it. This profoundly important work included legal research by Charles Hamilton Houston, Phineas Indritz, and other attorneys as well as academic research by sociologist E. Franklin Frazier, economist Robert Weaver, and other scholars who collaborated to produce the blockbuster *Segregation in Washington* in 1948. Such studies were, above all, utilitarian histories penned by liberal activists seeking reform and journalists trying to explain a fast-changing world to anxious readers. They could be achingly beautiful—Haynes Johnson's *Dusk at the Mountain: The Negro, the Nation, the Capital* (1963) is a poetic snapshot of the still segregated world inhabited by black Washingtonians. And they could be strikingly clear-eyed and entertaining—Sam Smith's *Captive Capital* (1974) brims with indignation at the ongoing powerlessness that D.C. residents experienced.

During the 1960s and early 1970s award-winning studies by two pioneering scholars established D.C. history as a legitimate academic subfield. Constance McLaughlin Green's two-volume *Washington* appeared in 1962, setting a high standard of scholarship and making it clear that D.C. history no longer could consist simply of hoary chestnuts told and retold by aging white men. Her *Secret City: A History of Race Relations in the Nation's Capital* (1967) provided a panoramic view of the "interplay between the races," though she struggled to describe the lives of the poor and focused instead on the "Negroes at the upper socio economic strata" for whom data were more prevalent. Its shortcomings aside, *Secret City* is a deeply researched and remarkably perceptive book that set the tone for studies of race relations for decades to come. Green was followed quickly by Letitia Woods Brown, whose *Free Negroes in the District of Columbia, 1790–1846* (1972), provided a granular view of early republican and antebellum black life in the city. Brown meticulously chronicled the efforts of enslaved and free black Washingtonians alike to secure a greater share of freedom. Her study remains a standard in the field.

Brown's work was an early example of what came to be known as the "new social history," a movement among historians nationwide to focus attention on local history and the lives of everyday people, rather than national policy-makers and elites. This movement coincided with the triumph of D.C.'s home rule movement, which also spurred interest in local D.C. history. Together, these developments inspired historians to look more deeply and critically into the past and to question assumptions about power and privilege, both in historical figures and in historical sources. The result was a generation's worth of interpretations that upended our understanding of D.C. history and unearthed new stories and themes that resonate throughout *Chocolate City*. An exemplar of the new approach was James Borchert's *Alley Life in Washington: Family, Community, Religion, and Folklife in the City, 1850–1970* (1980), which exploded the race- and class-inflected caricatures of "alley dwellers" created by Progressive Era reformers and sought to understand alley communities in all their complexity and richness.

Subsequent scholars used a similar approach to write a new D.C. history "from the bottom up." Kathleen Menzie Lesko, Valerie Babb, and Carroll R. Gibbs collaborated on a ground-breaking study, *Black Georgetown Remembered* (1991), that revealed the deep roots of the black experience in Georgetown. Elizabeth Clark-Lewis conducted dozens of in-depth oral histories to tell the story of early twentieth-century Washington from the perspective of female migrant domestic workers in *Living In, Living Out: African American Domestics in Washington, D.C., 1910–1940* (1994), and several related articles. The anthology *Urban Odyssey: A Multicultural History of Washington D.C.* (1996) challenged D.C. historians not to overlook the city's many ethnic minorities, including the largely forgotten white working classes. Two particularly important articles in the anthology were Olivia Cadaval's pioneering work on the Latino community and Megan McAleer's excellent piece on the Irish in D.C. This scholarship has complicated and enriched our understanding of the city's past.

Area museums and universities contributed to the flood of local history by creating new archives and encouraging new research on the city. The Smithsonian Institution opened the Anacostia Community Museum under Director John Kinard in 1967, and in the 1970s it began collecting oral histories and created a neighborhood-specific archive. The publications it sponsored filled a gaping hole in the field of D.C. history, which had all but ignored the neighborhoods east of the Anacostia River. George Washington University opened a

Center for Washington Area Studies in 1980, and the Urban Studies Department at the University of the District of Columbia initiated a D.C. History and Public Policy Project the following year. All three gained funding through the Humanities Council of Washington, D.C., an affiliate of the National Endowment for the Humanities, and used it to publish a rich assortment of neighborhood histories and reports on everything from housing and education to the struggle for self-determination. The apotheosis of local studies appeared in 1988 with the publication of editor Kathryn Schneider Smith's *Washington at Home*, a richly illustrated and well-researched collection of concise neighborhood histories.

The crack epidemic of the late 1980s and Marion Barry's 1990 conviction for drug use shifted the focus of D.C. history away from social history and neighborhood studies as many journalists rushed to pen accounts about the mayor and the city's descent into dysfunction. Jonathan Agronsky's angry *Marion Barry: The Politics of Race* (1991), Tom Sherwood and Harry Jaffe's riveting *Dream City: Race Power and the Decline of Washington D.C.* (1994) — arguably the most influential treatment of late twentieth-century D.C. in circulation today — and Jonetta Rose Barras's perceptive *The Last of the Black Emperors: The Hollow Comeback of Marion Barry in a New Age of Black Leaders* (1998) all offered detailed and insightful accounts of the Barry years. Their focus on the mayor, however, obscured the city's rich social movement history and crowded out other political actors.

By the late twentieth century, D.C. history looked vastly different than it had a half-century before. The emphasis on local people and neighborhood-level history brought a variety of new voices and stories unheard in traditional histories. These granular studies showed how the city's history has been shaped not just by powerful leaders but also by poor and working-class men and women, acting both on their own and collectively. At times, however, such studies could be disconnected from the larger context in which historical actors lived. A new generation of university-trained historians worked to combine the local with the national, helping readers understand complex struggles for power, rights, and access between the federal government and various local actors. These works have been essential to our understanding of race and democracy in the nation's capital.

One indispensable example of this combined approach is Howard Gillette's brilliantly named *Between Justice and Beauty* (1994), which explores how race and urban planning have shaped the development of the city. Much of *Chocolate City*'s discussions about urban planning, including late nineteenth-century real estate development and mid-twentieth-century urban renewal, build on Gillette's insights.

While Gillette covered the broad, two-hundred-year sweep of D.C. history, other late twentieth- and early twenty-first-century scholars have contributed tightly focused studies of particular eras. Our early chapters reflect the impact of Ken Bowling's careful work on the city's founding, including *Creating the Federal City, 1774–1800: Potomac Fever* (1988) and *The Creation of Washington D.C.: The Idea and Location of the American Capital* (1991). Our interpretation of antebellum Washington's antislavery community draws significantly from Stanley Harrold's excellent study, *Subversives: Antislavery Community in Washington, D.C., 1828–1865* (2003), which details the challenges and triumphs of D.C.'s interracial network of antislavery activists. Mary Beth Corrigan's important 1996 dissertation, "A Social Union of Heart and Effort," and related articles reveal the complex kin networks and community building efforts among free and enslaved black Washingtonians. William G. Thomas's recent work on freedom suits and black family networks in antebellum Washington emphasizes the agency that enslaved black Washingtonians showed in combating slavery. Thomas also has helped develop an extraordinary website, "Oh Say Can You See" (http://earlywashington.org), that digitizes and analyzes hundreds of legal files and court cases involving slavery in the nation's capital.

The Civil War and Reconstruction eras have earned the close attention of many serious scholars. Our chapters on that era draw immeasurably from the insights of Kate Masur's masterful *An Example for All the Land: Emancipation and the Struggle over Equality in Washington, D.C.* (2011). Masur places local black activism at the center of her study, showing how black activists such as George Hatton pushed for an expansive definition of equality even as conservative opponents mounted an effective counterrevolution. Kenneth J. Winkle's *Lincoln's Citadel: The Civil War in Washington, DC* (2013), offers a wonderfully readable account of the turbulent era and situates the nation's capital in the broader context of the war. Winkle also has been a driving force behind "Civil War Washington" (www.civilwardc.org), an important website that offers researchers a trove of primary sources and thoughtful interpretive essays. Alan Lessoff's *The Nation and Its City: Politics, "Corruption," and Progress, 1861–1902* (1994), remains the standard for understanding the regime of Alexander Shepherd and the white businessmen who followed him in ruling Washington.

The long era of Jim Crow in Washington—stretching from the imposition of commissioner rule in the 1870s to the modern civil rights movement of the 1940s and 1950s—has not received as much scholarly attention as it deserves. One exception is Eric Yellin's *Racism in the Nation's Service: Government Workers and the Color Line in Woodrow Wilson's America* (2013). Yellin's thorough study shows not only how the Wilson administration rolled back decades of black advances but also how the city's black community organized to defend their claims to the city.

Some of the best research on the era has been published in article form, including Michele Pacifico's work on the New Negro Alliance, or remains unpublished, including Marya Annette McQuirter's excellent dissertation, "Claiming the City: African Americans, Urbanization, and Leisure in Washington, D.C., 1902–1957" (2000). McQuirter reveals the fluidity of the city's segregation boundaries and highlights the various ways that black Washingtonians asserted themselves on the streets of the city. Promising new research on the era has emerged in recent years, including Tikia K. Hamilton's fine dissertation, "Making a 'Model' System: Race, Education and Politics in the Nation's Capital before *Brown*, 1930–1950" (2015), Treva Lindsey's *Colored No More: Reinventing Black Womanhood in Washington, D.C.* (2017), and Mary-Elizabeth Murphy's forthcoming *A National and Local Affair: African American Women's Politics in Washington, D.C., 1920–1945*.

The civil rights and Black Power eras of Washington history, stretching roughly from the end of World War II until the fall of Marion Barry in the early 1990s, merit more scholarly scrutiny. Our understanding of the era has been enriched by two extraordinary articles on the desegregation era that appeared in *Washington History* in 2004–5. Bell Clement's "Pushback: The White Community's Dissent from Bolling" examines how white Washingtonians resisted the civil rights movement, particularly during a failed effort to "save" Central High School as a white school. Marya McQuirter's "Our Cause Is Marching On: Parent Activism, Browne Junior High School, and the Multiple Meanings of Equality in Post-War Washington" describes the grassroots movement among black parents to force city officials to deal with the various problems caused by maintaining dual school systems. Two dissertations completed in 2013 examine the people and organizations involved in the civil rights and home rule struggles: Gregory M. Borchardt's "Making D.C. Democracy's Capital: Local Activism, the 'Federal State,' and the Struggle for Civil Rights in Washington, D.C.," and Lauren Pearlman's "Democracy's Capital: Local Protest, National Politics, and the Struggle for Civil Rights in Washington, D.C., 1933–1978." Other important works that have influenced our interpretations of this era are Anne M. Valk's *Radical Sisters: Second-Wave Feminism and Black Liberation in Washington, D.C.* (2008), which explores the outsized role that women played in the New Left activist communities that dotted Shaw and Columbia Heights, and Dana Flor's wonderful documentary, *The Nine Lives of Marion Barry* (2009), perhaps the best encapsulation of Barry's tumultuous career.

Since 2000, a massive wave of gentrification and the subsequent end of the city's black majority have created a unique subset of contemporary D.C. scholarship that has influenced our later chapters: gentrification studies. A critical precursor for this transformation was the federally directed restructuring of D.C.

government in the late 1990s under the Financial Control Board. Jahi Baruti's important dissertation, "The Control Board Era in the District of Columbia Government and Politics, 1995–2001" (2003), and Michael Fauntroy's *Home Rule or House Rule: Congress and the Erosion of Local Governance in the District of Columbia* (2003) are critical guideposts in our efforts to understand this process. Dennis Gale's *Washington DC: Inner City Revitalization and Minority Suburbanization* (1987) remains perhaps the most wide-ranging and thoughtful treatment of demographic change in the District. The talented cohort of scholars whose work Derek Hyra and Sabiyha Prince collected into the anthology *Capital Dilemma: Growth and Inequality in Washington, D.C.* (2016), have built on Gale's insights to explain gentrification as it continues to affect the city today.

Chocolate City seeks both to synthesize the important research on race and democracy in the nation's capital that has appeared in the half-century since Green's *Secret City* and to offer new research and analysis on understudied people, events, and eras. With the proliferation of specialized studies, we see the need for an accessible, one-volume narrative history that melds the powerful stories and insights of local history with the essential context and scope of broader studies. Although written primarily for a general readership, *Chocolate City* also contributes to scholarly conversations about race, democracy, and social change.

Ours is a study of *race* in Washington—not a study of black D.C. alone. White Washingtonians, too, have a "race," so we look seriously at how race affected the worldview and actions of white Washingtonians, including immigrants and the white working class, and we explore how their racial identity, racial fears, and sense of racial power have changed over time. We also seek to shift the field of D.C. history away from the black-white binary framework that undergirds much writing about the city. Though Washington's population has been largely white and black for much of its history, we incorporate Native American, Latino, Asian American, and Ethiopian stories that can get submerged in popular discussions of race in D.C.

We expand on the work of historians who have identified the deep and politically consequential class divisions in the city's various populations. These intraracial divisions are crucial to understanding group cohesion or dissension, the spaces for interracial cooperation, and the intense disagreements between governing elites and the "grassroots." Such divisions became particularly important during periods of racial flux or tension, as during Reconstruction and its aftermath or during the post–World War II civil rights era.

Chocolate City explores the critical role that race plays in Congress's refusal to grant self-determination to the nation's capital, and conversely how Washington's lack of self-government has exacerbated local racial mistrust through-out the city's history. The lack of political democracy has been a double-edged sword. Local activists at times have leveraged the federal government to achieve their ends, and national political actors have used D.C. to pursue their national policy agendas or play to their constituents' prejudices.

Our work digs deep into little-known or poorly understood episodes in D.C. history, including the struggles for power before the city's founding, how ante-bellum black residents used the courts to defend their interests, the role of the Irish in D.C.'s racial history, the importance of Perry Carson and his working-class coalition in the late nineteenth century, the movement against police bru-tality in the 1930s, the decline of the white working class in the desegregation era, the interracial movement to stop freeways, the statehood effort from the 1970s to the 1990s, and the persistent popularity of Marion Barry. These stories illuminate our larger themes about the enduring significance of race and the shifting dynamics of racial power, the debilitating effect of D.C.'s undemocratic political status on race relations in the city, and the catalyzing and demoralizing effect of being the nation's capital on local racial struggles.

The twenty-first century will provide ample fodder for future historians. The city's history is being documented every day, not only in the pages of the *Washington Post*, the *City Paper*, and the *Washington Informer*, but also on countless blogs and websites that reflect Washingtonians' ongoing love for the District's past. We hope that *Chocolate City* deepens that love for the city and inspires readers to engage in thoughtful conversations about race and democracy.

NOTES

Abbreviations

AA	*Afro-American*
CA	*Colored American*
CCEADL	Coordinating Committee for the Enforcement of the D.C. Anti-Discrimination Laws
CD	*Chicago Defender*
CFP	Cook Family Papers, Moorland-Spingarn Research Center, Howard University, Washington, D.C.
CHHP	Charles Hamilton Houston Papers, Moorland-Spingarn Research Center, Howard University, Washington, D.C.
CMID	Correspondence of the Military Intelligence Division Relating to "Negro Subversion," 1917–1941, National Archives and Records Administration, Washington, D.C.
CML-OHP	Celebración de la Mujer Latina Oral History Project, Community Archives, Washingtoniana Division, Martin Luther King Memorial Library, Washington, D.C.
DCCA	D.C. Community Archives, Washingtoniana Division, Martin Luther King Memorial Library, Washington, D.C.
DCSML	D.C. Statehood Movement Leaders Oral History Project, Washingtoniana Division, Martin Luther King Memorial Library, Washington, D.C.
ECTCP	Emergency Committee on the Transportation Crisis Papers, Washingtoniana Division, Martin Luther King Memorial Library, Washington, D.C.
EFFP	E. Franklin Frazier Papers, Moorland-Spingarn Research Center, Howard University, Washington, D.C.
ES	*Evening Star*
GWBTR	Greater Washington Board of Trade Records, Special Collections Research Center, Gelman Library, George Washington University, Washington, D.C.
JHP	Julius Hobson Papers, Washingtoniana Division, Martin Luther King Memorial Library, Washington, D.C.
KRL-HSW	Kiplinger Research Library, Historical Society of Washington, D.C.
LC	Library of Congress, Washington, D.C.
MBOE	Minutes of the Board of Education of the District of Columbia
MCTP	Mary Church Terrell Papers, Library of Congress, Washington, D.C.

NAACP-DC	Papers of the NAACP–D.C. Branch, Moorland-Spingarn Research Center, Howard University, Washington, D.C.
NARA	National Archives and Records Administration, Washington, D.C.
NCSNC	National Committee on Segregation in the Nation's Capital
NI	*National Intelligencer*
NR	*National Republican*
NYS-DC	Negro Youth Study, Washington, D.C.
NYT	*New York Times*
RB-OHC	Ralph Bunche Oral History Collection, Moorland-Spingarn Research Collection, Howard University, Washington, D.C.
RDCC	Records of the District of Columbia Commissioners and of the Offices Concerned with Public Buildings, National Archives and Records Administration, Washington, D.C.
RG	Record Group
RSCI	Records of the Select Committee to Inquire into the Existence of an Inhuman and Illegal Traffic in Slaves in the District of Columbia, Library of Congress, Washington, D.C.
SCRC-GL	Special Collections Research Center, Gelman Library, George Washington University, Washington, D.C.
SNCCP	Student Nonviolent Coordinating Committee Papers
USBC	United States Bureau of the Census
USGPO	United States Government Printing Office
WAA	*Washington Afro-American*
WB	*Washington Bee*
WBOT	Washington Board of Trade
WCP	*Washington City Paper*
WD	Washingtoniana Division, Martin Luther King Memorial Library, Washington, D.C.
WEFP	Walter E. Fauntroy Papers, Special Collections, Gelman Library, George Washington University, Washington, D.C.
WI	*Washington Informer*
WOD	William Owner Diary, Library of Congress, Washington, D.C.
WP	*Washington Post*
WPTH	*Washington Post and Times Herald*
WS	*Washington Star*
WT	*Washington Times*
WTR	*Washington Tribune*

Introduction

1. Washington, *Testament of Hope*, 217–18.

2. Martin Luther King, "I Have a Dream," speech transcript accessible online: https://kinginstitute.stanford.edu/king-papers/documents/i-have-dream-address-delivered-march-washington-jobs-and-freedom.

3. USBC, "Historical Census Statistics on Population Totals by Race," table 23.

4. "Ike Gets Letter from Dr. Butcher," *AA*, 14 Mar. 1953.

Chapter 1

1. On Anacostia, see Cantwell, "Anacostia"; Hutchinson, *Anacostia Story*; and Wennersten, *Anacostia*.

2. Nacotchtank was the largest of the three Native American settlements within the ten-mile square that would become the District of Columbia. Humphrey and Chambers, *Ancient Washington*, 23; Gardner, "Native Americans," 3–19; Rice, *Nature and History*, 56–69; Merrell, "Cultural Continuity," 550–53.

3. Humphrey and Chambers, *Ancient Washington*, 5; Rice, *Nature and History*, 52–56; Wennersten, *Anacostia*, 6, 9–10.

4. Rice, *Nature and History*, 48, 52–56; Merrell, "Cultural Continuity," 549–50.

5. Rice, *Nature and History*, 71–73.

6. Gardner, "Native Americans," 6–7; Roundtree, *Pocahontas, Powhatan, Opechancanough*, 47–49; Kupperman, *Captain John Smith*, 1–12.

7. Smith, *True Relation*; Roundtree, *Pocahontas, Powhatan, Opechancanough*, 63–66.

8. Strachey quoted in Roundtree, *Pocahontas, Powhatan, Opechancanough*, 31, 47–49; Rice, *Nature and History*, 59–60.

9. Smith, *True Relation*.

10. Strachey quoted in Vaughan, "Expulsion of the Savages," 72; Fausz, "Merging and Emerging Worlds," 50; Roundtree, *Pocahontas, Powhatan, Opechancanough*, 76–83; Rice, *Nature and History*, 80–81, 86–99.

11. John Smith, "The Accidents That Hap'ned in the Discovery of the Bay of Chisapeack" (1608), Captain John Smith Four Hundred Project, http://www.johnsmith400.org/journalfirstvoyage.htm; Hutchinson, *Anacostia Story*, 3.

12. Roundtree, *Pocahontas, Powhatan, Opechancanough*, 107–10; Smith, "Accidents That Hap'ned"; Mooney, "Indian Tribes," 259–66.

13. Gardner, "Native Americans," 6–7; Roundtree, *Pocahontas, Powhatan, Opechancanough*, 47–49; Smith landed at Nacotchtank on 16 July 1608. Smith, "Accidents That Hap'ned"; Mooney, "Indian Tribes," 259–66.

14. Merrell, "Cultural Continuity," 553, n18; Fausz, "Merging and Emerging Worlds," 47–52; Rice, *Nature and History*, 71–73, 93.

15. Kupperman, *Captain John Smith*, 11; Fausz, "Merging and Emerging Worlds," 52.

16. Roundtree, *Pocahontas, Powhatan, Opechancanough*, 208–15.

17. Edward Waterhouse, "A DECLARATION of the State of the Colony and Affaires in VIRGINIA. With a Relation of the Barbarous Massacre in the Time of Peace and League, Treacherously Executed upon the English by the Infidels, 22 March Last . . . ," in Kingsbury, *Records of the Virginia Company of London*, 541–64.

18. Rice, *Nature and History*, 78–79, 90–91; Fausz, "Merging and Emerging Worlds," 54–55.

19. Roundtree, *Pocahontas, Powhatan, Opechancanough*, 153, 156–57.

20. Roundtree, *Pocahontas, Powhatan, Opechancanough*, 153, 156–57. Wyatt quoted in

Humphrey and Chambers, *Ancient Washington*, 25; Castle, "Washington Area," 1–2; Henry Fleet, "A Brief Journal of a Voyage Made in the Bark 'Warwick' to Virginia and Other Parts of the Continent of America," in Neill, *English Colonization*, 226–27, 237; Fausz, "Merging and Emerging Worlds," 57; Rice, *Nature and History*, 87–90.

21. Fleet quoted in Semmes, *Captains and Mariners*, 94–95, 542; Fleet, "Brief Journal," 227–35; Pendergast, *Massawomeck*, 14–18; Fausz, "Merging and Emerging Worlds," 60–66, 74; Neill, *English Colonization*, 240.

22. Aubrey C. Land, "Provincial Maryland," in Walsh and Fox, eds., *Maryland, a History*, 2–3; Merrell, "Cultural Continuity," 554–55.

23. Fausz, "Merging and Emerging Worlds," 74–88; Merrell, "Cultural Continuity," 556–67; Semmes, *Captains and Mariners*, 445–46.

24. Castle, "Gisborough as Land Grant," 282–92; *Proceedings and Acts of the General Assembly, April 1666–June 1676*, 2:25–26, http://msa.maryland.gov; Hutchinson, *Anacostia Story*, 7–8; Gardner, "Native Americans," 14.

25. Castle, "Washington Area," 1–18; Merrell, "Cultural Continuity," 567; Wennersten, *Anacostia*, 14, 18–19; Castle, "Gisborough as Land Grant," 282–92.

26. Castle, "Gisborough as Land Grant,," 282–92.

27. Andrews, *History of Maryland*, 197–98; Castle, "Washington Area," 7; quotations from *Proceedings of the Council of Maryland, 1693–1697*, 13:251–52, 20:68, http://msa.maryland.gov.

28. Merrell, "Cultural Continuity," 569; Castle, "Washington Area," 7–16.

29. Castle, "Washington Area," 9–12; Merrell, "Cultural Continuity," 568–59.

30. Merrell, "Cultural Continuity," 569–70; Hutchinson, *Anacostia Story*, 7–8; Gardner, "Native Americans," 14; Mooney, "Indian Tribes," 265.

31. Castle, "Washington Area," 15; Kulikoff, *Tobacco and Slaves*, 39–41.

32. Melder, *City of Magnificent Intentions*, 18–19; Lesko, Babb, and Gibbs, *Black Georgetown Remembered*, 1–2.

33. Kulikoff, *Tobacco and Slaves*, 39–41, 270–72; Land, "Provincial Maryland," in Walsh and Fox, *Maryland, a History*, 27–28; Castle, "Blue Plains and Bellevue," 24–25; Jordan, "Political Stability," 270; Castle, "Washington Area," 16.

34. Humphrey and Chambers, *Ancient Washington*, 23–24. Though the name Anacostia River would not be included in L'Enfant's 1792 "Plan for the City of Washington," Ellicott included it in a 1793 map of the "Territory of Columbia" at Jefferson's insistence. Hutchinson, *Anacostia Story*, xix.

Chapter 2

1. Patrice Gaines, "After Reversal of Decline, Banneker Park Rededicated," *WP*, 15 Nov. 1997; *AA*, 4 Dec. 1971.

2. Henning, "Mansion and Family of Notley Young," 1–6; O'Connor quoted in Arnebeck, *Fiery Trial*, 20; Philibert, *Saint Matthew's of Washington*, 11; Downing, *Catholic Founders*, 4.

3. USBC, "Statistics on Slaves," table 65, "Per Cent Distribution of Slaveholding Families According to Number of Slaves Held: 1790 and 1850": http://www2.census.gov /prod2/decennial/documents/00165897ch14.pdf; Downing, *Catholic Founders*, 4.

4. Sawvel, *Complete Anas of Jefferson*, 33–34; Chernow, *Alexander Hamilton*, 324–31.

5. Alexander Hamilton, "Report on the Public Credit," in Hamilton, *Writings*, 533. Thanks to Erich Martel for pointing out Hamilton's clever intentions.

6. Bowling, *Creation of Washington*, esp. ix–x.

7. Sawvel, *Complete Anas of Jefferson*, 32.

8. Bowling, *Creation of Washington*, 31–33.

9. Bowling, "From 'Federal Town' to 'National Capital,'" 8–25; Harris, "Washington's 'Federal City,' Jefferson's 'Federal Town,'" 49–53; Bowling, *Creation of Washington*, 3; Young, *Washington Community*, 17.

10. Bowling, *Creating the Federal City*, 23–32; Bordewich, *Washington*, 5, 15.

11. Berlin, *Many Thousands Gone*, 369–70; Thomas, *Slave Trade*, 270–72, 480.

12. Inter-University Consortium for Political and Social Research, "Census Data for Year 1790," http://mapserver.lib.virginia.edu/php/start.php?year=V1790.

13. Thomas, *Slave Trade*, 470–73; Inter-University Consortium for Political and Social Research, "Census Data for Year 1790"; Johnson, *Taxation No Tyranny*.

14. Quoted in Horton, "Alexander Hamilton," 19; Alexander Hamilton to John Jay, April 1779, in Hamilton, *Writings*, 56–57.

15. Ketcham, *James Madison*, 148; Horton, "Genesis of Washington's African American Community," 28; Thomas Jefferson, "Notes on the State of Virginia," in Jefferson, *Writings*, 288; Washington, "Letters of Washington Bearing on the Negro," 417; George Washington, "Reflection on Slavery," in Washington, *Writings*, 701–2.

16. Madison quoted in Ketcham, *James Madison*, 248.

17. Hunt and Scott, *Debates in the Federal Convention*, 257.

18. Newman, *Transformation of American Abolitionism*, 48–49; George Washington to David Stuart, 15 June 1790, in Twohig, Mastromarino, and Warren, *Papers of Washington*, 525; Bordewich, *Washington*, 39–40.

19. Gordon-Reed, *Hemingses of Monticello*, 26, 164–69, 489–92; Bordewich, *Washington*, 45–46.

20. Thomas Jefferson, "The Anas. 1791–1806," in Jefferson, *Writings*, 669.

21. Terrell, *Colored Woman in a White World*, 427.

22. Seale, *President's House*, 40–45; Bryan, *History of the National Capital*, 1:194–95.

23. NI, 27 Mar. 1832; Arnebeck, *Fiery Trial*, 138, 255; USBC, *Fifth Census*; Bushong, "Imagining James Hoban," 50; Warner, *At Peace with All Their Neighbors*, 131.

24. Washington to Mrs. S. Fairfax (Sarah Cary Fairfax), 16 May 1798, Washington to Arthur Young, 12 Dec. 1793, in Sparks, *Writings of Washington*, 11:233, 12:310; Weld, *Travels*, 69.

25. George Washington, "Proclamation Concerning the Location of the Permanent Seat of Government," in Sparks, *Writings of Washington*, 12:121–23; USBC, *Heads of Families at the First Census*, 10.

26. Arnebeck, *Fiery Trial*, 34–35.

27. Arnebeck, *Slave Labor*, 45.

28. Thomas Jefferson to Major Ellicott, 2 Feb. 1791, in Padover, *Jefferson and the National Capital*, 40.

29. Bedini, "Survey of the Federal Territory," 83.

30. "Boundary Stones of the District of Columbia," http://www.boundarystones.org; Bedini, "Survey of the Federal Territory," 84–86.

31. Ellicott's daughter quoted in Bedini, "Survey of the Federal Territory," 87; *Georgetown Weekly Ledger*, 12 Mar. 1791, quoted in Tindall, *Standard History*, 60.

32. Benjamin Banneker to Jefferson, 19 Aug. 1791, in Cullen, *Papers of Jefferson*, 49–54.

33. Jefferson to Banneker, 30 Aug. 1791, in Cullen, *Papers of Jefferson*, 97–98; Sinha, *Slave's Cause*, 144–45.

34. "Thomas Jefferson Expresses His Ideas about the Capital City" and "L'Enfant Dislikes Grid Plan for Federal City," in "Primary Sources: The Federal City": http://www.ourwhitehouse.org/primaryfedcity.html; Commissioners to Municipality of Bordeaux, 4 Jan. 1793, RDCC, 1791–1867.

35. Young, *Washington Community*, 19.

36. Commissioners to Jefferson, 11 Apr. 1792, RDCC, 1791–1867; Jefferson to Commissioners, 6 Mar. 1792, Commissioners to Jefferson, 2 June 1792, in Padover, *Jefferson and the National Capital*, 106, 142.

37. Brandenburg and Brandenburg, "La Rochefoucauld-Liancourt's Visit," 59.

38. Commissioners to Jefferson, 5 Jan. 1793, in Padover, *Jefferson and the National Capital*, 165–66.

39. Commissioners quoted in Baker, "Erection of the White House," 131–32.

40. Arnebeck, *Slave Labor*, 49; Arnebeck, *Fiery Trial*, 205, 229; Bordewich, *Washington*, 190; Snethen, *Black Code*, 49.

41. Surveyor quoted in Arnebeck, *Slave Labor*, 24; Williams quoted in Arnebeck, *Fiery Trial*, 149.

42. Niemcewicz, *Under Their Vine and Fig Tree*, 93.

43. Arnebeck, *Fiery Trial*, 302.

44. Brown, *Incidental Architect*, 21–22.

45. Bell, "'Negroes Alone Work,'" esp. chap. 2.

46. La Rochefoucauld-Liancourt, *Travels through the United States of America*, 610; Brown, *Free Negroes*, 44; Arnebeck, *Slave Labor*, 29.

47. Horton, "Genesis of Washington's African American Community," 24; advertisement quoted in Arnebeck, *Fiery Trial*, 283.

48. McAleer, "'Green Streets,'" 49; Arnebeck, *Fiery Trial*, 456.

49. Smith quoted in Teute, "'Wild, Desolate Place,'" 48; Janson, *Stranger in America*, 209.

50. James Madison, "Federalist No. 43," in Rossiter, *Federalist Papers*, 272–73. Whit Cobb argues that most national leaders believed that the District was set up as an "implicit compact" in which residents would give up their political rights in return for the "political and economic benefits of proximity to the seat of government." See Cobb, "Democracy in Search of Utopia," 533–34. This view, however, ignores local residents' vehement objection to the loss of political rights.

51. diGiacomantonio, "'To Sell Their Birthright,'" 30–48.

52. Ibid. 42.

53. Moore, "Augustus Brevoort Woodward," 114–15.

54. NI, 29 Dec. 1800.

55. Bayard quoted in Richards, "Debates over Retrocession," 58.

56. Clark, "Mayoralty of Robert Brent," 268; Woodward quoted in diGiacomantonio, "'To Sell Their Birthright,'" 37; Newman and DePuy, "Bringing Democracy," 42.

57. Oliver Wolcott to Mrs. Wolcott, 4 July 1800, in Gibbs, *Memoirs*, 377–78.

58. Young, *Washington Community*, 25–26; Hunt, *First Forty Years*, 11.

59. Warden, *Chorographical and Statistical Description*, 27.

60. McAleer, "'Green Streets,'" 44–45; Clephane, "Local Aspect of Slavery," 232; Adams quoted in Withey, *Dearest Friend*, 277.

61. Corrigan, "Making the Most of an Opportunity," 95.

62. Warden, *Chorographical and Statistical Description*, 47; Callcott, *Mistress of Riversdale*, 10.

63. Horton, "Genesis of Washington's African American Community," 23–25.

64. Ball, *Slavery*, 13, 27–28.

65. Ball, *Slavery*, 13, 27–28.

66. Callcott, *Mistress of Riversdale*, 85; Corrigan, "Whether They Be Ours or No," 170, 180; Ball, *Slavery*, 28.

67. Ball, *Slavery*, 27–29, 36–37.

68. NI, 22 Dec. 1800; Brown, *Free Negroes*, 65.

69. NI, 19 Oct. 1801, 12 Jan. 1810.

70. Vandervelde, *Redemption Songs*, 195–96.

71. Documents concerning the Queen case, including Mina Queen's Petition for Freedom and the "Defendant's Bill of Exceptions" indicating Simon Queen's testimony, may be found on the extraordinary "O Say Can You See: Early Washington, D.C., Law & Family" website produced by the Center for Digital Research in the Humanities at the University of Nebraska, Lincoln, http://earlywashingtondc.org/cases/oscys.caseid.0011; William G. Thomas III, "The Timing of *Queen v. Hepburn*: An Exploration of African American Networks in the Early Republic," http://earlywashingtondc.org/stories/queen_v _hepburn.

72. Mima Queen v. Hepburn, 11 U.S. (7 Cranch) 290 (1813); Newmyer, *John Marshall*, 426–29; though the courts spelled the plaintiff's name as "Mima," attorney Key and Queen family naming traditions use the spelling "Mina." See "Mima Queen and Louisa Queen v. John Hepburn," http://earlywashingtondc.org/cases/oscys.caseid.0011. See also Thomas, "'They Brought Me Away.'"

73. Tanner portrait, Box 20-1, Folder 1, CFP.

74. Department of Education, *Special Report*, 195–97; John G. Sharp, "George Bell" and "Sophia Browning Bell," in Washington D.C. Genealogy Trails, http://genealogytrails .com/washdc/biographies/bio4.html#George_Bell; Smith, *Notable Black Women*, 624–25.

75. Provine, *District of Columbia Free Negro Registers*, 154; Department of Education, *Special Report*, 197–98; John G. Sharp, "Alethia 'Lethe' Browning Tanner," in Washington D.C. Genealogy Trails, http://genealogytrails.com/washdc/biographies/bio6.html.

76. USBC, "Historical Census Statistics on Population Totals by Race," table 23.

77. Department of Education, *Special Report*, 195–205; Ingle, *Negro in the District of Columbia*, 22–23, 199, 205; Russell, *Operation of the Underground Railroad*, part 4, 11; Corrigan, "Ties That Bind," 77; Horton, "Genesis of Washington's African American Community," 35–36.

78. *Acts of the Corporation of Washington*, 29–35; Alfers, *Law and Order*, 6.

79. Hunt, *First Forty Years*, 89–90.

Chapter 3

1. This quotation and much of the ensuing description come from Andrews, *Slavery and the Domestic Slave-Trade*, 135–38; and Abdy, *Journal*, 179–80. See also Bancroft, *Slave-Trading*, 60–63.

2. Featherstonhaugh, *Excursion*, 38; Deyle, "Rethinking the Slave Trade," 107–9.

3. Abdy, *Journal*, 179; Andrews, *Slavery and the Domestic Slave-Trade*, 135–38.

4. Andrews, *Slavery and the Domestic Slave-Trade*, 117; Tadman, *Speculators and Slaves*, 6, 12; Goldfield, "Antebellum Washington in Context," 9–10; Sturge, *Visit to the United States*, 74; Harrold, *Subversives*, 6.

5. Andrews, *Slavery and the Domestic Slave-Trade*, 148–49; Abdy, *Journal*, 179–80; Sturge, *Visit to the United States*, 74; Crothers, "1846 Retrocession," 159; Harrold, *Subversives*, 30.

6. J. B. C., A Mississippian, "Slavery and the Slave Trade in the District of Columbia," *American Whig Review*, 1 Apr. 1850, 339.

7. *Globe*, 11 Jan. 1836; Garrison and Garrison, *William Lloyd Garrison*, 199.

8. Torrey, *Portraiture of Domestic Slavery*, 42–44; Jesse Torrey to John Randolph, 29 Apr. 1816, RSCI, RG 233, HR 14A-C.17.4.

9. George Gleig, "Recollections of the Expedition to the Chesapeake, and against New Orleans, in the Years 1814–1915," *United Service Journal* (May 1840): 27–28; "Proclamation of Vice Admiral Sir Alexander F. I. Cochrane, R.N.," 2 Apr. 1814, https://maryland1812 .wordpress.com/2011/05/01/a-corps-of-colonial-marines-april-1814/; Kimmel, "Battle of North Point," 7; Taylor, "American Blacks in the War of 1812," 197–98; Blackburn, *Overthrow of Colonial Slavery*, 288; Lindsay, "Diplomatic Relations," 410. All twenty-first-century price and labor values are calculated using the purchasing power calculators found at http://www.measuringworth.com.

10. Mary Bayard Smith to Mrs. Kirkpatrick, Aug. 1814, in Hunt, *First Forty Years*, 111.

11. Teute, "'Wild, Desolate Place,'" 76–78; deposition of Francis Scott Key, RSCI, RG 233, HR 14A-C.17.4.

12. Torrey to Randolph, RSCI, RG 233, HR 14A-C.17.4.

13. Deposition of Francis Scott Key, RSCI, RG 233, HR 14A-C.17.4. Two decades later, a Georgetown slave named Dorcas Allen killed two of her children and maimed her other two rather than let them be sold south by a notorious slave trader. Allen was found not guilty reason of insanity and, with the help of former president John Quincy Adams, gained her freedom. Her remarkable story is told in Mann, "'Horrible Barbarity.'"

14. 14 Annals of Cong. 93–95 (1805); Tremain, *Slavery in the District of Columbia*, 58–59.

15. Torrey, *Portraiture of Domestic Slavery*, 33–34.

16. Torrey, *Portraiture of Domestic Slavery*, 34–35.

17. "Famous Duels: Henry Clay and John Randolph," *NYT*, 4 Aug. 1856; Thomas, "'They Brought Me Away'"; Crawford, "John Randolph of Roanoke."

18. 29 Annals of Cong. 1115–18 (1816); Fearon, *Sketches of America*, 288; Ames and Lundy, *Legion of Liberty*, 23; *Genius of Universal Emancipation* 10, no. 1 (January 1831).

19. Torrey, *Portraiture of Domestic Slavery*, 45; deposition of Judge William Cranch, 7 Mar. 1816, RSCI, RG 233, HR 14A-C.17.4; on Cranch, see Kramer, "Half a Century Past Midnight."

20. Key married a member of the slaveholding gentry—Mary Tayloe Lloyd's wealthy

father owned dozens of slaves, including Frederick Douglass at one point. Fischer, *Liberty and Freedom*, 167–68; Morley, *Snow-Storm in August*, 52–53; on Key's reputation, see, e.g., *African Repository* 47 (1871): 149; on his sense of Christian duty, see Fox, "American Colonization Society," 18–19; deposition of Francis Scott Key, RSCI, RG 233, HR 14A-C.17.4.

21. Key quoted in Fox, "American Colonization Society," 18; Leepson, *What So Proudly We Hailed*, 192; Thomas, "'They Brought Me Away.'"

22. Key quoted in Fox, "American Colonization Society," 18; NI, 24 Dec. 1816.

23. NI, 24 Dec. 1816.

24. Sherwood, "Formation of the American Colonization Society," 211–12.

25. Gurley, "A Discourse, Delivered on the Fourth of July, 1825, in the City of Washington," 12–17, KRL-HSW; Clay quoted in NI, 24 Dec. 1816; Sherwood, "Formation of the American Colonization Society," 209–28; Walton-Hanley, "Reversing the Middle Passage," 19–66.

26. NI, 17, 24 Dec. 1816; Costanzos, "Federal Town, Local City," 215; Seaton, *William Winston Seaton*, 264.

27. NI, 24 Dec. 1816.

28. USBC, *Historical Statistics of the United States, 1789–1945*, Ser. B, 13-23: "Population, Decennial Summary—Sex, Urban-Rural Residence, and Race: 1790–1940," 25.

29. NI, 14 Oct. 1817; "Resolution of the Colored Citizens of Washington re Liberia Colony," Box 20-1, Folder 40, CFP.

30. Powers-Greene, *Against Wind and Tide*, xviii; Ripley, *Black Abolitionist Papers*, 2:380.

31. Brown, *Free Negroes in the District of Columbia*, 141; "First Annual Report of the American Society for Colonizing the Free People of Color of the United States," in William Thornton Papers, LC; Smallwood, *Narrative*, 14–16; Abdy, *Journal*, 89.

32. Walton-Hanley, "Reversing the Middle Passage."

33. Levey, "Segregation in Education," 26–27; Corrigan, "Social Union of Heart and Effort"; Curry, *Free Black in Urban America*, 159; Krislov, *Negro in Federal Employment*, 9–10; newspaper quoted in Pacheco, *Pearl*, 16.

34. USBC, "Historical Census Statistics on Population Totals by Race," table 23; Curry, *Free Black in Urban America*, 251; Brown, *Free Negroes in the District of Columbia*, 65.

35. Brown, *Free Negroes in the District of Columbia*, 130–38.

36. *Southern Patriot*, 25 Aug. 1835; Morley, *Snow-Storm in August*, 3–35; Carol Gelderman, *Free Man of Color*, 6–11; Provine, "Economic Position of the Free Blacks," 68.

37. Corrigan, "Ties That Bind," 75; Jones, "Their Chains Shall Fall Off," 21–22; Greene, "Mount Zion, Washington's Oldest Black Church, Turns 200," 65; Williams, "Blueprint for Change," 366.

38. Department of Education, *Special Report*, 195–97; Russell, *Operation of the Underground Railroad*, part 4; Fitzpatrick and Goodwin, *Guide to Black Washington*, 201–2; Corrigan, "Making the Most of an Opportunity," 96; Corrigan, "Whether They Be Ours or No," 173. On black Catholicism in D.C., see: MacGregor, *The Emergence of a Black Catholic Community*.

39. NI, 29 Aug. 1818, quoted in Department of Education, *Special Report*, 197–98; Williams, *History of the Negro Race*, 193–94; Green, *Secret City*, 23.

40. This and the following two paragraphs are based on Sharp, *Diary of Michael Shiner*; John Sharp, "Michael Shiner," in Washington Genealogy Trails, http://genealogytrails

.com/washdc/michaelshiner/shiner.html; and Naval History and Heritage Command, "Introduction to the Diary of Michael Shiner Relating to the History of the Washington Navy Yard 1813–1869," https://www.history.navy.mil/research/library/online-reading-room/title-list-alphabetically/d/diary-of-michael-shiner/introduction.html.

41. Kerr, *Paper Bag Principle*, 39–40.

42. Royall, *Mrs. Royall's Pennsylvania*, 267; Royall, *Black Book*, 182–84; NI, 24 Nov. 1824.

43. Department of Education, *Special Report*, 312.

44. Burch, *Digest of the Laws*, 127–33.

45. Department of Education, *Special Report*, 203–4; Wiencek, *Imperfect God*, 282–90.

46. Department of Education, *Special Report*, 203–4; Provine, *District of Columbia Free Negro Registers*, 52.

47. Costin v. Corporation of Washington, 2 Cranch C. C. 254, Fed. Cas. No. 3,266.

48. *Costin v. Corporation of Washington*.

49. Schultz, *Mrs. Mattingly's Miracle*, 69–71; Clark, "Mayors of the Corporation of Washington," 61–98.

50. Clark, "Mayors of the Corporation of Washington," 91; Hickey, "Irish Catholics in Washington," 41–42.

51. MacGregor, *Parish for the Federal City*, 29; Dolan, *Irish Americans*, 16–17; Grassi, "Catholic Religion in the United States," 109.

52. Altenhofel, "Keeping House," 36–58; Ignatiev, *How the Irish Became White*, 38; Warner, *At Peace with All Their Neighbors*, 95.

53. Green, *Washington: Village and Capital*, 88–89.

54. "To the Voters of the City of Washington" (Washington, D.C., 1822), Printed Ephemera Collection, Portfolio 191, Folder 19, LC; "Doubts Having Been Entertained with Regard to the Truth of Some Rumors" (Washington, D.C., 1822), Printed Ephemera Collection, Portfolio 191, Folder 18, LC; U.S. v. Carbery, 2 Cranch 356–61;, 358–61; *Alexandria Herald*, 12 June 1822; NI, 15 June 1822.

55. NI, 24 June 1825; *United States' Telegraph*, 2 June 1826.

56. NI, 10 Jan. 1820; Crothers, "1846 Retrocession," 141–42; Goode, *Capital Losses*, 290–92.

57. Crothers, "1846 Retrocession," 146–48.

58. *National Journal*, 12 May 1824; NI, 20 Nov. 1818, 17 Mar. 1824; *National Messenger* (Georgetown), 12 Jan. 1820; Crothers, "1846 Retrocession," 149.

59. NI, 12 Apr. 1822.

60. Gatewood, *Aristocrats of Color*, 38–39; Provine, *District of Columbia Free Negro Registers*, 154.

61. Department of Education, *Special Report*, 200–201; Box 20-1, Folder 8, CFP; Morley, *Snow-Storm in August*, 24–25.

62. Harrold, *Subversives*, 14–15.

63. Walker, *Walker's Appeal*, 64; Hinks, *To Awaken My Afflicted Brethren*, 85; Sinha, *Slave's Cause*, 195–204; Hodges, *David Ruggles*, 3–4.

64. United States v. Prout, 4 Cranch C. C. 301, Fed. Cas. No. 16,094; *Freedom's Journal*, 30 Mar. 1827; Russell, *Operation of the Underground Railroad*, part 4, iv; Box 20-1, Folder 8, CFP.

65. Russell, *Operation of the Underground Railroad*, part 2, 21; "Free Negroes—District of

Columbia," Committee of the District of Columbia, H.R., 19th Cong., 2nd Sess., Rep. no. 48, 1–2.

66. Jay, *Miscellaneous Writings on Slavery*, 241; Blassingame, *Slave Testimony*, 341, 396; Corrigan, "Imaginary Cruelties?," 12.

67. "Free Negroes—District of Columbia," 1; Tremain, *Slavery in the District of Columbia*, 49.

68. Auslander, "Enslaved Labor and Building the Smithsonian."

69. Northup, *Twelve Years a Slave*, 21–22.

70. Abdy, *Journal*, 96–97; Bancroft, *Slave-Trading in the Old South*, 54; Fiske, Brown, and Seligman, *Solomon Northup*, 51–53.

71. Davis, "Civil War Recollections," 59; Fitzpatrick and Goodwin, *Guide to Black Washington*, 40; Holland, *Black Men Built the Capitol*, 28–29; Winkle, *Lincoln's Citadel*, 15–17.

72. Laprade, "Domestic Slave Trade in the District of Columbia," 17–34; Brown, *Free Negroes in the District of Columbia*, 13; USBC, "Historical Census Statistics on Population Totals by Race," table 23.

73. Finkelman, "Slavery in the Shadow of Liberty," 3–15; Lusane, *Black History of the White House*, esp. chaps. 1–4; Davis, "Impact of British Abolitionism," 20.

74. See, e.g., NI, 13 June, 7 Aug., or 12 Aug. 1835; Snethen, *Black Code*, 43; Tremain, *Slavery in the District of Columbia*, 51; Lewis, *Washington*, 101; Curran, *Bicentennial History of Georgetown University*, 120. For more on slavery at Georgetown, see http://slavery.george town.edu/.

75. *Freedom's Journal*, 1 Feb. 1828.

76. Andrews, *Slavery and the Domestic Slave-Trade*, 124.

77. Only Baltimore could claim a similarly active antislavery community. See Harrold, *Subversives*, chap. 1; *Freedom's Journal*, 6 Apr. 1827; and Hall, *Travels*, 3:42–43, 47.

78. Corrigan, "Imaginary Cruelties?," 4–27; Hamilton, *Men and Manners in America*, 142.

79. Quoted in Jay, *Miscellaneous Writings*, 240–41.

80. *Freedom's Journal*, 9 May 1828; MacGregor, *Parish for the Federal City*, 99; "Memorial of Inhabitants of the District of Columbia Praying for the Gradual Abolition of Slavery in the District of Columbia," 24 Mar. 1828, 20th Cong., 1st Sess., Doc. 215, in Pohl and Wennersten, *Abraham Lincoln and the End of Slavery*, 10.

81. Janney, *Memoirs*, 32–33; Ricks, *Escape on the Pearl*, 64.

82. Mayer, *All on Fire*, 100–101; *Genius of Universal Emancipation*, Vol. 1, 3rd Ser., 97; Lundy, *Life*, 30.

83. "A Voice from Washington," 4 May 1831, in Garrison, *Thoughts on African Colonization*, 22–23; Harrold, *Subversives*, 34; *Genius of Universal Emancipation*, Vol. I, 3rd Ser., 194–95.

84. Davis, "Impact of British Abolitionism," 31; Russell, *Operation of the Underground Railroad in Washington, D.C.*, part 2, 23; Department of Education, *Special Report*, 200, 270.

85. Miller, *Arguing About Slavery*, esp. Chapters 3, 5, 16, and 17.

86. *Genius of Universal Emancipation*, Vol I, Third Series, 114.

87. Cole, "Changes for Mrs. Thornton's Arthur," 367–79.

88. This description comes from: NI, beginning 7 Aug. 1835; *Niles Weekly Register*, 26 Dec. 1835, 281. An in-depth though imagined and at times fictionalized look at this incident can be found in Morley, *Snow-Storm in Aug.*, 171–204.

89. NI, 7 Aug. 1835; *Diary of Michael Shiner*, 61–62.

90. *Diary of Michael Shiner*, 61–62.

91. NI, 5, 7, 10 Aug. 1835; Kramer, "Trial of Reuben Crandall," 125; NI, 10 Aug. 1835.

92. NI, 28 Apr. 1836; Crandall, *Trial of Crandall*, 3.

93. Crandall, *Trial of Crandall*, 34.

94. *Southern Patriot*, 25 Aug. 1835; for more on Snow's background, see: Morley, *Snow-Storm in August*, 3–35; *Globe*, 11 Oct. 1833; Kramer, "Trial of Reuben Crandall," 124; William T. Steiger to Andrew Shriver, 13 Aug. 1835, in Hoyt, "Washington's Living History," 61–62.

95. Box 20-1, Folder 1, CFP; Steiger to Shriver, 13 Aug. 1835, 62; Department of Education, *Special Report*, 212.

96. MacGregor, *Parish for the Federal City*, 94; Dilts, *Great Road*, 133; Andrews, *Slavery and the Domestic Slave-Trade*, 94; Bryan, *History of the National Capital*, 2:239; Provine, "Economic Position of the Free Blacks," 62.

97. Hickey, "Irish Catholics," 61; Grimsted, "Rioting in Its Jacksonian Setting," 361–62; Steiger to Shriver, 11 Aug. 1835, in Hoyt, "Washington's Living History," 61; Department of Education, *Special Report*, 65.

98. *United States' Telegraph*, 29 Aug. 1835.

99. Ignatiev, *How the Irish Became White*, 96; Grimsted, "Rioting in Its Jacksonian Setting," 361–62, 386.

100. *Washingtonian*, 5 Aug. 1836; *Washingtonian & Farmers, Mechanics, and Merchants Gazette*, 10 Dec. 1836.

101. Kramer, "Trial of Reuben Crandall," 127–28.

102. Morley, *Snow-Storm in August*, 179–92, 224–34; *Washingtonian*, 25 July 1836.

103. "Mr. Key on the Colonization Society: Note A," *African Repository and Colonial Journal* 12, no. 11 (November 1836): 1.

104. "Mr. Key on the Colonization Society," 7.

105. *Emancipator*, 8 Mar. 1838, 175.

106. *Washingtonian*, 14, 23 Sept. 1836; NI, 15 Sept. 1835; Snethen, *Black Code*, 39–45; Russell, *Operation of the Underground Railroad*, part 2, 21.

107. "The Pinckney Resolutions," Cong. Globe, 25, 26 May 1836, in Pohl and Wennersten, *Abraham Lincoln and the End of Slavery*, 15.

108. *Washingtonian*, 6 June 1836.

109. Cary's name was misspelled in court documents.

110. Carey v. Washington, 5 Cranch C.C. 13; Provine, "Economic Position of the Free Blacks," 66.

Chapter 4

1. National Building Museum, "Our Historic Building," http://www.nbm.org/about -us/about-the-museum/our-historic-building.html; "National Building Museum Facts": http://www.nbm.org/about-us/about-the-museum/nbm-quick-facts.html.

2. The blue color had been ordered by Architect of the Capitol Thomas U. Walter to give the facade the appearance of blue granite. Historic American Buildings Survey, "Judiciary Square (Reservation No. 7)," HABS No. DC-690 (Washington, D.C.: National

Park Service, n.d.), 5; Goode, *Capital Losses*, 304; Milburn, "Fourth Ward," 61; Wright, *Language of the Civil War*, 35; Pasonneau, *Washington through Two Centuries*, 70–73.

3. Much of the western end of what we now call the Mall, including the site of the Lincoln Memorial, had been part of the Tiber's mouth. Department of Interior, *Washington, D.C.'s Vanishing Springs and Waterways*, 6–9; Ames, *Ten Years in Washington*, 68.

4. Melder, *City of Magnificent Intentions*, 93–95.

5. USBC, Table 1: Rank by Population of the 100 Largest Urban Places, Listed Alphabetically by State: 1790–1990, http://www.census.gov/population/www/documentation/twps0027/tab01.txt; Table 5: Population of the 61 Urban Places: 1820, http://www.census.gov/population/www/documentation/twps0027/tab05.txt; Table 8: Population of 100 Largest Urban Places: 1850, http://www.census.gov/population/www/documentation/twps0027/tab08.txt.

6. Dickens, *American Notes*, 135; Weld, *Vacation Tour*, 258.

7. Dickens, *American Notes*, 269–70.

8. Jay, *Miscellaneous Writings*, 240–42.

9. William Sawyer, *Speech of Hon. William Sawyer of Ohio, on the Slave Trade in the District of Columbia, Delivered . . . January 10, 1849* (Washington, D.C.: Congressional Globe Office, 1849), 3.

10. Much of the preceding and following paragraphs derives from Smallwood, *Narrative*, and Lovejoy, *Memoir of Torrey*, esp. 90–99. See also Harrold, *Subversives*, 78–85.

11. Russell, "Underground Railroad Activists in Washington, D.C.," 29; Sinha, *Slave's Cause*, 396; Giddings quoted in Winkle, *Lincoln's Citadel*, 24.

12. Woodson, *History of the Negro Church*, 180–81; Simmons, *Men of Mark*, 662–65; Sinha, *Slave's Cause*, 396; Blackett, *Making Freedom*, 1–2.

13. *Provincial Freeman*, 18 June 1859; "Proceedings of the North American Convention Convened at St. Lawrence Hall, Toronto, Canada West 11–13 Sept. 1851," *Voice of the Fugitive*, 24 Sept. 1851.

14. Russell, *Operation of the Underground Railroad*, Intro., 3, part 4, ii; Fitzpatrick and Goodwin, *Guide to Black Washington*, 201–2.

15. Slave owner quoted in Harrold, *Subversives*, 52; Cong. Globe, 28th Cong., 1st Sess., 78 (1843).

16. Winkle, *Lincoln's Citadel*, 21–24.

17. Letter writer quoted in Crothers, "1846 Retrocession," 155. Crothers differs significantly with Mark David Richards, who concludes that slavery played a minimal role in the retrocession debates. Richards, "Debates over Retrocession."

18. Retrocession advocate quoted in Crothers, "1846 Retrocession," 156.

19. This political divide eventually led to the creation of West Virginia as its own state in 1863.

20. Hepburn quoted in Richards, "Debates over Retrocession," 71–72.

21. *Friends' Review*, 14 Oct. 1848; Stowe, *Key to Uncle Tom's Cabin*, 310–11.

22. Edmonson's mother was enslaved. For more on Jennings, see Jennings, *Colored Man's Reminiscences*; for more on the Edmonsons, see Ricks, *Escape on the Pearl*, esp. 9–10.

23. Stowe, *Key to Uncle Tom's Cabin*, 310–11; Harrold, "Pearl Affair," 140–41; Ricks, *Escape on the Pearl*, 25–27; Pacheco, *Pearl*, 113–15.

24. Letter from S. G. Howe reprinted in *North Star*, 28 Sept. 1848; Russell, "Under-

ground Railroad Activists," 34–35; Stowe, *Key to Uncle Tom's Cabin*, 312; *New York Herald*, 20 Apr. 1848.

25. *National Era*, 7 Jan. 1847. Bailey later made his case in NI, 20 Apr. 1848; Harrold, "Gamaliel Bailey"; for more on the riots, see Harrold, "Pearl Affair," esp. 146–58.

26. *Friends' Review*, 14 Oct. 1848; *Christian Advocate and Journal*, 22 Nov. 1848; Russell, *Operation of the Underground Railroad*, part 3, 22–23; Stowe, *Key to Uncle Tom's Cabin*, 418–19.

27. Chaplin quoted in Harrold, *Subversives*, 144–45, 148; Rohrs, "Antislavery Politics"; *North Star*, 26 May 1848.

28. *North Star*, 5 May 1848; Giddings, *Speeches in Congress*, 451; Winkle, *Lincoln's Citadel*, 48–49.

29. Winkle, *Lincoln's Citadel*, 57–58; Burlingame, *Abraham Lincoln*, 289–90; Miller, *Life and Works of Lincoln*, 26–27.

30. Abraham Lincoln, "A Bill for Abolishing Slavery in the District of Columbia," draft, January 1849, Abraham Lincoln Papers, LC; Medford, "'Some Satisfactory Way,'" 5–22; Pohl, "Abraham Lincoln on Capitol Hill"; Winkle, *Lincoln's Citadel*, 48–57.

31. Jay, *Miscellaneous Writings*, 624.

32. Olmsted, *Journey*, 16; Harrold, *Subversives*, 163–66; Harrison, *Washington during Civil War and Reconstruction*, 7.

33. ES, 5 June 1861; YMCA of Metropolitan Washington, "Honoring 150 Years of Service," 2003 Annual Report, 5, WD; Fitzpatrick and Goodwin, *Guide to Black Washington*, 45.

34. Still, *Underground Railroad*, 180–85; Russell, *Operation of the Underground Railroad*, part 3, 18–21.

35. Harrold, *Subversives*, 146–47; Pacheco, *Pearl*, 220–21. Chaplin's and Allen's arrest and capture are memorialized in a historical marker in Jesup Blair Park in Silver Spring.

36. Corrigan, "'It's a Family Affair," 163–91.

37. Harrold, *Subversives*, 203–24; Wormley, "Myrtilla Miner," 452; O'Connor, *Myrtilla Miner*, 17.

38. Null, "Myrtilla Miner's 'School for Colored Girls,'" 259; O'Connor, *Myrtilla Miner*, 56.

39. For a hagiographic account of Lenox, see Clark, "Walter Lenox," 167–93.

40. Clark, "Colonel William Winston Seaton," 13–14.

41. Harrold, *Subversives*, 5–6.

42. UCSB, "Historical Census Statistics on Population Totals by Race," table 23; Addison quoted in Corrigan, "Social Union of Heart and Effort," 68.

43. *Appendix to the Congressional Globe for the First Session, Thirty-First Congress*, vol. 22, part 2 (Washington, D.C.: John C. Rives, 1850), 1,669; NI, 28 Oct. 1850.

44. Green, *Secret City*, 47–48.

45. Corrigan, "Social Union of Heart and Effort," 68; Green, *Secret City*, 48; Olmsted, *Journey*, 16–17.

46. UCSB, "Historical Census Statistics on Population Totals by Race," table 23.

47. NI, 6 May 1857; O'Connor, *Myrtilla Miner*, 65–66.

48. Warner, *At Peace with All Their Neighbors*, 208.

49. Altenhofel, "Washington, D.C., to 1900," 944; Corrigan, "Social Union of Heart and Effort," 70–71; Olmsted, *Journey*, 15–16; Berlin and Gutman, "Natives and Immigrants," 1176.

50. Denis A. Lane, "Story of the Passing of Historic Swampoodle," WP, 1 Jan. 1922.

51. Bonacich, "Abolition," 601.

52. "The Petition of Citizens of Washington City Remonstrating against the Employment of Negroes in the Public Services as Messengers, Laborers &c.," 10 Mar. 1852, RG 233, HR 32A-G5.6, NARA.

53. Winkle, *Lincoln's Citadel*, 137; Corrigan, "Social Union of Heart and Effort," 80; Douglass, *Life and Times*, 366–67.

54. Winkle, *Lincoln's Citadel*, 137–38; Olmsted, *Journey*, 4.

55. Warden, *Chorographical and Statistical Description*, 45; Gordon, "Recollections"; Olmsted, *A Journey in the Seaboard Slave States*, 11.

56. Gordon, "Recollections of a Boyhood in Georgetown," 121–40; Olmsted, *Journey*, 12.

57. MacGregor, *Parish for the Federal City*, 121.

58. NI, 3 June 1854; ES, 3 June 1856; Warner, *At Peace with All Their Neighbors*, 216; MacGregor, *Parish for the Federal City*, 118–19; Winkle, *Lincoln's Citadel*, 79–80.

59. MacGregor, *Parish for the Federal City*, 122.

60. NI, 29 May 1854.

61. *New York Daily Times*, 14 June 1855.

62. ES, 4 June 1856.

63. In 1807, President Jefferson had used the military against American citizens to enforce an embargo. Grimsted, *American Mobbing*, 241–42; NI, 2, 3 June 1857; Berret, "Address," 206–10; NI, 2 June 1867; Warner, *At Peace with All Their Neighbors*, 225–26.

64. *Weekly Anglo-African*, 10 Dec. 1859; Leech, *Reveille in Washington*, 18–19; Winkle, *Lincoln's Citadel*, 78–80; Gouvernor, *As I Remember*, 312.

65. USBC, *Population of the United States in 1860*, 589; Leech, *Reveille in Washington*, 15; Whyte, "Divided Loyalties," 104; owner quotation: WOD, cover page, vol. 8; Ellis, *Sights and Secrets*, 49; Poore, *Perley's Reminiscences*, 72.

66. Lomax, *Leaves from an Old Washington Diary*, 132.

67. ES, 16 Apr. 1861; George William Bagby, "Washington City," *Atlantic Monthly* 7 (January 1861): 8; Scott quoted in Lockwood and Lockwood, *Siege of Washington*, 27.

68. Laas, *Wartime Washington*, 1–6.

69. Montgomery Blair to Committee of Instruction, ES, 19 Mar. 1862; Elizabeth Blair Lee to Phillips Lee, 15 Dec. 1861, in Laas, *Wartime Washington*, 5, 91; MacGregor, *Parish for the Federal City*, 150; Gleeson, *Irish in the South*, 190.

70. Winkle, *Lincoln's Citadel*, 65.

71. Lomax, *Leaves from an Old Washington Diary*, 141; Whyte, "Divided Loyalties," 107–17; Harrison, *Washington during the Civil War and Reconstruction*, 23; Leech, *Reveille in Washington*, 18–19; Clark, "Richard Wallach," 209–10; Winkle, *Lincoln's Citadel*, 84–89.

72. Lincoln quoted in Lockwood and Lockwood, *Siege of Washington*, 27.

73. Bergman, "Negro Who Rode with Fremont," 31–32; ES, 15 Apr. 1856; George Reasons and Sam Patrick, "Jacob Dodson Helped Open the West," ES, 4 Jan. 1969; Jacob Dodson to Hon. Simon Cameron, 23 Apr. 1861, Cameron to Dodson, 29 Apr. 1861, in War Department, *War of the Rebellion*, 107, 133.

74. For a day-by-day account of the siege of Washington, see Lockwood and Lockwood, *Siege of Washington*.

75. Brooks, *Washington in Lincoln's Time*, 2–3; "Washington as a Camp," *Atlantic Monthly*

8, no. 45 (July 1861): 105–10; Adams and Leasher, *Letter from Washington, 1863–1865*, 33; Harrison, *Washington during the Civil War and Reconstruction*, 26.

76. Harrold, *Subversives*, 228–30; Bowen quoted in Masur, *Example for All the Land*, 23.

77. Whyte, "Divided Loyalties," 117; NR quoted in Harrold, *Subversives*, 228.

78. Keckly's name is often spelled "Keckley," including in her own 1868 book, *Behind the Scenes: Life of a Colored Woman Thirty Years a Slave, Four Years at the White House*. But Jennifer Fleischner has shown that Keckly herself spelled it without the second "e." Fleischner, *Mrs. Lincoln and Mrs. Keckly*.

79. The preceding paragraph was based on Keckly's *Behind the Scenes* and Fleischner, *Mrs. Lincoln and Mrs. Keckly*, 3 (quotation), 28–44, 65–88, 118–48.

80. Winkle, *Lincoln's Citadel*, 327; Fleischner, *Mrs. Lincoln and Mrs. Keckly*, 222–23; "Great Influx of Contrabands," NR, 12 Mar. 1862.

81. Terry, "Brief Moment in the Sun," 74.

82. "The Contrabands at Fortress Monroe," *Atlantic Monthly* 8, no. 49 (November 1861): 626–41; Masur, "Rare Phenomenon of 'Philological Vegetation,'" 1050–84.

83. Calvert quoted in Harrison, *Washington during the Civil War and Reconstruction*, 30–31.

84. Elizabeth Blair Lee to Phillips Lee, 18 Mar. 1862, in Laas, *Wartime Washington*, 112–13; Terry, "Brief Moment in the Sun," 76.

85. Winkle, *Lincoln's Citadel*, 241–42.

86. Winkle, *Lincoln's Citadel*, 243–44; Akers, "Freedom without Equality," 12.

87. NI, 12 Apr. 1862; ES, 21 Mar. 1862.

88. ES, 25 Mar. 1862; "Joint Resolution of Instruction," Cong. Globe, 2 Apr. 1862, in Pohl and Wennersten, *Abraham Lincoln and the End of Slavery*, 56.

89. NI, 4 Apr. 1862; Cong. Globe, 37th Cong., 2nd Sess., 1525 (1862).

90. Medford, "Some Satisfactory Way," 16–17; Cong. Globe, 37th Cong., 2nd Sess., 1191 (1862); Harrison, *Washington during the Civil War and Reconstruction*, 115.

91. Medford, "Some Satisfactory Way," 4–5; Allen C. Guelzo, *Lincoln's Emancipation Proclamation: The End of Slavery in America* (New York: Simon and Schuster, 2004), 87–88; NI, 17 Apr. 1862.

92. "An Act for the Release of Certain Persons Held to Service or Labor in the District of Columbia," in Pohl and Wennersten, *Abraham Lincoln and the End of Slavery*, 63–66.

93. McKean, *National Almanac and Annual Record*, 259; *Harper's Weekly*, 24 May 1862, 323; Harrison, *Washington during the Civil War and Reconstruction*, 117.

94. *Liberator*, 23 May, 11 July 1862; Masur, *Example for All the Land*, 41; "Welcome to the Ransomed; or, Duties of the Colored Inhabitants of the District of Columbia" (Baltimore: Bull & Tuttle, 1862), African American Pamphlet Collection, LC, 6–9; ES, 28 Apr. 1862.

95. Poore, *Perley's Reminiscences of Sixty Years in the National Metropolis*, 107; Alexander Crummell and L. D. Johnson to Caleb B. Smith, 16 May 1862, RG 48 M160, NARA; Isaac N. Cary to A. J. H. White, 24 Apr. 1863, RG 48, M 160, NARA. Kate Masur argues that "thousands" of black Washingtonians applied to emigrate. Masur, *Example for All the Land*, 35–37; *Harper's Weekly*, 12 Dec. 1863, 796.

96. *Pacific Appeal*, 13 Sept. 1862.

97. *Pacific Appeal*, 20 Sept. 1862; Walton-Hanley, "Reversing the Middle Passage."

98. Todd, *Story of Washington*, 149; "Report of the Commissioners," 17 Feb. 1864, 38th Cong., 1st Sess., Doc. 42, in Pohl and Wennersten, *Abraham Lincoln and the End of Slavery*,

75; Winkle, *Lincoln's Citadel*, 271; Wennersten, "'First Freed': Emancipation, Apr., 1862," 4; Elizabeth Blair Lee to Phillips Lee, 4 Apr. 1862, in Laas, *Wartime Washington*, 122; Provine, *Compensated Emancipation*, 142.

99. Provine, *Compensated Emancipation*, 86.

100. Reidy, "Winding Path to Freedom," 18–22.

101. Winkle, *Lincoln's Citadel*, 273–75. Most accounts spell Reed's name as "Reid," but Megan Smolenyak Smolenyak argues convincingly that Reed himself preferred the "Reed" spelling and used it throughout his postemancipation life. Smolenyak, "Slave Who Rescued Freedom," 54–56.

Chapter 5

1. *Harper's Weekly*, 12 May 1866, 300.

2. Howard, *Autobiography*, 320; *Harper's Weekly*, 12 May 1866, 300; NI, 19 Apr. 1866.

3. King, "Henry Highland Garnet," 143–50; Garnet quoted in Howard, *Autobiography*, 321.

4. *Harper's Weekly*, 12 May 1866, 300.

5. WOD, 19 Apr. 1866, vol. 9.

6. Sumner, *Works of Charles Sumner*, 13:351. Sumner urged Washingtonians to pursue integrated schools to "complete" the march to full "equality of rights."

7. Ingle, *Negro in Washington*, 8; Harrison, "Experimental Station for Lawmaking," 29–53; *Daily Patriot*, 26 Sept. 1872.

8. This paragraph is based on John Washington's memoir, "Memorys of the Past," which is reproduced in Blight, *Slave No More*, 165–212. Blight also includes a chapter on Washington's upbringing and escape on pages 16–54.

9. Washington, "Memorys of the Past," 212.

10. For an 1854 list of members of Fredericksburg's Shiloh Baptist Church, see http://www.shiloholdsite.org/early-members.htm; Blight, *Slave No More*, 94; Masur, *Example for All the Land*, 27.

11. Ethiop [William J. Wilson], "Letters from 'Ethiop,'" Nos. 2, 3 *Anglo-African*, 5, 19 Sept. 1863, http://civilwardc.org/texts/letters/; ES, 7 Apr. 1862; USBC, "Historical Census Statistics on Population Totals by Race," table 23.

12. Horton, "Development of Federal Social Policy," 16, 120–21; Keckly, *Behind the Scenes*, 111; Johnston, *Surviving Freedom*, 92; Poore, *Perley's Reminiscences*, 2:165–66.

13. *Weekly Anglo-African*, 30 Nov. 1861; *Christian Recorder*, 1 Nov. 1862; Keckley, *Behind the Scenes*, 114; "First Annual Report of the Contraband Relief Association, Presented at the Fifteenth Street Presbyterian Church, Washington, D.C., 9 Aug. 1863," in *Christian Recorder*, 22 Aug. 1863; "First Annual Report of the National Freedman's Relief Association of the District of Columbia," 6.

14. Harriet A. Jacobs, "Life among the Contrabands," *Liberator*, 5 Sept. 1862; "First Annual Report of the National Freedman's Relief Association of the District of Columbia," 5–6; "Memorial of Surgeon Thomas Antisell, 24 June 1864," RG 233, HR 38A-G4.1, NARA; Downs, *Sick from Freedom*, 95–96, 99–100.

15. *Weekly Anglo African*, 30 Nov. 1861; "Assistant Quartermaster at the Washington Depot to the Chief Quartermaster of the Depot," 31 July 1863, in Pohl and Wennersten,

Abraham Lincoln and the End of Slavery, 93–95; military official quoted in Harrison, *Washington during the Civil War and Reconstruction*, 34–35; D. B. Nichols, "From the Washington Contraband Depot," in *Facts Concerning the Freedmen: Their Capacity and Their Destiny* (Boston: Press of Commercial Printing House, 1863), 10.

16. Harrison, *Washington during the Civil War and Reconstruction*, 38.

17. Reidy, "'Coming from the Shadow of the Past,'" 406.

18. Winkle, *Lincoln's Citadel*, 307–10.

19. Howard, *Autobiography*, 195–96; NFRA quoted in Winkle, *Lincoln's Citadel*, 310; *First Annual Report of the National Freedman's Relief Association of the District of Columbia* (Washington, D.C., 1863), 4.

20. Nichols, "From the Washington Contraband Depot," 9; Winkle, *Lincoln's Citadel*, 314.

21. Manning, *Troubled Refuge*, 50; Reidy, "'Coming from the Shadow of the Past,'" 403–28; Winkle, *Lincoln's Citadel*, 342–47.

22. Nichols quoted in Harrold, *Subversives*, 227.

23. Danforth Nichols claimed of the freed slaves at Camp Barker that "not one in a hundred could read before they came inside the Union lines." Nichols, "From the Washington Contraband Depot," 10; Harrold, *Subversives*, 246.

24. Brown quoted in Reidy, "'Coming from the Shadow of the Past,'" 413.

25. *Christian Recorder*, 4 June 1864; Winkle, *Lincoln's Citadel*, 347.

26. De Boer, "The Role of Afro-Americans in the Origin and Work of the American Missionary Association, 1839–1877," 304–7; for Wilson's correspondence, see http://civilwardc.org/texts/letters/about#bodyn20.

27. De Boer, "The Role of Afro-Americans in the Origin and Work of the American Missionary Association, 1839–1877," 304–7; ES, 2 Dec. 1865.

28. Keckley, *Behind the Scenes*, 112.

29. *Christian Recorder*, 18 July 1863; Adams, *Letter from Washington*, 51; Doster quoted in Winkle, *Lincoln's Citadel*, 308.

30. *Weekly Anglo-African*, 30 Jan. 1864.

31. Masur, *An Example for All the Land*, 28; Winkle, *Lincoln's Citadel*, 307; NR, 23, 24 May 1862; *Christian Recorder*, 8 Aug. 1863.

32. Manning, *Troubled Refuge*, 211–12.

33. Adams, *Letter from Washington*, 35.

34. Thomas H. C. Hinton, "Grand Emancipation Celebration," *Liberator*, 8 May 1863; Parade participant quoted in Masur, *Example for All the Land*, 48.

35. "Welcome to the Ransomed," 8; Harriet A. Jacobs, "Life among the Contrabands," *Liberator*, 5 Sept. 1862; Horton, "Development of Federal Social Policy, 122–24.

36. Roe, "Dual School System," 28; Ingle, *Negro in the District of Columbia*, 25; Du Bois, *Black Reconstruction in America*, 661; Levey, "Segregation in Education," 197–98.

37. Clark-Lewis, *First Freed*, xiii; Harrold, *Subversives*, 232–33; Fitzpatrick and Goodwin, *Guide to Black Washington*, 202–3.

38. *Liberator*, 12 June 1863.

39. *Liberator*, 12 June 1863; Gibbs, *Black, Copper, and Bright*, iv; Terry, "Brief Moment in the Sun," 80; ES, 21 Sept. 1864.

40. Richard Wallach to Hon. James Harlan, Secretary of the Interior, "Letter from the

Mayor of Washington in Reference to the Relations of the General Government to the City of Washington," November 1865, Ser. 1248, 39th Cong., 1st Sess., 2:870; Adams, *Letter from Washington*, 272.

41. *Liberator*, 8 May 1863; reporter quoted in Masur, *Example for All the Land*, 45.

42. *Toronto Globe*, 22 Feb. 1864; *Harper's Weekly*, 2 July 1864.

43. *Constitutional Union* quoted in Masur, *Example for All the Land*, 46; Terry, "Brief Moment in the Sun," 81.

44. Masur, *Example for All the Land*, 43–44; Thomas H. C. Hinton, "Grand Emancipation Celebration," *Liberator*, 8 May 1863.

45. Adams, *Letter from Washington*, 233; Garnet, "Memorial Discourse," 89, italics in original.

46. National Lincoln Monument Association, *Celebration by the Colored People's Educational Monument Association*, 3; ES, 5 July 1865.

47. McKim quoted in Masur, *Example for All the Land*, 50.

48. Ellis, *Sights and Secrets*, 48; Maury, "Alexander 'Boss' Shepherd and the Board of Public Works," 1; Lessoff, *Nation and Its City*, 25; F. B. Hough, "Census of the District of Columbia," in Department of Education, *Special Report*, 28, 37.

49. Adams, *Letter from Washington*, 238; Green, *Secret City*, 83.

50. "An Act to Establish a Bureau for the Relief of Freedmen and Refugees," *Statutes at Large, Treaties, and Proclamations of the United States of America*, vol. 13 (Boston, 1866), 507–9; Horton, "Development of Federal Social Policy," 35–36; Harrison, "Welfare and Employment Policies," 76.

51. National Capital Planning Commission, *Worthy of the Nation*: 63; Adams, *Letter from Washington*, 271.

52. WOD, 10 Nov. 1865, vol. 9; Horton, "Development of Federal Social Policy," 70, 93–94; Downs, *Sick from Freedom*, 120–21; Green, *Secret City*, 81.

53. Message of the Mayor, 24 June 1867, *Journal of the Sixty-Fifth Council of the City of Washington, 1867–68* (Washington: Joseph L. Pearson, 1868), 30; Howard, *Autobiography*, 214; Downs, *Sick from Freedom*, 122–26.

54. Harrison, "Welfare and Employment Policies," 93–96.

55. Latham, *Black and White*, 66; Harrison, "Welfare and Employment Policies," 104.

56. Johnson, "City on the Hill," 169.

57. Johnson, "City on the Hill," 169–70; Carpenter, *Sword and Olive Branch*, 185–87.

58. Carpenter, *Sword and Olive Branch*, 113; Harrison, "Welfare and Employment Policies," 84–85; Dianne Dale, "Barry Farm/Hillsdale," in Smith, *Washington at Home*, 162–63. Thanks to Trish Savage for tracing Emily Edmonson to Barry Farms.

59. Williams, "Blueprint for Change," 374; Barnard, *Special Report of the Commissioner of Education*, 222.

60. Henry Highland Garnet, "The Colored People's National Lincoln Monument Institute," *Anglo-African*, 18 Nov. 1865; *Anglo-African* 12 Aug. 1865; *Elevator*, 28 July 1865; Logan, *Howard University*, 17–44.

61. Harrison, "Welfare and Employment Policies," 89–92; Melder, "Angel of Mercy in Washington," 256–62.

62. A. C. Richards, 6 Mar. 1866, cited in *Journal of the Sixty-Fourth Council of the City of Washington, 1866–67* (Washington: Joseph L. Pearson, 1867), 714–15.

63. Bureau officials quoted in Harrison, "Welfare and Employment Policies," 82.

64. Wallach to Harlan, November 1865; Speech of Mr. Sam'l A. Peugh, 5 Feb. 1866, *Journal of the Sixty-Third Council of the City of Washington, 1865–66* (Washington: Joseph L. Pearson, 1866), 3–5.

65. WOD, vol. 9.

66. Harrison, "Welfare and Employment Policies," 86–87.

67. Provine, *Compensated Emancipation*, 14; Records of the U.S. District Court for the District of Columbia Relating to Slaves, 1851–63, including emancipation and manumission papers, NARA: http://www.fold3.com/image/185262159.

68. *Liberator*, 12 June 1863; Hatton quoted in Masur, *Example for All the Land*, 45; Biddle and Dubin, *Tasting Freedom*, 287–88.

69. George W. Hatton, Orderly Sergeant, 1st USCI, Hampton Hospital, 1 July 1864, *Christian Recorder*, 16 July 1864, in Redkey, *Grand Army of Black Men*, 256–57. See also *Christian Recorder*, 13 June 1864.

70. Harrold, *Subversives*, 241–42.

71. NR, 16 Dec. 1864; NI, 7 May 1864; Abraham Lincoln, Last Public Address, Washington, D.C., 11 Apr. 1865, http://www.abrahamlincolnonline.org/lincoln/speeches/last.htm.

72. National Lincoln Monument Association, *Celebration by the Colored People's Educational Monument Association*, 31–32; ES, 5 July 1865; Masur, *Example for All the Land*, 132.

73. ES, 12 Dec. 1865; Terry, "Brief Moment in the Sun," 83–85; Du Bois, *Black Reconstruction*, 285.

74. Cong. Globe, 39th Cong., 2nd Sess., 38, 107 (1866).

75. ES, 18 Dec. 1865, 19 Jan. 1866; Johnson, "City on the Hill," 46.

76. David quoted in Johnson, "Reconstruction Politics in Washington," 181.

77. Kate Masur makes this point clear in *Example for All the Land*.

78. NI, 20 Dec. 1865.

79. Dr. William Boyd to Hon. L. F. S. Foster and Members of the Senate, 12 Dec. 1866, Petitions and Manuscripts, KRL-HSW; *Journal of the Sixty-Third Council*, 476–77.

80. NI, 4, 12, 22 Jan. 1866; Johnson, "City on the Hill," 42.

81. Briggs, *Olivia Letters*, 24.

82. NI, 15 Nov. 1865, 4 Jan. 1866; "Suffrage in the District of Columbia," 15 Dec. 1865, H.R. Rep. 2, 39C, 1st Ser., 1272; Terry, "Brief Moment in the Sun," 83–84.

83. Address of the Central Executive Committee of Irish Citizens, at Washington, D.C., by Thomas Antisell (President), James R. O'Beirne and P. A. Flynn (Secretaries), published in NI, 4 Sept. 1866; WOD, 6 June 1865, vol. 9.

84. Cong. Globe, 39th Cong., 1st Sess., 259 (1865); Masur, *Example for All the Land*, 139–40; Johnson, "City on the Hill," 50; Green, *Secret City*, 79–80; Du Bois, *Black Reconstruction*, 337.

85. *Elevator*, 7 July 1865.

86. Richardson, *Compilation*, 477.

87. *Harper's Weekly*, 9 Mar. 1867, 147; Johnson, "City on the Hill," 53–54; ES, 26 Feb. 1867; Terry, "Brief Moment in the Sun," 87.

88. "Breaking Ground for the Municipal Election," ES, 23 Jan. 1867; Terry, "Brief Moment in the Sun," 87; Johnson, "City on the Hill," 58.

89. NI, 3 June 1867; Terry, "Brief Moment in the Sun," 89.

90. *Harper's Weekly*, 22 June 1867, 397–98; Moore quoted in Masur, *Example for All the Land*, 148.

91. "The Petition of Daniel Burrows & 4871 Others, Colored Laborers of the City of Washington D.C.," 15 Jan. 1868, RG 233, HR 40A-H4.1, NARA.

92. "Resolution of the Republican Citizens of the 4th Ward of Washington D.C.," 16 July 1867, RG 46 Sen 40A-H5.1, NARA.

93. ES, 22, 27 May 1868.

94. ES, 30 May, 1 June 1868.

95. NI, 1 June 1868; ES, 25 May 1868; Johnson, "Reconstruction Politics in Washington," 182–83; Collins, "Mayor Sayles J. Bowen," 295–97; Masur, *Example for All the Land*, 153; Johnson, "City on the Hill," 66–67; *Journal of the Sixty-Fifth Council*, 687–88.

96. ES, 4, June 1868; *Georgetown Courier* quoted in Johnson, "City on the Hill," 71–72.

97. Johnson, "City on the Hill," 77; Masur, *Example for All the Land*, 154–55; Alfers, *Law and Order*, 35.

98. *Journal of the Sixty-Sixth Council of the City of Washington, 1868–69*, vol. 1 (Washington: Chronicle Print, 1869), 29; Green, *Secret City*, 92; WP, 20 Dec. 1896.

99. Bowling, "From 'Federal Town' to 'National Capital'" 9; Green, *Secret City*, 94; Masur, *Example for All the Land*, 159.

100. Johnson, "City on the Hill," 105.

101. ES, 8 June 1869.

102. ES, 8 June 1869.

Chapter 6

1. NR, 1 Apr. 1870; Mattingly, "Early Recollections and Reminiscences of South Washington," 106–107; Goode, *Capital Losses*, 215; Garfinkle, *The Jewish Community of Washington, D.C.*, 20; Melder, "Southwest Washington," 88–91.

2. Melder, "Southwest Washington," 90; Groves, "The Development of a Black Residential Community in Southwest Washington," 263–72.

3. WP, 7 Oct. 1878; Webb, Wooldridge, and Crew, *Centennial History of the City of Washington, D.C.*, 566; NR 16 & 20 Dec. 1865, 28 & 31 May, 17 Oct., and 13 Dec. 1867; 23 Apr. and 3 Aug. 1868; ES, 20 May 1864; *Twenty-Fourth Report of the Board of Trustees of Public Schools of the City of Washington, 1870-'71* (Washington City: M'Gill and Witherow, 1871), 178; Harper, *History of the Grand Lodge and of Freemasonry in the District of Columbia*, 212; U.S. Senate, 55th Congress, 1st Session. *Joint Select Committee to Investigate the Charities and Reformatory Institutions in the District of Columbia*. U.S. Congressional Serial Set, Issue 3565, 35;

4. ES, 17 & 20 Apr. 1871.

5. NR, 26 May 1869.

6. NR, 20 May 1869.

7. On Shepherd, see Johnson, "City on the Hill," 81; Maury, "Alexander R. Shepherd and the Board of Public Works," 394–410; Richardson, "Alexander R. Shepherd and the Race Issue in Washington," 18–35; for a hagiographic depiction, see Tindall, "A Sketch of Alexander Robey Shepherd," 49–66; ES, 9 June 1862.

8. ES, 1 Apr. 1862; Provine, *Compensated Emancipation*, 191; NR, 29 Apr. 1862, 22 Mar. 1864.

9. ES, 18 Jan. 1868,

10. ES, 23 Nov. 1865.

11. ES, 23 Nov. 1865.

12. ES, 26 Jan. 1866, 26 Feb. 1867, 18 Jan. 1868.

13. "Resolution in Favor of Continuing the Charter of the City," 17 Feb. 1868, RG 233, HR 40A-H4.1, NARA; "Petition [of] Citizens of Washington City, D.C., Praying for the Speedy Passage of a Bill Rechartering Said City," 19 Feb. 1868, RG 46, Sen 40A-H5.1, NARA.

14. Masur, Example for All the Land, 157; ES, 5 May 1869; Daily NI, 1 June 1868. On Irish Republicans, see NR, 9 Mar., 26 June 1869.

15. "The Great Meeting," ES, 25 May 1870.

16. ES, 14 May 1870.

17. ES, 24, 25 May 1870.

18. New Era, 19 May 1870; ES, 13 June 1870.

19. ES, 25 May 1870.

20. Maury, "Boss Shepherd," 4.

21. Daily Patriot quoted in Lessoff, Nation and Its City, 55.

22. NI, 7 Dec. 1865; ES, 15 Jan. 1869.

23. New Era, 27 Jan. 1870; Laws of the Corporation of the City of Washington Passed by the Sixty-Seventh Council (Washington, D.C.: McGill and Witherow, 1870), 194.

24. Masur, Example for All the Land, 208–13.

25. Johnson, "City on the Hill," 195.

26. George Alfred Townsend, "New Washington," Harper's New Monthly Magazine 50, no. 297 (February 1875): 322; Masur, Example for All the Land, 232.

27. Courier quoted in Whyte, "District of Columbia Territorial Government," 94.

28. "William Wilson Corcoran," Harper's Weekly, 3 Mar. 1888, 148–49.

29. Daily Patriot, 26 Sept. 1872; Reports of Committees of the House of Representatives for the Second Session of the Forty-Second Congress (Washington, D.C.: USGPO, 1872), 692.

30. Adams, Our Little Monarchy, 7.

31. Petition of the Lamplighters of the Cities of Washington and Georgetown, 14 Dec. 1874, RG 233, HR 43A-H5.4, NARA.

32. "How Shall We Govern the National Capital?," Nation, 11 June 1874, 375.

33. Osthaus, Freedmen, Philanthropy, and Fraud, 201–24; Richardson, "Alexander R. Shepherd," 30.

34. "The District of Columbia," Harper's Weekly, 4 July 1874, 554–55.

35. Lessoff, The Nation and Its City, 72–83; Masur, Example for All the Land, 248–50; Whyte, "The District of Columbia Territorial Government, 1871–1874," 98–102.

36. "The District of Columbia," Harper's Weekly, 4 July 1874, 554–55; Diner, Democracy, Federalism, 24–29.

37. Lessoff, Nation and Its City, 101–29; Newman and DePuy, "Bringing Democracy," 546–47.

38. "The Crime against Suffrage in Washington," Nation, 27 June 1878, 415; ES, 27 Feb. 1878; Logan, Thirty Years in Washington, 518.

39. Most historians, following the lead of contemporary editorial writers and ob-

servers, take this incident at face value and depict it as a looting episode. Kate Masur argues convincingly that it was an act of political theater and symbolic protest.

40. NR, 18 Dec. 1874.

41. "How Shall We Govern the National Capital?," 375–76; "The District of Columbia," Harper's Weekly, 9 Jan. 1875, 27.

42. Senate Exec. Journal, 43d Cong., 1st Sess., 370–71 (1874); "A. R. Shepherd Dead," WP, 13 Sept. 1902.

43. "Alexander R. Shepherd," WP, 4 Oct. 1885; "Statue of 'Boss' Shepherd," NYT, 4 May 1909; "Honor Shepherd," WP, 4 May 1909; Tindall, "Sketch of Alexander Robey Shepherd," 66; Du Bois, Black Reconstruction, 563.

44. "Letter from Washington," Baltimore Sun, 31 Oct. 1879; Tindall, "Sketch of Mayor Sayles J. Bowen," 38.

45. Andy Hall, "George W. Hatton, Soldier," http://www.theatlantic.com/national /archive/2011/01/george-w-hatton-soldier/69659/; "Sergeant George W. Hatton, 1st U.S.C.T.," http://deadconfederates.com/2011/03/02/sergeant-george-w-hatton-1st-u-s-c -t/; "Hatton Enters Politics," http://deadconfederates.com/2011/03/04/george-w-hatton -enters-politics/; "George Hatton's Long Road," http://deadconfederates.com/2011/03/09 /george-hattons-long-road/.

46. Army provost marshal general George Davis, quoted in McCoy, Policing America's Empire, 71.

47. USBC, 1860 Census of the United States, NARA microfilm publication M653, Roll 1002, 225; Morris, Oberlin.

48. For a fascinating exploration of Wall's life, see Sharfstein, Invisible Line.

49. Wm. H. Boyd, Boyd's Directory of Washington and Georgetown (Washington, D.C., 1869), 461; USBC, 1870 Census of the United States, NARA microfilm publication M593, Roll 127, 647.

50. USBC, 1870 Census of the United States, NARA microfilm publication M593, Roll 127, 647; WP, 1 Mar. 1879, 18 Apr. 1882, 12 Apr. 1891; Johnson, "City on the Hill," 195; Boyd, Boyd's Directory, 461.

51. UCSB, "Historical Census Statistics on Population Totals by Race," table 23; Townsend, "New Washington," 309.

52. Cary quoted in Moore, Leading the Race, 21.

53. Rhodes, Mary Ann Shadd Cary, 170–211; Streitmatter, Raising Her Voice, 25–36; Johnson, "Mary Ann Shadd."

54. Roe, "Dual School System," 28–29.

55. On some standardized tests, black students at M Street High outperformed their peers in white D.C. high schools. Robinson, "M Street High School," 119–43; Stewart, First Class.

56. Masur, "Patronage and Protest," 1048; Yellin, Racism in the Nation's Service, 39–60; Riley, Philosophy of Negro Suffrage, 83.

57. Yellin, "'It Was Still No South to Us,'" 25.

58. Moore, Picturesque Washington, 248; Du Bois, Negro Common School, 49–50.

59. "Frederick Douglass," Harper's Weekly, 21 Apr. 1877; Masur, Example for All the Land, 200; Dale, "Barry Farm/Hillsdale," 158–59, 163; Mark G. Emerson, "Charles Remond

Douglass," "Frederick Douglass, Jr.," and "Lewis Henry Douglass," in Finkelman, *Encyclopedia of African American History*, 407–8, 422–25.

60. Gatewood, *Aristocrats of Color*, 39.

61. CA, 20 Feb. 1904; Rhodes, *Mary Ann Shadd Cary*, 175; Kerr, *Paper Bag Principle*, 40; *People's Advocate*, 10 July 1880.

62. *People's Advocate*, 21 Apr. 1883; Moore, *Leading the Race*, 31.

63. WB, 15 Mar. 1884.

64. ES, 16 Feb. 1878; Green, *Secret City*, 136–48.

65. Alfers, *Law and Order*, 47, 51n25; Green, *Secret City*, 128; Between 1879 and 1890, only one black person won appointment to the police force: Schmidt, "On Being Black"; "Talk in a Fiery Vein," WP, 22 Dec. 1891; WT (morning), 23 July 1895; "Seeking Green's Arrest," WP, 9 Mar. 1895.

66. ES, 23 Dec. 1879; Tindall, "Sketch of Mayor Sayles J. Bowen," 30; WP, 22 Oct. 1878, 2 Dec. 1879, 21 Feb. 1907; NR, 10 Dec. 1860, 11 June 1861, 28 Jan. 1880, 14 July 1883; ES, 17 Dec. 1861.

67. WB, 21 Apr. 1883.

68. Four of the first five civilian commissioners were not from the city. Lessoff, *Nation and Its City*, 134–35; WB, 5 Feb. 1887; NR, 13 Dec. 1879, 14 July 1883.

69. WP, 11 Feb. 1892; ES, 18 Mar. 1892; ES, 15 Apr. 1895; Julian Ralph, "Our National Capital," *Harper's New Monthly Magazine* 90, no. 539 (April 1895): 673; WT, 15 July, 26 Nov. 1894; ES, 10 Mar. 1896.

70. "The Crime against Suffrage in Washington," *Nation*, 27 June 1878, 415.

71. WP, 4 Feb. 1878.

72. WBOT, *Annual Report* (1895), 20; ES, 19 Jan. 1878, 15 Apr. 1895.

73. ES, 30 Jan. 1878; Townsend, "New Washington," 309.

74. Ingle, *Negro in the District of Columbia*, 81.

75. Morgan quoted in Ingle, *Negro in the District of Columbia*, 85; ES, 6 Dec. 1890.

76. ES, 30 Jan. 1878, 13 Jan. 1880, 9 Aug. 1895; Logan, *Thirty Years in Washington*, 524.

77. "Surplus Negroes," WP, 25 Sept. 1878; ES, 16 Mar. 1895.

78. WT, 26 June 1894; WP, 7 Apr. 1889, 5 Mar. 1890.

79. *Bee*, 7 July 1883; ES, 6 Dec. 1892.

80. ES, 25 Apr. 1896.

81. Wm. H. Boyd, *Boyd's Directory of Washington and Georgetown* (Washington, D.C., 1880), 197; "Perry Carson Is Dead," WP, 1 Nov. 1909; "Col. Perry Carson Passes Away," AA, 6 Nov. 1909; NR, 1, 26 Aug. 1868; *Baltimore Sun*, 19 Nov. 1873; WB, 6 Nov. 1909.

82. "Colored Leader Dead," ES, Nov. 1, 1909; WP, 17 Sept. 1879, 17 Apr. 1883, 11 Apr. 1884, 1 Nov. 1909; CA, 27 Jan. 1900.

83. Johnson, "City on the Hill," 155.

84. Borchert, *Alley Life in Washington*, 6.

85. Borchert, *Alley Life in Washington*, 18, 42; Wm. H. Boyd, *Boyd's Directory of Washington and Georgetown* (Washington, D.C., 1869), 19–20, 27–31; Johnson, "City on the Hill," 178; Borchert finds 210 alleys in 1880, while a count of named alleys in *Boyd's Directory* finds 231.

86. NR, 29 May 1862; Board of Health report quoted in Borchert, *Alley Life in Washington*, 28.

87. Borchert, *Alley Life in Washington*, esp. 219–23.

88. WP, 9 Feb. 1880, 15 Apr. 1884, 26 Jan. 1888.

89. Simmons, *Men of Mark*, 118–32.

90. WB, 12 Apr. 1884.

91. WB, 8 Mar., 12 Apr. 1884.

92. WP, 16 Nov. 1890.

93. Bruce quoted in Gatewood, *Aristocrats of Color*, 55; Chestnutt quoted in Hobbs, *Chosen Exile*, 116.

94. P. H. Carson to R. H. Singleton, 30 Oct. 1888, *Reports of Committees of the House of Representatives, 51st Congress, 1st Session, 1889–'90* (Washington, D.C.: GPO, 1890), 34–35; ES, 19 Oct. 1895.

95. Kachun, *Festivals of Freedom*, 207–32.

96. WB, 22 Mar. 1884.

97. WB, 24 Mar. 1888.

98. Reporter quoted in Kachun, *Festivals of Freedom*, 225; WB, 21 Apr. 1888.

99. WP, 18 Feb. 1901.

Chapter 7

1. The first "suburb" was Uniontown, founded across the Anacostia River in 1854; Amzi Barber obituary, NYT, 19 Apr. 1909; W. Ray Luce, "A Brief History of LeDroit Park" (Washington, D.C.: National Park Service, 1975), in WD; Logan, *Howard University*, 60.

2. ES, 19 Sept. 1874; John Claggett Proctor, "Exclusive LeDroit Park Once Contributed to Beauty of City," *Sunday Star*, 1 July 1928.

3. WP, 31 July 1888; "How Le Droit Park Came to Be Added to the City," WT, 31 May 1903.

4. WP, 26 Nov. 1888.

5. WP, 3 Dec. 1886, 1 Aug. 1888, 30 Dec. 1890, 1 Aug. 1891.

6. Woody West and Earl Byrd, "Place of Dreams and Nightmares," WS, 28 Feb. 1974; Osceola Madden, "A Color Phase of Washington," *World To-Day* 14, no. 1 (January 1908): 550; Johnson, "From Romantic Suburb to Racial Enclave," 264–70; Kerr, *Paper Bag Principle*, 42–44.

7. WP, 17 Feb. 1893, 25 Mar. 1929; Spofford and Henry, *Eminent and Representative Men*, 238–41; Ullery, *Men of Vermont*, 118–20.

8. USBC, "Historical Census Statistics on Population Totals by Race," table 23; Lessoff, *Nation and Its City*, 19.

9. Julian Ralph, "Our National Capital," *Harper's New Monthly Magazine* 90, no. 539 (April 1895): 657; McCardle, "Development of the Business Sector, 1800–1973," 567.

10. Jacob, "'Like Moths to a Candle,'" 79–96.

11. WBOT, *Annual Report* (1890), 14.

12. Williams, "Blueprint for Change," 362.

13. Jacob, "'Like Moths to a Candle,'" 83–84.

14. Jacob, *Capital Elites*, 80–84.

15. George Alfred Townsend, "New Washington," *Harper's New Monthly Magazine* 50, no. 297 (February 1875): 309; Logan, *Thirty Years in Washington*, 523–24.

16. Weller, *Neglected Neighbors*, 215–18.

17. Lessoff, *Nation and Its City*, 160–62.

18. "Race Issue Plank for the Democrats," NYT, 17 June 1912; French, "Chevy Chase Village," 323.

19. Lampl and Williams, *Chevy Chase*, 138; Marc Fisher, "Chevy Chase, 1916: For Everyman, a New Lot in Life," WP, 15 Feb. 1999.

20. "James Wormley Dead," WP, 19 Oct. 1884; Helm, *Tenleytown*, 97, 129, 168, 174, 202–3.

21. French, "Chevy Chase Village," 310.

22. "East Washington Citizens' Association," pamphlet, 1891, LC; Hatcher, "Washington's Nineteenth-Century Citizens' Associations," 78; "The Color Line," WB, 7 May 1910; Mike DeBonis, "In 'One City,' Two D.C. Civic Federations," WP, 3 Mar. 2013.

23. Meriwether, "Washington City Government," 416; Dodd, *Government of the District of Columbia*, 265, 273.

24. ES, 12 Sept. 1889; Hatcher, "Washington's Nineteenth-Century Citizens' Associations," 90.

25. WP, 9 Dec. 1886, 4 Apr. 1887.

26. Spofford and Henry, *Eminent and Representative Men of Virginia*, 412–14; Hood, "In Memoriam: Michael Ignatius Weller," 197–98; WP, 2 Mar. 1892.

27. This board of trade was a new organization unconnected to an earlier, short-lived board of trade founded by Alexander Shepherd and others in 1865.

28. ES, 5 Nov. 1890. A similar organization had been founded by Alexander Shepherd and other businessmen in 1865 but lasted only a few years. ES, 23, 29 Nov. 1865; WP, 5 May 1909; Hatcher, "Washington's Nineteenth-Century Citizens' Associations," 77.

29. ES, 29 Nov. 1889; WBOT, *Annual Report* (1890), 7, 14.

30. Lessoff, *Nation and Its City*, 213–16; WBOT, *Annual Report* (1890), 3, 21–24; P. L. Dunbar, "Negro Life in Washington," *Harper's Weekly*, 13 Jan. 1900; Elfenbein, *Civics, Commerce, and Community*, 2.

31. Meriwether, "Washington City Government," 417–18; WP, 9 Feb. 1896; Lessoff, *Nation and Its City*, 210–21; Elfenbein, *Civics, Commerce, and Community*, 2.

32. Elfenbein, *Civics, Commerce, and Community*, 6; WBOT, *Annual Report* (1890), 20; WBOT, *Annual Report* (1899), 31; Lessoff, *Nation and Its City*, 222.

33. WBOT, *Annual Report* (1891), 3; WT (morning), 7 Mar. 1896.

34. Meriwether, "Washington City Government," 419; ES, 18 Nov. 1901; Henry B. F. MacFarland, "The Development of the District of Columbia," Address at the Executive Mansion, 12 Dec. 1900 (WBOT, 1900), WD; Henry B. F. MacFarland, "The District of Columbia," Address at the District of Columbia Day, 3 Sept. 1901 (Committee of Arrangements, 1901), WD.

35. Wilcox, *Great Cities in America*, 66.

36. Lessoff, "Washington Insider," 64–80.

37. Prout, "Hope, Fear, and Confusion," 1–19.

38. Chudacoff and Smith, *Evolution of American Urban Society*, 121.

39. Jacobs, *Death and Life of Great American Cities*, 24; Teaford, *Twentieth-Century American City*, 4; National Capital Planning Commission, *Worthy of the Nation*, 113; Daniel Burn-

ham, "White City and Capital City," *Century Illustrated Magazine* 63, no. 4 (February 1902): 619–20.

40. Francis E. Leupp, "Washington, a City of Pictures," *Scribner's Magazine* (February 1902), cited in Oppel and Meisel, *Washington, D.C.*, 363.

41. Charles Moore, "The Improvement of Washington, Second Paper," *Century Illustrated Magazine* 63, no. 5 (March 1902): 757; Montgomery Schuyler, "The New Washington," *Scribner's Magazine* (February 1912), cited in Oppel and Meisel, *Washington, D.C.*, 414.

42. *Report of the Commissioners of the District of Columbia 1901*, vol. 1 (Washington, D.C.: USGPO, 1901), 8; Gillette, *Between Justice and Beauty*, 92; Charles Moore, ed., "The Improvement of the Park System of the District of Columbia," U.S. Senate Committee on the District of Columbia, S. Rep. 166, 57th Cong., 1st Sess. (Washington, D.C.: USGPO, 1902), 8; National Capital Planning Commission, *Worthy of the Nation*, 113–14.

43. Charles Moore, "The Improvement of Washington," *Century Illustrated Magazine* 63, no. 4 (February 1902): 622; National Capital Planning Commission, *Worthy of the Nation*, 199–21.

44. National Capital Planning Commission, *Worthy of the Nation*, 123–25.

45. Moore, "Improvement of the Park System," 10–12.

46. Gillette, *Between Justice and Beauty*, 102–8; National Capital Planning Commission, *Worthy of the Nation*, 119, 130–33.

47. Schuyler, "New Washington," 395; Isaac F. Marcosson, "The New Washington," *Munsey's Magazine* 16, no. 3 (December 1911): 311–28.

48. Associated Charities quoted in Gillette, *Between Justice and Beauty*, 109.

49. Burnham, "White City and Capital City," 619–20; *Washington Life* quoted in Polter, "Dreams, Schemes, and Plat Maps," 40; Henry Loomis Nelson, "The Washington Negro," *Harper's Weekly*, 9 July 1892.

50. *WP*, 30 Aug. 1957.

51. *WP*, 29 Nov. 1903, 1 Jan. 1922; Coílín Owens, "Washington, D.C., 20th Century," in Glazier, *Encyclopedia of the Irish in America*, 946–47.

52. Testimony of Clare de Graffenried, "Typical Alley Houses in Washington," in S. Rep. 1297, "Stables in Union Court," 54th Cong., 2nd Sess., 378–79 (1896); Gillette, *Between Justice and Beauty*, 112–13.

53. Hannold, "'Comfort and Respectability,'" 20–39; Paige and Reuss, "Safe, Decent and Affordable," 75–77.

54. *WP*, 16, 17 Dec. 1903.

55. Weller, *Neglected Neighbors*, 11; *WP*, 2 Sept. 1903; "A Capital City of Broad Streets but Evil Alleys," *Charities* 10 (13 June 1903): 585.

56. Clare de Graffenried, "Typical Alley Houses," 378–79; Monday Evening Club, *Directory of the Inhabited Alleys of Washington, D.C.* (Washington, D.C.: n.p., 1912), map on p. 5, available at http://lcweb2.loc.gov/service/gdc/scd0001/2001/20011126001di/2001112600 1di.pdf.

57. *WP*, 28 Apr. 1901; Kolker, "Migrants and Memories," 53–54; Weller, *Neglected Neighbors*, 254.

58. Weller, *Neglected Neighbors*, 257, 319.

59. Ibid., 316–17.

60. *ES*, 14 Nov. 1914. See also *WP*, 24 May 1912, 12 Nov. 1914; "Mrs. Wilson's Death

and Washington's Alleys," *Survey* 31 (22 Aug. 1914): 515; and Borchert, *Alley Life in Washington*, 47.

61. Jones, *Housing of Negroes in Washington*, 42.

62. Weller, *Neglected Neighbors*, 268.

63. Harley, "Mary Church Terrell," 309–10; Fitzpatrick and Goodwin, *Guide to Black Washington*, 88–89; for more on Terrell, see Terrell, *Colored Woman in a White World*; and Quigley, *Just Another Southern Town*.

64. Davis quoted in Clark-Lewis, "'For a Real Better Life,'" 99; Baker, *Following the Color Line*, 113.

65. McQuirter, "Claiming the City," 8–9, 75; USBC, *Thirteenth Census*, 292, 839,1045.

66. Yellin, *Racism in the Nation's Service*, 21.

67. I. K. Friedman, "The Negroes of Washington," *Collier's Weekly* 30, no. 10 (6 Dec. 1902): 35–36.

68. Nelson, "Washington Negro"; Logan, *Thirty Years in Washington*, 524.

69. Madden, "Color Phase of Washington," 550; Yellin, *Racism in the Nation's Service*, 29.

70. Clark-Lewis, "Duty and 'Fast Living,'" 47; Clark-Lewis, "'For a Real Better Life,'" 99–100; Belle La Follette, "Colored Folk of Washington," *La Follette's Weekly Magazine*, 5 Aug. 1911, 11.

71. Plessy v. Ferguson, 163 U.S. 537, 545, 551 (1896); *WP*, 21 July 1904.

72. *WP*, 20 Feb. 1908.

73. *WP*, 28, 29 Mar., 12 May 1908; *AA*, 4 Apr. 1908; William E. Chancellor, "Washington's Race Question," *Collier's* 42, no. 2 (3 Oct. 1908): 24–25.

74. Mary Church Terrell, "What It Means to Be Colored in the Capital of the United States," *Independent*, 24 Jan. 1907.

75. Dunbar, "Negro Life in Washington."

76. Moore, *Leading the Race*, 3–6; Madden, "Color Phase of Washington," 549.

77. Moore, *Leading the Race*, 188; *CA*, 25 Nov. 1899.

78. Hilyer, *Twentieth Century Union League Directory*.

79. Ingham, "Building Businesses, Creating Communities," 639–47; Fitzpatrick, "'Great Agitation for Business,'" 61.

80. Harley, "Black Goddess of Liberty," 62–71; Higginbotham, "Nannie Helen Burroughs," 174–78.

81. Hammond, *Vanguard of the Race*, 47–62; McCluskey, *Forgotten Sisterhood*, 101–16; Higginbotham, "Nannie Helen Burroughs," 174–78; Hine, *Hine Sight*, 115.

82. *CA*, 7 Apr. 1900; Kendrick quoted in Yellin, *Racism in the Nation's Service*, 150.

83. Bernard, "These Separate Schools," 35; Thurber, "Negro at the Nation's Capital," 146; Moore, *Leading the Race*, 22.

84. Harries quoted in Bernard, "These Separate Schools," 43.

85. Marshall quoted in Bernard, "These Separate Schools," 49.

86. Robinson, "M Street High School," 123–24; Bernard, "These Separate Schools," 55–61.

87. Bernard, "These Separate Schools," 31.

88. Harlan and Strock, *Booker T. Washington Papers*, 1904–6, 304–5.

89. Terrell, "What It Means to Be Colored."

Chapter 8

1. WP, 15 Mar. 1915; "New Edifice Opens with Flag Raising," ES, 19 Mar. 1915; Lisa Lyman of Bureau of Engraving and Printing, email exchange with Chris Myers Asch, 7 Feb. 2014.

2. Washington Herald, 20 July 1913; WP, 15 Mar. 1914; Historical Resource Center, "BEP History" (Washington, D.C., 2004), 7.

3. Historical Resource Center, "BEP History," 6–7; Bureau of Engraving and Printing, Annual Report, 32.

4. Altenhofel, "Keeping House," 94–95; Altenhofel, "Washington, D.C., to 1900," 945; for a great description of the turn-of-the-century printing process and pictures of the bureau's printing floor, see http://www.streetsofwashington.com/2010/04/sweatshop-bureau-of-engraving-and.html; WP, 5 Apr. 1909; Mary Anderson, "Organizing the Bureau of Engraving and Printing Girls," Life and Labor 8 (January 1918): 11–12; Yellin, "'It Was Still No South to Us,'" 37.

5. CA, 6 Sept. 1906; WP, 7 June 1908.

6. Yellin, Racism in the Nation's Service, 4, 24–25, 63. Napier was also John Mercer Langston's son-in-law.

7. Hayes, Negro Federal Government Worker, 19–36; WP, 12 Feb. 1890; WB, 15 Feb., 20 Sept. 1890, 31 Oct. 1891; Harley, "Black Women in a Southern City," 63–64.

8. NYT, 17 Feb. 1895; WP, 17 Feb. 1895, 7 June 1908; WB, 2, 16 Dec. 1893.

9. USBC, 1910 Census of the United States, Census Place: Precinct 2, Washington, District of Columbia, Roll: T624_149, Page: 10A, Enumeration District: 0015, FHL microfilm: 1374162; Belle Case La Follette, "Color Line to Date," La Follette's Magazine 6, no. 4 (24 Jan. 1914): 6–7; "About Us," Barber-Scotia College website, http://www.b-sc.edu/about.html; WT, 19 July 1908; ES, 15 Jan. 1907; Yellin, "'It Was Still No No South to Us,'" 40.

10. "Segregation in Government Departments," Crisis 6, no. 1 (November 1913): 343–44; Green, Secret City, 156–66, 171; Johnson, Dusk at the Mountain, 226; Thurber, "Negro at the Nation's Capital," 26–38; Woodrow Wilson to Oswald Garrison Villard, 23 July 1913, in Link, Papers of Woodrow Wilson, 65; Yellin, Racism in the Nation's Service, 132–72; Schaffer, "New South Nation," esp. chap. 4.

11. Crisis 5, no. 5 (March 1913): 221; Crisis 5, no. 6 (April 1913): 270; Crisis 5, no. 8 (June 1913): 60; Belle Case La Follette, "The Color Line," La Follette's Magazine 5, no. 34 (23 Aug. 1913): 6–7; Unger, "'When Women Condemn the Whole Race,'" 281, 287; Booker T. Washington to Oswald Garrison Villard, 10 Aug. 1913, in Harlan and Smock, Booker T. Washington Papers, Vol. 12: 1912–1914, 248.

12. King, Separate and Unequal, 3.

13. Yellin, Racism in the Nation's Service, 118; Belle Case La Follette, "Segregation in the Civil Service," La Follette's Magazine, 5, no. 50 (13 Dec. 1913): 6; Oswald Garrison Villard to Woodrow Wilson, 21 July 1913, in Link, Papers of Woodrow Wilson, 28:60–61; King, Separate and Unequal, 10, 29, 234–35.

14. La Follette, "Color Line," 6–7; Crisis 6, no. 6 (October 1913): 275–76; La Follette, "Color Line to Date," La Follette's Magazine 6, no. 4 (24 Jan. 1914): 6–7.

15. "Bureau of Engraving and Printing," WB, 3 May 1913.

16. Yellin, *Racism in the Nation's Service*, 136–37; *Crisis* 6, no. 6 (October 1913): 276; La Follette, "Color Line," 6–7.

17. Sullivan, *Lift Every Voice*, 1–24; Walker, "Struggles and Attempts to Establish Branch Autonomy and Hegemony."

18. Terrell, *Colored Woman in a White World*, 191; *WT*, 3 Oct. 1903.

19. Coulibaly, "Kelly Miller," 40.

20. *Crisis* 3, no. 6 (April 1912): 259; *WT*, 7 Dec. 1912; Thurber, "Negro at the Nation's Capital," 10–11; Montgomery, "Intellectual Profile of Belle Case La Follette," 114; *Crisis* 5, no. 10 (August 1913): 190.

21. La Follette, "Color Line," 6–7; Montgomery, "Intellectual Profile of Belle Case La Follette," 117; Villard quoted in Walker, "Struggles and Attempts to Establish Branch Autonomy and Hegemony," 38.

22. Bruce, *Archibald Grimké*, 185–86; *WP*, 9 June 1916; *ES*, 28 Mar. 1913; *Richmond Times-Dispatch*, 26 Mar. 1913; *Crisis* 5, no. 10 (August 1913): 190; Thurber, "Negro at the Nation's Capital," 12; Walker, "Struggles and Attempts to Establish Branch Autonomy and Hegemony," 10–64.

23. *AA*, 15 Mar. 1930; *New York Amsterdam News*, 5 Mar. 1930; Thurber, "Negro at the Nation's Capital," 13–16; Chase quoted in Bruce, *Archibald Grimké*, 197.

24. *Crisis* 7, no. 4 (February 1914): 192–93; *Crisis* 7, no. 2 (December 1913): 89; "Honor or Dishonor," Box 19-19, Folder 373, Archibald H. Grimké Papers, Moorland-Spingarn Research Center, Howard University; Work, *Negro Year Book*, 36; Bruce, *Archibald Grimké*, 189.

25. "Race Discrimination at Washington," *Independent* (20 Nov. 1913): 330.

26. Thurber, "Negro at the Nation's Capital," 74–78.

27. Yellin, *Racism in the Nation's Service*, 2, 130–31.

28. Varel, "John Davis versus Woodrow Wilson," 3–20.

29. USBC, "Historical Census Statistics on Population Totals by Race," table 23; Thurber, "Negro at the Nation's Capital," 149–50; Sullivan, *Lift Every Voice*, 29–33.

30. A. R. Pinci, "The New Washington," *Munsey's Magazine* 64, no. 3 (August 1918): 485; "Women Crowding to Washington to Fill Government Jobs of Men Gone to Fight Nation's Battles," *WP*, 17 June 1917; Harrison Rhodes, "War-Time Washington," *Harper's* 136 (March 1918), cited in Graham, *Katherine Graham's Washington*, 257; Edward Hungerford, "In Wartime Washington," *Travel* 29, no. 4 (August 1917): 16; Green, *Washington: Capital City*, 237.

31. Derthick, *City Politics*, 6; Harley, "Black Women in a Southern City," 66.

32. "Profiteers and Red Tape Worms," *Good Government* 35, no. 3 (March 1918): 37–38; Ellen Maury Slayden, "The Capital at War," cited in Graham, *Katherine Graham's Washington*, 275.

33. "Living in War-Swollen Washington Is a Serious Problem," *Literary Digest* 57 (27 Apr. 1918): 56; Buchholz and Lehmann, "Josephine," 18.

34. John R. Hawkins to Hon. Newton D. Baker, 8 Oct. 1917, in Scott, *American Negro in the World War*, 48; *WT*, 17 Apr. 1917; "District Gave 17,945 Men to Nation during War, and Best Records of 9 States," *WP*, 6 Feb. 1919.

35. Scott, *Scott's Official History*, 34–36; "Harvey Takes Command of the Mobilization Here," *WP*, 26 Mar. 1917; Krugler, *1919*, 67.

36. Williams, *Torchbearers of Democracy*, 128–34, 250.

37. ES, 10 Apr. 1917.

38. Archibald Grimké to Emmett J. Scott, 17 Sept. 1918, in Scott, *Scott's Official History*, 452; "Jim Crow Camp? Maybe. That or Nothing." AA, 5 May 1917; Bruce, *Archibald Grimké*, 217–18.

39. "Extract from an Open Letter to the President," *Crisis* 14, no. 10 (August 1917): 164–65; Mellis, "'Monsters We Defy,'" 133–34; Bruce, *Archibald Grimké*, 216.

40. Terrell, *Colored Woman in a White World*, 251–59.

41. Mellis, "Monsters We Defy," 47–48.

42. McKaine and Lane quoted in Krugler, *1919*, 68; "Demonstrations in Colored High School," Major Walter H. Loving to Chief, Military Intelligence Section, 17 Dec. 1917, CMID, 1917–1941, RG 165, File 10218-70; Bruce, *Archibald Grimké*, 219–24.

43. F. R. Cotton, "Alleged Negro Activity," 16 Jan. 1918, CMID, RG 165, File 10218-91; R. H. Van Deman to Maj. W. H. Loving, 28 Feb. 1918, CMID, RG 165, http://www.fold3.com/image/1/179488225/; J. E. Cutler, "Pro-German Propaganda among Negroes," memo for Captain Taylor, 18 Oct. 1918, CMID, RG 165, File 10218-254; K. A. Wagner to Captain Henry G. Pratt, "Negro Propaganda," 4 Nov. 1918, CMID, RG 165, File 10218-254; Captain C. J. Harvey quoted in Krugler, *1919*, 67.

44. Major Walter H. Loving, "Conditions among Colored People of the District," memo to Chief, Military Intelligence Section, 30 June 1918, CMID, RG 165, File 10218-415; Cunningham, "Loving Touch," 4–25.

45. Archibald Grimké, "The Shame of America," in Marable, *Freedom on My Mind*, 543; W. E. B. Du Bois, "An Essay toward a History of the Black Man in the Great War," *Crisis* 18, no. 2 (June 1919): 72; "Returning Soldiers," *Crisis* 18, no. 1 (May 1919): 14.

46. Scott, *Scott's Official History*, 458, emphasis in original; Mary White Ovington, "Reconstruction and the Negro," *Crisis* 17, no. 4 (February 1919): 169–70.

47. Brownlow, *Passion for Anonymity*, 83; Asch, *Senator and Sharecropper*, 50–51.

48. A. R. Pinci, "The New Washington," *Munsey's Magazine* (August 1918): 485; Waskow, *From Race Riot to Sit-In*, 21–22; Krugler, "Mob in Uniform," 52.

49. "Attacks Teacher of Reno School near Connecticut Avenue," ES, 26 June 1919; Mellis, "Monsters We Defy," 160.

50. "Screams Save Girls from 2 Negro Thugs," WT, 19 July 1919. Most media reports used Williams's married name, Mrs. John Stephnick, but she was working under her maiden name. "Race War in Washington," NYT, 23 July 1919; "Series of Brutal Assaults Led to Race Riots at Capital," *Baltimore Sun*, 23 July 1919; Krugler, "Mob in Uniform," 56–57.

51. Mellis, "Monsters We Defy," 157; Waskow, *From Race Riot to Sit-In*, 24; "Detective Sergeant Wilson Victim," WP, 22 July 1919. For coverage of the violence, see WP, ES, *Washington Herald*, and WT from 19 July to 23 July 1919. See also Krugler, "Mob in Uniform," 57–59.

52. "Negro Pastors and Citizens Call on the President and Officials for Protection," WP, 22 July 1919; "Mobilization for Tonight," WP, 21 July 1919.

53. E. G. M., "The Washington Riots," *Nation* 109 (9 Aug. 1919): 173; Herbert J. Seligmann, "Race War?," *New Republic* 20 (13 Aug. 1919): 49; "Women Arms Buyers," WP, 23 July 1919; Krugler, "Mob in Uniform," 61; Krugler, *1919*, 80; "The Riots: An N.A.A.C.P. Investigation," *Crisis* 18, no. 5 (September 1919): 241–43.

54. "Four Dead, Scores, Wounded in Night of Red Terror Here," WT, 22 July 1919.

55. "Gen. Haan in Command after Wilson Confers with Bake on Riots," WP, 23 July 1919; Seligmann, "Race War?," 49.

56. Waldron quoted in Krugler, 1919, 97; Thomas quoted in Krugler, "Mob in Uniform," 61; "Riots: An N.A.A.C.P. Investigation," 241–43. See also "Our Own Subject Race Rebels," Literary Digest 62 (2 Aug. 1919): 25.

57. "Carrie Johnson Given Freedom in Murder Case," WTR, 25 June 1921; "Washington Newspaper Helped to Incite Riot," AA, 1 Aug. 1919.

58. Seligmann, "Race War?," 49.

59. "Race War in Washington," NYT, 23 July 1919.

60. J. E. Cutler, "Race Riots in Washington, D.C.," memorandum for the Director of Military Intelligence, 23 July 1919, CMID, RG 165, File 10218-350; J. E. Cutler, "The Negro Situation," memorandum for the Director of Military Intelligence, 15 Aug. 1919, CMID, RG 165, File 10218-361.

61. M. Churchill, "The Negro Situation," memorandum for the Chief of Staff, 20 Aug. 1919, CMID, RG 165, File 10218-361; W. H. Loving, "Final Report on Negro Subversion," memorandum to Director of Military Intelligence, 6 Aug. 1919, CMID, RG 165, File 10218-361, 12–14.

62. "Reaping the Whirlwind," CD, 2 Aug. 1919.

63. E. A. Chace, "My Appeal," WB, 2 Aug. 1919.

64. "Neval Holland Thomas," National Archives, U.S. World War I Draft Registration Cards, 1917–1918, Registration State: District of Columbia, Registration County: Washington, Roll: 1556844, Draft Board: 8; Introduction to Neval H. Thomas, "The District of Columbia—a Paradise of Paradoxes," Messenger 5, no. 10 (October 1923), cited in Lutz and Ashton, These "Colored" United States, 76; "Neval Thomas Heads Capitol NAACP," AA, 24 Jan. 1925; Wm. Pickens, "NAACP Has Effective Lobbyist in Neval Thomas," AA, 26 Oct. 1926; "Neval Thomas, Militant N.A.A.C.P. Leader Mourned," AA, 19 Apr. 1930; Kelly Miller, "A Living Sacrifice," New York Amsterdam News, 23 Apr. 1930.

65. Kelly Miller, "Kelly Miller Says," AA, 6 June 1925.

66. "The Inspired Beginning," WTR, 28 May 1921; Langland, Chicago Daily News Almanac, 702; Beverly Gage, "Our First Black President?," NYT, 6 Apr. 2008.

67. "Harding Shows His Hand," WTR, 2 July 1921; "Discrimination in Washington," WTR, 16 July 1921; "Harding Must Not Be Re-Elected," WTR, 18 Sept. 1921; "Discrimination Continues in Government," WTR, 11 June 1921; "Eat Lunch Where Spittoons Are Cleaned," WTR, 25 Feb. 1922; "Jim Crow Signs Posted in Rock Creek Park by Harding Appointee," WTR, 22 Apr. 1922; "Col. Sherill and Race Prejudice," WTR, 22 Apr. 1922; "Southern Prejudice in Washington," WTR, 11 June 1921.

68. "Near Fight as Citizens Are Jim Crowed," WTR, 3 June 1922.

69. "Dr. R. R. Moton Tells Nation the Negro Has Justified His Emancipation by Lincoln," WTR, 3 June 1922; Fairclough, "Civil Rights and the Lincoln Memorial," 408–16.

70. Thomas, "District of Columbia," 85.

71. "Klan Has Many Members Here," ES, 25 Sept. 1921; CD, 3 Jan. 1925; WP, 19 June 1927; "White-Robed Klan Cheered on March in Nation's Capital," WP, 9 Aug. 1925; "Ku Klan in Colorful Review as Conclave Opens," WP, 14 Sept. 1926.

72. Thomas, "District of Columbia," 82, 87; Miller, "Kelly Miller Says."

73. "U Street Survey Shows Big Business Boom," *WTR*, 25 June 1921; Fitzpatrick, "Great Agitation for Business," 50; Lillian Gordon quoted in Joyce and Reid, "Remembering Washington," 57.

74. Johnson, "Those Who Stayed," 219–41.

75. Hutchinson, "Jean Toomer," 683–92; Kerr, *Paper Bag Principle*, 45; Hobbs, *Chosen Exile*, 181–97.

76. Hobbs, *Chosen Exile*, 178–80, 268.

77. Hobbs, *Chosen Exile*, 4–27.

78. Marita Bonner, "On Being Young—a Woman—and Colored," *Crisis* 31, no. 2 (December 1925): 1244–47.

79. Langston Hughes, "Our Wonderful Society: Washington," *Opportunity* 5, no. 8 (August 1927): 226–27, cited in De Santis, *Collected Works of Langston Hughes*, 41–44. Brenda Ray Moryck offered a caustic rebuttal to Hughes several months later, claiming that he was "gullible" and "hasty" in his denunciations of the black elite. Moryck, "I, Too, Have Lived in Washington" (August 1927), in Wilson, *Opportunity Reader*, 368–77; Alain Locke, "Beauty and the Provinces," *Stylus* 2 (1929), cited in Molesworth, *Works of Alain Locke*.

80. Kerr, *Paper Bag Principle*; Jones, *Housing of Negroes*, 42; Collins, "'Substance of Things Hoped For,'" 155–75.

81. Heard, "'Bad' Black Consumer," v–vi; Feggans quoted in Collins, "'Substance of Things Hoped For,'" 135; "Interview with Mrs. Anna E. Murray," 2 Nov. 1938, Community Reports, Box 131-111, Folder 20, NYS-DC, Research Projects, EFFP; Kelly Miller, "Where Is the Negro's Heaven?" (December 1926), in Wilson, *Opportunity Reader*, 425–26.

82. Otis quoted in Elizabeth Clark-Lewis, "'For a Real Better Life,'" 107.

83. Clark-Lewis, "'This Work Had a End,'" 196.

84. Clark-Lewis, *Living In, Living Out*, 123–46; Clark-Lewis, "'For a Real Better Life,'" 111; Clark-Lewis, "'This Work Had a End,'" 211.

85. Jones, *Housing of Negroes*, 59, 74–78, 93.

86. U.S. Commission on Civil Rights, *Understanding Fair Housing*, Clearinghouse Publication 42 (February 1973), 4; French, "Chevy Chase Village," 309; Jones-Correa, "Origins and Diffusion of Racial Restrictive Covenants," 550.

87. Jones, *Housing of Negroes*, 70.

88. Corrigan v. Buckley, 271 U.S. 323 (1926); Cherkasky, "'For Sale to Colored,'" 46–49.

89. *Corrigan v. Buckley*. The *Corrigan* case received widespread coverage in the press, including the *WP*, *WTR*, *NYT*, *AA*, and *CD*. See, e.g., "Bar Mrs. Helen Curtis from Home," *CD*, 25 Nov. 1922; "Washington Judge Favors Segregation," *CD*, 14 June 1924; "Mass Meeting on Segregation on Sunday," *WTR*, 12 Apr. 1924; "Segregation Case Goes to U.S. Supreme Court," *WP*, 1 Nov. 1925; "Race Segregation Appeal Is Argued in Supreme Court," *Baltimore Sun*, 9 Jan. 1926; "'Would Drive Colored Folk out of Washington, D.C.," *AA*, 16 Jan. 1926; "Court Upholds Ban on Sale to Negroes," *NYT*, 25 May 1926; "Right to Restrict Realty Sales to Negroes Upheld," *WP*, 26 May 1926.

90. Cherkasky, "'For Sale to Colored,'" 46–49; Gonda, *Unjust Deeds*; "Residential Segregation: Discriminatory Housing in the Nation's Capital," Confidential Report for the NCSNC, Box 131-107, Folder 2, EFFP; Modan, *Turf Wars*, 51–54. Thank you to Sarah Shoenfeld of Prologue DC for noting how quickly covenants spread in Mount Pleasant.

91. "Outwits D.C. Whites," *AA*, 20 Apr. 1923; Louis R. Lautier, "While Lawyers Argue Block Becomes Black," *AA*, 16 Jan. 1926; Kelly Miller, "Separate Communities for Negroes," *Current History* 25 (March 1927): 830; "District Court Decision Aids Segregation," *WTR*, 7 June 1924.

92. Joyce and Reid, "Remembering Washington," 31, 54; Jones, *Housing of Negroes*, 80; Collins, "'Substance of Things Hoped For,'" 123; "Re: You Street, N.W.," 6 May 1938, Box 131-112, Folder 7, NYS-DC, Research Projects, EFFP; McQuirter, "Claiming the City," 3, 80–81.

93. Warnke, "Greek American Community," 87–88, 153–54.

94. "Re: Fourth Street Southwest," 9 May 1938, Box 131-112, Folder 7, NYS-DC, Research Projects, EFFP.

95. Much of the preceding paragraph is based on Carole Abrams Kolker's wonderful exploration of Southwest culture: Kolker, "Migrants and Memories." See also Evelyn Levow Greenberg, "Life in the Old Southwest," *Record* 3, no. 2 (November 1968), 3–10; and Robert Shosteck, "An Economic Study of the Southwest Jewish Community, 1855–1955," *Record* 3, no. 2 (November 1968), 21–35.

96. Kelly Miller, "Where Is the Negro's Heaven?" (December 1926), in Wilson, *Opportunity Reader*, 429.

Chapter 9

1. Ruben Castaneda, "In City's Toughest Areas, a Worn Path to Violence," *WP*, 21 June 1994; Darcy Courteau, "The Generous Soul beneath the Chaos of Carter Langston," *WP*, 2 Aug. 2014; Michael Massing, "D.C.'s War on Drugs: Why Bennett Is Losing," *NYT*, 23 Sept. 1990; Linda Wheeler, "League Lits Endangered D.C. Properties," *WP*, 21 July 2001; Maria Adebola, "Northeast D.C. Housing Complex Hosts Annual Health Day Bash," *WP*, 5 Sept. 2015.

2. "Assign Julius Gardner to Langston Terrace Housing Project in Washington," *Atlanta Daily World*, 27 Feb. 1937.

3. Robinson quoted in 1950s interview in Benjamin Forgey, "The Enduring Ideals of Langston Terrace," *WP*, 4 June 1988; Alice Graeme, "Young Sculptor Given Rare Opportunity," *WP*, 28 Feb. 1937; "Photo News," *AA*, 29 May 1937; Nelson M. Shepard, "Thousands to Be Turned Away in Langston Rent Scramble," *ES*, 23 Jan. 1938.

4. Shepard, "Thousands to Be Turned Away"; Quinn, "Making Modern Homes," 14, 32, 35 (Middleton quotation), 53; "Housing Project Marks First Year," *CD*, 13 May 1939.

5. Oliver McKee Jr., "Washington as a Boom Town," *North American Review* 239, no. 2 (February 1935): 177, 183; "Washington D.C.," *Fortune* 10, no. 6 (December 1934): 133; David L. Cohn, "Washington the Blest," *Atlantic Monthly* 163, no. 5 (May 1939): 609.

6. McKee, "Washington as a Boom Town," 183; "Washington D.C.," *Fortune*, 133; "Washington Has 25,000 Employed in Domestic Service," *WP*, 22 Sept. 1930; USBC, *Negroes in the United States*, Introduction; "847 Men and Women Are Cared for by Transient Bureau Here," *WTR*, 30 Mar. 1935; George T. Waugh, "Washington at Random," *WTR*, 13 Jan. 1933.

7. Paul Dickson and Thomas B. Allen, "Marching on History," *Smithsonian Magazine* (February 2003); Barber, *Marching on Washington*, 75–107.

8. McKee, "Washington as a Boom Town," 177; USBC, 1940 Census of the United States.

9. Cohn, "Washington the Blest," 609.

10. "Areas of Racial Tension," Box 163-16, Folder 13, CHHP; Turner Catledge, "Problem of Negro Worries Capital," NYT, 25 July 1943.

11. Fant, "Slum Reclamation and Housing Reform," 153–54.

12. "To Build Model Homes," WP, 30 Jan. 1916; Dorrie Davenport, "John Ihlder, 82, Fought Slums," WPTH, 20 May 1958; Fant, "Slum Reclamation and Housing Reform," 147–68; Paige and Reuss, "Safe, Decent and Affordable," 78–79; Clement, "Wagner-Steagall and the D.C. Alley Dwelling Authority," 434–48.

13. "Washington's Chest Expansion," Survey 66, no. 2 (15 Apr. 1931): 99.

14. "Survey of Housing Here Shows Deplorable Conditions," WTR, 6 Jan. 1933; interview with clerk at Aitkens Realty Office, 19 July 1938, Box 131-112, Folder 7, NYS-DC, Research Projects, EFFP.

15. Felix Bruner, "Alleys Survive 60-Year Fight," WP, 13 Jan. 1934; Jones, Housing of Negroes, 25–40; Ihlder quoted in Gillette, Between Justice and Beauty, 140.

16. John Ihlder, "Washington Alleys," WP, 23 Dec. 1930; "Bill to Ban Alley Homes Is Pushed," ES, 21 Mar. 1931; Gillette, Between Justice and Beauty, 137–38.

17. Fant, "Slum Reclamation and Public Housing," 213–14; Borchert, Alley Life in Washington, 52–54; Gillette, Between Justice and Beauty, 138–40; Quinn, "Making Modern Homes," 14–15.

18. Gillette, Between Justice and Beauty, 140.

19. "2 New Projects Announced by Alley Group," WP, 19 June 1937; Tract 54, 29 Nov. 1938, Community Reports, Box 131-111, Folder 20, NYS-DC, Research Projects, EFFP; "Plan to Exclude Colored in Area Meets Protest," WP, 22 July 1937; "ADA Is Criticized," WP, 21 Dec. 1937; "Alley Fund's Legal Basis Is Outlined," WP, 24 Dec. 1937; "Citizens Protest Restricted Zone," CD, 31 July 1937; "Lincoln Park Citizens Assail Daylight Time," WP, 18 May 1937; "Whites Aid Civic Body in Alley Housing Fight," AA, 31 July 1937; "Housing Project Opened to Colored," ES, 24 Dec. 1937.

20. Collins quoted in Green, Secret City, 247.

21. Hannold, "'Comfort and Respectability,'" 35–36.

22. Grant quoted in Gillette, Between Justice and Beauty, 139; "Housing Project Opened to Colored"; "On Reclaiming Slums," WP, 28 Feb. 1936.

23. Harris quoted in Gillette, Between Justice and Beauty, 142.

24. "Building Program Drives Chinese to Seek a New Center," Star, 16 Aug. 1931; "Connally Backs $9,000,000 Bill for Auditorium," WP, Apr. 21, 1938; "Chinatown Is Small, but Area Buzzes with Activity," ES, 21 May 1951; Gillette, Between Justice and Beauty, 142; Hathaway and Ho, "Small but Resilient," 43–48; Alison K. Hoagland, "Seventh Street/Downtown," in Smith, Washington at Home, 64–65.

25. Gillette, Between Justice and Beauty, 142; "Negro Housing Plight Here to Grow Worse, Women Shoppers Told," ES, 5 Jan. 1944; "Isolated Negro Community; Interview with Mr. Carter, Negro Resident, Chain Bridge Road," 7 Nov. 1938, Community Reports, Box 131-111, Folder 20, NYS-DC, Research Projects, EFFP.

26. Helm, Tenleytown, 129, 174; "Residential Segregation: Discriminatory Housing in the Nation's Capital," Confidential Report for the NCSNC, Box 131-107, Folder 2, 29,

EFFP; Federal Writers' Project, *Washington*, 75; Charles Moore, ed., *The Improvement of the Park System of the District of Columbia*, U.S. Senate Committee on the District of Columbia, S. Rep. 166, 57th Cong., 1st Sess. (Washington, D.C.: USGPO, 1902), 91–92; "Plans for New Junior High Call for Model Institution," *WP*, 15 Mar. 1929.

27. Doyle quoted in Helm, *Tenleytown*, 479–84; "Interview with White Resident Worker at the Reno Reservoir," November 1938, Community Reports, Box 131-111, Folder 20, NYS-DC, Research Projects, EFFP.

28. Reno Neighborhood Project Records, KRL-HSW: Elizabeth J. Miller, "Report on the Neighborhood History Project, 1977," Box 1, Folder 1; "Interview with Frank Coupe and Pete Toatly," 28 July 1977, Box 1, Folder 6; and "Interview at Rock Creek Baptist Church," 2 Aug. 1977, Box 1, Folder 7. Several black families on the 4800 block of 41st Street stayed in their homes until the 1970s. Ronald Taylor, "Five Houses Are Renovated and Neighborhood Changes," *WP*, 15 May 1975; Alma Guillermoprieto, "A Tender Tribute to Old Tenleytown," *WP*, 15 Sept. 1983; Helm, *Tenleytown*, 479–84.

29. Fant, "Slum Reclamation and Housing Reform," 150; Ecker, *Portrait of Old George Town*, chap. 14.

30. NCSNC and Landis, *Segregation in Washington*, 32; "Residential Segregation: Discriminatory Housing," 28; Gale, *Washington, D.C.*, 51–57.

31. Asch and Musgrove, "'We're Heading for Some Bad Trouble,'" 127–28.

32. Fant, "Slum Reclamation and Housing Reform," 284; "Interview with Mr. Gray, of Budget Committee," Community Chest, 1 June 1938, Community Reports, Box 131-112, Folder 7, NYS-DC, Research Projects, EFFP.

33. Ihlder diary quoted in Fant, "Slum Reclamation and Housing Reform," 287.

34. Ihlder diary quoted in Fant, "Slum Reclamation and Housing Reform," 287.

35. Yellin, *Racism in the Nation's Service*, 53, 138; "Messenger for War Department Dies," ES, 22 Apr. 1928.

36. In 2012, the Multicultural Center at Williams College was renamed in honor of Davis and his brother, Allison Davis, who also graduated from Williams. "Williams College Honors Two Black Alumni," *Journal of Blacks in Higher Education*, 29 Oct. 2012; Alfred E. Smith, "Adventures in Race Relations," *CD*, 3 Feb. 1945.

37. John A. Davis, "The Negro Outlook Today," *Survey Graphic* 31 (November 1942): 500; Bart Barnes, "John Aubrey Davis, Sr.: Scholar, Rights Activists Who Led Boycotts," *WP*, 21 Dec. 2002; Wolfgang Saxon, "John A. Davis, 90, Advocate in Major Civil Rights Cases," *NYT*, 21 Dec. 2002; Pacifico, "'Don't Buy Where You Can't Work,'" 71–72.

38. "Boycott Forces Hamburger Grill to Rehire Three," *WTR*, 31 Aug. 1933; "Alliance to Launch Campaign against Peoples Drug Stores," *WTR*, 7 Sept. 1933; "The New Negro Alliance," *WTR*, 28 Sept. 1933; Pacifico, "'Don't Buy Where You Can't Work,'" 68–69.

39. "A & P Hires Two Clerks," *WTR*, 28 Sept. 1933; "The New Negro Alliance," *WTR*, 28 Sept. 1933; Portia James, "New Negro Opinion Newspaper," *Smithsonian Collections Blog*, http://si-siris.blogspot.com/2011/05/new-negro-opinion-newspaper.html; press release, 16 May 1941, Box 78-50, Folder 1095, NAACP-DC.

40. "Peoples Drug Store—14th and U Streets, N.W.," 14 July 1938, Box 131-113, Folder 1, NYS-DC, EFFP.

41. New Negro Alliance v. Sanitary Grocery Co., 303 U.S. 552, 552–63 (1938); Pacifico, "'Don't Buy Where You Can't Work,'" 82–84.

42. Press release, 16 May 1941, and "If you are a wise owl . . . ," both in Box 78-50, Folder 1095, NAACP-DC.

43. "Washington D.C.," *Fortune* 10, no. 6 (December 1934): 132–33.

44. "Interview with Bookkeeper of the Cafritz Construction Company," 14 June 1938, Box 131-113, Folder 1, NYS-DC, EFFP.

45. "Coppers Pummel 10,000 Women Seeking 2,000 Jobs," AA, 15 Oct. 1938; NCSNC and Landis, *Segregation in Washington*, 54–55; Murphy, *National and Local Affair*, chap. 4.

46. Harding, "Eleanor Nelson, Oliver Palmer," 54; "Interview with Mr. Lester," 13 May 1938, Box 131-113, Folder 1, NYS-DC, EFFP.

47. "Interview with Annie Stein, Paid Employee of the Restaurant Alliance of A.F. of L.," 13 May 1938, Box 131-112, Folder 7, NYS-DC, Research Projects, EFFP; "Interview with Business Agent of the Waitresses Local—A.F. of L.," 13 May 1938, Box 131-112, Folder 7, NYS-DC, Research Projects, EFFP.

48. "Interview with Mr. Lester," 13 May 1938, Box 131-113, Folder 1, NYS-DC, EFFP.

49. Willie Evans, "Group Has a Mere 80 of 60,000 on Federal Pay-Roll," *Atlantic Daily World*, 7 Sept. 1936; "Washington D.C.," *Fortune* 10, no. 6 (December 1934): 133.

50. Harding, "Eleanor Nelson, Oliver Palmer," 17, 91–92; "Oliver T. Palmer, 79, D.C. Union, Civic Leader," WP, 9 Jan. 1975.

51. "Washington D.C.," *Fortune*, 130.

52. "Interview with Inez Robertson," 24 May 1938, Box 131-113, Folder 1, NYS-DC, EFFP.

53. Gellman, *Death Blow to Jim Crow*, esp. 109–42.

54. "Civic Association Committee Protests Police Brutality," WTR, 24 Mar. 1933.

55. Gellman, *Death Blow to Jim Crow*, 111; officer quoted in Murphy, *National and Local Affair*, chap. 3.

56. Murphy, *National and Local Affair*, chap. 3.

57. Gellman, *Death Blow to Jim Crow*, 118.

58. "Coffins Barred as Reds March against Police," AA, 16 July 1938; letter to editor, AA, 2 July 1938; "How Washington Protests Police Brutality," AA, 16 July 1938; "Pickets Protest Police Murders in Washington," CD, 16 July 1938.

59. "Stop Police Brutality," Petition Circulated in Negro Churches during Month of August 1938, Community Reports, Box 131-111, Folder 21, NYS-DC, Research Projects, EFFP; John Lovell Jr., "Washington Fights," *Crisis* 46, no. 9 (September 1939): 276; Gellman, *Death Blow to Jim Crow*, 122–26; Murphy, *National and Local Affair*, chap. 3.

60. "Re: You Street, N.W.," 6 May 1938, Box 131-112, Folder 7, NYS-DC, Research Projects, EFFP; Victor R. Daly, "Washington's Minority Problem," *Crisis* 46, no. 6 (June 1939): 171.

61. Merlo J. Pusey, "District Confronted by Financial Chaos: Washington's Revenues Are Spent for Upkeep of Federal Interests in City While Local Needs Are Neglected," WP, 17 Jan. 1937; "Washington, D.C.," *Fortune* 10, no. 6 (December 1934): 129; Merlo J. Pusey, "Observer Sees Capital as Political Step-Child," WP, 11 Jan. 1937; Merlo J. Pusey, "Unified Civil Regime First Stage of Reform," WP, 14 Jan. 1937.

62. ES, 4 July 1946; WP, 5 July 1946, 6 Jan. 1921; Noyes, *Our National Capital*, 15–23; Zigas, "Left with Few Rights," 24.

63. "D.C. Votes 7–1 for Self-Rule, 13–1 for Seats in Congress," WP, 2 May 1938; Noyes,

Our National Capital, 167; "84 Per Cent of District Residents Favor Home Rule, Right to Vote in U.S. Elections," WP, 19 Nov. 1945.

64. "Speech Delivered over WMAL," 21 Nov. 1935, in "Federation of Civic Associations," Vertical File, WD; ES, 20 May 1934; Pinchback quoted in Hering, "Voice of the Voteless," 10.

65. Grover Ayers, "D.C. 'City State' Might Be First of 40, Wrecking U.S.," WP, 30 Apr. 1938; Turner quoted in Hering, "Voice of the Voteless," 10.

66. Zigas, "Left with Few Rights," 27; Merlo J. Pusey, "Right to Vote in D.C. Held a National Issue," WP, 3 June 1934; U.S. Congress, Senate Committee on the District of Columbia, *Reorganization of the Government of the District of Columbia*, 151; Ward, *Defending White Democracy*, 75–76.

67. Noyes quoted in Hering, "Voice of the Voteless," 10.

68. The "white artists only" policy had been demanded by a major donor before the building was even constructed, and DAR began enforcing it after white patrons complained about black tenor Roland Hayes's appearance at the facility in 1932. Arsenault, *Sound of Freedom*, 90–91.

69. Victor R. Daly, "Washington's Minority Problem," *Crisis* 46, no. 6 (June 1939): 170–71.

70. Hamilton, "Making a 'Model' System," 77–133; Arsenault, *Sound of Freedom*, 126; Report of the Committee of the Board of Education on the Community Use of Buildings, 3 Mar. 1939, Box 78-41, Folder 763, NAACP-DC.

71. Black, "A Reluctant but Persistent Warrior," 233–50.

72. Edward T. Folliard, "Ickes Introduces Contralto at Lincoln Memorial; Many Officials Attend Concert," WP, 10 Apr. 1939; Sandage, "Marble House Divided," 492–535; Savage, *Monument Wars*, 256–57.

73. Lovell, "Washington Fights," 276; Mary McLeod Bethune to Charles Hamilton Houston, 10 Apr. 1939, cited in Melder, *City of Magnificent Intentions*, 452.

74. New Negro Alliance quoted in Arsenault, *Sound of Freedom*, 167.

75. Alden Stevens, "Washington: Blight on Democracy," *Harper's Magazine* 184 (December 1941): 50; Gueli, "'Girls on the Loose,'" 44; James Reston, "L'Enfant's Capital—and Boomtown, Too," NYT *Magazine* (1 June 1941): 6.

76. USBC, "Historical Census Statistics on Population Totals by Race," table 23.

77. Washington Urban League, "Race Relations in the Nation's Capital, 1939–1940," KRL-HSW; A. Philip Randolph, "Why and How the March Was Postponed," undated press release [1941], Box 163-18, Folder 27, CHHP.

78. "Negroes' Parade Called Off after Executive Order," ES, 26 June 1941; Asch, "Revisiting Reconstruction," 4–5; Kryder, *Divided Arsenal*, 60–65; Murray quoted in Bell-Scott, *Firebrand and First Lady*, 102–3.

79. Joseph Lohman and Edwin W. Embree, "The Nation's Capital," *Survey Graphic* 36 (January 1947): 34; Gooding "Dream Deferred," 22; King, *Separate and Unequal*, 258–59.

80. Stevens, "Washington: Blight on Democracy," 50, 54.

81. Ralph Matthews, "Social Frills Hold No Thrills for Her," AA, 29 Mar. 1958; "Charming Lobbyists," CD, 6 June 1942; "Famed D.C. Medic, Mazique, Wins Hot Divorce Battle," *Jet* 26, no. 25 (24 Sept. 1964): 23; Ridlon, *Black Physician's Struggle for Civil Rights*, 89, 103–4, 130–32, 183–84; Orbach and Natanson, "Mirror Image," 7–14.

82. Orbach and Natanson, "Mirror Image," 7–14; Chandler Owen, *Negroes and the War* (Washington, D.C.: Office of War Information, n.d. [ca. 1943]), 15.

83. Parks, *Choice of Weapons*, 222–26.

84. Parks, *Choice of Weapons*, 230–31; Orbach and Natanson, "Mirror Image," 16–25.

85. Roger G. Kennedy, "Introduction," in Federal Writers' Project, *WPA Guide*, xxiii.

86. Murray quoted in Bell-Scott, *Firebrand and First Lady*, 103; Lauren, *Power and Prejudice*, esp. chaps. 4–5; Dower, *War without Mercy*, 119–20; Asch, *Senator and Sharecropper*, 114–15.

87. Lucia M. Pitts, "The Federal Diary," WP, 25 July 1942.

88. "The Job Color-Line in the Nation's Capital," Box 78-66, Folder 1462, NAACP-DC; "Hearing Set Tuesday in Case involving Colored Bus Drivers," ES, 16 May 1943; "Citizens Committee on Race Relations, Inc.: First Annual Report," 1 Aug. 1944, Box 163-19, Folder 2, CHHP; "D.C. Transit Still Dodges FEPC Order," 9 Jan. 1943.

89. Robert Paul, "Hiring Negroes," WP, 1 Oct. 1942; "Still Late to Work?," ES, 11 Mar. 1943; "Drive to Ban Jim Crow on Washington Buses," *New York Amsterdam News*, 7 Nov. 1942; "Cooperation Promised Job Body by ODT," AA, 14 Nov. 1942; "Unit Formed to Fight for Transit Co. Jobs," AA, 22 Aug. 1942; "Capital Transit Co. Accused of Barring Negro Employees," WP, 2 Apr. 1943; FEPC chairman quoted in Green, *Secret City*, 258.

90. Harry McAlpin, "D.C. Bus Firm Insists on Barring Negro Drivers," CD, 28 Nov. 1942; "Negroes 'Not Cultured' So They Can't Be Bus Drivers," CD, 30 Jan. 1943.

91. "Capital Transit Agrees to Open Trolley, Bus Jobs to Negroes," WP, 16 Dec. 1942; "Capital Bus Official Bows; Hires Negroes," CD, 26 Dec. 1942; "Whites Refuse to Aid Bus Driver Learn D.C. Job," CD, 13 Feb. 1943; Fred Brandeis, "Transit Firm's 'Strike' Fears in Hiring Policy Challenged," WP, 16 Jan. 1945; "Hearing Set Tuesday."

92. "Transit Company Job Pickets," AA, 15 May 1943; "Hearing Set Tuesday"; "Rumors of Riot Give Capital War of Nerves," AA, 15 May 1943; "Marcantonio Scores Policy of Transit Co.," AA, 15 May 1943; Harry McAlpin, "Riot Rumors Keep D.C. on Edge for Entire Week," CD, 15 May 1943; Harry McAlpin, "Week-Long Drive Blasts Job Ban on Capital Buses," CD, 8 May 1943; "Protest, Parade Mark Transit Work Request," WP, 8 May 1943; "Colored Bus Drivers Demanded at Rally," ES, 8 May 1943; "Minutes of Meeting of the Citizens Committee on Race Relations," 3 Feb. 1944, Box 78-57, Folder 1290, NAACP-DC; "Job Color-Line in the Nation's Capital"; "Race Relations," WP, 24 Sept. 1945.

93. Murray, *Song in a Weary Throat*, 200–201.

94. Bell-Scott, *Firebrand and First Lady*, esp. 113–19; Pauli Murray Project, http://pauli murrayproject.org/; Gilmore, *Defying Dixie*, 264–73, 384–93.

95. Gilmore, *Defying Dixie*, 384–93.

96. Murray, *Song in a Weary Throat*, 224–27; Pauli Murray, "A Blueprint for First Class Citizenship," *Crisis* 51, no. 2 (November 1944), cited in Honey, *Bitter Fruit*, 276–77.

97. Brown, "NAACP Sponsored Sit-Ins," 274–86.

98. Fleegler, "Theodore G. Bilbo," 13–14; Morgan, *Redneck Liberal*, 2–4; Ward, *Defending White Democracy*, 68–69; Brown, "NAACP Sponsored Sit-Ins," 274–86.

99. Turner Catledge, "Problem of Negro Worries Capital," NYT, 25 July 1943; Sitkoff, "African American Militancy," 87.

100. "Citizens Committee on Race Relations, Inc.: First Annual Report," 1 Aug. 1944, Box 163-19, Folder 2, CHHP; "Report of the Alley Dwelling Authority for the District of

Columbia," 1941, Box 78-56, Folder 1272, NAACP-DC, 1; Stevens, "Washington: Blight on Democracy," 51; Meyer, *Journey through Chaos*, 316–17.

101. "Family Housing Shortage Most Acute," *WP*, 23 Dec. 1941.

102. John Ihlder, "Nine Projects Now Being Developed," *Sunday Star*, 16 June 1940; Meyer, *Journey through Chaos*, 318; Nancy Perry, presentation at the Arlington Historical Society, 13 Feb. 2014; Brinkley, *Washington Goes to War*, 235–36.

103. "Citizens Committee on Race Relations, Inc.: First Annual Report," 1 Aug. 1944, in Box 163-19, Folder 2, CHHP; Green, *Secret City*, 261–67.

104. Green, *Secret City*, 238–40.

105. Ihlder quoted in Barnes, "National Controversy in Miniature," 91.

106. "First Lady Hits Segregation in Federal Housing," *CD*, 18 Dec. 1943.

107. Frank Diggs, "White, Colored Unite to Map Cooperation," *WP*, 20 Apr. 1941; "Wender Says Roosevelt Gave U.S. Housing 'Death Kiss,'" *ES*, 10 June 1944; "Senate Hearings on Slums End on Race Issue," *Sunday Star*, 11 June 1944; see also Barnes, "Origins of Urban Renewal," 114–17.

108. Height, *Open Wide the Freedom Gates*, 99.

109. Gueli, "'Girls on the Loose,'" 102; Wright, *Far from Home*, 5; Height, *Open Wide the Freedom Gates*, 99–100; Slowe Hall is now part of Howard's campus. "Howard Gets Two Government Halls," *CD*, 10 July 1948; "U.S. to Sell Capital Dorms," *WP*, 2 Feb. 1944.

110. "Residential Segregation: Discriminatory Housing," 35, 46–47; Valentine quoted in Barnes, "Origins of Urban Renewal," 124; "Senate Hearings on Slums End on Race Issue."

Chapter 10

1. The fort was named in honor of Admiral Samuel F. Dupont, the same Union leader memorialized by Dupont Circle in Northwest Washington. V. Dion Hayes, "From Obsolete to State of the Art," *WP*, 21 Aug. 2008; "50 Years Later, Sousa Still Struggling over Brown," *WT*, 13 May 2004; Salvatore and Sprinkle Jr., *National Historic Landmark Nomination*, 4–15; Turner Construction, "John Philip Sousa Middle School," http://www.turner construction.com/experience/project/2F6/john-philip-sousa-middle-school.

2. "Suburbs Gain Attraction," *WP*, 13 Jan. 1907; "Valley Realty Company," *WP*, 24 Feb. 1907.

3. "Report of the Alley Dwelling Authority for the District of Columbia," 1941, Box 78-56, Folder 1272, 17, NAACP-DC; John Ihlder, "Nine Projects Now Being Developed," *Sunday Star*, 16 June 1940; Benedetto, Donovan, and Duvall, *Historical Dictionary of Washington*, 31–33; Elsie Carper, "Rising Enrollments Tax Seating Space, Teachers," *WP*, 11 Sept. 1949.

4. Cantwell, "Anacostia," 354–55.

5. Cantwell, "Anacostia," 348.

6. Issac Franck, "Racial Integration in the Nation's Capital—An Introductory Statement," in National Association of Intergroup Relations Officials, *Civil Rights in the Nation's Capital*, 3.

7. Williams, *Torchbearers of Democracy*, 42–43, 133–34, 250; Charles H. Houston, "Saving the World for Democracy," Pittsburgh Courier, 14 Sept. 1940; McNeil, *Groundwork*, 13, 45; Kluger, *Simple Justice*, esp. 105–31.

8. Kluger, *Simple Justice*, 125–28.

9. "Minutes of Meeting of the Citizens Committee on Race Relations," 26 Oct. 1945, Box 78-57, Folder 1290, NAACP-DC.

10. Venice T. Spraggs, "Houston Quits FEP," CD, 8 Dec. 1945; Asch, "Revisiting Reconstruction," 1–28.

11. J. A. O'Leary, "Bilbo Appeals for Re-Election So He Can Block D.C. Suffrage," ES, 8 May 1946; "Mayor of Washington," WP, 4 July 1946.

12. Mrs. Werner W. Moore quoted in "Statements or Excerpts of Committee against Segregation in Recreation before the Board of Education," 17 July 1945, Box 78-74, Folder 1575, 11, NAACP-DC.

13. "Race Segregation 'Natural' Here, Newell Tells Citizens," WP, 15 Oct. 1947; *Neighborhood News*, the organ of the Rhode Island Avenue Citizens Association, quoted in "Residential Segregation: Discriminatory Housing in the Nation's Capital," Confidential Report for the NCSNC, Box 131-107, Folder 2, 43, EFFP; "Text of Federation Report on Racial Survey," *Sunday Star*, 5 Jan. 1947; "No Discrimination Here, Declares Citizens' Head," *Washington Daily News*, 9 Dec. 1947.

14. Jack Eisen, "Gen. Ulysses S. Grant III Dies," WP, 30 Aug. 1968; Grant quoted in King, *Making Americans*, 340–41; Murray Marder, "Segregation Report Assailed as Distorted 'Special Plea,'" WP, 22 Dec. 1948; William D. Nixon, "Ghettoized Housing," letter to the editor, WP, 8 Jan. 1949.

15. USBC, "Current Population Reports Series P25-139, Years 1940–1949," http://www2.census.gov/programs-surveys/popest/tables/1980-1990/state/asrh/st4049ts.txt; Gillette, *Between Justice and Beauty*, 153.

16. Jackson, "Federal Subsidy and the Suburban Dream," 430–32; "Residential Segregation: Discriminatory Housing," 62.

17. Derthick, *City Politics*, 3; "Residential Segregation: Discriminatory Housing," 3, EFFP.

18. Derthick, *City Politics*, 2–5; "Residential Segregation: Discriminatory Housing"; Grier, *Understanding Washington's Changing Population*, 3–12; Gillette, *Between Justice and Beauty*, 168; FHA report quoted in Jackson, "Federal Subsidy and Suburban Dream," 439; NCSNC and Landis, *Segregation in Washington*, 40–41.

19. "Russian Newspaper Hits Treatment of Negroes Here," ES, 21 Aug. 1947; Phineas Indritz, "Racism in the Nation's Capital," *Nation* (18 Oct. 1952): 355.

20. "Statements or Excerpts of Committee against Segregation in Recreation," 4–6.

21. For more on the Cold War and the civil rights movement, see Borstelmann, *Cold War and Color Line*; and Dudziak, *Cold War Civil Rights*; Harry Truman, "Special Message to the Congress on Civil Rights," 2 Feb. 1948, http://www.presidency.ucsb.edu/ws/?pid=13006.

22. President's Committee on Civil Rights, *To Secure These Rights*, 89–95.

23. "Resolution," 22 Nov. 1947, Box 78-75, Folder 1589, NAACP-DC.

24. "Minutes of Meeting of the Citizens Committee on Race Relations," 18 Dec. 1945, Box 78-57, Folder 1290, NAACP-DC; "A Message of Good Will," Box 78-57, Folder 1290, NAACP-DC; "Bilbo Picket Set for Long Crusade," AA, 22 Dec. 1945; "Thirty in Mixed Groups Turned Away at National," ES, 4 Dec. 1946.

25. "Mrs. Alice Hunter Named on New Recreation Board," AA, 30 May 1942; "Alice Callis Hunter," WP, 10 July 1989; "Final Report of Citizens Committee against Segregation

in Recreation," 20 May 1948, Box 78-14, Folder 248, 8, NAACP-DC; Hamilton, "Making a 'Model' System," 134–90.

26. "Residential Segregation: Discriminatory Housing," 15–17; Sam Stavisky, "500 Attend Rally to Prevent Sale of Homes to Negroes," WP, 9 Nov. 1947.

27. Charles H. Houston, "The Highway," AA, 13 Sept. 1947; NCSNC and Landis, *Segregation in Washington*, 30; Vose, *Caucasians Only*, 77; "Residential Segregation: Discriminatory Housing," 43; "White Citizens' Association Violated Rule by Holding 'Hate' Parley in School," AA, 27 Sept. 1947; Congress Heights Citizens' Association quoted in Clement, "Pushback," 91.

28. Stavisky, "500 Attend Rally"; Gilligan quoted in Vose, *Caucasians Only*, 81; "White Citizens' Association Violated Rule."

29. J. Y. Smith, "Lawyer Raphael G. Urciolo Dies; Fought Racially Biased Covenants," WP, 7 Oct. 1994; John J. O'Connor, "Washington Reporter," *Interracial Review* (June 1947): 95; Vose, *Caucasians Only*, 80, 89–90.

30. Frank Wilder, "Race Covenant Rule Disappoints Many," WP, 4 May 1948.

31. "Henry Gilligan Quitting Post on School Board after 11 Years," WP, 4 Apr. 1937; Henry Gilligan, "Citizens' Rights," WP, 22 Mar. 1944; "Henry Gilligan Rites to Be Held Monday; Attorney Was 69," ES, 7 Oct. 1950; Vose, *Caucasians Only*, 78, 84.

32. "D.C. Property Covenants Upheld by Appellate Court," AA, 3 Feb. 1945.

33. Mays v. Burgess, 147 F.2n 869, 873–78 (12th Cir. 1945).

34. McNeil, *Groundwork*, 177–80; Alan Barth, "'Militant Liberal' Molding Our Laws," WPTH, 12 June 1955; Vose, *Caucasians Only*, 99.

35. "'Racism Must Go,' High Court Told by Houston," AA, 24 Jan. 1948; McNeil, *Groundwork*, 181.

36. Dillard Stokes, "High Court Voids Racial Ban in Realty Transactions," WP, 4 May 1948; Frank Wilder, "Race Covenant Rule Disappoints Many," WP, 4 May 1948.

37. Jean M. White, "Southwest Design Wins on Merit—and Then Comes Big Question," WPTH, 22 Oct. 1961. For examples of violence accompanying black people moving into white neighborhoods, see "Stones Greet Negroes Moving into White Neighborhood Here," WP, 4 Apr. 1949; and "Minority Group Getting Fed Up," AA, 17 Sept. 1949.

38. Jones, *Radical Line*, 16–32; Asch, "Annie Stein," 79–80.

39. "Farewell Reception in Honor of Mrs. Annie Stein," 8 Mar. 1953, Box 1, Folder 1, CCEADL Papers, 1949–1954, KRL-HSW; Caplan, "Trenton Terrace Remembered," 47; Jones, *Radical Line*, 31, 100.

40. NCSNC and Landis, *Segregation in Washington*, 31, 87, 88; Pritchett, "National Issue."

41. "The Executive Board of the Federation of Citizens Associations of the District of Columbia on 'Segregation in Washington,'" Vertical Files, WD, 1–2.

42. Indritz, "Racism in the Nation's Capital," 355–57; Murray Teigh Bloom, "Democracy Comes to Washington," *Pageant* 7, no. 2 (August 1951): 38.

43. Pauli Murray, *Song in a Weary Throat*, 229–30; "Suggested Outline for Speakers on the 1872 Law," CCEADL, Reel 14, MCTP; NCSNC and Landis, *Segregation in Washington*, 18.

44. "Suggested Outline for Speakers on the 1872 Law"; Borchardt, "Making D.C. Democracy's Capital," 28–29; Caplan, *Farther Along*, 114.

45. "Maher to Study 1872 Race Law," WT, 3 June 1949.

46. "Farewell Reception in Honor of Mrs. Annie Stein," 8 Mar. 1953, Box 1, Folder 1,

CCEADL Papers, 1949–1954, KRL-HSW; "Suggested Outline for Speakers on the 1872 Law"; Jones, *Radical Line*, 7–8, 93–105; Caplan, *Farther Along*, 109–10, 113; Borchardt, "Making D.C. Democracy's Capital," 16–54.

47. "Suggested Outline for Speakers on the 1872 Law."

48. The committee chose to demonstrate at the 14th Street NW location of Thompson's, which was in the same building as the office of National Lawyers' Guild attorneys Joe Forer and David Rein, who were working on the case. Stein, "Thompson Case," 105; "Affidavit of Mary Church Terrell," and "Background of the Complaint Filed with Corporation Counsel," 30 Jan. 1950, both in CCEADL, Reel 14, MCTP.

49. "Press Release: From PMs, Thursday, March 30," CCEADL, Reel 14, MCTP; Caplan, "Eat Anywhere!," 32; Bloom, "Democracy Comes to Washington," 38–43; District of Columbia v. John R. Thompson Co., Inc., 346 U.S. 100 (73 S.Ct. 1007, 97 L.Ed 1480); Borchardt, "Making D.C. Democracy's Capital," 42–43.

50. Caplan, "Eat Anywhere!," 32; "Victory at Kresge's," 15 Jan. 1951, CCEADL, Reel 14, MCTP.

51. Annie Stein to Edna J. Coker, 6 Nov. 1951, and "Progress Report," July 1951, both in Box 1, Folder 16, CCEADL Papers, 1949–1954, KRL-HSW; Press release, 19 Jan. 1952, Box 1, Folder 17, CCEADL Papers, 1949–1954, KRL-HSW; "Progress Report," 1 June 1951, "Summary of Enforcement Day Survey," 9 June 1951, and "Memorandum Re Boycott against the Hecht Co.," 8 Oct. 1951, all in CCEADL, Reel 14, MCTP; Caplan, "Eat Anywhere!," 34.

52. District of Columbia v. John R. Thompson Company, Inc., Municipal Court for the District of Columbia, Criminal no. 99150; "Factsheet on Frank H. Myers Decision in the Thompson Restaurant Case," Box 1, Folder 8, CCEADL Papers, 1949–1954, KRL-HSW; "Donohue Poses Plan to Curb Segregation," ES, 23 Jan. 1953.

53. Borchardt, "Making D.C. Democracy's Capital," 47–48.

54. "Freedom for All," WP, 3 Feb. 1953; Nichols, "'Showpiece of Our Nation,'" 45.

55. District of Columbia v. John R. Thompson Co., Inc.

56. Caplan, "'Eat Anywhere!'" 39; Alice Dunnigan, "Resents Ike's Taking Credit for Winning DC Restaurant Case," New York Amsterdam News, 20 Jan. 1953; "Obituaries," WPTH, 25 July 1954; "Annie Stein of Progressive Party," WP, 16 May 1981.

57. "NCHA Sees D.C. Still Short of Low-Rent Units," ES, 13 Apr. 1953; "Segregation in 9 More Housing Projects to End," ES, 11 Sept. 1953; "While Politicians Talk, Washingtonians Are Working Out Their Own Problems," Sunday Star, 19 Oct. 1952.

58. Indritz, "Racism in the Nation's Capital," 356.

59. "D.C. Afro Honor Roll Pays Tribute to 10," AA, 10 Feb. 1951; Juan Williams, "Puzzling Legacy of 1954," WP, 17 May 1979; Bob Levey, "Going, Going, Gone Condo: Neighborhood Nostalgia," WP, 4 Dec. 1980; J. Y. Smith, "D.C. Desegregation Activist Gardner L. Bishop Dies at 82," WP, 27 Nov. 1992; Kluger, Simple Justice, 513–20.

60. Kluger, Simple Justice, 514; Williams, "Puzzling Legacy of 1954."

61. Williams, "Puzzling Legacy of 1954"; Kluger, Simple Justice, 515.

62. "Educational Segregation: The Denial of Opportunity to Youth," Confidential Report for the NCSNC, Box 131-107, Folder 3, 23, EFFP; Roe, "Dual School System," 28; Wolters, Burden of Brown, 9–10; Hamilton, "Making a 'Model' System," 20–76.

63. "Educational Segregation: The Denial of Opportunity to Youth," 22–23; Diner,

Crisis of Confidence, 14. White enrollment in 1935–36 was 58,644; black enrollment was 32,472. In 1947–48, white enrollment was 49,877, while black enrollment was 41,612. U.S. Congress, Subcommittees on District of Columbia Appropriations, Senate and House of Representatives, *Report of a Survey of the Public Schools of the District of Columbia*, 308; Knoll, *Truth about Desegregation*, 13.

64. Agnes E. Meyer, "Modern' Browne Junior High Far behind White Schools," WP, 9 Mar. 1947; U.S. Congress, Subcommittees on District of Columbia Appropriations, Senate and House of Representatives, "*Report of a Survey of the Public Schools of the District of Columbia*," 343–45.

65. Meyer, "Modern' Browne Junior High"; McQuirter, "'Our Cause Is Marching On,'" 68, 76; Hansen, *Danger in Washington*, 10.

66. Coit Hendley Jr., "Our Dual School System: Validity of Segregation May Be Tested on Complaint That It also Means Discrimination," ES, 13 Oct. 1947; Knoll, *Truth about Desegregation*, 5.

67. "Colored Pupil Barred from White School," ES, 3 Feb. 1944; "D.C. School Jim Crow Suit Revised," AA, 3 June 1944; "School Board, in Answer to Suit, Denies Responsibility," AA, 29 July 1944; "Three Women and Seven Men Named to Afro's Honor Roll," AA, 27 Jan. 1945; "Educational Segregation: The Denial of Opportunity to Youth."

68. Joe Shepherd, "Girl Jolts D.C. School System," CD, 12 Apr. 1947; "Father of Expelled Girl Assails School Segregation," ES, 2 June 1947; "Court Case to Test Right of School Board to Bar Girl," AA, 31 May 1947; "Segregated School Law Facing Test," AA, 12 Apr. 1947; Harry Keelan, "Voice in the Wilderness," AA, 31 May 1947; "Educational Segregation: The Denial of Opportunity to Youth," 48–49; Carlos Munoz Jr., "Punto Final! In Praise of Ernesto Galarza," *Hispanic Outlook in Higher Education* 10, no. 5 (19 Nov. 1999): 92.

69. "Educational Segregation: The Denial of Opportunity to Youth," 52; Meyer, "Modern' Browne Junior High."

70. "Parents Petition Board to Abandon Segregated Policy," *Washington Pittsburgh Courier*, 26 Apr. 1947; "Suit in District Court Challenges Legality of School Segregation," ES, 8 Oct. 1947; McQuirter, "'Our Cause Is Marching On,'" 70–71.

71. "Civic Group Critical of Reported Plan to Remove Students," ES, 25 Oct. 1947; "20 Groups Will Testify at Hearing on Shift of 5 Schools to Negroes," ES, 12 Nov. 1947; Greene quoted in McQuirter, "'Our Cause Is Marching On,'" 76; "Negroes Assail Handed-Down Schoolhouses," WP, 22 Dec. 1947; Hamilton, "Making a 'Model' System," 191–241.

72. "Parents Picket in Protest of Three School Transfers," AA, 13 Dec. 1947; "Parents Attend Browne School to Back Protest," ES, 15 Dec. 1947; McQuirter, "'Our Cause Is Marching On,'" 74–75.

73. V. R. Montanari, "Parent-Pupil Strike Reduces Attendance from 1427 to 190 at Browne School, Annexes," WP, 9 Dec. 1947; Elsie Carper, "New School Plans to Ease Jam at Browne," WP, 6 Dec. 1947; "School Strike Ultimatum Laid Down by Parents," WP, 16 Dec. 1947; "Parents' Group Fails in Effort to See Truman," ES, 13 Dec. 1947; "Browne Strike Parley Ends in Stalemate," WP, 23 Dec. 1947; "Officials Warn Parents to Stop School Strike," WP, 31 Dec. 1947; "D.C. School Head Cool Amid Fury," AA, 13 Dec. 1947; Geo. W. Johnson, "Attitude of Poor Citizenship," letter to editor, ES, 24 Dec. 1947; "Corning Letter Urges Parents to Cease Boycott of School," ES, 31 Dec. 1947.

74. Charles H. Houston, "The Highway," AA, 17 Jan. 1948; "Browne School Strike Ends; Two Suits to Decide 'Issues,'" WP, 2 Feb. 1948; "Pupils Return to Browne as Strike Ends," WP, 3 Feb. 1948; McQuirter, "'Our Cause Is Marching On,'" 78–79.

75. McQuirter, "'Our Cause Is Marching On,'" 79; Kluger, Simple Justice, 518.

76. Sam Stavisky, "Browne Strike Brings Inquiry into D.C. School Situation," WP, 14 Dec. 1947; "Dirksen Asks for Full Report on Strike at Browne Jr. High," WP, 10 Dec. 1947; U.S. Congress, Subcommittees on District of Columbia Appropriations, Senate and House of Representatives, Report of a Survey of the Public Schools of the District of Columbia, 401, 610, 979. "Inadequate" appears seventy-seven times in the report.

77. U.S. Congress, Subcommittees on District of Columbia Appropriations, Senate and House of Representatives, Report of a Survey of the Public Schools of the District of Columbia, 375–77.

78. U.S. Congress, Subcommittees on District of Columbia Appropriations, Senate and House of Representatives, Report of a Survey of the Public Schools of the District of Columbia, 332–40.

79. Hansen, Miracle of Social Adjustment, 24; Clement, "Pushback," 90–91.

80. Hamilton, "Making a 'Model' System," 264–74.

81. "CENTRAL for CARDOZO," ES, 14 Feb. 1950; John B. Duncan, Gardner L. Bishop, and E. B. Henderson, separate letters to the editor, ES, 15 Sept. 1949; "Hearing Slated on Congestion at Cardozo High," ES, 21 July 1949; "Use of Wilson College to Relieve Crowding at Cardozo Studied," ES, 1 July 1949; Hamilton, "Making a 'Model' System," 281–83.

82. "Federation Splits on Central Use as Negro School," ES, 2 Oct. 1949; Edward T. Dunlap to members of the Alumni Association and Friends of Central High School, 20 Aug. 1949, Dunlap to Melvin C. Sharpe, 13 Dec. 1949, and Dunlap to Stephen G. Spottswood, Aug. 1949, all in Central High School Alumni Association, Box 1, Harry S. Wender Papers, KRL-HSW.

83. Coit Hendley Jr., "School Heads Prepare to Shift Central High to Colored Use," ES, 9 Mar. 1950.

84. Irene Osborne, "The Public School System," in National Association of Intergroup Relations Officials, Civil Rights in the Nation's Capital, 65–72.

85. Carr v. Corning, Superintendent of Public Schools, 182 F.2d 14 (D.C. Cir. 1950); American Bar Association Journal 36 (April 1950): 313.

86. Carr v. Corning.

87. Gardner L. Bishop to Board of Education, 6 Sept. 1950, "Minutes of the Fourth Meeting of the Board of Education, Sept. 6, 1950," MBOE, 70:171.

88. "Minutes of the Fourth Meeting of the Board of Education, Oct. 4, 1950," MBOE, 71:4.

89. Crooms, "Race, Education and the District of Columbia," 16; Kurland and Casper, Landmark Briefs, 397, 440.

90. Richard Pearson, "Milton Korman Dies; Was Judge, Top D.C. Official," WP, 29 Sept. 1983; "Milton Daniel Korman," WP, 2 Oct. 1983; Kurland and Casper, Landmark Briefs, 429, 438–39.

91. "America's Most Fascinating Women," AA, 21 July 1951; Ethel L. Payne, "Maggie Butcher—D.C.'s Magnificent Militant," CD, 5 June 1954; Jeanne Rogers, "Integration a

Unique Problem Here: Some Schools Won't Change Very Much," *WP*, 23 May 1954; Margaret Just Butcher, "School Board Members Says Issue of Child's Education Should Transcend Racial and Religious Differences," *WP*, 16 Feb. 1954; Clement, "Pushback," 99–100.

92. Bolling v. Sharpe, 347 U.S. 497 (1954); "Ethel Meets Boy Made Immortal by Supreme Court Decision," *CD*, 29 May 1954.

93. Rogers, "Integration a Unique Problem Here"; Bess Furman, "Schools in Capital Prepared for Segregation Ban; Superintendent Foresees Fast, Smooth Transition," *NYT*, 18 May 1954; Nichols, *Matter of Justice*, 66; Clement, "Pushback," 100.

94. John N. Popham, "Shift in Opinion on Bias Stressed," *NYT*, 2 July 1954.

95. "Minutes of the Recessed Session of Special Board Meeting of May 25, 1954, Held on June 2, 1954," MBOE, 89:A-42–A-73; Bess Furman, "Capital's Schools Begin Racial Integration Smoothly," *NYT*, 14 Sept. 1954; Douglass Cater, "Washington: 'A Model for the Rest of the Nation,'" *Reporter* (30 Dec. 1954): 12.

96. "Chinese Youth Integration Foe," *CD*, 16 Oct. 1954; Bess Furman, "Smooth Start Is Disrupted by Hundreds in Capital—Police on Extra Duty," *NYT*, 5 Oct. 1954; Marie Smith and Harry Gabbett, "Two-Way Ultimatum Given Pupils," *WPTH*, 7 Oct. 1945; "Students at Anacostia and McKinley Stage Protest on Integration," *ES*, 4 Oct. 1954; Clement, "Pushback," 100–101.

97. James G. Deane, "Success Is Surprise to School Officials," *ES*, 6 Sept. 1955; James G. Deane, "Some Students Found Worries Exaggerated," *ES*, 8 Sept. 1955; James G. Deane, "Rumors Were Worse Than What Happened," *ES*, 9 Sept. 1955; Eve Edstrom, "D.C. Feels Integration Works, Study Shows," *WPTH*, 31 Aug. 1955.

98. "Federation Asks Ban on Integration," *WP*, 8 Sept. 1954; "Supreme Court Blocks Federation's Move to Halt School Integration," *WPTH*, 11 Jan. 1955; "12,648 Petition for Mrs. Butcher," *WPTH*, 21 Feb. 1956; "Homework Neglected," *WPTH*, 28 Apr. 1956; Borchardt, "Making D.C. Democracy's Capital," 92–94.

99. USBC, *Statistical Abstract of the United States*, 1959, 121; Hansen, *Danger in Washington*, 26, 56; Horowitz, *Courts and Social Policy*, 108.

100. Hansen, *Danger in Washington*, 55–58.

101. Martin Well, "John McMillan Dies, Opposed Home Rule as Congressman," *WP*, 4 Sept. 1979; Ward, "1956 D.C. School Hearings," 82–110; Wolters, *Burden of Brown*, 13–14.

102. Cater, "Washington: 'A Model,'" 15; Eve Edstrom and Grace Bassett, "Integration Too Rapid, Say Sharpe and Gerber," *WPTH*, 20 Sept. 1956; Clement, "Pushback," 103–4.

103. U.S. House Committee on the District of Columbia, *Investigation of Public School Conditions* (Washington, D.C.: USGPO, 1957), 44–46, quoted in Diner, "Black Majority," 251; Johnson, *Dusk at the Mountain*, 130–31; Ward, "1956 D.C. School Hearings," 82–110; Clement, "Pushback," 103–4; Walker, "Blackboard Jungle," esp. 1932–34; Borchardt, "Making D.C. Democracy's Capital," 94–106.

104. "Hatchet Job," *WPTH*, 20 Sept. 1956; "Return to Segregation 'Unthinkable,'" *Atlanta Daily World*, 29 Dec. 1956; Knox, *Democracy and District of Columbia Public Schools*, vii; Hansen, *Miracle of Social Adjustment*; Richard L. Lyons and Eve Edstrom, "Integration Called a Miracle of Social Adjustment Here," *WPTH*, 11 Feb. 1957.

105. "Mrs. Butcher Assails Critics of Negro Pupils," *WPTH*, 3 Feb. 1956.

106. Erwin Knoll, "Desegregation Here Is 'Complete,' Corning Announces," *WPTH*, 31 Oct. 1957; Cater, "Washington: 'A Model,'" 12–15.

107. Cater, "Washington: 'A Model,'" 15.

108. Luther A. Huston, "Acting with More Than 'Deliberate Speed,' the Capital Swiftly Set Pace for Nation," NYT, 13 Mar. 1956.

Chapter 11

1. Jacobs quoted in Howes, "Crisis Downtown," 3.

2. Chalmers Roberts, "Progress or Decay: I—'Downtown Blight' in the Nation's Capital," WP, 27 Jan. 1952; Farrar, Building the Body Politic, 78–81.

3. Howes, "Crisis Downtown," 2–3; Gutheim, Worthy of the Nation, 233, 317; Ammon, "Commemoration amid Criticism," 179–80; National Park Service, Historic American Buildings Survey, 15; Gillette, Between Justice and Beauty, 161.

4. Farrar, Building the Body Politic, 89–91; Gutheim, Worthy of the Nation, 235; Ammon, "Commemoration amid Criticism," 182; Gillette, Between Justice and Beauty, 155.

5. James W. Rouse and Nathaniel S. Keith, No Slums in Ten Years, quoted in Gutheim, Worthy of the Nation, 324.

6. Future D.C. Commissioner John B. Duncan articulated some of the homeowners' concerns. "District Urged to Clear Slums while Building," ES, 25 Feb. 1949; "Commissioners Study Redevelopment Plans for Marshall Heights," ES, 26 Mar. 1949; Paige and Reuss, "Safe, Decent and Affordable," 85–88; Courier quoted in Gillette, Between Justice and Beauty, 163.

7. Ammon, "Commemoration amid Criticism," 182–83.

8. Ammon, "Commemoration amid Criticism," 183–84; Gutheim, Worthy of the Nation, 315.

9. National Capital Park and Planning Commission, Housing and Development, 1.

10. Gillette, Between Justice and Beauty, 161–62.

11. Berman v. Parker, 348 U.S. 26 (1954). For an excellent legal analysis of the decision, see Lavine, "Urban Renewal and the Story of Berman v. Parker," 423–75.

12. Wolf Von Eckardt, "New Southwest a Bundle of Boons," WPTH, 28 Oct. 1962; Howes, "Crisis Downtown," 2, 6; Ammon, "Commemoration amid Criticism," 187.

13. D.C. Redevelopment Land Agency, "Questions and Answers about Relocation in Southwest Washington," brochure, "Residential Sections—Southwest," Vertical Files, WD; Howes, "Crisis Downtown," 29; Ammon, "Commemoration amid Criticism," 185–86.

14. Howes, "Crisis Downtown," 7, 10; Gillette, Between Justice and Beauty, 163; Ammon, "Commemoration amid Criticism," 187–88, 196–98.

15. Howes, "Crisis Downtown," 10; Derthick, City Politics, 19; Thursz, Where Are They Now?, 93, 97–103.

16. Robert E. Baker, "Housing Restrictions Top Grievance List of Washington Negroes," WPTH, 12 Aug. 1963; Federation of Citizens Associations, "Minutes of Feb. 28 Meeting," 1963, Box 1, Folder 7, Chillum Heights Citizens Association Collection, DCCA.

17. "Urban Renewal Hit at NAACP Rally," WPTH, 15 Aug. 1960; James R. Carberry, "Renewal Seen Free of Race Discrimination," WPTH, 30 Jan. 1961.

18. Caplan, Farther Along, 1–12, 73–75, 107–9; Adam Bernstein, "D.C. Integrationist Marvin Caplan Dies at 80," WP, 14 Jan. 2000; Marvin Caplan, interview with Katherine Shannon, 14 Nov. 1967, RB-OHC, 1–34.

19. Neighbors Inc., newsletter, May 1962, Box 1, Folder 9, Chillum Heights Citizens Association Collection, DCCA; Johnson, *Dusk at the Mountain*, 48–53; Caplan, *Farther Along*, 152.

20. James G. Banks et al., "Civil Rights in Washington, D.C., 1948–1958: Status and Trends in Housing," in National Association of Intergroup Relations Officials, *Civil Rights in the Nation's Capital*, 42; Thomas B. Kendrick, "New Suburban Group to Help Negroes Get Equal Housing," WPTH, 20 Nov. 1962; John Maffre, "Interracial Group Is Trying to Set Example for Capital," WPTH, 6 June 1963; Baker, "Housing Restrictions Top Grievance List."

21. USBC, "Historical Census Statistics on Population Totals by Race," table 23.

22. Stephen S. Rosenfeld, "Interracial Group Tries to Make Living Easier in Changing NW Neighborhood," WPTH, 28 Jan. 1962; testimony of George Grier, in U.S. Commission on Civil Rights, *Housing in Washington*, 20; Maffre, "Interracial Group."

23. Marvin Caplan, "The Last White Family on the Block," *Atlantic Monthly* (July 1960), reprinted in Caplan, *Farther Along*, 145–50.

24. Caplan, "Last White Family," 145–50.

25. Rosenfeld, "Interracial Group"; Caplan, *Farther Along*, 158–63; Palmer, *Living as Equals*, esp. chaps. 3, 4; testimony of Marvin Caplan, in U.S. Commission on Civil Rights, *Housing in Washington*, 381.

26. See NI "Home Seekers" ads in ES and other local newspapers, e.g., 20 May 1959; Palmer, *Living as Equals*, 111; Caplan, "Last White Family," 145–50.

27. Fundraising letter, 1960, "Miscellaneous" folder, Box 15, Neighbors, Inc. Collection, WD; "9 Homes to Be Shown by 'Neighbors,'" WPTH, 26 May 1962.

28. Marvin Caplan, "Classified Complaint," letter to the editor, WPTH, 1 Jan. 1959; Caplan, *Farther Along*, 172; Palmer, *Living as Equals*, 101–2; Gilbert, "Toward a Color-Blind Newspaper," 9; "Block Plan Revealed by 'Neighbors,'" WPTH, 30 Oct. 1960; "NW Group Protests Harassment to Sell," WPTH, 3 Dec. 1961; "District Crime Data Called Inaccurate, Misleading," WPTH, 24 Apr. 1960.

29. Susanna McBee, "Integrated Neighborhood Loses Self-Consciousness about Race," WPTH, 17 July 1964; Haynes Johnson, "Neighbors, Inc.: The Story of an Effort to Build an Integrated Community," ES, 13 Jan. 1965; Caplan, *Farther Along*, 167–72; Sarah Booth Conroy, "Neighbors, Inc.," WPTH, 7 May 1972; "League to Get Rights Award," CD, 11 Mar. 1961; Jean White, "'New Nations' Families to Get Welcome Party,'" WPTH, 12 May 1961; "Prescription against Panic," WPTH, 31 Jan. 1962; William J. Raspberry, "500 Neighbors Sip Tea at Integrated Parties," WPTH, 16 Sept. 1963; "Neighbors, Inc., Scores with Art, Book Festival," WPTH, 7 June 1964.

30. "Neighbors Inc., Third Annual Report—1961," Box 17, oversize folder, Neighbors, Inc. Collection, WD; Caplan interview with Shannon, 67–70; "Anti-Bias Group Cites Progress," ES, 28 Jan. 1962; "Area Group Sees White Panic Halted," WPTH, 19 May 1963; Johnson, "Neighbors, Inc."

31. "The Junior High School Question and Integration in the Neighbors, Inc. Area," in "Public Schools—1961–1964" folder, and "What about Schools?," n.d., in "Miscellaneous" folder, both in Box 15, Neighbors, Inc. Collection, WD.

32. "Neighbors, Inc., Area Schools Show Drop in White Students," WPTH, 4 Nov. 1965; Johnson, "Neighbors, Inc."

33. Caplan, *Farther Along*, 176–78.

34. Eddie Dean, "A Brief History of White People in Southeast," *WCP*, 16 Oct. 1998; Carl Bernstein, "Whites in Far Southeast Bitter, Estranged," *WPTH*, 4 Aug. 1970.

35. Susanna McBee et al., "Dropouts Are Called Major Problems," *WP*, 13 Jan. 1963.

36. Gail S. Lowe, "Congress Heights: A Many-Layered Past," in Smith, *Washington at Home*, 338; Richard Severo, "This Is Anacostia," *WPTH*, 8 May 1966; James Welsh, "Flow of Negroes to Suburbs Dramatic," *Sunday Star*, 26 Oct. 1969.

37. Bernstein, "Whites in Far Southeast Bitter, Estranged"; Office of Assistant to the Mayor for Housing Programs, Community Renewal Program, *Washington's Far Southeast 70* (Washington, D.C., 1970), viii, 20, 22.

38. Bernstein, "Whites in Far Southeast Bitter, Estranged."

39. Grier, *Understanding Washington's Changing Population*, 19–22; Andrew Kopkind and James Ridgeway, "Washington: The Lost Colony," *New Republic* 154, no. 17 (23 Apr. 1966): 13.

40. During Hobson's lifetime, contemporary sources indicated that he was born in 1922. census records are incomplete, but the 1920 census shows an infant son named Julius Hobson born in Birmingham to Erma and Julius Hobson in 1919. The 1930 census, however, states that he is only nine years old (for a 1920 or 1921 birth year). "David Eaton Interview with Julius Hobson 1974," transcript of Tape 1, Box 73, JHP; "Julius Hobson: A Goad for Change," *WPTH*, 2 July 1972; "Hobson: Just an Unlucky Guy," *WPTH*, 5 July 1972; Sam Smith, "Place," from "Multitudes: An Unauthorized Memoir," http://prorev.com/mmplace.htm; Solomon, *Washington Century*, 62–65, 73–74; Julius Hobson, interview with Katherine Shannon, 3 July 1967, RB-OHC.

41. Simeon Booker, "Washington's Civil Rights Maverick," *Ebony* 20, no. 7 (May 1965): 145; "Julius Hobson: A Goad for Change."

42. "A Last Angry Man," *Time* 100, no. 23 (4 Dec. 1972): 32–33.

43. "Sterling Tucker: Veteran Crusader for Negro Cause," *WP*, June 8, 1968; LaBarbara Bowman, "D.C. Council Vice Chairman Tucker Seeks Step-Up: Tucker Knows Key to Survival in D.C." *WP*, Oct. 26, 1974; Kenneth Bredemeier, "Council Chairman's Background and Steady Way Appeal to Many," *WP*, Sept. 7, 1978.

44. George Lardner Jr., "Fauntroy: Builder of 'Creative Tension,'" *WP*, May 27, 1965. Alex Poinsett, "How Blacks Can Gain Two Senators," *Ebony* 33, no. 8 (June 1978); Daniel Donaghy, "Walter Fauntroy," in Finkelman, *Encyclopedia of African American History*.

45. Robert E. Baker, "Fragmented Leadership Frustrates Achievement of D.C. Negroes' Goals," *WPTH*, 16 Aug. 1963; Derthick, *City Politics*, 85, 140–42; Diner, "Black Majority," 254–55; Chuck Stone Oral History Interview, 11 Apr. 1999, DCSML, OHP 20-9, DCCA, 1, 8.

46. "Commissioner Duncan," *WPTH*, 25 July 1961; Claudia Levy, "D.C. Commissioner John Duncan Dies," *WP*, 22 June 1994; Derthick, *City Politics*, 132–39; Ross, *Outside the Lines*, 143–58; Smith, "Civil Rights on the Gridiron," 189–207.

47. Robert E. Baker, "Job Picture Far from Rosy to Negroes Here," *WPTH*, 13 Aug. 1963; Robert E. Baker, "Negro-Police Hostility Less but Remnants of Old Habits Remain," *WPTH*, 15 Aug. 1963; Chuck Stone, "U.S. Govt Color Bar Worse than District's: Urban League," *WAA*, 4 June 1963; Kim Willenson, "Small Progress Seen in Hiring Negroes Here," *WPTH*, 6 Nov. 1962.

48. "Segregated Schools Laid to Housing," ES, 8 June 1963; Baker, "Housing Restrictions Top Grievance List"; "Tucker Cites Housing Cost for Negroes," WPTH, 17 Nov. 1960; Russell Baker, "Behind Washington's Postcard Facade: Change, Trouble and Danger Afflict Capital," NYT, 10 June 1963; Grier, Understanding Washington's Changing Population, 9–12; see U.S. Commission on Civil Rights, Housing in Washington."

49. Tucker, Beyond the Burning, 20, 129.

50. Derthick, City Politics, 48; "Interview: Former D.C. Police Office Talks about Relations with the Community," WAMU, 22 Aug. 2014.

51. John McKelway, "Senators Are Cold to D.C. Funds Plea," ES, 18 Mar. 1961; Grace Bassett, "Welfare Told to Take Closer Look at Budget," ES, 19 Aug. 1961; Baker, "Behind Washington's Postcard Facade"; Louis Cassels, "Integration Foes Help Make Capital Time Bomb," CD, 27 Feb. 1963; Harry Ernst, "Robert C. Byrd—A 'Villain' to Poor of D.C.?," Charleston (W.Va.) Gazette, 12 May 1965; Kopkind and Ridgeway, "Washington: The Lost Colony," 14.

52. Alvin Shuster and Ben A. Franklin, "How a Race Riot Happened," Saturday Evening Post, 4 May 1963, 15–19; Les Ledbetter, "Drunken Adults Started Riot Say Eastern High Students," WAA, 27 Nov. 1962.

53. "Complete Text of Citizens Committee Report on Stadium Melee," WPTH, 11 Jan. 1963; "33 Injured in Fights at Stadium," WPTH, 23 Nov. 1962; Gerald Grant, "Student Leaders Meet, Deplore Stadium Melee," WPTH, 25 Nov. 1962; "Miss. Racist Orders Probe of Holiday Riot at D.C. Grid Game," CD, 11 Dec. 1962; Russell Baker, "Fear of Racial Violence Haunts Capital," NYT, 11 June 1963; Flamm, Law and Order, 28–29.

54. "Complete Text of Citizens Committee Report."

55. Stephen S. Rosenfeld, "CORE Unit to Protest Job Bias," WPTH, 22 July 1961; "Picket Captains," n.d., Box 1, "CORE Memoranda" folder, JHP; "Merit Hiring Statement Falls Short, Negroes Say," ES, 27 Sept. 1961; Edward Peeks, "D.C. CORE Says Jobs or Else," "Defensive and Angry," 20 Nov. 1962; Julius W. Hobson to H. I. Romnes, 17 Apr. 1963, and Hobson to Percy Williams, 9 Apr. 1963, both in Box 1, "CORE Memoranda" folder, JHP; Simeon Booker, "Work in Ghetto Gets Confidence of Negroes," Jet, 16 Feb. 1967; Booker, "Washington's Civil Rights Maverick," 142; "CORE Planning Continued Drive against Utilities," ES, 15 Oct. 1962; Solomon, Washington Century, 123–26.

56. "Recent and Prospective Activities of the Housing Committee of the Congress of Racial Equality, Washington, D.C. Chapter," Box 1, "CORE Minutes" folder, JHP; "Diggs Joins Pickets at Downtown Building," ES, 16 May 1963; John B. Willmann, "Race Policy Defended by Cafritz," WPTH, 26 May 1963; Sam Eastman, "Cafritz Backs Housing Open to All Races," ES, 1 July 1963; "Cafritz Supports Proposal to Outlaw Housing Discrimination in District," WPTH, 2 July 1963; "Transition by Law," WPTH, 3 July 1963; Solomon, Washington Century, 136–38.

57. Chuck Stone, "NAACP, CORE, SCLC, in Mass Protest Here on Fri.," WAA, 11 June 1963; Phil Casey, "3000 in Peaceful March Here," WPTH, 15 June 1963.

58. Chuck Stone, "CORE, SCLC, NAACP Join Hands," WAA, 18 June 1963; Casey, "3000 in Peaceful March Here"; Peter Kumpa, "3,000 Stage Civil Rights March in D.C.," Baltimore Sun, 15 June 1963.

59. Washington, Testament of Hope, 217–18; Jones, March on Washington; Clarence Hunter, "Early-In, Early-Out Plan for Marchers," ES, 12 July 1963; Gray and Krafchik, "'Its Fingers

Were Crossed and Its Guard Was Up,'" 22; "Memorandum re: Free D.C. Movement and Organizing in Washington, D.C.," Marion Barry to SNCC Educational Workshop, 3 Sept. 1966, SNCCP, Reel 61, Subgroup C, Series V:17; "Washington Home Rule Committee, Inc." Minutes, 10 Oct. 1963, Box 1, "CORE Minutes" folder, JHP; Hobson's role as an FBI informant was first revealed publicly by the *Post*'s Paul Valentine in 1982: Paul W. Valentine, "FBI Records List Julius Hobson as 'Confidential Source' in '6os," *WP*, 22 May 1981; "Letter to Washington Field re: Julius Wilson Hobson," in "FBI Papers" folder, Box 75, JHP.

60. "11 Negro Leaders Hit School Boycott Plan," *WPTH*, 11 Mar. 1964; "School Head Meets with Core Chief," *WPTH*, 24 Mar. 1964; "Foolish Boycott," *ES*, 11 Mar. 1964; "Disruptive Force Seen as Threat to CORE," *ES*, 18 Apr. 1964; "Julius Hobson: A Goad for Change"; "Minutes of the May 22, 1964 Steering Committee Meeting," and Julius W. Hobson to James Farmer, 22 June 1964, both in Box 1, "CORE Memoranda" folder, JHP, 7.

61. "Disruptive Force Seen as Threat to CORE"; "Strategy and Tactics Committee—Aug. 8, 1965 Meeting," Box 4, "ACT—Minutes of Meetings" folder, JHP.

62. John Mathews, "Julius W. Hobson: The Gadfly for District's Negro Militants," *Sunday Star*, 16 Apr. 1967; Bart Barnes, "ACT Chapter Here Planned by Hobson," *WPTH*, 7 July 1964; "Confidential FBI Report re Julius W. Hobson," "FBI Papers" folder, Box 75, JHP; Hobson interview with Shannon, 6; "Hobson Specialty: Successful Hoaxes," *WPTH*, 4 July 1972; "'Rat Rally' Nets 100 Spectators but No Rats," *WPTH*, 23 Aug. 1964; Mathews, "Julius W. Hobson."

63. Gerald Grant, "Track Plan Assailed by Tobriner," *WPTH*, 27 Oct. 1965.

64. "Anti 'Track' Committee Set," *WAA*, 13 Apr. 1965; "Backtracking," *WPTH*, 28 Oct. 1965.

65. Hobson v. Hansen, 269 F. Supp. 401 (D.C. 1967).

66. Susan Filson, "Civil Rights Case Here Is Held Vital," *WPTH*, 23 July 1966; Susan Jacoby, "The Superintendent Simply Stood Still," *WPTH*, 9 July 1967.

67. Smith, *Captive Capital*, 237.

68. Arthur S. Brisbane, "Marion Barry Just Wants to Be Loved," *WP*, 26 Apr. 1987; Marion Barry, interview with Katherine M. Shannon, 3 Oct. 1967, RB-OHC, 42.

69. Asch and Musgrove, "Marion S. Barry"; Jaffe and Sherwood, *Dream City*, 35–41.

70. Randolph quoted in Jones, *March on Washington*, Epilogue; Jesse Lewis, "King Begins Tour Here on Call for Home Rule," *WPTH*, 5 Aug. 1965; Maddison, "'In Chains 400 Years.'" 169–71.

71. On Carmichael, see Joseph, *Stokely*.

72. "Memorandum re: Free D.C. Movement (FDCM)," SNCCP, Reel 61, Subgroup C, Series V:1; "A Proposal for an Action Project in Washington, D.C.," SNCCP, Reel 61, Subgroup C, Series I:166.

73. "Memorandum re: Free D.C. Movement," Marion Barry Jr. to SNCC Executive Committee and SNCC Staff, 14 Mar. 1966, SNCCP, Reel 61, Subgroup C, Series V:1.

74. "Washington Home Rule Committee, Inc.," Minutes, 8 Aug., 10 Oct. 1963, Box 1, "CORE Minutes" folder, JHP.

75. Frederick L. Scott, "The Home Rule Issue in the District of Columbia," Legislative Research Service, 25 July 1961, SNCCP, Reel 61, Subgroup C, Series V:1.

76. Johnson, *Dusk at the Mountain*, 6–7, 210–11, 233; Carl P. Leubsdorf, "Voting Rights Bill Won't Help Washingtonians," *Owosso (Mich.) Argus-Press*, 21 June 1965.

77. Martin F. Nolan, "The Negro Stake in Washington Home Rule," *Reporter* (11 Aug. 1966), 18; "Board of Trade Stand on Home Rule Fought," ES, 17 Jan. 1966; Andrew Kopkind and James Ridgeway, "Washington: Life in the Lost Colony—II," *New Republic* 154, no. 18 (30 Apr. 1966): 20; "Apathy Blamed for Home Rule Defeat," WPTH, 30 Oct. 1965.

78. Elsie Carper, "LBJ Spurs Leaders on Home Rule," WPTH, 11 Oct. 1965; "Statement by Marion Barry," 26 Feb. 1966, SNCCP, Reel 61, Subgroup C, Series V:1; "The District of Columbia Coalition of Conscience: Constitution and By-Laws," SNCCP, Reel 61, Subgroup C, Series III:92; "Minutes of Meeting of D.C. Coalition, Dec. 16, 1965," WEFP, Part 1, Box 21, Folder 10, SCRC-GL; Kopkind and Ridgeway, "Washington: Life in the Lost Colony—II," 22.

79. Louie Estrada and Martin Weil, "O. Roy Chalk, D.C. Transit Owner before Metro System, Dies at Age 88," WP, 2 Dec. 1995; Edmund V. Haffman to Student Non-Violent Coordinating Committee, 3 Nov. 1965, and "Statement of Marion Barry," 2 Nov. 1965, and "Statements before Washington Metropolitan Area Transit Commission," all in SNCCP, Reel 61, Subgroup C, Series II:79; "Memorandum re: Free D.C. Movement and Organizing in Washington, D.C.," Marion Barry to SNCC Educational Workshop, 3 Sept. 1966; "Statement of Marion Barry, Jr.," 18 Jan. 1966, SNCCP, Reel 61, Subgroup C, Series II:79.

80. "Council Offers New Cardozo Plan," WPTH, 20 May 1966; Yvonne Shinhoster Lamb, "Willie J. Hardy: Activist, 2-Term D.C. Council Member," WP, 23 Aug. 2007; "Statement of Marion Barry, Jr.," 18 Jan. 1966; Rohal, "Mobilizing the Community in an Era before Social Media," 49–52.

81. Richard Corrigan, "SNCC Claims Bus Boycott Was a 90 Per Cent Success," WPTH, 25 Jan. 1966; "75,000 Riders Boycott Buses in Protest," WAA, 25 Jan. 1966; "Further Local Boycotts Are Considered by SNCC," WPTH, 28 Jan. 1966; Kopkind and Ridgeway, "Washington: Life in the Lost Colony—II," 21; "Memorandum re: Free D.C. Movement," Marion Barry Jr. to SNCC Executive Committee and SNCC Staff, 14 Mar. 1966.

82. "Memorandum re: Free D.C. Movement," Marion Barry Jr. to SNCC Executive Committee and SNCC Staff, 14 Mar. 1966.; "Statement by Marion Barry, Jr.," 21 Feb. 1966, SNCCP, Reel 61, Subgroup C, Series V:8.

83. Larry A. Still, "'Free D.C.' Drive Opens, Picketing Set Tomorrow," ES, 4 Mar. 1966; Larry Still and S. Z. Fahnestock, "Boycott Leaders Beam Plea at Shoppers, Delay Picketing," ES, 6 Mar. 1966.

84. "Threat of Boycott to Get Home Rule Is Assailed by Sisk," ES, 23 Feb. 1966; "President F. Elwood Davis Expresses Concern over Coalition Actions," *Board of Trade News* (April 1966), GWBTR, Series 17, Box 368, Folder 7, SCRC-GL.

85. Mary Stratford, "NE Shopping District Boycott Target," WAA, 1 Mar. 1966; "NE Shoppers Suggest Protest Move Downtown," WAA, 8 Mar. 1966; Willard Clopton and John Carmody, "Free D.C.'ers End Drive in Northeast: Merchants Report Slight Impact," WPTH, 13 Mar. 1966; William Raspberry, "Tactics Meant Failure for Free D.C. Movement," WPTH, 22 Mar. 1966; Nolan, "Negro Stake in Washington Home Rule," 20–21.

86. Press release, n.d., SNCCP, Reel 61, Subgroup C, Series V:1; Jack Eisen, "Trade Board Names Negro as Director," WPTH, 19 Apr. 1966; Willard Clopton, "The Genesis and the Exoduses of Free D.C. Movement," WPTH, 26 Apr. 1966. For internal Board of Trade concerns about the boycott, see memos and letters in GWBTR, Series 17, Box 368,

Folder 8, SCRC-GL; Dan Morgan, "Barry Finds Home Rule a Frustrating Battle," *WPTH*, 25 July 1966.

87. "Memorandum re: Free D.C. Movement and Organizing in Washington, D.C.," Marion Barry to SNCC Educational Workshop, 3 Sept. 1966; Clopton, "Genesis and Exoduses."

88. "Memorandum re: Free D.C. Movement and Organizing in Washington, D.C.," Marion Barry to SNCC Educational Workshop, 3 Sept. 1966.

89. Paul A. Schuette, "New Agency to Combat Delinquency," *WPTH*, 16 Dec. 1962; Wiley Austin Branton, interview with James Mosby, 20 Oct. 1969, RB-OHC; James Banks, interview with James Mosby, 2 Nov. 1969, RB-OHC, 27.

90. Julius Hobson to James G. Banks, Oct. 23, 1964, Box 4, "ACT—Memoranda" folder, JHP; Banks and Banks, *Unintended Consequences*; James G. Banks, interview with William McHugh, 14 Dec. 1966, John F. Kennedy Library Oral History Program; Joe Holley, "D.C. Housing Official James Banks, 84, Dies," *WP*, 15 June 2005; William Raspberry, "Progress of Youth Program Highlights Poverty War," *WPTH*, 6 Mar. 1967; Jean R. Hailey, "Barry Quits SNCC Post to Aid Poor," *WPTH*, 19 Jan. 1967; "'It Shows the Cops Were Wrong'—Barry," *WAA*, 5 Sept. 1967.

91. Kopkind and Ridgeway, "Washington: The Lost Colony," 13–14; Maddison, "'In Chains 400 Years,'" 187; Valk, *Radical Sisters*, 27; Branton interview with Mosby; William Raspberry, "Successor to Banks Risks Reputation," *WPTH*, 19 May 1967.

92. Harry B. Anderson, "Meet Your Neighbor," *AA*, 26 Feb. 1938; "Dorothy Boulding Ferebee," *WP*, 18 Sept. 1990; Vanessa M. Gamble, "Dorothy Boulding Ferebee," in Ware, *Notable American Women*, 203–5; Valk, *Radical Sisters*, 28–36.

93. Kopkind and Ridgeway, "Washington: Life in the Lost Colony—II," 22; Valk, *Radical Sisters*, 32.

94. "How Does It Feel to Be on Welfare?," *WAA*, 31 May 1966; Ruth Jenkins and Bernard Garnett, "Long Suffering Welfare Clients Raise Their Voices," *WAA*, 31 May 1966; Caroline Heck, "Etta Horn and Life," *WPTH*, 6 Sept. 1970; J. Y. Smith, "Welfare Activist Moves from Street to Office," *WP*, 17 May 1975; Haskins, "Behind the Headlines," 65.

95. "By-Laws of the Model Inner City Community Organization, Inc.," SNCCP, Reel 61, Subgroup C, Series III:94; Wolf Von Eckhardt, "Shaw Area Will Launch New-Style City Renewal," *WPTH*, 8 Apr. 1966; Kevin Klose, "Ghetto Held City Church Key," *WPTH*, 12 Aug. 1967; Jim Hoagland, "Shaw Area Told to Aid in Renewal," *WPTH*, 4 Dec. 1966; "What MICCO Is/What MICCO Does," SNCCP, Reel 61, Subgroup C, Series III:94; Derthick, "Defeat at Fort Lincoln," 8.

96. "Renewal Aid by Citizens Seen in Shaw," *WPTH*, 9 July 1966; Willard Clopton Jr., "$18 Million Grant Goes to Shaw Area," *WPTH*, 24 Oct. 1966; "MICCO Theme Song," SNCCP, Reel 61, Subgroup C, Series III:94; "Housing Focus of Greatest Interest at Shaw Meeting," *WAA*, 30 Jan. 1968; John Carmody, "Dr. King Pushes Shaw-Area Renewal," *WPTH*, 13 Mar. 1967.

97. Leonard Downie Jr. and Robert G. Kaiser, "City Wants Shaw Group to List Realty Holdings," *WPTH*, 10 Sept. 1967; Ernest Holsendolph, "Board Adopts Plan to Meet School Ruling," *ES*, 29 July 1967.

98. Martin Weil, "Willard Wirtz, Labor Secretary for JFK and LBJ, Dies at 98," *WP*, 25 Apr. 2010.

99. Paul Delaney, "Mayfield Heading $300,000 Project," ES, 3 Aug. 1967; Hollie I. West, "600 Pride, Inc., Volunteers Prepare for Work," WPTH, 6 Aug. 1967; Barry interview with Shannon, 54–56; "Pride, Inc.: DC.'s Cool Answer to Hot Summers," Ebony 23, no. 2 (December 1967): 82–89; Tucker, Beyond the Burning, 120–21; Robert G. Kaiser, "Pride Leaders Are Looking Ahead," WPTH, 7 Sept. 1967.

100. William Raspberry, "Pride Turns to Job Skills for Youths," WPTH, 24 Nov. 1967; Carl Bernstein, "Officials Praise Pride for Rat War Victories," WPTH, 3 Sept. 1967; Jim Hoagland, "Mayfield Quits Pride, Claims Betrayal," WPTH, 25 Nov. 1967.

101. Elsie Carper and Peter Milius, "House Accepts New D.C. Rule," WPTH, 10 Aug. 1967; Lyndon B. Johnson, "Special Message to the Congress Transmitting Reorganization Plan 3 of 1967: Government of the District of Columbia," Item no. 247, Office of the Federal Register, Public Papers of the Presidents: Lyndon B. Johnson, 585–88; Lyndon B. Johnson, "Test of Message on City Rule, War on Crime," WPTH, 28 Feb. 1967; Elsie Carper, "Johnson Orders New D.C. Rule," WPTH, 2 June 1967; Raoul Kulberg, "The Last Colony–II," Concern (1 Sept. 1967); Diner, Democracy, Federalism, 53–55.

102. "Biographies of Nominees for New D.C. City Council," ES, 29 Sept. 1967.

103. Milton Coleman and Craig Timberg, "Unifier Led D.C. Into Home Rule," WP, 28 Oct. 2003; Ken Ringle, "A Leader Defined Dignity," WP, 28 Oct. 2003; Robert L. Asher, "Walter Washington: Back Home," WPTH, 7 Sept. 1967; Johnson quoted in Diner, "Black Majority," 258.

104. Department of Justice, Federal Bureau of Investigation, Uniform Crime Reporting Statistics, "Estimated Crime in District of Columbia," http://www.ucrdatatool.gov /Search/Crime/State/RunCrimeStatebyState.cfm.

105. Dan Morgan, "Barry's Arrest Sparks Dispute on 'Loitering,'" WPTH, 28 May 1966; "Uniformed Policemen," Box 4, "ACT—Police" folder, JHP; "City Warned of Rise in Ghetto Tensions," WPTH, 22 Sept. 1967; Commissioners' Council on Human Relations, "Human Relations Program in the Metropolitan Police Department—A Progress Report," 22 May 1966, 1, Box 4, "ACT—Police" folder, JHP; Robert L. Asher, "They Advance in Silence: Capital's Human Relations Council Works for Interracial Harmony without Fuss or Fanfare," WPTH, 31 Jan. 1965.

106. Hannerz, Soulside, 162–69.

107. "Synopsis of Southeast disturbance," WAA, 23 Aug. 1966; Julius Hobson, undated letter re D.C. Police, Box 4, "ACT—Police" folder, JHP.

108. Hechinger and Taylor, "Black and Blue," 6–7; "Mayor Unsure of Right to Probe Policeman," ES, 16 Nov. 1967; Charles Conconi, "Council's Action in Police Probe Is Ruled Illegal," Sunday Star, 26 Nov. 1967.

109. "Black United Front: Statement of Purpose," Box 4, "ACT—Black United Front" folder, JHP; Robert C. Maynard, "Negroes to Drive for Unity," WPTH, 11 Jan. 1968; Robert C. Maynard, "D.C. Negro Leaders Work to Maintain Uneasy Coalition," WPTH, 12 Jan. 1968; "Ministers' Group Opposes Movement," WAA, 16 Jan. 1968; Robert C. Maynard, "Urban League Wary of Black United Front," WPTH, 18 Jan. 1968;

110. "Proposal for an Action Project in Washington, D.C.," SNCCP, Reel 61, Subgroup C, Series I:166; Monroe W. Karmin, "Calm in the Capital," Wall Street Journal, 23 June 1967.

111. Gilbert, *Ten Blocks from the White House*, 1; Fauntroy quoted in Pearlman, "Democracy's Capital," 89; Karmin, "Calm in the Capital,"; Hannerz, *Soulside*, 159, 165.

Chapter 12

1. Martin Luther King Jr., "Remaining Awake through a Great Revolution," speech delivered at the National Cathedral, Washington, D.C., 31 Mar. 1968, http://king encyclopedia.stanford.edu/encyclopedia/documentsentry/doc_remaining_awake_through _a_great_revolution/; Orville Green, "King Admits Cards Stacked against Poor People's March," *WAA*, 2 Apr. 1968; Pearlman, "More Than a March," 24–41.

2. Risen, *Nation on Fire*, 54–58; Gilbert, *Ten Blocks from the White House*, 13–30; Haskins, "Behind the Headlines," 57.

3. Schaffer, "1968 Washington Riots," 4.

4. Pearlman, "Democracy's Capital," 110.

5. Michael Adams, "D.C. Leaders Show Grief, Ire," ES, 5 Apr. 1968; Gilbert, *Ten Blocks from the White House*, 31; Paul Delaney, "Mayor Witnesses Looting," ES, 5 Apr. 1968; "The Second Sacking of Washington," *U.S. News and World Report* 64, no. 17 (22 Apr. 1968): 32–33; Risen, *Nation on Fire*, 67.

6. Gilbert, *Ten Blocks from the White House*, 44; "Epitaph and Legacy," *Washington Daily News*, 5 Apr. 1968; "The Face of the City," *Washington Daily News*, 6 Apr. 1968; "Mindless Mob Spurns Dr. King's Creed," *Sunday Star*, 7 Apr. 1968; Adams, "D.C. Leaders Show Grief,"; Phil Oliver, "Carmichael Warns of 'Retaliation,'" WP, 6 Apr. 1968; Carmichael quoted in Pearlman, "Democracy's Capital," 115.

7. "Troops Fail to Halt Looting; 5 Dead, over 2,000 Arrested," ES, 6 Apr. 1968; Richard Sarro, "How the Decision Was Reached to Bring in Troops," *Sunday Star*, 7 Apr. 1968; Gilbert, *Ten Blocks from the White House*, 88–102; Schaffer, "1968 Washington Riots," 15.

8. "Troops Fail to Halt Looting"; Haynes Johnson, "A Resident Tours His City," *Sunday Star*, 7 Apr. 1968; Gilbert, *Ten Blocks from the White House*, 179–81, 186; Schaffer, "1968 Washington Riots," 19–21; Ben A. Franklin, "Capital Put under 4 P.M. Curfew," NYT, 7 Apr. 1968.

9. Schaffer, "1968 Washington Riots," 17; "Estimated Impact on Washington's Economy Resulting from the Civil Disorders during the Period Apr. 4–15, 1968," 10 June 1968, GWBTR, Series 11, Box 285, Folder 32, SCRC-GL; Dobrovir, "Justice in Time of Crisis," app. F, 143; Gilbert, *Ten Blocks from the White House*, 119, 224.

10. "The City's Response," ES, 9 Apr. 1968; Pearlman, "Democracy's Capital," 119; National Capital Area Civil Liberties Union, "A Police Department in Trouble: Racial Discrimination and Misconduct in the Police Department of Washington, D.C.," Aug. 1, 1968, Box 4, "ACT—Police" folder, JHP; Burton M. Langhenry to Ramsey Clark, 13 May 1968, GWBTR, Series 11, Box 284a, Folder 34, SCRC-GL; Crosby S. Noyes, "District Deserves High Marks in Riot Control," ES, 20 Apr. 1968; Gilbert, *Ten Blocks from the White House*, 178; Connecticut Avenue Association, "Order from White House—'Don't Shoot Looters,'" GWBTR, Series 11, Box 287, Folder 17, SCRC-GL.

11. Schaffer, "1968 Washington Riots," 9; Haskins, "Behind the Headlines," 64; Carol Honsa, "Shaw Unit Asks Renewal Voice," WPTH, 14 Apr. 1968.

12. Gilbert, *Ten Blocks from the White House*, 153–54.

13. "Sees City's Chance for New Identity," *WAA*, 16 Apr. 1968; "Riots Signal Need for Change," *WAA*, 16 Apr. 1968.

14. Government of the District of Columbia City Council, "Report of the City Council Public Hearings on the Rebuilding and Recovery of Washington, D.C. from the Civil Disturbances of Apr., 1968," 7; and "Statement by John W. Hechinger, Chairman of the Council, at a News Conference on Rebuilding and Recovery of the City," 10 May 1968 (stapled to cover of council report), 3, both in WD.

15. Gilbert, *Ten Blocks from the White House*; Smith, *Captive Capital*, 125–26; Sam Smith Oral History Interview, 2 Nov. 1998, DCSML, OHP 20-7, DCCA; Smith, *Captive Capital*, 248–49; Jo-Ann Armao, "Legendary Takoma Park Mayor Dies," *WP*, 18 Dec. 1990; Retha Hill, "Takoma Park's 'Angry' Mayor Remembered," *WP*, 6 Jan. 1991; Matt Schudel, "Ruth Abbott, 89; Takoma Park, MD., Activist, Mayor's Wife," *WP*, 15 Nov. 2009; Bob Levey and Jane Freundel Levey, "End of the Roads," *WP Magazine*, 26 Nov. 2000; Borchardt, "Making D.C. Democracy's Capital," 212–13.

16. Jack Eisen, "100-Lane Road Web Forecast," *WP*, 9 Nov. 1958; Schrag, *Great Society Subway*, 36–40; Schrag, "Freeway Fight in Washington," 649–50.

17. "The Revolt against Big-City Freeways," *U.S. News and World Report*, 1 Jan. 1962, 48.

18. George Lardner Jr., "The Game in Upper Northwest," *WPTH*, 28 Dec. 1964; Schrag, *Great Society Subway*, 41–44.

19. "Group Opposes Renewal without Resettlement," *WPTH*, 28 Nov. 1964; Robert E. Baker, "Housing Restrictions Top Grievance List of Washington Negroes," *WPTH*, 12 Aug. 1963; Williams quoted in Borchardt, "Making D.C. Democracy's Capital," 213; J. Y. Smith, "Bishop Smallwood Williams, Founder of Bible Way, Dies," *WP*, 30 June 1991.

20. Schrag, *Great Society Subway*, 44–48; George Lardner Jr., "Northeast Freeway Urged Here," *WPTH*, 10 Nov. 1964.

21. "Remarks by Alan S. Boyd, Secretary of Transportation, Prepared for Delivery before the Washington Board of Trade," 26 Sept. 1967, and "A Statement to the Bishops in the Washington Area," 26 Feb. 1968, both in Box 23, "Chronological 1967" folder, ECTCP; "Victory Rally and Celebration," flyer, Box 41, "Flyers 1965–68" folder, ECTCP.

22. ECTC fund-raising letter, Apr. 1968, Box 23, "Chronological April 1968" folder, ECTCP.

23. The Committee of 100 was not connected to the earlier Committee of One Hundred. Craig quoted in Bob Levey and Jane Freundel Levey, "End of the Roads," *WP Magazine*, 26 Nov. 2000.

24. Reginald Booker, interview by Robert Wright, 24 July 1970, RB-OHC; "Minutes of the Black United Front, Feb. 13, 1968," WEFP, Part 1, Box 16, Folder 14, SCRC-GL; Borchardt, "Making D.C. Democracy's Capital," 222.

25. "A Basic List for Freeway Fighters," Box 23, "Chronological 1966" folder, ECTCP; "Homeowners and Tenants in Proposed Freeway Route Organize for Action," Box 41, "Flyers 1965–68" folder, ECTCP; R. H. Booker to Mayor, Deputy Mayor, and Members of the City Council of the District of Columbia, 19 Mar. 1968, Box 23, "Chronological March 1968" folder, ECTCP; "A Communication to the Conference of the American Institute of Planners," 1 Oct. 1967, Box 23, "Chronological 1967" folder, ECTCP; B. D. Colen, "Bridge

Foes Protest, Plan March Today," *WPTH*, 20 Oct. 1969; William Raspberry, "Recipe for Action: Support 'Insanity,'" *WP*, 2 Feb. 1970.

26. Drew Pearson, "D.C. Mayor on Spot in Freeway Fight," *WPTH*, 21 Feb. 1968; 656; D.C. Federation of Civic Associations et al. v. Thomas F. Airis, as Director of the District of Columbia Department of Highways and Traffic, et al., 391 F.2d 478; "The Interstate System in the District of Columbia," *Hearings before the Subcommittee on Roads of the Committee on Public Works, U.S. House of Representatives*, 2–4 Apr. 1968, 3; David Jewell and Robert G. Kaiser, "Freeway Halt Is Ordered," *WPTH*, 16 Feb. 1968.

27. Schrag, "The Freeway Fight in Washington, D.C.," 653–55; "Interstate System in the District of Columbia," *Hearings before the Subcommittee on Roads of the Committee on Public Works, U.S. House of Representatives*, 2–4 Apr. 1968, 1–3; Smith, *Captive Capital*, 212–13.

28. Jack Eisen and Ina Moore, "Fists Fly at Voting on Roads," *WPTH*, 10 Aug. 1969; Walterene Swanston and Ronald Sarro, "Bridge OKd, Foes Threaten Suits," *ES*, 10 Aug. 1969.

29. Paul Delaney, "District of Columbia, to Gain Subway, Accepts Bridge and Freeway It Did Not Want," *NYT*, 24 Aug. 1969; "The Fight Goes On!," flyer, Aug. 1969, Box 35, "Transportation—Misc. Papers," JHP; Jack Eisen, "Natcher Links Funds for Subway to Settlement of All Freeway Suits," *WPTH*, 12 Aug. 1969.

30. B. D. Colen, "Nearly 100 Bridge Foes 'Occupy' Three Sisters Islands," *WPTH*, 13 Oct. 1969; "Protest Delays Bridge Work," *WPTH*, 15 Oct. 1969; Paul W. Valentine, "Police Club Protestors at 3 Sisters Bridge Site," *WPTH*, 21 Oct. 1969; "Police, Militants Skirmish," *WPTH*, 17 Nov. 1969; Borchardt, "Making D.C. Democracy's Capital," 226.

31. Jack Eisen, "Bridge Project Halted," *WPTH*, 8 Aug. 1970.

32. Smith, *Captive Capital*, 216.

33. National Conference of Christians and Jews, Inc., "Police-Community Relations in the District of Columbia" (Washington, D.C., July 26, 1968), WEFP, Part 1, Box 18, Folder 6, SCRC-GL; Ruth Bates Harris, interview with Robert Wright, 16 Mar. 1971, RB-OHC, 7.

34. Black United Front, "Proposal for Neighborhood Control of the Police in the Black Community," 25 Sept. 1968, WEFP, Part 1, Box 18, Folder 7, SCRC-GL; Ronald Sarro, "Black United Front Presents Demands on Police Control," *ES*, 17 Oct. 1968; Robert G. Kaiser, "Black Front Presents Police-Control Plan," *WPTH*, 18 Oct. 1968; "City to Weigh Front Proposal," *WPTH*, 23 Oct. 1968; "Police Control Plea Renewed," *WPTH*, 11 Oct. 1968; Arthur I. Waskow, "Community Control of the Police" (Institute for Policy Studies), Box 4, "ACT—Police" folder, JHP.

35. Department of Justice, Federal Bureau of Investigation, Uniform Crime Reporting Statistics, "Estimated Crime in District of Columbia": http://www.ucrdatatool.gov/Search/Crime/State/RunCrimeStatebyState.cfm; Jones and Flax, "The Quality of Life in Metropolitan Washington (D.C.)," 24; "Statement to D.C. Council's Public Safety Committee on Its Report on Police-Community Relations," 16 Aug. 1968, "Office Files, 1968–1969, Book 1," Box 2, Federation of Citizens Associations Collection, DCCA; Robert L. Asher, "Nixon Labels D.C. a 'Crime Capital,' Blames Johnson," *WPTH*, 23 June 1968.

36. Ronald Sarro, "Model Precinct Hotly Debated," *ES*, 19 Oct. 1968; John Fialka, "Meet the Author of the Precinct Plan," *ES*, 15 June 1968; Barry Kalb, "'Police Relations' a Two-Way Street," *ES*, 29 Oct. 1968; Carl Bernstein, "How to Not Model a Precinct," *WPTH*,

16 Mar. 1969; Kelly, "Generalizations from an OEO Experiment," 58; Johnson, *Study of Police-Community Relations Programs*," 13–16.

37. William Raspberry, "D.C. Model Precinct in Trouble," *WPTH*, 22 July 1968; Ronald Sarro, "Police-Citizen Project Wins Federal Grant," *ES*, 29 June 1968.

38. Kelly, "Generalizations from an OEO Experiment," 59; Wiley Branton, "UPO and Pilot Precincts," letter to the editor, *ES*, 19 July 1968.

39. "Five Quit Planning Group for Pilot Police Precinct," *WAA*, 12 Nov. 1968; John Fialka, "'Tough' 13th Precinct Picked for Police Citizens Project," *ES*, 23 Jan. 1969.

40. "Extremes—Affluence and Poverty—Rub Shoulders in 13th," *Sunday Star*, 26 Jan. 1969; Bernstein, "How to Not Model a Precinct."

41. Carl Bernstein, "Rights Groups United in Fight on Chief of Model Precinct," *WPTH*, 12 Apr. 1969; Carl Bernstein, "Model Precinct Talks Disrupted," *WPTH*, 20 Feb. 1969; "Project Data Will Be Given Citizens of 13th," *ES*, 21 Feb. 1969; "Barry to Seek Model Precinct Ban," *WPTH*, 27 Feb. 1969; Peter Braestrup, "Pilot Police Project Seen as a Fraud," *WPTH*, 10 Sept. 1969.

42. "Bias Panel Calls for Ouster of Shellow," *Sunday Star*, 13 Apr. 1969; "Extremes—Affluence and Poverty—Rub Shoulders in 13th"; Peter Braestrup, "Police-Community Relations Still a Major Problem in D.C.," *WPTH*, 1 Aug. 1969.

43. Peter Braestrup, "'Good Faith' Asked on Pilot Precinct," *WPTH*, 25 June 1969; "Pilot Precinct Work 'in Limbo,'" *WPTH*, 1 Aug. 1969; "6 in Pilot Police Project Seem Sure of Election," *ES*, 30 Jan. 1970; Carl Bernstein, "Hill Leaders Fight Police Pilot Project," *WPTH*, 12 Feb. 1970; "Participation, Not Control," *ES*, 18 Feb. 1970; Kelly, "Generalizations from an OEO Experiment," 78.

44. Kelly et al., *Pilot Police Project*, 320; Kelly, "Generalizations from an OEO Experiment," 60–62; Johnson, *Study of Police-Community Relations Programs*, 15–16; Paul W. Valentine, "Pilot District Project, Nearly Out of Money, Seeks Extension," *WPTH*, 6 Aug. 1972.

45. Betty James, "Role of Police, Reformers Reversed on Pilot Precinct," *ES*, 24 July 1968; Charles Cassell, interview with Robert Wright, 31 Dec. 1968, RB-OHC, 9; Tucker, *Beyond the Burning*, 126.

46. Carlos Sanchez, "The Old Man's Hispanic Honor," *WP*, 10 Feb. 1987; Joseph D. Whitaker, "Hispanic Leader Carlos Rosario Dies," *WP*, 4 Feb. 1987.

47. Cadaval, "The Latino Community: Creating an Identity in the Nation's Capital," 233; Repak, *Waiting on Washington*, 61; Richard Critchfield, "New Latin Arrivals Often Victimized Here," *ES* 3 Apr. 1972; Cadaval, "Latino Community," 235–36; Marcela Davila, Oral History Interview, and Casilda Luna, Oral History Interview, CML-OHP, Community Archives, WD.

48. Lunn, "Community at a Crossroads," 60–61; Repak, *Waiting on Washington*, 2–3.

49. Philip Shandler, "The Silent Minority," *Sunday Star*, 5 Jan. 1969, 5; "Our Latin Quarter," *WPTH*, 27 Jan. 1969; Bill Bancroft, "Afternoon in the Teatro," *WPTH*, 29 Nov. 1971; John DeFerrari, "The Ontario Theatre's Many Past Lives," Streets of Washington (blog), http://www.streetsofwashington.com/2011/10/ontario-theatres-many-past-lives.html; Betty Medsger, "Latins Form Largest Immigrant Group," *WPTH*, 4 Dec. 1972.

50. Casilda Luna, Oral History Interview; Rosario quoted in Cadaval, "Latino Community," 235.

51. Medsger, "Latins Form Largest Immigrant Group"; "YWCA Classes Set for All

Ages," *WPTH*, 30 Dec. 1960; Susan Jacoby, "Spanish Pupils Pose Problem," *WPTH*, 23 Sept. 1967; Sanchez, "Old Man's Hispanic Honor"; "Carlos Manuel Rosario," *WP*, 7 Feb. 1987; Lunn, "Community at a Crossroads," 65–66.

52. Medsger, "Latins Form Largest Immigrant Group"; "No Old World Flavor Here," *Sunday Star*, 8 Apr. 1973; Marcela Davila, Oral History Interview; Jim Hoagland, "The Spanish-Speakers Are Isolated," *WPTH*, 17 Dec. 1967.

53. Hoagland, "Spanish-Speakers Are Isolated,"; Jacoby, "Spanish Pupils Pose Problem"; Isabel West, "Ferment in the Barrio," *ES*, 11 Nov. 1973.

54. Paul Delaney, "D.C. Poverty Aid Asked for Spanish-Speaking," *ES*, 20 Dec. 1967; Martha Hamilton, "Many Spanish Children in D.C. Don't Go to School," *WPTH*, 23 Nov. 1973; Hoagland, "Spanish-Speakers Are Isolated"; Philip Shandler, "Police, D.C. Latin Leaders Act to Close Language Gap," *Sunday Star*, 12 Dec. 1966.

55. Shandler, "Silent Minority"; Critchfield, "New Latin Arrivals Often Victimized Here."

56. Shandler, "Silent Minority."

57. Delaney, "D.C. Poverty Aid Asked for Spanish-Speaking"; Charles Koprowski, "Spanish-Speaking Community Protests Poverty Fund Cuts," *WPTH*, 12 Dec. 1966; Jesse W. Lewis Jr., "Group Criticizes Curb on Antipoverty Aides," *WPTH*, 14 Oct. 1966; Lunn, "Community at a Crossroads," 60–61; Cadaval, "Latino Community," 234–35; "D.C. Latins Protest Lack of Funding for Center," *ES*, 12 July 1969; Martin Weil, "Group Urges Pilot Project to Teach Spanish to Police," *WPTH*, 5 Dec. 1969; John Fialka, "Train Police in Spanish, Educational Group Asks," *ES*, 5 Dec. 1969; Martin Weil, "23 Policemen Learn Spanish," *WPTH*, 1 Mar. 1970.

58. Marcela Davila, Oral History Interview, 4; Casilda Luna, Oral History Interview, 5; Cadaval, "Latino Community," 237.

59. Medsger, "Latins Form Largest Immigrant Group."

60. Repak, *Waiting on Washington*, 61–68; Medsger, "Latins Form Largest Immigrant Group"; "Spanish Panel Named," *WPTH*, 31 July 1970.

61. Fialka, "Train Police in Spanish"; Medsger, "Latins Form Largest Immigrant Group."

62. Shandler, "Silent Minority"; Hoagland, "Spanish-Speakers Are Isolated"; West, "Ferment in the Barrio."

63. Susan Jacoby, "Vocal Cardozo Unit Wins City Hall Ear," *WPTH*, 11 Apr. 1969.

64. Philip Shandler, "2 Feuding Latin Factions in District Reach Truce," *ES*, 20 Nov. 1966; Hoagland, "Spanish-Speakers Are Isolated"; Jacoby, "Vocal Cardozo Unit Wins City Hall Ear."

65. Richard E. Prince, "D.C. Spanish Minority Finds Ally in Montoya," *WPTH*, 15 Dec. 1969; William Raspberry, "Council Learns What It's Like to Belong to Latin Minority," *WPTH*, 30 Jan. 1970.

66. "Spanish Panel Named"; "No Old World Flavor Here"; Betty Medsger, "Latins Form Largest Immigrant Group."

67. Cadaval, "Hispano-American Festival and Latino Community," 95–96.

68. West, "Ferment in the Barrio"; Simpatia Novale, "Latinos Get Cold Shoulder," *D.C. Gazette* (March 1975); Antonio Welty to D.C. Chief of Police, 19 Mar. 1976, in "Latino," Box 5, Columbian Files Collection, DCCA; West, "Ferment in the Barrio."

69. Anita F. Allen, "Remembering Anacostia as It Was," *WP*, 10 July 1986.

70. Peter Milius, "School Board Bill Offered," *WPTH*, 16 Aug. 1967; William Raspberry, "Bill to Elect School Unit Languishes," *WPTH*, 21 Feb. 1968; Ellen Hoffman, "School Election Bill Signed," *WPTH*, 23 Apr. 1968; Ellen Hoffman, "School Board Contest Begins," *WPTH*, 29 July 1968; Robert L. Asher, "Last-Minute Entries Join City School Race," *WPTH*, 22 Sept. 1968; "Mrs. Allen Enters School Board Race," *WPTH*, 11 Aug. 1968; "64 Beat Deadline, Enter School Race," *WPTH*, 23 Sept. 1968; Susan Jacoby, "Key Election Issue: Education of Poor," *WPTH*, 3 Nov. 1968; Susan Jacoby, "Until School Board Runoff, Hobson's the One," *WPTH*, 7 Nov. 1968; "School Board Elections—Final Round," *WPTH*, 24 Nov. 1968; Susan Jacoby, "Anita Allen, Sessions Lead in School Race," *WPTH*, 27 Nov. 1968.

71. Lawrence Feinberg, "Mrs. Allen Airs Views on School Needs," *WPTH*, 8 Feb. 1970; Peter Milius, "Schools' Leaders Assailed," *WPTH*, 22 May 1969.

72. Karlyn Barker, "School Board Rivalry on Air," *WPTH*, 24 Oct. 1971; "Allen Backs Police in Schools, Barry Disagrees," *WPTH*, 4 Oct. 1971; Richard E. Prince, "Mrs. Allen, Allies Lose D.C. Vote," *WPTH*, 3 Nov. 1971.

73. Richard E. Prince, "D.C. Delegate Bill Signed by Nixon," *WPTH*, 23 Sept. 1970; "4 Delegate Hopefuls Air Views," *WPTH*, 7 Mar. 1971.

74. "Want a New State," *WP*, 18 Aug. 1893; Paul Valentine, "Bill for D.C. Statehood Backed," *WP*, 26 Feb. 1976; Smith, *Multitudes*; Sam Smith, "The Case for Statehood," in Smith, *Statehood Papers*; Smith, *Captive Capital*, 271; Sam Smith Oral History Interview, 2 Nov. 1998, DCSML, OHP 20-7, DCCA, 5–11.

75. "Declaration of the DC Statehood Party: Towards a Cooperative Community," in "Home Rule, Misc. Papers," Box 34, JHP, DCCA; David Boldt, "District Home Rule, Not Crime, Is Main Issue in Campaign," *WP*, Mar. 19, 1971; "Fauntroy Attacks Plan on Statehood," *WP*, July 15, 1971.

76. Walter E. Fauntroy, interview with Edward Thompson III, 23 Feb., 5 Mar. 1973, RB-OHC, 16.

77. Alex Poinsett, "How Blacks Can Gain Two Senators," *Ebony* 33, no. 8 (June 1978); Kenneth Bredemeier, "Fauntroy Sets Political Mission," *WP*, 24 Aug. 1978; Martin Well, "John McMillan Dies, Opposed Home Rule as Congressman," *WP*, 4 Sept. 1979; Fauntroy, *Home Rule or House Rule*, 24–25; Diner, *Democracy, Federalism*, 59.

78. Fauntroy, *Home Rule or House Rule*: 53–56.

79. Walter E. Washington and Washington, D.C., City Council, *Ten Years since Apr. 4, 1968: A Decade of Progress for the District of Columbia; A Report to the People* (Washington, D.C.: District of Columbia, 1978), 1–5; Fauntroy, *Home Rule or House Rule*, 24–25; Stephen Green, "Diggs Says Home Rule a 'Partnership,'" *WP*, 16 Feb. 1974; Sam Smith, "Outlying Precincts," *D.C. Gazette* 5, no. 3 (March 1974).

80. Sam Smith Oral History Interview, 18 Nov. 1998, DCSML, OHP 20-7, DCCA, 2.

81. Milton Coleman, "The District: Careers, Political Structures Face Test," *WP*, 10 Sept. 1978; LaBarbara Bowman, "D.C. Council Vice Chairman Tucker Seeks Step-Up: Tucker Knows Key to Survival in D.C." *WP*, 26 Oct. 1974.

82. Paul W. Valentine, "Candidates Leap into Arena: D.C. Political Hopefuls Jockeying for Position," *WP*, 9 May 1974; "56 Seek Office in D.C. Election," *Washington Afro American*, 8 July 1978; "Stands of Candidates in Ward Five Primary," *WP*, 1 Sept. 1974; Douglas B.

Feaver, "Leaders Emerge in City Council Races," WP, 11 Sept. 1974; "David Clarke, 53; Led City Council in Washington," NYT, 29 Mar. 1997; Eric Pianin, "From Protest to Power," WP, 27 Aug. 1983.

83. "Self-Determination for DC," fundraising letter to supporters, 28 Mar. 1973, Ephemera Collection, Home Rule and Representation Ephemera, KRL-HSW; "Lobby Corps," Series 1, Box 2, and "Memorandum Re: D.C. Home Rule Strategies," 28 Oct. 1971, both in Box 1, Folder I-1, Self-Determination for D.C. Collection, DCCA; "Coalition Strategy: How to Win Votes for DC Voice in Congress," WP, 5 Mar. 1978.

84. Donald Baker, "Full D.C. Representation Debated; House Vote Today," WP, 2 Mar. 1978; Schrag, Behind the Scenes, 246; "Senate Sets Decision on D.C. Voting," WP, 22 Aug. 1978; "Filibuster Greets Senate Debate on Voting Rights Act," WP, 17 Aug. 1978; Vose, "When District of Columbia Representation Collides," 124; Diner, Democracy, Federalism, 62.

85. John Sansing, "Can Whites Survive in DC? Or Are We Going toward a 'Chocolate City' and 'Vanilla Suburbs'?," Washingtonian 12, no. 1 (October 1976): 133–39, 180–90.

86. Wells, "Decent Place to Stay."

87. The Post first used the term "gentrification" in 1973 in an article about revitalization in London, the city where the term was coined in 1964. The Post first used the term to refer to the process in Washington, D.C., in 1977. See "Londoners v. Developers," WP, 25 Mar. 1973; "Will 'Saved' Cities Mean Suburban Slums?," WP, July 30, 1977; and Asch and Musgrove, "'We're Headed for Some Bad Trouble,'" in Hyra and Prince, Capital Dilemma,

88. "Is There a National Back-to-the-City Trend? Probably Not," WP, 4 Sept. 1978; Logan, "Mrs. McCain's Parlor," 959–60, 970–71; Milton Coleman, "Paranoia Politics," WP Magazine, 27 Aug. 1978, 10.

89. Huron, "Creating a Commons in the Capital," 58–59; "Tenant Revolt Fueled by Increases in Rent, Evictions," WP, 21 Dec. 1978; "The Battling Tenants," WP, 19 Nov. 1979; "Adams-Morgan House Prices Soaring: Row House Prices Soaring in Adams-Morgan Boom," WP, 24 Mar. 1974; "Gambles in 'No Man's Land' Have Paid Off for Investors," WP, 11 Sept. 1979; "Poor Again Feel Pressure from Developers," WP, 15 Feb. 1977; Huron, "Work of the Urban Commons," 11.

90. Logan, "Mrs. McCain's Parlor," 969–70; Huron, "Creating a Commons in the Capital," 58–59; "Ward 1 Race Splits an Old Alliance," WP, 21 July 1982; Henig, Gentrification in Adams Morgan, 31–32; Frank Smith and Marie Nahikian, "The AMO Coop Housing Trust," "Adams Morgan Organizations," Box 1, Columbian Files Collection, DCCA.

91. "District Mayor Signs Rent Control Measure," WP, 2 Aug. 1974; Wells, "Decent Place to Stay," esp. chap. 4.

92. "Seaton Place Project Eyed by NCPC," WP, 2 May 1965. "City Charges 959 Housing Violations," WP, 20 May 1976; "A Neighborly Party to Aid the Seaton Street Fund, WP, 7 Oct. 1976; "Team Effort on Seaton Place, WP, 13 Apr. 1977; "Tenant Revolt Fueled by Increases in Rent, Evictions."

93. "Tenant Revolt Fueled by Increases in Rent, Evictions"; "Tenants Groups to Organize Residents of Adams-Morgan," WP, 29 Mar. 1979; D.C. Advisory Committee to the U.S. Commission on Civil Rights, Neighborhood Renewal—Reinvestment and Displacement in D.C.; Wells, "Decent Place to Stay"; "In D.C. Loan Program, Mortgage Defaults Abound," WP, 15 Jan. 2012; Huron, "Work of the Urban Commons"; "Battling Tenants."

94. Milton Coleman, "Mayor Cites Record in Campaign Kickoff,'" WP, 27 May 1978; William H. Jones, "Mayor Washington: 'Something Good Is Happening,'" WP, 8 Jan. 1978; Milton Coleman, "Tucker Formally Enters Mayor Race: Charges District Poorly Managed," WP, 23 Apr. 1978; Eugene L. Meyer and LaBarbara Bowman, "D.C. Slates Aim at Council Race: 2 D.C. Slates Gear Up for Council Race," WP, 16 Apr. 1976; Philip Shandler, "Fauntroy for Tucker over Barry," WS, 8 Sept. 1977.

95. Philip Shandler, "The Talk of the District," WS, 18 Jan. 1977; Jaffe and Sherwood, *Dream City*, 105–7.

96. Reporter Maurice Williams died on the scene, and security guard Mack Cantrell suffered a bullet wound to the face. Jaffe and Sherwood, *Dream City*, 107–11; King, *Breeding of Contempt*, 109–22; William Greider and Richard Harwood, "Hanafi Muslim Bands Seize Hostages at 3 Sites; 1 Slain, Others Wounded," WP, 10 Mar. 1977; "Mack W. Cantrell, 46, Shot in Hanafi Raid," WP, 6 July 1977; Phil McCombs, "The Hanafi Takeover: One Year Later: Hanafi Takeover Altered the Lives of Many," WP, 5 Mar. 1978.

97. Kathy Sawyer, "Barry a 'Very Lucky Man'; Bullet Stopped near Heart," WP, 10 Mar. 1977; Jaffe and Sherwood, *Dream City*, 112; Leon Dash, "D.C. Election Unit Auditing Reports of '76 Barry Campaign," WP, 20 Aug. 1978; Marion Barry, "A Homemade Agenda for the City," WP, 24 Apr. 1977.

98. Milton Coleman, "Tucker Gains Support in D.C. Political Move," WP, 23 Oct. 1977; Fauntroy quoted in Jaffe and Sherwood, *Dream City*, 112–13; Milton Coleman, "Barry Enters Mayor Race," WP, 22 Jan. 1978.

99. Milton Coleman, "56 File to Run in D.C. Primary Election," WP, 6 July 1978; Coleman, "Mayor Cites Record in Campaign Kickoff"; Kenneth Bredemeier, "Big D.C. Contributors Hedging on Mayoral Race: Big Contributors Hedging on D.C. Mayoral Race," WP, 13 Aug. 1978; Milton Coleman, "Who Is for Whom? Endorsements Reflect Confusing City Politics," WP, 7 Sept. 1978; Coleman, "The District: Careers, Political Structures Face Test"; Leon Dash, "Teamsters Union Endorses Tucker in Mayoral Race," WP, 21 June 1978.

100. Coleman, "Paranoia Politics," 8–9.

101. Donia Mills, "Gay Political Experience in Washington," WS, 31 Oct. 1977; Sam Smith, "Despite It All, Barry's the Best," *D.C. Gazette* 9, no. 4 (April 1978); "Barry's Victory: The Racial Questions in District Politics," WP, 19 Oct.1978; Thomas Morgan, "Gays Hope to Cast the Deciding Votes for Barry," WP, 4 Sept. 1978; Milton Coleman, "Marion Barry: The Activist Denies He's Changed," WP, 2 Jan. 1979.

102. Milton Coleman, "ADA Endorses Marion Barry for Mayor," WP, 12 Apr. 1978; "Marion Barry for Mayor," WP, 20 Aug. 1978; Milton Coleman and Kenneth Bredemeier, "Rivals Blame Each Other for Calif. Defeat," WP, 6 Sept. 1978; "Marion Barry for Mayor," WP, 30 Aug. 1978; "Mr. Barry's School-Board Days," WP, 5 Sept. 1978; "The Housing Issue," WP, 7 Sept. 1978; "A Vote for Marion Barry," WP, 8 Sept. 1978; "A Vote for Something Better," WP, 10 Sept. 1978.

103. Milton Coleman and Kenneth Bredemeier, "Dixon Victor in D.C. Council Chairman Race: Marion Barry Hangs onto Narrow Lead in Ballot Count," WP, 13 Sept. 1978; Stephen Lynton, "Tucker to Ask Court for New D.C. Election," WP, 23 Sept. 1978; Paul W. Valentine and Karlyn Barker, "7,000 Votes Uncounted in D.C. Race," WP, 22 Sept. 1978; Paul Valentine, "Mayor Says Barry Won D.C. Vote," WP, 28 Sept. 1978; Laura Kiernan, "Tucker Says Barry Won City Primary," WP, 27 Sept. 1978; Donald Baker, "Tucker Pledges

to Back Barry for Mayor," *WP*, 29 Sept. 1978; William Raspberry, "D.C. Election Snafu," *WP*, 27 Sept. 1978.

104. Jaffe and Sherwood, *Dream City*, 116; "Barry's Victory"; Judy Bachrach, "'The Power Is in the Appraisal,'" *WS*, 10 Oct. 1978.

105. Harry Jaffe has written the most thorough explorations of Wiggins's "The Plan" idea, and nearly all the extensive discussion of the idea is rooted in his work, though in both sources cited below he mistakenly lists the date for Wiggins's postprimary articles as 1979 not 1978. See Jaffe and Sherwood, *Dream City*, 132–33. Harry Jaffe, "So-Called 'Plan' for White Supremacy Lives on in D.C.," *Washington Examiner*, 30 Aug. 2010. Although Wiggins briefly mentions a "plan" in a 1975 column, the five columns in which Wiggins thoroughly articulates the ideas that would come to constitute "The Plan" are: Lillian Wiggins, "'Master Plan' for Washington," *WAA*, 30 Sept. 1978; Wiggins, "Will the Election Strategy Work?," *WAA*, 23 Sept. 1978; Wiggins, "Who Really Did 'Take a Stand'?," *WAA*, 7 Oct. 1978; Wiggins, "Lack of Strategy Really Hurts," *WAA*, 14 Oct. 1978; and Wiggins, "Will We Cause Our Own Demise?," *WAA*, 28 Oct. 1978. Wiggins's last column covered the gentrification that had enveloped much of the center city. Though marginal to her thinking in the fall of 1978, these two issues later would become stock elements of "The Plan" idea.

106. Joe Holley, "Affirmative Action Pioneer Advised GOP Presidents," *WP*, 14 July 2005; Milton Coleman and Kenneth Bredemeier, "Barry Wins Mayor Race in a Breeze," *WP*, 8 Nov. 1978; Paul Valentine, "Poor Blacks Built Landslide for Barry, Analysis Shows," *WP*, 9 Nov. 1978.

107. Agronsky, *Marion Barry*, 184.

108. Robert F. Levey, "Old-Time Ward Fight Marks Election," *WPTH*, 2 Nov. 1970.

109. Nicholas Lemann, "Marion Barry: The Question Is: Will He Deliver?," *WP Magazine* (16 Dec. 1979): 21.

Chapter 13

1. "Real Estate, Changing Hands," *Hill Rag* (August 2011).

2. Rader, *Signal through the Flames*, 49–60. Colman McCarthy, "J. Edward Guinan, Former Catholic Priest Who Ministered to the Homeless, Dies at 78," *WP*, 3 Jan. 2015; Schrag, *Behind the Scenes*, 18–19.

3. Rader, *Signal through the Flames*, 35–48, 63–66.

4. Columbia Heights Citizens' Association, *A Statement of the Some of the Advantages of the Beautiful Columbia Heights, a Neighborhood of Homes* (Washington, D.C., 1904), available at http://ia601409.us.archive.org/13/items/statementofsomeooocolum/statementof someooocolum.pdf; Brian Kraft et al., *Cultural Convergence: Columbia Heights Heritage Trail* (Washington, D.C.: Cultural Tourism DC, 2009); Anne H. Oman and Michel McQueen, "Group Home Growth May Bring Controversy to All Neighborhoods," *WP*, 4 Sept. 1980.

5. In 1970, 1345 Euclid was valued at $11,548. Lusk's Realty Assessment Directory, District of Columbia, 1970, WD; William L. Claiborne, "Halfway Houses Stir Feud: Police, Penal Aides Differ," *WPTH*, 19 Sept. 1971; Philip McCombs, "3 Freed in Street Slaying: U.S. Withholds Details in Death of Policeman," *WP*, 7 Dec. 1971; Anne Oman, "Group Home Growth May Bring Controversy to All Neighborhoods," *WP*, 4 Sept. 1980;

"Crime and Justice," *WP*, 27 June 1973; Patricia Camp, "Group Occupies Apartments in Housing Protest," *WP*, 16 Sept. 1978; Patricia Camp, "Area Blighted by Vacant Houses," *WP*, 6 Feb. 1979.

6. Christopher Wright, "Black Groups Accuses D.C. of Neglecting '68 Riot Areas," *WS*, 6 Feb. 1971; Toni House, "Just the Beginning," *WS*, 13 Jan. 1971; William Delaney, "Barry and Anita—Two Different Worlds," *WS*, 3 Nov. 1971; Kenneth Turan and Laton McCartney, "You Are What You Read: Sketches of Six Special Bookstores," *WPTH*, 12 Nov. 1972.

7. Hombs and Snyder, *Homelessness in America*, 92; Juan Williams, "Antiwar Unit of '60s Helps Poor in 70s," *WP*, 20 Sept. 1976.

8. Neil Henry, "A Washington Winter's Tale: Fear Hunger, Loathing Abuse," *WP*, 5 May 1980.

9. Carol Fennelly, interview with author (Musgrove); Paul Valentine, "See City Agrees to Provide More Homeless Shelters," *WP*, 16 Dec. 1978; Paul Valentine, "Barry Backs Small Shelters, Centers for Street People," *WP*, 15 Feb. 1979; Hombs and Snyder, *Homeless in America*, 97; Rader, *Signal through the Flames*, 123.

10. Jaqueline Trescott, "Ivanhoe Donaldson, Stage Manager in the Political Drama," *WP*, 3 Nov. 1978; Garrett Epps, "Aide-de-Camp: Ivanhoe Donaldson," *WP*, 31 Dec. 1978; Martin Weil, "Donaldson: Troubleshooter for City, Mayor," *WP*, 18 Dec. 1984; Halberstam, *Children*, 618–19; Ewing, "Garvey or Garveyism," 130–45.

11. Larry Rubin to author (Musgrove), email, 22 Jan. 2014; Jaffe and Sherwood, *Dream City*, 104–5.

12. LaBarbara Bowman, "'Congregate Care' Facility for Elderly Proposed at Garfield Terrace Project," *WP*, 5 Nov. 1979; Jaffe and Sherwood, *Dream City*, 104–5, 126–28.

13. Milton Coleman, "Paranoia Politics," *WP Magazine*, 27 Aug. 1978, 11.

14. Jack Eisen, "Mayor Barry Sets Fast Pace for Employees," *WP*, 6 Jan. 1979; Milton Coleman, "100 Days," *WP*, 15 Apr. 1979; Milton Coleman, "Barry Polishing District's Image," *WP*, 24 May 1979; Milton Coleman, "Barry Names Top Aides: Most of 13 Appointees Share His Background," *WP*, 30 Dec. 1978; Milton Coleman, "Barry's First Year," *WP*, 7 Jan. 1980; Milton Coleman, "Mayoral Appointments: The Importance of Race," *WP*, 19 Apr. 1979; Milton Coleman, "Barry, Hispanos Parting Ways?," *WP*, 13 Dec. 1979; Milton Coleman, "Washington's Gay Vote," *WP*, 21 Apr. 1979; Jaffe and Sherwood, *Dream City*, 140–42; Agronsky, *Marion Barry*, 185–86.

15. Milton Coleman, "Barry's Knights of the Round Tables," *WP*, 2 Mar. 1979; Milton Coleman, "Stokely Carmichael Pays Call on Barry," *WP*, 25 Jan 1979; Milton Coleman, "Barry to Attend July Africa Summit," *WP*, 22 June 1979; Alice Bonner, "African Journal: Barry Is Cheered by Villagers in Senegal," *WP*, 17 July 1979.

16. Coleman, "100 Days"; Lemann, "Marion Barry: The Question Is: Will He Deliver?"; "A Step toward Success," *WP*, 21 Aug. 1981.

17. Thompson, "'60s Activist Now Sees 'The System' as MBOC Director," *WP*, 15 Mar. 1979.

18. Thompson, "'60s Activist Now Sees 'The System'"; "Mayor Announces New Thrust for Minority Businesses," *WI*, 22 Mar. 1979; Jaffe and Sherwood, *Dream City*, 152.

19. LaBarbara Bowman, "Bates Street Project Bungled, Developers At Fault, Report Says," *WP*, 20 Aug. 1982; "Step toward Success"; Coleman, "100 Days."

20. Lawrence Meyer, "Report on D.C. Cites Millions in Lost Funds," *WP*, 20 June 1976;

Merrill Brown, "City Unveils Computerized Budget Plan," WP, 28 Sept. 1979; Alphonse Hill, interview with author (Musgrove); Thomas Lippman, "D.C. Audit: Big Deficit, a Way Out," WP, 3 Feb. 1981.

21. Jack Eisen, "City Surplus Fund Exceeded by Need to Pay Past Bills," WP, Feb. 7 1979; Jack Eisen and Eugene Robinson, "'81 Barry Budget Sets More Cuts, Rise in 2 Taxes," WP, 21 May 1980; Jaffe and Sherwood, Dream City, 129.

22. Eisen and Robinson, "'81 Barry Budget Sets More Cuts"; Rader, Signal through the Flames, 134–36.

23. Judith Valente and Eugene Robinson, "Youth, Labor Groups Criticize Barry for Proposed Cuts in City's Budget," WP, 11 Apr. 1980; Jack Eisen, "Barry Booed by Crowd at Budget Rally," WP, 4 May 1980; Eugene Robinson, "Mayor, Once Full of Confidence, Now Echoes Walter Washington," WP, 4 Jan. 1981.

24. Valente and Robinson, "Youth, Labor Groups Criticize Barry"; Judith Valente, "Barry Asks Blacks to Curb Criticism," WP, 11 May 1980; Barry Sussman, "Barry Rated Unfavorably in Poll of City Residents," WP, 28 Dec. 1980; "Barry's Fiscal Plan Stresses Austerity," WP, 20 July 1980.

25. Easton, Gang of Five; Stephanic and Delgado, No Mercy; Mike McIntire, "Conservative Nonprofit Acts as a Stealth Business Lobbyist," NYT, 21 Apr. 2012; neither the WP nor the NYT mentions ALEC before 1980. "Former ALEC National Chairs," http://alec.devhm .net/about-alec/history/former-alec-national-chairmen/; Phyllis Schlafly, "The D.C. Ripoff Amendment," Phyllis Schlafly Report 12, no. 3 (October 1978); Patrick Buchanan, "Scuttle the D.C. Amendment," New Orleans Times Picayune, 9 Sept. 1978; Frank van der Linden, "Many States Cool, to D.C. Amendment," Nashville Banner, 7 Oct. 1978; Margaret Aylward, "Is or Is Not the American Legislative Exchange Council a Lobbying Organization," 11 Feb. 1979, in Collection 3, Series 1, Box 4, Folder "Opposition Organizations 2 of 2," DCCA; Elena Hess to District Director of the Internal Revenue Service, Mar. 31, 1979, in Collection 3, Series 1, Box 4, Folder "Opposition Organizations 1 of 2," DCCA; "House in Wyoming Votes Down DC Voting Rights Amendment," WP, 20 Jan. 1979; Donald P. Baker, "D.C. Amendment Drive Moribund after 6 Months," WP, 3 Mar. 1979; Jackson Diehl, "Fauntroy Offers to Criticize PLO to Gain Votes for Amendment," WP, 30 Jan. 1980.

26. Edsall and Edsall, Chain Reaction, 99–115; Pearlman, "Democracy's Capital," 199–200; Buchanan, "Scuttle the D.C. Amendment"; "Notes on Presentations Given on the ALEC Meeting," 2 Dec. 1978, Collection 3, Series 1, Box 4, Folder "Opposition Organizations 1 of 2," DCCA; Donna Carlson, "Heritage Foundation Forum: DC Amendment: Bad Public Policy," Atlanta Daily World, 8 Dec. 1978.

27. Joseph Rauh and Harold Himmelman, "Turning the Tide on DC Voting Rights," WP, 21 Aug. 1979; "Capital's Statehood Vote Gets Scant Notice," NYT, 10 Nov. 1980; T. R. Reid, "Conservatives Devise Strategy to Kill D.C. Amendment," WP, 11 Feb. 1979; Keith Richburg, "DC Voting Rights Plank Dies Quietly in Detroit," WP, 12 July 1980; Keith Richburg, "Rebuilders in Control at Detroit," WP, 14 July 1980; American Presidency Project, "Political Party Platforms, 1840–2012," http://www.presidency.ucsb.edu; Kalman, Right Star Rising, 354–55; Shade and Campbell, American Presidential Campaigns and Elections; Ira Shapiro, "The Year the Senate Fell," NYT, 6 Jan. 2010; Marjorie Hunter, "Conservative House Democrats Seek Bigger Voice," NYT, 8 Nov. 1980.

28. Fauntroy, *Home Rule or House Rule*, 12–13; Howie Kurtz and Michael Isikoff, "Congress Still Rules the Roost in DC," *WP*, 25 Oct. 1981.

29. Fauntroy, *Home Rule or House Rule*, 69–70, 81–87; Kurtz and Isikoff, "Congress Still Rules the Roost."

30. "Downtown Is Back," *WP*, 23 Oct. 1986; Gale, *Washington, D.C.*, 37–49; Schrag, *Great Society Subway*, 171–220; Jaffe and Sherwood, *Dream City*, 146–51; Solomon, *Washington Century*, 308–9, 319–20; Thomas Lippman, "Backers of City's New Convention Center Optimistic," *WP*, 3 May 1981; Bob Levey, "Our Town: Friendly, but in Flux," *WP*, 8 Jan. 1981.

31. Juan Williams, "Ward 7: New Stronghold for Marion Barry," *WP*, Aug. 2, 1982.

32. Williams, "Ward 7"; Jaffe and Sherwood, *Dream City*, 186–87.

33. Juan Williams, "Begins Campaign with Attack on Barry," *WP*, 4 Apr. 1982; Juan Williams, "Barry Pushes Self as Only Real 'Black' Candidate," *WP*, 28 July 1982; Juan Williams, "A Mayoral Platform Based on Frustration," *WP*, 7 Apr. 1982; Juan Williams, "Patricia R. Harris Dies at 60," *WP*, 24 Mar. 1985.

34. Juan Williams, "Wards 4, 5: Key Battlegrounds in D.C. Mayoral Race," *WP*, 17 Aug. 1982; Juan Williams and Eric Pianin, "Clarke Will Head D.C. Council," *WP*, 15 Sept. 1982; Eric Pianin and Juan Williams, "Barry Credits Winning Race to Personality," *WP*, 16 Sept. 1982.

35. Riguer, *Loneliness of the Black Republican*, 261–310.

36. Claudia Levy, "Teodis 'Ted' Gay Dies at 52," *WP*, 14 Jan. 1995; Jaffe and Sherwood, *Dream City*, 181.

37. Wilson quoted in Jaffe and Sherwood, *Dream City*, 181; Guyot quoted in Durrin, *Promises to Keep*.

38. Arthur S. Brisbane and Tom Sherwood, "Mayor Barry Defeats Schwartz, Wins Third Term," *WP*, 5 Nov. 1986; Levy, "Teodis 'Ted' Gay Dies at 52"; Eugene Robinson, "Our Own Boss Barry," *WP*, 10 June 1984.

39. Juan Williams, "The Mind of Rayful Edmond," *WP Magazine*, 24 June 1990.

40. The preceding paragraphs were based on: A. Smith, *American Gangster: Rayful Edmond*; Williams, "Mind of Rayful Edmond"; Mike Folks and Jim Keary, "Edmond Linked to Mob Family," *WT*, 20 Nov. 1989; Jaffe and Sherwood, *Dream City*, 200–204.

41. Ronald Kessler, "The Heroin Economy: Millions a Day," *WP*, 12 May 1970; Lusane, *Pipe Dream Blues*, 153–64; Joe Paull and Matt McDade, "Million-Dollar Dope Ring Defied Society in This 'Cool City,'" *WP*, 4 Jan. 1953; Philip Carter, "Nixon Acts to Curb Drug Traffic Here," *WP*, 23 Feb. 1969; William Claiborne, "Heroin Problem Peaks in D.C., to Ease in 2 Years, Doctor Says," *WP*, 11 Apr. 1972.

42. Gordon Chaplin, "Cocaine in Washington," *WP*, 5 June 1977; "Drug Probes on Capitol Hill End Quietly," *WP*, 15 Jan. 1984; Robert Meyers, "4 Sentenced in Virginia Cocaine King," *WP*, 11 Aug. 1979; "Maryland Police Smash Alleged Regional Cocaine Smuggling Ring," *WP*, 9 Oct. 1982; John Mintz, "30 Arrested in N. Va. on Drug Charges," *WP*, 19 July 1984.

43. R. H. Melton and Linda Wheeler, "Once for Elite, Cocaine Now an Equal-Opportunity Vice," *WP*, 22 June 1986; Meyers, "4 Sentenced in Virginia Cocaine King"; "Maryland Police Smash Alleged Regional Cocaine Smuggling Ring"; Mintz, "30 Arrested in N. Va. on Drug Charges"; Lewis and Reeves, *Slugg*; Linda Wheeler, "Gunfights

Heighten Danger at Drug-Plagued Hanover Place," *WP*, 25 Nov. 1985; Fenston et al., *Crack, the Drug That Consumed the Nation's Capital*.

44. Lawrence Feinberg, "Census Shows Loss of Middle-Income Blacks to Suburbs," *WP*, 2 Feb. 1984; Margaret Shapiro, "Blacks in the Suburbs: D.C. Is Still Home," *WP*, 5 Oct. 1981.

45. Cole, *Never Too Young to Die*; Smith, *Lenny, Lefty, and the Chancellor*; Sally Jenkins and Michael Wilbon, "The Strange Final Weeks of Len Bias' Life," *Los Angeles Times*, 19 Aug. 1986; Keith Harrison, "'I Couldn't Blame Tribble,' Juror Says," *WP*, 5 June 1987; Judith Havemann, "Reagan Signs Antidrug Bill," *WP*, 28 Oct. 1986.

46. Frasier, *Without Bias*; Weinreb, "The Day Innocence Died"; Harrison, "'I Couldn't Blame Tribble,' Juror Says"; Havemann, "Reagan Signs Antidrug Bill"; Lauralyn Sasaki and Gabe Fuentes, "Administration Efforts to Curb 'Crack' Assailed as Inadequate," *Los Angeles Times*, 16 July 1986; Zita Arocha, "Ex-Addict Says He Cooked Cocaine at 10 Houses," *WP*, 16 July 1986.

47. Arthur S. Brisbane, "Barry Calls 'Summit' on Drugs," *WP*, 4 Oct. 1986; Linda Wheeler and Sari Horowitz, "Operation Clean Sweep's Future Uncertain," *WP*, 26 Jan. 1988; "Crack's Rapid Rise Brought Chaos to DC," in Fenston et al., *Crack: The Drug That Consumed the Nation's Capital*; Sari Horwitz and Linda Wheeler, "D.C. Operation Clean Sweep to Resume," *WP*, 29 Apr. 1987; unnamed dealers quoted in Kofie, *Race, Class and the Struggle for Neighborhood in Washington, DC*, 84.

48. Wheeler and Horowitz, "Operation Clean Sweep's Future Uncertain"; John Ward Anderson, "330 Rearrested in Clean Sweep," *WP*, 13 Dec. 1986; Eugene Robinson, "'Clean Sweep' Doesn't Work," *WP*, 21 Dec. 1986; Courtland Milloy, "Clean Sweep's Dirty Trail," *WP*, 22 Mar. 1988; Nancy Lewis and Victoria Churchville, "Turner Says Clean Sweep Has Failed," *WP*, 8 Dec. 1988; Lusane, *Pipe Dream Blues*, 170.

49. Lewis and Reeves, *Slugg*; Melton and Wheeler, "Once for Elite, Cocaine Now an Equal-Opportunity Vice"; Cole, *Never Too Young to Die*, 67–69; Fenston et al., *Crack, the Drug That Consumed the Nation's Capital*.

50. Williams, "Mind of Rayful Edmond."

51. Michael Issikoff and Nancy Lewis, "By Highway and Air, California Connection Supplied D.C. Series," *WP*, 4 Sept. 1989; Williams, "Mind of Rayful Edmond."

52. Wheeler, "Gunfights Heighten Danger at Drug-Plagued Hanover Place"; Linda Wheeler and Keith Harriston, "Jamaican Gangs Wage War over Drugs, Area Police Say," *WP*, 19 Nov. 1987; Jaffe and Sherwood, *Dream City*, 218–23.

53. Vernon Loeb, "Barry Brings End to Turbulent D.C. Saga," *WP*, 22 May 1998.

54. Athelia Knight and Tom Sherwood, "'We've Got to Find a Way to Stop All of This,'" *WP*, 16 Feb. 1989; Debbie Price, "Murder Capital' Label Has Long Stalked D.C." *WP*, 4 Apr. 1989; Malcolm Gladwell, "Murder Capital We're Not," *WP*, 16 Apr. 1989; Jaffe and Sherwood, *Dream City*, 221–23; Castaneda, *S Street Rising*, 163.

55. Patrice Gaines-Carter, "The Nation of Islam: A Close-Knit Society," *WP*, 18 Sept. 1988; Sari Horowitz and Patrice Gaines-Carter, "Muslim Leader Says D.C. Police 'Involved' in Drug Activity," *WP*, 28 Apr. 1988; "The Muslims to the Rescue," *Ebony* 44, no. 10 (August 1989): 136–40.

56. Sonsyrea Tate, "Residents Take Stand against Drugs in Shaw," *WP*, 12 Jan. 1989;

Linda Wheeler, "Anti-Drug Crusade Intensifies in Shaw," *WP*, 3 June 1989; Lusane, *Pipe Dream Blues*, 184; DeNeen L. Brown, "Residents Have Drug Sellers on the Run," *WP*, 4 June 1989; Linda Wheeler, "Burning of 6 Crack Houses in Northwest Cheers Neighbor," *WP*, 3 Mar. 1989; "D.C. Churches and Civic Groups Joined the Fight against Crack," in Fenston et al., *Crack: The Drug That Consumed the Nation's Capital*; Cindy Loose, "Standing Tall on Upshur St.," *WP*, 30 May 1993.

57. Vernon Loeb, "A Turbulent Era That Defined D.C. Comes to an End," *WP*, May 22, 1998; Jaffe and Sherwood, *Dream City*, 108, 137–38, 166, 169.

58. Jaffe and Sherwood, *Dream City*, 164–65; Joe Pichirallo and Eric Pianin, "Ex-Deputy Mayor Donaldson Pleads Guilty to City Thefts," *WP*, 11 Dec. 1985; Joe Pichirallo and Arthur Brisbane, "Donaldson Gets Seven Years for Defrauding the District," *WP*, 28 Jan. 1986; Joe Pichirallo and Arthur Brisbane, "Hill Quits as D.C. Deputy Mayor," *WP*, 16 Mar. 1986.

59. Agronsky, *Marion Barry*, 198–99; Musgrove, *Rumor Repression and Racial Politics*, 131; Edward D. Sargent, "City Gives Pitts Hotel $1 Million Contract to Shelter Homeless," *WP*, 3 June 1982; Marianne Szegedy-Maszak, "How the Homeless Bought a Rolls for Cornelius Pitts," *Washington Monthly*, 1 July 1987; Patrice Gaines-Carter, "Audit Asked of D.C. Contract with Hotel for Homeless Families," *WP*, 22 May 1986; Sharon LaFraniere, "Auditor Hits Shelter Contract: D.C. Officials Called 'Grossly Derelict,'" *WP*, 20 Nov. 1986; Mauro Craig, "A Possible Rebirth for Pitts Hotel," *WP*, 31 July 2003.

60. William Raspberry, "DiGenova Had Better Have Something," *WP*, 12 June 1987; Gwen Ifill, "Black Officials: Probes and Prejudice," *WP*, 28 Feb. 1988; Jaffe and Sherwood, *Dream City*, 190–93; Musgrove, *Rumor Repression and Racial Politics*, 184–85.

61. Sharon LaFraniere and Tom Sherwood, "Barry Denies Drug Use, Criticizes U.S. Officials; Leaks Intended to Run Me out of Office'" *WP*, 19 June 1987; Tom Sherwood, "District Building Rally Backs Barry," *WP*, 26 June 1987; Nancy Lewis and Tom Sherwood, "Judge Dismisses Barry Suit Accusing diGenova of Leaks," *WP*, 25 July 1987.

62. Jaffe and Sherwood, *Dream City*, 180–84; Ed Bruske, "Taylor, Gurley Focus Campaigns on Corruption Issue," *WP*, 29 Aug. 1986; Courtland Milloy, "We Need a Good Dose of Machine Politics," *WP*, 9 Nov. 1986; Phil McCombs, "Regardie, Zeroing in on Barry," *WP*, 3 Mar. 1989; "Mayor Barry: Beyond the Victory," *WP*, 7 Nov. 1986; Loeb, "Turbulent Era That Defined D.C."

63. Michael Isikoff, "Bennett Unveils Plan to Combat Washington Drug Crisis," *WP*, 11 Apr. 1989; Tom Sherwood, "GOP Woos Turner for D.C. Mayor," *WP*, 27 Apr. 1989; Tom Sherwood and Sari Horowitz, "Moving toward Mayoral Bid, Turner Joins GOP," *WP*, 28 July 1989.

64. Isikoff, "Bennett Unveils Plan"; George H. W. Bush, address from the White House, 5 Sept. 1989, http://www.c-span.org/video/?8921–1/presidential-address-national-drug-policy; Lusane, *Pipe Dream Blues*, 176–79; Michael Isikoff, "Drug Buy Set Up for Bush Speech," *WP*, 22 Sept. 1989; James Gerstenzang and Ronald Ostrow, "Bush Defends Drug Purchase Set Up to Aid His Speech," *WP*, 23 Sept. 1989; Tracey Thompson, "Drug Purchase for Bush Speech Like 'Keystone Kops,'" *WP*, 15 Dec. 1989; Barton Gellman, "Mistrial Declared in Cocaine Arrest near White House," *WP*, 22 Dec. 1989.

65. Tracey Thompson, "Portrait of 'Rasheeda' Emerges on Stand," *WP*, 1 July 1990; Chris Spolar, "Vista Hotel Incident Tarnishes Rasheeda Moore's Glossy Image," *WP*, 21 Jan. 1990.

66. Agronsky, *Marion Barry*, 9.

67. Marlene Cimons, "Capital Youths Venting Ire over Mayor Barry Drugs," *Los Angeles Times*, 26 Jan. 1990; Roxanne Robert and David Mills, "Sadness and Hurt in a Stunned City," *WP*, 20 Jan. 1990; Richard Morin, "57 Percent of Poll Respondents Say the Mayor Should Resign," *WP*, 21 Jan. 1990.

68. Jaffe and Sherwood, *Dream City*, 273–75; Agronsky, *Marion Barry*, 71.

69. Morin, "57 Percent of Poll Respondents"; R. H. Melton and Michael York, "Barry Acknowledges Using Crack at Vista," *WP*, 30 May 1990.

70. Musgrove, *Rumor Repression and Racial Politics*, 145, 179–208; Ann Devroy, "Selective Enforcement' Issue Raised by NAACP; Hooks Says Group Sees Emphasis on Black Officials, *WP*, 23 Jan. 1990.

71. Elsa Walsh and Barton Gellman, "Chasm Divided Jurors in Barry Drug Trial," *WP*, 23 Aug. 1990.

72. Burton Gellman, "Barry's 'High Public Office' Led Judge to Stronger Sentence," *WP*, 27 Oct. 1990; Williams, "Mind of Rayful Edmond"; Christopher Daly, "Barry Judge Castigates Four Jurors," *WP*, 31 Oct. 1990; Agronsky, *Marion Barry*, 373–74.

73. R. H. Melton and Mary Ann French, "For Council Campaign, a Blessing and a Curse," *WP*, 27 Oct. 1990; Jaffe and Sherwood, *Dream City*, 299–301.

74. Toni-Michelle Travis, "Sharon Pratt Kelly: The Reform Mayor," in Walters and Travis, *Democratic Destiny*, 89–90; "Arrington Dixon, Wife Are Getting a Divorce," *WP*, 6 Jan. 1982; Eric Pianin, "Sharon Pratt Dixon Steps Up Bid for DNC Post," *WP*, 16 Nov. 1984; Tom Sherwood, "Bests, Worsts, Almosts from the Convention," *WP*, 28 July 1988.

75. Tom Sherwood and Richard Morin, "Poll Show Jackson over Barry," *WP*, 10 May 1989; Nathan McCall, "Sharon Dixon Gets 1st Endorsement," *WP*, 20 Mar. 1990; Tom Sherwood, "Sharon Pratt Dixon Said Preparing to Run for D.C. Mayor," *WP*, 20 Apr. 1988; Sherwood, "GOP Woos Turner"; Sherwood and Horowitz, "Moving toward Mayoral Bid"; Michael Abramowitz, "Poll Says 54 Percent in D.C. Want Barry to Quit," *WP*, 24 Oct. 1989; "Enter Maurice Turner," *WP*, 3 Apr. 1990; Sari Horowitz, "Turner Hopes to Walk the Beat to Mayor's Office," *WP*, 1 Sept. 1990; "Bush Joins Efforts by GOP to Win DC Mayoral Race," *Baltimore Sun*, 23 Sept. 1990; "Maurice Turner, 57, Former Police Chief in Nation's Capital," *NYT*, 18 June 1993; Jaffe and Sherwood, *Dream City*, 297–98.

76. Mary Ann French, "Dixon Takes Office with Open Arms," *WP*, 3 Jan. 1991; B. Drummond Ayres Jr., "Woman Nominated for Capital Mayor," *NYT*, 12 Sept. 1990.

77. Jaffe and Sherwood, *Dream City*, 305–7; Solomon, *Washington Century*; Ann Swardson, "Area's Go-Go Years Likely to Be Gone for Good," *WP*, 27 Jan. 1991; Jacqueline Salmon, "Condo Sales Drop 25 Percent in D.C. Area," *WP*, 10 Aug. 1991.

78. Cadaval, "Latino Community," 231–49; Modan, *Turf Wars*, 58–88; Alma Guillermoprieto, "District's Growing Hispanic Community Seeks Political Clout to Match Numbers," *WP*, 11 Sept. 1983; Henig, *Gentrification in Adams Morgan*, 16–17; Carlos Sanchez, "A New Voice for District Hispanics," *WP*, 2 June 1991; Richard Morin and Nell Henderson, "Miles Apart in Mt. Pleasant," *WP*, 19 May 1991; Joel Glenn, "Depositors May Recoup 25 on $1," *WP*, 1 Feb. 1991.

79. Rudolph Gannascoli, "Roots of a Riot," *WP*, 12 May 1991; Christine Spolar, "The Painful Lessons of Mount Pleasant," *WP*, 12 May 1991; Skip Kaltenheueer, "How to Kill a Neighborhood," *WP*, 12 May 1991.

80. Nancy Lewis, "Mt. Pleasant Case Sent to Grand Jury," WP, 21 May 1991; Ruben Castenada, "Four Months Later, Learning from Mount Pleasant's Turmoil," WP, 8 Sept. 1991.

81. Ruben Castaneda and Nell Henderson, "Simmering Tension between Police, Hispanics Fed Clash," WP, 6 May 1991; Nancy Rupert and James Lewis, "D.C. Neighborhood Erupts after Officer Shoots Suspect," WP, 6 May 1991; Carlos Sanchez and Rene Sanchez, "Police, Latino Youths Clash in 2nd Night of Violence," WP, 7 May 1991.

82. Spolar, "Painful Lessons of Mount Pleasant"; Nell Handerson, "We're Angry 'Cause of Being Hassled,' Youths Say," WP, 8 May 1991; "Mayor Dixon and Mount Pleasant," WP, 9 May 1991; Morin and Henderson, "Miles Apart in Mt. Pleasant."

83. Travis, "Sharon Pratt Kelly," 95; Juan Williams, "Black Power's New Dilemma," WP, 12 May 1991; Carlos Sanchez, "Dixon Picks Acting Latino Affairs Chief," WP, 25 May 1991.

84. Williams, "Black Power's New Dilemma"; Repak, Waiting on Washington, 69–71; Sanchez, "Dixon Picks Acting Latino Affairs Chief"; Sanchez, "New Voice for District Latinos"; Nell Henderson, "Small Likelihood Seen of Latino Advances," WP, 13 Sept. 1991; Travis, "Sharon Pratt Kelly," 95; Pamela Constable, "Fighting to Keep a Foot in the Door," WP, 16 Dec. 1994.

85. Howard Kurtz, "Estranged Encounters of the Word Kind," WP, 17 Dec. 1992; Travis, "Sharon Pratt Kelly," 92–93; "Bond's Bear Hug Grips 'Bloated Bureaucracy,'" WT, 25 Mar. 1991; James Ragland, "Apparent Rift at the Top Adds to Dixon Staff Woes," WP, 20 Aug. 1991; Adrianna Flynn, "Kelly Says Her Undoing Was Politics," WT, 1 Jan. 1995.

86. Mary Ann French, "Dixon's First 100 Days," WP, 12 Apr. 1991; Courtland Milloy, "The Honeymoon Is Over," WP, 4 July 1991; Nell Henderson, "Kelly Is Making Progress on Her Work-Force Pledge," WP, 21 Jan. 1993; Bill Rice, "The Incredible Shrinking Sharon Pratt," WP, 18 July 1993; Morin Nell, "Poll Finds a Pessimistic D.C.," WP, 5 Feb. 1992.

87. Milton Coleman, "Statehood Party Loses Political Clout," WP, 1 Mar. 1979; Rader, Signal through the Flames, 49–60; McCarthy, "J. Edward Guinan, Former Catholic Priest"; Schrag, Behind the Scenes, 16–19; Cynthia Gorney, "Julius Hobson Sr. Dies," WP, 24 Mar. 1977; Jack Eisen, "Referendums Bill Wins Support of D.C. Council," WP, 14 Mar. 1979; Eugene Meyer, "Group Opens Drive for D.C. Statehood," WP, 26 Nov. 1970; Schrag, Behind the Scenes, 18–22.

88. Schrag, Behind the Scenes, 18–24, 44–45; "Capitol's Statehood Vote Gets Scant Notice," NYT, 10 Nov. 1980.

89. Tom Sherwood, "D.C. Statehood: Liberals Could Scuttle Statehood Chances," WP, 20 Oct. 1980; Schrag, Behind the Scenes, 24–26, 68–89, 112–20.

90. The text of the Constitution for the State of New Columbia can be found in Schrag, Behind the Scenes, 259–94; Charles Cassell, "Looking to Statehood," WP, 6 June 1982; Sam Smith, "The Constitution," WTR (1982), in Smith, Statehood Papers.

91. Sandra Evans Teeley, "Barry Ready to Submit Petition for Statehood," WP, 8 Sept. 1983; Alma Guillermoprieto, "Advocates of Statehood Rap Skeptics," WP, 24 May 1984; Sandra Teeley, "Barry Ready to Submit Petition"; "Passage of Statehood Bill by House in '87 Predicted," WP, 17 Mar. 1987; "D.C. Statehood Fauntroy's Big Loss; Colleagues Blame His Tactics for Bill's Failure," WP, 12 Nov. 1987.

92. Patrice Gaines-Carter, "LeDroit Park Reawakening as Prime City Neighborhood,"

WP, 31 May 1986; "Where We Live; LeDroit Park's Hallmark: Grand Past, New Appeal," *WP*, 11 Nov. 1989; Watkins interview.

93. Barras, *Last of the Black Emperors*; Watkins interview; David Shribman, "Jackson Is Now Faced with Dilemma of Running for Mayor and Giving Up 'National Leverage,'" *Wall Street Journal*, 22 Jan. 1990; Nathan McCall, "Backing Grows for Shadow Election," *WP*, 27 Feb. 1990; Tom Sherwood and Althea Knight, "Jackson Defeats Dukakis 4-to-1 in District Primary," *WP*, 4 May 1988; Nathan McCall, "D.C. Votes 'Shadow' Lobbyist," *WP*, 28 Mar. 1990; Nathan McCall, "Jackson Tops Field, Poised for 1st Office," *WP*, 12 Sept. 1990; Nathan McCall, "Jackson Poised to Win 6-Year Lobbyist's Term," *WP*, 7 Nov. 1990.

94. Kent Jenkins Jr., "Ground Rules Laid for District's Shadow Senators," *WP*, 17 Feb. 1991; Jaffe and Sherwood, *Dream City*, 319.

95. Nell Henderson, "The Naysayers: 'Perhaps the Most Common Concern Is the Economic Viability of the Proposed State,'" *WP*, 4 July 1993; "Jesse, out of the 'Shadow,'" *WT*, 3 Dec. 1992.

96. Executive Office of the Mayor, "Mayor Kelly Declares Apr. as DC Statehood Month," press release, 1 Apr. 1993; "1993 Statehood 'Plan of Action' Activities," undated, "Statehood" binder, WD; "DC Abortion Funding Restrictions Eased," *CQ Almanac* (1993): 584; Kent Jenkins Jr., "Mayor, 37 Others Arrested after Statehood Protest," *WP*, 27 Aug. 1993; Paul Duggan, "Courting D.C. Statehood," *WP*, 2 Sept. 1993; Cindy Loose, "D.C. Shuns Case of Statehood Demonstrators," *WP*, 20 Oct. 1993; email correspondence with Citizens for New Columbia leader Bernard Demczuk, 3 Sept. 2015.

97. Henderson, "Naysayers"; Kent Jenkins, "House Turns Down Statehood for D.C.," *WP*, 22 Nov. 1993; Jaffe and Sherwood, *Dream City*, 325; Jeffrey Itell, "Eleanor's Etiquette: How to Thank the Shadow Senator Who Has Done Nothing," *WCP*, 5 Jan. 1996.

98. Barras, *Last of the Black Emperors*, 13, 26, 32–49; Jaffe and Sherwood, *Dream City*, 314; Rene Sanchez, "Barry Rides Home on Wave of Support," *WP*, 24 Apr. 1992; Rene Sanchez, "Barry to Formally Declare in Ward 8," *WP*, 18 June 1992.

99. Sam Fullwood III, "He's Back and Feeling the Power," *Los Angeles Times*, 29 Oct. 1992.

100. Patricia Sullivan, "D.C. Council Member, Home Rule Soldier Wilhelmina J. Rolark," *WP*, 15 Feb. 2006; Rene Sanchez, "Wilhelmina Rolark, Standing Tough," *WP*, 20 May 1992; Barras, *Last of the Black Emperors*, 49.

101. Barras, *Last of the Black Emperors*, 56, 79. Fullwood, "He's Back and Feeling the Power"; Sanchez, "Wilhelmina Rolark, Standing Tough"; Rene Sanchez, "Barry Wins by Landslide in Ward 8," *WP*, 16 Sept. 1992; "The Council Election in Ward 8," *WP*, 12 Sept. 1992; "Former Mayor's Victory Worries Many in Capital," *NYT*, 17 Sept. 1992.

102. Barras, *Last of the Black Emperors*, 66–71; Rene Sanchez, "No Borders for Barry," *WP*, 10 May 1993; Laurie Goodstein, "School Prayer Initiative Gains in D.C." *WP*, 7 Apr. 1994; Yolanda Woodlee, "Promoter Bucks to Boost Voter Rolls," *WP*, 21 July 1994; Rene Sanchez, "Barry Troops Enlisting Low-Income Voters," *WP*, 15 Aug. 1994; Rene Sanchez, "Voter Sign-Up Makes Ward 8 A Match for 3," *WP*, 28 Oct. 1994.

103. Howard Blum, "Behind the Criminal Behavior of D.C. Cops," *WP*, 9 Jan. 1994; Eddie Dean, "Almost Blue: Carl T. Rowan Jr. walks a self-assigned beat of D.C. police corruption," *WCP*, 23 Jan. 1998; Jaffe and Sherwood, *Dream City*, 321.

104. Jaffe and Sherwood, *Dream City*, 321.

105. DeNeen Brown and James Ragland, "Barry Win Transcends City's Barriers," WP, 15 Sept. 1994.

106. Jaffe and Sherwood, *Dream City*, Afterword; "Barry Victory Reveals Widening Racial Rift," NYT, 15 Sept. 1994; Yolanda Woodlee, "I'm the Best . . . for Washington,'" WP, 15 Sept. 1994; "Wealthy Ward in the Capital Talks Secession," NYT, 27 Oct. 1994; Michael Janofsky, "Republican Strives against Brutal Odds in Her Quest against Marion Barry," NYT, 14 Oct. 1994.

107. "Marion Barry's Inaugural Address," WP, 5 Jan. 1995.

108. Howard Schneider and David Vise, "Barry Says Home Rule Government Unworkable, Urges U.S. Takeover of Courts, Prisons, Welfare," WP, 3 Feb. 1995; Blaine Harden, "Barry Defends His Turf Against Congress," WP, 11 Mar., 1995; David A. Vise and Blaine Harden, "Race and the Bottom Line in D.C.," WP, 19 Mar. 1995; "Board to Oversee D.C. Finances," *CQ Almanac* (1995): 3–25; Howard Schneider, "Clinton Signs D.C. Control Board Bill,'" WP, 18 Apr. 1995.

109. Schneider and Vise, "Barry Says Home Rule Government Unworkable"; Harden, "Barry Defends His Turf"; Vise and Harden, "Race and the Bottom Line"; "Board to Oversee D.C. Finances"; Schneider, "Clinton Signs D.C. Control Board Bill."

110. Nnamdi quoted in Siegel, *Future Once Happened Here*, 65–66.

Chapter 14

1. E. C. Kohn, "Chinatown Has Own Spirit of Exclusiveness," *Sunday Star*, 14 Aug. 1927; "Census in Chinatown," WP, 7 June 1900; "A Bit of the Orient on the Capital's Main Avenue," *Washington Times Herald*, 14 Dec. 1902.

2. "Chinamen at School," WP, 5 Nov. 1893; Kohn, "Chinatown Has Own Spirit of Exclusiveness"; Lee, "Asian and Asian American Students," 34–53.

3. J. B. McDonnell, "Ancient Landmarks Disappear in Plans of Greater Capital," WP, 9 Aug. 1931; "Building Program Drives Chinese to Seek a New Center," WP, 10 Aug. 1931; "Where Will Chinatown Locate?," *Washington Times Herald*, 25 May 1931.

4. "Chinatown Is Small, but Area Buzzes with Activity," ES, 21 May 1951; "Ousted by U.S. Project on Avenue," *Washington Times Herald*, 8 Oct. 1931; "Chinese Invasion of H Street Irks Property Owners," WP, 10 Oct. 1931; "Chinatown Blackout Perfect," WP, 26 Aug. 1942.

5. "A New Day for Chinatown," ES *Sunday Magazine*, 25 Oct. 1964.

6. Saundra Saperstein, "Chinatown: Dreams for a Better Life," WP, 24 Feb. 1985; Betty Medsger, "Chinatown Not Home to Most Chinese," WP, 5 Dec 1972.

7. William Fuchs, "A New Day for Chinatown," *Washington Star Sunday Magazine*, 25 Oct. 1964; Bart Barnes, "Sports Arena Fight: Progress vs. People," WP, 31 Feb. 1972; Saperstein, "Chinatown."

8. Stephen J. Lynton, "Far East Center to Be Built in D.C.'s Chinatown," WP, 13 May 1983; Saperstein, "Chinatown"; David S. Hilzenrath, "Dream of Chinatown Center Fades amid Revisions, Setbacks," WP, 9 Apr. 1988.

9. Hilzenrath, "Dream of Chinatown Center Fades"; Marc Fisher, "'If the Price Is Right, We Sell,'" WP, 29 Jan. 1995.

10. Peter Perl, "Wizards Owner Helped Transform D.C.," *WP*, 25 Nov. 2009; Jane Leavy, "Abe Pollin Tries to Make Business a Family Affair," *WP*, 29 Nov. 1981; Valerie Strauss, "'Special Chemistry' Expedited Arena Deal Pollin Liked Barry's Alacrity, Sources Say," *WP*, 30 Dec. 1994.

11. William Gildea, "Positive Reaction Greets Pollin's New Arena Plan," *WP*, 29 Dec. 1994; Michael A. Fletcher, "Chinatown Says It's Neglected in Arena Plans," *WP*, 30 June 1995; Fisher, "'If the Price Is Right.'"

12. Doug Struck, "Pollin's Arena Proves a Winner with the Fans," *WP*, 3 Dec. 1997; Yanan Wang, "D.C.'s Chinatown Has Only 300 Chinese Americans Left, and They're Fighting to Stay," *WP*, 18 July 2015; Chinatown Cultural Development Strategy, 2009, http://planning.dc.gov/page/chinatown-cultural-development-strategy.

13. William Chapman, "Brimmer Is Selected for Reserve Board," *WP*, 27 Feb. 1966; Matt Schudel, "Andrew F. Brimmer, Fed Governor and Head of D.C. Control Board, Dies at 86," *WP*, 10 Oct. 2012; Stephanie Strom, "Andrew Brimmer, First Black Member on Fed Board, Dies at 86," *NYT*, 12 Oct. 2012.

14. Hobart Rowen, "Negro Separatism Rejected by Fed Governor Brimmer," *WP*, 4 June 1968; Robert J. Samuelson, "Brimmer Cool to Black Capitalism," *WP*, 30 Dec. 1969; Hobart Rowen, "Brimmer Urges Jobs Plan," *WP*, 14 Apr. 1972; James L. Rowe Jr., "Brimmer to Leave Fed," *WP*, 15 May 1974. Association for the Study of African American Life and History, "Our Presidents," https://asalh100.org/our-presidents/.

15. Andrew F. Brimmer, "It Will Take More to Keep Business in D.C.," *WP*, 23 Aug. 1981; Tom Sherwood, "Financial Gain Seen from Statehood," *WP*, 30 Sept. 1986; James Ragland, "Kelly Pledges Renewed Effort to Get Commuter Tax," *WP*, 9 Oct. 1992; Rowen, "Brimmer Urges Jobs Plan"; Rowe, "Brimmer."

16. David A. Vise and Howard Schneider, "Norton Seeks Control Board for D.C.," *WP*, 17 Feb. 1995; David A. Vise and Blaine Harden, "Race and the Bottom Line in D.C.," *WP*, 19 Mar. 1995.

17. It was officially called the D.C. Financial Responsibility and Management Assistance Authority, though that name was never used in common parlance.

18. David A. Vise and Howard Schneider, "D.C. Control Board Approved by House," *WP*, 4 Apr. 1995.

19. The five members of the first Control Board were Brimmer, Ladner, Constance Newman, Stephen Harlan, and Edward Singletary. David A. Vise and Howard Schneider, "Economist in Lead for D.C. Board," *WP*, 19 Apr. 1995; David A. Vise and John F. Harris, "Clinton Set to Seat 3 on D.C. Board," *WP*, 31 May 1995; Brimmer quoted in Barras, *Last of the Black Emperors*, 187; "Brimmer/Barry Get Together," *Afro-American Red Star*, 25 Nov. 1995.

20. Harden and Vise, "Race and the Bottom Line in D.C."

21. Barras, *Last of the Black Emperors*, 182–95; Baruti, "Control Board Era," 87–88; David A. Vise and Hamil R. Harris, "City Workers Block Streets in Protest," *WP*, 5 Dec. 1995; David A. Vise, "Barry Goes Toe to Toe with Control Board," *WP*, 8 Feb. 1996.

22. David A. Vise and Howard Schneider, "Control Board to Take Lead on D.C. Cuts," *WP*, 3 Feb. 1996.

23. Barras, *Last of the Black Emperors*, 227–33; Yolanda Woodlee and David A. Vise, "Barry Promises to Back Hawkins to the Bitter End," *WP*, 4 June 1996; Vanessa Williams, "Government Employees, Public Split on Hawkins," *WP*, 6 June 1996.

24. Barras, *Last of the Black Emperors*, 217–18, 207–13, 221, 226–28; Castaneda, *S Street Rising*, 230–31; Toni Locy and Yolanda Woodlee, "Home of Barry Associate Searched by Federal Fraud Task Force," *WP*, 9 June 1996.

25. Michael Powell and David A. Vise, "Key Republican Typically Blunt on Plans for D.C.,'" *WP*, 3 Mar. 1997.

26. David A. Vise, "Clinton's Plan for D.C. Meets with Resistance," *WP*, 15 Jan. 1997. Fauntroy, *Home Rule or House Rule*, 189; O'Cleireacain, *Orphaned Capital*.

27. David A. Vise, "Congressional Oversight of D.C.'s Finances Takes a Conservative Turn," *WP*, 9 Jan. 1997; David A. Vise, "D.C. Takeover May Not Go Far Enough, Brimmer Says," *WP*, 16 May 1997.

28. David A. Vise, "Hill Leaders Considering City Manager," *WP*, 16 July 1997; "Control Board's New Power Exceeds a City Manager's," *WP*, 9 Aug. 1997.

29. Vernon Loeb, "A Weakened D.C. Mayor's Strong Words," *WP*, 11 Aug. 1997; Knight Chamberlain, "600 Protesters Picket for D.C. Outside Faircloth's Front Door," *WP*, 24 Aug. 1997; "A Big Thank You: D.C. Residents Helped Oust N.C. Sen. Lauch Faircloth," *Afro-American Red Star*, 14 Nov. 1998; Vernon Loeb, David Montgomery, and Hamil A. Harris, "For Barry, the Web Has Some Sticky Spots," *WP*, 14 Aug. 1997; David A. Vise and Michael Powell, "Faircloth Invokes D.C. Power Shift in N.C. Campaign," *WP*, 4 June 1998.

30. Michael Powell and Vanessa Williams, "High Hopes and Home Rule Fears," *WP*, 10 Aug. 1997.

31. Vernon Loeb, "Survey Shows Barry Ahead of the Pack," *WP*, 19 May 1998; "Mayor Retirement Announcement," C-SPAN, 22 May 1998.

32. Loeb, "Turbulent Era That Defined D.C."

33. Loeb, "Turbulent Era That Defined D.C."

34. Peter Perl, "Behind the Bowtie," *WP*, 4 June 2000.

35. Barras, *Last of the Black Emperors*, 202–8; Perl, "Behind the Bowtie"; Yolanda Woodlee, "Residents Push for Mayoral Bid by Williams," *WP*, 15 May 1998; Beth Berselli, "Going for Broke," *WP*, 17 June 1998; Jaffe and Sherwood, *Dream City*, Epilogue.

36. David A. Vise, "Financial Officer to Run for D.C. Mayor," *WP*, 31 May 1998; Jonetta Rose Barras, "Getting the Job Done," *Washingtonian* (October 1996); Harris, "High Tide of Pragmatic Black Politics," 103–20.

37. Michael Powell, "Williams Wins Mayoral Primary," *WP*, 16 Sept. 1998; "Mayoral Race by Ward," *WP*, 17 Sept. 1998; Michael H. Cottman and Yolanda Woodlee, "Williams Wins Big in D.C. Mayor's Race," *WP*, 4 Nov. 1998.

38. Michael Janofsky, "Head of Financial Control Board for District of Columbia Resigns under Fire," *NYT*, 21 Mar. 1998; David A. Vise, "Rivlin Vows to Work for D.C. Home Rule," *WP*, 20 June 1998; David A. Vise, "Restore Home Rule in '99, Brimmer Says," *WP*, 1 Sept. 1998; David A. Vise, "D.C. Mayor to Regain Powers on Jan. 2," *WP*, 21 Dec. 1998.

39. Michael H. Cottman, "Mayor Seeks His Stride," *WP*, 2 Jan. 2000.

40. Michael H. Cottman, "Williams's Wary Approach to Race," *WP*, 13 Mar. 1999.

41. Avram Goldstein, "D.C. General Sends Off Its Last Patient," *WP*, 24 June 2001; Jacob Fenston, "From Public Hospital to Homeless Shelter: The Long History of D.C. General," WAMU, 30 May 2014.

42. Colbert I. King, "More Than D.C. General," *WP*, 3 Mar. 2001; Jaffe and Sherwood,

Dream City, Epilogue; Robert E. Pierre and Avram Goldstein, "D.C. General Battle Focuses on Williams as Much as Medicine," *WP*, 11 Mar. 2001.

43. Avram Goldstein, "D.C. Inspectors Urge Closure of Southeast's Only Hospital," *WP*, 25 July 2003; Avram Goldstein, "Creditors Threaten Greater Southeast," *WP*, 24 Oct. 2003.

44. Chan Sewall, "Windfall, Shortfall at Last Meeting of D.C. Control Board," *WP*, 27 Sept. 2001; Baruti, "Control Board Era," 109.

45. Craig Timberg and Richard Morin, "Williams Unhurt by Scandal, Poll Finds," *WP*, 1 Sept. 2002; Yolanda Woodlee and Craig Timberg, "Panic Led to Dubious Signatures, Collector Says," *WP*, 19 July 2002.

46. Yolanda Woodlee and Craig Timberg, "Williams Kept Off Democratic Ballot," *WP*, 27 July 2002; Craig Timberg, "D.C. Pastor Challenges Mayor," *WP*, 13 Aug. 2002; Craig Timberg, "Barry Backs Wilson for Mayor," *WP*, 30 Aug. 2002; Craig Timberg and Yolanda Woodlee, "Williams Claims Win in Primary," *WP*, 13 Sept. 2002; Johanna Neuman, "Tainted Petition Muddles Race for D.C. Mayor," *Los Angeles Times*, 4 Aug. 2002.

47. Erika Blount Danois, "Standing Their Ground," *Crisis* 112, no. 3 (May–June 2005): 28–32; on gentrification in Georgetown, see Gale, "Restoration in Georgetown"; and Lesko, Babb, and Gibbs, *Black Georgetown Remembered*.

48. On "stalled gentrification" in Mount Pleasant, see Williams, *Upscaling Downtown*.

49. Carol D. Leonnig, "Tenants' Suit Accuses D.C. of Prejudice in Evictions," *WP*, 14 Apr. 2004; Serge F. Kovaleski, "No Slumlord Trials Despite Crackdown," *WP*, 11 Nov. 2001; Bill Miller, "Judge Urges D.C. to Consult Tenants in Slum Crackdown," *WP*, 28 Apr. 2000; Kovaleski, "No Slumlord Trials"; Sue Ann Pressley Montes, "City to Pay $700,000 in Settlement with Hispanic Tenants," *WP*, 14 Dec. 2006.

50. Sewall, "Windfall, Shortfall"; David Nakamura, "D.C. Council to Join Suit against Commuter Tax Ban," *WP*, 15 July 2003; Spencer S. Hsu, "Federal Land Could Be Shifted to D.C. Control," *WP*, 7 Feb. 2005.

51. Susanna F. Schaller, "Situating Entrepreneurial Place Making in DC," in Hyra and Prince, *Capital Dilemma*, 146–47.

52. Craig Timberg, "Williams Makes a Promising Start," *WP*, 3 Jan. 2003; "Mr. Mayor, Try a Really Big Magnet," *WP*, 4 Jan. 2003; Brookings Institute, "Neighborhood 10: Ten Strategies for a Stronger Washington" (Washington, D.C., 17 Apr. 2003); Hsu, "Federal Land Could Be Shifted."

53. Virginia Mansfield, "H Street Rebuilding Sparked," *WP*, 30 May 1985; "Better Times at 14th and U," *WP*, 18 Apr. 1987; Yolanda Woodlee, "Arena Deal Seen as 'Coup' for Barry Administration," *WP*, 23 Oct. 1995; Ann Mariano, "A Winning Way to Own a Home in D.C." *WP*, 13 Aug. 1993.

54. Robert Suro, "Drop in Murder Rate Accelerates in Cities: District, P.G. County among Leaders in Trend," *WP*, 31 Dec. 1997; "District of Columbia Crime Rates, 1960–2014," http://www.disastercenter.com/crime.

55. Anne Gowen, "D.C. Enclaves Reap Rewards of Contracting Boom as Federal Dollars Fuel Wealth," *WP*, 15 Aug. 2011; Joel Kotkin, "The Expanding Wealth of Washington," *Forbes*, 19 Mar. 2012; Dylan Matthews, "Is the Government Making Washington Rich? (In Charts, of Course)," *WP*, 25 Sept. 2012; Brad Plumer, "America's Staggering Defense

Budget, in Charts," WP, 7 Jan. 2013; "The Federal Outsourcing Boom and Why It's Failing Americans," WP, 31 Jan. 2014.

56. For a discussion of the new urbanism, see Osman, *Invention of Brownstone Brooklyn*; Debbi Wilgoren, "At Core of City, Old-Timers, Recent Arrivals Seek a New Balance," WP, 10 July 2003.

57. "355: The Giant Pool of Money," *This American Life*, WBEZ, 9 May 2008; Mary Clare Fleury et al., "Tales from the Boom and Bust," *Washingtonian Magazine* (April 2010).

58. "The Forgotten Neighbor on Florida Ave.," WP, 16 Oct. 2005.

59. Flor, *Nine Lives of Marion Barry*.

60. Fleury et al., "Tales from the Boom and Bust"; Danois, "Standing Their Ground."

61. Jason Cherkis et al., "Gentrification and Its Discontents," WCP, 4 Feb. 2005; Bryan Westley, "Blacks' Majority in D.C. Slipping," *Associated Press*, 12 Sept. 2007.

62. Wilgoren, "At Core of City"; Chan Sweall, "Tenants Decry Study Urging End to D.C. Rent Control," WP, 12 Oct. 2000; Benny L. Kass, "New Law Keeps Rent Control Strong in the District," WP, 12 Aug. 2006; Ruble, *Washington's U Street*, 272–84; "Living with the Tensions of Gentrification," WP, 12 Nov. 2005.

63. By the first decade of the new millennium the Ethiopian and Eritrean population in the Washington, D.C., area had exceeded one hundred thousand. Singer et al., *World in a Zip Code*; Paul Schwartzman, "Shaw Shuns 'Little Ethiopia,'" WP, 25 July 2005.

64. Lori Montgomery and Yolanda Woodlee, "Opponents of New Stadium Seek to Keep Team at RFK," WP, 3 Oct. 2004.

65. Debbi Wilgoren and Lori Montgomery, "Williams Details Stadium Funding," WP, 28 Sept. 2004.

66. David Nakamura, "Williams Faces Stadium Skeptics," WP, 13 Oct. 2004; Lori Montgomery and Yolanda Woodlee, "Barry In, 3 D.C. Council Incumbents Out," WP, 15 Sept. 2004.

67. Lori Montgomery and Yolanda Woodlee, "Stadium Backers in Line for Reward," WP, 10 Nov. 2004; David Nakamura and Thomas Heath, "Accord Reached on D.C. Stadium," WP, 21 Dec. 2004.

68. For a discussion of displacement by the HOPE VI program, see Bockman, "Home Rule from Below," 75–78. Vernon Loeb, "At Wilson Dwellings, a Dream Gets Hope," WP, 23 Jan. 1997; Robert Samuels, "In District, Affordable-Housing Plan Hasn't Delivered," WP, 7 July 2013; Mark Anderson, "House Broken: How DC's Plan to Save Low-Income Housing Went Wrong," WCP, 31 Oct. 2014.

69. Samuels, "In District, Affordable-Housing Plan Hasn't Delivered"; Anderson, "House Broken."

70. Danois, "Standing Their Ground." By 2015, some of the condos in Thomas's old building were selling for more than $400,000. See Perry Stein, "The Complicated History of a D.C. Block Smeared by Rep. Schock's Former Adviser," WP, 9 Feb. 2015.

71. Jura Koncius, "Campaign Stop," WP, 3 Aug. 2006; Harry Jaffe, "Adrian Fenty, Born to Run," *Washingtonian*, Nov. 1, 2008; "Adrian Fenty," The Black Past.org, http://www.blackpast.org/aah/fenty-adrian-m-1970.

72. "A Good Deal for the District?," WP, 10 Sept. 2006.

73. Marc Fisher, "Fenty Emerges as Action Hero," WP, 24 Aug. 2006; Michael Grunwald, "A Good Deal for the District?," WP, 10 Sept. 2006; Elissa Silverman, "Fenty Alters the Race

a Doorstep at a Time," *WP*, 27 June 2006; Libby Copeland, "See How He Runs," *WP*, 31 Aug. 2006; David Nakamura, "Fenty Trounces Foes in Mayoral Race," *WP*, 8 Nov. 2006.

74. Nakamura, "Fenty Trounces Foes in Mayoral Race"; Robert Barnes and Lori Montgomery, "Fenty Emerges from D.C. Pack," *WP*, 23 July 2006; Lori Montgomery, "In Sweep, Fenty Draws on Uniting to Conquer," *WP*, 14 Sept. 2006.

75. Jarrett A. Zafran, "What's So New about Obama?," *Harvard Crimson*, 1 Oct. 2007; Matt Bai, "Is Obama the End of Black Politics?," *NYT Magazine*, 6 Aug. 2008; Andra Gillespie, "Meet the New Class: Theorizing Young Black Leadership in a 'Postracial' Era," in Gillespie, *Whose Black Politics?*, 9–42; Fisher, "Fenty Emerges as an Action Hero."

76. David Nakamura, "Cropp and Fenty Have Pursued Their Legislative Agendas Opposite Means," *WP*, 1 Aug. 2006; Montgomery, "In Sweep, Fenty Draws on Uniting to Conquer."

77. Harry Jaffe, "Adrian Fenty: His Own Worst Enemy?," *Washingtonian Magazine*, 1 Mar. 2010; David Nakamura and Elissa Silverman, "Fenty Stays Close to Home for Top Aides," *WP*, 7 Dec. 2006; David Nakamura, Yolanda Woodlee, and Hamil R. Harris, "Color of Cabinet Has Fenty on the Defensive," *WP*, 3 July 2007; David Nakamura, "A High-Profile Start," *WP*, 18 Apr. 2007; Ian Urbina, "Starting Fast, with an Eye on the Long Run," *NYT*, 10 Sept. 2007.

78. Nakamura, "High-Profile Start"; "Fenty Commits to Increased, Customized Community Policing," *WI*, 11 Jan. 2007; Allison Klein, "Violence Rises Despite Police Presence," *WP*, 7 Nov. 2007.

79. Nakamura, "Fenty Trounces Foes in Mayoral Race"; Nikita Stewart and David Nakamura, "Council Set for 'Big Risk' on Fenty's Schools Plan," *WP*, 4 Mar. 2007; "D.C. City Council Gives Fenty Power over Schools," *Afro-American Red Star*, 7 Apr. 2007.

80. Lori Montgomery and Jay Mathews, "The Future of D.C. Public Schools: Traditional or Charter Education?," *WP*, 22 Aug. 2006; Spencer S. Hsu and Justin Blum, "D.C. School Vouchers Win Final Approval," *WP*, 23 Jan. 2004; National Alliance for Public Charter Schools, "A Growing Movement: America's Largest Charter School Communities" (November 2015), http://www.publiccharters.org/wp-content/uploads/2015/11/enrollmentshare_web.pdf; Montgomery and Mathews, "Future of D.C. Public Schools."

81. Rhee claimed to have taken seventy students who were "at almost rock bottom on standardized tests" to "absolutely at the top" in two years. Evan Thomas, "Can Michelle Rhee Save D.C.'s Schools?," *Newsweek*, 22 Aug. 2008; She said repeatedly (including on her résumé) that 90 percent of her students scored at the 90th percentile or above. Nick Anderson, "Rhee Faces Renewed Scrutiny over Depiction of Students' Progress When She Taught," *WP*, 11 Feb. 2011. Those numbers were based, not on actual data, but on a conversation Rhee had with her principal in which she was told that her students' scores had improved. Rhee fabricated the specific numbers. Former teacher and education blogger Guy Brandenburg revealed her repeated fabrications in 2011: https://gfbrandenburg.wordpress.com/2011/01/31/the-rhee-miracle-examined-again-by-cohort/; Whitmire, *Bee Eater*, 7–64; Alexandra Hootnick, "Teachers Are Losing Their Jobs but Teach for America Is Expanding; What's Wrong with That?," *Nation*, 15 Apr. 2014.

82. Congressional Research Service, "K-12 Education: Highlights of the No Child Left Behind Act of 2002," RL-31284 (15 Jan. 2003), 1–3.

83. Joseloff, "Education of Michelle Rhee."

84. V. Dion Haynes and Yolanda Woodlee, "D.C. Schools Chief Fires 98 Workers," *WP*, 8 Mar. 2008; Theola Labbe and V. Dion Haynes, "Rhee Blasts Textbook Process for Letting Supplies Languish," *WP*, 4 Aug. 2007.

85. Bill Turque, "Rhee Fires Her Children's Principal," *WP*, 9 May 2008.

86. Bill Turque, "Rhee Bypasses Talks, Imposes Dismissal Plan," *WP*, 3 Oct. 2008; Joseloff, "Education of Michelle Rhee"; V. Dion Haynes and Dan Keating, "Some D.C. Principals Credit Rhee for Big Gains in Test Scores," *WP*, 11 July 2008; Emma Brown, "Teachers in 18 D.C. Classrooms Cheated on Tests Last Year, Probe Finds," *WP*, 12 Apr. 2013; John Merrow, "Michelle Rhee's Reign of Error," Taking Note (blog), 11 Apr. 2013, http://takingnote.learningmatters.tv/?p=6232.

87. June Kronholz, "D.C.'s Braveheart," *EducationNext* 10, no. 1 (Winter 2010): http://educationnext.org/d-c-s-braveheart/.

88. Bill Turque, "Up Close, Rhee's Image Less Clear," *WP*, 8 Dec. 2008; Amanda Ripley, "Can She Save Our Schools?," *Time*, 8 Dec. 2008.

89. Jaffe, "Adrian Fenty: Born to Run"; Jaffe, "Adrian Fenty: His Own Worst Enemy?"

90. "Process of School Closings Is Criticized," *Afro-American Red Star*, Jan. 19, 2008; Bill Turque, "Rhee's Need to Hurry Runs into Parents' Fear of Change," *WP*, 7 May 2008.

91. Marc Fisher, "Success of Closings Plan Hangs on Rhee's Resolve," *WP*, 6 Jan 2008.

92. Jonetta Rose Barras, "Recruiting Diversity," *WCP*, 27 Aug. 2010; Jonetta Rose Barras, "Neighborhood Schooled," *WCP*, 26 Aug. 2011.

93. Bill Turque, "Not Eager to March to Rhee's drum," *WP*, 13 Nov. 2009; Whitmire, *Bee Eater*, 171–76; Ann E. Marimow, "Schools Chancellor Catches Flak for Unpopular Moves," *WP*, 16 Mar. 2010; Petrillli, *Diverse Schools Dilemma*.

94. Lyndsey Layton, "The Number of Black Teachers Has Dropped in Nine U.S. Cities," *WP*, 15 Sept. 2015.

95. "District Teachers Protest Unfair Firings by Fenty Administration," *WI*, Oct. 15, 2009; Bill Turque, "D.C. Council, Rhee Tensions Grow over Budget Cuts," *WP*, 20 Oct. 2009; "Update: Michelle Rhee vs. the D.C. Teachers' Union," *Fast Company*, 1 Feb. 2010; Mike DeBonis, "Michelle Rhee Explains Fast Company Quote," *WCP*, 26 Jan. 2010; Bill Turque, "Rhee Helps, Hinders Fenty's Reelection Bid," *WP*, 1 Sept. 2010.

96. Alejandro Lazo, "Fenty Wants to Use Public Funds for SW Waterfront," *WP*, 16 Jan. 2008; David Nakamura, "Fenty Eyes Public Funds for Soccer Stadium," *WP*, 14 Feb. 2008.

97. Jonathan O'Connell and Kathy Orton, "Far from the City, Far from Recovery," *WP*, 6 May 2016; Rachel L. Swarns, "A Trendy Turn in Obama's Town," *NYT*, 18 Jan. 2013; Lydia DePillis, "Why It's So Hard to Find a Cheap Apartment in Washington, D.C.," *WP*, 19 Aug. 2014; Adrienne LaFrance, "New Apartment Buildings Are Geared for Millennials," *WP*, 18 Apr. 2014; Perry Stein, "Gymnauseum: Does D.C.'s New Wealth Explain the Boutique-Fitness Boom?," *WCP*, 3 Oct. 2014.

98. Eugene L. Meyer, "A Comeback Story Decades in the Making," *NYT*, 30 Jan. 2008.

99. Jenny Reed, *Disappearing Act: Affordable Housing in D.C. Is Vanishing amid Sharply Rising Housing Costs* (Washington, D.C.: Center on Budget and Policy Priorities, May 2012).

100. Elissa Silverman, "Fenty's Relocation Plan Angers Some Temple Courts Residents," *WP*, 7 June 2007; Mark Anderson, "How D.C.'s Plan to Save Low-Income Housing Went Wrong," *WCP*, 29 Oct. 2014.

101. Robert Samuels, "In District, Affordable Housing Plan Hasn't Delivered," *WP*,

7 July 2013; Tyler Currie, "A Long Way Home," WP Magazine, 17 Dec. 2006; Hamil R. Harris, "Bible Way Church Continues Community Legacy along New York Ave.," WP, 12 Apr. 2013; Quadel Consulting and Training LLC, "Policy Advisor's Recommendations on the District of Columbia's New Communities Initiative" (August 2014), http://dcnew communities.org/wp-content/uploads/2014/09/Policy-Advisors-Recommendations-on -the-NCI-Program.pdf; "District of Columbia Housing Authority FY2010 MTW Annual Report" (Revised), D.C. Housing Authority, 21 Mar. 2012, http://portal.hud.gov/hud portal/documents/huddoc?id=dcha-fy10rpt.pdf.

102. Jaffe, "Adrian Fenty: His Own Worst Enemy?"

103. Ann E. Marimow and Jennifer Agiesta, "Blacks' Disillusionment a Challenge for Fenty," WP, 1 Mar. 2010.

104. Mike DeBonis, "After '06 Landslide, an Apparent Reversal," WP, 30 Aug. 2010; Nikita Stewart, "Fenty Won't Evict Cora Barry's Group," WP, Oct. 2, 2009; Jaffe, "Adrian Fenty: His Own Worst Enemy?"

105. Nikita Stewart and Jon Cohen, "Fenty's Approval Ratings Plummet," WP, 31 Jan. 2010; Robert McCartney, "Black Residents Fault Fenty on Housing, Jobs," WP, 4 Feb. 2010.

106. Tim Craig, Nikita Stewart, and Paul Schwartzman, "Gray Jump-Starts D.C. Mayor's Race," WP, 30 Mar. 2010.

107. Robert McCartney, "Adrian Fenty, Vincent Gray and the Politics of Race and Class in D.C.," WP, 29 Aug. 2010; DeBonis, "After '06 Landslide, an Apparent Reversal."

108. "After Moving D.C. in the Right Direction, Mayor Fenty Rejected by Voters," Sun Reporter, 23 Sept. 2010.

109. Courtland Milloy, "Ding-Dong, Fenty's Gone; the Wicked Mayor Is Gone," WP, 16 Sept. 2010.

Epilogue

1. Todd Kliman, "Rainbow Room: The Busboys and Poets Controversy," Washingtonian, 1 Dec. 2005; Mai Abdul Rahman, "Peace Activists Welcomed in DC," Washington Report on Middle East Affairs (December 2005): 56–58; "D.C. Restaurant Becomes Hub of Anti-War Activity," Voice of America, 23 Sept. 2005.

2. David Montgomery, "Andy Shallal, Owner of Busboys and Poets, Is 'Democracy's Restauranteur,'" WP, 8 Dec. 2011.

3. Vermont came the closest to matching D.C.'s vote total, with 67 percent of its ballots going to Obama. "Election Results 2008," NYT, 9 Dec. 2008; Bill Turque, "Emotional Day Ends in Jubilation for Some, Stoicism for Others," WP, 5 Nov. 2008.

4. Michael D. Shear and Anne E. Kornblut, "A Historic Inauguration Draws Throngs to the Mall," WP, 21 Jan. 2009.

5. "Bargaining away the District's Rights," WP, 11 Apr. 2011; Arthur Delany, "DC for Obama Furious over Budget Deal," Huffington Post, 12 June 2011; Tim Craig, "Obama to Use D.C. 'Taxation without Representation' License Plates," WP, 15 Jan. 2013; David Nakamura and Aaron Davis, "In D.C., Disappointment with Obama over His Silence on Statehood," WP, 26 July 2016.

6. Kijakazi et al., "The Color of Wealth in the Nation's Capital," 2; Rachael Swarns, "A Trendy Turn in Obama's Town," NYT, 18 Jan. 2013.

7. Carol Morello and Dan Keating, "Blacks' Majority Status Slips Away," WP, 25 Mar. 2011.

8. Elizabeth Change et al., "The March of the Millennials," WP, 18 Oct. 2013; Erin Carlyle, "Washington, D.C., Tops Forbes 2014 List of America's Coolest Cities," Forbes, 6 Aug. 2014.

9. Mike DeBonis, "D.C., Where Blacks No Longer Are a Majority, Has a New African American Affairs Director," WP, 5 Feb. 2015.

10. Erika Niedowski, "D.C. Is Continuing to Whiten," WCP, 7 Jan. 2010; "D.C., Long a 'Chocolate City' Becoming More Vanilla," NPR, 15 Feb. 2011, http://www.npr.org/2011/02/15/133754531/d-c-long-chocolate-city-becoming-more-vanilla.

11. Natalie Hopkinson, "Farewell to Chocolate City," NYT, 23 June 2012; Morello and Keating, "Blacks' Majority Status Slips Away."

Essay on Sources

1. Asch and Levey, "Washington, D.C."

SELECTED BIBLIOGRAPHY

Archives

Bowdoin College, Brunswick, Maine
    Student Nonviolent Coordinating Committee Papers (microfilm)
Charles Sumner School Museum and Archives, Washington, D.C.
    Minutes of the Board of Education of the District of Columbia
George Washington University, Special Collections Research Center, Washington, D.C.
    Greater Washington Board of Trade Records
    Walter E. Fauntroy Papers
Historical Society of Washington, D.C., Kiplinger Research Library, Washington, D.C.
    Coordinating Committee for the Enforcement of the D.C. Anti-Discrimination Laws
    Harry S. Wender Papers
Howard University, Moorland-Spingarn Research Center, Washington, D.C.
    Archibald H. Grimké Papers
    Charles Hamilton Houston Papers
    Cook Family Papers
    E. Franklin Frazier Papers
    Papers of the NAACP—D.C. Branch
    Ralph Bunche Oral History Collection
Library of Congress, Washington, D.C.
    Abraham Lincoln Papers
    Mary Church Terrell Papers
    Records of the Select Committee to Inquire into the Existence of an Inhuman and
        Illegal Traffic in Slaves in the District of Columbia
    William Owner Diary
    Martin Luther King, Jr., Memorial Library, Washingtoniana Division, Washington,
        D.C.
    Celebración de la Mujer Latina Oral History Project
    Chillum Heights Citizens Association Collection
    D.C. Community Archives
    D.C. Statehood Movement Leaders Oral History Project
    Emergency Committee on the Transportation Crisis Papers
    Julius Hobson Papers
    Neighbors, Inc., Collection
    Self-Determination for D.C. Collection
National Archives and Records Administration, Washington, D.C.
    Records of the District of Columbia Commissioners and of the Offices Concerned
        with Public Buildings

Records of the House of Representatives
Records of the Office of the Secretary of Interior
Records of the United States Senate
Records of the War Department General and Special Staffs

Newspapers

Afro-American Red Star	Pacific Appeal
Alexandria Herald	People's Advocate
Atlanta Daily World	Pittsburgh Courier
Baltimore Sun	Provincial Freeman
Charleston (W.Va.) Gazette	Reporter
Chicago Defender	Richmond Times-Dispatch
Christian Advocate and Journal	Southern Patriot
Christian Recorder	Sunday Star
Colored American	(San Francisco) Sun Reporter
Congressional Globe	Telegraph
Daily Patriot	Toronto Globe
D.C. Gazette	United States' Telegraph
Emancipator	Voice of the Fugitive
Evening Star	Wall Street Journal
Freedom's Journal	Washington Afro American
Friends' Review	Washington Bee
Genius of Universal Emancipation	Washington City Paper
Georgetown Courier	Washington Critic
Globe	Washington Daily News
Hill Rag	Washington Herald
Independent	Washington Informer
Liberator	Washington Journal
Nashville Banner	Washington Pittsburgh Courier
National Intelligencer	Washington Post
National Republican	Washington Star
New Era	Washington Times
New Orleans Times Picayune	Washington Times Herald
New York Amsterdam News	Washington Tribune
New York Daily Times	Washingtonian
New York Herald	Washingtonian & Farmers, Mechanics, and
New York Times	Merchants Gazette
North Star	Weekly Anglo-African
Owosso (Mich.) Argus-Press	Weekly Register

Magazines

American Mercury	Century Illustrated Magazine
Atlantic Monthly	Collier's Weekly

Congressional Quarterly	Munsey's Magazine
Crisis	Nation
Ebony	Pageant
ESPN Magazine	The Phyllis Schlafly Report
Evening Star Sunday Magazine	Scribner's Magazine
Forbes	Smithsonian Magazine
Fortune	Stylus
Good Government	Survey
Harper's New Monthly Magazine	Survey Graphic
Harper's Weekly	Time
Interracial Review	World To-Day
Jet	Washingtonian
La Follette's Magazine	Washington Monthly
Life and Labor	Washington Post Magazine
The Messenger	

U.S. Government Documents

Bureau of the Census. *Fifth Census; or Enumeration of the Inhabitants of the United States, 1830.* Washington, D.C.: Census Office, 1830.

———. *Heads of Families at the First Census of the United States Taken in the Year 1790: Virginia.* Washington, D.C.: USGPO, 1908.

———. "Historical Census Statistics on Population Totals by Race, 1790 to 1990, and by Hispanic Origin, 1970 to 1990, for the United States, Regions, Divisions, and States." Population Division, Working Paper No. 56. Washington, D.C., September 2002.

———. *Historical Statistics of the United States, 1789–1945.* Washington, D.C.: USGPO, 1949.

———. *Negroes in the United States, 1920–1932.* Washington, D.C.: USGPO, 1935.

———. *Population of the United States in 1860.* Washington, D.C.: USGPO, 1864.

———. *Statistical Abstract of the United States, 1959.* Washington, D.C.: USGPO, 1959.

———. *Thirteenth Census of the United States.* Vol. 2. Washington, D.C.: USGPO, 1910.

Bureau of Engraving and Printing. *Annual Report of the Director of the Bureau of Engraving and Printing.* Washington, D.C.: USGPO, 1914.

Commissioners of the District of Columbia. *Report of the Commissioners of the District of Columbia 1901.* Vol. 1. Washington, D.C.: USGPO, 1901.

Department of Education. *Special Report of the Commissioner of Education on the Condition and Improvement of the Public Schools in the District of Columbia.* Washington, D.C.: USGPO, 1871.

Department of Interior. *Washington, D.C.'s Vanishing Springs and Waterways.* Geological Survey Circular 752. Washington, D.C.: USGPO, 1977.

District of Columbia Advisory Committee to the United States Commission on Civil Rights. *Neighborhood Renewal—Reinvestment and Displacement in D.C.* Washington, D.C.: USGPO, February, 1981.

District of Columbia. Emergency Justice Project Task Force. *Justice in Time of Crisis: A Staff*

Report to the District of Columbia Committee on the Administration of Justice under Emergency Conditions. Washington, D.C.: USGPO, 1969.

Federal Writers' Project. *Washington, City and Capital*. Washington, D.C.: USGPO, 1937.

————. *The WPA Guide to Washington, D.C.* New York: Pantheon, 1983.

National Capital Park and Planning Commission. *Housing and Development: A Portion of the Comprehensive Plan for the National Capital and Its Environs*. Monograph No. 3. Washington, D.C., June 1950.

National Park Service. *Historic American Buildings Survey: Southwest Washington, Urban Renewal Area*. Washington, D.C., 2004.

Office of War Information. *Negroes and the War*. Washington, D.C.: USGPO, 1943.

President's Committee on Civil Rights. *To Secure These Rights*. Washington, D.C.: USGPO, 1947.

Office of the Federal Register. *Public Papers of the Presidents of the United States: Lyndon B. Johnson. Containing the Public Messages, Speeches and Statements of the President*. 1967, book 1. Washington, D.C.: USGPO, 1968.

U.S. Commission on Civil Rights. *Housing in Washington: Hearings before the United States Commission on Civil Rights, April 12–13, 1962*. Washington, D.C.: USGPO, 1962.

U.S. Congress. House. *Reports of Committees of the House of Representatives for the Second Session of the Forty-Second Congress*. Washington, D.C.: USGPO, 1872.

————. *Reports of Committees of the House of Representatives, 51st Congress, 1st Session, 1889–90*. Washington, D.C.: USGPO, 1890.

————. Committee on the District of Columbia. *Investigation of Public School Conditions*. Washington, D.C.: USGPO, 1957.

U.S. Congress, Senate. Committee on the District of Columbia. *Senate Report No. 166, 57th Congress, First Session*. Washington, D.C.: USGPO, 1902.

————. *Reorganization of the Government of the District of Columbia: Hearings before a Subcommittee of the Committee on the District of Columbia*. Washington, D.C.: USGPO, 1943.

U.S. Congress. Subcommittees on District of Columbia Appropriations, Senate and House of Representatives. *The Report of a Survey of the Public Schools of the District of Columbia*. Washington, D.C.: USGPO, 1949.

War Department. *The War of the Rebellion: Compilation of the Official Records of the Union and Confederate Armies*. Ser. 3, Vol. 1. Washington, D.C.: USGPO, 1880.

Interviews

In 2014–15, the authors worked with the SNCC Legacy Project to conduct a census of the SNCC veterans who moved to Washington, D.C., between 1965 and 1985. We did not count members of the Nonviolent Action Group who left the city after graduating from Howard University because we were interested in the community of SNCC veterans who came to the city and had a decisive impact on its culture and politics after 1965. We counted thirty-five.

Barnes, Johnny. Interview with George Derek Musgrove. Washington, D.C., 4 October 2012.

Hill, Alphonse. Interview with George Derek Musgrove. Washington, D.C., 19 January 2015.

Watkins, Frank. Interview with George Derek Musgrove. Washington, D.C., 6 September 2012.

Published Sources

Abdy, Edward S. *Journal of a Residence and Tour in the United States of America, from April, 1833, to October, 1834*. London: John Murray, 1835.

Acts of the Corporation of Washington, Passed by the Tenth Council. Washington, D.C.: A. and G. Way, 1813.

Adams, F. C. *Our Little Monarchy: Who Runs It, and What It Costs*. Washington, D.C.: F. A. Fills, 1873.

Adams, Lois, and Evelyn Leasher, eds. *Letter from Washington, 1863–1865*. Detroit, Mich.: Wayne State University Press, 1999.

Agronsky, Jonathan. *Marion Barry: The Politics of Race*. Latham, N.Y.: British American, 1991.

Alfers, Kenneth G. *Law and Order in the Capital City: A History of the Washington Police, 1800–1886*. Washington, D.C.: George Washington University, 1976.

Altenhofel, Jennifer. "Washington, D.C., to 1900." In *The Encyclopedia of the Irish in America*, edited by Michael Glazier, 944. Notre Dame, Ind.: University of Notre Dame Press, 1999.

Altshuler, David, ed. *The Jews of Washington, D.C.: A Communal Anthology*. Chappaqua, N.Y.: Rossel Books, 1985.

Ames, Julius Rubens, and Benjamin Lundy. *The Legion of Liberty: And Force of Truth, Containing the Thoughts, Words, and Deeds of Some Prominent Apostles, Champions and Martyrs*. New York: American Anti-Slavery Society, 1857.

Ames, Mary Clemmer. *Ten Years in Washington: Life and Scenes in the National Capital, as a Woman Sees Them*. Hartford, Conn.: A. D. Worthington, 1873.

Ammon, Francesca Russello. "Commemoration amid Criticism: The Mixed Legacy of Urban Renewal in Southwest Washington, D.C." *Journal of Planning History* 8, no. 3 (August 2009): 175–220.

Andrews, Ethan Allen. *Slavery and the Domestic Slave-Trade in the United States*. Boston: Light and Stearns, 1836.

Andrews, Mathew Page. *History of Maryland: Province and State*. New York: Doubleday, Doran, 1929.

Arnebeck, Bob. *Slave Labor in the Capital: Building America's Iconic Landmarks*. Mount Pleasant, S.C.: History Press, 2014.

———. *Through a Fiery Trial: Building Washington, 1790–1800*. Lanham, Md.: Madison Books, 1991.

Arsenault, Raymond. *The Sound of Freedom: Marian Anderson, the Lincoln Memorial, and the Concert That Awakened America*. New York: Bloomsbury, 2009.

Asch, Chris Myers. "Annie Stein." *Washington History* 28, no. 2 (Fall 2016): 79–80.

———. "Revisiting Reconstruction: James O. Eastland, the FEPC, and the Struggle to

Rebuild Germany, 1945–1946." *Journal of Mississippi History* 67, no. 1 (Spring 2005): 1–31.

———. *The Senator and the Sharecropper: The Freedom Struggles of James O. Eastland and Fannie Lou Hamer*. Chapel Hill: University of North Carolina Press, 2011.

Asch, Chris Myers, and Jane Freundel Levey. "Washington, D.C." In *Encyclopedia of Local History*, edited by Carol Kammen. Lanham, Md.: Rowan and Littlefield, forthcoming.

Asch, Chris Myers, and George Derek Musgrove. "Marion S. Barry." *Washington History* 27, no. 1 (Spring 2015): 66–67.

Auslander, Mark. "Enslaved Labor and Building the Smithsonian." *Southern Spaces* (December 12, 2012), http://southernspaces.org/2012/enslaved-labor-and-building -smithsonian-reading-stones.

Baker, Abby Gunn. "The Erection of the White House." *Records of the Columbia Historical Society* 16 (1913): 120–49.

Baker, Ray Stannard. *Following the Color Line: An Account of Negro Citizenship in the American Democracy*. New York: Doubleday, Page, 1908.

Ball, Charles. *Slavery in the United States: A Narrative of the Adventures of Charles Ball, a Black Man*. New York: John S. Taylor, 1837.

Bancroft, Frederic. *Slave-Trading in the Old South*. Baltimore: J. H. Furst, 1931.

Banks, James G., and Peter S. Banks. *The Unintended Consequences: Family and Community, the Victims of Isolated Poverty*. Lanham, Md.: University Press of America, 2004.

Barber, Lucy G. *Marching on Washington: The Forging of an American Political Tradition*. Berkeley: University of California Press, 2002.

Barnes, William R. "A National Controversy in Miniature: The District of Columbia Struggle Over Public Housing and Redevelopment, 1943–1946." *Prologue* 9 (Summer 1977), 90–104.

Bedini, Silvio A. "The Survey of the Federal Territory: Andrew Ellicott and Benjamin Banneker." *Washington History* 3, no. 1 (Spring–Summer 1991): 76–95.

Bell-Scott, Patricia. *The Firebrand and the First Lady: Pauli Murray, Eleanor Roosevelt, and the Struggle for Social Justice*. New York: Alfred A. Knopf, 2016.

Benedetto, Robert, Jane Donovan, and Kathleen Duvall. *Historical Dictionary of Washington*. Lanham, Md.: Scarecrow Press, 2003.

Bergman, G. M. "The Negro Who Rode with Fremont in 1847." *Negro History Bulletin* 28, no. 2 (November 1964): 31–32.

Berlin, Ira. *Many Thousands Gone: The First Two Centuries of Slavery in North America*. Cambridge, Mass.: Harvard University Press, 1998.

Berlin, Ira, and Herbert G. Gutman. "Natives and Immigrants, Free Men and Slaves: Urban Workingmen in the Antebellum American South." *American Historical Review* 88, no. 5 (December 1983): 1175–1200.

Berret, James G. "Address of Ex-Mayor James G. Berret." *Records of the Columbia Historical Society* 2 (1899): 206–18.

Biddle, Daniel, and Murray Dubin. *Tasting Freedom: Octavius Catto and the Battle for Equality in Civil War America*. Philadelphia: Temple University Press, 2010.

Black, Allida M. "A Reluctant but Persistent Warrior: Eleanor Roosevelt and the Early Civil Rights Movement." In *Women in the Civil Rights Movement: Trailblazers and*

Torchbearers, 1941–1965, edited by Vicki L. Crawford, Jacqueline Anne Rouse, and Barbara Woods, 233–50. Bloomington: Indiana University Press, 1993.

Blackburn, Robin. *The Overthrow of Colonial Slavery, 1776–1848*. London: Verso, 2000.

Blackett, R. J. M. *Making Freedom: The Underground Railroad and the Politics of Slavery*. Chapel Hill: University of North Carolina Press, 2013.

Blassingame, John W. *Slave Testimony: Two Centuries of Letters, Speeches, Interviews, and Autobiographies*. Baton Rouge: Louisiana State University Press, 1977.

Blight, David W. *A Slave No More: Two Men Who Escaped to Freedom*. New York: Harcourt, 2007.

Bonacich, Edna. "Abolition, the Extension of Slavery, and the Position of Free Blacks: A Study of Split Labor Markets in the United States, 1830–1863." *American Journal of Sociology* 81, no. 3 (November 1975): 601–28.

Borchert, James. *Alley Life in Washington: Family, Community, Religion, and Folklife in the City, 1850–1970*. Urbana: University of Illinois Press, 1980.

Bordewich, Fergus. *Washington: The Making of the American Capital*. New York: Amistad, 2008.

Borstelmann, Thomas. *The Cold War and the Color Line: American Race Relations in the Global Arena*. Cambridge, Mass.: Harvard University Press, 2003.

Bowling, Kenneth R. *Creating the Federal City, 1774–1800: Potomac Fever*. Washington, D.C.: American Institute of Architects Press, 1988.

———. *The Creation of Washington, D.C.: The Idea and Location of the American Capital*. Fairfax, Va.: George Mason University Press, 1991.

———. "From 'Federal Town' to 'National Capital': Ulysses S. Grant and the Reconstruction of Washington, D.C." *Washington History* 14, no. 1 (Spring–Summer 2002): 8–25.

Brandenburg, David J., and Millicent H. Brandenburg. "The Duc De La Rochefoucauld-Liancourt's Visit to the Federal City in 1797: A New Translation." *Records of the Columbia Historical Society* 49 (1973–74): 35–60.

Briggs, Emily Edson. *The Olivia Letters: Being Some History of Washington City for Forty Years as Told by the Letters of a Newspaper Correspondent*. Washington, D.C.: Neale, 1906.

Brinkley, David. *Washington Goes to War*. New York: Ballantine Books, 1996.

Brooks, Noah. *Washington in Lincoln's Time*. New York: Century, 1895.

Brown, Clifford W., Jr., and Rachel Seligman. *Solomon Northup: The Complete Story of the Author of "Twelve Years a Slave."* Santa Barbara, Calif.: Praeger, 2013.

Brown, Flora Bryant. "The NAACP Sponsored Sit-Ins by Howard University Students in Washington, D.C., 1943–1944." *Journal of Negro History* 85, no. 4 (Autumn 2000): 274–86.

Brown, Gordon S. *Incidental Architect: William Thornton and the Cultural Life of Early Washington, D.C., 1794–1828*. Athens: Ohio University Press, 2009.

Brown, Letitia Woods. *Free Negroes in the District of Columbia*. New York: Oxford University Press, 1972.

Brownlow, Louis. *A Passion for Anonymity: The Autobiography of Louis Brownlow (Second Half)*. Chicago: University of Chicago Press, 1958.

Bruce, Dickson D., Jr. *Archibald Grimké: Portrait of a Black Independent*. Baton Rouge: Louisiana State University Press, 1993.

Bryan, Wilhelmus Bogart. *A History of the National Capital: From Its Foundation through the Period of the Adoption of the Organic Act*. 2 vols. New York: MacMillan, 1914.

Buchholz, Margaret Thomas, and Josephine Lehmann. "Josephine: The Washington Diary of a War Worker, 1918–1919." *Washington History* 10, no. 2 (Fall–Winter 1998–99): 4–23.

Burch, Samuel, comp. *A Digest of the Laws of the Corporation of the City of Washington to the First of June, 1823*. Washington, D.C.: James Wilson, 1823.

Burlingame, Michael. *Abraham Lincoln: A Life*. Vol. 1. Baltimore: Johns Hopkins University Press, 2008.

Bushong, William. "Imagining James Hoban: Portraits of a Master Builder." *White House History*, no. 22 (Spring 2008): 49–57.

Cadaval, Olivia. "The Latino Community: Creating an Identity in the Nation's Capital." *Urban Odyssey: A Multicultural History of Washington, D.C.*, edited by Francine Curro Cary, 231–49. Washington, D.C.: Smithsonian Institution Press, 1996.

Callcott, Margaret Law, ed. *Mistress of Riversdale: The Plantation Letters of Rosalie Stier Calvert, 1795–1821*. Baltimore: Johns Hopkins University Press, 1991.

Cantwell, Thomas J. "Anacostia: Strength in Adversity." *Records of the Columbia Historical Society* 49 (1973–74): 330–70.

Caplan, Marvin. "Eat Anywhere! A Personal Recollection of the Thompson's Restaurant Case and the Desegregation of Washington's Eating Places." *Washington History* 1, no. 1 (Spring 1989): 24–39.

———. *Farther Along: A Civil Rights Memoir*. Baton Rouge: Louisiana State University Press, 1999.

———. "Trenton Terrace Remembered: Life in a 'Leftist Nest.'" *Washington History* 6, no. 1 (Spring–Summer 1994): 46–65.

Carpenter, John A. *Sword and Olive Branch: Oliver Otis Howard*. 1964. New York: Fordham University Press, 1999.

Cary, Francine Curro, ed. *Urban Odyssey: A Multicultural History of Washington, D.C.* Washington, D.C.: Smithsonian Institution Press, 1996.

Castaneda, Ruben. *S Street Rising: Crack, Murder, and Redemption in D.C.* New York: Bloomsbury, 2014.

Castle, Guy. "Blue Plains and Bellevue: Two Early Plantations of the Washington Area." *Records of the Columbia Historical Society* 63/65 (1963–65): 19–31.

———. "Gisborough as a Land Grant, Manor and Residence of the Dents, Addisons, Shaaffs and Youngs." *Records of the Columbia Historical Society* 53/56 (1953–56): 282–92.

———. "The Washington Area between 1608 and 1708, with a Biographical Note on Prince George of Denmark." *Records of the Columbia Historical Society* 63/65 (1963–65): 1–18.

Cherkasky, Mara. "'For Sale to Colored': Racial Change on S Street, N.W." *Washington History* (Fall–Winter 1996–97): 40–57.

Chernow, Ron. *Alexander Hamilton*. New York: Penguin, 2004.

Chudacoff, Howard P., and Judith E. Smith. *The Evolution of American Urban Society*. 5th ed. Upper Saddle River, N.J.: Prentice Hall, 2000.

Clark, Allen C. "Colonel William Winston Seaton and His Mayoralty." *Records of the Columbia Historical Society* 29/30 (1928): 1–102.

———. "The Mayoralty of Robert Brent." *Records of the Columbia Historical Society* 33/34 (1932): 267–305.

———. "The Mayors of the Corporation of Washington: Thomas Carbery." *Records of the Columbia Historical Society* 19 (1916): 61–98.

———. "Richard Wallach and the Times of His Mayoralty." *Records of the Columbia Historical Society* 21 (1918): 195–245.

———. "Walter Lenox, the Thirteenth Mayor of the City of Washington." *Records of the Columbia Historical Society* 20 (1917): 167–93.

Clark-Lewis, Elizabeth. "'For a Real Better Life': Voices of African American Women Migrants, 1900–1930." In *Urban Odyssey: A Multicultural History of Washington, D.C.*, edited by Francine Curro Cary, 97–112. Washington, D.C.: Smithsonian Institution Press, 1996.

———. *Living In, Living Out: African American Domestics in Washington, D.C., 1910–1940.* Washington, D.C.: Smithsonian Institution Press, 1994.

———. "'This Work Had a End': African-American Domestic Workers in Washington, D.C., 1910–1940." In *"To Toil the Livelong Day": America's Women at Work, 1780–1980*, edited by Carol Groneman and Mary Beth Norton, 196–212. Ithaca, N.Y.: Cornell University Press, 1987.

———, ed. "Duty and 'Fast Living': The Diary of Mary Johnson Sprow, Domestic Worker." *Washington History* 5, no. 1 (Spring–Summer 1993): 46–65.

———, ed. *First Freed: Washington, D.C., in the Emancipation Era.* Washington, D.C.: Howard University Press, 2002.

Clement, Bell. "Pushback: The White Community's Dissent from Bolling." *Washington History* 16, no. 2 (Fall–Winter 2004–5): 86–109.

———. "Wagner-Steagall and the D.C. Alley Dwelling Authority." *Journal of the American Planning Association* 78, no. 4 (Autumn 2012): 434–48.

Clephane, Walter C. "The Local Aspect of Slavery in the District of Columbia." *Records of the Columbia Historical Society* 3 (1900): 224–56.

Cobb, Whit. "Democracy in Search of Utopia: The History, Law, and Politics of Relocating the National Capital." *Dickinson Law Review* 99 (Spring 1995): 533–34.

Cole, Lewis. *Never Too Young to Die: The Death of Len Bias.* New York: Pantheon Books, 1989.

Cole, Stephanie. "Changes for Mrs. Thornton's Arthur: Patterns of Domestic Service in Washington, DC, 1800–1835." *Social Science History* 15, no. 3 (Autumn 1991): 367–79.

Collins, Carolyn B. "Mayor Sayles J. Bowen and the Beginnings of Negro Education." *Records of the Columbia Historical Society* 53/56 (1953–56): 293–308.

Corrigan, Mary Beth. "Imaginary Cruelties? A History of the Slave Trade in D.C." *Washington History* 13, no. 2 (Fall–Winter 2001–2): 4–27.

———. "'It's a Family Affair': Buying Freedom in the District of Columbia, 1850–1860." In *Working toward Freedom: Slave Society and Domestic Economy in the American South*, edited by Larry E. Hudson Jr., 163–91. Rochester, N.Y.: University of Rochester Press, 1994.

———. "Making the Most of an Opportunity: Slaves and the Catholic Church in Early Washington." *Washington History* 12, no. 1 (Spring–Summer 2000): 90–101.

———. "The Ties That Bind: The Pursuit of Community and Freedom among Slaves and Free Blacks in the District of Columbia, 1800–1860." In *Southern City, National*

Ambition: *The Growth of Early Washington, D.C.*, ed. Howard Gillette Jr., 69–90. Washington, D.C.: George Washington University Center for Washington Area Studies, 1995.

———. "'Whether They Be Ours or No, They May Be Heirs of the Kingdom': The Pursuit of Family Ties among Enslaved People in the District of Columbia." In *In the Shadow of Freedom: The Politics of Slavery in the National Capital*, edited by Paul Finkelman and Donald R. Kennon, 169–94. Athens: Ohio University Press, 2011.

Crandall, Reuben. *The Trial of Reuben Crandall, M.D.* New York: H. R. Piercy, 1836.

Crooms, Lisa A. "Race, Education and the District of Columbia: The Meaning and Legacy of Bolling v. Sharpe." *Washington History* 16, no. 2 (Fall–Winter 2004–5): 14–22.

Crothers, A. Glenn. "The 1846 Retrocession of Alexandria: Protecting Slavery and the Slave Trade in the District of Columbia." In *In the Shadow of Freedom: The Politics of Slavery in the National Capital*, edited by Paul Finkelman and Donald R. Kennon, 141–68. Athens: Ohio University Press, 2011.

Cullen, Charles T., ed. *The Papers of Thomas Jefferson.* Vol. 22: *6 August 1791–31 December 1791.* Princeton, N.J.: Princeton University Press, 1986.

Cunningham, Roger D. "The Loving Touch: Walter H. Loving's Five Decades of Military Music." *Army History*, no. 64 (Summer 2007): 4–25.

Curran, Robert Emmett. *The Bicentennial History of Georgetown University: From Academy to University, 1789–1889.* Vol. 1. Washington, D.C.: Georgetown University Press, 1993.

Curry, Leonard P. *The Free Black in Urban America, 1800–1850: The Shadow of the Dream.* Chicago: University of Chicago Press, 1981.

Davis, David Brion. "The Impact of British Abolitionism on American Sectionalism." In *In the Shadow of Freedom: The Politics of Slavery in the National Capital*, edited by Paul Finkelman and Donald R. Kennon, 19–35. Athens: Ohio University Press, 2011.

Davis, Harriet Riddle. "Civil War Recollections of a Little Yankee." *Records of the Columbia Historical Society* 44/45 (1942–43): 55–75.

Derthick, Martha. *City Politics in Washington, D.C.* [Cambridge, Mass.]: Joint Center for Urban Studies of the Massachusetts Institute of Technology and Harvard University, 1962.

———. "Defeat at Fort Lincoln." *Public Interest*, no. 20 (Summer 1970): 3–39.

De Santis, Christopher, ed. *The Collected Works of Langston Hughes.* Vol. 9. Columbia: University of Missouri Press, 2002.

Deyle, Steven. "Rethinking the Slave Trade: Slave Traders and the Market Revolution in the South." In *The Old South's Modern Worlds: Slavery, Region, and Nation in the Age of Progress*, edited by L. Diane Barnes and Brian Schoen and Frank Towers, 104–19. Oxford: Oxford University Press, 2011.

Dickens, Charles. *American Notes for General Circulation.* London: Chapman and Hall, 1874.

diGiacomantonio, William C. "'To Sell Their Birthright for a Mess of Potage': The Origins of D.C. Governance and the Organic Act of 1801." *Washington History* 12, no. 1 (Spring–Summer 2000): 30–48.

Dilts, James D. *The Great Road: The Building of the Baltimore & Ohio, the Nation's First Railroad, 1828–1853.* Palo Alto, Calif.: Stanford University Press, 1993.

Diner, Steven J. "The Black Majority: Race and Politics in the Nation's Capital." In

Snowbelt Cities: Metropolitan Politics in the Northeast and Midwest since World War II, edited by Richard M. Bernard, 247–68. Bloomington: Indiana University Press, 1990.

————. *Crisis of Confidence: The Reputation of Washington's Public Schools in the Twentieth Century*. Studies in D.C. History and Public Policy, no. 1, Washington, D.C.: Center for Applied Research and Urban Policy, University of the District of Columbia, 1982.

————. *Democracy, Federalism, and the Governance of the Nation's Capital, 1790–1974*. Studies in D.C. History and Public Policy, no. 10. Washington, D.C.: Center for Applied Research and Urban Policy, University of the District of Columbia, 1987.

Dodd, Walter Fairleigh. *The Government of the District of Columbia: A Study in Federal and Municipal Administration*. Washington, D.C.: John Byrne, 1909.

Dolan, Jay P. *The Irish Americans: A History*. New York: Bloomsbury, 2008.

Douglass, Frederick. *The Life and Times of Frederick Douglass*. Hartford, Conn.: Park, 1881.

Dower, John. *War without Mercy: Race and Power in the Pacific War*. New York: Pantheon, 1986.

Downing, Margaret B. *The Catholic Founders of the National Capital*. New York: Paulist Press, 1917.

Downs, Jim. *Sick from Freedom: African-American Illness and Suffering during the Civil War and Reconstruction*. Oxford: Oxford University Press, 2012.

Du Bois, W. E. B. *Black Reconstruction in America, 1860–1880*. 1935. New York: Athenaeum, 1962.

————. *The Negro Common School*. Atlanta: Atlanta University Press, 1901.

Dudziak, Mary. *Cold War Civil Rights: Race and the Image of American Democracy*. Princeton, N.J.: Princeton University Press, 2002.

Easton, Nina. *Gang of Five: Leaders at the Center of the Conservative Ascendancy*. New York: Touchstone, 2000.

Ecker, Grace Dunlop. *A Portrait of Old George Town*. Richmond, Va.: Dietz, 1951.

Edsall, Thomas, and Mary Edsall. *Chain Reaction: The Impact of Race, Rights and Taxes on American Politics*. New York: W. W. Norton, 1992.

Elfenbein, Jessica I. *Civics, Commerce, and Community: The History of the Greater Washington Board of Trade 1889–1989*. Dubuque, Iowa: Kendall/Hunt, 1989.

Ellis, John B. *The Sights and Secrets of the Nation's Capital*. New York: U.S. Publishing, 1869.

Ewing, Adam. "Garvey or Garveyism? Colin Grant's *Negro with a Hat* (2008) and the Search for a New Synthesis in UNIA Scholarship." *Transition*, no. 105 (2011): 130–45.

Fairclough, Adam. "Civil Rights and the Lincoln Memorial: The Censored Speeches of Robert R. Moton (1922) and John Lewis (1963)." *Journal of Negro History* 82, no. 4 (Autumn 1997): 408–16.

Farrar, Margaret E. *Building the Body Politic: Power and Urban Space in Washington, D.C.* Urbana: University of Illinois Press, 2008.

Fauntroy, Michael. *Home Rule or House Rule: Congress and the Erosion of Local Governance in the District of Columbia*. New York: University Press of America, 2003.

Fausz, J. Frederick. "Merging and Emerging Worlds: Anglo-Indian Interest Groups and the Development of the Seventeenth-Century Chesapeake." In *Colonial Chesapeake Society*, edited by Lois Green Carr, Philip D. Morgan, and Jean B. Russo, 47–98. Chapel Hill: University of North Carolina Press, 1988.

Fearon, Henry Bradshaw. *Sketches of America*. London, 1819.

Featherstonhaugh, G. W. *Excursion through the Slave States*. New York: Harper and Brothers, 1844.

The Federal Cases, Comprising Cases Argued and Determined in the Circuit and District Courts of the United States, Book 6. St. Paul, Minn.: West, 1894.

Finkelman, Paul, ed. *Encyclopedia of African American History, 1619–1895*. New York: Oxford University Press, 2006.

Finkelman, Paul, and Donald R. Kennon, eds. *In the Shadow of Freedom: The Politics of Slavery in the National Capital*. Athens: Ohio University Press, 2011.

Fischer, David Hackett. *Liberty and Freedom: A Visual History of America's Founding Ideas*. Oxford: Oxford University Press, 2005.

Fitzpatrick, Michael Andrew. "'A Great Agitation for Business': Black Economic Development in Shaw." *Washington History* 2, no. 2 (Fall–Winter 1990–91): 48–73.

Fitzpatrick, Sandra, and Maria R. Goodwin. *The Guide to Black Washington: Places and Events of Historical and Cultural Significance in the Nation's Capital*. New York: Hippocrene Books, 1999.

Flamm, Michael W. *Law and Order: Street Crime, Civil Unrest, and the Crisis of Liberalism in the 1960s*. New York: Columbia University Press, 2005.

Fleegler, Robert L. "Theodore G. Bilbo and the Decline of Public Racism, 1938–1947." *Journal of Mississippi History* 68 (Spring 2006): 1–27.

Fleischner, Jennifer. *Mrs. Lincoln and Mrs. Keckly: The Remarkable Story of the Friendship between a First Lady and a Former Slave*. New York: Broadway Books, 2004.

Fletcher, Patsy Mose. *African American Leisure Destinations around Washington, D.C.* Charleston, S.C.: History Press, 2015.

French, Roderick S. "Chevy Chase Village in the Context of the National Suburban Movement, 1870–1900." *Records of the Columbia Historical Society* 49 (1973–74): 300–329.

Gale, Dennis. *Washington, D.C.: Inner-City Revitalization and Minority Suburbanization*. Philadelphia: Temple University Press, 1987.

Gardner, William M. "Native Americans: Early Encounters." In *Urban Odyssey: A Multicultural History of Washington, D.C.*, edited by Francine Curro Cary, 1–19. Washington, D.C.: Smithsonian Institution Press, 1996.

Garfinkle, Martin. *The Jewish Community of Washington, D.C.* Charleston, S.C.: Arcadia, 2005.

Garnet, Henry Highland. "A Memorial Discourse." Philadelphia: Joseph M. Wilson, 1865.

Garrison, Wendell Phillips, and Francis Jackson Garrison. *William Lloyd Garrison, 1805–1879: The Story of His Life, Told by His Children*. New York: Century, 1885.

Garrison, William Lloyd. *Thoughts on African Colonization*. Boston: Garrison and Knapp, 1832.

Gatewood, William. *Aristocrats of Color: The Black Elite, 1880–1920*. Bloomington: Indiana University Press, 1990.

Gelderman, Carol. *A Free Man of Color and His Hotel: Race, Reconstruction, and the Role of the Federal Government*. Washington, D.C.: Potomac Books, 2012.

Gellman, Eric S. *Death Blow to Jim Crow: The National Negro Congress and the Rise of Militant Civil Rights*. Chapel Hill: University of North Carolina Press, 2012.

Gibbs, C. R. *Black, Copper, and Bright: The District of Columbia's Black Civil War Regiment.* Silver Spring, Md.: Three Dimensional Publishing, 2002.

Gibbs, George. *Memoirs of the Administrations of Washington and John Adams, Edited from the Papers of Oliver Wolcott, Secretary of the Treasury.* Vol. 2. New York: W. Van Norden, 1846.

Giddings, Joshua R. *Speeches in Congress.* Boston: John P. Jewett, 1853.

Gilbert, Ben W. *Ten Blocks from the White House: Anatomy of the Washington Riots of 1968.* New York: Frederick A. Praeger, 1968.

———. "Toward a Color-Blind Newspaper: Race Relations and the *Washington Post.*" *Washington History* 5, no. 2 (Fall–Winter 1993–94): 4–27.

Gillette, Howard, Jr. *Between Justice and Beauty: Race, Planning, and the Failure of Urban Policy in Washington, D.C.* Philadelphia: University of Pennsylvania Press, 1996.

———, ed. *Southern City, National Ambition: The Growth of Early Washington, D.C., 1800–1860.* Washington, D.C.: George Washington University Center for Washington Area Studies, 1995.

Gillespie, Andra. *Whose Black Politics? Cases in Post-Racial Black Leadership.* New York: Routledge, 2010.

Gilmore, Glenda. *Defying Dixie: The Radical Roots of Civil Rights, 1919–1950.* New York: W. W. Norton, 2008.

Glazier, Michael. *The Encyclopedia of the Irish in America.* Notre Dame, Ind.: University of Notre Dame Press, 1999.

Gleeson, David T. *The Irish in the South, 1815–1877.* Chapel Hill: University of North Carolina Press, 2001.

Goldfield, David R. "Antebellum Washington in Context: The Pursuit of Prosperity and Identity." In *Southern City, National Ambition: The Growth of Early Washington, D.C., 1800–1860,* ed. Howard Gillette Jr., 1–20. Washington, D.C.: George Washington University Center for Washington Area Studies, 1995.

Gonda, Jeffrey D. *Unjust Deeds: The Restrictive Covenant Cases and the Making of the Civil Rights Movement.* Chapel Hill: University of North Carolina Press, 2015.

Goode, James M. *Capital Losses: A Cultural History of Washington's Destroyed Buildings.* Washington, D.C.: Smithsonian Institution Press, 1979.

Gordon, William A. "Recollections of a Boyhood in Georgetown." *Records of the Columbia Historical Society* 20 (1917): 121–40.

Gordon-Reed, Annette. *The Hemingses of Monticello: An American Family.* New York: W. W. Norton, 2008.

Gouvernor, Marian. *As I Remember: Recollections of American Society during the Nineteenth Century.* New York: D. Appleton, 1911.

Graham, Katherine. *Katherine Graham's Washington.* New York: Vintage Books, 2002.

Grassi, John. "The Catholic Religion in the United States in 1818." In *The American Catholic Historical Researches,* edited by Martin I. J. Griffin, vol. 8, 98–112. Philadelphia: M. I. J. Griffin, 1891.

Gray, Derek, and Jennifer Krafchik. "'Its Fingers Were Crossed and Its Guard Was Up': Washington Prepares of the March for Jobs and Freedom." *Washington History* 25 (Summer 2013): 20–35.

Green, Constance McLaughlin. *Secret City: A History of Race Relations in the Nation's Capital.* Princeton, N.J.: Princeton University Press, 1967.

————. *Washington: Capital City, 1879–1950*. Princeton, N.J.: Princeton University Press, 1963.

————. *Washington: Village and Capital, 1800–1878*. Princeton, N.J.: Princeton University Press, 1962.

Greene, Dolores Dunmore. "Mount Zion, Washington's Oldest Black Church, Turns 200." *Washington History* 8, no. 2 (Fall 2016): 65–66.

Grier, Eunice S. *Understanding Washington's Changing Population*. Washington, D.C.: Washington Center for Metropolitan Studies, 1961.

Grimsted, David. *American Mobbing, 1828–1861: Toward Civil War*. New York: Oxford University Press, 1998.

————. "Rioting in Its Jacksonian Setting." *American Historical Review* 77, no. 2 (April 1972): 361–97.

Groves, Paul A. "The Development of a Black Residential Community in Southwest Washington: 1860–1897." *Records of the Columbia Historical Society* 49 (1973–74): 260–75.

Guelzo, Allen C. *Lincoln's Emancipation Proclamation: The End of Slavery in America*. New York: Simon and Schuster, 2004.

Gurley, Ralph Randolph. "A Discourse, Delivered on the Fourth of July, 1825, in the City of Washington." Washington, D.C.: Gales and Seaton, 1825.

Halberstam, David. *The Children*. Robbinsdale, Minn.: Fawcett Books, 1999.

Hall, Basil. *Travels in North America, in the Years 1827 and 1828*. Vol. 3. Edinburgh: R. Cadell, 1830.

Hamilton, Alexander. *Writings*. New York: Library of America, 2001.

Hamilton, Thomas. *Men and Manners in America*. Edinburgh: William Blackwood, 1833.

Hammond, L. H. *The Vanguard of the Race*. New York: Council of Women for Home Missions, 1922.

Hannerz, Ulf. *Soulside: Inquiries into Ghetto Culture and Community*. New York: Columbia University Press, 1969.

Hannold, Elizabeth. "'Comfort and Respectability': Washington's Philanthropic Housing Movement." *Washington History* 4 (Fall–Winter 1992–93): 20–39.

Hansen, Carl F. *Danger in Washington: The Story of My Twenty Years in the Public Schools in the Nation's Capital*. West Nyack, N.Y.: Parker, 1968.

————. *Miracle of Social Adjustment: Desegregation in the Washington, D.C., Schools*. Washington, D.C.: Anti-Defamation League of B'nai B'rith, 1957.

Harlan, Louis R., and Raymond W. Strock, eds. *The Booker T. Washington Papers*. Vol. 8: 1904–6. Urbana: University of Illinois Press, 1979.

Harley, Sharon. "The Black Goddess of Liberty." *Journal of Negro History* 81, no. 1–4 (Winter–Autumn 1996): 62–71.

————. "Black Women in a Southern City: Washington, D.C., 1890–1920." In *Sex, Race, and the Role of Women in the South*, edited by Joanne V. Hawks and Sheila L. Skemp, 59–74. Jackson: University Press of Mississippi, 1983.

————. "Mary Church Terrell: Genteel Militant." In *Black Leaders of the Nineteenth Century*, edited by Leon F. Litwack and August Meier, 307–22. Urbana: University of Illinois Press, 1988.

Harper, Kenton N. *History of the Grand Lodge and of Freemasonry in the District of Columbia*. Washington, D.C.: R. Beresford, 1911.

Harris, C. M. "Washington's 'Federal City,' Jefferson's 'Federal Town.'" *Washington History* 12, no. 1 (Spring–Summer 2000): 49–53.

Harrison, Robert. "An Experimental Station for Lawmaking: Congress and the District of Columbia, 1862–1878." *Civil War History* 53, no. 1 (March 2007): 29–53.

———. *Washington during Civil War and Reconstruction: Race and Radicalism.* Cambridge: Cambridge University Press, 2011.

———. "Welfare and Employment Policies of the Freedmen's Bureau in the District of Columbia." *Journal of Southern History* 72, no. 1 (February 2006): 75–110.

Harrold, Stanley. "Gamaliel Bailey, Antislavery Journalist and Lobbyist." In *In the Shadow of Freedom: The Politics of Slavery in the National Capital,* edited by Paul Finkelman and Donald R. Kennon, 58–82. Athens: Ohio University Press, 2011.

———. "The Pearl Affair: The Washington Riot of 1848." *Records of the Columbia Historical Society* 50 (1980): 140–60.

———. *Subversives: Antislavery Community in Washington, D.C., 1828–1865.* Baton Rouge: Louisiana State University Press, 2003.

Haskins, Faye P. "Behind the Headlines: The *Evening Star's* Coverage of the 1968 Riots." *Washington History* 19–20 (2007–8): 50–67.

Hatcher, Ed. "Washington's Nineteenth-Century Citizens' Associations and the Senate Park Commission Plan." *Washington History* 14, no. 2 (Fall–Winter 2002–3): 70–95.

Hathaway, David, and Stephanie Ho. "Small but Resilient: Washington's Chinatown over the Years." *Washington History* 15, no. 1 (Spring–Summer 2003): 42–61.

Hayes, Laurence J. W. *The Negro Federal Government Worker.* Washington, D.C.: Howard University, 1941.

Hechinger, John W., Sr., and Gavin Taylor. "Black and Blue: The D.C. City Council vs. Police Brutality, 1967–69." *Washington History* 11, no. 2 (Fall–Winter 1999–2000): 4–23.

Height, Dorothy. *Open Wide the Freedom Gates.* New York: Public Affairs, 2003.

Helm, Judith Beck. *Tenleytown, D.C.: Country Village into City Neighborhood.* Hagerstown, Md.: Tennally, 1981.

Henig, Jeffrey R. *Gentrification in Adams Morgan: Political and Commercial Consequences of Neighborhood Change.* Washington, D.C.: Center for Washington Area Studies, George Washington University, 1982.

Henning, George C. "The Mansion and Family of Notley Young." *Records of the Columbia Historical Society* 16 (1913): 1–24.

Hering, Katharina. "Voice of the Voteless: The District of Columbia League of Women Voters, 1921–1941." *Washington History* 28, no. 1 (Spring 2016): 3–13.

Higginbotham, Evelyn Brooks. "Nannie Helen Burroughs." In *Black Women in America: An Historical Encyclopedia,* edited by Dorothy C. Hine, vol. 1, 201–4. Oxford: Oxford University Press, 2005.

Hilyer, Andrew F., ed. *The Twentieth Century Union League Directory.* Washington, D.C.: Union League, 1901.

Hine, Darlene Clark. *Hine Sight: Black Women and the Re-Construction of American History.* Bloomington: Indiana University Press, 1994.

Hinks, Peter P. *To Awaken My Afflicted Brethren: David Walker and the Problem of Antebellum Slave Resistance.* University Park: Pennsylvania State University Press, 1997.

Hobbs, Allyson. *Chosen Exile: A History of Racial Passing in America*. Cambridge, Mass.: Harvard University Press, 2014.

Holland, Jesse. *Black Men Built the Capitol: Discovering African-American History in and around Washington, D.C.* Guilford, Conn.: Globe Pequot, 2007.

Hombs, Mary Ellen, and Mitch Snyder. *Homeless in America: A Forced March to Nowhere*. Washington, D.C.: Community for Creative Nonviolence, 1982.

Honey, Maureen, ed. *Bitter Fruit: African American Women in World War II*. Columbia: University of Missouri Press, 1999.

Hood, James Franklin. "In Memoriam: Michael Ignatius Weller, 1846–1915." *Records of the Columbia Historical Society* 19 (1916): 197–203.

Horowitz, Donald L. *The Courts and Social Policy*. Washington, D.C.: Brookings Institution, 1977.

Horton, James O. "Alexander Hamilton: Slavery and Race in a Revolutionary Generation." *New-York Journal of American History* 3 (Spring 2004): 16–24.

———. "The Genesis of Washington's African American Community." In *Urban Odyssey: A Multicultural History of Washington, D.C.*, edited by Francine Curro Cary, 20–41. Washington, D.C.: Smithsonian Institution Press, 1996.

Howard, O. O. *Autobiography of Oliver Otis Howard, Major General United States Army*. Vol. 2. New York: Baker and Taylor, 1908.

Howes, Robert G. "Crisis Downtown: A Church Eye-View of Urban Renewal." Washington, D.C.: National Conference of Catholic Charities, December 1959.

Hoyt, William D. "Washington's Living History: The Post Office Fire and Other Matters, 1834–39." *Records of the Columbia Historical Society* 46/47 (1944–45): 49–69.

Humphrey, Robert, and Mary Elizabeth Chambers. *Ancient Washington: American Indian Cultures of the Potomac Valley*. Washington, D.C.: George Washington University, 1977.

Hunt, Gaillard, ed. *The First Forty Years of Washington Society: In the Family Letters of Margaret Bayard Smith*. 1906. New York: Frederick Ungar, 1965.

Hunt, Gaillard, and James Brown Scott, eds. *The Debates in the Federal Convention of 1787, Which Framed the Constitution of the United States of America* . . . . New York: Oxford University Press, 1920.

Huron, Amanda. "Creating a Commons in the Capital: The Emergence of Limited-Equity Cooperatives in Washington, D.C." *Washington History* 56, no. 1 (Fall 2014): 56–67.

Hutchinson, George B. "Jean Toomer and the 'New Negroes' of Washington." *American Literature* 63, no. 4 (December 1991): 683–92.

Hutchinson, Louise Daniel. *The Anacostia Story, 1608–1930*. Washington, D.C.: Smithsonian Institution Press, 1977.

Hyra, Derek, and Sabiyha Prince, eds. *Capital Dilemma: Growth and Inequality in Washington, D.C.* New York: Routledge, 2015.

Ignatiev, Noel. *How the Irish Became White*. New York: Routledge, 1995.

Ingle, Edward. *The Negro in the District of Columbia*. Baltimore: Johns Hopkins University Press, 1893.

Ingham, John N. "Building Businesses, Creating Communities: Residential Segregation and the Growth of African American Business in Southern Cities, 1880–1915." *Business History Review* 77, no. 4 (Winter 2003): 639–65.

Jackson, Kenneth T. "Federal Subsidy and the Suburban Dream: The First Quarter-Century of Government Intervention in the Housing Market." *Records of the Columbia Historical Society* 50 (1980): 421–51.

Jacobs, Jane. *The Death and Life of Great American Cities*. New York: Vintage Books, 1961.

Jacob, Kathryn Allamong. *Capital Elites: High Society in Washington, D.C., after the Civil War*. Washington, D.C.: Smithsonian Institution Press, 1995.

———. "'Like Moths to a Candle': The Nouveaux Riches Flock to Washington, 1870–1900." In *Urban Odyssey: A Multicultural History of Washington, D.C.*, edited by Francine Curro Cary, 79–96. Washington, D.C.: Smithsonian Institution Press, 1996.

Jaffe, Harry S., and Tom Sherwood. *Dream City: Race, Power, and the Decline of Washington, D.C.* Kindle ed. New York: Simon and Schuster, 1994.

Janney, Samuel M. *Memoirs of Samuel M. Janney*. Philadelphia: Friends' Book Association, 1881.

Janson, Charles Williams. *The Stranger in America, 1793–1806*. London, 1807.

Jefferson, Thomas. *Writings*. New York: Library of America, 1984.

Jennings, Paul. *A Colored Man's Reminiscences of James Madison*. Brooklyn, N.Y.: George Beadle, 1865.

Johnson, Clifton H. "Mary Ann Shadd: Crusader for the Freedom of Man." *Crisis* 78, no. 3 (April–May 1971): 89–90.

Johnson, Haynes B. *Dusk at the Mountain: The Negro, the Nation, and the Capital; A Report on Problems and Progress*. New York: Doubleday, 1963.

Johnson, Ronald. "From Romantic Suburb to Racial Enclave: LeDroit Park, Washington, D.C., 1880–1920." *Phylon* 45, no. 4 (1984): 264–70.

———. "Those Who Stayed: Washington Black Writers of the 1920s." *Records of the Columbia Historical Society* 50 (1980): 484–99.

Johnson, Samuel. *Taxation No Tyranny*. London: T. Cadell, 1775.

Johnson, Thomas R. "Reconstruction Politics in Washington: 'An Experimental Garden for Radical Plants.'" *Records of the Columbia Historical Society* 50 (1980): 180–90.

Johnson, Wanda B. *A Study of Police-Community Relations Programs in Washington, D.C.* Washington, D.C.: National Institute of Law Enforcement and Criminal Justice, 1972.

Johnston, Allen. *Surviving Freedom: The Black Community of Washington, D.C., 1860–1880*. New York: Garland, 1993.

Jones, Martin V., and Michael J. Flax. "The Quality of Life in Metropolitan Washington (D.C.)." Washington, D.C.: Urban Institute, March 1970.

Jones, Thai. *A Radical Line: From the Labor Movement to the Weather Underground, One Family's Century of Conscience*. New York: Free Press, 2004.

Jones, Walter H. *Recreation and Amusements among Negroes in Washington D.C.* New York: Praeger, 1927.

Jones, William Henry. *Housing of Negroes in Washington, D.C.: A Study in Human Ecology*. Washington, D.C.: Howard University Press, 1929.

Jones, William P. *The March on Washington: Jobs, Freedom, and the Forgotten History of Civil Rights*. New York: W. W. Norton, 2013.

Jones-Correa, Michael. "The Origins and Diffusion of Racial Restrictive Covenants." *Political Science Quarterly* 115, no. 4 (2000–2001): 541–68.

Jordan, David W. "Political Stability and the Emergence of a Native Elite in Maryland." In *The Chesapeake in the Seventeenth Century: Essays on Anglo-American Society and Politics*, edited by Thad W. Tate and David L. Ammerman, 243–73. New York: W. W. Norton, 1979.

Joseph, Peniel E. *Stokely: A Life*. New York: Basic Civitas, 2014.

Joyce, Carleen, and Virginia Reid. "Remembering Washington." Washington, D.C.: IONA Senior Service, 1993.

Justesen, Benjamin R. "George Henry White and the End of an Era." *Washington History* 15, no. 2 (Fall–Winter 2003–4): 34–51.

Kachun, Mitch. "Celebrating Emancipation and Contesting Freedom in Washington, D.C." In *In the Shadow of Freedom: The Politics of Slavery in the National Capital*, edited by Paul Finkelman and Donald R. Kennon, 220–38. Athens: Ohio University Press, 2011.

———. *Festivals of Freedom: Memory and Meaning in African American Emancipation Celebrations, 1808–1915*. Amherst: University of Massachusetts Press, 2003.

Kalman, Laura. *Right Star Rising: A New Politics, 1974–80*. New York: W. W. Norton, 2010.

Keckly, Elizabeth. *Behind the Scenes: Life of a Colored Woman Thirty Years a Slave, Four Years at the White House*. New York: G. W. Clareton, 1868.

Kelly, Rita Mae. "Generalizations from an OEO Experiment in Washington, D.C." *Journal of Social Issues* 31, no. 1 (1975): 57–86.

———, et al. *The Pilot Police Project: A Description and Assessment of a Police-Community Relations Experiment in Washington, D.C.* Kensington, Md.: American Institutes for Research, 1972.

Kerr, Audrey Elisa. *The Paper Bag Principle: Class, Colorism, and Rumor and the Case of Black Washington, D.C.* Knoxville: University of Tennessee Press, 2006.

Ketcham, Ralph Louis. *James Madison: A Biography*. Charlottesville: University of Virginia Press, 1971.

Kijakazi, Kilolo, et al. *The Color of Wealth in the Nation's Capital*. Durham, N.C.: Duke University; Washington, D.C.: Urban Institute; New York: New School; Oakland, Calif.: Insight Center for Community Economic Development, 2016.

Kimmel, Ross M. "The Battle of North Point: A Little-Known Battle from a Scarcely Remembered War." *Maryland Natural Resource* (Fall 2008): 5–8.

King, Cynthia P. "Henry Highland Garnet." In *African-American Orators: A Bio-Critical Sourcebook*, edited by Richard W. Leeman, 143–49. Westport, Conn.: Greenwood, 1996.

King, Desmond. *Making Americans: Immigration, Race, and the Making of Diverse Democracy*. Cambridge, Mass.: Harvard University Press, 2000.

———. *Separate and Unequal: African Americans and the U.S. Federal Government*. 1995. Oxford: Oxford University Press, 2007.

King, John W. *The Breeding of Contempt*. Bloomington, Ind.: Xlibris, 2003.

Kingsbury, Myra, ed. *The Records of the Virginia Company of London*. Vol. 3. Washington, D.C.: USGPO, 1906.

Kluger, Richard. *Simple Justice: The History of Brown v. Board of Education and Black America's Struggle for Equality*. New York: Alfred A. Knopf, 2004.

Knoll, Erwin. *The Truth about Desegregation in Washington's Schools*. Annandale, Va.: Turnpike Press, 1959.

Knox, Ellis O. *Democracy and the District of Columbia Public Schools: A Study of Recently Integrated Public Schools*. Washington, D.C.: Judd and Detweiler, 1957.

Kofie, Nelson. *Race, Class and the Struggle for Neighborhood in Washington, DC*. New York: Garland, 1999.

Kramer, Neil S. "The Trial of Reuben Crandall." *Records of the Columbia Historical Society* 50 (1980): 123–39.

Krislov, Samuel. *The Negro in Federal Employment: The Quest for Equal Opportunity*. Minneapolis: University of Minnesota Press, 1967.

Krugler, David. "A Mob in Uniform: Soldiers and Civilians in Washington's Red Summer, 1919." *Washington History* 21 (2009): 49–77.

———. *1919, the Year of Racial Violence: How African Americans Fought Back*. Cambridge: Cambridge University Press, 2014.

Kryder, Daniel. *Divided Arsenal: Race and the American State during World War II*. Cambridge: Cambridge University Press, 2001.

Kulikoff, Allan. *Tobacco and Slaves: The Development of Southern Cultures in the Chesapeake, 1680–1800*. Chapel Hill: University of North Carolina Press, 1986.

Kupperman, Karen, ed. *Captain John Smith: A Selected Edition of His Writings*. Chapel Hill: University of North Carolina Press, 1988.

Kurland, Philip B., and Gerhard Casper, eds. *Landmark Briefs and Arguments of the Supreme Court of the United States: Constitutional Law*. Vol. 49. Arlington, Va.: University Publications of America, 2008.

Laas, Virginia Jeans. *Wartime Washington: The Civil War Letters of Elizabeth Blair Lee*. Urbana: University of Illinois Press, 1991.

Lampl, Elizabeth Jo, and Kimberly Prothro Williams. *Chevy Chase: A Home Suburb for the Nation's Capital*. Crownsville: Maryland Historical Trust Press, 1998.

Langland, James, ed. *The Chicago Daily News Almanac and Year-Book for 1921*. Chicago: Chicago Daily News, 1920.

Laprade, William T. "The Domestic Slave Trade in the District of Columbia." *Journal of Negro History* 11, no. 1 (January 1926): 17–34.

La Rochefoucauld-Liancourt, François-Alexandre-Frédéric, Duc de. *Travels through the United States of America: The Country of the Iroquois, and Upper Canada, in the Years 1795, 1796, and 1797*. Vol. 2. London: R. Phillips, 1800.

Latham, Henry. *Black and White: A Journal of a Three-Months' Tour in the United States*. London: Macmillan, 1867.

Lauren, Paul Gordon. *Power and Prejudice: The Politics and Diplomacy of Racial Discrimination*. Boulder, Colo.: Westview, 1996.

Lavine, Amy. "Urban Renewal and the Story of *Berman v. Parker*." *Urban Lawyer* 42, no. 2 (Spring 2010): 423–75.

Lee, Antoinette J. "Asian and Asian American Students in the Washington, D.C., Public Schools during the Segregation Era." *Washington History* 28, no. 2 (Fall 2016): 34–53.

Leech, Margaret. *Reveille in Washington, 1860–1865*. 1942. New York: New York Review of Books, 2011.

Leepson, Marc. *What So Proudly We Hailed: Francis Scott Key, a Life*. New York: Palgrave MacMillan, 2014.

Lesko, Kathleen, Valarie Babb, and C. R. Gibbs. *Black Georgetown Remembered: A History of Its Black Community from the Founding of the "Town of George" in 1751 to the Present Day*. Washington, D.C.: Georgetown University Press, 1991.

Lessoff, Alan. *The Nation and Its City: Politics, "Corruption," and Progress, 1861–1902*. Baltimore: Johns Hopkins University Press, 1994.

———. "Washington Insider: The Early Career of Charles Moore." *Washington History* 6, no. 2 (Fall–Winter 1994–95): 64–80.

Lewis, Tom. *Washington: Our National City*. New York: Basic Books, 2015.

Lewis, Tony, Jr., and K. L. Reeves. *Slugg: A Boy's Life in the Age of Mass Incarceration*. Washington D.C.: Hanover Place Press, 2015.

Lindsay, Arnett J. "Diplomatic Relations between the United States and Great Britain Bearing on the Return of Negro Slaves, 1783–1828." *Journal of Negro History* 5, no. 4 (October 1920): 391–419.

Link, Arthur S., ed. *The Papers of Woodrow Wilson*. Vol. 28. Princeton, N.J.: Princeton University Press, 1978.

Lockwood, John, and Charles Lockwood. *The Siege of Washington: The Untold Story of the Twelve Days That Shook the Union*. Oxford: Oxford University Press, 2011.

Logan, Cameron. "Mrs. McCain's Parlor: House and Garden Tours and the Inner-City Restoration Trend in Washington, D.C." *Journal of Urban History* 39, no. 5 (2013): 956–74.

Logan, Mary. *Thirty Years in Washington*. Hartford, Conn.: A. D. Worthington, 1901.

Logan, Rayford W. *Howard University: The First Hundred Years, 1867–1967*. New York: New York University Press, 1969.

Lomax, Elizabeth Lindsay. *Leaves from an Old Washington Diary, 1854–1863*. New York: E. P. Dutton, 1943.

Lovejoy, J. C. *J. C. Lovejoy's Memoir of Charles T. Torrey*. Boston: John P. Jewett, 1847.

Lundy, Benjamin. *The Life, Travels, and Opinions of Benjamin Lundy*. Philadelphia: William D. Parrish, 1847.

Lusane, Clarence. *The Black History of the White House*. San Francisco: City Light Books, 2011.

———. *Pipe Dream Blues: Racism and the War on Drugs*. Boston: South End Press, 1991.

Lutz, Tom, and Susanna Ashton. *These "Colored" United States: African American Essays from the 1920s*. New Brunswick, N.J.: Rutgers University Press, 1996.

MacGregor, Morris J. *A Parish for the Federal City: St. Patrick's in Washington, 1794–1994*. Washington, D.C.: Catholic University of America Press, 1994.

Maddison, Catherine. "'In Chains 400 Years . . . and Still in Chains in DC!': The 1966 Free DC Movement and the Challenges of Organizing in the City." *Journal of American Studies*, 41 (2007): 169–92.

Mann, Alison T. "'Horrible Barbarity': The 1837 Murder Trial of Dorcas Allen, a Georgetown Slave." *Washington History* 27, no. 1 (Spring 2015): 3–14.

Manning, Chandra. *Troubled Refuge: Struggling for Freedom in the Civil War*. New York: Alfred A. Knopf, 2016.

Marable, Manning, ed. *Freedom on My Mind: The Columbia Documentary History of the African American Experience*. New York: Columbia University Press, 2003.

Masur, Kate. *An Example for All the Land: Emancipation and the Struggle for Equality in Washington, D.C.* Chapel Hill: University of North Carolina Press, 2011.

———. "Patronage and Protest in Kate Brown's Washington." *Journal of American History* 99, no. 4 (March 2013): 1047–71.

———. "A Rare Phenomenon of 'Philological Vegetation': The Word 'Contraband' and the Meanings of Emancipation in the United States." *Journal of American History* 94, no. 4 (2007): 1050–84.

Mattingly, Robert E. "Early Recollections and Reminiscences of South Washington: The Island." *Records of the Columbia Historical Society* 37/38 (1937): 101–22.

Maury, William M. *Alexander "Boss" Shepherd and the Board of Public Works.* Washington, D.C.: George Washington University, 1975.

Mayer, Henry. *All on Fire: William Lloyd Garrison and the Abolition of Slavery.* New York: St. Martin's Griffin, 1998.

McAleer, Margaret H. "'The Green Streets of Washington': The Experience of Irish Mechanics in Antebellum Washington." In *Urban Odyssey: A Multicultural History of Washington, D.C.,* edited by Francine Curro Cary, 42–62. Washington, D.C.: Smithsonian Institution Press, 1996.

McCardle, William. "The Development of the Business Sector, 1800–1973." *Records of the Columbia Historical Society* 73/74 (1973–74): 556–94.

McCluskey, Audrey Thomas. *A Forgotten Sisterhood: Pioneering Black Women Educators and Activists in the Jim Crow South.* Lanham, Md.: Rowman and Littlefield, 2014.

McCoy, Alfred. *Policing America's Empire: The United States, the Philippines, and the Rise of the Surveillance State.* Madison: University of Wisconsin Press, 2009.

McKean, William Vincent, ed. *The National Almanac and Annual Record for the Year 1863.* Philadelphia: George W. Childs, 1863.

McNeil, Genna Rae. *Groundwork: Charles Hamilton Houston and the Struggle for Civil Rights.* Philadelphia: University of Pennsylvania Press, 1983.

McQuirter, Marya Annette. "'Our Cause Is Marching On': Parent Activism, Browne Junior High School, and the Multiple Meanings of Equality in Post-War Washington." *Washington History* 16, no. 2 (Fall–Winter, 2004–5): 66–82.

Medford, Edna Greene. "'Some Satisfactory Way': Lincoln and Black Freedom in the District of Columbia." *Washington History* 21 (2009): 5–22.

Melder, Keith E. "Angel of Mercy in Washington: Josephine Griffing and the Freedmen, 1864–1872." *Records of the Columbia Historical Society* 63/65 (1963–65): 243–72.

———. *City of Magnificent Intentions.* Washington, D.C.: Intac, 1997.

Meriwether, C. "Washington City Government." *Political Science Quarterly* 12, no. 3 (September 1897): 407–19.

Merrell, James. "Cultural Continuity among the Piscataway Indians of Colonial Maryland." *William and Mary Quarterly,* 3rd ser., 36, no. 4 (October 1979): 548–70.

Meyer, Agnes E. *Journey through Chaos: America's Home Front.* New York: Harcourt, Brace, 1944.

Milburn, Page. "Fourth Ward." *Records of the Columbia Historical Society* 33/34 (1932): 61–69.

Miller, James. "Black Washington and the New Negro Renaissance." In *Composing Urban History and the Constitution of Civic Identities,* edited by John J. Czaplicka and Blair A.

Ruble, 219–41. Washington, D.C.: Woodrow Wilson Center and Johns Hopkins University Press, 2003.

Miller, Marion Mills, ed. *Life and Works of Abraham Lincoln.* Vol. 2. New York: Current Literature, 1907.

Miller, William Lee. *Arguing about Slavery: The Great Battle in the United States Congress.* New York: Alfred A. Knopf, 1996.

Modan, Gabriella Ghalia. *Turf Wars: Discourse Diversity, and the Politics of Place.* Malden, Mass.: Blackwell, 2007.

Molesworth, Charles. *The Works of Alain Locke.* New York: Oxford University Press, 2012.

Mooney, James. "Indian Tribes of the District of Columbia." *American Anthropologist* 2, no. 3 (July 1889): 259–66.

Moore, Charles. "Augustus Brevoort Woodward: A Citizen of Two Cities." *Records of the Columbia Historical Society* 4 (1901): 114–27.

Moore, Jacqueline M. *Leading the Race: The Transformation of the Black Elite in the Nation's Capital, 1880–1920.* Charlottesville: University Press of Virginia, 1995.

Moore, Joseph West. *Picturesque Washington.* Providence, R.I.: J. A. and R. A. Reid, 1887.

Moore, Thomas. *Epistles, Odes, and Other Poems.* Philadelphia: John Watts, 1806.

Morgan, Chester. *Redneck Liberal: Theodore G. Bilbo and the New Deal.* Baton Rouge: Louisiana State University Press, 1985.

Morley, Jefferson. *Snow-Storm in August: Washington City, Francis Scott Key, and the Forgotten Race Riot of 1835.* New York: Nan A. Talese, 2012.

Morris, J. Brent. *Oberlin: Hotbed of Abolitionism.* Chapel Hill: University of North Carolina Press, 2014.

Murphy, Mary-Elizabeth. *A National and Local Affair: African American Women and Political Activism in Washington, D.C., 1920–1945.* Chapel Hill: University of North Carolina Press, forthcoming.

Murray, Pauli. *Song in a Weary Throat: An American Pilgrimage.* New York: HarperCollins, 1987.

Musgrove, George Derek. *Rumor Repression and Racial Politics: How the Harassment of Black Elected Officials Shaped Post–Civil Rights America.* Athens: University of Georgia Press, 2012.

National Association of Intergroup Relations Officials. *Civil Rights in the Nation's Capital: A Report on a Decade of Progress.* Annandale, Va.: Turnpike Press, 1959.

National Capital Planning Commission, Frederick Gutheim, consultant. *Worthy of the Nation: The History of Planning for the National Capital.* Washington, D.C.: Smithsonian Institution Press, 1977.

National Committee on Segregation in the Nation's Capital and Kenesaw Mountain Landis. *Segregation in Washington: A Report.* Chicago, 1948.

National Freedman's Relief Association of the District of Columbia. *First Annual Report of the National Freedman's Relief Association of the District of Columbia.* Washington, D.C.: M'Gill and Witherow, 1863.

National Lincoln Monument Association. *Celebration by the Colored People's Educational Monument Association in Memory of Abraham Lincoln on the Fourth of July, 1865, in the Presidential Grounds, Washington, D.C.* Washington, D.C.: McGill and Witherow, 1865.

Neill, Edward D. *The English Colonization of America during the Seventeenth Century.* London: Strahan, 1871.

Newman, Jason, and Jacques B. DePuy. "Bringing Democracy to the Nation's Last Colony: The District of Columbia Self-Government Act." *American University Law Review* 24, no. 3 (Spring 1975): 537–747.

Newman, Richard S. *The Transformation of American Abolitionism: Fighting Slavery in the Early Republic.* Chapel Hill: University of North Carolina Press, 2002.

Newmyer, R. Kent. *John Marshall and the Heroic Age of the Supreme Court.* Baton Rouge: Louisiana State University Press, 2001.

Niemcewicz, Julian. *Under Their Vine and Fig Tree: Travels through America in 1797–1799, 1805.* Elizabeth, N.J.: Grassman, 1965.

Nichols, David A. *A Matter of Justice: Eisenhower and the Beginning of the Civil Rights Revolution.* New York: Simon and Schuster, 2007.

———. "'The Showpiece of Our Nation': Dwight D. Eisenhower and the Desegregation of the District of Columbia." *Washington History* 16, no. 2 (Fall–Winter 2004–5): 44–65.

Northup, Solomon. *Twelve Years a Slave.* 1853. New York: Penguin, 2013.

Noyes, Theodore W. *Our National Capital and Its Un-Americanized Americans.* Washington, D.C.: Washington Loan and Trust, 1951.

Null, Druscilla J. "Myrtilla Miner's 'School for Colored Girls': A Mirror on Antebellum Washington." *Records of the Columbia Historical Society* 52 (1989): 254–68.

O'Cleireacain, Carol. *The Orphaned Capital: Adopting the Right Revenues for the District of Columbia.* Washington, D.C.: Brookings Institution Press, 1997.

O'Connor, Ellen. *Myrtilla Miner: A Memoir.* Cambridge, Mass.: Riverside, 1885.

Olmsted, Frederick Law. *A Journey in the Seaboard Slave States in the Years 1853–1854.* Vol. 1. New York: J. P. Putnam and Sons, 1904.

Oppel, Frank, and Tony Meisel, eds. *Washington, D.C., a Turn-of-the-Century Treasury.* Seacaucus, N.J.: Castle, 1987.

Orbach, Barbara, and Nicholas Natanson. "The Mirror Image: Black Washington in World War II–Era Federal Photography." *Washington History* 4, no. 1 (Spring–Summer 1992): 4–25.

Osman, Suleiman. *The Invention of Brownstone Brooklyn: Gentrification and the Search for Authenticity in Postwar New York.* New York: Oxford University Press, 2012.

Osthaus, Carl R. *Freedmen, Philanthropy, and Fraud: A History of the Freedman's Savings Bank.* Urbana: University of Illinois Press, 1976.

Pacheco, Josephine F. *The Pearl: A Failed Slave Escape on the Potomac.* Chapel Hill: University of North Carolina Press, 2005.

Pacifico, Michelle. "'Don't Buy Where You Can't Work': The New Negro Alliance of Washington." *Washington History* 6, no. 1 (Spring–Summer 1994): 71–72.

Padover, Saul K. *Thomas Jefferson and the National Capital.* Washington, D.C.: USGPO, 1946.

Paige, Jerome S., and Margaret M. Reuss. *Safe, Decent and Affordable: Citizen Struggles to Improve Housing in the District of Columbia.* Washington, D.C.: Department of Urban Studies, University of the District of Columbia, 1983.

Palmer, Phyllis. *Living as Equals: How Three White Communities Struggled to Make Interracial*

Connections during the Civil Rights Era. Nashville, Tenn.: Vanderbilt University Press, 2008.

Parks, Gordon. *A Choice of Weapons*. St. Paul: Minnesota Historical Society Press, 1986.

Pasonneau, Joseph R. *Washington through Two Centuries: A History in Maps and Images*. New York: Monacelli, 2004.

Pearlman, Lauren. "More Than a March: The Poor People's Campaign in the District of Columbia." *Washington History* 26, no. 2 (Fall 2014): 24–41.

Pendergast, James F. *The Massawomeck: Raiders and Traders into the Chesapeake Bay in the Seventeenth Century*. Philadelphia: American Philosophical Society, 1991.

Petrilli, Michael. *The Diverse Schools Dilemma: A Parent's Guide to Socioeconomically Mixed Public Schools*. Washington, D.C.: Thomas B. Fordham Institute, 2012.

Philibert, Helene, Estelle, and Imogene. *Saint Matthew's of Washington, 1840–1940*. Baltimore: A. Hoen, 1940.

Pohl, Robert S. "Abraham Lincoln on Capitol Hill." In *Abraham Lincoln and the End of Slavery in the District of Columbia*, edited by Robert S. Pohl and John R. Wennersten, 17–26. Washington, D.C.: Eastern Branch Press, 2009.

Pohl, Robert S., and John R. Wennersten, eds. *Abraham Lincoln and the End of Slavery in the District of Columbia*. Washington, D.C.: Eastern Branch Press, 2009.

Polter, Julie. "Dreams, Schemes, and Plat Maps: Mary Logan and Columbia Heights." *Washington History* 19–20 (2007–8): 30–49.

Poore, Benjamin Perley. *Perley's Reminiscences of Sixty Years in the National Metropolis*. 2 vols. Philadelphia: Hubbard Brothers, 1886.

Powers-Greene, Ousmane. *Against Wind and Tide: The African American Struggle against the Colonization Movement*. New York: NYU Press, 2014.

Pritchett, Wendell E. "A National Issue: Segregation in the District of Columbia and the Civil Rights Movement at Mid-Century." Faculty Scholarship, Paper 1226. 2005. http://scholarship.law.upenn.edu/faculty_scholarship/1226.

Prout, Jerry. "Hope, Fear, and Confusion: Coxey's Arrival in Washington." *Washington History* 25 (Summer 2013): 1–19.

Provine, Dorothy. *Compensated Emancipation in the District of Columbia: Petitions under the Act of April 16, 1862*. Westminster, Md.: Willow Bend Books, 2005.

———. *District of Columbia Free Negro Registers, 1821–1861*. Bowie, Md.: Heritage Books, 1996.

———. "The Economic Position of the Free Blacks in the District of Columbia, 1800–1860." *Journal of Negro History* 58, no. 1 (January 1973): 61–72.

Quigley, Joan. *Just Another Southern Town: Mary Church Terrell and the Struggle for Racial Justice in the Nation's Capital*. New York: Oxford University Press, 2016.

Rader, Victoria. *Signal through the Flames: Mitch Snyder and America's Homeless*. Kansas City, Mo.: Sheed and Ward, 1986.

Rampersad, Arnold, and David Roessel, eds. *The Collected Poems of Langston Hughes*. New York: Alfred A. Knopf, 2004.

Redkey, Edwi, ed. *A Grand Army of Black Men: Letters from African-American Soldiers in the Union Army, 1861–1865*. Cambridge: Cambridge University Press, 1992.

Reidy, Joseph P. "'Coming from the Shadow of the Past': The Transition from Slavery to

Freedom at Freedmen's Village, 1863–1900." *Virginia Magazine of History and Biography* 95, no. 4 (October 1987): 403–28.

———. "The Winding Path to Freedom under the District of Columbia Emancipation Act of April 16, 1862." *Washington History* 26, no. 2 (Fall 2014): 18–22.

Repak, Terry A. *Waiting on Washington: Central American Workers in the Nation's Capital.* Philadelphia: Temple University Press, 1995.

Rhodes, Jones. *Mary Ann Shadd Cary: The Black Press and Protest in the Nineteenth Century.* Bloomington: Indiana University Press, 1998.

Rice, James D. *Nature and History in the Potomac Country: From Hunter-Gatherers to the Age of Jefferson.* Baltimore: Johns Hopkins University Press, 2009.

Richards, Mark David. "The Debates over the Retrocession of the District of Columbia, 1801–2004." *Washington History* 16, no. 1 (Spring–Summer 2004): 54–82.

Richardson, James D. *A Compilation of the Messages and Papers of the Presidents, 1789–1908.* Vol. 6. Washington, D.C.: Bureau of Literature and Art, 1909.

Richardson, John. "Alexander R. Shepherd and the Race Issue in Washington." *Washington History* 22, no. 1 (2010): 17–35.

Ricks, Mary Kay. *Escape on the Pearl: The Heroic Bid for Freedom on the Underground Railroad.* New York: HarperCollins, 2007.

Ridlon, Florence. *A Black Physician's Struggle for Civil Rights: Edward C. Mazique, M.D.* Santa Fe: University of New Mexico Press, 2005.

Riguer, Leah Wright. *The Loneliness of the Black Republican: Pragmatic Politics and the Pursuit of Power.* Princeton, N.J.: Princeton University Press, 2014.

Riley, Jerome. *The Philosophy of Negro Suffrage.* Washington, D.C.: The Author, 1897.

Ripley, C. Peter, ed. *The Black Abolitionist Papers.* Vol. 2. Chapel Hill: University of North Carolina Press, 2015.

Risen, Clay. *A Nation on Fire: America in the Wake of the King Assassination.* New York: John Wiley and Sons, 2009.

Robinson, Henry S. "The M Street High School, 1891–1916." *Records of the Columbia Historical Society* 51 (1984): 119–43.

Roe, Donald. "The Dual School System in the District of Columbia, 1862–1954: Origins, Problems, Protests." *Washington History* 16, no. 2 (Fall–Winter 2004–5): 26–43.

Rohal, Brian. "Mobilizing the Community in an Era before Social Media." *Washington History* 28, no. 1 (Spring 2016): 49–52.

Rohrs, Richard C. "Antislavery Politics and the Pearl Incident of 1848." *Historian* 56, no. 4 (Summer 1994): 711–24.

Ross, Charles K. *Outside the Lines: African Americans and the Integration of the National Football League.* New York: New York University Press, 1999.

Rossiter, Clinton, ed. *The Federalist Papers.* New York: Mentor, 1961.

Roundtree, Helen. *Pocahontas, Powhatan, Opechancanough: Three Indian Lives Changed by Jamestown.* Charlottesville: University of Virginia Press, 2005.

Royall, Anne. *The Black Book, or a Continuation of Travels in the United States.* Vol. 3. Washington, D.C.: The Author, 1829.

———. *Mrs. Royall's Pennsylvania, or Travels Continued in the United States.* Vol. 1. Washington, D.C.: The Author, 1829.

Ruble, Blair. *Washington's U Street: A Biography*. Baltimore: Johns Hopkins University Press, 2010.

Russell, Graham, and Gao Hodges. *David Ruggles: A Radical Black Abolitionist and the Underground Railroad in New York City*. Chapel Hill: University of North Carolina Press, 2010.

Russell, Hilary. *The Operation of the Underground Railroad in Washington, D.C., c. 1800–1860*. Washington, D.C.: Historical Society of Washington D.C. and the National Park Service, July 2001.

———. "Underground Railroad Activists in Washington, D.C." *Washington History* (Fall–Winter 2001–2): 28–49.

Salvatore, Susan Cianci, and John H. Sprinkle Jr. *National Historic Landmark Nomination: John Philip Sousa Junior High School*. Washington, D.C.: National Park Service, 2001.

Sandage, Scott. "A Marble House Divided: The Lincoln Memorial, the Civil Rights Movement, and the Politics of Memory, 1939–1963." In *Time Longer Than Rope: A Century of African American Activism, 1850–1950*, edited by Charles M. Payne and Adam Green, 492–535. New York: New York University Press, 2003.

Savage, Kirk. *Monument Wars: Washington, D.C., the National Mall, and the Transformation of the Memorial Landscape*. Berkeley: University of California Press, 2009.

Sawvel, Franklin B., ed. *The Complete Anas of Thomas Jefferson*. New York: Round Table Press, 1903.

Schaffer, Dana Lanier. "The 1968 Washington Riots in History and Memory." *Washington History* 15, no. 2 (Fall–Winter 2003–4): 4–33.

Schrag, Philip G. *Behind the Scenes: The Politics of a Constitutional Convention*. Washington, D.C.: Georgetown University Press, 1985.

Schrag, Zachary. "The Freeway Fight in Washington, D.C.: The Three Sisters Bridge in Three Administrations." *Journal of Urban History* 30 (July 2004): 648–73.

———. *The Great Society Subway: A History of the Washington Metro*. Baltimore: Johns Hopkins University Press, 2006.

Schultz, Nancy Lusignan. *Mrs. Mattingly's Miracle: The Prince, the Widow, and the Cure That Shocked Washington City*. New Haven, Conn.: Yale University Press, 2011.

Scott, Emmett Jay. *Scott's Official History of the American Negro in the World War*. New York: Andesite Press, 1919.

Seale, William. *The President's House: A History*. 1986. Baltimore: Johns Hopkins University Press, 2008.

Seaton, Josephine. *William Winston Seaton of the "National Intelligencer."* Boston: James R. Osgood, 1871.

Semmes, Raphael. *Captains and Mariners of Early Maryland*. Baltimore: Johns Hopkins University Press, 1937.

Shade, William, and Ballard Campbell, eds. *American Presidential Campaigns and Elections*. Vol. 3. Armonk, N.Y.: M. E. Sharpe, 2003.

Sharfstein, Daniel J. *The Invisible Line: Three American Families and the Secret Journey from Black to White*. New York: Penguin, 2011.

Sharp, John G., transcriber. *The Diary of Michael Shiner Relating to the History of the Washington Navy Yard, 1813–1869*. Washington, D.C.: Department of the Navy, 2007.

Sherwood, Henry Noble. "The Formation of the American Colonization Society." *Journal of Negro History* 2, no. 3 (July 1917): 209–28.

Siegel, Fred. *The Future Once Happened Here: New York, D.C., L.A., and the Fate of America's Big Cities*. New York: Free Press, 1997.

Simmons, William J. *Men of Mark: Eminent, Progressive and Rising*. Cleveland: Geo. M. Rewell, 1887.

Singer, Audrey, et al. *The World in a Zip Code: Greater Washington, D.C. as a New Region of Immigration*. Washington, D.C.: Brookings Institution, 1998.

Sinha, Manisha. *The Slave's Cause: A History of Abolition*. New Haven, Conn.: Yale University Press, 2016.

Sitkoff, Harvard. "African American Militancy in the World War II South: Another Perspective." In *Remaking Dixie: The Impact of World War II on the American South*, edited by Neil McMillen, 70–92. Jackson: University Press of Mississippi, 1997.

Smallwood, Thomas. *A Narrative of Thomas Smallwood (Coloured Man)*. . . . Toronto: James Stephens, 1851.

Smith, C. Fraser. *Lenny, Lefty, and the Chancellor: The Len Bias Tragedy and the Search for Reform in Big-time College Basketball*. Baltimore: Bancroft, 1992.

Smith, Jessie Carney, ed. *Notable Black Women*. Book 2. New York: Gale Research, 1996.

Smith, John. *A True Relation of Such Occurrences and Accidents of Note as Hath Hapned in Virginia since the First Planting of That Colony*. . . . London: John Tappe, 1608.

Smith, Kathryn Schneider, ed. *Washington at Home: An Illustrated History of Neighborhoods in the Nation's Capital*. Baltimore: Johns Hopkins University Press, 2010.

Smith, Sam. *Captive Capital: Colonial Life in Modern Washington*. Bloomington: Indiana University Press, 1974.

———. *Multitudes: The Unauthorized Memoir*. N.d., http://prorev.com/mmintrol.htm.

———. *The Statehood Papers: Articles on Statehood by Sam Smith, 1970–1991*. Washington, D.C.: Progressive Review, 1993.

Smith, Thomas G. "Civil Rights on the Gridiron: The Kennedy Administration and the Desegregation of the Washington Redskins." *Journal of Sports History* 14, no. 2 (Summer 1987): 189–208.

Smolenyak, Megan. "The Slave Who Rescued Freedom." *Ancestry* 27, no. 3 (May–June 2009): 54–56.

Snethen, Worthington G. *The Black Code of the District of Columbia, in Force September 1st 1848*. New York: American and Foreign Anti-Slavery Society, 1848.

Solomon, Burt. *The Washington Century: Three Families and the Shaping of the Nation's Capital*. New York: William Morrow, 2004.

Sparks, Jared, ed. *The Writings of George Washington*. 12 vols. Boston: Russell, Shattuck, and Williams, 1833–37.

Spofford, Ainsworth, and William Wirt Henry. *Eminent and Representative Men of Virginia and the District of Columbia of the Nineteenth Century*. Madison, Wis.: Brant and Fuller, 1893.

Stein, Annie. "The Thompson Case: A Real Life Bread-and-Butter Struggle." In *The National Lawyers Guild: From Roosevelt through Reagan*, edited by Ann Fagan Ginger and Eugene M. Tobin, 104–6. Philadelphia: Temple University Press, 1988.

Stephanic, Jean, and Richard Delgado. *No Mercy: How Conservative Think Tanks and Foundations Changed America's Social Agenda.* Philadelphia: Temple University Press, 1996.

Stewart, Alison. *First Class: The Legacy of Dunbar, America's First Black Public High School.* Chicago: Chicago Review Press, 2013.

Stewart, James B. "Christian Statesmanship, Codes of Honor, and Congressional Violence: The Antislavery Trials and Triumphs of Joshua Giddings." In *In the Shadow of Freedom: The Politics of Slavery in the National Capital,* edited by Paul Finkelman and Donald R. Kennon, 36–57. Athens: Ohio University Press, 2011.

Still, William. *The Underground Railroad.* Philadelphia: Porter and Coates, 1872.

Stowe, Harriet. *Key to Uncle Tom's Cabin.* Boston: John P. Jewett, 1853.

Streitmatter, Rodger. *Raising Her Voice: African-American Women Journalists Who Changed History.* Lexington: University Press of Kentucky, 1994.

Sturge, Joseph. *A Visit to the United States in 1841.* London: Hamilton, Adams, 1842.

Sullivan, Patricia. *Lift Every Voice: The NAACP and the Making of the Civil Rights Movement.* New York: New Press, 2009.

Sumner, Charles. *The Works of Charles Sumner.* 15 vols. Boston: Lee and Shepard, 1880.

Tadman, Michael. *Speculators and Slaves: Masters, Traders, and Slaves in the Old South.* Madison: University of Wisconsin Press, 1989.

Taylor, Alan. "American Blacks in the War of 1812." In *The Routledge Handbook of the War of 1812,* edited by Donald R. Hickey and Connie D. Clark, 193–207. New York: Routledge, 2016.

Teaford, Jon C. *The Twentieth-Century American City.* Baltimore: Johns Hopkins University Press, 1993.

Terrell, Mary Church. *A Colored Woman in a White World.* 1940. Amherst, N.Y.: Humanity Books, 2005.

Thomas, Hugh. *The Slave Trade: The Story of the Atlantic Slave Trade, 1440–1870.* New York: Touchstone Books, 1997.

Thursz, Daniel. *Where Are They Now?* Washington, D.C.: Health and Welfare Council of the National Capital Area, 1966.

Tindall, William. "A Sketch of Alexander Robey Shepherd." *Records of the Columbia Historical Society* 14 (1911): 49–66.

———. "A Sketch of Mayor Sayles J. Bowen." *Records of the Columbia Historical Society* 18 (1915): 25–43.

———. *Standard History of the City of Washington.* Knoxville, Tenn.: H. W. Crew, 1914.

Todd, Charles Burr. *The Story of Washington: The National Capital.* New York: G. P. Putnam's Sons, 1889.

Torrey, Jesse. *A Portraiture of Domestic Slavery, in the United States. . . .* Philadelphia: John Bioren, 1817.

Tremain, Mary. *Slavery in the District of Columbia.* New York: G. P. Putnam's Sons, 1892.

Tucker, Sterling. *Beyond the Burning: Life and Death of the Ghetto.* New York: Association Press, 1968.

Twohig, Dorothy, Mark A. Mastromarino, and Jack D. Warren, eds. *The Papers of George Washington. Presidential Series.* Vol. 5. Charlottesville: University Press of Virginia, 1996.

Ullery, Jacob, comp. *Men of Vermont: An Illustrated Biography of Vermonters and Sons of Vermont.* Brattleboro, Vt.: Transcript, 1894.

Unger, Nancy C. "'When Women Condemn the Whole Race': Belle Case La Follette's Women's Column Attacks the Color Line." In *Women in Print: Essays on the Print Culture of American Women from the Nineteenth and Twentieth Centuries,* edited by James P. Dany and Wayne A. Wiegand, 281–98. Madison: University of Wisconsin Press, 2006.

Valk, Anne M. *Radical Sisters: Second-Wave Feminism and Black Liberation in Washington, D.C.* Urbana-Champaign: University of Illinois Press, 2008.

Vandervelde, Lea. *Redemption Songs: Suing for Freedom before Dred Scott.* Oxford: Oxford University Press, 2014.

Vaughan, Alden. "Expulsion of the Savages: English Policy and the Virginia Massacre of 1622." *William and Mary Quarterly,* 3rd ser., 35, no. 1 (January 1978): 57–84.

Vose, Clement E. *Caucasians Only: The Supreme Court, the NAACP, and the Restrictive Covenant Cases.* Berkeley: University of California Press, 1959.

————. "When District of Columbia Representation Collides with the Constitutional Amendment Institution." *Publius* 9, no. 1 (Winter 1979): 105–25.

Walker, Anders. "Blackboard Jungle: Delinquency, Desegregation, and the Cultural Politics of Brown." *Columbia Law Review* 110, no. 7 (2010): 1911–53.

Walker, David. *Walker's Appeal, in Four Articles; Together with a Preamble, to the Coloured Citizens of the World.* 1830. Chapel Hill, N.C.: DocSouth Books, 2011.

Walters, Ronald, and Toni-Michelle Travis, eds. *Democratic Destiny and the District of Columbia: Federal Politics and Public Policy.* Lanham, Md.: Lexington Books, 2010.

Walsh, Richard, and William Lloyd Fox, eds. *Maryland, a History, 1632–1974.* Baltimore: Maryland Historical Society, 1974.

Ward, Jason Morgan. *Defending White Democracy: The Making of a Segregationist Movement and the Remaking of Racial Politics, 1936–1965.* Chapel Hill: University of North Carolina Press, 2011.

————. "The 1956 D.C. School Hearings and the National Vision of Massive Resistance." *Journal of Civil and Human Rights* 1 (Spring–Summer 2015): 82–110.

Warden, D. B. *A Chorographical and Statistical Description of the District of Columbia.* Paris: Smith Rue Montmercy, 1816.

Ware, Susan, ed. *Notable American Women: A Biographical Dictionary.* Vol. 5. Cambridge, Mass.: Harvard University Press, 2004.

Warner, William W. *At Peace with All Their Neighbors: Catholics and Catholicism in the Nation's Capital, 1787–1860.* Washington, D.C.: Georgetown University Press, 1994.

Washington, George. "Letters of George Washington Bearing on the Negro." *Journal of Negro History* 2, no. 4 (October 1917): 411–22.

————. *Writings.* New York: Library of America, 1997.

Washington, James M., ed. *A Testament of Hope: The Essential Writings and Speeches of Martin Luther King, Jr.* San Francisco: HarperSanFrancisco, 1986.

Waskow, Arthur I. *From Race Riot to Sit-In, 1919 and the 1960s: A Study in the Connections between Conflict and Violence.* New York: Doubleday, 1966.

Webb, William Benning, John Wooldridge, and Harvey W. Crew. *Centennial History of the City of Washington, D.C.* Dayton, Ohio: United Brethren, 1892.

Weld, Charles Richard. *A Vacation Tour in the United States and Canada*. London: Longman, Brown, Green, and Longmans, 1855.

Weld, Issac, Jr. *Travels through the States of North America and the Provinces of Lower Canada, during 1795, 1796, and 1797*. 4th ed. London: John Stockdale, 1800.

Weller, Charles Frederick. *Neglected Neighbors*. Philadelphia: John C. Winston, 1909.

Wennersten, John. *Anacostia: The Death and Life of an American River*. Baltimore: Chesapeake Book, 2008.

Whitmire, Richard. *The Bee Eater: Michelle Rhee Takes on the Nation's Worst School District*. New York: Jossey-Bass, 2011.

Whyte, James H. "The District of Columbia Territorial Government, 1871–1874." *Records of the Columbia Historical Society* 51/52 (1951–52): 87–102.

———. "Divided Loyalties in Washington during the Civil War." *Records of the Columbia Historical Society* 60/62 (1960–62): 103–22.

Wiencek, Henry. *Imperfect God: George Washington, His Slaves, and the Creation of America*. New York: Farrar, Straus and Giroux, 2003.

Wilcox, Delos F. *Great Cities in America: Their Problems and Their Government*. New York: MacMillan, 1910.

William, Jay. *Miscellaneous Writings on Slavery*. Boston: John P. Jewett, 1853.

Williams, Brett. *Upscaling Downtown: Stalled Gentrification in Washington, D.C.* Ithaca, N.Y.: Cornell University Press, 1988.

Williams, Chad L. *Torchbearers of Democracy: African American Soldiers in the World War I Era*. Chapel Hill: University of North Carolina Press, 2010.

Williams, George Washington. *The History of the Negro Race in America, from 1619 to 1880*. Vol. 2. New York: G. P. Putnam's Sons, 1883.

Williams, Melvin R. "A Blueprint for Change: The Black Community in Washington, D.C., 1860–1870." *Records of the Columbia Historical Society* 71/72 (1971–72): 359–93.

Wilson, Sondra Kathryn, ed. *The Opportunity Reader: Stories, Poetry, and Essays from the Urban League's Opportunity Magazine*. New York: Modern Library, 1999.

Winkle, Kenneth J. *Lincoln's Citadel: The Civil War in Washington, DC*. New York: W. W. Norton, 2013.

Withey, Lynne. *Dearest Friend: A Life of Abigail Adams*. New York: Touchstone, 2002.

Wolters, Raymond. *The Burden of Brown: Thirty Years of School Desegregation*. Knoxville: University of Tennessee Press, 1984.

Woodson, Carter G. *The History of the Negro Church*. Washington, D.C.: Associated Publishers, 1921.

Work, Monroe N., ed. *Negro Year Book: An Annual Encyclopedia of the Negro, 1914–1915*. Tuskegee, Ala.: Negro Year Book, 1915.

Wormley, G. Smith. "Myrtilla Miner." *Journal of Negro History* 5, no. 4 (October 1920): 448–57.

Wright, James D. *The Language of the Civil War*. Westport, Conn.: Oryx, 2001.

Wright, Mary Herring. *Far from Home: Memories of World War II and Afterward*. Washington, D.C.: Gallaudet University Press, 2005.

Yellin, Eric S. *Racism in the Nation's Service: Government Workers and the Color Line in Woodrow Wilson's America*. Chapel Hill: University of North Carolina Press, 2013.

————. "'It Was Still No South to Us': African American Civil Servants at the Fin de Siècle." *Washington History* 21 (2009): 22–47.

Young, James Sterling. *The Washington Community, 1800–1828.* New York: Columbia University Press, 1966.

Zigas, Eli. "Left with Few Rights: Unequal Democracy and the District of Columbia." Washington, D.C.: D.C. Vote, Creative Commons, 2008.

Theses, Dissertations, and Unpublished Papers

Altenhofel, Jennifer Lynn. "Keeping House: Irish and Irish-American Women in the District of Columbia, 1850–1890." Ph.D. diss., American University, 2004.

Barnes, William Robert. "The Origins of Urban Renewal: The Public Housing Controversy and the Emergence of a Redevelopment Program in the District of Columbia, 1942–1949." Ph.D. diss., Syracuse University, 1977.

Baruti, Jahi. "The Control Board Era in the District of Columbia Government and Politics, 1995–2001." Ph.D. diss., Howard University, 2003.

Bell, Felicia. "'The Negroes Alone Work': Enslaved Craftsmen, the Building Trades, and the Construction of the U.S. Capitol, 1790–1800." Ph.D. diss., Howard University, 2009.

Bernard, Rachel Deborah. "These Separate Schools: Black Politics and Education in Washington, D.C., 1900–1930." Ph.D. diss., University of California—Berkeley, 2012.

Borchardt, Gregory M. "Making D.C. Democracy's Capital: Local Activism, the 'Federal State,' and the Struggle for Civil Rights in Washington, D.C." Ph.D. diss., George Washington University, 2013.

Cadaval, Olivia. "The Hispano-American Festival and the Latino Community: Creating an Identity in the Nation's Capital." Ph.D. diss., George Washington University, 1989.

Collins, Donald E. "'A Substance of Things Hoped For': Multiculturalism, Desegregation, and Identity in African American Washington, D.C., 1930–1960." Ph.D. diss., Carnegie Mellon University, 1997.

Corrigan, Mary Beth. "A Social Union of Heart and Effort: The African-American Family in the District of Columbia on the Eve of Emancipation." Ph.D. diss., University of Maryland, 1996.

Costanzos, Adam Robert. "Federal Town, Local City: Building a Home and a National Capital in Early Washington, DC, 1790–1850." Ph.D. diss., University of California–Davis, 2012.

Coulibaly, Sylvie. "Kelly Miller, 1895–1939: Portrait of an African American Intellectual." Ph.D. diss., Emory University, 2006.

Crawford, Aaron Scott. "John Randolph of Roanoke and the Politics of Doom: Slavery, Sectionalism, and Self-Deception, 1773–1821." Ph.D. diss., University of Tennessee, 2012.

De Boer, Clara Merritt. "The Role of Afro-Americans in the Origin and Work of the American Missionary Association, 1839–1877." Ph.D. diss., Rutgers University, 1973.

Fant, Barbara Gale Howick. "Slum Reclamation and Housing Reform in the Nation's Capital, 1890–1940." Ph.D. diss., George Washington University, 1982.

Fox, Early Lee. "The American Colonization Society, 1817–1840." Ph.D. diss., Johns Hopkins University, 1917.

Gale, Dennis. "Restoration in Georgetown, Washington, D.C. 1915 to 1965." Ph.D. diss., George Washington University, 1982.

Gooding, Frederick W. "A Dream Deferred: Black Federal Workers in Washington, D.C., 1941–1981." Ph.D. diss., Georgetown University, 2013.

Gueli, Cynthia. "'Girls on the Loose'? Women's Wartime Adventures in the Nation's Capital, 1941–1945." Ph.D. diss., American University, 2006.

Hamilton, Tikia K. "Making a 'Model' System: Race, Education and Politics in the Nation's Capital before Brown, 1930–1950." Ph.D. diss., Princeton University, 2015.

Harding, Mary Elizabeth. "Eleanor Nelson, Oliver Palmer and the Struggle to Organize the CIO in Washington, D.C., 1937–1950." Ph.D. diss., George Washington University, 2002.

Heard, Sandra Rena. "The 'Bad' Black Consumer: A Study of African-American Consumer Culture in Washington, D.C., 1910s–1930s." Ph.D. diss., George Washington University, 2010.

Hickey, Matthew Edward. "Irish Catholics in Washington up to 1860: A Social Study." M.A. thesis, Catholic University of America, 1933.

Horton, Lois E. "The Development of Federal Social Policy for Blacks in Washington, D.C., after Emancipation." Ph.D. diss., Brandeis University, 1977.

Huron, Amanda. "The Work of the Urban Commons: Limited-Equity Cooperatives in Washington, D.C." Ph.D. diss., City University of New York, 2012.

Johnson, Thomas Reed. "The City on the Hill: Race Relations in Washington, D.C., 1865–1885." Ph.D. diss., University of Maryland, 1975.

Kolker, Carole Abrams. "Migrants and Memories: Family, Work, and Community among Blacks, Eastern European Jews, and Native-Born Whites in an Early Twentieth Century Washington, D.C., Neighborhood." Ph.D. diss., George Washington University, 1997.

Kramer, Neil. "Half a Century Past Midnight: The Life and Times of William Cranch." Ph.D. diss., Claremont Graduate School, 1978.

Levey, Jane Freundel. "Segregation in Education: A Basis for Jim Crow in Washington, D.C., 1804–1880." M.A. thesis, George Washington University, 1991.

Lunn, Maxine Pitter. "Community at a Crossroads: Latino Community Participation in Agenda Setting in Washington, D.C." Ph.D. diss., George Mason University, 1996.

McQuirter, Marya Annette. "Claiming the City: African Americans, Urbanization, and Leisure in Washington, D.C., 1902–1957." Ph.D. diss., University of Michigan, 2000.

Mellis, Delia Cunningham. "'The Monsters We Defy': Washington, D.C., in the Red Summer of 1919." Ph.D. diss., City University of New York, 2008.

Montgomery, Dee Ann. "An Intellectual Profile of Belle Case La Follette: Progressive Editor, Political Strategist and Feminist." Ph.D. diss., Indiana University, 1975.

Pearlman, Lauren. "Democracy's Capital: Local Protest, National Politics, and the Struggle for Civil Rights in Washington, D.C." Ph.D. diss., Yale University, 2013.

Quinn, Kelly Anne. "Making Modern Homes: A History of Langston Terrace Dwellings, a New Deal Housing Program in Washington, D.C." Ph.D. diss., University of Maryland, 2007.

Schaffer, Samuel Lonsdale. "New South Nation: Woodrow Wilson's Generation and the Rise of the South, 1884–1920." Ph.D. diss., Yale University, 2010.

Schmidt, Sandra K. "On Being Black in an Overwhelmingly White Police Department." Paper presented at the 38th Annual Conference on D.C. Historical Studies, November 5, 2011.

Terry, David. "A Brief Moment in the Sun: The Aftermath of Emancipation in Washington, D.C." Paper presented at the annual meeting of the Association for the Study of African American Life and History, Charlotte, N.C., 15 Dec. 2013.

Thomas, William G., III. "'They Brought Me Away': A Slave Sale and the Ordeal of Ann Williams." Paper presented at the D.C. Historical Studies Conference, Washington, D.C., November 2015.

Thurber, Bert H. "The Negro at the Nation's Capital, 1913–1921." Ph.D. diss., Yale University, 1973.

Varel, David A. "John Davis versus Woodrow Wilson: Racism and Resilience in the Nation's Civil Service, 1882–1928." Unpublished manuscript in the possession of the author.

Walker, Lewis Newton, Jr. "The Struggles and Attempts to Establish Branch Autonomy and Hegemony: A History of the DC Branch of the NAACP, 1912–1942." Ph.D. diss., University of Delaware, 1979.

Walton-Haley, Jennifer A. "Reversing the Middle Passage: The American Colonization Society and Race Relations, 1816–1964." Ph.D. diss., University of Kentucky, 2009.

Warnke, Christine Matilda. "Greek American Community of Washington, D.C. (1890–1935): Implications of Ingrouping." Ph.D. diss., University of Maryland College Park, 1993.

Wells, Katie. "A Decent Place to Stay: Housing Crises, Failed Laws, and Property Conflicts in Washington D.C." Ph.D. diss., Syracuse University, 2013.

Films and Radio

A. Smith and Co. *American Gangster: Rayful Edmond.* Documentary. BET, 2007.

Chappelle, Dave. *Killin' Them Softly.* Comedy special. HBO, 2000.

Durrin, Ginny. *Promises to Keep.* Documentary. WETA, 1988.

Fenston, Jacob, et al. *Crack: The Drug That Consumed the Nation's Capital.* Five-part radio series. WAMU, January 27, 2014.

Flor, Dana. *The Nine Lives of Marion Barry.* Documentary. HBO, 2009.

Frasier, Kirk. *Without Bias.* Documentary. ESPN, 2009.

Joseloff, Michael. "The Education of Michelle Rhee." *Frontline,* WBGH/Boston, 3 January 2013.

INDEX

commissioner, 335; and United Planning
Organization, 347; and Lyndon Johnson, 351
Commission of Fine Arts, 200
Committee against Segregation in Recreation, 293
Committee for Racial Democracy in the Nation's
Capital, 292–93, 307
Committee for the Aid and Development of
Spanish-Speaking Disadvantaged Minority in
the District of Columbia, 373
Committee of One Hundred, 193–94
Committee of 100 Ministers, 100
Committee of 100 on the Federal City, 363, 366
Committee on Jobs for Negroes in Public Utilities,
278
Committee to Recall Mayor Barry, 433–34
Communist Party, 265, 267, 297–98
Community Chest, 252, 255, 260
Community control (of police), 366–70
Commuter tax, 440
Compromise of 1850, 93, 96, 97, 99
Compromise of 1877, 167, 171
Confederacy: and enslaved people, 111, 122;
prisoners from, 125; Republican views of, 136;
and Andrew Johnson, 146; sympathizers of,
146; government of, 171; and D.C. suffrage,
176; comparison to segregationists after
World War II, 288
Confederate army, 108, 111, 122, 124, 126, 176:
D.C. residents join, 107; D.C. fears of invasion
by, 107–8, 124
Confiscation Act, 111
Congress: D.C. lack of representation in, 1,
49, 344, 380; controls D.C., 2–3, 34–38,
122, 149, 187, 194, 198, 336, 353, 388, 398;
strips D.C. residents of voting power, 18;
chooses site of capital, 18–20, 24–26, 34;
stinginess of, 30, 66–67, 158, 199, 269; and
black codes, 45, 62; and slave trade in D.C.,
55–56; and colonization, 57, 116; black
visitors to, 58; and black Washingtonians,
62–63, 69; and city vagrants, 65; changes
city charter, 66; considers relocating capital,
66; and retrocession, 67–68, 89; and slavery,
71–76, 81–82, 86–89, 91–93, 97–99; and
suffrage, 97, 173–76, 181, 184; and
development in D.C., 99–100, 135–36, 158;
and Know-Nothings, 103; and fugitives
from slavery, 111; and Blue Jug, 111, 114; and
emancipation, 114–18; and black suffrage,
121, 141–46; and public schools, 131, 170, 208,
214–16, 309, 311–13, 317, 377; and streetcars,
134; Henry Highland Garnet speaks to,
134–35, 238; and Radical Reconstruction,
136–41, 156, 164; and black employment, 148;
and black office holding, 148, 154, 208; and
consolidation movement, 157, 160; and city
charter, 158; investigates Alexander Shephard,
163, 165; revokes D.C. self-government,
165–68, 172–73; and Board of Trade, 194–95,
213; and McMillan Plan, 200–201; and alleys,

203–5, 254–56, 263; and segregation in D.C.,
209, 220, 225, 247–48, 286, 288–89, 292–93,
299, 301–2; and Bureau of Engraving and
Printing, 218; and World War I, 228; and Great
Depression, 250; and Chinatown, 257; and
local reformers, 260; and D.C. police, 267,
369–70; and home rule, 270, 303, 318, 344,
346–47, 351, 379–80; and Marian Anderson
concert, 272; and D.C. civil rights bill, 279;
segregationists in, 317, 336–37; and urban
renewal, 321–22; fears racial violence, 352;
and highway funding, 360–66 passim; and
Latino residents, 375; and nonvoting delegate,
378; and statehood, 378–79, 417–20; and D.C.
Voting Rights Amendment, 380–81; and white
fears of black power, 381–82; and drugs,
402, 404; funds D.C. government, 413; takes
over D.C., 422–23, 429–37; and D.C. General
Hospital, 436; and commuter tax, 440; and
charter schools, 448–49
Congress Heights (neighborhood), 330–31, 353,
442
Congress Heights Citizens Association, 295
Congressional Cemetery, 167
Congress of Industrial Organizations, 263,
265–66, 268
Congress of Racial Equality (CORE), 333–34,
337–39
Congress of the Confederation, 19
Connaughton, John, 290
Connecticut Avenue, 161, 164, 247
Conococheague Creek, 24
Consolidated Parent Group, 308, 310–12
Constitution, D.C., 417–418
Constitution, U.S.: and creation of D.C., 2, 18–20;
and slavery, 22–23, 51, 54; and D.C. suffrage,
35, 174, 380; and free black residents, 58, 61,
63–64; and Civil War, 107; and black suffrage,
154; and racial equality, 206, 267, 301, 313
Constitutional Convention (D.C.), 417–18
Constitutional Convention of 1787, 20, 22–23
Constitutional Union, 134
Constitution Hall, 271–72
Continental Army, 19
"Contraband,", 110–11, 137
"Contraband" camps, 125–26
Contraband Fund, 125
Contraband Relief Association, 124
Cook, George F. T., 214
Cook, John F., 44, 68–70, 76, 78, 83, 96, 172
Cook, John F., Jr.: and Social, Civil, and Statistical
Association, 116; education of, 128–29; and
Civil War, 129; and post–Civil War politics,
132, 135, 143, 147, 150–51; and Sayles
Bowen, 158; in territorial government, 161;
prominence of, 171; and black suffrage, 173–
74; and George F. T. Cook, 214
Cooke, Henry, 160–61, 164–65
Cooke, Jay, 164–65
Cooke, Paul, 310

Hodge, Lena, 296
Holland, Jerry, 31
Holy Trinity Church, 45
Homebuilders' Association of Metropolitan Washington, 321
Home Defense League, 232
Home Owners Committee of the Citizens Association of Georgetown, 259
Home rule: lack of, 1, 49, 194, 337, 344; loss of, 18, 35–38, 167–68, 172–73, 184, 433–34, 438; expansion of, 66; and black codes, 82–83; and racial equality, 144; D.C. residents considered incapable of, 152, 163; controversies over, 154; consolidation movement undermines, 156–58; advocates support, 160–61, 174–75, 181, 193–94; arguments against return of, 175–76; racial divisions in perceptions of, 175–76, 270, 381–82; and citizens associations, 192–93; and Board of Trade, 195; presidential endorsements of, 303, 344, 351; and racial integration, 318; and Congress, 318, 398, 423, 431; activists push for, 325, 393, 421, 462; and Marion Barry / Free D.C., 343–47; and 1967 government reorganization, 351; city regains, 376, 379–80, 388; and campaign for D.C. Voting Rights Amendment, 380–81; and fight against displacement, 383; and elections, 385; and city bureaucracy, 395; and Republicans, 400, 422; diminished hopes for, 424; and Financial Control Board, 430–34, 436; uneasy return to, 434–38
Hooks, Benjamin, 411
Hoover, Herbert, 251
Hope Division, 153
Hopkins, Charlotte, 222
Hopkinson, Natalie, 461
Horn, Etta Mae, 348–49
House Committee on the District of Columbia, 72–73, 145, 309, 316, 336, 379
House Committee on Un-American Activities, 298
House of Delegates: D.C., 160, 163, 166; Virginia, 89
Housing: activists push for, 2, 136, 251, 260, 283, 294, 396; as social problem, 4, 280, 318; for enslaved workers, 32–33; for Irish immigrants, 100; shortage of, 123, 189, 227; for freedpeople, 125; and Freedmen's Bureau, 136–38; in Southwest D.C., 153, 247, 321–22; in alleys, 179, 202, 227, 252–57, 445; discrimination in, 209, 227, 243–44, 272, 281, 294–304, 326, 335–38, 440; and benefit of passing, 240–41; restrictive covenants on, 244–46, 281, 294–97; during Depression, 250; segregation of, 258–59, 286, 290, 299; conditions of, 280–81; and federal government, 281; white resistance to integrated, 282; during World War II, 282–83; and fears of displacement, 283; redlining of, 290–91; and urban renewal, 322–25;

desegregation of, 326, 331; and Neighbors, Inc., 328–29; Walter Washington's experience with, 352; and riots, 359; for Latino residents, 372–73; and statehood activists, 378; and gentrification, 382–84, 439–46; and Bates Street Project, 394–95; in Chinatown, 428; in suburbs, 429; and new development, 429, 454–55
Housing and Home Finance Agency, 323
Housing reform movement: and private investment, 202; effort to eliminate alleys, 200–206 passim, 222, 227, 252–57, 445
Houston, Charles Hamilton: and World War I, 228, 287; and 1930s protests, 251; and New Negro Alliance, 262; and Marian Anderson Citizens' Committee, 271; background of, 287–88; and NAACP legal strategy, 288–89; and Cold War, 292; and housing segregation, 295–97; and *Segregation in Washington*, 298; and antidiscrimination laws, 300; death of, 300, 311–12; and Gardner Bishop, 308–9; legacy of, 388
Hovey, Charles, 177
Howard, Clinton, 270
Howard, Clyde, 443
Howard, O. O., 120, 136, 138–39, 270
Howard, Thomas, 61
Howard Hill Aid Society, 169
Howard Players, 240
Howard Theater, 230, 242
Howardtown, 186–87, 204
Howard University: founding of, 139; first professor at, 160; as magnet for black migration, 169; educator Amzi Barber of, 185; reputation of, 186; graduates of, 211, 240, 275, 347, 351, 412; sociologist Kelly Miller of, 223; historian Rayford Logan of, 228; and administrator Emmett Jay Scott, 232; and 1919 riot, 233; and U Street, 239; sociologist William Henry Jones of, 243; architect Hilyard Robinson of, 249; 1930s activism at, 266; and Marian Anderson concert, 271; and 1943–44 sit-ins, 279–80, 399; dean Lucy Diggs Slowe of, 283; housing segregation near, 295; president Mordecai Johnson of, 298; interim president Joyce Ladner of, 431; poet E. Ethelbert Miller of, 461
Howard University Law School, 151, 168, 169, 211, 279, 287–88, 296, 299–300, 312, 412, 446
Howes, Robert G., 324
Hughes, Cathy, 410
Hughes, Langston, 241, 458, 461
Hughes, Percy, 215
Humphrey, Hubert, 298, 362
Hunter, Alice, 293
Hunter, Diana, 456
Hunter College, 279, 297
Hunting Creek Warehouse, 14
Hurd, James, 295–97

with black families, 193; and Board of Trade, 195; descent into, 226; of immigrants, 246; and housing, 252; of black workers, 277; of former Southwest residents, 324; and War on Poverty, 347; and antipoverty organizations, 347–51; and Poor People's Campaign, 355; and Latino community, 372; and antiwar activists, 390; in urban areas, 394; and race, 440; concentrated, 445; and market-based solutions to, 448–49

Powell, Ruth, 279

Powhatan, 6–10

Powhatan Confederacy, 6–10

President's Committee on Civil Rights, 292

President's Homes Commission, 204

President's Square (present-day Lafayette Square), 43

Pride, Inc., 350–51, 353, 355, 358, 369, 391, 407

Prince George's County, Md., 6, 13, 43–44, 86, 141, 332, 402, 420, 456, 461

Private schools: in antebellum D.C., 44–45, 131; School for Colored Girls, 95–96, 99; during Civil War, 131; white children attend, 305; growth of, 330; and D.C. Opportunity Scholarship Program, 449

Proctor and Gamble, 386

Prout, John W., 68–69, 74, 80, 83

Public housing: Langston Terrace Dwellings, 249–50; and integration, 259–60, 297, 303, 319; conditions of, 281; white resistance to, 282; in Southeast D.C., 325, 331; and Etta Mae Horn, 348–49; and Bates Street Project, 394–95; in Ward 7, 399; and Pride, Inc., 407; and political organizing, 421; in Chinatown, 429; and New Communities Initiative, 445, 455–56

Public schools: black public school system, 115, 131–32; and Sayles Bowen, 148–49, 169–70; and Emancipation Day, 184; black control of segregated, 214–16; overcrowding in, 304–7; black parent strike of, 308–9; Strayer report on conditions of, 309; transfer of Central to black school system, 310–11; Carr v. Corning decision and, 311; Bolling v. Sharpe decision and, 312–13, 323; desegregation of, 314–19, 326–27; white flight from, 330–31; Julius Hobson lawsuit against, 339–41; and Latino families, 372–74; community control of, 377; and Chinese students, 426; Adrian Fenty's reform of, 448–54

Public Works Administration, 249–50

Pullman, Raymond, 234

Purvis, Charles, 174

Pusey, Merlo, 269–70

Quartermaster Department, 124–25

Quayle, Dan, 409

Queen, Mina, 42–43, 54, 59

Queen, Simon, 42

Queen v. Hepburn (1813), 42–43, 59

Racial discrimination and racism: in churches, 60; in D.C., 131, 209, 216, 225, 226–31, 271–75, 276, 277, 287–94 passim, 301, 333, 372; in Union army, 141; in politics, 148; in employment, 148, 212, 218, 263–66, 283, 294, 299, 335–37, 372; in public places, 150–51; and memory of Reconstruction, 175–76; and Washington Post, 181; challenges to, 213, 232, 236, 241; in schools, 214, 308, 311; in federal government, 220, 338; during World War I, 229; within black community, 242; and Socialist and Communist Parties, 263; during World War II, 277; on streetcars, 278; and national security, 292; in housing, 294–304, 335–38, 440; emotional toll of, 334; in the law, 342; against white minority, 381; against Latinos, 415–16

Radcliffe College, 241

Radical Republicans: in D.C., 109, 120–22; and postwar agenda, 136; and black suffrage, 141–48; opposition to, 154–57; and disfranchisement, 157–59, 166; after Reconstruction, 176, 182; and biracial democracy, 184, 462

Ralph, Joseph, 221–22

Ramos, Rudolfo, 372

Randolph, A. Philip, 231, 266, 273–74, 342

Randolph, John, 53–54, 57

Raspberry, William, 348, 363, 368, 375

Ray, John, 422

Reagan, Ronald, 398, 400, 404, 408, 411

Reagan National Airport, 26

Reagon, Bernice Johnson, 381

Real estate development: lucrative nature of, 96, 185, 190, 194, 197; and Alexander Shepherd, 156–57; boom in, 162, 187–88; in alleys, 179; size of industry, 188; and Chevy Chase, 191; and residential segregation, 192, 243–44, 295, 297, 299, 328; and suburbs, 197; values of, 201; and destruction of black communities, 258; and redlining, 290–91; and restrictive covenants, 294; in Southwest, 322, 332; and racially changing neighborhoods, 327–28, 399; west of Rock Creek Park, 332; and gentrification, 382–84; in 2000s, 390, 448, 460; and drugs, 402; during recession, 413; in Chinatown, 427–29; and Adrian Fenty, 454–56

Reconstruction: in D.C., 122; retreat from, 164–69 passim, 211, 220, 238, 394; Radical (Congressional), 136–46; and black opportunity, 170, 173, 180, 184, 207, 266, 270, 278; end of, 171, 184, 210; black leadership during, 172–73, 178, 241, 249; memory of, 175–77, 299; and black unity, 182–83; residential diversity during, 187; and citizens associations, 192; antidiscrimination laws from, 208, 300–301; extent of racial change during, 284, 287

school desegregation appeal, 316; *Berman v. Parker* (1954), 323
Susquehanocks, 6
Swampoodle, 85, 100, 103, 178, 201–4, 332
Synagogues, 152, 247, 328

Takoma (neighborhood), 243, 253, 258, 327–28, 330
Takoma Park, Md., 360, 362
Talmud Torah Synagogue, 152
Tanner, Alethia Browning, 43–44, 60, 68
Tappan, Lewis, 94
Taxation: without representation, 3, 18, 34, 37, 174, 196, 459; racial dimensions of, 121; "contraband" tax, 125; and schools, 131; and democracy, 155–57, 160, 175–76; fears of excessive, 156, 270; during Reconstruction, 158; and economic development, 161; and territorial government, 164; and Congress, 165; and black property owners, 190; and citizens associations, 192; poll taxes, 208; and Chinatown, 257, 428; and urban blight, 361; and home rule, 379; and real estate development, 382, 413, 440; and gentrification, 383, 398–99, 428–29; during Barry administration, 396; conservative opposition to, 397; during Dixon administration, 417; and population decline, 422; city's limited taxing authority, 433; and commuter tax, 440
Taylor, Charles, 432
Taylor, Robert, 283
Teach For America, 449, 453
Temple Courts, 445, 455–56
Temple Courts Tenant Association, 456
Ten Miles Square Club, 270
Tennallytown (now "Tenleytown"), 191–92, 253, 257–59
Terra Rubra plantation, 54
Terrell, Mary Church: LeDroit Park address of, 187; background of, 206; anger at discrimination, 209; and racial solidarity, 210–11; as teacher, 212; articulates black concerns, 213; and Anna Julia Cooper, 215; on symbolism of D.C., 216; on Du Bois–Washington split, 223; and discrimination during World War I, 229–30; and traveling, 236; and New Negro Alliance, 262; and Coordinating Committee for the Enforcement of the D.C. Anti-Discrimination Laws, 297, 300–303; and black leadership, 377
Terrell, Robert, 187, 207, 211
Territorial government: establishment of, 160; black opposition to, 160–61; and Alexander Shepherd, 161–62; critics of, 162–63; investigations of, 163–65; financial difficulties of, 164–65; end of, 165–66; legacy of, 167–68, 184
Thatcher, Margaret, 448
Third Baptist Church, 352

Third Street Church of God, 460
Thomas, Deborah, 445–46
Thomas, Louise, 439–40, 443, 445–46
Thomas, Neval, 234, 236–39, 261
Thompson's Restaurant, 280, 283, 301–3
Thoreau, Henry David, 63
Thornton, Anna, 32, 76–77, 80
Thornton, William, 32, 56, 76
Thorpe, Leroy, Jr., 406
372nd Infantry Regiment, 228
Three Sisters Bridge, 362, 365–66
Thurmond, Strom, 381
Tiber Creek, 84–85, 100
Tie-Sheng, Dai, 428
Tifereth Israel, 328
Tillman, Ben, 209
Tin Cup Alley, 179
Tobriner, Walter, 338
Tolbert, John, 39
Toomer, Jean, 240–41
Torrey, Charles T., 86–90
Torrey, Jesse, 52–54, 74
To Secure These Rights (1947), 292–93
Touré, Ahmed Sékou, 353
Townsend, George, 176
Tracking (in education), 340
Transient camps, 250
Treadwell, Mary, 407
Trenton Terrace, 298
Trinidad, 50, 342
Trinidad, D.C. (neighborhood), 442
Truman, Harry, 286, 292, 303, 308, 351
Trumbull, Lyman, 120
Tucker, Sterling: arrives in D.C., 334; and March on Washington, 338; appointed to city council, 351; joins Black United Front, 354; on police issues, 369–70; and 1974 election, 380; loses 1978 election, 384–86
Turner, Henry McNeal, 116, 124, 132
Turner, John, 270
Turner, Letha, 189
Turner, Maurice, 404, 408–9
Turner, Nat, 74
Tuskegee Institute, 208, 223, 238, 333–34, 430
Twain, Mark, 189
Tweed, "Boss," 164
Twenty-Third Amendment, 344

Uline Arena, 293
Uncle Tom's Cabin (Stowe), 91
Underground Railroad, 87–89, 93–95, 132, 153
Unification Church, 419
Union army, 108, 110, 122, 130, 132–34, 137, 141, 153, 169, 178, 349
Union Directory, 211
Union League, 142
Unions: segregation in, 209, 259; in Bureau of Engraving and Printing, 218; and interracial organizing, 251, 263–71; and *New Negro Alliance* ruling, 263; Jewel Mazique and, 275; during